CHINA TODAY

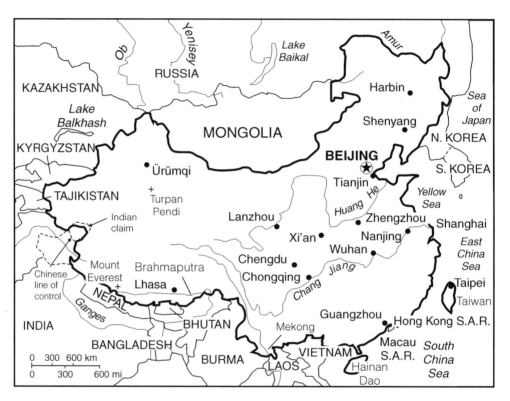

China.

CHINA TODAY

AN ENCYCLOPEDIA OF LIFE IN THE PEOPLE'S REPUBLIC

VOLUME II: M–Z

Edited by Jing Luo

Aimin Chen, Associate Editor, Economics
Shunfeng Song, Associate Editor, Economics
Baogang Guo, Associate Editor, Labor Relations
Ronghua Ouyang, Associate Editor, Education

GREENWOOD PRESS
Westport, Connecticut • London

Library of Congress Cataloging-in-Publication Data

Encyclopedia of contemporary Chinese civilization / edited by Jing Luo ; Aimin Chen, associate editor, economics ; Shunfeng Song, associate editor, economics ; Baogang Guo, associate editor, labor relations ; Ronghua Ouyang, associate editor, education.
    p. cm.
  Includes bibliographical references and index.
  ISBN 0-313-32170-1 (set : alk. paper)—ISBN 0-313-32768-8 (v.1: alk. paper)—ISBN 0-313-32769-6 (v.2 : alk. paper) 1. China—Civilization—1949—Encyclopedias. I. Luo, Jing, 1960-
  DS777.6.E52 2005
  951.05'03—dc22   2004022532

British Library Cataloguing in Publication Data is available.

Library of Congress Catalog Card Number: 2004022532
ISBN: 0-313-32170-1 (set code)
        0-313-32768-8 (vol. I)
        0-313-32769-6 (vol. II)

First published in 2005

Greenwood Press, 88 Post Road West, Westport, CT 06881
An imprint of Greenwood Publishing Group, Inc.
www.greenwood.com

Printed in the United States of America

The paper used in this book complies with the
Permanent Paper Standard issued by the National
Information Standards Organization (Z39.48-1984).

10 9 8 7 6 5 4 3 2 1

CONTENTS

M

Macao

See One Country, Two Systems.

Management Education

Management education has evolved synchronically with the development of China's economy since the People's Republic of China (PRC) was established in 1949. It has transformed through a path of rise, fall, and rise again during the past half century, just as China's economy has.

Stage I (1949–1958)

Soon after the Chinese Communist Party took over power in mainland China in 1949, the new government nationalized all universities and colleges and completely restructured its higher-education system, copying the USSR's model as China's economy did. In 1952, the government began to break up comprehensive universities and reorganized them according to professional fields, such as liberal arts, engineering, agriculture, medicine, and so on. Under the new system, the economic and management programs established before 1949 in a handful of universities, though all on a small scale, were either disbanded or restructured. Two new management education models based on two corresponding USSR institutions were introduced. The first one was represented by Remin University of China in Beijing, a Chinese version of the Moscow National Economy College, which trained officials of various ranks in the planning and control of the centrally planned economy. The second model was represented by Harbin Institute of Technology, Harbin, Heilongjiang Province, and Shanghai Jiaotong University, Shanghai, both of which were modeled on then Leningrad Engineering Economy College of the USSR, which trained mainly "economic engineers" for production administration in enterprises. Russian professors were invited to either directly teach or act as senior advisers to Chinese instructors in these model schools. Hundreds of Chinese students and scholars from fellow universities around the country were sent to the model schools to learn the USSR-style management practice or receive management educational training. The programs of the model schools then acted as the basis on which dozens of colleges and universities built their own management programs. Thousands of prospective managers and governmental cadres were trained under the two USSR models. They became the backbone of management teams in **state-owned enterprises (SOEs)** and governmental agencies in charge of economic affairs in the years to come.

Stage 2 (1958–1978)

The ideology of orthodox Communists, primarily Maoism, gradually prevailed and maintained dominance in both the Party and the government during this period. **Mao Zedong** and his orthodox colleagues prioritized "revolution" over "production" and declared that they would even prefer "Communist grass" to "capitalist crops" (the Communist doctrine over economic development). Correspondingly, the criteria for managerial candidacy were identified with "redness" (political credentials and ideological loyalty) rather than "expertise" (technical or managerial skills). As a result, most management education programs were gradually weakened and eventually dismissed by the government. Subsequently, when the **Great Cultural Revolution** began in 1966, most universities and colleges were eventually shut down. Management education programs based on the two USSR models were replaced by various Communist Party schools or cadre schools, both of which primarily taught Marxism, Leninism, and Maoism doctrines, with little managerial skill training.

Stage 3 (1978–Present)

The turnaround of China's economy, as well as its management education, began in late 1978 under Deng Xiaoping's leadership. One main objective of the "Reform and Opening" policy was to delegate more autonomy to SOEs and make them more efficient in production by having them run more like independent firms in the marketplace. This new economic policy caused profound and broad changes in every aspect of China's social and economic life. Due to the dismissal of management education programs during the Cultural Revolution, most Chinese managers then lacked the necessary managerial training. Even those who had been trained under the USSR models during the 1950s lacked the comprehensive knowledge and skills to run an independent firm and create revenue for the firm's own sake. China experienced a shortage of highly educated managers at all levels. Therefore, management education was one of the first areas where the reform policy was initially implemented. This time, however, the Chinese government decided to learn from the West rather than from Communist Russia, which had been the "big brother."

As soon as China and the United States restored their diplomatic relations in 1979, Deng Xiaoping became the first top leader of China who officially visited the United States. A key mission of his visit was to ask President Jimmy Carter for assistance in developing management education in China. The result was the establishment of the first Western-style business school in the People's Republic's history, the National Center for Industrial Science and Technology Management Development (known as the Dalian Center), located on the campus of Dalian Institute of Technology (now renamed Dalian University of Technology) in Dalian, Liaoning Province. The Dalian Center was cosponsored by three ministries of China and the Department of Commerce of the United States. Each year from 1980 to 1989, more than a dozen American professors from top U.S. business schools came to teach various executive training programs at the Dalian Center. Participants in these training programs included SOE managers, government officials, and university faculty from all over the country. They later became the major forces in China's economic reform and management education development. Encouraged by the success of the Dalian Center, the government soon established several other major training centers in different cities around the country in the 1980s, cooperating with other major developed countries such as Canada, Germany, Japan, the United Kingdom, the Netherlands, and the European Community. Moreover, hundreds of managerial cadres institutes were also established at the ministerial, provincial, and municipal levels. These centers and institutes primarily provided management training to management practitioners. Degree programs in management education also mushroomed throughout the country under the leadership of those faculty members trained at the Dalian Center. By 1988, around 350 universities had established various management-related undergraduate and graduate programs, and at least 40 of the universities had created their own management or business schools. Beginning in 1990, MBA programs were run on an experimental basis in nine universities authorized by the government. Such programs were soon extended to twenty-six universities in 1994, fifty-six in 1998, and sixty-two by 2001.

Dual System of Management Education

During the past two decades, management education has been managed by two systems in China: the State Economic Commission (SEcC) system and the State Education Commission (SEdC) system. The SEcC (renamed the State Economic and Trade Commission in 1998) is the controlling authority of China's national economy. The SEcC system of management education includes Chinese-Western cooperative training centers around the country and various managerial cadres institutes at the ministerial, provincial, or municipal levels. They are primarily in charge of the training and development of existing managers in SOEs, more like continuing education or on-the-job training in nature. Moreover, they do not have the authority to run degree programs, especially graduate degrees. The SEdC (renamed the Ministry of Education in 1998) is the state authority that administers education affairs of the country, including degree granting. The SEdC system of management education is the ordinary higher-education system—universities and colleges with bachelor's, master's, and/or Ph.D. degree programs. Since the early 1980s, these universities and colleges have benefited from the pioneering work of several key centers under the SEcC system, as well as from sending their own faculty to study abroad. They have gradually established their own departments or schools of management/business with degree programs from bachelor's to master's and Ph.D. However, they could not decide how many students they would admit for their programs. Instead, they had to follow the SEdC's quota, as the tuition for these programs (as well as all other degree programs) was partially or fully paid by the government. Their graduates used to be assigned jobs in SOEs (i.e.,the buyers) by the government according to its central plan. Today, however, students have gained more autonomy in choosing their employers, but universities and colleges still cannot decide their enrollments.

Since 1990, the focus of management education in China has been shifted from nondegree programs and undergraduate and academic graduate degree programs to MBA programs. This trend has benefited Chinese universities in revenue and management practitioners in career development. Those centers and institutes under the SEcC system tend to establish alliances with universities and colleges for cosponsorship of MBA programs. However, in order to enhance their own capabilities of management education, Chinese universities and colleges are also seeking partnerships with foreign business schools for joint MBA programs (granting Chinese MBA degrees). Moreover, some entrepreneurial foreign business schools have explored the Chinese MBA market with their own degrees. The pioneer in this respect is the State University of New York at Buffalo, which had joint MBA programs with the Dalian Center in the late 1980s and Remin University of China in the 1990s. More recent cases have involved MIT, Thunderbird University, Washington University, Rutgers University, Boston University, and others. After all the hardship and struggles during the past half century, management education in China reached its golden era in the late 1990s and is catching up with international trends.

See also Corporate Governance; Deng Xiaoping (1904–1997), Reforms of; Human Resource Management (HRM); Open Door Policy (1978).

Bibliography

Chan, M.W.L., "Management Education in the People's Republic of China," in *Management Issues in China*, ed. D. Brown and R. Potter, 1:237–257 (London and New York: Routledge, 1996); Deng, S., and Y. Wang, "Management Education in China: Past, Present, and Future," *World Development* 20, no.6 (1992): 873–880; Warner, M., *How Chinese Managers Learn: Management and Industrial Training in China* (London: Macmillan, 1992).

Wei He

Mandarin

See Putonghua, Promotion of.

Mao Zedong (1893–1976)

Mao Zedong was one of the great twentieth-century revolutionaries. He was an organizer of the Chinese Communist Party (CCP) and the founder of the

Chairman Mao Zedong shakes hands with members of the
Red Guards in September 1966. © Bettmann/Corbis.

People's Republic of China. He left an indelible imprint on modern history
and, in many ways, determined the course of China's national development.

Mao was born on December 26, 1893, the son of a rich peasant in Shaoshan
Village, Xiangtan County, Hunan Province. When he was young, he received several years of traditional Chinese education in the village. His father was abusive
and treated him harshly. At the age of thirteen, he threatened to throw himself
into a pond and forced his father to back down. He brought this lesson to his political life, and scholars agree that Mao's childhood trained him as a rebel.

Like all Chinese children of the time, Mao's marriage was arranged. However, the early death of his wife freed him from this family obligation. In 1910,
he left the village to study at a school in Xiangtan, where he broadened his vision by wide reading of journals, newspapers, and books. The new ideas and
knowledge he gained had a profound impact on him. He then studied in
Changsha, the provincial capital, and took part in the 1911 Revolution by joining the Republican army for six months.

In the following years, Mao further dedicated himself to study. He absorbed
ideas not only from Chinese tradition but also from Western philosophy, politics, ethics, history, and economics. It was during this period that Mao started
to publish his radical opinions and organize students into groups searching for
solutions to China's problems. In 1918, he graduated from the First Provincial
Normal School in Changsha. While many of his friends chose to study in
France, Mao decided to stay. Mao was a domestic product. He did not travel to
a foreign county until after the establishment of the People's Republic, and
then only twice to the Soviet Union. This does not mean that he was not
stirred by foreign influences. Mao studied in Beijing and worked in Changsha

searching for a new theory for national salvation. He found Marxism. In the meantime, he courted and married Yang Kaihui, the daughter of his teacher.

In 1921, Mao was one of twelve founders of the CCP. In the following years, Mao worked in Hunan to recruit members for the Party. During the CCP-KMT (Kuomintang) alliance (1924–1927), Mao developed his political and organizational skills, especially while serving as head of the KMT peasant department. He regarded the peasantry as the real force of revolution. He envisioned, as he wrote in a famous tract of 1927, that millions of peasants would rise "like a fierce wind or tempest" and "in the end, send all the imperialists, warlords, corrupt officials, local bullies, and bad gentry to their graves." Throughout his life, Mao kept his faith in the peasants and regarded them as the backbone of the Chinese revolution.

Jiang Jieshi's (Chiang Kai-shek's) purge of the Communists in 1927 almost destroyed the CCP. Mao had to seek refuge in the remote rural areas, and there he remained for the next two decades. It was during these years that Mao formulated a sinified interpretation of Marxism appropriate to the unique characteristics of the Chinese revolution. At the same time, he developed strategies for the military struggle against the KMT. Mao first led the Red Army in the Jinggang Mountains, on the Jiangxi-Hunan border, and then in southern Jiangxi, where he built a soviet government and served as its chairman from 1931 to 1934. These bases allowed Mao to put his theories into practice. One of his boldest modifications of Marxism was that Chinese social and political conditions meant that the revolution would proceed by "encircling the cities from the countryside." This unorthodox theory altered the fundamental Marxist notion that the Communist revolution must proceed from the cities under the leadership of the urban working class. Mao consolidated his support among the mass of the poor peasantry by implementing **land reform**. Mao also initiated strict discipline within the Red Army and turned it into a model force that maintained close ties with the peasants. It was during these years that his second wife was killed by the KMT. He then married He Zizhen, a fellow revolutionary.

From 1931 to 1934, Jiang Jieshi launched five encirclement and annihilation campaigns against the Communists. Mao's military tactics were successful against the first four campaigns, but the fifth could not be repelled. Communist historians attribute this to party rivals who had pushed Mao aside and to the overwhelming numerical superiority of the KMT forces. Some 100,000 Communists managed to break out of the encirclement and set off on the famous flight known as the Long March. At the Zunyi Conference, held in 1935 in the course of the retreat, Mao became the supreme leader of the CCP, the position he held until his death. Although Mao lost 90 percent of his men, the Long March became a symbol of the heroism and invincibility of the Red Army. One year after evacuating Jiangxi, Mao's forces reached northern Shaanxi. For the next decade this served as the CCP's principal base area, with its capital in the small dusty town of Yan'an.

It may be an overstatement to say that the outbreak of war with Japan in 1937 saved Mao from another KMT campaign, but it was indeed during the war that the CCP was able to enlarge its military strength and territorial presence throughout northern and eastern China. In 1937, Mao entered into a second united front with the KMT, this time to deal with the common enemy,

Japan. Between 1937 and 1945, the CCP waged guerrilla warfare and established many base areas behind Japanese lines. By the time of Japan's surrender, Mao commanded 1 million troops and 2 million militiamen and controlled nineteen "liberated areas" of more than 100 million people. In his personal life, during the war Mao divorced his third wife and married a well-known movie star, Jiang Qing, later known in the West as Madame Mao.

The balance of power in China in 1945 was radically different from that in 1937. The CCP had emerged as a major player in the national political arena. Although the Americans endeavored to mediate between Mao and Jiang in the hope of setting up a coalition government, the effort was fruitless. In the ensuing civil war, the CCP gained the victory in a series of major battles in northern China. Jiang Jieshi and the remnants of the KMT fled to Taiwan. In Beijing, on October 1, 1949, Mao proclaimed the establishment of the People's Republic of China and declared to the world that the "Chinese people have stood up."

Mao had proven himself a great revolutionary leader in bringing the CCP to power, but now an entirely new challenge confronted him, that of ruling and transforming a country of more than 500 million people. China was "poor and blank," Mao was confident that "poverty gives rise to the desire for change as well as the desire for action and the desire for revolution. On a blank sheet of paper free from any mark, the freest and most beautiful pictures can be painted." Mao's plans for the reconstruction of China contained pronounced romantic and utopian elements. The future China was to be a people's democratic dictatorship, and Mao envisioned a populace pure in its revolutionary commitment. There must be constant vigilance against enemies of the revolution. People must be indoctrinated with proletarian ideas and guided by strict Communist discipline. People should strive for a proletarian class identity, possess one mind, and live a common style of life. Mao pursued absolute equality for his people. Although the old ruling class had been overthrown, Mao warned that enemies might be lurking and conspiring within the ranks of the people. People might be influenced by old ideas and traditions, as well as by outside enemies, and thus wittingly or unwittingly go over to the enemy camp. Hence Mao developed the theory of continuing revolution and launched a number of political movements designed to maintain the purity of the revolution. The Anti-Rightist Campaign in 1957 subjected 400,000 to 700,000 intellectuals to a purge. The ten years of the **Great Cultural Revolution (1966–1976)** constituted a national mobilization against supposed enemies inside the Party, government, and army. Because these people held such important positions, Mao warned that they were the most dangerous of all. In the course of the Cultural Revolution, millions of officeholders were purged and hundreds of thousands of citizens lost their lives in the violence that gripped the cities. The Cultural Revolution was the culmination of Mao's attempt to create a permanent revolutionary society. With Mao's death in 1976, the Cultural Revolution was quickly brought to an end by his successors.

Mao's utopianism also characterized his approach to China's economic development. In the early years of the People's Republic, the Soviet Union served as the model for Chinese economic planning. Mao, however, believed that China could exceed the growth rates achieved by cautious Soviet central planners. He dreamed of catching up with Britain in fifteen years and the United

States in thirty. To realize these goals, he launched a mass mobilization of the population to accelerate industrial and agricultural production, the **Great Leap Forward** of 1958. Mao spoke of a thousand years of Communist happiness after a few years of hard work. He ordered both urban dwellers and peasants to produce iron and steel so that China might overtake the West. The "backyard iron and steel" proved of no use for industrial purposes, and the mobilization was highly wasteful of manpower and resources. Villages were organized into mammoth communes in order to better utilize labor power and break down parochial local identities. Massive irrigation, tree-cutting, and grain-planting campaigns were launched. The result was an ecological disaster and three years of famine. The Great Leap Forward took a toll of some 20 million people in rural China between 1959 and 1962.

In foreign policy, Mao first "leaned" toward the Soviet Union, but distanced himself from Moscow after Joseph Stalin's death in 1953. An open rift with the Soviets in the early 1960s reached a dangerous climax in 1969, when a serious border incident led some Chinese and Soviet leaders to believe that war was imminent. From the late 1950s to the early 1970s, China was almost an isolated nation, sustained by Mao's self-reliance principle. Although Mao often denounced American imperialism as a paper tiger, in his late years he moved toward the United States to balance off a threatening Soviet Union. This change of policy suited American interests, and in 1972 Richard Nixon readily responded to Mao's invitation to come to China. Normalization of relations between China and the United States began that year, ending more than two decades of mutual hostility.

The death of Mao on September 9, 1976, not only brought an end to the Cultural Revolution but also presaged the end of mass campaigns as a feature of Chinese life. However, Mao's legacy persisted. Even if Deng Xiaoping's reforms negated most of Mao's domestic policies, Mao's name was still revered, and Mao Zedong Thought was upheld as a guiding principle for the nation. To a large degree, Deng's intent was to change the content of the Maoist political and economic model while retaining Mao as a symbol of the achievements of the Communist revolution. The formula adopted in the official evaluation of Mao is 70 percent success and 30 percent failure. For many Chinese, Mao's place in Chinese history is assured by his central role in leading the revolution to victory in 1949. However, his attempts once in power to bring about a total transformation of Chinese society are regarded as much less successful, particularly his economic policies, of which the Great Leap Forward was the most tragic in its results. Mao offers contrasting images: for some, he was a great leader, a prolific writer, and an erudite scholar; for others, he was a power-hungry dictator, an evil emperor, and a detestable tyrant. All agree on Mao's epic stature in China's twentieth-century history. That it was Mao who brought his nation from humiliating weakness to global power alone ensures him a continuing place in the annals of contemporary China.

See also Gang of Four; Korean War (1950–1953); Nixon's Visit to China/Shanghai Communiqué (1972); Ping-Pong Diplomacy; Sino-American Relations, Conflicts and Common Interests; Sino-American Relations since 1949; Sino-Soviet Alliance; Zhou Enlai.

Bibliography

Cheek, Timothy, *Mao Zedong and China's Revolutions: A Brief History with Documents* (Boston and New York: Bedford/St. Martin's, 2002); Mao, Zedong, *Selected Works of Mao Zedong* (Beijing: Peoples Publishing House, 1969); Schram, Stuart, *Mao Tse-tung* (New York: Simon and Schuster, 1966); Spence, Jonathan, *Mao Zedong* (New York: Viking, 1999); Wilson, Dick, ed., *Mao Tse-tung in the Scale of History* (Cambridge: Cambridge University Press, 1977).

Patrick Fuliang Shan

Marriage and Divorce

Since the early days of Chinese civilization, marriages have been performed to join families who see their union as advantageous for various reasons: to have economic gain, to continue the family line, and to protect the children that come after the couple's union so that they will make sacrifices to their parents after their deaths. Since the middle of the twentieth century, marriages have become more the couple's issue. People marry for reasons that include mutual affection, personal security, family building, companionship, and social and family expectations.

Because Chinese culture is far from homogeneous, with more than fifty ethnic nationalities constituting and enriching it, marriages vary greatly in terms of beliefs, values, customs, and rituals. The Marriage Law (May 1, 1950), the first law adopted after the founding of the New China, serves as the basic code that governs and regulates marriage and family relations. It aims at abolishing the patriarchal marriage and family system that featured compulsory arranged marriages and superior social status of men over women. Later amendments in 1980 and 2001 further stipulate principles such as freedom of marriage, monogamy, equality, and protection of women's rights and interests.

For the majority of the Chinese people, marriage is on a legal basis only. When two persons of opposite sexes want to get married, they each get a letter from their workplace affirming that neither is already married, undergo a health check, and then present themselves at a civil affairs department where they fill out a form. For many people, this registration with the civil staff and obtaining a marriage certificate indicate the beginning of their married life. Unlike many cultures elsewhere, this moment of legal acknowledgment of the union does not require the couple to vocally pledge their fidelity and commitment to one another. The bride and groom may also choose to perform a religious ceremony. For instance, people with Christian beliefs may have an additional wedding ceremony at the church. As the society is opening up, family relationships are undergoing many changes. As table 5 shows, the divorce rate is on the rise, while, at the same time, the marriage rate is hovering at around the same level.

Most people marry, though a small urban population chooses not to, a practice in head-on collision with tradition. The legal marriage age is twenty-two for men and twenty for women. Increased career opportunities, longer life expectancy, and a stronger sense of individualism join with government propaganda efforts for late marriages, especially in urban areas. In the year 2001, the

TABLE 5
Marriage and Divorce Statistics

Year	Registered Marriages of Mainland China (10,000 couples)	Divorces (10,000 couples)	Divorce Rate (percent per 1,000)
1980	719.8	34.1	0.7
1988	899.2	65.9	1.2
1997	914.1	119.8	1.9
2001	805.0	125.0	2.0

Source: *China Statistical Yearbook 2002* and *China Population Statistics Yearbook 1999*.

average female age at first marriage rose to 23.4. In rural areas, however, the practice is typically more a continuation of tradition. In the mid-1990s, about a third of marriages overall involved at least one partner who was below the legal minimum age.

Interethnic and interracial marriages are on a steady rise, though they are not very popular. There were altogether more than 16 million people in China registered for marriages in 1982. Some 20,000 registered for marriages with a foreigner or a citizen of Hong Kong, Macao, or Taiwan that same year. In the year 2001, that figure had jumped to around 80,000.

Arranged marriages are banned in the new Marriage Law. Marriage for love has struck a chord with the general public. Yet limited social mobility and inconvenient transportation make romantic love still a luxury for many. Proposals initiated by parents and go-betweens, with the consent of the prospective bride and groom, remain the most popular form of marriage in rural areas.

The traditional concept of a "good match" between male and female—talents for the man and good looks for the woman—still has considerable influence at present, though it is expressed in somewhat different forms. In choosing prospective partners, men typically prefer women who will look up to them. Accordingly, women often favor men who are taller, two or three years older, and better educated. Gentle temperament is definitely a desirable quality in the choice of female dates.

In addition to the emotional investment the couple may put in, marriage is also a big financial investment, more so for the parents than for the couple. Young couples, especially in rural areas, often depend on their parents' savings to start a new family. They typically expect to get a new house or renovate the old one belonging to parents for the marriage, though this often means that the parents move in with them. In urban areas, parents are expected to provide the couple with daily necessities from furniture and transportation vehicles to cooking utensils. The climax comes with a glamorous wedding banquet, to which relatives and friends are invited to witness the marriage. Under the urging of parents and peer pressure, the newlyweds may find the marriage a financial burden too heavy to bear alone. For instance, getting married in Shanghai in 2001 might cost eight years' salary for an average worker. This has caused social concern among the general public.

Young married couples are expected to live with their parents in the first few years after marriage. They give emotional support to the parents while they are financially still dependent on the elders. A nuclear family is often formed when the first and in most cases only child has grown beyond infancy. Premarital sex and extramarital affairs are still generally unacceptable for morality reasons, though there is greater public tolerance of them.

The splendor of the wedding and affection for each other do not always guarantee a lifelong marriage. The national divorce rate has nearly tripled in the last two decades. Large **cities** and more economically developed areas have even higher divorce rates. In 2001, Shanghai's divorce rate was 4.86 per thousand marriages. The same year, in the capital city, Beijing, 79,385 couples registered for marriage, while 27,683 couples got divorced.

There are two ways to obtain a divorce in China. Couples who have reached consensus can register at local civil affairs departments. Otherwise, they have to file for divorce at family courts.

Common reasons for divorce include extramarital affairs of the spouse, desertion, disputes over finance and child care, incompatible or unsatisfactory sex life, and domestic abuse and violence. Quality of marriage and individual happiness rather than pleasing of the extended family and "social stability" have become important considerations for possible divorces.

Today, divorce is no longer regarded as shameful, and divorced persons are actively seeking new love. This is in sharp contrast to the situation a quarter of a century ago, when divorce was a social taboo. It used to be one of the hardest challenges facing those couples who longed to end their marital relations. Loss of mutual affection was not a good enough reason for terminating the marriage. They typically had to go through formal mediations that could last for years. The couple's patience and desire usually would wear out before they could actually obtain the official permission to divorce. From 1980 on, the amendments have allowed for no-fault divorce, thus simplifying the procedure for those couples in which both partners desire it. However, these new and perceivably more liberal amendments also take some blame for the current high divorce rate.

Women nowadays enjoy greater equality with men than their mothers and grandmothers, thanks to the revolution and the Marriage Law. They have more say in whom they want for a spouse. They do not have to change their maiden names after marriage, and they have greater freedom to decide if they want to divorce. Currently, about 60 to 70 percent of divorce cases are filed by women as they acquire more education, economic responsibility, and career opportunities. Legal efforts have been made to ensure that women who are deserted by their husbands are protected and compensated. Nevertheless, traditions often hinder them from their free will. After divorce, the father is often given custody of the children when they have grown beyond infancy. Typically better economic conditions and the traditional value of the children carrying on the father's family name favor the father in custody. On the practical side, the woman may find herself homeless after divorce, for in urban areas, the house or apartment was often given by the man's work unit when the two got married.

Like everything else that is happening in China, the public concepts of marriage, family, and divorce are undergoing rapid changes. Demands for same-sex marriage are on the rise. Lesbians and gays are making their voices heard in legislative bodies. Male superiority and authority over marriage and family life are beginning to give way, and in some areas have given way, to gender equality. The old cliché that divorce would affect social stability and shatter faith in the family is arguably being replaced by greater concern for individual happiness. As the social trend of decentralization of both the government and the extended family continues, it remains an open question whether significant numbers of people will voice their counteropinion and use legislative means to place curbs on some of the more liberal (meaning more westernized) practices concerning family life.

See also Ethnic Marriage Customs; Family Collectivism; Great Cultural Revolution, Impact of on Woman's Social Status; Mosuo People, Matriarchal Tradition of; Women, Role as Mothers; Women, Social Status of.

Bibliography

Liu, Dalin, Lun Ng, Zhou Liping, and Erwin J. Haeberie, *Sexual Behavior in Modern China: Report on the Nationwide Survey of 20,000 men and women* (London and New York: Continuum International Publishing Group, 1997); *Marriage Law* (revised) (Standing Committee of the National People's Congress, April 28, 2001); National Bureau of Statistics, *China Population Statistics Yearbook* (Beijing: China Statistics Press, 1999); National Bureau of Statistics, *China Statistical Yearbook 2002* (Beijing: China Statistics Press, 2002).

Hong Wang

Marriage Customs

See Ethnic Marriage Customs; Marriage and Divorce.

Matriarchal Tradition

See Mosuo People, Matriarchal Tradition of.

Media Bodies, Central and Local

In the area of media coverage, contemporary China has tremendously changed. There has been a leap in the development of media infrastructure since 1978, when China's reform toward a market economy began. By 2001, more than 2,000 newspapers and 8,000 magazines and periodicals were circulating. The number of magazines and periodicals is 8.6 times the number in 1978, when there were only 930 magazines and periodicals. There was an annual production of 154,526 kinds of books and 5,000 volumes per 1,000 people in 2001, whereas in 1978 there were only 14,987 books published. Wired and wireless broadcasting reach 92.9 percent of the total population, leaving about 90 million people with no access to it. In 1998, there were about 340 million **television** sets and 3,240 television stations, an average of one television set for every three viewers. There were 673 radio stations in 1998. By

2001, there were thirty-one film studios, compared with four film studios in 1952, with an annual production of approximately 600 to 800 films of all kinds between the late 1970s and the end of the 1990s.

Since the end of the twentieth century, the **Internet** has experienced a boom time. There were only 2,000 Internet users in China in 1993. By 2003, the number is estimated to have reached 57 million, more than 25,000 times more than in 1993. Most governmental units at all levels have a Web presence. Universities and companies are connected, and some are presented through both Chinese and English interfaces. China is now regarded as the second-largest Internet country, with 125.6 million computers online, second only to the United States. It is the number one cell phone country in the world. The number of people working in the advertising industry in 2000 reached 640,000, up from 16,000 in 1982, a fortyfold increase in eighteen years. The nation's economy, politics, and culture are becoming more and more dependent on communication and media. A few Chinese Internet companies, such as Sohu (www.sohu.com.cn), Xing Lang (www.xinglang.com.cn), and Zhonghua (www.zhonghua.com.cn), are listed on the New York Stock Exchange.

Between 1949 and 1978, before the beginning of Deng Xiaoping's economic reform, the Chinese media were only used by the Communist Party as tools to maintain its power and to propagate its ideology to the people. Media were called "the mouthpiece of the Party." During the **Great Cultural Revolution (1966–1976)**, the media were used largely as tools in power struggles among different political factions within the Chinese Communist Party. The number of newspapers was reduced from 200 in the 1950s to 40. Many other media such as television and radio were paralyzed. Since Deng started the economic reform in 1978, the Chinese media have been serving multiple functions. In addition to being tools of the Party in exercising control, the Chinese media have been playing an increasingly important role in China's economic reform and development. In particular, the media's entertainment and socialization functions have been a driving force in many aspects. For example, the newspaper industry directly controlled by the Party makes up two-thirds of the total national newspaper industry, with one-third not under the Party's direct control. Before 1978, the industry was 100 percent directly controlled by the Party. The situation has given rise to a wide range of popular culture.

The Chinese media are increasingly internationally and globally oriented. For example, the Xinhua News Agency has established ninety-eight news bureaus around the world, with daily news reports of as many as 200,000 words. The *People's Daily* and *Guangming Daily* have also established numerous news bureaus in major metropolitan areas of the world. *China Daily,* an English newspaper in Beijing, has subscribers widely around the world. A global audience tunes in CCTV International. *Peking Review,* a weekly magazine in many foreign-language versions, such as English, Russian, and German, has remained a classic weekly for the international audience since 1949. *China's Women* and *China Pictorial,* with an international audience as their focus, have also been well known. Since the economic reform in 1978, a few newspapers in Chinese have been established by pro–People's Republic businesspeople, such as *Overseas Chinese Daily* on the east coast of the United States and *Sing Tao Daily* on the west coast.

Most media in China are owned by the state at various levels of administration, although a few Internet newspaper companies such as Netease and Sohu are exceptions. While all of the Party-owned media bodies such as the *People's Daily* and the Xinhua News Agency are fully subsidized by the state and the Party, most media bodies survive largely on their own revenue from sales and advertising. A few media bodies owned by the state have received private investment, which includes foreign investment. *Business Week* in the United States, for example, runs a joint-venture magazine in Chinese in China. A private Internet media company called Media China Net Ltd. (www.Media China.net) that is completely owned by a private media entrepreneur from Hong Kong now functions in Beijing. Increased foreign investment in the sector is expected in the coming years due to China's entrance into the World Trade Organization (WTO). Regardless of this, the relationship between Chinese media entities and the Chinese government is similar to the relationship between manager and boss: the latter holds the ultimate power. More specifically, China's national media czar is the Ministry of Propaganda, which supervises the practices of media entities from a macro perspective and reports to a standing member of the Poliburo (currently Li Changchun) in charge, who further reports to the Party general secretary (currently Hu Jintao). Media entities owned or registered within a province, a city, or a county, while being managed by the personnel of the media entities themselves, are supervised by a director of propaganda who reports to a Party secretary at each respective level. The current situation of the Chinese media is best described as one head with many mouths.

The media in contemporary China are much freer than before the economic reform began in 1978, when there was one head with only one mouth. This is especially true in the social and economic spheres. There is still strong censorship in the political sphere, especially with regard to the political system, national policies, past and current key political leaders, and politically sensitive domestic and international issues. The Chinese media are allowed to diversify and localize in covering economic news. They are allowed to reveal violations, flaws, and corruption. Call-in radio hot lines and television talk shows have begun to air in the metropolitan centers such as Shanghai and Beijing. Members of the audience are encouraged to call in to talk about their psychological issues of social import, such as depression and suicidal instincts. While political saloons were fashionable but banned from being covered in the 1980s, economic saloons or forums mushroomed in urban centers in the 1990s, which attracted as much media coverage as possible. However, if the media cover Party- and state-censored topics such as prodemocracy activists and issues related to the Falun Gong religious cult, journalists run the risk of being reprimanded. Chinese citizens in and outside China are banned from posting censored messages such as intellectual debates on taboo topics online or setting up their own Web sites for "politically incorrect" goals. The state and Party have been implementing "the Golden Shield" project to set up "the Internet Firewall" to defend China's "information sovereignty" from being violated, and 30,000 Internet police persons have been hired to guard against "politically incorrect" information being made available to Chinese online users in China on a daily basis. A few "Internet dissidents" have been put on trial and imprisoned.

With its goal to develop into a media giant, an economic giant, and a cultural giant, China is now undergoing two media revolutions, a media management revolution and a media education revolution. The Chinese media industry has been faced with serious challenges in the world media market since China's entrance into the World Trade Organization in December 2001. On the one hand, media bodies in China are in isolation from each other and thus lack competitiveness in the world media market. On the other hand, most global media giants are entering the Chinese market, with thirty-four of their television channels available in China. In response to such challenges, the Chinese media have been consolidated into sixty-eight media groups: thirty-eight newspaper management groups, thirteen television and radio management groups, nine publishing groups, five media advertising and sales groups, and three film-production groups. To make Chinese media more competitive in the long term, about 300 universities have established undergraduate and graduate programs of communication/media in the form of colleges or departments.

The question remains whether Western media freedom will be allowed in China, and if so, what the time frame will be. While such questions are largely topics of speculation, under the push of the economic reform, much progress has indeed been made with respect to media freedom.

See also Film Production; Media Distribution; Media Reform; Press Control; Press Freedom; Telecommunications Industry; Television Institute and Self-Learning.

Bibliography

Keatley, Robert L., *The Role of the Media in a Market Economy*, Conference Report, China Policy Series no. 19 (New York: National Committee on United States–China Relations, 2003); Lee, Chin-chuan, ed., *China's Media, Media's China* (Boulder, CO: Westview Press, 1994); Tong, Bing, *Rushi Yinian de Zhongguochuanmei Shichang Xingeju* (The loss of normalcy of media China a year after china's entrance into WTO), Beijing, China, www.mediachina.net, accessed on June 12, 2003.

Wenshan Jia

Media Distribution

Chinese media distribution should be understood in the context of press or information control—how much and what information the government allows its people to have access to. Placed in this context, media distribution is to be seen as the government's unyielding effort to control not only the amount but also the content of information. For these purposes, the government has long been a beneficiary of a system to centralize distribution through several designated agencies or organizations. However, the opening-up of Chinese society as a result of the economic reform, the increased need for more and unfettered information on the part of the Chinese people, and the media organizations' pressure to survive with less or even no government subsidies in a market economy have given rise to a complex and evolving landscape for Chinese media distribution.

For a long time, print materials—newspapers, magazines, and books—dominated the Chinese media market. Their distribution patterns were one-dimensional. The post office meant everything to the distribution of newspapers and magazines. Not only did the post office transport these print media to individuals and units, but it was also the designated agent for newspaper and magazine subscriptions. Book distribution was a little different: while the post office was still responsible for transporting books to various venues, books were distributed through the nationwide network of the Xinhua Bookstore.

Since the late 1980s, several significant changes have appeared in the distribution of the print media. Even though the post office remains the major distributor for newspapers and magazines, newsstands operated by private citizens have sprouted all over China to compete with the post office and give individuals unprecedented choices for information consumption. Some newspapers and magazines, dissatisfied with the post office's monopoly and high distribution fees, have set up their own distribution networks. For instance, a magazine associated with a women's federation may ask its local branches to carry out the distribution. Book publishers have also diversified their system of distribution. Instead of solely relying on the Xinhua Bookstore, they have also decided to set up their own distribution department, to conduct their own market surveys, and to establish their own distribution networks, which consist of privately owned bookstores or individual distributors. Recently, the distribution of books has also taken advantage of the **Internet**.

Internationally, the importation and exportation of print materials used to be less diversified, since it was handled or monopolized by one single, centralized company. Since the late 1980s, exportation rights have been decentralized slightly by giving provincial press bureaus the power to export the products from their local publishing houses. The Chinese government has not relaxed its rigid control of importation: it permits the importation of some foreign-language newspapers and news periodicals to be circulated only to expensive hotels and Chinese government and academic units, but no Chinese-language newspaper or news magazine may be legally imported from abroad, except for certain Chinese-controlled Hong Kong publications.

Like the print media, the distribution of electronic products, mainly films and radio and **television** programs, was for a long time one-dimensional, similar to a structure of vertical monopoly. Studios produced films, a centralized, state-owned company managed the circulation, and theaters were obliged to project the movies on the screen. Since the early 1990s, there have been encouraging signs of loosening of the control in distribution and allowing more competition. **Film production** studios have secured the right to sell directly to newly decentralized provincial and subprovincial film-distribution companies and even to individual theaters.

One centralized company also monopolized the importation, exportation, and distribution of foreign films, including those that originated in Hong Kong. While in theory this company still retains its monopoly over international transactions, the present situation is much more favorable for the international flow of domestic and foreign films. On the one hand, more and more foreign films are allowed to come to the Chinese market, and the decision on what kinds of films to import is no longer made on the basis of ideological standards. On the other hand, an increasing number of domestic films are coproduced with overseas companies, and these films form a unique category that takes advantages of loopholes in distribution. Additionally, many Western movies, often bootlegged, are available in numerous small-scale, privately owned theaters.

A similar situation appears in the television world. Chinese television stations exist in a hierarchical structure, as do their programs: stations on lower rungs of the ladder should carry certain programs from the stations above. For example, the CCTV news channel is required to be relayed by local stations. With regard to international programming, theoretically, only a handful of stations have the right to directly import foreign programs, and all other stations must secure their rights from these stations. The government has repeatedly issued memorandums to warn stations to keep a certain proportion of foreign programs in the total programming. However, local stations often defy these rules. The relaxation in programming reached a new level when cable television arrived since the government exhibited less persistence in applying the same level of control.

Media distribution in China is changing. The Chinese government strives to officially open its book, newspaper, and magazine distribution market to overseas investment, as announced in 2003. Even though this flow of foreign capital is only restricted in distribution, one can expect that distribution, driven by economic interests, will translate into message production. The government has also given permission for residents in certain areas of China to receive programs from Rupart Murdock's Hong Kong–based television networks. Some see this as a precursor of a full-fledged commitment to opening to the international media market.

See also Hong Kong, Return of; Media Bodies, Central and Local; Media Reform; Press Control; Press Freedom; Telecommunications Industry; Television Institute and Self-Learning.

Bibliography

Lynch, D., *After the Propaganda State: Media, Politics, and "Thought Work" in Reform China* (Stanford, CA: Stanford University Press, 1999); *2002 Chinese Media Yearbook and Directory* (Beijing: CMM Intelligence, 2002).

Changfu Chang

Media Reform

Media reform in China refers to changes in or about the media. It is often regarded as an area where change is slowest and hardest. The dynamism of the media reform came from several forces, including the Chinese Communist Party, journalists and **intellectuals**, and the public. However, the goals of the media reform for each of these forces were different, and the importance of these forces was also different during different times, depending on the political climate of the time. Nevertheless, the decisive force always resided in the power of the Party, and to the Party, the ultimate purpose of the media reform is to strengthen its leadership and to better execute its policies, not to discard them.

China modeled its political, economic, and media institutions after the Soviet Union when Communist China was established in 1949. Ever since then, the Party has been concurrently the owner, the manager, and the practitioner of the media. All key positions of the media are occupied by loyal Party members, and nationwide a Party unit corresponding to each administrative level is charged with supervising the media. As a propaganda tool, the media are considered a mouthpiece of the Party and are used as a vehicle of the Party to broadcast the government/Party line. Thus the fundamental role of the media is twofold: (1) to propagate Communist ideals and (2) to execute Party and government policies. Therefore, no editorial independence is allowed. Instead, the media are required to keep their focus of work and tone of propaganda always in accordance with the Party's policy emphasis and "basic task."

Media reform began shortly after the end of the **Great Cultural Revolution** when the Party embarked on openness and the transition of the focus from class struggle to economic development in 1978. On the one hand, the media reform was a product of the economic reform; on the other hand, the media reform was also used as a tool to promote the economic reform. But in the past two and a half decades, the media reform has had several ups and downs, and each of the ups and downs resulted from changes in the nation's political climate and the Party's policies, particularly after the anti–bourgeois-liberalization campaign in 1983, the anti-spiritual-pollution campaign in 1987, and the campaign against peaceful evolution by Western countries and overseas enemy forces after 1989.

The media reform since the late 1970s can be divided into four stages. The first stage was from the late 1970s to the early 1980s, with a focus on media development and technical improvement of media performance. The second stage was from the early 1980s to the mid-1980s and centered on the operation of the media and media organizations' financial structures. The third stage was from the mid-1980s until the Tiananmen prodemocracy event in 1989 and started to address the issues related to the role of media in political democratization. The fourth stage began after the Tiananmen prodemocracy event and lasted throughout the 1990s, with a new direction toward marketization and commercialization of the media industry.

In the late 1970s and early 1980s, changes first occurred in the form of renouncing the drab writing and reporting style that had marked the ultraleftist reign during the Great Cultural Revolution, with an attempt to return to the earlier ideals of the Party media and to more effectively promote the Party's new "reform" and **Open Door** policies. The definition of media as instruments of class struggle was officially dropped; instead, the media were considered instruments of economic and cultural construction, and a new stress was placed on economic information and entertainment. Not only did reporters begin to emphasize truthfulness, brevity, timeliness, liveliness, and readability, but also the scope of reporting was broadened—human interest stories, accident/disaster news, and crime reportage appeared in the media. News reports that were critical of the daily work and wrongdoing of low-ranking Party and government officials became available.

Media reform reached a new stage around the mid-1980s. Although operational changes were the most conspicuous, demands for greater editorial independence were raised, and some fundamental structural and even ideological changes were also taking shape. The Party even once declared that editorial autonomy would be permitted so long as editorial decisions were in line with the Party's policies. Thus operational, structural, and ideological changes were seen as intertwined. News organizations were given more editorial autonomy, Party control over the media was relatively relaxed, and unprecedentedly, **press freedom** even became an overt issue for advocates of media reform.

After the mid-1980s, media reform became critical of the Soviet model and began overtly or covertly involving fundamental Communist concepts as to whether media are the Party's tool or whether the people should take precedence over the Party. Also, press legislation was one of the hot topics of debate. Articles that questioned the Party's monopoly of the media appeared publicly. In this stage, democratization became a key issue in the struggle for media reform. In the meanwhile, concepts and practices from Western countries and from Hong Kong and Taiwan, whose media had formerly been condemned as negative examples, were being partially adopted. Particularly, the media's role as a watchdog of the people and a surveillance and supervision force of the Party and the government was brought up. For years, these concepts had been taboos in China. Shifting from seeing them as the major features of "decadent" Western media, some journalists and intellectuals championed these concepts for their positive contribution to China's political development.

Since the Tiananmen prodemocracy event in 1989, the media reform has suffered a major setback that was apparent both in journalistic practice and in theoretic discussion. Combating the "peaceful transformation" by the West remained a priority until the early 1990s. The media were again instructed to fulfill didactic and exhortatory responsibilities by providing "correct" direction to the public and arousing people's confidence in and enthusiasm for the Communist system. At the same time, restrictions on editors and reporters increased. Media reform then turned to a new direction: marketization and commercialization of the media industry. Editorial independence and political liberalization of the media were stopped. One by one, various restrictions have been issued. In the meantime, market forces have rapidly penetrated every aspect of media operations. Although the market mechanism had been part of media reform from the beginning, the issue of media commercialization was not a focus of the movement. In recent years, commercialization has assumed an astonishing pace in every aspect of the media. Although the media, except for a very few, still remain state owned, they have become self-sustaining, and the pressures from market competition have forced most media organizations to focus only on revenues and profits. In the name of media reform, various kinds of commercial sponsorships, sensational reporting and lurid description of crimes, and vulgar tabloids surfaced. Corruption in journalism, such as exchanging "red bags," a trade of favors, for airing one another's promotional pieces, is rampant and has replaced the earlier years' efforts to reveal social and Party problems and to denounce government officials' wrongdoings.

In spite of all these twists and turns, and regardless of whether the media reform should really be called a "reform" or merely an "adjustment," overall it has had a profound impact on China's media. The media have changed so much during the past two and a half decades that they are now conspicuously distinguishable from the media of the past in the following aspects: (1) the media are much more developed and modernized; (2) the media are much more accessible to average people; (3) the media are much more internationalized; (4) the media are much more commercialized; (5) the media are much more professional; and (6) the media are much more diversified. Changes in all these aspects swept across all media organizations in China, which moved steadfastly away from the nearly total politicization and regimentation that characterized the prereform years. Nevertheless, the most important impact of the media reform is one that may not be as visible: the media reform has actually contributed to erosion of the Party's power and the Communist ideology. Although the Party's original purpose in the media reform was to consolidate the Communist system, all these changes have liberalized the system. However, the media reform has not changed the Party's fundamental concept of media, and the essential role of the media has remained static. The media are still considered the Party's mouthpiece, and the Party continues to exercise blunt forms of media censorship. The media reform still goes on, but most of the efforts are once again concentrated on operational and technical levels. The media are in the process of a reform that must weather sporadic setbacks.

See also Internet; Media Bodies, Central and Local; Media Distribution; Press Control; Telecommunications Industry; Television; Television Institute and Self-Learning.

Bibliography

Chu, Leonard, "Continuity and Change in China's Media Reform," *Journal of Communication* 44, no. 3 (summer 1994): 4–21; Hong, Junhao, *The Internationalization of Television in China: The Evolution of Ideology, Society, and Media since the Reform* (Westport, CT: Praeger, 1998); Zhao, Yuezhi, *Media, Market, and Democracy in China: Between the Party Line and the Bottom Line* (Urbana: University of Illinois Press, 1998).

Junhao Hong

Mediation Practices

Chinese mediation, or *tiaojie*, refers to a conventional use of intermediaries (usually social elites such as gentry and government officials) in resolving interpersonal/intergroup conflicts and in maintaining harmony at various levels of Chinese society. Unlike the function of mediation in the West, Chinese mediation is a dominant approach to **conflict resolution**. It is preferred over litigation. In the cultural tradition, while litigation is endorsed by legalism, mediation is the way of Confucianism. With the triumph of Confucianism over legalism in the second century B.C. by becoming the government-endorsed philosophy, it is understandable why mediation has become the established approach to conflict resolution in Chinese society.

Chinese mediation can be described as a process of mediated compromise or win-win solution via active and sometimes "coercive" moral education/persuasion by the mediator in conjunction with a mix of Confucian, Marxist, Maoist, and capitalist ideologies in the context of communal pressure. The disputants are expected to rise up to selflessness, to forgive one another, and to begin to treat one another like members of the same family through the mediation process. To be neutral, to respect individual choice, and to respect the privacy of disputants are not on the priority list of the Chinese mediator. His/her goal is to teach each disputant a moral lesson, end the dispute, and keep the community and the state in a state of harmony and stability. Sometimes, when necessary, the mediator involves the significant others of each disputant, such as parents, spouses, friends, and supervisors, in the process of persuading/coercing the disputing parties to end the dispute for the communal good. Self-sacrifice for the good of the community is thought to be more honorable than seeking an individual's justice.

In contrast, mediation in the West, particularly in the United States and Canada, is proconflict rather than proharmony. It puts special emphasis on the individual goals of fairness, justice, equality, equity, and the disputants' autonomy in finding their own solution to the conflict. In China, mediation is used as a civic approach to conflict resolution to achieve humanistic ends of molding disputants into more morally conscious gentlemanhood, a concept derived from the Confucian concept of an ideal personality that is peaceful, relational, public-good oriented, community conscious, and loyal to the state. In the West, mediation is conceptualized primarily as a means to maximize legitimate individual interests such as saving time, money, and emotional strains, instead of persuading both sides to be more sensitive to the needs and interests of the opponent.

While mediation in the West emphasizes assertiveness rather than aggressiveness and avoidance, mediation in China stresses humility, avoidance, tolerance, forgiving, and pardon. While Western mediation is largely based on moderate individualism and rationalism, Chinese mediation is largely based on collectivism and Confucian relationalism.

In fact, Chinese culture can be regarded as a culture of mediation. Chinese mediation practice reflects the principles of Confucianism. Mediation is a part of the refinement expected of every educated member of the society. It is in conformity with the Confucian principle of "the middle path" or *zhongyong-zhidao*, which means avoiding going to extremes in handling a conflict. With the goal of maintaining or repairing the interpersonal relationship, mediation is consistent with the Confucian values of social harmony or *hexie* and benevolence or *ren*. As an indirect form of conflict resolution, mediation is consistent with the Confucian preference for indirectness in handling a conflict and avoidance of confrontation, sensitivity to mutual concerns about face, and respect for mutual human dignity and honor.

In using social elites and persons of good moral standing as mediators, Chinese mediation reflects the Confucian view of social hierarchy and its value of elites' rule. Because Chinese mediation is based on the Confucian value of moral refinement, social hierarchy, and relative justice, it does not strive to establish a professional process. Mediators do not seek absolute justice and equality in resolving conflicts, which characterize mediation in the West, but rather mutual forgiving. As an equivalent of a combination of Western analytical concepts and practices such as mediation, arbitration, education, therapy, counseling, consulting, and negotiation, Chinese mediation is a holistic cultural practice consistent with the holistic nature of Confucianism and the Chinese worldview.

Given the process and nature of Chinese mediation, Chinese mediators employ techniques and strategies with unique Chinese characteristics to mediate conflicts. Some of the most common techniques include using general moral/ideological education/persuasion on both the parties, convincing disputing parties to make concessions, and inducing disputing parties to engage in mutual apology and self-criticism. The mediator, in facilitating the process, provides assistance in reducing the conflict. In the case of a dispute between husband and wife, where a wife wants to divorce a husband who has lost his job, for example, the mediator may have the woman ponder the stressful jobless situation of her unfortunate husband. The mediator may even involve friends and relatives and let them add additional moral lessons and pressure so as to end the conflict. Western mediators do not usually explicitly moralize. They try to maintain neutrality and guide the process on the basis of laws and regulations. Typical Western mediation techniques include listening, paraphrasing, summarization, and presenting all available options to the disputing parties to choose from. These Western techniques of mediation are rarely found in Chinese mediation.

Chinese mediation has a long history. As early as the Ming dynasty (1368–1644), rulers required village leaders and elders to mediate interpersonal, interfamily, and interclan disputes. Disputants were encouraged by the county magistrate to use mediation to handle their conflict peacefully rather than through litigation. Both the disputants who brought the case to the magistrate for a legal resolution would be caned fifty times before they would be allowed to tell their stories, regardless of who was right or wrong. The assumption was that the two disputing parties who brought the case to the magistrate were morally incompetent members of the community who needed to be penalized. As a result, very few cases were brought to them. In the Kangxi era (1662–1722) of the Qing dynasty, the Kangxi emperor and his ministers scared people into avoiding the use of litigation.

In Communist China, mediation was transformed to be class differentiated in light of Marxism and Maoism. During the early times of the revolution, in the areas under the Chinese Communist Party's control such as Yan'an and other Red bases years before 1949, class camaraderie was the ground for forgiveness. This later became an institutionalized practice after the founding of the People's Republic of China. Because the Chinese Communist Party's Marxist and Maoist ideology was the official ideology, the Confucian foundation of mediation was also transformed. Mediation after 1949 used the Marxist and Maoist ideology as the formal and official guidance, but the Confucian principles were nonetheless deeply embedded in mediation practices. For example, mediation was used only as a civic means to resolve conflicts among the people. Conflicts between the people and the enemy classes, such as the "five kinds" that include landlords, rich peasants, reactionaries, the bad elements, and rightists (*di, fu, fan, huai*, and *you*), could only be resolved through class struggle. In 1954, mediation committees became official at the national level with the passage of the Provisional Organizational Principles for the People's Mediation Committees. In the mid-1950s, after communes were established in rural areas and neighborhood committees in **cities**, these units were often the final mediators and arbitrators of local conflicts. There were about 950,000 mediation committees that consisted of 6,000,000 mediators in China in 1987, and 133,000 workplace mediation committees that consisted of 1 million voluntary employee mediators. The figures probably remain about the same today.

Since Deng Xiaoping's economic reform began in 1978, mediation, as a practice and an institution, has been reshaped to bridge Confucianism, Marxism, and capitalism. For the first time in Chinese history, mediation has begun to use the economic scale as a complementary tool in addition to the Marxist ideological framework and the Confucian moralization. More than half the disputes are resolved through mediation. Mediation is also preferred and practiced in dealing with China's disputes with foreign counterparts. The Provisional Rules of Procedure of the Maritime Arbitration Commission of the China Council for the Promotion of International Trade, for example, stipulate that the Maritime Arbitration Commission may use mediation in dealing with related conflicts. China's Foreign Economic and Trade Arbitration Commission also values mediation in resolving international economic and trade conflicts.

In a way, China remains a nation of mediation. As China has moved deeper into the process of globalization, there has been a stronger and stronger demand to adopt the rule of law to protect disputants' rights and interests and to maintain equality and justice. Therefore, mediation for face, relational harmony, and social stability is under pressure to change. However, the Chinese preference for mediation is expected to remain strong regardless of such pressures because of the country's vibrant cultural tradition.

See also Confucian Tradition and Christianity; Corporate Governance; Human Resource Management (HRM); Legal Infrastructure Development and Economic Development; Management Education.

Bibliography

Clarke, Donald C., "Dispute Resolution in China," in *Contract, Guanxi, and Dispute Resolution in China*, ed. Tahirih V. Lee, 369–420 (New York: Garland Publishing, 1997); Jia, Wenshan, "Chinese Mediation and Its Cultural Foundation," in *Chinese Conflict Management and Resolution*, ed. Guo-Ming Chen and Ringo Ma, 289–295 (New York: Garland Publishing, 2002); Ren, Jianxin, "Mediation, Conciliation, Arbitration, and Litigation in the People's Republic of China," *International Business Lawyer*, October 1987, 363–367; Wall, James A., Jr., and Michael Blum, "Community Mediation in the People's Republic of China," *Journal of Conflict Resolution* 35 (1991): 3–20.

Wenshan Jia

Medical Provision, Structure of

According to official statistics, the Chinese population reached nearly 1.3 billion in 2002. There were 330,348 medical institutions and 4,507,700 health professionals, including 2,099,658 physicians, in the country in 2001. The current life expectancy of the Chinese population is 68.7 years for males and 73.0 years for females. Since the establishment of the People's Republic of China, health care provision in China has made significant improvement, as shown in table 6.

Composition of Hospitals

The hospital system in China is composed of following types of hospitals:

- General hospitals are the backbone of the Chinese hospital system. A general hospital is a full-service hospital with a full range of medical specialties within its organization. The bigger a general hospital is, the more specialized its departments become. There are four levels of general hospitals, including the national level (A-1 or A-2 levels), provincial level (A-3 or A-4 levels), municipal level (B level), and county level (C level). The national-level general hospitals are the largest hospitals, are equipped with advanced medical equipment, and recruit the best medical experts in the nation. They are the national clinical and medical training centers. Many medical college or university-affiliated hospitals are also national-level general hospitals. Each province, municipality, or county has at least one provincial-, municipal-, or county-level hospital, respectively, that is the largest and the best in equipment and personnel

TABLE 6
Improvement of Medical Provision in China

	No. of Hospitals	No. of Hospital Beds	No. of Physicians
1949	2,600	80,000	363,400
1957	4,179	295,000	546,300
1965	42,711	766,000	762,800
1975	62,425	1,598,000	877,700
1980	65,450	1,982,000	1,153,200
1985	59,614	2,229,000	1,413,300
1990	62,454	2,624,000	1,763,100
1992	61,352	2,744,000	1,808,200
1993	60,800	2,794,800	1,831,700
1995	68,000	2,331,300	1,913,200
2001	65,424	3,201,248	2,099,658

Note: The falling number of hospitals in 2001 is a result of the government's effort to merge small hospitals into larger and better-equipped ones.

Source: Ministry of Public Health.

in its locality. In general, provincial-level hospitals have 500 to 800 patient beds, municipal-level hospitals have 300 to 500 patient beds, and county hospitals have 150 to 300 patient beds.

- Specialized hospitals specialize in certain major medical specialties such as tumors, plastic surgery, and so on. Specialized hospitals are usually large A-level hospitals.

- Teaching hospitals are hospitals affiliated with medical colleges and universities. These are also usually large A-level hospitals.

- Enterprise-affiliated employee hospitals are hospitals affiliated with and run by large **state-owned enterprises (SOEs)** with more than 5,000 employees or state-owned enterprises in remote areas with more than 3,000 employees. They are often open to the public especially if they are large. Large, medium, and small enterprise-affiliated employee hospitals in general are equivalent to provincial-, municipal-, and county-level hospitals, respectively, in terms of their size, equipment, and medical expertise.

According to Chinese medical theory, these black beetles can enrich a liquor that is used to improve potency.

- Military hospitals: The army has its own medical care system, and its hospitals, where workload allows, also accept civilian patients.

- Traditional Chinese medicine hospitals treat patients using traditional Chinese medical theory, therapies, and medicines.

- Traditional Chinese and Western medicine integration hospitals attempt to treat patients by combining Western and traditional Chinese medical theories, therapies, and medicines. Recent developments, as indicated in table 7, show that the total number of facilities is trending lower. However, local and preventive facilities are on a rising trend.

The technical capabilities of all Chinese hospitals have been assessed by the government in recent years and divided in A, B, and C levels, with the A level being the largest and the C level being the smallest. Hospitals are classfied based on their size, medical services, and research and teaching facilities. A-, B-, and C-level hospitals have 500+, 300+, and 150+ patient beds, respectively.

Since 2000, medical institutions in China have also been subjected to new classified administration by the government as either nonprofit or profit-making medical institutions. Different fiscal and taxation policies have been developed for these two different categories of medical institutions.

Nonprofit medical institutions continue to be the primary providers of health care in the country and enjoy preferential fiscal and taxation policies. State-owned profit-making medical institutions can enjoy some fiscal assistance, but their fee structure must reflect this assistance. Other nonprofit medical

TABLE 7
Number of Medical Institutions in China in 2001

Type of Medical Institution	Number in 2001	Number in 2003
Total medical institutions*	330,348	291,323
Hospitals (General)	16,781	17,764
Rehabilitation centers	461	305
Health centers	48,643	45,204
Outpatient clinics	3,716	3,584
Other clinics, health centers, and enterprise clinics	244,345	204,468
Mother and child health care facilities	2,548	3,033
Specialized disease-prevention stations	1,783	1,749

*This is a partial list. Local institutions, such as Immunization Administration stations and R & D centers, are not listed although they are included in the "Total medical institutions" number.

Source: Ministry of Public Health.

institutions that do not receive government funding support are allowed to set their fees freely and pay taxes accordingly.

Medical and Health Care Provision in Urban Areas

Medical and health care provision in urban areas is a three-level network. Level 1 is composed of neighborhood clinics or enterprise-affiliated clinics; level 2 is composed of municipal-level general hospitals, specialized prevention or health centers, and enterprise-affiliated employee hospitals; and level 3 is composed of provincial-level general hospitals, teaching hospitals, and large enterprise-affiliated employee hospitals. Patients are treated first by the level 1 health centers and are, if necessary, transferred to level 2 and 3 hospitals based on a referral system.

Medical and Health Care Provision in Rural Areas

Medical and health care provision in rural areas is also a three-level network. Level 1 is composed of village clinics; level 2 is township health centers; and level 3 is county hospitals. Patients are treated first by the level 1 village clinics and are, if necessary, transferred to level 2 or 3 hospitals based on a referral system.

Sanitariums and Rehabilitation Hospitals/Centers

The network of sanitariums and rehabilitation hospitals in China treats patients with a variety of therapies based on traditional Chinese medicine and Western medicine. While sanitariums have been built since the 1950s mainly to treat war veterans, senior officials, and workers involved in work-related accidents, rehabilitation hospitals/centers have been built only since the early 1980s, when rehabilitation medicine received the attention of the medical profession and the government. Most of the sanitariums and rehabilitation hospitals/centers are owned and operated by the state. Many larger hospitals have now established their own rehabilitation medicine departments. According to statistics of the Ministry of Public Health, there were 582 sanitariums with 115,983 beds in China in 1995 and 204,468 beds in 2003.

See also Health Care Reform; Pharmaceutical Industry, Administrative and Regulatory Structures of; Pharmaceutical Products, Sales and Marketing of.

Bibliography

Editorial Committee, State Drug Administration, *State Drug Administration Yearbook 2002* (Beijing: State Drug Administration Yearbook Press, 2003); Editorial Committee of the China Health Yearbook, *China Health Yearbook* (Beijing: People's Health Publishing House, 2002 and 2003); Editorial Committee of the China Pharmaceutical Yearbook, *China Pharmaceutical Yearbook* (various issues, 2001–2003) (Beijing: China Publishing House); Shen, James, *Marketing Pharmaceuticals in China* (Whippany, NJ: Wicon International, 2001).

Jian Shen

Migrant Population

The migrant population in China can be categorized into two groups: the migrant population and the floating population. The term "migrant population" refers to those who must obtain governmental permission, undergo certain procedures of official household registration, move from a place of departure

Many migrant workers are hired for construction projects, like the one shown here.

to a place of destination, and then permanently settle down. That is, to migrate, one needs an official change of permanent residence. The Chinese terminology for this kind of migrant is *renkou qianyi*. In contrast, the "floating population" consists of people who have in fact not migrated but simply "float and move." Floating people may engage in partial temporary relocation but maintain ties with their original place of abode, where their permanent residence registration stays. Thus the floating population is not, and will not become, a permanently settled group. In Chinese parlance, the floating population is called *renkou liudong*. Both *renkou qianyi* and *renkou liudong* are referred to as internal migration because the migration takes place within the Chinese political territory, either within a province, across provinces, or between rural and urban areas.

Three major flows of the migrant population have occurred during the period from 1950 to the present. The first two occurred during the 1960s and 1970s, and the third took place in the late 1990s. During the 1960s, a nationwide urban-rural migration flow occurred through which thousands of educated young people (primarily high-school students) answered the call from the Communist Party and Chairman **Mao Zedong** to go down to the countryside to "receive education from the poor and lower-middle class." This flow occurred during the **Great Cultural Revolution (1966–1976)**. These young people came basically from urban areas and moved to rural areas within or across provinces. Their purpose was not to move away from their urban families permanently but only to "receive education from the peasants." However, over time many of these urban young people got married and settled down in the countryside, thus becoming part of the migrant population. The second major migration was just the opposite, the counterflow to the urban-rural migration. In other words, the young people who had previously moved from urban areas to rural areas were now starting to move back to urban areas. This rural-urban migration took place as a combined result of the end of the Great Cultural Revolution, the advent of the economic reform, and the Open Door policy adopted by the Chinese government since the late 1970s and early 1980s. The third major migration began in the late 1990s and continues into the present decade in response to the construction of the Three Gorges Dam on China's Yangtze River, because of which an estimated 1.4 to 1.9 million migrants have to relocate.

A geographic landscape of an overall distribution of a migrant population can be shown by the net in-migration rates among three districts, each encompassing provinces and autonomous regions: the eastern regions (ten), the central regions (twelve), and the western regions (five). During the thirty-year period from 1950 to 1980, the eastern provinces remained the district with the most in-migrants, followed by the central provinces, while the western provinces had the fewest in-migrants. In spite of disparities in the volume of migration, a common feature of these districts was that the net rates of in-migration increased during the period. According to Chinese government statistics (1991), the net in-migration rates for the eastern provinces, for example, rose from 60 percent in 1955 to 70 percent in 1980; the net in-migration rates for the central provinces went up from 67 percent in 1955 to 75 percent in 1980; the rates for the western provinces increased from 60 percent in 1955 to 71 percent in 1980. In the country as a whole, the net in-migration rates rose from 63 percent in 1955 to 72 percent in 1980. Mean-while, the net out-migration rates decreased from 37 percent in 1955 to 27 percent in 1980.

Like the patterns of migration in the rest of the world, the characteristics of the migrant population in China are selective in gender, age, occupation, and educational attainment. An overview of the total interprovincial migrant popu-lation in the country demonstrates that the male migrant population outnum-bers the female migrant population. The dominance of male migration over female suggests relative gender inequality in terms of employment, job re-allocation, doing business, receiving education, and retirement. Of all age groups, three appear to be the peak groups who migrate. According to a sur-vey conducted in the city of Beijing in 1987, the age group twenty to twenty-four was ranked first with about 38.6 percent of all migrants, followed by the age group fifteen to nineteen with 18.7 percent and the age group thirty to thirty-four with 10.3 percent. In terms of the occupations of the inter-provincial migrants, workers engaged in production and transportation were the most likely migrants, with 32.7 percent, followed by laborers engaged in farming, forestry, animal husbandry, and fishery, with 31.2 percent. Profes-sional and technical personnel ranked third in the migrant population at 14.5 percent. Last, people who were engaged in commerce and services were the fourth-largest migrant population, accounting for about 11.7 percent.

Apart from the migrant population (*renkou qianyi*) mentioned earlier, the floating population (*renkou liudong*) has obtained great momentum since the economic reform in the late 1970s. As reported by the state statistical bureau, in the year 1982 the estimated volume of the floating population in the coun-try reached 30 million. By 1985, the number rose to 40 million. In 1987, this figure rose to 60 million. On average, the net growth of the floating population has been around 10 million every year and has a tendency to increase. With re-gard to the directions of these "floaters," the donor areas are the rural areas, whereas the host areas are **cities**, in general, and the metropolitan areas, in par-ticular. The general pattern of the floating population is that the bigger the city, the larger the volume. The motivations and reasons for the floating migrants are multifaceted. Prior to 1980, population floating was social in nature, for ex-ample, a visit to friends or relatives, an appointment with a doctor, or hospital-ization. After 1980, however, people floated primarily for economic and business purposes and included but were not limited to job seekers, contract workers, cleaners, baby-sitters, businessmen, and family housekeepers. With regard to the sex and age compositions of the floating population, men, at 72 percent, outnumber women, at 28 percent. The dominant age group is pro-duction laborers aged fifteen to fifty-four years. These floaters are primarily sur-plus laborers from the vast countryside.

The occurrence and the volume of the migrant population in China are char-acterized by selection, strict control, and limitation. The specific characteris-tics of the Chinese migration lie in and are largely determined by the country's social, economic, and political system, which is characterized by **central plan-ning**. That is, theoretically, migration goes as planned. For example, the Chi-nese government has adopted a policy that controls the development of bigger cities, seeks to moderately develop medium-sized cities, but actively promotes the development of small cities. This policy provides direction and sets limits to rural-urban migration. This explains partially why the country's rural-urban migration tends to be slower and fluctuates over time.

In general, the migrant population in the country during the last half century has been affected by two major factors: the central planning system and the market system. Under the central planning system during the thirty years from 1950 to 1980, the migrant population was based on governmental planning that was strictly enforced nationwide. The economic reform since the late 1970s set the stage for a potential flow of migration. The shift of the governmental focus to economic construction and the adoption of the audacious **Open Door policy** have provided a political, social, and economic environment for interprovincial, rural-urban, or even urban-rural migration, including floating migration, especially during the last two decades of the twentieth century. However, the volume of the permanent migrant population is still controlled except for a dramatic surge of the "floating population." In fact, China's economic reform has not led to much change in policy on rural-urban migration, nor is it having a great impact on permanent migration. China's migration policy is still based on central planning even under the present market system.

See also International Migration and Overseas Chinese; Urbanization and Migration.

Bibliography

Agarwal, Anil, and Narain S. Agarwal, "Global Warming in an Unequal World: A Case of Environmental Colonialism," in *Green Planet Blues*, ed. Michael Alberty and Geoffrey D. Dabelko (Boulder, CO: Westview Press, 1997); Solinger, Dorothy J., *Contesting Citizenship in Urban China: Peasant Migrants, the State, and the Logic of the Market* (Berkeley: University of California Press, 1999); Weeks, John R., *Population: An Introduction to Concepts and Issues*, 9th ed. (Belmont, CA: Thompson Wadsworth Learning, 2004); Yuan, Yongxi, Li Muzhen, Zhang Xuexin, Fang Litian, and Xu Shaoyu, eds., *Chinese Population (Zhongguo Renkou)* (Beijing: China Finance and Economics Publishing House, 1991).

Jianjun Ji

Migration

See International Migration and Overseas Chinese; Migrant Population; Urbanization and Migration.

Military Ranking and Promotion

China's army, air, naval, and strategic missile forces are collectively known as the Chinese People's Liberation Army (PLA). During the Chinese civil war of 1946–1949, the Chinese Communist Party (CCP) reorganized its armed forces into the PLA in September 1949. Since the founding of the People's Republic of China (PRC) in October 1949, the PLA has experienced some major changes in its ranking and promotion systems.

After the **Korean War** ended in 1953, the PLA reorganized its services into a Soviet-style structure. As part of his effort to reform the PLA, Marshal Peng Dehuai, vice chairman of the CCP Central Military Commission (CMC), established a Soviet-style system of military ranks in 1955. Some of the CCP leaders opposed the new ranking system because it changed the PLA tradition of equality among soldiers and commanders. **Mao Zedong**, chairman of the CCP and the CMC, approved the new ranking system and awarded for the first and only time in PLA history the rank of marshal to ten of the PLA's top commanders in September 1955. In May 1992, the last marshal, Marshal Nie Rongzhen, died. Currently the highest military rank in China is full general.

Besides the ten marshals, the PLA named ten chief generals, fifty-seven full generals, 175 lieutenant generals, and 800 major generals among its commanders in September 1955. The ranking system survived after Peng was accused by Mao of forming a "right opportunist clique" and conducting "unprincipled factional activity," charges that often meant pro-Soviet political positions, and removed him from his post as minister of defense in 1959. Before 1965, two more lieutenant generals and 560 more major generals were named in the Chinese services.

At the beginning of the **Great Cultural Revolution (1966–1976)**, Marshal Lin Biao criticized Peng's reform and the PLA ranking system as part of the "Soviet revisionist military structure." As the defense minister and vice chairman of the CMC, Lin abolished the ranking system in 1966. Lin was killed in a plane crash in Mongolia after his anti-Mao plot, or "counterrevolutionary clique," failed in September 1971. Although Lin's military doctrine was abandoned and his top commanders were purged in the early 1970s, no ranking and promotion system was resumed in the PLA until 1988.

In June 1981, Deng Xiaoping replaced **Hua Guofeng** as chairman of the CMC and chief of the PLA General Staff. Deng launched a large-scale military reform. In 1982, Deng established a Military System Reform Leading Group in the CMC. In 1985, Deng declared that the threat of a major war with the Western powers was remote. A new world war or a major nuclear war no longer seemed imminent. Instead, Deng forecast a more likely scenario that the PLA would be fighting a "limited war" and "local war." Deng's reforming efforts focused on the development and improvement of PLA technology and weaponry and the reduction of PLA troops. He downsized the PLA forces by 1 million troops in 1985–1987. By the late 1980s, the PLA reduced its size down to about 3 million. In 1988, after the personnel reduction was complete, the PLA reintroduced the ranking system in all its services.

In 1989, Jiang Zemin became the chairman of both the CCP and the CMC. In the early 1990s, Jiang launched a new military reform known as the "two transformations." According to Jiang, the PLA should be transformed from an army prepared to fight local wars under ordinary conditions to an army prepared to fight and win "local wars under modern high-tech conditions," and from an army based on quantity to an army based on quality. This recent effort at comprehensive reform and modernization appears to be cutting across every facet of PLA activity, especially affecting organizational structure and personnel appointments. Jiang paid close attention to personnel policy and has promoted more than fifty officers to the rank of full general. It was reported that in the

1990s, Jiang himself insisted on reviewing the files of any officer recommended for promotion down to the level of division commander. By the end of 1999, the PLA had forty-two full generals.

During the 1990s reform, Jiang also emphasized regulation and standardization of PLA ranking and promotion. The Standing Committee of the Ninth **National People' Congress** revised the existing Regulations on Active-Service Officers of the Chinese People's Liberation Army. In December 2000, Jiang issued the Active-Service Officers Law of the People's Republic of China. In the past, officers up for promotion had been required to undergo training at only three command levels: company, regimental, and army. The new law requires training prior to promotion at every level.

The CMC has established a series of procedures for officer promotion evaluations that employ more uniform and standardized evaluation criteria. According to the Regulations on Appointments and Removals of Military Officers on Active Service, an officer will be evaluated by superior officers, peer reviews, and unit Party committees. Despite increasing efforts to promote officers on the basis of skills and merit, political reliability remains an important factor in assessing an officer's promotion. In the 2000 Active Service Officers Law, "loyalty to the Communist Party" and "having firmly held revolutionary ideals" are requirements for all officers.

The selection and promotion processes of noncommissioned officers (NCOs) are more regularized and merit based. According to the Regulations on Military Service of Active-Duty Servicemen (1999) and the Regulations for Managing Noncommissioned Officers (2001), noncommissioned officers are selected through a process of application by the candidate. Then a "grassroots unit" (battalion and below) makes a recommendation. A military committee evaluates the application and recommendation. After the committee's approval, an examination is given by a military unit to the candidate. Selection is based on training and skills, with priority given to personnel who hold state-issued certifications for professional qualifications. There are six grades within the noncommissioned officer corps. Promotion from one grade to another involves increases in pay and benefits. The PLA General Staff Department is responsible for managing noncommissioned officers in all military units.

The current officers' ranking and promotion systems are designed to transform the PLA into a military force founded on quality. The scale of this endeavor is measured not just in the vast numbers involved, but also in the breadth of the intellectual leap the PLA officer corps, NCO corps, and enlisted troops have to make in this transformation from a labor-intensive to an expertise-intensive force.

See also Armed Forces, Reforms of; Jiang Zemin (1926–), Populism of; Military Service System.

Bibliography

Allen, Kenneth, Dean Cheng, David Finkelstein, and Maryanne Kivlehan, *Institutional Reforms of the Chinese People's Liberation Army: Overview and Challenges* (Alexandria, VA: CNA Corporation, 2002); Joffe, Ellis, *The Chinese Army after Mao* (Cambridge, MA: Harvard University Press, 1987); Shambaugh, David, ed., *China's Military in Transition* (Oxford: Clarendon Press, 1997); Xinhua News Agency, *China's National Defense*, China's Defense White Papers (Beijing, 1998, 1999, 2000, and 2001); Zhang, Jie, and Xiaobing Li, eds., *Social Transition in China* (Lanham, MD: University Press of America, 1998).

Xiaobing Li

Military Service System

The Chinese military services, collectively called the People's Liberation Army (PLA), had a total of more than 2.3 million troops on active duty in 2002. The military services include 1.6 million ground forces, 420,000 air force personnel, 250,000 naval personnel, and 110,000 strategic missile forces. The PLA service and recruitment system has experienced some major changes since the Chinese Communist Party (CCP) reorganized and centralized its armed forces into the PLA in September 1949.

During the Chinese civil war of 1946–1949, the PLA adopted a universal service system to recruit new soldiers for the Communist armed forces. When the PLA controlled China, except **Tibet** and Taiwan, it had a total of 5.5 million troops as of October 1949. After its victory, the PLA reduced its forces to 4 million by the summer of 1950.

In October 1950, the PLA became fully involved in the **Korean War** by sending troops to Korea. The Chinese troops in Korea were called the Chinese People's Volunteer Force (CPVF). In fact, the CPVF troops were PLA troops assigned to the Korean War. The CPVF command actually served as the PLA's front command in Korea. The CCP hoped that using the name "volunteers" instead of the PLA would convince the world that the CPVF troops were organized by Chinese volunteers, not the Chinese government, in order to avoid a direct state of war with the United States and the other fifteen nations that had joined the United Nations forces in Korea. A total of 3 million Chinese troops participated in the Korean War from 1950 to 1953. To meet the manpower needed in its foreign war, the PLA increased its forces to 6.11 million by January 1952.

After the Korean Armistice was signed in July 1953, the PLA began a mass demobilization. In 1954, the PLA replaced the universal military service system with the compulsory service system during peacetime. The State Council announced the New System of Compulsory Military Service on December 16, 1954. From 1956 to 1958, the PLA experienced another major reduction of its forces. By the end of 1958, there were about 2.4 million PLA troops in China. The length of mandatory service for soldiers in the ground forces was three years. Those assigned to the technical services in the PLA Navy and Air Force served four years. The PLA had

Military police patrol in Beijing's Tiananmen Square.

two mechanisms for maintaining technical expertise among enlisted personnel. First, there was the lengthy initial three- or four-year period of mandatory service. Second, conscripts were permitted to voluntarily extend their periods of service for up to six years. In some cases, these volunteers were then given the option to serve for up to an additional eight to twelve years.

In the 1960s, the tensions in the **Taiwan Strait crisis**, the Sino-Indian War, and the Sino-Soviet confrontation demanded more servicemen. The **Great Cultural Revolution** became a nationwide mass movement in China in the summer of 1966. **Mao Zedong**, chairman of the CCP, decided to employ the PLA to restore social and political order and prevent possible civil war in the country. Moving to center stage, the PLA took over the civilian governments at provincial, district, city, and township levels through its military administrations, or military administrative committees, in 1967–1970. The PLA units used their officers as representatives for schools, factories, companies, and farms. PLA involvement in local affairs contributed to another increase in the Chinese military services. By the middle of the 1970s, the PLA numbered more than 6 million troops.

In 1975, Deng Xiaoping became the chief of the PLA General Staff after his return from the Cultural Revolution (1966–1976), in which he had lost all of his positions in the Party, government, and military from 1966 to 1975. Deng started a new military reform by demobilizing 600,000 men. Thereafter, the PLA began a series of reductions. By 1982, active-duty servicemen were reduced to 4.2 million.

In 1985, the Chinese government announced that the PLA would once again reduce its troops by 1 million men. On April 4, 1987, the PLA spokesman made a public announcement that the PLA had accomplished its goal. According to China's national census of 1990, the PLA then had a total of 3.2 million servicemen and women.

In 1989, Jiang Zemin became the chairman of both the CCP and the CCP's Central Military Commission (CMC). In the early 1990s, Jiang launched a new military reform known as the "two transformations." Jiang announced that the PLA should be transformed from an army prepared to fight local wars under ordinary conditions to an army prepared to fight and win "local wars under modern high-tech conditions," and from an army based on quantity to an army based on quality. Jiang's reform effort of comprehensive modernization in the 1990s appears to be cutting across every facet of the PLA system. It has especially affected the service system and organizations. The reform was focused on reducing headquarters personnel by 20 to 50 percent.

In September 1997, Jiang announced at the CCP Fifteenth National Congress that the PLA would be reduced by 500,000 troops in the next year. On July 28, 1998, the *White Papers of China's Defense* stated that the PLA had accomplished its goal of reduction, and it would maintain the current 2.5 million troops. Almost half the total members were enlisted conscripts.

The current service system of the PLA is based on conscription. In December 1998, the Chinese government revised its Military Service Law. In July 1999, the PLA revised its Regulations on Military Service of Active-Duty Servicemen of the Chinese People's Liberation Army. According to the new law and regulations, the period of obligatory conscript service has been reduced from three years for soldiers in ground forces and four years for those in the

PLA's technical services to a standard two years for all of its services. These new laws and regulations were established because of domestic political pressures from rural areas, where farm families were complaining about the loss of their sons' labor for as long as four years.

According to the current service system, upon entry into the first year of service, a newly conscripted soldier is given the rank of private second class. Upon completion of the first year of service, the private second class is given the rank of private first class. For those second-year soldiers who decide to spend more than two years in the military, their promotion means selection as a noncommissioned officer. PLA recruitment and promotion are based predominantly on technical criteria in order to enforce the standards for qualification for conscription. However, the PLA's desire for high-tech troops and officers has to compete with a still vibrant private economic sector. The majority of the PLA's new recruits continue to come from poor rural areas. The reform and modernization of the PLA are taking place within the greater context of an ever-changing China and within the constraints of what Chinese society at large can contribute or support.

See also Armed Forces, Reforms of; Jiang Zemin (1926–   ), Populism of; Military Ranking and Promotion.

Bibliography

Allen, Kenneth, Dean Cheng, David Finkelstein, and Maryanne Kivlehan, *Institutional Reforms of the Chinese People's Liberation Army: Overview and Challenges* (Alexandria, VA: CNA Corporation, 2002); Jencks, Harlan, *From Muskets to Missiles: Politics and Professionalism in the Chinese Army, 1945–1981* (Boulder, CO: Westview Press, 1982); Li, Xiaobing, and Hongshan Li, eds., *China and the United States: A New Cold War History* (Lanham, MD: University Press of America, 1998); Lilley, James, and David Shambaugh, eds., *China's Military Faces the Future* (Armonk, NY: M. E. Sharpe, 1999); Xinhua News Agency, *China's National Defense*, China's Defense White Papers (Beijing, 1998, 1999, 2000, and 2001).

Xiaobing Li

Minority Women in Xinjiang and Taiwan

Xinjiang Uygur Autonomous Region is located in northwestern China and is in the central part of the Eurasian continent. Xinjiang as an autonomous region was established on October 1, 1953, and its capital city is Urumqi. The largest province in China, Xinjiang has an area of 1.66 million square kilometers, or 17 percent of the total territory of China. Its population is 17.47 million (according to the 1998 census), with 10.73 million persons of minority nationalities. The forty-six minority nationalities include Uygur, Han, Kazakh, Hui, Tartar, Daur, Man, Kirghiz, Mongolian, Russian, Sibo, Tajik, Uzbek, and others.

After the founding of the People's Republic of China in 1949, minority women in Xinjiang began to realize their status in society and to resume their active participation in social and political life. From then on, minority women in Xinjiang finally stepped out of the old family shadow and become a positive force in local economic construction. According to the Political Propaganda

Department of the Xinjiang Women's Federation, in December 1953, 90 percent of minority women in Xinjiang participated in the election during the first nationwide general election in China, and used their democratic right for the first time in history. In the people's congress of Xinjiang Uygur Autonomous Region, there were fifty-two women from different minority groups. There were three minority women in the national people's congress, the highest national legislative branch. As stated in Xinjiang's implementation of the Act of Protection of Women's Rights, among "the leaders in government agencies at all levels, there must be a certain percentage of females. The same is true in all state departments, social organizations, and government-run companies. It is the full responsibility of these government agencies and social organizations, as well as companies and departments, to pay attention and choose minority women in the leading positions."

The working population of minority women is 2.04 million, 45.02 percent of the total minority work force. Among them, there are some slight differences in employment percentage. The highest is among women of Dongxiang nationality, 79.2 percent; then Uygur, 76.08 percent; the third is Kirghiz, 71.72 percent; then Hui, 68.83 percent; and Kazakh and Xibo, 60.22 percent and 60.58 percent, respectively.

Birth control has a significant impact on minority women's social, political, and employment status in Xinjiang. Early marriage, early fertility, multiple births, and large families have kept women at home and have wasted their potential in the economic field. Early marriage and fertility have also reduced women's participation in society and are the main obstacle that prevents women from having more education and better professional training. According to Yili County's 1988 report, women's fatality rate in labor (giving birth) from 1985 to 1987 was 541.14 per 100,000 people. The main cause (51.9 percent) was bleeding resulting from birth complications and lack of medical facilities. Until 1990, only 26.9 percent of tribal Kazakh women gave birth in local hospitals.

Thanks to the supportive policies and regulations of the central government, the social and political status of minority women in Xinjiang has been greatly improved. Increased education and training programs for minority people not only enlarged their knowledge but also provided job opportunities. However, a small number of educated intellectuals are significantly influenced by wrongfully conceived ambitions to totally get rid of central government control and finally make Xinjiang independent. Among them are some high-ranking government officials and some so-called successful entrepreneurs. A by-product of more freedom and better economic conditions is increased nationalism and even separatism. While this is deemed undesirable, it is a fact that China must constantly deal with in the twenty-first century.

Like Xinjiang Uygur minority women, minority women in Taiwan have gone through stages toward liberation. The native Taiwan residents mainly belong to the Baiyue nationality, who used to live in southern areas of mainland China and moved to Taiwan some 6,000 years ago. It was not until 400 years ago that they had any communication with other nationalities.

At the highest level, Taiwan's minorities belong to two ethnic families, the Gaoshan nationality and the Pingpu nationality. The Gaoshan nationality is divided into nine nationalities, Taiya, Saixia, Bunong, Cao, Lukai, Paivin, Beinan, Yamei, and Saipu. They total 320,000 people, or 2 percent of Taiwan's population. The Pingpu nationality is divided into ten nationalities, Kaidajalan, Leilang, Gemalan, Daokasi, Babula, Maowajian, Bazehai, Hongya, Xilaya, and Shao. The total population is about 100,000.

In their marital systems, all of them keep their own special rituals and forms, but one thing in common and identical in all ethnic groups is that the young people base their marriage on true free love, the couple can freely have intimate association with each other and enjoy total freedom of communication, and young people can choose their own lovers and get permission from both families after they make their decision for marriage. However, when the marriage ceremony is over, they have to follow closely the formalities, disciplines, and family practices of the group.

With regard to minority women's political status and social position in Taiwanese society, because they represent a small population and because of the tradition they inherited, they are clearly ignored in today's Taiwanese politics. Women's political and social status as a whole is an increasing concern for the legislature and local governments. Because of their lack of political representation, they are obviously exploited. They have much less access to employment and educational opportunities and suffer from disadvantages in the welfare system and insurance coverage.

The structure of Taiwan's democratic system has been built from the top, unlike that in the mainland, where the government started this procedure from the bottom. Therefore, the agendas of interest groups gain much more attention than women's issues, particularly issues related to minority women. Taiwan's economic protection system favors working males. It appears that while Taiwan claims to be a free society, it lags far behind the government of the mainland in supporting women's rights. This may be due to the Communist tradition, in which equality between men and women is a foundation of the system. Nevertheless, governments on both sides of the strait need to make more efforts to improve women's social status.

See also Taiwan, Ethnicity and Ethnic Policies of; Women, Role as Mothers; Women, Social Status of.

Bibliography

The Research Study of Taiwan Native Residents (Beijing: Ethnic Publishing House, 2002); *Xinjiang Statistics Yearbook* (Beijing: China Statistics Press, 1996); *Xinjiang Yearbook* (Beijing: China Statistic Press, 1985, 1988, 1990, 1995); *Xinjiang's Forty Years* (Beijing: China Statistics Press, 1995).

Mei Zhou and Xiaoxiao Li

Misty Poetry

Misty poetry (*meng long shi*) is also translated into English as "poetry of opacity" or, in some other literatures, as "obscurist poetry." The misty school is characterized by oblique imagery and elliptical syntax and by its peculiar linguistic style, in which subject, verb tense, and the usages of number are elusive and transitions are unclear. The most important misty poetry writers are Bei Dao, Gu Cheng, Shu Ting, Duo Duo, Jiang He, Mang Ke, Yang Lian, Luo Gengye, and Liang Xiaobing.

In the beginning of the school's development, the names "misty" or "opacity" were used in a derogatory sense by some of the most traditional poets of the old generation, who found the new poetry to be incomprehensible, indirect, foggy, hazy, vague, gloomy, evasive, and confusing in meaning—in a word, misty. Another connotation of "opacity" arises from questions about the validity of this new poetic form, which, it was claimed, could not be understood by the people.

During the **Great Cultural Revolution (1966–1976)**, and particularly after 1972, Western creative works and literary theories began to be circulated among Chinese political leaders, who criticized them in the light of Marxist and Maoist doctrines. Chinese **intellectuals** and young people who belonged to or had connections with these political circles were thus exposed to contemporary Western literature, a circumstance that played an important role in subverting the authority of Maoist literary principles. **Mao Zedong**'s literary theories had become cast-iron orthodoxy during the Great Cultural Revolution, which ideologically sanitized Chinese literature and criticism, stripping both of human emotions. The imposition of this rigid conformity created symptoms of spiritual deprivation. After the onset of economic reform in 1978, the national response was a voracious appetite for personal freedom, which allowed for a modicum of individual diversity. Western capitalism and Western literature were equally attractive to a society weary of conformity. The post-Mao era was thus characterized by literary liberation and intellectual freedom, which created the social-psychological environment in which misty poetry was born.

The first New Poetry writer was Guo Lusheng, whose pen name was Index Finger (Shizhi). He started to write modern, premisty poems during the Cultural Revolution, when he was working in the countryside. At first, his poems were transmitted in handwritten versions, but they soon became popular with younger readers via various underground publications.

In 1974, a young underground poet named Yi Qun, whose works were profoundly influenced by European literature, gained popularity for the stylistic reforms exhibited by his poems. Between 1969 and 1976, such young poets as Mang Ke, Duo Duo, Lin Mang, Bei Dao, Yan Li, and Tian Xiaoqing, who at that time were blue-collar or agricultural workers, began writing poems that were influenced by Western literary styles. Many had not even finished high school or elementary school before being sent to work in the countryside by the Communist Party. They formed the Baiyangdian Group, which was named after Lake Baiyangdian. These young poets wrote with more freedom in rhyme and more opacity in semantics to express the dreams and fantasies of Chinese youth and to tell fairy tales. Seeking poetic aestheticism instead of rationalism and realism, both in form and in content, this group laid the foundation of the misty school.

Gu Cheng later pointed out that there is a reality in everything that is independent; hence the poet is free to explore his own world. Misty poetry first gained popularity, especially with the young, in the early 1970s. In 1976, when **Zhou Enlai** died, many people gathered in Tiananmen Square to protest the Cultural Revolution and indirectly condemn Mao Zedong's politics. Poetry was an important part of this protest. Bei Dao and other misty poets joined this so-called April 5 Movement and posted their poems in Tiananmen Square together with hundreds of other poems.

In 1978, Bei Dao, Gu Cheng, Jiang He, and Mang Ke self-published their first nonofficial magazine of poems, titled *Jintian* (Today), on the "Wall for Democracy" in the Xidan district of Beijing. At first, this publication circulated only among the people gathered around the Wall. Bei Dao was optimistic about China's democratic future. He pointed out that suppression could only give rise to more diligent pursuits of democracy. In the early 1980s, *Today* ceased publication, and a new generation of poets emerged as Bei Dao assumed leadership of the New Poetry movement from the mentally ill Guo Lusheng.

In 1979, the first misty poetry was published in the official literary magazine *Poetry*. Immediately after, several well-known Chinese publishers began printing such famous examples of misty poetry as Bei Dao's "Yiqie" (All of them) and "Xuangao" (Declaration); Shu Ting's "Zhi Xiangshu" (To oak tree) and "Zuguo A, Wo Qin'ai De Muqin" (My dear motherland); Gu Cheng's "Yidai Ren" (One generation); Luo Gengye's "Bu Man" (Not satisfied); and Liang Xiaobing's "Zhongguo, Wo De Yaoshi Diule" (China, I lost your key). In October 1980, *Poetry* published a number of poems by Shu Ting, Jiang He, and Xu Jingya. By the mid-1980s, many literature publishers and magazines in China were competing with each other to publish misty poems.

Misty poetry was the most controversial poetic phenomenon in the post-Mao era. Beginning in the early 1980s, newspapers and magazines controlled by the Communist Party strongly criticized misty poetry as unacceptable to the people, who could not interpret its real meaning. Criticism was both political and artistic. The former attacked misty poems as too far from socialist orthodoxy, and the latter claimed that the misty style could never be accepted by the common people. Because misty poems are full of indignation, protest, spiritual expression, and a new generation's desire for change, the misty school definitely marked a new age of poetry in China. Although experimental poetry is still marginalized inside China, the misty poets received some recognition overseas, in part because the introduction of Chinese poetry in the West has so far been very restricted. A quick look at the translation anthologies of contemporary Chinese poetry published in the United States in recent years shows that misty poetry still dominates.

The misty poets rebelled against the official artistic ideology, which held that the arts must serve politics and the people. The misty poets believed that socialist reality had been contaminated by excessive ideological propaganda, which had made ideology a kind of simulacrum that "served to alienate the human being from his or her true self." For Bei Dao, Mang Ke, Yang Lian, Shu Ting, and other misty poets of this first post-Mao generation, the function of poetry was to recover the human self. This emphasis on recovering and refining the self was accompanied in poetic practice by the imagist language the poets fashioned. Landscape was humanized, and poetry was a mirror with which to see the reader or the writer. By infusing landscape (sky, rain, mist, river) with personal emotions through an impressionistic prism and often turning these images into political allegories, the misty poets strove to transcend the confines of realism and form a new entity between the self and the external world.

The "New Generation" poets defied the misty school's belief in "heroism" and the "imagistic" method of writing. They criticized their predecessors for being "too historically conscious and too ornate in their poetic images." Not satisfied with the value, reality, and art in the existing world, they expressed support for the six "antis": antitradition, antisublimity, antilyricism, anticulture, antiaesthetics, and antipoetics. Facing the threat of losing their identity and subjectivity, they felt an urgent need to find a foothold in a local and global environment that is in constant and rapid transition. To the New Generation poets, the misty poets' single-minded belief in truth, perfection, and humanity and their imagistic, symbolic method of writing poetry were outdated. For them, the most important task was not to celebrate heroism and utopian idealism, but to strip off the facades of decency, beauty, and sublimity from language and art. Some of the misty poems of the New Generation tend to point to the eternal darkness and ugliness of human nature. They are characterized by a generalized sensitivity to breaks and discontinuities, by difference rather than identity, by gaps and holes rather then seamless webs, and by an emphasis on reestablishing the "pure" relationships between words and objects, spatial experience and exploration.

As far as linguistic expression is concerned, misty poems are characterized as paradoxical in their attitude. They are fully aware of the indispensability of language—"Poets live in language." At the same time, they realize that the nature of language is to cover. When it expresses, there's always something in between. . . . How difficult it is to write poetry, not only difficult, it is desperate. To these poets, being means writing, and writing means constant battles with language. The necessity of expressing and the impossibility of expressing have put these poets in a painful position. As Bei Dao pointed out, "Only language can redeem the collapsed and collapsing life," and the New Generation poets seek pure language, defying any symbolic meaning or imagistic juxtaposition that their misty predecessors may have forced on words. They believe that meaning is illusory and ideological and should not have power over language. The only meaning for language is its "meaninglessness," its resistance to human conceptualization and social and cultural value.

Poet Gu Cheng was born in Beijing in 1956. His father was the well-known Mao-era army poet Gu Gong. Gu Cheng spent four years in a remote zone of Shandong Province during the Cultural Revolution. He published his first collection of poetry, *Hei Yanjing* (Dark Eyes), in 1986. From the mid-1980s, his works became increasingly experimental and eschewed the brilliant lyricism and complex metaphoric textures of his early work. He wrote several extended series, such as *Bulin Dang'an* (The Bulin file), *Songge Shijie* (Eulogy worlds), and *Shuiyin* (Quicksilver). *Tonghua Shiren* (Fairy-tale poet) has been used extensively by both Chinese and Western critics to shed light on the poetry of Gu Cheng. The conceptual vagueness of his fairy-tale quality seriously limits the work's usefulness. Illusion played a key role in Gu Cheng's earliest attempts to formulate an individual poetics. In 1988, Gu Cheng moved to

Auckland, New Zealand, with his wife and son. In 1993, he committed suicide after killing his wife.

Bei Dao (pseudonym of Zhao Zhenkai), one of China's foremost misty school poets, was born in 1949 in Beijing. Both his father, an administrative cadre leader, and his mother, a medical doctor, came from traditional middle-class families in Shanghai. During the Cultural Revolution, Bei Dao joined the Red Guards. Like most other youths, he was sent to the countryside, where he became a construction worker. Living in total isolation in the mountains outside Beijing increased his youthful melancholy and prompted him to explore a more spiritual approach to life. By 1974, Bei Dao had finished the first draft of his novella *Waves* and had begun a sequence of poems. These poems became a guiding beacon for the youth of the April 5 Democracy Movement of 1976. In December 1978, Bei Dao and Mang Ke published the first issue of *Today*. Widely treasured by those who participated in China's democracy movement, Bei Dao's poetry is marked by the effort to reveal the nature of the self, to identify both public and private wounds, to trust in instinctive perceptions, and to reach out to other afflicted souls. It depicts the intimacy of passion, love, and friendship in a society where trust can literally be a matter of life and death.

In the early 1980s, Bei Dao worked at the Foreign Languages Press in Beijing. He was a key target in the government's Anti-Spiritual-Pollution Campaign, but in 1983 he managed to meet secretly with the American poet Allen Ginsberg, who had come to China as part of a group of American authors. Bei Dao was forced into exile following the Tiananmen Square massacre in 1989. He, along with other exiled writers and artists, has found a voice in a renewed version of *Today*, which was relaunched in Stockholm in 1990. Bei Dao was later inducted into the American Academy of Arts and Letters as an honorary member. In recent years, his name has been constantly reported by the media as being on the short list of Nobel candidates. In 1983, Bei Dao's poems were published in the East Asia Papers series of the Cornell University East Asia Program, and also in *Renditions* 19/20 in Hong Kong by the Chinese University Press. His poems also appeared in the *Bulletin of Concerned Asian Scholars* (1984) and in *Contemporary Chinese Literature* (1985). When the political situation changed in the mid-1980s, Bei Dao traveled in Europe and the United States. As political control of the public debate in China showed some signs of relaxation in the 1980s, his poetry became more pessimistic, culminating in 1986 in *Bai Ri Meng* (Nightmarish). In the same year, his anthology *Bei Dao Shi Xuan*, a collection of poems written between 1970 and 1986, was received with enthusiasm. However, the book was soon banned by the Chinese cultural authorities. After a year in England, followed by a tour in the United States, Bei Dao returned to China in late 1988.

Bei Dao's poetry cannot be separated from the disillusionment, the alienation, and the despair that arise from the attempt to reconstruct meaning in a meaningless world that many Chinese have experienced since the 1980s. Thus his verse touches the reader as gloomy and sad, perhaps more so than that of any other poet of his generation. Whereas his earlier poetry, written between 1970 and 1978, contained dreams of love, freedom, and happiness, such voices disappeared almost entirely in his later work of the mid-1980s.

This later poetry is filled with images of blood, barrenness, old age, incongruity, and coldness.

In 1989, when the demonstration in Tiananmen Square was suppressed in the massacre of June 4, Bei Dao was in Berlin. Because students circulated some of his poems during the democracy movement, he was accused of helping incite the events in the square. Bei Dao therefore decided to stay in exile. His friends Duo Duo, Yang Lian, and Gu Cheng also chose exile. With former contributors, he reestablished *Today*, which became one of the influential forums for Chinese writers abroad. After teaching in Sweden, Denmark, and Germany, Bei Dao moved to the United States and became a resident scholar at the University of Michigan. In his traveling isolation, Bei Dao discovered the extraordinary effect of the forces of history and history's cataclysmic events on the life of the individual, and he expressed this discovery in his *Can Xue* (Old snow). The volume is divided into three sections that coincide with the European cities where the exiled poet has resided—Berlin, Oslo, and Stockholm. Indeed, the title evokes images of the weight of repression over China, both old and new, by describing remnants of national upheavals in European cities.

Duo Duo was born in Beijing, China, on August 28, 1951. He was a reporter for the national newspaper *Farmer's Daily* from 1980 to 1989. He left China on June 4, 1989. He was a Chinese teacher in the Department of Far Eastern Languages, School of Oriental and African Studies, at the University of London from 1989 to 1990. He was also a writer-in-residence at Glendon College, York University, in 1990–1991.

Shu Ting's real name is Gong Peiyu. She was born in 1952 in Fujian Province. Like most of the misty poets, she was sent during the Cultural Revolution to the countryside, and she began to write poems during her rustication. Upon returning to the city, she became a blue-coller worker. She achieved prominence as the leading female misty writer. Her first poetry collection, *Shuangwei Chuan* (Double-matted boat), appeared in 1982. She also published a joint collection with Gu Cheng, but then stopped writing at the time of the anti-spiritual-pollution movement. She published another two books of poetry in the mid-1980s: *Hui Changge de Yiweihua* (The signing iris) and *Shizuniao* (Archaeopteryx). Afterwards, she also published some essays.

Given this widespread shift toward opacity, it is perhaps not surprising that by the start of the new millennium, writers of Chinese poetry were thought to outnumber readers. In the two decades since 1979, the aims of the misty poets have been largely achieved: to create a space for poetic experimentation within a political culture of literary utilitarianism. In this process, however, poetry has been transformed from the popular front line of thought liberation into an isolated, self-enclosed vanguard. At present, as China's political system is continuously reformed, poets can mostly find a way to publish what they want and enjoy their freedom in writing as long as they do not directly criticize government figures.

See also Anticorruption Literature and Television Dramas; Avant-garde Literature; Experimental Fiction; Great Cultural Revolution, Literature during; Intellectuals, Political Engagement of (1949–1978); Intellectuals, Political Engagement of (1978–Present); Literary Policy for the New China; Literature of the Wounded;

Modern Pop-Satire; Neorealist Fiction and Modernism; Pre–Cultural Revolution Literature; Revolutionary Realism and Revolutionary Romanticism; Root-Searching Literature; Sexual Freedom in Literature.

Bibliography

Guo, Zhigang, and Sun Zhongtian, eds., *Contemporary Chinese Literature—Second Part* (Beijing: Higher Education Press, 1993); Jin, Han, *Modern Chinese Novels* (Zhejiang, China: Zhejiang University Press, 1997); Zhang, Rongjian, ed., *Contemporary Chinese Literature* (Wuhan, China: University of Sciences and Technology of Central China Press, 2001); Zhang Rongjian, ed., *Contemporary Chinese Literature—Reference Materials* (Wuhan, China: University of Sciences and Technology of Central China Press, 2001); Zhang, Weizhong, *Transformations in the New Age Novels and the Chinese Traditional Culture* (Beijing: Xuelin Press, 2002).

Zhiyuan Chen

Modern Pop-Satire

There are many forms of modern pop-satire, including *xiaopin* (short plays and essays), *xiangsheng* (comic dialogues), and *minyao* (ballads and folk rhymes, often of a topical and political nature). The first two forms, which have been popularized by the annual Chinese New Year's Gala on CCTV watched by all Chinese families, belong to the performing arts. *Minyao*, popularly known as *shunkouliu* (rhymed talk), is anonymous and is becoming increasingly popular. The **Internet**, cellular phones, and, occasionally, paper media are venues of spread. Contemporary pop-satire is often performed in the form of rhymed talk or integrated into comedies, regional farces, and even rock songs.

Rhymed talk basically takes the form of narratives that touch all aspects of life. A typical function of this genre is to allow people to air their anger and complaints. In fact, some poems in *The Odes*, the earliest Chinese collection of folk poetry (1066–541 B.C.), are rhymed talks of the time. Chinese Confucian rulers sent officials into localities to collect folk songs as a means of detecting people's lives and their general mood.

The worsening situation of corruption in the government is a by-product of the economic transition. Since the late 1970s, many high-level officials have taken advantage of their privileges and filled their own pockets, often to the common people's detriment. This has inspired a wealth of rhymed talks where people express grievances in a sarcastic way. The six anonymous rhymed talks presented here have all been included in collections published in China.

> High-ranking officials amuse themselves with men and women; intermediate-ranking officials are cheaters and hypocrites; lower-level officials are hooligans in nature.

This passage may sound shocking, but speaks volumes of truth. The scandals of Chen Xitong, a Politburo member and Party secretary of the Beijing Committee, and his accomplice Wang Baosen, the deputy mayor of Beijing, both involved consorting with women at public expense, in addition to embezzling millions of dollars in money and material goods. The rhymed talk presented here emerged after the Chen and Wang case was exposed in 1995. In 2000, Hu Changqing, the deputy governor of Jiangxi, and Cheng Kejie, a vice chairman of the **National People's Congress** and also the governor of Guangxi, each accepted bribes and accumulated money and property worth millions of dollars by taking advantage of their positions in the government. Both officials had concubines, and Cheng's mistress was also his accomplice.

The Ten Classes of People

The first class are public servants.
  Their wives and children enjoy a happy life.
The second class are office holders.
  They take turns going abroad to have real fun.
The third class are government contractors.
  Their feasting and womanizing are reimbursed.
The fourth class are lenders of public banks.
  They travel from one scenic spot to another with their mistresses.
The fifth class live on kickbacks.
  Their embezzlement and bribe-taking know no end.
The sixth class are cops.
  Delicacies of every kind are never in shortage.
The seventh class handle scalpels.
  You must pass red packets if you want to stay alive.
The eighth class are chauffeurs of officials.
  They follow their leaders to wining and dining.
The ninth class are the self-employed.
  After deceiving Zhang, they cheat on Li.
The tenth class are masters of the country.
  They carry their lunch-boxes and learn from Lei Feng.

The message of this piece is that corruption has become an epidemic in which people at all strata of society are involved. Among them, cadres or officials take the lead, as targeted in classes one, two, and six. The broad masses, who were once elevated as the "masters" of the country by **Mao Zedong**, have sunk to the bottom during the reform era. Without power and privilege, they must live a plain life like Lei Feng, an ordinary soldier who served the people warmheartedly and sacrificed his young life at his post in 1963. There have been several versions of "The Ten Classes of People" since the 1970s; all seem to have sarcastically been modeled on Mao's well-known 1926 "Analysis of the Classes in Chinese Society," in which he maintained that class distinctions were essential for his revolution.

The theme of denouncing the scandalous behaviors of elements from various social strata has many variations. The following offers a different flavor:

The top-class police are the criminal police.
They get drunk before getting to a criminal case.
The second-class police are the traffic cops.

They show up in every corner to collect fees.
The third-class police are the pubic security police
Who chase away the johns and sleep with the girls themselves.

These lines satirize government functionaries specifically. Apparently, the corrupt police get on people's nerves more than anything else.

During the time of the **Great Cultural Revolution** of the 1960s, songs and poems were used to sing the praises of Party leaders and the Communist cause. These songs and poems were refurbished in the 1990s to denounce corruption. The following cynical verses are modeled on a famous poem written by Chairman Mao in the 1930s to encourage the heroism of the Red Army in bravely finishing the Long March.

Imitating the Long March

An official must not fear the challenges of drinkers,
A thousand cups are handled with ease.
The steaming "lover's hot pot" boils in five waves,
Seafood, barbecue, and fish balls are abundant.
Sauna and massage warm up the body,
At *Mahjong* table one forgets the cold dawn.
There comes the girl with snow-white skin;
The companionship adds infinite joy.

Many corrupt officials have a perverted logic and set limits to themselves, such that they can get away with whatever they do.

The New Four Basic Principles

Dine to the heart's content, but avoid being a drunkard.
Take gifts, but do not accept bribes.
Love the new (woman), but do not abandon the old.
Be romantic, but do not be obscene.

According to the *Jiancha Ribao* (Procurators' daily), out of the state fiscal revenues, billions of dollars were spent on wining and dining by public servants. The previously mentioned cases of Chen, Hu, and Cheng reflect the extent to which officials' bribe taking had risen. The four new basic principles sound cynical in that the real Four Basic Principles were declared by Deng Xiaoping in 1978 and include sticking to the Communist course, sticking to Marxism-Lennism–Mao Zedong Thought, safeguarding the Communist leadership, and holding on to the democratic dictatorship, all of which are sublime goals of the Party.

During the sudden acute respiratory syndrome (SARS) crisis in 2003, more rhymed talks emerged. This nightmare, which claimed hundreds of lives in China alone, seemed to have had a positive function, at least for a while:

Wining and dining could not be stopped; but SARS stopped it.
Tourism on public money could not be eliminated; but SARS stopped it.

Meetings and paper trails are endless; but SARS wiped them out.
Rampant fraud and deception could not be stopped; but SARS
    stopped it.
Prostitution and whoring could not be eradicated; but SARS cleaned
    it up.

The moral degeneration of Chinese officials reflected in these folk-art forms is blatant. However, thanks to the many forms of pop-satire, many behind-the-scenes maneuvers would probably never be exposed to the public in a country where the state controls the media and democratic channels are lacking. Therefore, one cannot understand official corruption without paying attention to pop-satire, without which society might well become even more corrupt. To date, most politically engaging pop-art forms make the authorities nervous, but the latter are powerless to do much about them because they are so popular. Their succinct, amusing style, skillful rhymes and rhythms, and straight-to-the-point plain language, among other characteristics, all contribute to the popularity of rhymed talks.

See also Anticorruption Literature and Television Dramas; Avant-garde Literature; Corruption and Fraud, Control of; Experimental Fiction; Great Cultural Revolution, Literature during; Intellectuals, Political Engagement of (1949–1978); Intellectuals, Political Engagement of (1978–Present); Literary Policy for the New China; Literature of the Wounded; Misty Poetry; Neorealist Fiction and Modernism; Pre–Cultural Revolution Literature; Revolutionary Realism and Revolutionary Romanticism; Root-Searching Literature; Sexual Freedom in Literature.

Bibliography

Link, Perry, and Kate Zhou, "*Shunkouliu*: Popular Satirical Sayings and Popular Thought," in *Popular China: Unofficial Culture in a Globalizing Society*, ed. Perry Link, Richard P. Madsen and Paul G. Pickowicz, 89–109 (Lanham, MD: Rowman & Littlefield, 2002); Lu, Wen, *Baixing Huati: Dangdai Shunkouliu* (Ordinary people's topics: Present-day shunkouliu) (Beijing: Zhongguo Dang'an, 1998); Yao, Siyuan, ed., *Bainian Minyao* (A century of folk rhymes), *Minzu Wenxue* qiannian jinian tekan (special millennium issue of National Literature) (Beijing: Chinese Writers' Association, 1999); *Yaogun Shunkouliu* (Rock and roll shunkouliu), audiotape (n.p.: Qianxi Jipin and Jinlong Changpian, 2001); Zhen, Yan, *Xiandai Liuxing Minyao* (Modern pop-rhymes) (Hohhot [Inner Mongolia]: Yuanfang, 2001).

Helen Xiaoyan Wu

Modern Standard Chinese (MSC)

See Putonghua, Promotion of.

Modernism

See Neorealist Fiction and Modernism.

Mosuo People, Matriarchal Tradition of

The Mosuo people comprise one of the most remarkable ethnic groups in China. Their ethnic identity includes the famous matriarchal system and the practice of the "walking marriage." This marriage system is also known as "Ahxia marriage" or "Ahzhu marriage," meaning the association of boys and girls. The tradition is regarded as a living fossil in the history of marriage. Some field studies have been done by anthropologists, ethnologists, sociologists, and historians. In addition, the walking marriage has been widely reported by the media, often with sensational exaggerations, to attract curious tourists. Scientists believe that walking marriage indeed represents the culture of a primitive stage that has long ceased to exist.

The Mosuo people are a branch of the Naxi people, according to the ethnic classification by the government. However, they prefer to call themselves Mosuo instead of Naxi. The Mosuo people live in the area around Lake Luguhu of Yongning, a township of Ninglang County, in northwestern Yunnan Province. Some of the Mosuo people live in the surrounding Yanyuan County, Yanbian County, and Muli County. They all keep the walking marriage system and matriarchal system. The total population of the Mosuo people is more than 10,000.

Among the Mosuo people who live around peaceful Lake Luguhu, the walking marriage has been practiced for many generations. The young man and the young woman involved in the relationship belong to two different families that are, however, both headed by the mothers of the families. Since the parties usually live in different villages, the husband or boyfriend needs to travel to his wife or girlfriend's house from his mother's home late in the afternoon or in the evening and return to his mother's home early the next morning to do

In this 1996 photo, mounted Mosuo tribeswomen wear traditional dress. © *Michael S. Yamashita/Corbis.*

farm work and to have breakfast. Since the travel often covers a substantial distance, the term "walking marriage" is well justified.

Walking marriage is apparently not marriage in the traditional sense. While it is called marriage, it is rather a kind of partnership. The words "Ahzhu" and "Ahxia" (or "Ahxiao") that are used to address one another by the lovers simply mean girlfriend and boyfriend. If the young people deeply fall in love, they stay together for an extended period of time, or permanently in some cases. If they fall out of love, however, they happily separate. Most partners do not register their relationships with government agencies. However, some began to register for their "marriage" after the founding of the People's Republic of China in 1949.

The husband and wife, or partners, of the walking marriage build their relationship on the basis of love instead of other factors. If the woman does not want to keep the relationship, she may simply call it off, and the man will not come to visit her any longer. If the man does not want to continue the relationship, he may also tell her his decision and can stop their relationship. There are no hard feelings involved. In the case where the woman initiates the separation, however, the man knows it when he returns and finds his belongings laid outside the woman's house.

A young Mosuo may have many Ahzhu or Ahxia (girlfriends or boyfriends) during his/her lifetime. Some may only have five or six, some may have a few dozen, and some may even have more than a hundred such walking relationships. Generally, at their younger age, the Mosuos change their girlfriends or boyfriends more frequently. As they grow older, the relationships become more stable. After middle age, especially after a child is born, the relationships are open and more like the widely practiced marriage. During the **Great Cultural Revolution (1966–1976)**, many people were forced to register to get married because their walking marriage was regarded as a bad custom by the government. However, as soon as the Cultural Revolution ended, most of the registered partners had to file for "divorce." For the Mosuos, a marriage without feeling is unbearable. This may be the reason why the Mosuo people stick to the walking marriage system and resist formal and legal marriage.

A Matriarchal system is a system in which women play more important roles than men and make the final decisions in both social and family life. In such a system, women are powerful and play the role of leaders of society and heads of families. Therefore, men are subordinated to women. According to historians, the matriarchal system existed in primitive ages, possibly the Neolithic period. The features of the matriarchal system of the Mosuo people are as follows:

1. The walking marriage belongs to pairing marriage in anthropological terms. The pairing marriage of the Mosuo people has been categorized into the early pairing marriage with an important rule, however, that close matrilineal kin relatives are excluded from the pairing marriage. For example, people within close matrilineal kinship are not given permission to visit one another. However, it is not uncommon for close patrilineal kin relatives to enter the pairing game due to the fact that in a matrilineal system it is often difficult to tell the relationships on the father's side.

2. The original family bonding remains predominant even after the part-nership starts. The man and the woman involved primarily belong to their respective mothers' families. Hence they stay together at night and separate in the daytime. They work and live with their own fam-ilies.

3. All the children born from the walking marriage belong to the wife's family, which has the responsibility to foster and educate the chil-dren. While children know who their mothers are, they may not know who their fathers are. But this does not matter, because they are counted according to the maternal line and inherit only the matri-lineal property, but nothing patrilineal.

4. The head of a family is the oldest or the most capable woman instead of a man. She is in charge of the economic affairs and housework of the family. Her brothers are her assistants and sometimes help her handle family affairs. Men in the families are subordinate and follow orders.

5. Family property is owned by all members of the family, and the means of livelihood are usually distributed equally among all the fam-ily members. The style of family life is one of democracy; that is, it is based on discussions and consensus.

6. Women play main roles in most of the farming work, as well as house chores, although labor-intensive jobs such as plowing or tilling are normally done by men.

The Mosuo matriarchal system is in a transitional phase, since about 40 per-cent of the total Mosuo families share both matriarchal and patriarchal sys-tems. In this kind of family, some men may bring their wives to live with them in their mothers' families, while some women may still practice their tradi-tional walking marriage. Consequently, in the same household, children from both traditions live together. The children of the men and their Ahxia (girl-friend or boyfriend) are counted according to the patriarchal line, and the chil-dren of the women and their Ahxia (boyfriend) are counted according to the matriarchal line, but the wife and children are family members of the matriar-chal family. All the family members, whether matrilineal or patrilineal, have equal rights to property and inheritance. It is common that a bilineal family changes into a matriarchal or patriarchal family in one generation, and in the next generation it changes back. It can also happen that for several generations the family follows a bilineal tradition, but for the next few generations the sys-tem reverses to a matriarchal or patriarchal family. Changes such as these have been typical for more than a century. Despite all the volatility, however, most of the heads of bilineal families are women. In some families, after a man gets married, he moves out with his wife to set up a new family and starts a patriar-chal family branch.

Acculturation sometimes happens among tourists and even some researchers when they live a relatively long time with Mosuo people in the Lake Luguhu area. It is said that some outsiders from big cities such as Shanghai and Beijing admire the local culture so much that they marry local people and settle down in this beautiful place. Many say that it is heavenly love that man should pursue. For the Mosuos, while walking marriage is not authentic marriage, love is based on real feeling.

See also Ethnic Kinships; Ethnic Marriage Customs; Ethnic Minorities, Political Systems of; Ethnicity and Ethnic Policies; Minority Women in Xinjiang and Taiwan; Taiwan, Ethnicity and Ethnic Policies of; Women, Role as Mothers; Women, Social Status of.

Bibliography

Song, Shuhua, ed., *An Introduction to Chinese Ethnic Minorities* (Beijing: Central University for Nationalities Press, 2001); Xu, Wanbang, and Qi Qingfu, eds., *An Introduction to Chinese Ethnic Minority Cultures* (Beijing: Central University for Nationalities Press, 1996).

Yinghui Wu

Mothers in Modern China

See Women, Role as Mothers; Women, Social Status of.

N

National People's Congress (NPC), Structure and Functions of

The National People's Congress (NPC) is the highest legislative body of the People's Republic of China. It consists of a standing committee and several special committees. It has its seat in the Great Hall of the People in Beijing's Tiananmen Square and represents China's thirty provinces, autonomous regions, municipalities directly administered by the central government, and the military. Its main functions and powers include the formulation of laws, the delegation of authority, policy creation, and supervision of governing activities. Each NPC lasts for a term of five years. Annual sessions are held in between the general sessions. The First Session of the First National People's Congress was held in September 1954. It adopted the Constitution of the People's Republic of China. The latest, the Tenth NPC, was held in March 2003.

The Standing Committee is a permanent organ of the NPC. Composed of a chairman, multiple vice chairmen, a secretary-general, and on average 135 members, it exercises daily functions between the general assembly sessions. It has the responsibility to report on its work to the Congress. The chairman and vice chairmen of the committee serve no more than two consecutive terms of five years. The first chairman of the committee was **Liu Shaoqi**. The chairman as of 2004 was Wu Banguo.

Special committees, both permanent and provisional, are major components of the NPC. Permanent committees include the Committee on Nationalities and Law, the Financial and Economic Committee, the Educational, Science, Culture, and Public Health Committee, the Committee of Foreign Affairs, and the Overseas Chinese Committee. The Committee for Internal and Judicial Affairs and the Committee on Environmental and Resource Protection are also permanent. Provisional committees or commissions are inquiry bodies set up to resolve special issues. Special committees work under the direction of the NPC Standing Committee on behalf of the NPC while it is not in session.

Almost 3,000 delegates meet in the Grand Hall of the People in Beijing for the opening of the Chinese National People's Congress (NPC) on March 5, 2004. © Guang Niu/Reuters/Corbis.

The NPC has the legislative power to enact and amend the Constitution of the People's Republic of China and laws concerning criminal offenses and civil affairs. Its delegating authority allows the Congress to select, empower, and remove officials of the state organs. It has the power to select the members of the Standing Committee of the NPC, to elect the president and vice president of the People's Republic of China, and to appoint the premier and vice premiers of the State Council and ministers. It also has the power to elect the chairman of the Central Military Commission, the president of the Supreme People's Court, and the procurator-general of the Supreme People's Office of Procurator.

The NPC devises policies and approves national economic and social development plans. It examines and approves the state budget and its implementation. It has the power to approve the establishment of provinces, autonomous regions, and municipalities directly under the central government and to decide on the establishment of **special administrative regions** and the systems to be instituted within these regions. It also has the power to declare war and approve treaties with other nations.

The NPC exercises its supervisory role to oversee the activities of the government on behalf of the people. According to the Constitution, the State Council, the Supreme People's Court, and the Supreme People's Office of Procurator are all under the supervision of the NPC.

The NPC is composed of about 2,900 delegates and meets for about two weeks each year. Delegates to the NPC are elected for a term of five years. They come from different classes and social strata, represent various parties, organizations, and nationalities, and have the right to vote. Members of the State Council and the Central Military Commission, the president of the Supreme People's Court, and the procurator general of the Supreme People's Procuratorate attend sessions of the NPC as nonvoting delegates.

The National People's Congress has been seen as a symbolic and powerless rubber-stamp legislature for predetermined Communist Party decisions. Particularly during the era of **Mao Zedong**, bills and proposals presented to the Congress used to be approved by a show of raised hands unanimously without debate. It never overturned a resolution proposed by the Chinese Communist Party. Changes took place in the mid-1980s when Deng Xiaoping launched the economic reform that liberalized the Chinese legal system to a significant extent. Being aware of problems of bureaucracy and corruption, Deng made many changes to address the abuses of the system. In April 1986,

Deng, in a speech, suggested the separation of the Party from the government, believing that the NPC should be sovereign. However, the separation of the Party and the state will be a prolonged process and a core target of the reform.

The Seventh National People's Congress of 1988 marked a departure from its traditional image of obedience, because it functioned powerfully as a supreme state authority. Delegates felt an urgency to forge ahead with China's economic reforms and for the first time spoke their minds. The Seventh Congress became a starting point for real debate and discussion that changed the habitual action of blind approval. In the Seventh Congress, 71 percent of the delegates were newly elected, and many of them expressed independent and assertive views. In a total break with precedent, in which an automatic show of raised-hand unanimity had terminated all policy discussion, delegates now began to speak up and cast negative votes. For example, the Seventh NPC approved policies to accelerate the Four Modernizations. It passed a bill to provide constitutional protection to the freedom of people to buy and sell their land-use rights or their stakes in enterprises. It also supported a policy that provided legal protection to the free sale of housing. These decisions challenged the system of Party patronage.

With regard to system reform, the Seventh NPC endorsed an institutional change. It approved the reorganization of four central ministries of railways, petroleum, coal, and nuclear power that were in charge of managing China's energy and transportation systems and a 20 percent cut in administrative personnel. With its approval of letting enterprises set up their own management free from interventions of the Party committee, the NPC ended the control of the Party over production.

Embracing a new style of openness, NPC session discussions have begun to be aired on Chinese national **television**. Foreign journalists are permitted, in many circumstances, to attend all the main sessions, and there are frequent press conferences and public discussions.

The NPC now exerts much more influence on decision making than formerly. Although legislation still usually originates from the State Council and is overseen by the Politburo, the Congress assumes its power to propose amendments. It is empowered to oversee the application of laws passed, and it has specialized committees to investigate the implementation of approved projects. Votes are no longer unanimous. In many cases, negative votes can be significantly large. The NPC is playing an increasingly significant role in balancing the government and the Party and in guaranteeing the current economic transition.

See also Administrative Structure of Government.

Bibliography

Goldman, Merle, *Sowing the Seeds of Democracy in China: Political Reform in the Deng Xiaoping Era* (Cambridge, MA: Harvard University Press, 1994); O'Brien, Kevin J., *Reform without Liberalization: China's National People's Congress and the Politics of Institutional Change* (Cambridge: Cambridge University Press, 1990); Pu,

Xingzu, Ding Rongsheng, Sun Guanhong, and Hu Jinxing, *Zhong Hua Renmin Gong He Guo Zhengzhi Zhidu (The political system of the People's Republic of China)* (Hong Kong: Sanlian, 1995).

Jingyi Song

Nationalism in Modern China

Historically, Chinese officials and the populace believed that China was the center of the universe and other states the Middle Kingdom's tributaries. This myth led to arrogance and chauvinism. The sense of dominance diminished after a series of invasions by Western powers, starting with the Opium War between Britain and China in 1840. On the Chinese side, the period from 1840 to 1945 is a history of national humiliation: China was invaded, bullied, looted, and humiliated by "the Eight Allied Western Powers" and later by Japan. The defenselessness and helplessness in that part of Chinese history have left an indelible and humiliating scar on the Chinese mentality. The defeat, however, has contributed to a strong bonding between the Chinese public and the Chinese Communist Party (CCP), which led the war against the Japanese invasion from 1937 to 1945 and stood up to the U.S.-led international embargo and threats of nuclear attacks against China in the 1950s. The CCP constantly reminds the nation of the humiliation the Chinese people suffered at the hands of foreign nations and foreigners since 1840. While this patriotic education does have the self-serving purpose of reinforcing the political legitimacy of the CCP, these campaigns also helped the Chinese people perceive themselves and others from a perspective of history and in the context of the world community.

Historical experience determines that the priority of the Chinese leadership, government, and people is to build a "rich country and strong army" to guarantee that China will never again face a similar experience. Other objectives are part of and subordinate to this central goal. China defines its identity and relations with the United States in light of the needs of building China into an independent, powerful, and rich nation. Given this history, it is not surprising that Beijing's foreign policy is state centered, exhibits a strong nationalist tendency, and aims to safeguard national independence and sovereignty to ensure a long-term peaceful and stable international environment conducive to its economic development and all-around modernization drive. The CCP is determined to restore China to its rightful position in the world.

Modern Chinese nationalism and national independence were first advocated by Chinese **intellectuals** in the late nineteenth century, followed by major antiforeign nationalist movements such as the Boxer Rebellion of 1900, the May 4 Movement of 1919, and the Anti-Japanese War of the 1930s and 1940s. After the CCP took over China in 1949, it advocated opposition to U.S. imperialism and Soviet hegemonism until Chinese leader Deng Xiaoping shifted China's attention to the economy and reform in 1978. The government's patriotism movement aims to revitalize the nation and unify all Chinese people. The government's anti-Western propaganda, Chinese intellectuals' anti-American works, and the public anti-U.S. sentiment mainly focus on avenging China's past. This has greatly impacted the Chinese people's consciousness and nationalistic feelings, especially among Chinese intellectuals and government officials. In the 1980s, the nationalist feelings of most Chinese people, especially the youth, were reinforced on the heels of the Japanese textbook controversy. In 1982, Japan's Ministry of Education used "entered" instead of "invaded" in Japanese school textbooks to describe its aggression in China and Asia in the 1930s and 1940s. This revision provoked widespread protests in China and East Asia. Beijing launched a full-scale campaign to force Tokyo to review the disputed terminology. The compliance has been an on and off, dragged-out process, one reason being that Japanese textbooks are published by multiple publishers.

Since the 1990s, the rise of global ethnic and national conflicts has further awakened the Chinese sense of national identity and has fueled the public's sense of nationalism. Official and public anti-American sentiment over the political and economic barriers set up by the United States, such as the blocking of the Chinese bid for the 2000 Olympic Games, linking trade to politics, and the bombing of the Chinese embassy in Yugoslavia in 1999, led to China's call to change the international order. Emphasis on Chinese ethnic identity grows with the widespread success and the rapid expansion of the Chinese economy, trade, diplomacy, sports, education, arts, the military, and other fields. Believing that the United States is conspiring to suppress the rise of China on the world stage with a double standard in human rights, trade, and nuclear weapons proliferation, China accuses the United States of selling weapons to Taiwan and supporting its independence. From time to time, these dormant sentiments erupt into symbolic displays of Chinese displeasure such as the 2001 spy plane incident.

Nationalism is an identity represented by individuals but expressed by institutions. Unless they are organized and expressed, individual nationalistic ideas or feelings matter little in international relations. Expressed more successfully through the state, nationalism is about national identity associated with the uniqueness of the nation-state. The rise of China and Chinese nationalism coincides with China's rapid economic growth, military modernization, and cultural and educational expansions, as well as growing anti-Western sentiment and self-assertiveness. Nationalism has become the common denominator between the government and the public in China, at times replacing the official ideology. The recoveries of Hong Kong in 1997 and Macao in 1999 were carefully orchestrated to underscore the collective past and future of the Chinese nation. Portraying the recoveries of Hong Kong and Macao as the symbolic end of "a century of shame" at the hands of Western powers in modern Chinese history, the government strategically set Macao's handover for the last day of the millennium to indicate the end of an era, as well as the beginning of a new one. Similarly, the failed bid for the 2000 Olympics was an emotional blow to the national psyche that was corrected only by the proud success of the 2008 Olympic bid. History and nationalism played an important role in escalating the 2001 U.S. spy plane incident to an international crisis. Like American "patriotism" displayed in the war on terrorism, Chinese "nationalism" during the crisis also drew rhetoric from politicians and the media alike. Yet the word "nationalism" can conjure up an image of a villain, while "patriotism" evokes that of a hero.

See also Anti-Western Nationalism in China (1989–1999); June 4 Movement; One Country, Two Systems.

Bibliography

Lam, Tong, "Identity and Diversity," in *China beyond the Headlines*, ed. T. B. Weston and L. M. Jensen (Lanham, MD: Rowman & Littlefield, 2000); Xu, Guangqiu, "Anti-American Nationalism in China: Causes and Formation," in *Image, Perception, and the Making of U.S.-China Relations*, ed. Hongshan Li and Zhaohui Hong (Lanham, MD: University Press of America, 1998); Zhao, Quansheng, "Modernization, Nationalism, and Regionalism in China," in *Comparative Foreign Policy*, ed. S. Hook (Englewood, NJ: Prentice Hall, 2002); Zheng, Yongnian, *Discovering Chinese Nationalism in China: Modernization, Identity, and International Relations* (New York: Cambridge University Press, 1999).

Yu Zhang

Neorealist Fiction and Modernism

Neorealist fiction, which appeared in 1988, has its roots in traditional Chinese realism before the **Great Cultural Revolution (1966–1976)**. Pre–Cultural Revolution Chinese fiction (1949–1966) was the result of a kind of grafting between pre-Communist modern Chinese literature from 1919 to 1949 and Western literature. In 1841, China's "Bamboo Gate" was opened by the Western gunboat, and this opening had a predominant influence on pre–Cultural Revolution literature. Also, pre-Communist modern Chinese literature was profoundly influenced by Western European and Russian realism. Post–Cultural Revolution literature marked the death of **Mao Zedong**'s literary policy as a result of more literary freedom for Chinese writers together with the introduction of the capitalist market system in China. In the post-Mao era, the so-called traditional writers started to follow the general principles of René Wellek's realism as a regulative idea in European literature in a more faithful way and almost totally abandoned Mao's principle of literature as serving blue-collar workers, peasants, and soldiers. Very few Chinese writers still insist on following Mao's instructions in writing.

Besides the literal criticism of political persecution and social injustice during the so-called Proletarian Cultural Revolution, writers expanded their vision to include present and future socioeconomic and sociopolitical changes and their consequences in Chinese society after the introduction of the capitalist market system into the Chinese economy. Chinese early realism rejuvenated in modern literature, which grasped social reality as a systematic evolution through a combination of serious concerns about society and a strong demand for social justice. In the early 1980s, the names of Habermas, Derrida, and Foucault suddenly became familiar to Chinese **intellectuals**, along with those of other Western writers and thinkers who had been banned for half a century. As a result, humanitarianism and individualism have gained their fullest expression in the contemporary realist fictions of China. In its stylistic features, the new realism of China incorporated many contemporary Western literary tools to enrich its forms of expression.

Neorealism differs from traditional realism in its content, form, and way of expression. On the basis of a wider consideration of literary categorization, this subclassification can be enlarged in such a way as to cover all new forms of realistic literal expression. Chinese contemporary new realism or neorealism should cover more subcomponents than used to be defined by both Chinese and Western literary critical worlds. According to stylistic, semantic, and logical considerations, neorealist fiction can further be subcategorized into report-style fiction (*jishi xiaoshuo*), fiction with historical topics (*lishi ticai xiaoshuo*), protofiction (*yuansheng xiaoshuo*), stream-of-consciousness fiction (*yishi liu xiaoshuo*), reflection fiction (*fansi xiaoshuo*), and new fiction of local customs (*fengsu xiaoshuo*).

Historical episodes and criticisms again became popular topics in modern novels, short stories, and dramas. Both before and after the Cultural Revolution, historical topics for novels were considered the most welcomed topics in contemporary literature of China. However, before the Cultural Revolution, Mao Zedong always considered historical topics as a kind of symbolism that his political opponents used to attack his policies. Therefore, many historians and writers were very careful when they wrote about these topics. The most obvious example is the drama titled *Hairui's Dismissal*, written by Wu Han, a famous Chinese historian. During his time in power, Mao persecuted all other Communist leaders who disagreed with his economic and political policies. Mao considered *Hairui's Dismissal* a drama intentionally written by Wu Han to criticize his policy during the 1958–1961 period and the dismissal of Peng Dehuai, a famous Chinese general who had been the commander of the Chinese army in the **Korean War**. Wu Han taught at Qinghua University before 1952 and became the vice mayor of Beijing during Mao's regime because of his strong support for the Chinese socialist revolution. Mao and his followers thought that Wu Han wanted to use the dismissal of Hairui, a high-ranking governmental official who served a Chinese emperor in the Qing dynasty, to allude to Mao's dismissal of Peng Dehuai, minister of national defense of China. Since Mao was interested in studying Chinese history, he was extremely sensitive to any type of criticism of historical events that might be applied to contemporary Chinese politics, whose principal author and authority must be Mao himself. That is one of the reasons why historical topics for novels, dramas, and soap operas suddenly became very popular immediately after Mao's death.

Post–Cultural Revolution historical realism has been characterized by its truthfulness to historical reality, in opposition to Mao's combination of **revolutionary realism and revolutionary romanticism**, that is, an exaggeration of revolutionary idealism by ignoring to some extent the historical reality. Among the most important writers in post–Cultural Revolution historical realism are Ling Li, Jiefang (Chinese readers know him as Er-yue, his pen name), Yao Xueyin, Zhou Xi, Li Dingxing, Jiang Hesen, Ba Ren, Bao Chang, Li Ruqing, Gu Wenguang, and Gu Puguang. The topics of their historical narratives are related to some of the most important empires and peasant uprising leaders in different dynasties of China. Generally speaking, what the majority of these writers expressed in their works were their deep concerns, sadness, and silent protests against the social reality and the imperial dictatorship that dominated China for more than 2,500 years. However, post–Cultural Revolution neorealistic historical narrative somehow escaped historical reality, created some unrealistic characters in order to focus more on the sentimental sides of the stories, and started to use some contemporary literary languages for their writing. For instance, Yang Shu'an's *Jiuyue Ju* (September chrysanthemum), Feng Jicai's *Shen Deng Quanzhuan* (Magical lantern profile), Bao Chang's *Gengzi Fengyun* (Vicissitude in 1900), and Gu Hua's *Dadu Hun* (Dadu spirit) do not follow a "bibliographic style," that is, shopping-list style, nor a totally historical perspective, but are a kind of fiction related to their historical background. Romanticism, surrealism, and modern fantasy guide parts of the narration of the stories, together with imagination, exaggeration, legendary color, and some stream-of-consciousness.

Fiction of local customs refers to those writings that carry strong denotative, connotative, and linguistic expressions of Chinese local cultural flavors. Since China is a large country whose different regions have been separated by geographic and topographic barriers, local dialects, customs, traditions, sentiments, and societies have always been topics for Chinese writers throughout history. In modern Chinese literature, several writers can be considered authors of this school, such as Lao She, Mao Dun, Zhao Shuli, and Liu Shaotang. In the post–Cultured Revolution era, Gu Hua, Deng Youmei, Ye Weilin, He Shiguang, Li Kuanding, He Liwei, Wang Zengqi, and Lu Wenfu also joined this school. Among them, Gu Hua's *Furong Zhen* (A Town named Hibiscus), *Futu Lin* (The Mountain Futu), and *Jin Ye Mulian* (Magnolia with golden leaves) and Liu Shaotang's *Pu Liu Ren Jia* (A family of willow and cattail) constitute representative works of fiction of local customs in this period. Gu Hua's short and long fiction after the 1980s showed a strong tendency toward a neorealistic school.

Gu Hua, a well-known contemporary Chinese novelist, is the pen name of Luo Hongyu. He was born on June 20, 1942, in a small town called Erxian in Jiashu District, Hunan Province. In 1953, when he was a teenager, his father died of persecution in a political campaign against reactionaries led by the Communist Party because he had been a district governor during Jiang Jieshi's (Chiang Kai-Shek's) regime before 1949. When he was an elementary-school student, he was kicked out of school three times because of the political problems of his father. In 1952, he was forced to abandon high school because of poverty and to start work in the fields together with his mother. After many years of agricultural work, he managed to enter a school of agriculture. During his study, he began to be interested in literature and write short stories and novels. Upon graduating from this school, he became an agricultural worker on a government-owned farm. Gu Hua farmed for fourteen years until the Cultural Revolution in 1966, when he was punished and pursued by the "Red terrorism" as a political reactionary.

Because of his personal interest in arts and literature, at the end of the Cultural Revolution in 1975, he was selected as a writer for a local opera company. In 1980, he was sent to study in a series of intensive courses organized by the National Association of Chinese Writers. His first novel published in China was *A Town Called Hibiscus* (1981), which described the tragedy of a local opera writer and director during the Cultural Revolution. His peculiar writing style, through which readers can smell the wildflowers and grass in the countryside, and his great sense of humor under the "Red terrorism" impressed the public so much that this novel was highly esteemed throughout the entire country. When this novel was adapted into a movie, he became famous nationwide. Afterwards, he published *Pa Man Qing Teng de Xiao Wu* (A hut Covered by Vines, 1983), *Jin Ye Mulian* (Magnolia with golden leaves, 1983), *Mill at the Cattail Stream* (1983), and other works. He won the National Award of Short Stories, the Mao Dun Literature Prize (the most prestigious prize in Chinese literature), the Furong Literature Prize of China, and the Lunlung Literature Prize of China. In June 1986, he attended the International Symposium of Gu Hua's Writing in Holland. In 1987, he was a visiting scholar at the University of Aiwa in the United States and took part in an international writers' training program at the same university. When Gu Hua was in China, he was the director of the Pen Association of China, vice president of the Association of Writers of Hunan Province, executive chairman of the Artists' Association of Hunan Province, an executive member of the Sixth People's Congress of Hunan Province of China, and a member of the Seventh National Chinese People's Political Consultative Conference.

In 1984, some of his works were criticized by the Chinese government because his writings reflect some sociopolitical realities that differ from the guidelines of the propaganda of the Chinese Communist Party. For that reason, in 1988 he moved to Canada and settled in Vancouver.

Many of Gu Hua's novels and short stories published in the last twenty years, such as *Zhen Nu* (Virtuous woman, 1987) and *Taowang* (Escaping, 1989), use modern literary tools like stream of consciousness, fantasy, and absurdity. His publications include more than twenty novels and short stories, three essays, and literature commentaries. Many of his important works have been translated into English, French, German, Japanese, Korean, Italian, Spanish, Hungarian, Dutch, and other languages. Eight of his novels were adapted into movies, dramas, and different types of local operas such as Shouxin opera, Huangmei opera, Putian opera, Ping opera, Huaden opera, and Huagu opera.

Reflection fiction (*fansi xiaoshuo*) may cover a very wide range of post–Cultural Revolution narrative. Almost immediately after Mao's death in 1976, many Chinese writers of both the old generation and the new generation started to enjoy their temporal freedom of expression and attempted to come to grips with the enormity of the events of the past decade of the Cultural Revolution and all the incidents that occurred after 1949. On the basis of a short period of rethinking about what had happened during the previous decades of political vicissitudes of the People's Republic of China, for the first time, Chinese writers had the opportunity to write about the reality and the long-suffering of the Chinese people during a series of political movements after 1949. Among the most outstanding writers of reflection fiction are Shi Tiesheng, Dai Houying, Han Han and Zhang Jie, who followed the traditional path of realism. However, there is also a group of young writers who tried to show incidental reality with imaginative, fantastic, and magic artistic tools. Instead of reflecting the past with real photographic pictures, they use surrealistic brushes and imaginative colors to digest the past. Among these neorealistic writers are Wang Xiaobo and Yu Jie. Their short and long narratives and essays contain profound reflections of Chinese contemporary episodes.

Wang Xiaobo (1952–1997) was born in Beijing. When he was a high-school student, the Chinese Cultural Revolution started, and he became an agricultural worker in a kind of farm owned by the Chinese army and then an elementary-school teacher. After several years of hard work as a blue-collar worker, in 1978 he was selected to study at the college level, even though he had never had the opportunity to finish high-school study. He studied business administration and political economy at the People's University of China and received his undergraduate degree in 1982. In 1984, he received a scholarship from the University of Pittsburgh in the United States and conducted East Asian studies at the graduate level. In 1988, he received his master's degree and returned to China. He taught at the Department of Sociology of Peking University for three years and accounting at the People's University of China for one year. Tired of college teaching jobs, in 1991 he started to write short and long stories. His stories are full of the fight for justice and equity. He was a very sensitive and thoughtful but romantic and liberal writer. His motto was "looking for the truth, because the truth is simple, beautiful, interesting, and new." His most important publications are *Golden Age*, *Romantic Knight*, *Looking for In-pair*, *Legibility Temple*, *Love in the Revolutionary Time*, *Silver Age*, *The Future World*, *My Yin and Yang*, and *Neo Histograms and Critics*. He died in Beijing at age forty-five on April 10, 1997.

Yu Jie (1972–   ) was born in a beautiful village of Pujiang District near Chengdu, the capital of Sichuan Province, in October 1972. His father was a famous doctor of Chinese traditional medicine. In 1996, he entered Beijing University to study Chinese language and literature at the graduate level, and he received a master's degree in 2000. He became a famous Chinese contemporary writer upon the publication of his first novel, *Bing he Huo* (Ice and fire), in 1998. This novel achieved a publication record of 600,000 copies nationwide. He is considered the most productive, talented, and popular young writer in China. He has published thirty-three books, including novels and political commentaries. Besides *Ice and Fire*, the most popular of his novels are *Outcry from an Iron House*, *Wounds of Civilization*, *Say or Not Say*, *Embarrassing Age*, *Wings Wishing to Fly*, *Rats Like Rice*, *The Frontier between Love and Wound*, and *The Mountain of Aromatic Herb*.

New report-style fiction (*jishi xiaoshuo*) writers include Liu Xinwu, Zhang Xinxing, Sang Hua, Liang Xiaosheng, Feng Jicai, and Liu Yazhou. New report-style fiction differs from the traditional 4-W (where, when, what, why) reports or news because it intends to tell stories the way journalists report news. However, in order to make up a story that looks like a real news event and fabricate a character who does not look like a fictitious character, the writer tries to show the where, when, what, and why of an occurrence with a pseudoreport in a newspaper. In this way, the writer will have more liberty in literary creation by using his or her imagination. Perhaps the first new report-style short-story writer was Liu Yazhou. Two of his well-known report-style narratives from 1983 are *Nuren de Mingzi Shi Ruozhe?* (Is woman synonymous with weakness?) and *Zhongguo Xin* (Chinese heart).

In *5.19 Chang Jingtou* (Zoom lens of May 19), Liu Xinwu created a fictitious character named Hua Zhiming to show the conscious process of soccer fans of modern China and their psychological status in Chinese contemporary culture. Zhang Xinxing and Sang Hua's *Beijing Ren* (People in Beijing) purports to be the "reproduction of their record" of the voices of 100 people of Beijing regarding their ideals, attitudes toward life, and beliefs. With this fabricated narrative, the authors intend to show the social-psychological reality of Chinese people, above all those who live in the metropolitan **cities**, and the cultural changes in the last two decades. Other famous report-style stories published in the last twenty years are Feng Jicai's *Yibai Ren de Shi Nian* (Ten years of one hundred people), Dai Qing's *Dangdai Nuxing Xilie* (Contemporary feminine series), Liu Xinwu's *Gonggong Qiche Yongtandiao* (Bus aria) and *Wangfujing Wanghuatong* (Kaleidoscope on Wangfujing), and Lao Gui's *Xuese Huanghun* (The bloody dusk).

Protofiction (*yuansheng xiaoshuo*) refers to a kind of novel that reveals a prototype of people, their thinking, and their lifeways without exaggeration and romantic or sentimental description. After 1988, the avant-garde school started to decline in China, and writers sought to write in a more realistic way without too much stylistic overdoing. This way of writing differs from traditional realism, magic realism, and surrealism. The most representative writers of this school are Liu Heng, Fang Fang, Li Zhi, Liu Zhengyun, Ye Zhaoyan, Li Qi, Sun Li, Jia Ping'ao, A Cheng, and He Liwei. According to international criticism on Chinese literature, in a so-called protosituation, writers are looking for antirationalism, antihumanitarianism, and antisentimental descriptions. For most protofiction writers, this world is too complicated, too real, and too ambiguous and, at the same time, too simple, too absurd, too unreal, and too clear. Therefore, it is better to describe this world and the people living in it in a more direct, plain, simple, and clear way without any redundancy and exaggeration. Since a writer is not an omnipotent god who can realize all the realities and what people are thinking about the realities, it is better to avoid the complicated side of reality and our reflections about reality and reduce our sentiment to zero. Literary criticism also names this type of narrative "life notes" (*renjian biji*), which actually is a combination of modern Western spontaneous literary techniques and Taoist naturalist philosophy. The name "life notes" originally comes from the well-known novel of the same name written by Li Qingxi, which describes the common life of three cigarette smokers.

Combining realism and allegory, in his novel *Heihei* (Blacks), Shi Tiesheng tried to describe a moving presentation of rural poverty by showing a "good dog" Blacks as a powerful symbol for the trusting and longtime suffering of Chinese people during the **Great Leap Forward** and the Cultural Revolution. Dai Houying's novel *Ren, a Ren!* (People, ah people!), published in 1980, constituted an attempt to fathom the existential meaning of the socialist period of China from 1957 to 1976. The author uses the modernist technique of nonlinear time sequences together with a multiple first-person narration and internal monologues to explore the fate of human nature and the problematic aspects of individual responsibility. The author also focuses on the relationship between the individual and history as the way to interpret the internal world of the main characters. Chinese political authorities criticized this novel during the political campaign against "spiritual pollution" (1983–1984) under the leadership of Deng Xiaoping.

Other important short and long narratives of this subcategory of the neorealist school are Liu Heng's *Gou Ri De Liangshi* (Damned grains, 1986),

Li Qi (Energy, 1987), *Lianhua Tao* (A chain of rings, 1989), and *Sitiao Hanzi* (Four men, 1988); Liu Zhengyun's *Danwei* (Entity, 1989), *Touren* (Leader, 1989), Liu Heng's *Tapu* (Tapu, 1987), *Guanchang* (Officialdom, 1989), and *Xin Bing Lian* (New recruits company, 1987); Fang Fang's *Da Peng Che Shang* (On a big covered truck, 1987) and *Fengjing* (Landscape, 1987); Li Qi's *Bu Tan Aiqing* (Do not speak about love, 1988) and *Fannao De Rensheng* (Vexed life, 1987); and Ye Zhaoyan's *Hong Fangzi Jiudian* (Red public house, 1989) and *Yang Ge* (Love song, 1989).

Stream-of-consciousness fiction (*yishi liu xiaoshuo*) was initiated in Chinese contemporary narrative at the end of the 1970s. Wang Meng, the minister of culture of China during the period immediately after Mao's era, was actually the initiator of this literature school in China. Although his publications immediately after the Cultural Revolution incorporated only some stream-of-consciousness methodology into his typically traditional realistic narrative, he had a profound influence on contemporary Chinese neorealist fiction in all aspects. Among his first literary creations with some modern stream-of-consciousness flavor are Buddha *Ye De Yan* (Night eyes), *Chun Zhi Sheng* (Spring voice), *Hai De Meng* (Sea dream), and *Hudie* (Butterfly). In his short stories, he rearranges time and space in their natural narrative sequence by focusing more on psychological development and sentimental ups and downs of the characters than on the chronological order. His new writing style constitutes a challenge to traditional Chinese realism.

Other important works with stream-of-consciousness techniques after the 1980s are Li Guowen's *Yueshi* (Lunar eclipse) and *Dongtian li de Chuntian* (A spring inside the winter), Ru Zhijuan's *Caoyuan Shang De Xiaolu* (A path through grasslands), and Chen Rong's *Ren Dao Zhongnian* (The middle age). As has been pointed out throughout this entry, in many contemporary Chinese novels and short stories that belong to the neorealistic school, the stream-of-consciousness method is commonly used to enlarge the expressive power of literal semantics. One of the most important contemporary poets, Bei Dao, also used this technique in his famous novel *Bodong* (Undulation, 1981), also known by English speakers as *Waves*. In Bei Dao's short stories, collected in *Waves*, the images are often equally powerful as his own style, but the form lets Bei Dao explore his own self and his own society with more leisure. *Waves* is Bei Dao's most ambitious work; it was published first in 1979 for his own journal, *Today*. Like many of Bei Dao's stories, it is about people who insist on believing in love, even when society and those around them make such a belief seem folly. The novella made Bei Dao one of the prominent figures in Chinese modernist fiction. The stories in the book about the "lost generation" of the Cultural Revolution are seemingly disjointed. Bei Dao uses multiple narrators and interior monologue, breaking away from the traditional ways of expression. The book also introduces the underside of Chinese society in the 1970s, the crooks and thugs who managed to add an extra level of despair for those Chinese already harried or driven almost mad by the state. Bei Dao's vision is not totally despairing, although he has seen and heard much that might justify such an attitude, but it is certainly dark, and the flashes of light that cut through the haze of anguished memory seem at times too frail to make up for all the loss. At their best, his stories are almost unbearably poignant. The stream-of-consciousness method is also used in many of his poems.

In conclusion, in the broad context of reform, Chinese literature has experienced tremendous changes. The traditional concern for distinguishing right from wrong has been replaced by the creation of new ways of expression. There has been a revolution of expression.

See also Anticorruption Literature and Television Dramas; Avant-garde Literature; Experimental Fiction; Great Cultural Revolution, Literature during; Intellectuals, Political Engagement of (1949–1978); Intellectuals, Political Engagement of (1978–Present); Literary Policy for the New China; Literature of the Wounded; Misty Poetry; Modern Pop-Satire; Pre–Cultural Revolution Literature; Root-Searching Literature; Sexual Freedom in Literature.

Bibliography

Guo Zhigang, and Suen Zhongtian, eds., *Contemporary Chinese Literatur—Second Part* (Beijing: Higher Education Press, 1993); Jin Han, *Modern Chinese Novels* (Hangzhou, China: Zhejiang University Press, 1997); Zhang Rongjian, ed., *Contemporary Chinese Literature* (Wuhan, Hubei Province, China: University of Sciences and Technology of Central China Press, 2001); Zhang Rongjian, ed., *Contemporary Chinese Literature—Reference Materials* (Wuhan, Hubei Province: University of Sciences and Technology of Central China Press, 2001); Zhang Weizhong, *Transformations in the New Age Novels and the Chinese Traditional Culture* (Beijing: Xuelin Press, 2002).

Zhiyuan Chen

New Party (NP) (Taiwan)

Taiwan's New Party was born in 1993 with goals such as political reforms in Taiwan and unification of China. As the third-largest political force, the New Party played a significant role in Taiwanese politics in the 1990s.

Until July 1987, Taiwan was ruled under the Temporary Provisions Effective during the Period of National Mobilization for Suppression of the Communist Rebellion, which came into effect in 1948. The martial law that followed gave the ruling Nationalist Party (Kuomintang, KMT) absolute power without worrying about the terms in the Constitution. This continued when the KMT government retreated to Taiwan after 1949. In the late 1960s, things began to change. The government became more tolerant of different ideas, and opposition developed. In the 1980 national election, opposition candidates openly criticized the ruling KMT. In December 1986, some opposition politicians organized the Democratic Progressive Party (DPP). The next year, President Jiang Jingguo (Chiang Ching-guo) abandoned martial law. In early 1991, the National Assembly officially abolished the Temporary Provisions and adopted ten amendments to the Constitution. The following year, the second National Assembly further amended the Constitution, changing many rules for the National Assembly elections and instituting "direct election" for the president.

In the 1980s, the KMT began to show signs of weakening unity among its members. The conservative "hard-liners" against the Communists and for China's reunification began to feel doubtful about KMT leaders' move away from the party's principal lines. In the late 1980s, they charged that the party's leader, Li Denghui (Lee Teng-hui), was adopting more DPP ideas that preferred an independent Taiwan. In March 1993, these nonmainstream KMT factions registered to form the New Nationalist Party Line group, and several of their leaders resigned from their government offices to run for Legislative Yuan seats. On August 10, they declared the birth of the New Party.

In its declaration, the New Party criticized the ruling KMT's corruption and "refusing to learn from its past failure." It also labeled the DPP "nonresponsible," "exclusive," and the "champion of Taiwan's independence" that endangered the security of Taiwan. The New Party leaders claimed that they were the real representatives and spokesmen of the common people, the genuine democratic party determined to follow political reforms against government corruption and for stable social order. They claimed that they would regard the security of Taiwan as the highest principle and urged the KMT and DPP to start negotiations with mainland China.

From the beginning, the New Party was under attack from both the KMT and the DPP. The KMT party system never stopped giving its "traitors" a hard time. The DPP even used violence against the New Party. But the New Party kept on gaining popular support. During the 1994 elections, the New Party candidates won 6.09 percent of the popular vote. For the offices of provincial governor and mayor of Taipei, the NP performed better, gaining 7.7 percent in general votes and more than 30 percent in Taipei City. Altogether, the NP candidates captured two seats in the Provincial Assembly, eleven seats in the Taipei City Council, and two seats in the Kaohsiung City Council. The New Party's performance in the December 1995 election for the Legislative Yuan was the most impressive. Running on a platform of reconciliation and reunification with mainland China, the NP candidates won 12.95 percent of the popular vote and sent twenty-one representatives to the Legislative Yuan (12.8 percent of the chamber). Three months later, the New Party claimed another victory by sending forty-six of its members to the National Assembly (13.8 percent of the total seats) and claiming 13.67 percent of the popular vote.

The New Party leaders have been criticizing the KMT government's efforts to broaden Taiwan's international roles. President Li's visit in June 1995 to his alma mater, Cornell University, in the United States, NP leaders charged, offended the Beijing government, which regarded this move as proof that the Taiwanese leader was moving toward independence. During the summer, the People's Liberation Army conducted a series of military exercises, including missiles launched into the sea around Taiwan, to intimidate the Taipei government. The New Party charged the KMT with "unnecessarily antagonizing the mainland" and putting the security of the Taiwanese people at risk. This criticism seems to have won popular support. The New Party's progress can also be explained, at least partially, as the result of the party's advocacy of clean government and political reforms in Taiwan.

The New Party has always insisted that it represents the common folk against the KMT's political games and corruption and the DPP's "dangerous tricks" of Taiwan independence. The NP leaders stated that the situation was crying for a third political force to balance these two parties. They declared that the New Party would have "the National Assembly as its center, public opinion as its direction, general election as its means" to serve the people. The NP leaders claimed that they would keep an equal distance from the KMT or DPP, leaving cooperation with either a possibility so long as these two parties' policies were in the interests of the Taiwanese people. The party's "Three Parties, No Majority" doctrine states that the New Party will serve as a "balancer," watching over the other parties, forcing them to follow the rules of fair play, and helping rebuild people's confidence in Taiwan's democratic reforms.

The New Party's organization is different. It does not require its members to pledge, to pay dues, or to attend regular meetings. There are no chairpersons, central committee, or executive committee. There are only some "coordinators" to call the meetings, and all decisions are based on the results of democratic procedures. The party even welcomes so-called spiritual members, who do not have to register with the party so long as they support the New Party agenda. The New Party announces that it has nothing to do with the powerful financial cliques that have long been an active interest group in Taiwan's politics. This has reflected the desires of Taiwan's new middle-class urban population.

The New Party's "Mainland Policy" states that both Taiwan and the mainland are parts of China, and people on both sides of the Taiwan Strait should have this consensus. But the New Party does not promote a fast reunification with the mainland. "The unification should follow the strengthened communication, mutual trust, system adjustments, and the trial of time across the Strait. It should be achieved through peaceful means, and if necessary, accomplished by the future generations." The New Party supports the maintenance of the status quo of Taiwan-mainland relations while promoting more exchanges between the two sides. It insists that the final reunification with the mainland should take place after Beijing finally gives up its Communist authoritarianism and when the majority of the Taiwanese people consider that the time is ripe. The two sides should put aside the issue of sovereignty, which both are claiming now, and sincerely consider the possibility of a confederate system for a future "Greater China." For the near future, the "Mainland Policy" proposes to establish more channels of communication, including cultural, educational, athletic, and journalistic exchanges. The policy also suggests that some special "free economic and trade areas" be established on both sides of the Taiwan Strait to promote economic cooperation. Taipei should support the mainland's activities in international affairs. In return, Beijing should also respect Taiwan's role in the world.

Since the successful 1995 election, the New Party has suffered from many problems such as the lack of activity coordination and different opinions, as well as personalities, shortage of financial support, and other difficulties. In late 1997, the party launched intraparty reforms and "mass mobilization" campaigns aimed at the 1998 election for Taipei mayorship. But the results of the 1998 "three-in-one" election (the Legislative Yuan, the Taipei and Kaohsiung mayors' offices, and the two city councils' elections at the same time) were a big disappointment. Because of the lack of unity and coordination, the New Party lost about half its voters—only 7.09 percent of Taiwan voters supported the New Party candidates. Their Legislative Yuan seats dropped from twenty-one to eleven, while the KMT regained its majority control in the chamber and even won the Taipei mayor's office from the DPP. Facing the disappointing results, NP members criticized each other. Some even complained that they would never again work for the party.

But many people understand that the KMT victory in this election had something to do with the NP voters, especially in the competition for the Taipei mayor's office—about 77 percent of NP supporters actually voted for the KMT. Without the NP votes, the KMT candidate might well have lost the election to the DPP. The New Party members preferred to have the KMT rather than the proindependence DPP in office, since the KMT is still talking about China's reunification.

The New Party made some serious self-criticism and tried again during the 2000 presidential election. However, with the People First Party coming into being as the third-largest political party and the DPP winning the presidency, the influence of the New Party declined. Many New Party members actually changed their party affiliation. People wonder if the New Party will continue to play some role in Taiwan politics, since reunification will continue to be the core issue of mainland-Taiwan relations, which, in turn, will have a great impact on Taiwan's future.

See also Chen Shuibian (1950–); Taiwan, Constitutional Reform in; Taiwan, Development of Democracy in; Taiwan, Economic Transition of; Taiwan, Financial Relations with the Mainland; Taiwan, Trade Relations with the Mainland; Taiwan Strait Crisis, Evolution of.

Bibliography

Chin, Ko-Lin, *Heijin: Organized Crime, Business, and Politics in Taiwan* (Armonk, NY: M. E. Sharpe, 2003); Roy, Denny, *Taiwan: A Political History* (Ithaca, NY: Cornell University Press, 2003).

Xiansheng Tian

Newspapers

See Media Bodies, Central and Local; Media Distribution; Media Reform; Press Control; Press Freedom.

Nixon, Richard

See Nixon's Visit to China/Shanghai Communiqué (1972); Ping-Pong Diplomacy.

Nixon's Visit to China/Shanghai Communiqué (1972)

President Richard Nixon visited China on February 21–28, 1972. "The week that changed the world," as President Nixon called his historic 1972 visit, made for an eight-day television extravaganza and a public relations coup for hosts and guests alike. For eight days and nights, American television audiences tuned in to a spectacular parade of images from China, the first they had seen in more than twenty years. Nixon's trip received worldwide attention.

President Richard Nixon dines with Chinese Premier Zhou Enlai during Nixon's 1972 visit to China. © Bettman/Corbis.

Confronted with America's deep trouble in the **Vietnam War** and intense strategic rivalry with the Soviet Union, Nixon tried to build a relationship with China after he came to power in 1969. Chinese leaders felt an increased threat from the Soviet Union and responded positively to Nixon's message. In November 1970, Chinese premier **Zhou Enlai** told visiting leaders from Pakistan and Romania that "if the American side indeed has the intention to solve the Taiwan issue," Beijing would welcome the U.S. president's representative to Beijing for discussions. In April 1971, China invited U.S. Ping-Pong players to visit Beijing. The **Ping-Pong diplomacy** improved the political atmosphere between China and the United States. U.S. national security adviser Henry Kissinger's secret trip to Beijing in July 1971 and another trip in October 1971 paved the road for President Nixon's historic visit in 1972.

Soon after their arrival, Nixon and Kissinger were summoned to a meeting with Chairman **Mao Zedong**, which Kissinger later referred to as their "encounter with history." Next came a formal welcome banquet hosted by Premier Zhou Enlai. In the Great Hall of the People, as the band played such American favorites as "America the Beautiful," "Seize the hour! Seize the day!" Nixon quoted from Mao, raising his glass to his Chinese hosts. But beyond the pomp and spectacle, the banquet sent a clear and dramatic message to everyone watching that a new relationship was being forged.

On February 27, 1972, the two nations signed the Shanghai Communiqué. Leaders of both countries recognized that there are essential differences between China and the United States in their social systems and foreign policies. However, the two sides agreed that countries, regardless of their social systems, should conduct their relations on the principles of respect for the sovereignty and territorial integrity of all states, nonaggression against other states, noninterference in the internal affairs of other states, equality and mutual benefit, and peaceful coexistence. International disputes should be settled on this basis without resorting to the use or threat of force. The United States and the People's Republic of China are prepared to apply these principles to their mutual relations.

The communiqué stated: (*a*) progress toward the normalization of relations between China and the United States is in the interests of all countries; (*b*) both wish to reduce the danger of international military conflict; (*c*) neither should seek hegemony in the Asia-Pacific region and each is opposed to efforts by any other country or group of countries to establish such hegemony; and (*d*) neither is prepared to negotiate on behalf of any third party or to enter into agreements or understandings with the other directed at other states. When China and the United States declared their opposition to hegemony of any power in Asia, they clearly were referring to the Soviet Union. Thus Sino-American relations were established on a firm foundation of mutual self-interest.

The two sides reviewed the long-standing serious disputes between China and the United States. The Chinese side reaffirmed its position: the Taiwan question is the crucial question obstructing the normalization of relations between China and the United States; the government of the People's Republic of China is the sole legal government of China; Taiwan is a province of China that should have long been returned to the motherland; the liberation of Taiwan is China's internal affair in which no other country has the right to interfere; and all U.S. forces and military installations must be withdrawn from Taiwan. The Chinese government firmly opposes any activities that aim at the creation of "one China, one Taiwan," "one China, two governments," "two Chinas," or an "independent Taiwan" or advocate that "the status of Taiwan remains to be determined."

The U.S. side declared: The United States acknowledges that all Chinese on either side of the Taiwan Strait maintain that there is but one China and that Taiwan is a part of China. The U.S. government does not challenge that position. It reaffirms its interest in a peaceful settlement of the Taiwan question by the Chinese themselves. With this prospect in mind, it affirms the ultimate objective of the withdrawal of all U.S. forces and military installations from Taiwan. In the meantime, it will progressively reduce its forces and military installations on Taiwan as the tension in the area diminishes. The word "acknowledge" was translated into Chinese as *chengren*, which implies recognition of a legitimate claim.

The two sides agreed that it was desirable to broaden understanding between the two peoples. To this end, they discussed specific areas in such fields as science, technology, culture, sports, and journalism, in which people-to-people contacts and exchanges would be mutually beneficial. Each side undertook to facilitate the further development of such contacts and exchanges.

Both sides viewed bilateral trade as another area from which mutual benefit could be derived and agreed that economic relations based on equality and mutual benefit were in the interest of the peoples of the two countries. They agreed to facilitate the progressive development of trade between their two countries.

The two sides also expressed the hope that the gains achieved during this visit would open up new prospects for the relations between the two countries. They believed that the normalization of relations between the two countries was not only in the interest of the Chinese and American peoples but also would contribute to the relaxation of tension in Asia and the world.

President Nixon's trip to Beijing in 1972 symbolized a dramatic change in Sino-American relations, ending once and for all the irrationality of a situation in which the United States for almost a quarter of a century had ignored the existence of the world's most populous country, a nation with great potential power and a rival of the Soviet Union. Just as Washington during the 1950s feared the Sino-Soviet coalition, and Beijing during the 1960s frequently pointed to alleged Soviet-American collusion to isolate China, so Moscow now became apprehensive about closer Sino-American relations.

The Shanghai Communiqué established the basis for U.S.-China strategic cooperation, but Beijing refused to establish formal U.S.-China diplomatic relations as long as Washington recognized the Republic of China (ROC). Concerned about Soviet missile deployments and expansion in the Third World, the Carter administration in 1978 met China's conditions for normalization. The United States agreed to recognize the People's Republic of China as "the sole legal government of China," to remove all U.S. troops from Taiwan, and to abrogate the U.S.-ROC defense treaty. Nixon's 1972 visit to China was a major step toward the normalization of U.S.-China relations. China and the United States established diplomatic relations in January 1979.

See also Sino-American Relations, Conflicts and Common Interests; Sino-American Relations since 1949; Sino-Soviet Alliance; Taiwan Strait Crisis, Evolution of.

Bibliography

Harding, Harry, *A Fragile Relationship: The United States and China since 1972* (Washington, DC: Brookings Institution, 1992) (the Shanghai Communiqué is reprinted on pp. 373–377); Kissinger, Henry, *White House Years* (Boston: Little, Brown, 1979); Mann, James, *About Face: A History of America's Curious Relationship with China from Nixon to Clinton* (New York: Vintage Books, 2000); Tyler, Patrick, *A Great Wall: Six Presidents and China: An Investigative History* (New York: Public Affairs, 1999).

Guoli Liu

NP

See New Party (NP) (Taiwan).

NPC

See National People's Congress (NPC), Structure and Functions of.

O

Officialdom

See Corruption and Fraud, Control of.

Old-Age Insurance

China's **social security system** was first established in 1951. Under the old system, male workers retired at sixty and female workers retired at fifty-five. Work units bore the sole responsibility for providing retirees with pension benefits and other welfare services. In essence, China's old-age insurance worked through an employment security system.

China classifies work units into three categories: state owned, collective, and private. Before the reform, old-age insurance covered all employees in the state-owned sector. Their work units administered all aspects from determining eligibility to paying benefits. For urban collectives, there were no standard provisions. Benefits and coverage varied from trade to trade and from locality to locality. Employees in the private sector and rural farmers received no old-age insurance.

Reforming this old-age insurance system became necessary for at least three reasons. First, the Chinese economic structure had changed dramatically with the economic reform and **Open Door policy**. In 1978, the urban employment share of state-owned units was 78 percent. This share decreased to 38 percent in 2000. Therefore, the pension system, which was limited primarily to employees of government and party organizations, **state-owned enterprises**, and large urban collectives, was shrinking in its coverage of the labor force as self-employment and employment in private enterprises grew.

Second, the old system was pay-as-you-go in nature; that is, taxes were collected from the working generation to finance the benefits to the retired generation. Under this system, each generation benefits by population growth since there are more young people supporting the retirees. China's population, however, is aging rapidly because of strict family-planning controls, fast economic development and urbanization, and longer life expectancy. In 1999, the share of China's population aged sixty and over was 13.81 percent. Projections conducted by the United Nations (UN) indicated that the aged population in China will increase 111 percent between 2000 and 2025. In 1983, China had 38.76 million retirees. This number increased to 129.2 million in 2000. As a result, the dependency ratio of retirees to working employees increased from 1:8.9 in 1983 to 1:3.5 in 2000. The pay-as-you-go system obviously cannot be sustained in China.

Third, under the old system, enterprises bore the sole responsibility for providing retirees with pension benefits. Obviously, there was much disparity in pension burdens borne by older and newer enterprises. Some old enterprises had more retirees than active workers, and even those with good performance had difficulty allocating sufficient funds to pay for pension benefits. The decentralized old-age insurance system not only created inequality among enterprises but also lacked benefit portability and thus discouraged worker mobility across enterprises, industries, and sectors. Furthermore, the system demanded no contributions directly from employees and had no mechanism to share pension risk with other enterprises.

China's reform of old-age insurance started in 1984 with pension-pooling experiments in some cities and counties. Enterprises that participated in pooling programs put a portion of their total wages into a pension fund managed by a local old-age insurance bureau. A key objective of this reform is to relieve individual enterprises of full responsibility for their workers' retirement pensions by establishing funds that pool resources and share risks among enterprises. The ultimate goal is to establish a three-tier old-age insurance system. The first tier is basic insurance that will provide a basic pension to all workers in urban sectors. The second tier is enterprise supplementary insurance, which will consist of enterprises' additional contributions to the basic pension. The third tier is individual pension savings that are deposited in mandatory individual pension accounts. Once the three-tier system is established, the state, enterprises, and individual workers will share pension financing.

In 1997, the Chinese government adopted a Decision on Establishing a Uniform Basic Old-Age Insurance System for Enterprise Employees. The main points of the decision are as follows:

- A new system should cover employees in all urban sectors and the urban self-employed, including employees in state-owned enterprises and collective enterprises, Chinese employees in foreign-funded enterprises, employees and employers of private enterprises, and individual businesspeople and their hired hands.

- The responsibility for the operation of the pension scheme, including the keeping of employee records and payment of pensions, will be transferred from enterprises to social insurance agencies. A uniform scheme will be established for all sectors and labor forces, who are subject to a uniform standard, uniform administration, and uniform adjustment to use the funds.

- The old-age pension will be multitiered: a defined-benefit public pillar for redistribution, a mandatorily funded defined-contribution pillar for each worker, and a voluntary supplement pension pillar managed by each individual firm or private insurance company. The first pillar is to ensure a minimum living standard above the poverty line for all old people.

Pension financing is being diversified, and work units are no longer the sole contributors to the pension fund. Employees now also make contributions, and the government is to contribute as needed in its role as pension guarantor. Employee and employer contribution rates are levied on total wages, with a combined premium rate of 20 percent. Workers' contributions were to be a minimum of 4 percent of their wages by 1997 and were to increase 1 percentage point every two years from 1998 onwards until they reached 8 percent. All of the worker's contributions are to be allocated to the individual account, and the State Council has called for an interest rate based on bank savings rates to be credited to these accounts.

Under the new system, new workers who entered the labor force after 1997 will receive a combined pension income of social pool pension benefit and individual account-related monthly benefit, provided they have fifteen years of creditable service. Junior workers who started work before 1997 but had not retired by 1997 will get a mixture of the new and old systems of creditable service. They will receive the same two components as new workers plus a transition benefit, which is 1.72 percent of the average wage in the final working year of service before 1997. Older workers who retired prior to 1997 and are entitled to benefits defined by the former system will receive an average replacement rate of 80 percent.

After the adoption of the decision, employees participating in the old-age insurance program increased from 86.71 million in late 1997 to 94.33 million in 1999 and 106.3 million by the end of 2001. The number of retirees who enjoyed the basic old-age pension also increased from 25.33 million to 29 million and 33.46 million, respectively. Pensions are distributed through banks or postal offices. In 2001, the distribution rate of the socialized basic old-age insurance reached 98 percent, with a total of 205.41 billion yuan. The central government subsidized 34.2 billion yuan.

Some studies have proposed recommendations to improve China's old-age insurance. One recommendation is to invest pension funds in stocks. Interestingly, starting in June 2003, the social security fund entered the stock market. The first investment amount was 14 billion yuan. Another recommendation is to raise the official retirement ages (sixty for men and fifty-five for women), at least in the long run. Compared with countries that have similar life expectancies, retirement in China comes earlier. Early retirement causes a higher dependency ratio and makes the pension burden heavier on the working generation. A third recommendation is to unify pension programs across industries. Currently, eleven special state-owned enterprise (SOE) industrial sectors are running independent pension programs in parallel with provincial pooling systems. Their pension funds are pooled vertically at an industrial level. Hence money-losing industries cannot get help from profit-earning industries, which limits the base of risk sharing.

More important, China's old-age insurance should make a greater effort to cover the rural sector. In 2000, 499 million farmers were employed in the rural sector, accounting for 70 percent of the total working population in China. However, the rural sector shared only 11 percent of national social security benefits. Clearly, the development of the social security system has been delayed in the rural areas.

China began to try out old-age insurance in some of the rural areas in 1991. The rural pension program is administered by the Ministry of Civil Affairs of China. Currently, about 61 million rural farmers have participated in some kind of voluntary rural pension plan. Under most conditions, villages have organized funds to pay out old-age pensions for elders, to run old-age homes, and to provide all kinds of welfare for the villagers, according to the economic development situation of the village collective.

It is worth mentioning that most of the peasant households have carried on production and consumption on the scale of the family as a unit. The responsibility of providing for the aged is mainly met by their sons and daughters or their legal charges. This practice has fitted with the present countryside custom and old moral concepts of Chinese tradition and also has been protected by law.

See also Social Security Reform; Social Strata; Welfare Attainments since 1978.

Bibliography

Ministry of Labor and Social Security, *China Labor Statistical Yearbook* (Beijing: Labor Press, 2001); National Bureau of Statistics of the PRC, *China Statistical Yearbook* (various issues, 1994–2001) (Beijing: China Statistics Press); Song, Shunfeng, and George S-F Chu, "Social Security Reform in China: The Case of Old-Age Insurance," *Contemporary Economic Policy* 15 (1997): 85–93; Yin, Jason Z., Shuanglin Lin, and David F. Gates, eds., *Social Security Reform: Options for China* (Singapore: World Scientific, 2000).

Shunfeng Song

One Country, Two Systems

Deng Xiaoping's innovative, pragmatic political formula "one country, two systems" resulted in the British handover of Hong Kong as well as the Portuguese handover of Macao to the People's Republic of China (PRC) in 1997 and 1999, respectively. Originally, the concept was introduced to pave the way for China's reunification with Taiwan at the end of the 1970s. When the Sino-British negotiations began in 1982, it was adopted to resolve the Hong Kong and, later, Macao issues.

The concept was gradually developed by Deng Xiaoping and his followers from the late 1970s to 1984. It was a product of Deng's modernization programs for China. The "one country, two systems" idea provides for Hong Kong, Macao, and Taiwan to be incorporated into China under the central

A busy street in Hong Kong, which in 1997 ceased to be a British colony and became part of the People's Republic of China.

government in Beijing and essentially allows socialism and capitalism to coexist in a reunified China. The phrase itself was first introduced in reference to the Hong Kong and Macao issues in July 1982. During China's negotiations with Britain between 1982 and 1984, it became the guiding principle, and the concept was further elaborated. Although China has never clearly stated the precise contents of the concept, particularly with regard to the political system of Hong Kong, it characterized the concept as linkage: "A linkage of China's domestic politics with international issues; a linkage of the PRC's socialism with the capitalism of Hong Kong, Macao, and Taiwan; and a linkage of Hong Kong, Macao, and Taiwan in a framework of China's reunification."

The basic pledge was that China and Hong Kong would be "one country, two systems" for fifty years after 1997. "One country" refers to Chinese sovereignty and has always taken precedence where mainland China was concerned. "Two systems" involves complex histories and contradictory sentiments and is stressed by Hong Kong as more important than "one country."

The Sino-British Joint Declaration on the Question of Hong Kong and the Basic Law (enacted by China) embody the slogan in formal documentation. Both provide that Hong Kong will be a **special administrative region** of the People's Republic of China and will enjoy a high degree of autonomy, with executive, legislative, and independent judicial power, including that of final adjudication. It also means that Hong Kong and China have two separate customs entities and separate currencies. By guaranteeing fifty years of autonomy for Hong Kong, this formula holds out the promise of the continued prosperity of Hong Kong's capitalist economy while China undertakes its own capitalist transformation and political liberalization. In the best-case scenario, China and Hong Kong would converge at the same point along the same trajectory and merge to become "one country, one system." Indeed, by 1997, when Hong Kong was handed over to the mainland, very little of socialism remained in the mainland Chinese economic landscape. Nevertheless, China was far from being a modern capitalistic economy with an expanding democracy.

"One country, two systems" satisfied three interested parties at the negotiating table and was politically acceptable to all of them, with some trade-offs. China regained the sovereignty of Hong Kong. This symbolized the end of what Beijing considered a humiliation of a century and a half. The trade-off was Beijing's promise to maintain Hong Kong's capitalist system. For the British government, Hong Kong was no longer under its political control, but it could continue to exert influence through capitalistic competition and pluralist politics. The Hong Kong people were glad that their lifestyle could be preserved.

The biggest change in the political system was the replacement of a London-appointed governor by a locally elected chief executive blessed by Beijing. Besides the governor, the only other senior position discontinued after 1997 was that of the attorney general. This post has been renamed secretary of justice. All other senior posts remained unchanged.

While the years since the handover have not been free of problems, Beijing has been honoring its pledge to allow the people of Hong Kong to govern themselves. The rule of law and the independence of the judiciary have been upheld. Freedoms of press and religion are still parts of the reality of the Hong Kong people's daily life. Hong Kong has retained its distinct identity and strengths as an international business, financial, shipping, and aviation center. On the other hand, there are signs that one country is gradually overwhelming two systems, such as the resignation of Hong Kong chief secretary Anson Chan, the handling of Falun Gong (a religious cult) demonstrators, the controversy over the "right of abode," and the debate over English as the official language of instruction in secondary schools. Beijing has publicly stated that when "one country" is in conflict with the "two systems," "one country" should take priority.

On the basis of the success of "one country, two systems" in Hong Kong and Macao, China maintains that it is "the best mode for complete reunification of the motherland" and has promoted this as the model for Taiwan's reunification. Most notable is former Chinese president Jiang Zemin's speech on January 30, 1995, "Continue to Strive to Complete the Grand Cause of China's Reunification." Elaborating the concept of "one country, two systems," Jiang made an eight-point proposal for improving cross-strait relations and accelerating the process of China's peaceful reunification. Particularly in the arena of diplomatic relations, China has constantly reminded Taipei that if it subscribes to the "one country, two systems" model, the heads of Taiwan can be received everywhere as de facto leaders of state in a manner akin to the warm welcome Tung Cheehwa, the chief executive of Hong Kong, receives from many countries. Taipei has repeatedly rejected the model as a recipe for annexation. By suggesting different models such as "one China, two separate administrations," "one China, two governments," "one China, the federation," and "one China, the commonwealth of China," the Taiwanese insist that there is only one China, and that Taiwan and the mainland are on an equal footing. Although it is not clear how the stalemate between Beijing and Taipei will be broken, the success and prosperity of Hong Kong remain vital to shaping Taiwan's as well as the world's perception of "one country, two systems."

See also Administrative Structure of Government; Deng Xiaoping (1904–1997), Reforms of; Hong Kong, Return of; Jiang Zemin (1926–   ), Diplomacy of.

Bibliography

Ministry of Foreign Affairs of the People's Republic of China, "A Policy of 'One Country, Two Systems' on Taiwan," http://www.fmprc.gov.cn/eng/ziliao/3602/t18027.htm, accessed on November 25, 2004; Hamilton, Gary G., ed., *Cosmopolitan Capitalists: Hong Kong and the Chinese Diaspora at the End of the Twentieth Century* (Seattle: University of Washington Press, 1999); Kemenade, William van, *China, Hong Kong, Taiwan, Inc.: The Dynamics of a New Empire* (New York: Vintage Books, 1998); Wang, Enbao, *Hong Kong, 1997: The Politics of Transition* (Boulder, CO: Lynne Rienner, 1995); Wong, Yiu-chung, " 'Captive Colony' " in *Global Issues: China*, 9th ed., 199–201 (Guilford, CT: McGraw-Hill/Dushkin, 2002).

Ting Ni

One-Child Policy, History of

The "one-child policy" is a government family-planning policy, in place since 1980, to limit the number of children born to Chinese families. The goal of the policy is to avert the threat to the state of a population explosion. In the 1950s, the government urged mothers to provide more soldiers for the nation and purged economists who warned of looming troubles of an oversized population. The issue of family planning was brought up again in the 1970s, however, when major **cities** started to urge population control. The policy was only forcefully implemented after the **National People's Congress** in 1980 called for building family planning into China's long-term development strategy. In the same year, the Marriage Law was revised to restrict the age of marriage to twenty-two for men and twenty for women. The law also encourages late marriage and late childbearing. The 1982 census revealed that the population had crossed the 1 billion mark. Until then, the Chinese government had rejected "population explosion" as a real and significant threat to the socialist economy. Later, on Article 25 of the Constitution of 1982 was formulated to state, "The state promotes family planning so that population growth may fit the plans for economic and social development."

The family-planning policy, also called the "one-child policy," restricts urban families to one child and families in rural and pastoral areas to a maximum of two children. A government report released in 2001 claimed that the policy had effectively curbed the rapidly growing population. According to government data, without the one-child policy, China would have added 330 million people by 2001, more than the entire U.S. population. Benefits of family planning, according to the government, include better life for the people, liberation of women from frequent births, and the availability of more educational opportunities.

Since the implementation of family planning, the average fertility rate has dropped from six children per family in the 1970s to about two per family by the beginning of the year 2001. This is largely attributable to abortion, which has since been made widely available, and the compulsory use of long-term birth-control intrauterine devices (IUDs). Financial punishment has been forceful as well: violators pay a heavy fine equivalent to $300 in some areas and lose all benefits.

The one-child policy met tremendous resistance, especially before the 1990s, during its implementation. The traditional concept of having a son to carry on the family name is deeply rooted. Rural people still harbor the traditional concept of family happiness—the more children, the better. Violent protests often broke out in rural areas, where 800 million Chinese live. Because the policy was never formalized into law, local officials have had wide latitude in carrying out the policy and have resorted to brutal force at times. Measures such as coerced abortion and sterilization were among those most widely condemned by international human rights groups.

As the market reform has gained momentum, and as population aging has become a real pressure day by day since the late 1990s, the government has started to reform the stiff population pragmatism. In large cities, such as Shanghai, the experimental policy allows single-child couples to have two children. Some cities allow couples to have two children as long as the births are five years apart. In rural areas, some villages have abolished birth permits (a quota system) and allow couples to decide on their own when to have a baby. The government also encourages local officials to initiate and fund their own pilot projects on family planning, expecting to achieve both population reduction and stability.

Changes are happening in the marketing of birth-control devices. Notably since 2000, a variety of birth-control pills and devices have been put on the market as alternatives to IUDs. For some people, the forbidden area of family planning has been transformed from a simple arena of law enforcement to an attractive market of business opportunities. The prospect of profitability is attracting both state-owned and private enterprises. It is not rare for newspapers, media, and educational materials prepared by government agencies to include graphic instructions that used to be frowned upon. Analysts suspect, however, that the policy change may actually reflect a recent governmental effort in dealing with consequences of the overly harsh practices in the past, such as gender imbalance, rapid population aging, workforce deficiencies, and symptoms of a single-child society. In fact, some Chinese demographic scientists estimate that a "two-children plan" could safely be implemented in all of China. The first Family Planning Law, adopted in September 2002, allows provinces and municipalities to set up local regulations. It is clearly specified that couples that meet special provisions within the law be allowed a second child. Many local governments already had laws to that effect, and in 2003 Anhui Province passed regulations that allow thirteen categories of couples to apply to have a second child, while some can have a third or more. In many cities and regions families that meet local requirements may have a second child. Clearly, while the one-child policy remains dominant, many changes are taking place.

See also Marriage and Divorce; One-Child Policy, Social Issues of; Women, Role as Mothers; Women, Social Status of.

Bibliography

Information Office of the State Council of the People's Republic of China, *Family Planning in China* (Beijing: Information Office of the State Council of the People's Republic of China, 1995); State Family Planning Commission, *Population and Family Planning Law* (Beijing: State Family Planning Commission, September 1, 2002).

Jing Luo

One-Child Policy, Social Issues of

In 1979, the Chinese government established the one-child-per-couple population-control policy (one-child policy). The fast-growing Chinese population during the thirty-year period between 1949 and the late 1970s had put a serious strain on China's social and economic development. China's gross industrial and agricultural output could not keep up with rapid population growth; **unemployment** and surplus labor in rural areas were rampant; and education of the country's young was in jeopardy because of a fast-rising number of school-age children. In short, the Chinese government realized that in order

This billboard, photographed in Beijing in 1983, encourages couples to have only one child. © Bettmann/Corbis.

to feed its huge population for years to come, rapid population growth had to stop. Hence the goal of the one-child-per-couple population-control policy of 1979 was to set a demographic ceiling for China: the Chinese population was to stabilize at 1.2 billion people by the year 2000. China was to achieve zero population growth (ZPG) by that time. The policy was implemented at the local level through governmental agencies.

The one-child policy has been remarkably successful in achieving its original demographic goal. The crude birth rate dropped by 43 percent between 1972 and 1982. The total fertility rate was reduced from 5.81 children per woman in 1970 to less than 2 children per woman in 2000. In other words, the average Chinese woman has two children today, compared with six children thirty years ago. Population growth slowed down drastically, from 26 percent in 1970 to 8.8 percent in 2000. By reducing the fertility rate and therefore the population growth rate, China has been able to greatly improve its infant mortality rate, maternal mortality rate, and, accordingly, its life expectancy for both men and women. In the end, China was able to avoid population growth by 250 to 300 million by the year 2000. More than twenty years after the implementation of the one-child policy, China now has seen an entire generation of single children.

However, the generation of single children has spawned a host of social issues, both positive and negative, linked directly or indirectly to the implementation of the one-child population-control policy. For example, in the last twenty years, China has seen tremendous economic and social development, partly due to its effective population-control policy. The number of school-age children has been dropping steadily since the mid-1990s. Presumably, fewer children means better educational opportunities and maximal resources for each child. They are also healthier, more intelligent, more sociable, and more likely to make friends than nonsingle children.

With fewer children, parents can afford to invest in their children's education and have more time to devote to their own education and careers. Reduced fertility especially has helped rural women resist family pressure for bearing more children.

However, the one-child-per-couple population policy has met strong resistance, especially among the rural population, which makes up more than 70 percent of the total population. One obstacle is the strong preference for sons, which can be traced back to the traditional Chinese marriage pattern and family formation, as well as ancestor worship practices. Traditionally, Chinese families were patrilineal; that is, only male children could inherit their families' land. Chinese families were also patrilocal, meaning that exogamy was strictly observed. Women married into their husbands' families; those few men who married into their wives' families were usually subject to humiliation. Within a patrilocal system, responsibility for support of one's elder parents lay mainly with sons who lived with their parents after they got married. Rarely did this duty fall to daughters who went to live with their husbands' families when they married.

Ancestor worship also played an important role in son preference in traditional China. The purpose of ancestor worship was to ensure the continuity of the family lineage. To have sons and grandsons was to fulfill one's filial duty and secure one's afterlife. Historically, the strong desire for male offspring, coupled with economic hardships, made many Chinese families consciously limit the number of girls they would have. Unwanted female infants were either victims of infanticide or abandoned.

In recent decades, the one-child policy has made the "son preference" practice salient once again. Because contemporary China has no rural pension system and because of the persistence of the patrilocal and patrilineal family structure, some families, particularly rural ones, choose to have one son, not just one child. The result is a resurgence of female infanticide, abortion of female fetuses, and a large number of "missing" girls who are either dead, abandoned, or given up for adoption. In addition, women who cannot have a son may be abused.

Another consequence of "son preference" is an imbalance of the sex ratio in which men outnumber women significantly. According to the fifth national census data released in April 2002, China has a sex ratio at birth of 116.9 male newborns per 100 female newborns. The international standard sex ratio is about 105 male infants per 100 female infants at birth. As a result, an estimated 50 million Chinese men may not be able to find a wife in years ahead.

Guttentag and Secord (1983) suggest that an imbalance in the sex ratio (defined as the number of males over the number of females) in a society has serious social and cultural consequences. At the very least, over- or undersupply of one sex relative to the other shapes family structure, family relations, and the relative status of each sex. According to Guttentag and Secord (1983), an undersupply of women relative to men forces women into assuming more traditional gender roles such as those of wives and mothers because men who can afford to marry desperately attempt to keep and protect their women so that other men cannot "steal" them. Women in a society with a high sex ratio are less likely to be educated or permitted by their husbands to work outside the home.

Another serious consequence of a high sex ratio in China is the flourishing of illegal trafficking and trade of women on black markets. Most women who are kidnapped are sold to men who otherwise could not either find a wife or afford to marry one. The situation is compounded by poverty, because poor, mostly rural men find that purchasing a wife through a trafficker is far less expensive than paying for a wedding. Many have chosen the former. However, there are also women who are sold "voluntarily." These women look to escape poverty or an abusive husband.

The drastically reduced fertility has significantly increased the dependency ratio of the Chinese population—a graying of the Chinese population. For example, about 9 percent of the total population was over sixty in 2000; by 2030, this could reach 22 percent.

Still more consequences of the one-child population-control policy exist. The one-child policy is unevenly implemented: more urban and well-educated couples tend to have only one child, while poor and less educated rural couples and ethnic-minority couples have two or more children. As a result, urban fertility, especially that in Shanghai, is well below the replacement level of fertility, meaning that in the long run, China would have a negative population growth. This pattern may create further inequality in such areas as educational opportunities.

The one-child policy may also have some long-term implications for Chinese culture. If this policy continues indefinitely, there would be generations of Chinese who do not have any sisters, brothers, uncles, aunts, nieces, or nephews. The impact of social trends on family structure could be profound.

Given time, the patrilocal marriage pattern may have to change. Young people either set up their household right after their marriage or may have to choose which set of parents they would like to live with. Nevertheless, it becomes the responsibility of the two young people to eventually take care of two sets of parents.

Although single children have been found to be more social and intelligent, they are also more likely to be overpampered. They may show signs of selfishness and have little interest in marriage and having children themselves in the future. In fact, their rebellious attitudes toward family cause major concerns about whether the one-child generation will be willing and able to care for their elders in the future.

Recently, an interesting trend has emerged: more couples, mostly urban couples, prefer to have a daughter as their only child. The reason cited is that daughters tend to stay closer to their parents after marriage. Given that more and more urban young people tend to set up their own households upon marriage, instead of living with the husbands' families, married daughters have more freedom to visit their own parents and are more likely to contribute to their parents' care in the future.

China implemented its First National Family Planning Law on September 1, 2002. The new family-planning law consists of seven chapters and forty-seven articles that outline individuals' legal obligations and provide standardized provisions on measures that guarantee the national population and birth-control policy. Particularly, the new law stipulates women's rights and bans any discrimination and abuse of baby girls. It also calls for increased educational and employment opportunities for women. The new law has brought legislation into the family-planning area that has been abused over the years. Hopefully, the new family-planning law could reduce some high social and demographic costs of the one-child policy for China in the years ahead.

See also Marriage and Divorce; One-Child Policy, History of; Women, Role as Mothers; Women, Social Status of.

Bibliography

"China to Implement First National Family Planning Law," *People's Daily*, August 3, 2002; Chu, Henry, "China's Marriage Crisis," *Los Angeles Times*, March 3, 2001; Das Gupta, Monica, Jiang Zhenghua, Li Bohua, Xie Zhenming, Woojin Chung, and Bae Hwa-Ok, "Why Is Son Preference So Persistent in East and South Asia? A Cross-Country Study of China, India, and the Republic of Korea," Working paper 2942, World Bank, 2003; Guttentag, Marcia, and Paul F. Secord, *Too Many Women? The Sex Ratio Question* (Thousand Oaks, CA: Sage Publications, 1983); Li, Heng, "Men Outnumber Women, Population Structure Worries China," *People's Daily Online*, September 27, 2002, http:// english.people.com.cn/200209/27/eng20020927-104013.shtml, accessed on November 25, 2004.

Liying Li

Open Door Policy (1978)

The Open Door policy was officially proclaimed by Deng Xiaoping in 1978, but it was rooted in a fundamental shift in thinking and policy in both China and the outside world. China's opening to the outside world occurred because both its leaders and the industrial democracies concluded that the nation's isolation was costly and dangerous for China, the region, and the world. In the 1970s, **Mao Zedong, Zhou Enlai**, and Deng Xiaoping on the Chinese side and such Western leaders as Presidents Richard Nixon and Jimmy Carter, Germany's Helmut Schmidt, and Japan's Kakuei Tanaka had reached the same conclusion: The weak and divided China of the late 1960s and early 1970s invited foreign aggression from the Soviet Union and was a source of global and regional instability, but a modernizing and stable China could be a bulwark for regional peace and prosperity.

After intense struggle in the post-Mao succession, Deng Xiaoping emerged as the new paramount leader in 1978. Deng gave greater play to market forces, dismantled agricultural collectives, and encouraged foreign trade with and investment in China. The impressive economic growth of the newly industrialized countries in Asia, whose success was based largely on their strong links with the international economy, had an important influence on Chinese reformers. Deng claimed that China had opened its door and would never close it again. The heart of the pragmatist program was a top-priority commitment to economic development—the Four Modernizations, referring to the modernizations of industry, agriculture, science and technology, and national defense.

The Open Door foreign economic policy reflected a fundamental change in China's development strategy. The desire to get greater access to U.S. economic assistance and technology provided the impetus for Beijing to work for improved relations with Washington. A drive to improve relations with the United States from 1978 to 1981 was an important component of the opening to the outside world. Beijing wanted broad and generous U.S. support for the Four Modernizations and moved to improve relations with the United States to achieve this. The normalization of Sino-American relations on January 1, 1979, led to the rapid creation of an institutional and legal framework for expanded economic cooperation. These efforts paid off: the United States granted most-favored-nation trading status to China in July 1979, gradually loosened trade restrictions, and shifted the People's Republic of China (PRC) to the category of "friendly, nonallied" country in May 1983.

In the late 1970s and early 1980s, four special economic zones were set up at Shenzhen, across the border from Hong Kong, Zhuhai, opposite Macao, Xiamen, across from Taiwan, and Shantou, on the coast of northern Guangdong. Furthermore, fourteen "open cities" were designated along China's coast. Provided with special tax and investment incentives to lure foreign capital and technology, these special zones were the spearhead of China's new strategy of export-led development. The special zones were designed to import high technology, increase exports, earn foreign exchange, create jobs, assimilate foreign managerial and entrepreneurial skills, and attract foreign investment.

Utilization of foreign investment was a central component of the open door. Such investment was anathema during the first thirty years of the PRC's history, but in 1979 a law on foreign investment was promulgated. During the next several years, restrictions on the type, size, and operations of foreign investment were progressively relaxed. The permissible forms of foreign investment eventually included compensatory trade, processing of materials, assembly, joint ventures, and complete foreign ownership. Overseas Chinese were among the most enthusiastic respondents to Beijing's calls for foreign investment. After 1992, China further intensified its effort to attract foreign investment. In the 1990s, China ranked with the United States as one of the two largest recipients of **foreign direct investment**. In 2002, China became the top recipient of foreign direct investment in the world.

China's decision to participate in the global market has had a demonstrably powerful effect on domestic administrative structures, economic institutions, and legal norms. Once the decision to open up was made in 1978, for example, administrative decentralization, enterprise reform, and the creation of a legal framework to protect commercial transactions and property rights were needed to enhance China's competitiveness in the world market. The realization that rapid economic development and technological modernization would require large infusions of foreign capital similarly meant that Chinese leaders would need to pay greater attention to foreign concerns, in particular to ways of improving the local investment climate. Under such conditions, they had little choice but to undertake a liberalization of prevailing commercial norms and practices.

Market-oriented domestic reforms were also linked to the absorption of foreign technology. Technology transfers were now initiated and decided upon at the enterprise level, which made it more likely that any technology acquired would be appropriate and fully utilized. Direct interactions between Chinese enterprises acquiring technology and foreign firms selling it also facilitated technical training by the foreign partner. Market-oriented domestic reforms also were intended to encourage foreign businesses to undertake operations by providing a more economically rational and less bureaucratized environment in which foreign businesses could operate. Together with the rebuilding of the judicial and legal system, these reforms were intended to help create a more predictable environment for foreign businesses. As a result, the gap between the Chinese and the international business environment has been narrowed.

It is a national policy of China to open to the outside world in all directions. In the face of intense economic competition and rapid technological advances, China should take a stance in the world by improving the pattern of opening up in all directions, at all levels, and in a wider range, more effectively using domestic and international markets and resources, striving to open international markets, and taking an active part in regional economic cooperation and multilateral trade systems. Over the years, China has expanded its initial focus on opening to the West to opening to all countries, including its former strategic competitor, Russia.

The policy of opening to the outside world has produced significant results. The Open Door policy, coupled with China's domestic reforms, has prompted remarkable economic growth. China's gross national product more than quadrupled between 1978 and 2000. China's average annual rate of economic growth increased from about 6 percent between 1953 and 1978 to more than 9 percent between 1979 and 2000. The economic reforms have been extraordinarily successful at transforming China from a closed economy to a major trading nation. China's total foreign trade rose from $21 billion in 1978 to more than $300 billion in 1997 and more than $620 billion in 2002. The ranking of China in the world's trading nations jumped from thirty-second to sixth. By 2002, China's exports to the United States exceeded those of Japan.

In addition to fostering a series of domestic institutional and legal reforms, China's Open Door policy of 1979 has also resulted in wider Chinese participation in international regimes and organizations. China became the largest recipient of World Bank loans. One very significant development is China's entry into the World Trade Organization (WTO) in 2001. Hong Kong has become part of China, and Taiwan has developed extensive economic and cultural contacts with the mainland. As a result of the Open Door policy, China and the outside world have become truly interdependent.

See also Deng Xiaoping (1904–1997), Politics of; Deng Xiaoping (1904–1997), Reforms of; Hong Kong, Return of; One Country, Two Systems; Sino-American Relations, Conflicts and Common Interests; Sino-American Relations since 1949; Sino-Japanese Relations since 1949; Sino-Russian Relations since 1991; Sino-Soviet Alliance.

Bibliography

Economy, Elizabeth, and Michel Oksenberg, eds., *China Joins the World: Progress and Prospects* (New York: Council on Foreign Relations Press, 1999); Garver, John W., *Foreign Relations of the People's Republic of China* (Englewood Cliffs, NJ: Prentice Hall, 1993); Lardy, Nicholas R., *Integrating China into the Global Economy* (Washington, DC: Brookings Institution Press, 2002); Shirk, Susan L., *How China Opened Its Door: The Political Success of the PRC's Foreign Trade and Investment Reforms* (Washington, DC: Brookings Institution Press, 1994); Zweig, David, *Internationalizing China: Domestic Interests and Global Linkages* (Ithaca, NY: Cornell University Press, 2002).

Guoli Liu

Overseas Chinese

See International Migration and Overseas Chinese; United States, Chinese in.

P

Patent Protection

In today's capitalistic world, one of the most important topics in debate is patent protection and its enforcement. In the United States and other developed countries, most patent laws have seen little change in the past years due to a long history of capitalism. It is in China, where only since the 1980s has communism released its grasp to allow some capitalist ideas to flow in, that changes and additions to patent laws have been made and will continue to be made throughout China's development and accession to the World Trade Organization and beyond. These changes and additions are profound because until only a few decades ago China was run by a Communist government under which the state owned and operated everything and had no need for laws such as these. Copyright and trademark laws along with high rates of piracy are also tied directly to the continuously changing legal environment in which patent protection and enforcement reside.

Patent law is a relatively new topic in China. As a whole, China's modern legal environment began to appear after the reforms led by Deng Xiaoping in the late 1970s to revitalize China. Before this crucial turning point in its history, China was strictly a Communist state where everything was owned and operated by the Chinese government. In this society, there was no need for patent protections or other such laws, including laws on copyright infringement and trademark usage, because no business entity existed, hence no possible competition.

The main purpose of the reforms was to introduce some capitalistic principles while still maintaining the control of a Communist state, in effect creating a "socialist market economy." These principles led to the introduction of market competition, restructuring of **state-owned enterprises (SOEs)**, and the introduction of foreign investments. This also meant that the Communist Party's grasp on the people had to be compromised by means of more governing under the rule of law. As privatization began after the reforms, the need for protection of a person's own ideas and businesses through patents, copyrights, and trademarks arose because competing enterprises were duplicating and pirating to put money in their own pockets. This problem can be seen in any capitalist society and can often become hazardous to the well-being of that society unless action against it is taken through laws.

The People's Republic of China (PRC) Patent Law

The original Patent Law was passed by the **National People's Congress (NPC)** in 1984. It offered a rough sketch of patent protection and overall was poorly enforced. Because of this lack of enforcement and unclear articles, within eight years, it was amended. This amendment strengthened and enforced the law, but as time progressed (and capitalism expanded in people's minds), the realization that more must be added to make the law comparable to that of the United States or other international trade partners became apparent. Another important factor in the movement to make a second amendment to the law was to bring China one step closer to compliance with the World Trade Organization's (WTO) requirements. Being a partner in the WTO was a crucial step China needed to make to grow in the modern world. The second amended Patent Law was passed on August 25, 2000, and came into effect on July 1, 2001.

The Second Amended Patent Law

The major changes in the law can be divided into three categories: new judicial and administrative protections, improved application procedures, and simplified enforcement procedures. The new judicial and administrative protections are important because they eliminate problems dealing with the WTO requirements on trade-related aspects of intellectual property rights (TRIPs). Perhaps the most important article of the amended Patent Law regarding TRIPs is Article 11, which gives patent owners the right to prohibit unauthorized "offering for sale." This means that no one may advertise the patented products, display the products, or offer the products for sale without the authorization of the patent holder. The rights of the patent holder on this matter were not protected under previous laws. Other important articles regarding protections that were not present in previous laws are Articles 6, 60, 61, and 63. Article 6 deals with employment inventions and, under the new law, is more favorable to employers. Under the article, an employment invention is an invention made while performing the tasks of the employer or made by the employee using not just the employer's materials (as in the old law) but also technological resources. It should also be noted that this article, unlike other parts of the amended Patent Law, is different from the U.S. patent law. The U.S. patent law also provides employers the right to use the employee's patent royalty free. Article 60 pertains to patent infringement damages. These damages are now determined by the loss incurred by the patent owner and the profit received by the infringer. Under the old Patent Law, there was no standard for determining infringement damages. Under Article 61, if a patent owner can prove that someone is infringing or will infringe on his or her rights, he or she may seek an order of injunction from the court. This was also nonexistent in previous laws. Also, in previous laws, ignorance was sufficient to exempt a seller or user from prosecution for an infringement, which severely crippled the enforcement of patent rights. Article 63 helps rectify this. To further protect patent owners and enforce patent rights, possible infringers who use or sell patented products will not be liable for damages only if the infringer can prove that the products come from a legitimate source. The new protections expressed in these articles are all crucial to the well-being of patent owners and in the long run promote and encourage technicians and engineers to innovate new products and methods to be patented.

The second category of changes in the Patent Law is improvements in patent application procedures. In general, these procedures have now been simplified, and the filing requirements for foreign and international applicants have been reduced. Under Article 36, prior foreign research is no longer needed when an applicant has filed an application in a foreign country, although in some cases the applicant will be asked to furnish documents. This leniency is due in part to the fact that the China patent office, now called the State Intellectual Property Office (SIPO), has adequate searching capacity. In previous years (and laws), SIPO did not. Another key improvement not found in the old patent laws is that any Chinese entities or individuals who intend to file an international patent application shall first file an application with SIPO (Article 20). SIPO will then appoint a patent agent. This simplifies the application process and, more important, conforms with WTO requirements on TRIPs. Also, to protect possible patent owners who have yet to see their application approved, under Article 19 the agents assume the responsibility of keeping all information confidential.

The last category of major changes in the amended Patent Law is simplified enforcement procedures. Under Articles 45 and 46, the law removes revocation procedures found in the old laws to avoid overlap and conflict with the invalidation procedures and describes the proceedings of invalidation (interested parties can only challenge a patent's validity now through the invalidation procedure). Another enforcement procedure is the burden of proof found in Article 57. Where a process-invention patent for the manufacturing of a new product is involved, anyone manufacturing the identical product must prove that its process is different from the patented process (to disprove that infringement occurred). This article is similar to a U.S. law with the exception that U.S. courts may use their discretion to decide whether or not the process is different, but guidelines are tougher in Chinese courts. Another method to simplify enforcement procedures is using a statute of limitations of two years (Article 62). Jurisdiction of local authorities is another area that has gone through changes to simplify the enforcement procedures. The amended Patent Law gives provincial-level authorities that have jurisdiction the ability to handle any patent infringement dispute, as in the old laws, but now they have clearly written powers. The changes and additions implemented by the second amended Patent Law are designed to simplify and, at the same time, clearly define what is to be done in the process of issuing, enforcing, and protecting patents.

Copyrights and Trademarks

About the same time as the second amended Patent Law was passed, amendments to the Copyright and Trademark Laws were also created and passed. The most probable reason for these changes was again to satisfy WTO requirements. The Trademark Law was amended on October 27, 2001, and became effective on December 1, 2001 (other, less major provisions were passed in late 2002). A review of some of the major changes leads to outcomes similar to those of the amended Patent Law. Enforcement has been strengthened, the procedures for registration have been simplified, and infringements have definitive punishments. Similarities to U.S. trademark laws can also be seen. For example, individuals may now register more kinds of trademarks, including three-dimensional trademarks and trademarks with geographic indications. The Copyright Law was amended at the same time, on October 27, 2001. Once again, some similarities appear. Copyright enforcement has been strengthened, protection has been broadened, and more rights have been clearly defined for the copyright owner. In general, the amended laws that are being passed in China to deal with the legal environment surrounding patents and other capitalist materials are moving closer to what is seen in developed capitalist countries such as the United States.

The Future of Laws in China

Even though the newly amended laws in China are being enforced with greater rigor now than in the past, there is still much piracy to be dealt with. The piracy comes in many forms. The most talked about is copyrighted information through the **Internet** (patent infringement is also a large issue, but it remains behind the spotlight of copyright infringement, in the eyes of the public, because the average individual in today's society has more in common with online copyright issues). This is because even in the United States, piracy on the Internet is a major problem due to anonymity. In China, copyrighted software and Internet piracy alone cost companies more than U.S. $1 billion in 2000. It is estimated that China has more than 90 percent of its software pirated due to anonymity and the lack of qualified enforcement officers. Some problems have been addressed, mainly in Beijing and Shanghai, but without stricter amendments, laws, and enforcement practices, these problems will only get worse. Other areas where lawbreaking can be seen are vendors openly hawking DVDs for as little as a dollar on city streets and the selling of fake brand-name items such as Nike shoes and other consumer goods such as cosmetics.

Great leaps have been taken by China, especially in recent years, to strengthen patent and copyright laws, largely because of regulations on becoming a WTO member, which China strove to do in order to further advance in the world. The current challenges China faces in strengthening the laws are educating enforcement officers, increasing consumer awareness, and stopping the ignorance of lawbreakers. Now that China is a WTO member, the citizens of China will see more amendments, more publicity, and stricter laws dealing with the prosecution of patent and copyright infringements as the years progress because of pressure from fellow WTO members (to avoid sanctions), but also because of the natural course of becoming a more capitalistic society.

See also Legal Infrastructure Development and Economic Development; World Trade Organization (WTO), China's Accession to.

Bibliography

Chen, Jiwen, "The Amended PRC Patent Law," *China Business Review*, July–August 2001: 38–42; "China Urged to Intensify Piracy Crackdown," January 23, 2002, http://www.cnn.com/2002/BUSINESS/asia/01/23/china.piracy/index.html, accessed on March 1, 2004; Esler, Lindsay, and Paul Davies, "New Law Gives Hope to Patent Owners," http://www.legalmediagroup.com/mip/includes/print.asp?SID=1143, accessed on December 9, 2004; Feng, Peter, *Intellectual Property in China* (Hong Kong: Sweet & Maxwell Asia, 1997); Williams, Martyn, "U.S. Criticizes China over Copyrights," April 25, 2002, http://www.cnn.com/2002/TECH/industry/04/25/china.copyrights.idg/index .html, accessed on February 29, 2004; Yaozeng, Shen, "China Sweeps Away Outdated IP Laws," *Managing Intellectual Property*, January 2003, http://www.legalmediagroup .com/mip/includes/print.asp?SID=1763, accessed on December 8, 2004.

Steve Gentner

Pattern of Savings

See Savings, Pattern of.

People's Communes/Household Responsibility System

In 1958, nine years after the founding of the People's Republic of China, **Mao Zedong** and his supporters launched the **Great Leap Forward**, an ambitious movement to rapidly transform China into an economic power essentially through mobilizing the political enthusiasm and revolutionary fervor and releasing the creative energies of the masses. A radical economic program that aimed to drastically improve agricultural and industrial production, especially of iron and steel, mainly through utilizing moral incentives and mass mobilization with little regard to technological constraints, the Great Leap Forward ended a few years later in a total fiasco.

A high point of the Great Leap Forward in the rural areas was the formation of the "people's communes," promoted by Mao Zedong and officially endorsed by a Central Committee resolution in August 1958. According to the August resolution, rural communes could best mobilize peasants' production capability and would play a major role in facilitating socialist construction and accelerating China's transition to communism. Consequently, communes began to emerge all over the countryside. By the end of 1958, rural China was organized into roughly 26,000 communes that incorporated almost all peasant households. Although communes varied widely in size, they averaged 5,000 households and between 15,000 and 25,000 people each.

The establishment of communes led to a highly centralized rural economy and represented a radical effort to create large-scale yet self-contained rural communities. Based on Mao's notion of self-reliance, each commune was supposed to be a self-sufficient unit capable of producing its own basic necessities and complete with its own education and medical system, agricultural production, and industries. Virtually replacing the existing townships or county-level administrations, communes functioned as the new rural political and economic units and integrated almost all aspects of peasants' lives.

Communes were supposed to and did on many occasions provide more effective means of organizing an extensive labor force for large-scale construction and water-control projects. They were also further divided into production brigades consisting of several originally separate villages, which were in turn divided into smaller work units, known as production teams. A production team was in actual practice a reconstituted village and was often in direct charge of work assignments and the recording of work points gained by peasants. Work points accumulated by peasants would be tallied at year's end and would be converted mainly to payment in kind, usually in the form of grain, and partially to payment in cash.

A significant change brought about by the Great Leap Forward and the formation of communes was the enlistment of rural women into the work force. Many rural women had previously worked only sporadically or seasonally in the fields because their primary duties were in the households. They were now called upon to work full-time in the fields and received work points accordingly. Although the rate of their work points was lower than that for men, women's financial contributions to families were significant. To free them from household chores for work in the fields, communes set up day-care facilities and mess halls. Rural women thus became an integral part of the work force.

Caught up in the fervor of creating economic miracles during the Great Leap Forward, many communes plunged into agricultural disasters. Intent on pleasing their superiors or demonstrating their revolutionary enthusiasm, some overzealous rural cadres often resorted to foolhardy planting techniques, such as close planting, overuse of fertilizers, and deep plowing in the hope of achieving enormous crops, which in turn killed crops before they reached maturity. Unable to meet unrealistically high quotas, cadres often submitted highly inflated reports of productivity figures. Exaggerated reporting of grain production left China poorly prepared for 1959 and 1960 when bad weather, combined with seriously flawed policies, resulted in a devastating crisis with severe food shortages and massive famine.

The Great Leap Forward turned out to be a disaster. Meanwhile, communes also proved to be too large to function effectively. By the end of the Great Leap Forward, the size of communes was reduced, which resulted in an increase of the number of communes to 74,000. Furthermore, communes also turned over many of their functions to production brigades and production teams.

In the late 1970s, a few years after the death of China's revolutionary leader Mao Zedong, the new leader, Deng Xiaoping, and his supporters launched drastic economic reforms. The most significant of the new policies was the so-called household responsibility system, that is, to contract land to individual peasant households. At the famous Third Plenum of the Eleventh Central Committee convened in late 1978, two significant drafts concerning agricultural development and people's communes were passed. The documents suggested that peasants' payments should be directly related to work performed and that responsibility for tasks could be assigned to small work groups. Although the documents did not specify the size of small work groups, peasants increasingly viewed the household as such a small group. This marked the beginning of the trend toward returning to household farming. The resolutions passed at the Third Plenum resulted in a significant change in agricultural organization in the next few years that culminated in the reestablishment of household farming.

During the transitional period, production teams retained control of landownership. However, control over the inputs was gradually shifted to individual households. Initially, production teams signed contracts with individual peasant families on a yearly basis and distributed a certain amount of land along with farm tools to a family, which agreed to submit a designated amount of yield from the so-called responsibility land. Very quickly, almost all inputs became the responsibility of the household, and any surplus production from the responsibility land beyond taxes and collective dues belonged to the peasant families, which could then sell it on the free market. Toward the end of 1981, more than a third of rural households participated in the responsibility system. Two years later, the system applied to almost all rural households. In January 1983, the *People's Daily* proclaimed that "the People's Commune in the old sense no longer exists." Consequently, the collective agriculture that had been introduced in the late 1950s virtually disappeared and was succeeded by a system in which the household was again the basic unit of production. Meanwhile, the township authorities resumed administrative functions that had previously been assigned to communes or production brigades. In 1984, the central government approved assigning land leases on a fifteen-year term and sanctioned the transfer of such leases to other cultivators. In addition, peasants were allowed to hire wage laborers to work on their leased land. The impact of the reforms became more pronounced after early 1992, when Deng Xiaoping reaffirmed the government's determination to quicken the pace of modernization, which had suffered a setback since the Tiananmen Square incident of 1989.

Decollectivization and the introduction of the household responsibility system have resulted in greater farming efficiency and hence an increase in agricultural productivity. As a consequence, a surplus agricultural labor force has emerged. In the meantime, economic reforms also prompted the development of rural enterprises and private businesses, once condemned as capitalistic. Because nonagricultural opportunities are now available to peasants, many male peasants are often the first to abandon agricultural labor and to rush to towns and **cities** or rural enterprises for new job opportunities.

Peasants are now eager to seek nonagricultural sources of income. They are attracted to rural or township industry because it promises a relatively higher income. Income from agriculture is meager by comparison and is often not enough to ensure the economic prosperity of a rural family. In other words, a rural family cannot experience significant improvement in its living standard if it relies solely on agricultural income. Nevertheless, many peasants continue to view the responsibility land as their basic security and are reluctant to abandon it. Nonagricultural positions can be more lucrative, but less secure. If peasants lose their wage-earning jobs, they can always return to the land.

The availability of alternative forms of employment for peasants has led to notable changes in the gender division of labor. Because many male peasants are taking up higher-paying nonfarming jobs, work on the responsibility land often falls to rural women. Caught up in the national mood to get rich quickly and in order to improve their living standard, rural women often encourage their husbands to find wage-paying jobs elsewhere so they can bring home a regular and higher income. They themselves then spend much time working on the family responsibility land and take care of the domestic chores, which often include cooking, washing, cleaning, and raising the domestic livestock (usually a few chickens and one or two pigs).

In sum, the household responsibility system that was initiated in the late 1970s has resulted in unprecedented changes in the lives of peasants. Among other things, the system has generated higher incomes in many rural families. However, it has also caused problems, especially for rural women. For instance, the illiteracy rate among women is rising because families tend to favor their daughters' labor at the expense of their education. Married women often experience the so-called double burdens. One drastic outcome in gender division of labor following the implementation of the household responsibility system and other rural economic reforms is the new phenomenon of "men as wage earners and women as tillers" in many rural regions.

See also Agricultural Reform; Family Collectivism; *Hukou* System; Migrant Population; Rural Industrialization.

Bibliography

Saith, Ashwani, ed., *The Re-emergence of the Chinese Peasantry: Aspects of Rural Decollectivisation* (New York: Croom Helm, 1987); Zhou, Kate Xiao, *How the Farmers Changed China: Power of the People* (Boulder, CO: Westview Press, 1996).

Hong Zhang

People's Liberation Army (PLA)

See Armed Forces, Reforms of; Military Ranking and Promotion; Military Service System.

Pharmaceutical Industry, Administrative and Regulatory Structures of

The pharmaceutical industry is interpreted in China in a wider sense administratively and statistically and is composed of more than simply pharmaceuticals. It has five subindustries: pharmaceutical chemicals (including biochemical products), medical devices, health materials, pharmaceutical machinery, and pharmaceutical packaging materials.

Traditional Chinese medicines are considered to be separate from the pharmaceutical industry, which was under the industrial management of the State Pharmaceutical Administration of China and was regulated by the Ministry of Public Health of China until 1998. The traditional Chinese medicines industry is under the industrial management of the State Administration of Traditional Chinese Medicine and was also regulated by the Ministry of Public Health until 1998. Both the pharmaceutical industry and the traditional Chinese medicines industry are now regulated by the State Drug Administration, a new government agency formed in 1998 and modeled after the U.S. Food and Drug Administration (USFDA).

Old Administrative and Regulatory Structure

Unlike Western countries, China's pharmaceutical industry was built under the structure of a centrally planned economy. Though **central planning** has been deemphasized by the central government and the position of the administrative authority has been weakened, the structure continues to remain and function to a certain extent. The State Pharmaceutical Administration of China (SPAC) was the central government's arm for industrial administration of the pharmaceutical industry until 1998. Its major responsibilities included the following:

- Overall planning of the industry's products, output, and sales
- Research and development of new products
- Setting prices for the industry's products
- Managing the central government's investment in the pharmaceutical industry for new projects and upgrading projects
- Market research and statistics
- International exchange and collaboration
- Establishing a national quality assurance system, implementation of Regulations on Medicine Production Quality (GMP), Regulations on Quality Control of Medicine Distribution (GSP), and Regulations on Quality Control of Non-clinical Studies on Medicine (GLP), and appraisal of production facilities and quality assurance programs of enterprises
- Formulation and development of strategies, policies, and regulations for the Chinese pharmaceutical industry
- Implementation of the state's industrial strategies and policies and enforcement of pharmaceutical-related laws and regulations
- Coordination of pharmaceutical foreign trade and international exchange together with other central government departments
- Other administrative functions

The State Administration of Traditional Chinese Medicines (SATCM) was the central government's arm for industrial administration of the traditional Chinese medicines industry until 1998. Its major responsibilities were similar to those of SPAC but were exercised over traditional Chinese medicines.

The Ministry of Public Health (MPH) was the regulatory authority of the Chinese pharmaceutical industry until 1998. The MPH and SPAC had many overlapping responsibilities, particularly in areas such as quality control, GMP, GSP, and GLP implementation, appraisal of pharmaceutical plants and products, and licensing of manufacturers and distributors. Very often these two organizations disputed over administrative territories and ended up with each enforcing its own regulations. The Drug Administration Bureau within the Ministry of Health was responsible for overall regulatory control of the Chinese pharmaceutical industry. The principal functions of the Drug Administration Bureau were as follows:

- Execution of legislation and regulations pertaining to drug control and administration

- Examination, approval, and registration of drugs produced by local manufacturers and specifications thereof
- Examination and approval of new drugs
- Monitoring and control of the quality of drugs to eliminate drugs with uncertain efficacy, high toxicity, or adverse reactions
- Prohibition and disposal of fake and substandard drugs
- Supervision, examination, approval, and registration of imported drugs
- Management of narcotics, poisons, and psychotic drugs
- Administration of hospital pharmacies
- Imposition of administrative penalties on violators of legislation or regulations

Current Administrative and Regulatory Structure

As China moved toward a more market-oriented economy, the industrial administration role of the government in the country's industrial sector was reduced continuously as part of the government's overall reform policy. At the same time, there was a genuine need to reorganize China's drug regulatory system to ensure quality and safety of medicines and improve efficiency.

The fifteenth **National People's Congress** in 1998 approved a plan to reorganize China's industrial administrative and regulatory structure of pharmaceuticals and traditional Chinese medicines. Under the plan, the State Pharmaceutical Administration of China (SPAC), a part of the State Administration of Traditional Chinese Medicine (SATCM), and parts of the Ministry of Health (MOH) were merged into a single pharmaceutical government agency called the State Drug Administration (SDA). The reorganization was aimed at reducing bureaucracy and duplications of responsibilities of the three agencies.

The SDA was formed in 1998 to take over only the regulatory control of pharmaceuticals, traditional Chinese medicines, medical devices, pharmaceutical packaging materials, and pharmaceutical machinery. The industrial administration of the pharmaceutical and traditional Chinese medicine industries was minimized following the reorganization, which focuses more on regulation of medicines. The responsibilities for industrial administration of the pharmaceutical industry were moved to the State Economic and Trade Commission, and those for industrial administration of the traditional Chinese medicines remain with SATCM.

SDA's Responsibilities

The internal structure and responsibilities of the newly established State Drug Administration (SDA) were approved by the State Council in June 1998. The administration is a central government agency for administrative and technical supervision of research and development (R&D), as well as production, distribution, and application of drugs. These include herbal materials, herbal preparations, formulated Chinese medicines, bulk pharmaceutical chemicals and their formulations, antibiotics, biochemical drugs, diagnostic drugs, psychoactive drugs, medical devices, health materials, and pharmaceutical packaging materials. The main responsibilities of the SDA include the following:

- Formulation, revision, and enforcement of laws and regulations related to the administration of drugs
- Formulation, revision, and issuance of official specifications (or quality standards) of drugs and development of the national essential drugs bulletin
- Registration of new drugs, generics, imported drugs, and protected traditional Chinese medicines
- Development of the nonprescription drug system and evaluation and issuance of the nonprescription drug bulletin
- Reevaluation, adverse drug reaction monitoring, and registration withdrawal of approved drugs
- Evaluation of authorized clinical trials and clinical pharmacology centers
- Formulation, revision, and issuance (when authorized) of official specifications of medical device products and development of a medical device administrative classification bulletin
- Registration of imported medical devices and approval of clinical research centers of medical devices
- Issuance of registration and production permits of medical device products and certification of medical device quality and product safety
- Formulation, revision, and enforcement of administrative guidelines for preclinical and clinical drug research
- Supervision, inspection, and sampling of drug quality of pharmaceutical manufacturers, distributors, and medical institutions and announcement of quality survey results
- Prosecution of persons involved in production and sales of fake and substandard drugs, and supervision of rural herbal material trading markets
- Evaluation and approval of pharmaceutical advertisements, management of pharmaceutical administrative protection, and directing all institutes for control of drugs and biological products
- Management and supervision of narcotic drugs, psychoactive drugs, toxic drugs, radioactive drugs, and special drug devices
- Research on laws and regulations related to pharmaceutical distribution, introduction of a licensing system for pharmaceutical wholesaling and retailing, and formulation of guidelines for sale and purchase of prescription and nonprescription drugs, herbal materials, and herbal preparations
- Formulation of a licensing system for registered pharmacists (including traditional Chinese medicine pharmacists) and direction of the examination and registration of pharmacists

- Collaboration with other government departments in implementation of national pharmaceutical industrial policies through the use of administrative measures
- Organization and direction of international exchanges in drug administration areas between governments and international organizations
- Carrying out other administrative matters entrusted by the State Council

New Roles of the Ministry of Health

Following the reorganization of China's drug regulatory system, the MOH's responsibilities were reduced mainly to administration of medical institutions, the medical profession, disease control, blood banks, and health care promotion. However, it continues to retain regulatory authority over health-food products (nutritional or health supplements) and food products. The following previous responsibilities of the ministry were transferred to other central government agencies:

- Responsibilities for pharmaceutical regulatory control and inspection were transferred to the State Drug Administration. The responsibilities include approval for registration of new and imported drugs, the formulation of drug administration laws and regulations, and development and issuance of quality standards (specifications) of pharmaceutical and medical biological products and biomaterials. Also included are responsibilities for the reappraisal of approved drugs and adverse drug reaction surveillance, development of the national essential drugs bulletin, and licensing of hospital formularies.
- Responsibilities for border health quarantine and health examination of imported food at ports of entry were transferred to the State Administration of Border Quarantine and Examination.
- Responsibilities for administering the state free medical care system were transferred to the Ministry of Labor and Social Security.
- Responsibilities for implementing health-related state projects, quality control of these projects, examination and training of health care professionals, and the like were decentralized to other related government or nongovernmental organizations.

See also Health Care Reform; Medical Provision, Structure of; Pharmaceutical Products, Sales and Marketing of.

Bibliography

Editorial Committee, State Drug Administration, *State Drug Administration Yearbook 2002* (Beijing: State Drug Administration Yearbook Press, 2003); Editorial Committee of the China Health Yearbook, *China Health Yearbook* (Beijing: People's Health Publishing House, 2002 and 2003); Editorial Committee of the China Pharmaceutical Yearbook, *China Pharmaceutical Yearbook* (Beijing: China Publishing House, 2001, 2002, and 2003); Shen, James, *Marketing Pharmaceuticals in China* (Whippany, NJ: Wicon International, 2001).

Jian Shen

Pharmaceutical Products, Sales and Marketing of

To understand the current situation of pharmaceutical sales and marketing in China, it is necessary first to describe the traditional or conventional Chinese pharmaceutical distribution network as it existed before the reforms of the 1980s. Conventional Chinese pharmaceutical distribution and sales had a pyramid structure, as shown in Figure 3.

The China National Corporation of Medicines (CNCM) at the top of the pyramid was the manager of the entire pharmaceutical distribution network and had responsibilities of administration, supervision, planning and market survey, and others. It reported to the State Pharmaceutical Administration of China (SPAC). CNCM can be viewed as an administrative department of SPAC under the centrally planned economy before reform.

Level 1 and 2 pharmaceutical procurement and supply stations were responsible for procurement of pharmaceutical products from manufacturers in their territory and supplying to Level 3 stations within their territory or to Level 1 or 2 stations in other regions. These stations did not deal with retailers directly. There were six level 1 stations, twenty-nine provincial medicine corporations, and 218 level 2 stations nationwide.

Level 3 stations were responsible for procurement of pharmaceutical products from Level 1 or 2 and supplying to Level 4 stations and urban area retailers in their territory. There were more than 2,300 level 3 stations nationwide.

Level 4 stations were responsible for procurement from Level 3 and supplying to retailers in their territory. Level 4 included wholesalers and retailers

Herbal remedies are carefully stored, weighed, and measured.

FIGURE 3
Traditional Structure of the Chinese Pharmaceutical Distribution System

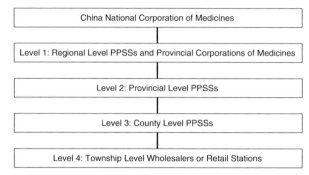

Note: PPSS = pharmaceutical procurement and supply station.

widespread in townships and serving mainly the needs of the rural areas. There were a total of nearly 76,000 such wholesalers and retailers throughout the country. No other companies were allowed to trade pharmaceutical products under the conventional system.

Manufacturers were not allowed to sell their products to anyone apart from Level 1 or 2 stations of their locality, and in fact they manufactured according to the plan and supplied their output at fixed prices to Level 1 or 2 stations. They were also not allowed to handle international marketing or export by themselves, but only through state foreign trade companies.

There were two retailing channels of pharmaceuticals in China: hospitals and drug stores. Hospitals and drug stores used not to control their own purchasing. Instead, the drugs were simply supplied to them by level 3 or 4 stations based on plans. They also had no financial interests in drug sales.

The reform policy pursued by the Chinese government since the early 1980s has brought fundamental changes to the Chinese economy and its structure. China has now the most decentralized administrative system and the most market-oriented economy it has ever had in its history. Local governments have much more authority than before, while companies and enterprises have received much greater autonomy in business management in such areas as long-term strategy, finance, purchasing, and sales and marketing. All **state-owned enterprises** and more and more government institutions have now become financially independent.

The pharmaceutical industry is no exception. All parties involved in pharmaceutical distribution, including manufacturers, distribution companies and supply and procurement stations, hospitals and drug stores, and even CNCM itself, have become financially independent one by one and have won more and more autonomy from their current or former superior departments.

With the loss of financial power and the fading of administrative authority over its subordinate companies and stations, CNCM can no longer maintain the pyramid structure of the conventional pharmaceutical distribution system. Former PPSSs gradually became independent companies, while a large number of pharmaceutical distribution companies were started in the 1990s by other industrial departments, local governments, and even private entrepreneurs.

The conventional pharmaceutical distribution and sales system finally collapsed in the late 1990s.

Following China's entry into the World Trade Organization (WTO) in 2001, the Chinese government made a commitment to open up its pharmaceutical distribution business to foreign investment by 2003. Along with the actual implementation of this commitment, local private investment were allowed officially in the pharmaceutical distribution sector. In addition, China has been encouraging the development of retail pharmacy chains in order to improve efficiency of pharmaceutical retailing.

Well before the final collapse of the conventional Chinese pharmaceutical distribution system in the late 1990s, manufacturers were allowed total freedom to make their own decisions as to what they produce and how much, and to whom, where, and how they sell. Motivated by the new pharmaceutical marketing practices introduced by Sino-foreign joint ventures and the growing bad-credit problem of the pharmaceutical distribution companies, many larger Chinese manufactures have began marketing and sales of their products directly to hospitals and drug stores in big **cities** since the mid-1980s.

Hospitals are now financially independent and suffer from a shortage of government funding for expansion, upgrading, employee welfare, and other needs. As a result, drug sales have become the primary source of income for hospitals. Hospitals now deal with manufacturers and all types of pharmaceutical distribution companies with no restrictions at all.

Despite fast recent growth of retail pharmacy sales, hospital pharmacies continue to be the dominant pharmaceutical retail distribution channel, representing 80 percent of the total pharmaceutical retail sales in China. Less than a decade ago, this channel controlled 95 percent of Chinese pharmaceutical retail sales.

As China's social economic structure changes and living standards improve, the demand for self-medication through retail pharmacies increases. The country has experienced rapid growth in pharmaceutical retail sales in recent years. Pharmaceutical retail sales used to represent only 5 percent of total pharmaceutical sales, but this figure grew to around 20 percent in 2002. Such sales represent 30 percent and 50 percent in Guangzhou and Shenzhen, respectively, where the local economy is booming and population movement is fast. Local observers believe that sales through retail pharmacies are set to grow in the next few years because of more intensive Western-style marketing with Chinese characteristics. Because the number of pharmaceutical manufacturers more than tripled in the past decade, competition in the Chinese pharmaceutical market has become overwhelmingly intensive.

Pharmaceutical marketing, especially in-hospital promotions, was introduced in China by Sino-foreign joint ventures such Shanghai Squibb and Xian Janssen in the 1980s. Local manufacturers quickly learned and started to sell and market their products directly to hospitals. However, as competition intensified, pharmaceutical manufacturers and distributors began to compete in offering monetary incentives such as "red bags," commissions, or "education funds" to hospitals and physicians in order to increase their sales. Hospitals and many physicians took advantage of the dominant position they have in pharmaceutical sales and became reliant on revenues from pharmaceutical sales. Typically, a Chinese hospital generates around 50 percent of its total income from drug sales, and "commissions" from drug sales can be a large share of income of many physicians.

See also Health Care Reform; Medical Provision, Structure of; Pharmaceutical Industry, Administrative and Regulatory Structures of; World Trade Organization (WTO), China's Accession to; World Trade Organization (WTO), Impact of on Service Industries.

Bibliography

Editorial Committee, State Drug Administration, *State Drug Administration Yearbook 2002* (Beijing: State Drug Administration Yearbook Press, 2003); Editorial Committee of the China Health Yearbook, *China Health Yearbook* (Beijing: People's Health Publishing House, 2002 and 2003); Editorial Committee of the China Pharmaceutical Yearbook, *China Pharmaceutical Yearbook* (Beijing: China Publishing House, 2001, 2002, and 2003); Shen, James, *Marketing Pharmaceuticals in China* (Whippany, NJ: Wicon International, 2001).

Jian Shen

Ping-Pong Diplomacy

In April 1971, amid the Cold War tension, the American table-tennis team visited China at the invitation of its long-time enemy, opening the era of "Ping-Pong diplomacy." A series of negotiations were conducted secretly during the ensuing months by Henry Kissinger, the secretary of state of the United States, who traveled to China to meet privately with Premier **Zhou Enlai**. On February 21, 1972, President Richard Nixon made his historic state visit to China and met with Chairman **Mao Zedong**. The visit paved the way for the resumption of formal Sino-American diplomatic relations in 1979.

Advocating for people-to-people contact, Ping-Pong diplomacy opened up a new way to establish relations based on mutual understanding and friendship. For decades after the establishment of the People's Republic, the Chinese government explored ways to enter the world community, although sanctions were imposed by Western nations. In 1953, Premier Zhou initiated the **Five Principles of Peaceful Coexistence**, which were later written into the declarations of the **Bandung Conference of 1955**. They became fundamental principles for all nations in dealing with international affairs. However, the world that China faced was one filled with tensions. Even before the end of World War II, in which the United States and the Soviet Union had fought together as allies, there were signs of tensions between the two nations. Once the war was over, these tensions grew to create what became known as the Cold War. Regional armed conflicts demonstrated the rivalries between the United States and the Soviet Union. The Cuban missile crisis in the 1960s brought the world closer to nuclear war than at any time since World War II. Wars in the Middle East and the **Vietnam War** increased the dangerous global situation. Many factors led China to resort to Ping-Pong diplomacy. One was the Western sanctions launched by the United States and its allies, which fostered China's stance of

President Richard Nixon greets the touring Chinese table tennis team in the rose garden of the White House on April 18, 1972. © *Bettmann/Corbis.*

hostility. Another was the internal conflict within the Communist bloc, which inspired the idea of "triangle diplomacy."

China fought as an allied power in World War II, but tensions and hostilities grew between the United States and China when the latter became a Communist country in 1949 after the war. Refusing to recognize the legitimacy of the People's Republic of China, the United States not only blocked the admission of China into the United Nations, but also imposed economic sanctions. In the meantime, the United States provided economic and military aid to the Kuomintang government in Taiwan. The patrolling of the U.S. Seventh Fleet in the Taiwan Strait posed a threat to China.

Although China joined the Soviet bloc after World War II, relations between the two countries remained tense due to Joseph Stalin's dictatorial manner of control. The situation intensified when Nikita Khrushchev came to power and dished out the theory of "peaceful transition." Ideological conflicts were followed by armed border conflicts. Even though both powers supported North Vietnam in its war against the United States, China's concern over the intentions of the USSR was heightened when the Soviet Union invaded Czechoslovakia in 1968 and when Communist Party secretary Leonid Brezhnev announced that the USSR had the right to intervene in socialist countries. The deployment of military forces along the border and the armed Sino-Soviet clash at Damansky Island on the Ussuri River in 1969 alarmed China and induced it to seek broad diplomatic contacts with the United States to put its hostile neighbor on notice about a possible shift in alliance so as to ease the tension.

The idea of opening some venues of contact with the United States was discussed by members of the Chinese leadership in order to offset pressure from the Soviets. Meanwhile, China was in pursuit of economic development. Members of the technically sophisticated staffs of the Daqing oilfield and the Ministry of Petroleum Industries lobbied for advanced Western technology because foreign skills and resources were essential if China were to continue to expand oil production and explore offshore oilfields.

Resumption of some relationships between the United States and China had been in the minds of the leadership on both sides. However, attempts were only made through roundabout ways and very brief meetings between diplomats. The first such contacts took place in Geneva and later in Warsaw. There were gestures by the Kennedy administration toward rethinking American intransigence toward China, but these efforts were halted after the president's assassination in 1963. In 1966, Secretary of State Dean Rusk suggested that Chinese scientists and scholars be allowed to visit the United States, but this was also put on hold because of the **Great Cultural Revolution** in China that was launched in that year.

The intention of the U.S. government to withdraw from the war in Vietnam revived the notion of thawing the tension with China in 1969. Pressed by the mounting anti–Vietnam War movement and by the economic decline in the United States, President Nixon recognized that the United States "simply cannot afford to leave China outside the family of nations" when it deals with global affairs. Nixon began to seek opportunities of negotiation. On one occasion, Henry Kissinger expressed willingness to open talks with China through the Pakistani and Romanian diplomatic delegations, admitting the significant role of "Communist China" in Asian and Pacific affairs. Both China and the United States edged toward renewing contacts with each other after this.

In January 1970, China offered the possibility of having further talks at a higher level or through other channels acceptable to both sides to discuss the Taiwan issues. In April 1971, the Chinese invited the U.S. table-tennis team, which was competing at the time in the Thirty-First World Table Tennis Championship in Nagoya, Japan, to visit China on a goodwill mission. On April 14, led by Graham Steenhoven, a group of fifteen American Ping-Pong players arrived in China and became the first American delegates to visit China after two decades of hostility since 1949.

On December 8, 1970, Henry Kissinger received a message, passed by Pakistani president Yahya Khan, about inviting a special envoy of President Nixon to discuss the Taiwan issues. On July 9, 1971, Kissinger met Premier Zhou Enlai privately and planned the details of a visit by President Nixon. To support such contacts, decisions were made by the U.S. Treasury and other government departments to end the ban on the transfer of U.S. dollars to China and to allow American ships under foreign flags to transport goods to China. On July 15, both sides made a public announcement of an American presidential visit to China at an unfixed date. On February 21, 1972, President Nixon arrived in Beijing.

The initiative of nongovernmental contact created a channel of communication that resulted in bilateral summit talks. In the Shanghai Communiqué, both sides hammered out differences and common grounds. The status of Taiwan was the top issue. China maintained its opposition to "two Chinas," while the

United States acknowledged that "all Chinese on either side of the Taiwan Strait maintain there is but one China and that Taiwan is a part of China." With this statement, the United States affirmed the ultimate objective of the withdrawal of all its forces and military installations from Taiwan.

The closing sections of the communiqué suggested the intention of developing more "people-to-people contacts and exchanges" in science, technology, culture, sports, and journalism. Both sides also agreed that trade between the two countries should be increased and diplomatic dialogues should be continued. Accordingly, the Chinese table-tennis team paid a return visit to the United States in April 1972. In January 1979, diplomatic relations were formally established with the opening of embassies in the capital cities of Beijing and Washington, D.C.

For the Chinese, Ping-Pong diplomacy characterized a remarkable moment in China's diplomatic history. The normalization of relations between the two countries contributed toward the relaxation of tension in Asia and in the world. It demonstrated to the world that two vastly different countries could meet on the grounds of common interests and in a spirit of mutual respect. Ping-Pong diplomacy became a popular topic in Chinese life as well. In schools, the coaches of Ping-Pong training never fail to mention how the small Ping-Pong ball could move the big earth ahead. On the international front, shortly after Nixon's visit to China, the General Assembly of the United Nations voted to grant China's seat to the People's Republic of China and remove Taiwan. Premier Zhou Enlai once expressed his admiration for Ping-Pong, saying that, Never before in history had a sport been used so effectively as a tool of international diplomacy.

See also Cold War and China; Nixon's Visit to China/Shanghai Communiqué (1972); Sino-American Relations, Conflicts and Common Interests; Sino-American Relations since 1949; Taiwan Strait Crisis, Evolution of; United Nations (UN) and China.

Bibliography

Kissinger, Henry, *White House Years* (Boston: Little, Brown, 1979); Ross, Robert S., *Negotiating Cooperation: The United States and China, 1969–1989* (Stanford, CA: Stanford University Press, 1995).

Jingyi Song

POEs

See Privately Owned Enterprises (POEs).

Poetry

See Avant-garde Literature; Great Cultural Revolution, Literature during; Misty Poetry.

Political Systems

See Ethnic Minorities, Political Systems of.

Pop-Satire

See Modern Pop-Satire.

Postsecondary Education

See Higher-Education Reform.

Pre–Cultural Revolution Literature

Chinese literature during the seventeen years from 1949, when the new state was founded, to the eve of the **Great Cultural Revolution** in 1965 was intertwined with politics. Therefore, it is generally agreed that there was hardly a single work of written literature produced in this period that had a genuine claim to literary distinction, although both Chinese and Western writers have also noted that the quality of literary works rose in periods of relaxation such as 1956–1957 and 1959–1962, when politics were not the sole criterion for the assessment of literary works.

In line with Chinese tradition, literature was mobilized to support the new state in early 1949, even before the formal promulgation of the new People's Republic. The first step in mobilizing writers and artists to support the new regime in Beijing was taken in 1949 with a congress in which prominent politicians participated, including **Mao Zedong**, Zhu De, and **Zhou Enlai**. At the congress, the Chinese National Federation of Writers and Artists was established. Distinguished writers, such as Ba Jin and Mao Dun, and performers were welcomed with assurance, and most of the May 4 writers stopped writing and confined themselves to administrative and ceremonial duties. The reasons were multifold: some stopped writing when faced with the difficulty of writing about the new prescribed topics or in the new style, while others were presumably satisfied that they had achieved their career goals. As a consequence, literature was left to younger writers whose careers were launched in Yan'an and whose works, almost without exception, were optimistic and didactic. Common themes included **land reform** and the 1950s Marriage Law.

For the wavering **intellectuals**, a succession of thought-reform and political study sessions took place in the early 1950s. Political campaigns involving criticism and self-criticism sessions following the Yan'an model—through criticism and self-criticism was formed at the beginning of the 1940s at the Communist red base Yan'an became an effective mechanism for remolding the ideological outlook of those who harbored uncertainties about the new era and those who were perceived to be subversive elements of society. As a result, writers were greatly intimidated during this period by endless political campaigns, namely, "the Hundred Flowers Campaign" (1956–1957), "the Anti-Rightist Campaign" (1957), and the **Great Leap Forward** (1958), together with the other great battles in literature and arts: "the Life of Wu Xun Campaign," "the Criticism of the Dream of the Red Mansion Studies," "the Campaign against Hu Feng," and "the Campaign against the Domination of Old Operas in the Theater" in 1961 and 1962.

The first full-scale campaign against a writer was the attack on Hu Feng in 1953 for supposedly advocating individualism and bourgeois ideas in literature. During the next two years, the campaign widened to include more than 80,000 writers and other intellectuals who were accused of supporting Hu Feng in anti-Party activities.

The purpose of the Hundred Flowers Campaign (1956–1957) was not simply to permit greater cultural variety and enjoyment; its chief aim was to throw light on problems within the Party by people from the outside to correct bureaucratic, sectarian, and subjective work styles among Party cadres. It therefore earnestly encouraged writers and other non-Party intellectuals to voice criticisms of Party policies. At the express invitation of the state, writers and intellectuals outpoured criticism of and outright opposition to the Party and its policies, so much so that the Party was taken aback at the vigor of the response. By mid-1957, Party conservatives forced a halt to the campaign, and those who had been active or outspoken were punished during the 1957 Anti-Rightist Campaign, when they were denounced and either imprisoned or sent to labor reform camps. Many, such as Wang Meng and Zhang Xianliang, remained confined for more than two decades. The campaign generated bitter divisions and resentment for many years to come.

During the Great Leap Forward movement of 1958–1959, which came out of necessity because of the international situation (tensions with the Soviet Union and continued U.S. support for Taiwan), literary writers were required to make their own leaps forward not only by increasing their output, but more significantly by renewed spells in the countryside among the peasants to collect materials and to compile folk-song collections. The populist policies of the Great Leap Forward were translated into literary terms in the Poetry Campaign of 1958–1959, in which millions of people in farms and factories all over China were encouraged to take time off from their work to compose poetry in the form of folk songs. A new upsurge in encouragement of amateur writers thus swept over the country. However, the Great Leap Forward did not bring prosperity but three hard years because of natural disasters, the break with the Soviet Union, and the leadership's erratic and irrational policies.

During this pre–Cultural Revolution period, the chief document for writers was the "Talks at the Yan'an Forum on Literature and the Arts," in which Mao unambiguously declared that all literature inevitably acts as a political tool, and that in all literary creations, politics comes before art for both readers and writers. Communist writers, the document stated, should not only be responsible to the masses, but more important, must serve the organizational needs of the Party. For the next forty years from the early 1950s, the document was reprinted with minor revisions as official policy for all writers and all readers in the new society. It had more weight than government policy or law, so that the history of literature in this period became defined in terms of adherence to or departures from the "Talks."

Along with this document, "socialist realism" was proclaimed to be the official doctrine for literature at the Second Congress of the Federation of Writers and Artists in 1953, signaling both dependence on the Soviet Union and the determination of the authorities to have the controlling voice in the production of a new socialist literature for the new age. The fiction of "socialist realism" written in the 1950s and early 1960s prescribed a generally optimistic picture of socialist reality and of the development of the Communist revolution. It was marked by strict adherence to Party doctrine and a narrow emphasis on the credible depiction of external reality and thus inhibited writers' creativity and led to stagnation.

In 1960, at the third conference of the federation, "socialist realism" was replaced by a call for the "combination of revolutionary realism plus revolutionary romanticism," a slogan that not only implied criticism of the former Soviet-based line but also gave leeway for even more idealized depictions of life in China since 1949. For most professional writers, it represented an even more pronounced retreat from the liberalization of the "Hundred Flowers" period.

A new literature thus gradually emerged in the 1950s and 1960s that was able to carry the Party's message in a way compatible with the mass audience's literary and artistic expectations. With the exception of a few short stories, most fiction from the 1950s and 1960s is considered to have little literary merit. Most of the highly publicized writers of the 1950s and 1960s gained prominence through their ability to write according to current policy. Other writers, including Ru Zhijuan, Hao Ran, Liu Bingyan, and Wang Meng, were not necessarily more skillful or creative but attracted more attention beyond China because of their challenges to political orthodoxy. What the two groups shared was a common preoccupation with politics, which led to a decline in writing skills and diversity.

Literature in this period is mainly characterized by the following literary devices: formal stylistic features such as the storyteller narrative voice; dialect and colloquial expressions in narrative as well as dialogue; heroic models instead of the more complex middle characters, the central and heroic position given to workers, peasants, and soldiers, and the forceful female characters; and traditional "realism" rather than May 4 naturalism or critical realism. Literature in this period became more and more a medium of programmed political education.

See also Anticorruption Literature and Television Dramas; Avant-garde Literature; Experimental Fiction; Great Cultural Revolution, Literature during; Intellectuals, Political Engagement of (1949–1978); Intellectuals, Political Engagement of (1978–Present); Literary Policy for the New China; Literature of the Wounded; Misty Poetry; Modern Pop-Satire; Neorealist Fiction and Modernism; Revolutionary Realism and Revolutionary Romanticism; Root-Searching Literature; Sexual Freedom in Literature.

Bibliography

McDougall, Bonnie S., ed., *Popular Chinese Literature and Performing Arts in the People's Republic of China, 1949-1979* (Berkeley: University of California Press, 1984); McDougall, Bonnie S., and Kam Louie, *The Literature of China in the Twentieth Century* (London: Hurst & Company, 1997).

Xiaoling Zhang

Press Control

The Communist Party's effective control of Chinese society and the people is often attributed to effective press control. Although the legitimacy of press control is often associated with a Marxist view of the press, it is quite doubtful whether Marx ever endorsed press control in his writings. Chinese Marxist theorists have often cited Lenin, regarded as the architect of socialism, who argued that in the socialist state, the press should be controlled. The Chinese Communist Party has produced a remarkable amount of literature to rationalize the control of the press. **Mao Zedong**'s articulation of the function of art in the 1940s is arguably the most influential treatise that still shapes the understanding of the press and its relationship to the Party and provides legitimacy for press control.

Press control in China is achieved through a well-implemented two-tier system, the propaganda tier and the administrative tier, each of which exists in a vertical structure from the top at the state level to the bottom at the local level. The propaganda tier starts from the Central Propaganda Department in the nation's capital and works through the various propaganda departments at provincial, district, county, and even township levels. These propaganda units usually set the agenda for the press—what can or cannot be reported and to what extent. The administrative tier, in addition to setting up technical standards, oversees whether or not the press follows the Party line. As in the structure of the propaganda tier, administrative agencies or units are also established hierarchically from the state to the local level, but unlike the propaganda tier, different administrative units are established to deal with different forms of the press. The Bureau of Press and Publication Administration is responsible for non-Party print media such as newspapers, magazines, journals, and books. The Ministry of Radio, Television, and Film keeps a close eye on programs on radio and **television**. The newly established Bureau of Network Information and Control is in charge of the **Internet** and computer-mediated communication.

In case one is confused about the concept of "Party media," it is necessary to note that propaganda departments at various levels directly control the major newspapers, the mouth organs of the party. The Xinhua News Agency and the *People's Daily*, for example, have status as separate government ministries and are directly controlled by the Party's Central Committee. Just below, hierarchically, are the two national newspapers under the control of the Central Propaganda Department, the *Guangming Daily* and the English-language *China Daily*, which have the rank of vice ministries. The national Propaganda Department appoints publishers, chief editors, and other key officials of the newspapers just mentioned, as well as a few others, while provincial and local Party leaders make similar appointments for Party newspapers in their jurisdiction.

A sophisticated censorship mechanism is strictly implemented. First, the press must be licensed and materials to be published or broadcast must be approved ahead of time by the respective propaganda tier and/or the administrative tier. For example, a book publisher must submit a proposal for a book and get an International Standard Book Number (ISBN) from the national Bureau of Press and Publication Administration before the publication of that book becomes legal. Second, a "cultural police force" often reads, reviews, or monitors programs or publications from the press and submits its reports to respective propaganda departments or administrative agencies. Third, announcements in the form of circulars, bulletins, or newsletters are issued on a weekly or monthly basis, updating new guidelines for specific issues, as well as warnings, or publicizing known offenders. It is common for newspapers to remove an article or for publishers to drop an item at the last minute under pressure from above. A recent example is the banning of the coverage of the scandal involving the Chinese Hope Project launched in 1996, which manages overseas donations for assisting basic education. Once a violation is found, punishment is imposed. For Party media, punishment may involve personnel changes such as demotion for the accused. For non-Party media, a huge fine may be imposed, and in some cases, the license may be revoked.

In general, the press is regarded as a propaganda tool. The media are required to uphold Communist ideology, stick to "the Party line" (*dangxing*), and play "the correct tone" (*zhuxuanlu*). The major goal of the media is not to expose the dark side of society but to depict a bright picture to instill confidence. A typical newscast often opens with upbeat stories such as leaders' or the Party's new directives, scientific advances, and economic achievements. There is a consensual seven-to-three ratio, which means that good news stories will take up 70 percent of the news hole. With regard to a breaking news story, the government often spares no effort to control information. The horrific story that hundreds of people allegedly died in 2002 of food poisoning in the city of Nanjing illustrates this kind of control. The Party did not allow the press to cover the story in the hours immediately after the incident. When it finally broke out, a news angle was prescribed. Instead of looking for accountability of the government, news frames would center on how the Party responded to the needs of the victim families and how the victim families were grateful to the Party.

Coverage of a number of areas and topics is expressly prohibited. Anything critical of the Party, socialism, and political leaders will not be tolerated. The issue of the one-child policy and its relationship to human rights is also taboo. Other areas such as the private lives of political leaders and corruption involving high-level officials are not allowed unless the coverage is designed as part of a political purge. What issues should be reported and in what way also depend on particular contexts. Propaganda departments and administrative units often inform the press of the "status" of a particular issue. Following the war with the Vietnamese in the late 1970s, the press produced many media products that glamorized the Chinese army and demonized the enemy soldiers. Nonetheless, when China and Vietnam resumed diplomatic relations in the early 1990s, a circular came to all the media stating that the press should stop publishing or broadcasting materials about the war with the Vietnamese.

Even though control is tight, signs of change are noticeable. In fact, a gap between the Party-owned media and non-Party media has widened considerably. Local newspapers enjoy much more freedom and less control as Chinese society moves toward a culture of consumerism. For many media practitioners, as long as one does not directly attack the Party and the system, flexibility in the press is allowed and expanded. Technological advances also make more dissemination of information possible. This is particularly true with the Internet. Even though the Chinese government has stepped up policing the Internet (e.g., installing filtering software, jailing violators, and blocking undesirable information), more and more people are able to circumvent the government control.

Practitioners and China watchers believe that more and more media organizations are playing "edge-ball" journalism to get away with censorship. For instance, while local newspapers are not allowed to write opinion pages for international affairs other than conforming to the Xinhua News Agency, local newspapers can create a smart alternative to defy this policy in the form of an "expert column" in which experts are invited to discuss international issues and thereby to express different opinions.

See also Media Bodies, Central and Local; Media Distribution; Media Reform; Press Freedom.

Bibliography

Lynch, D., *After the Propaganda State: Media, Politics, and "Thought Work" in Reform China* (Stanford, CA: Stanford University Press, 1999); Zhao, Y., *Media, Market, and Democracy in China: Between the Party Line and the Bottom Line* (Urbana: University of Illinois Press, 1998).

Changfu Chang

Press Freedom

The Chinese official attitude toward press freedom is different from the one adopted by most Western countries. The latter is primarily based on the fundamental principles of the United Nations Universal Declaration of Human Rights that everyone has the right to freedom of opinion and expression without interference and to seek, receive, and impart information and ideas through any media regardless of frontiers. Western practices are divisible along two kinds of criteria for press freedom, a broad approach and a local approach. The former mainly refers the structure of the news-delivery system, such as laws and regulations with regard to the content of the press. The latter refers to news gathering, such as the freedoms of expression, exchange of information, publication, and voicing criticism against the government.

In China, for most of the time since the founding of the People's Republic of China in 1949, the term "press freedom" has been conceived by the authorities as a Western and capitalist idea and has not been allowed to appear in publications. The authorities' stance toward press freedom has closely followed the doctrine of Marx, Lenin, and Stalin and has been practiced by the Chinese Communist Party (CCP) leaders in a relatively pragmatic way and with practical considerations in specific contexts.

In the Marxist view, press freedom in theory is very important, and without it all other freedoms would be "bubbles." However, Marx denounces the hypocrisy of press freedom in the capitalist system, stating that in capitalist society the theory of press freedom and the practice of press freedom contradict each other. Press freedom is used by the capitalists to maximally guarantee the

A newsstand in Beijing.

interest of the capitalist ruling class, and hence it is a perfect reflection of the nature of all capitalist freedoms, legal, political, and economic. Therefore, in the Marxist logic, press freedom is only the freedom of the capitalists; once press freedom endangers the interest of the capitalist class, it is immediately taken away. Likewise, Lenin praises press freedom as "a great goal," but criticizes that in capitalist society press freedom is built on the basis of monetary power and thus is just a mask or disguise of the capitalists. As a result, 99 percent of the press freedom is monopolized by the rich class. In the view of Stalin, like anything in class society, press freedom must bear the class attribute, and universal press freedom does not exist, because the capitalists have a capitalist press freedom and the proletarians have a proletarian press freedom. Therefore, a socialist society does not need to have a capitalist press freedom. Moreover, even a socialist press freedom is created with intended limitations—it should obey and serve the interest of the Communist Party; no press freedom should be given to the political dissidents.

While **Mao Zedong** and his successors Deng Xiaoping and Jiang Zemin faithfully inherited the principles of Marx, Lenin, and Stalin, they implemented these principles with their own interpretations based on China's political and social needs in different historical periods. Mao claimed that press freedom is the most important freedom of human beings, but there are different kinds of press freedom; press freedom in capitalist society is only a deceptive slogan because there is never a true press freedom for everyone; therefore, China should use a dichotomous policy on press freedom—press freedom only belongs to "the people," and "antirevolutionaries" should never be granted press freedom; instead, they should always be under the "proletarian dictatorship" and should not be permitted any freedom of speech or freedom of action. Even the reformist leader Deng Xiaoping emphasized that for "the people," press freedom still should have some boundaries; press freedom should never become an obstacle to society's political stability and the nation's direction. He further clarified that the priority of press freedom in China should be to serve the needs of the country's "Four Modernizations" and support the Communist Party's **"Four Cardinal Principles."** Ex-President Jiang Zemin warned that press freedom in China should never allow "a few people" to promote Western "bourgeois liberalization" and "spiritual pollution." The most authoritative Chinese dictionary of modern journalism published under Jiang's leadership insists that press freedom in contemporary capitalist society carries great deception. Press freedom in any society cannot be absolute, and it is a right that is accompanied by responsibility. Here, the foremost responsibility of the press is defined as to following the Party's policy and serving the Party's political and ideological needs.

As a result of these principles and practices, the Chinese press is allowed a freedom that is defined by the Party and must closely follow three guidelines: (1) the press must accept the Party's guiding ideology as its guidance; (2) it must propagate the Party's policies, directives, and programs; and (3) it must accept the Party's leadership and stick to the Party's organizational principles and press policies. Press freedom in China thus has four distinctive "Chinese characteristics." First, it is a freedom that is given by the Party, not one that belongs to the press. Second, the freedom is compromised by political and ideological requirements of the Party. Third, the degree of freedom is not guaranteed but changeable based on the needs of the Party and the political climates of the nation. Fourth, press freedom is more bound by politics than by laws and regulations. Thus press freedom in China is sometimes referred to as "press freedom within a cage" or "a caged press freedom," though the size of the cage may vary due to domestic and international situations.

Despite the fact that press freedom is a forbidden issue in the public forum, and the Party's policy on press freedom must not be challenged, from the 1950s to the present, there has always been a persistent pursuit of a genuine press freedom. As early as the mid-1950s, a number of **intellectuals** and journalists boldly proposed that China needed a true press freedom. The Party smashed this proposal and severely punished its authors by labeling them "rightists" and "antirevolutionaries." The concept of press freedom completely disappeared for a decade during the **Great Cultural Revolution** from the mid-1960s to the mid-1970s. With the end of the Great Cultural Revolution and China's embarkation on openness and reform in the late 1970s, the demand for press freedom was revived throughout the 1980s. Especially during the 1989 Tiananmen Square prodemocracy movement, press freedom was one of the three slogans, and for the first time in the history of Communist China, many reporters and editors from the Party-owned press joined the demonstration with a banner stating, "We Want Press Freedom." Press freedom, along with democracy, once again became the focus of growing aspirations among journalists and intellectuals.

From the 1990s to the present, the driving force for press freedom has mainly come from three sectors: (1) an increasing group of intellectuals who are becoming more and more dissident against the political system and Communist ideology; (2) a growing number of media practitioners who want to have less Party control over the press and more freedom to reveal and fight all kinds of corruption, injustice, and social problems; and (3) a newly emerged middle class whose members not only want more uncensored political and economic information but also outlets for voicing their views and opinions. Unlike before, the Party no longer simply rejects the notion and importance of press freedom; instead, on the one hand, the Party defines and interprets press freedom in its own way and claims that China must develop its own form of "socialist press freedom," rather than simply follow the Western model. On the other hand, the Party has given the press more freedom than before, such as the freedom of financial and marketing operations and administrative operations. However, citizens still cannot publish or broadcast criticism of senior officials or voice opinions that challenge the Party. There are still many legal and nonlegal guidelines that require journalists to avoid covering sensitive topics. While press freedom in some aspects has increased, press controls have become more subtle. Evidently, from theory to practice, press freedom in China is still very different from the same concept in many other countries. In the Western sense, there is no press freedom in China. According to a study of press freedom in 139 countries released by Reporters without Borders, the degree of press freedom in China is still ranked 138th, only better than North Korea. A long march still awaits China to achieve a true press freedom.

See also Internet; Media Bodies, Central and Local; Media Distribution; Media Reform; Press Control; Telecommunications Industry; Television.

Bibliography

Chen, Lidan, *Marxian Journalism* (Beijing: China Radio and Television Press, 2002); He, Zhou, and Huailin Chen, *The Chinese Media: A New Perspective* (Hong Kong: Pacific Century Press, 1998); Hong, Junhao, "The Role of Media in China's Democratization," *Media Development* 49 no. 1 (2000): 18–22; Reporters without Borders, *World Press Freedom Index* (Paris: Reporters without Borders Publishing, 2002).

Junhao Hong

Primary Education

In China, primary education includes preschool education and elementary education. Preschool, or kindergarten, lasts up to three years, and children enter as early as age three until age six. Elementary education is usually formally named primary education. It spans either five or six years and, together with lower secondary school education, fulfills the requirements of the Law of Compulsory Education. The entry age of primary education is six or seven. According to the law, all children who have reached the age of six are to enroll in school and receive compulsory education. In certain areas, the beginning of school may be postponed to the age of seven; however, the state, the local community, and the families should strictly guarantee the enrollment. Statistics show that by 2001 the net enrollment ratio of primary school–age children reached 99.1 percent, compared with about 20 percent in the pre–1949 days. There were 111,706 kindergartens with a total enrollment of 20,218,400 children and 491,273 primary schools with a total enrollment of 125,434,700 students (Ministry of Education 2002).

Primary education aims to foster the children's physical, cognitive, and psychosocial development. The ideal objective is to have every child fully developed into a "complete student" with excellence of morality, intelligence, and physical health (*san hao xue sheng*). Morality is measured in terms of his or her patriotism, behaviors in and out of school, and performance in a sense of responsibility, diligence, honesty, frugality, school discipline, respect for elders, care for youngsters, and adherence to acceptable social and community norms. Intelligence is evaluated on the basis of students' mastery of knowledge and skills in reading, writing, mathematics, social studies (history, geography) and nature science, and music and arts, as well as students' initiatives in learning and positive attitudes toward schooling. Excellence of physical health is examined through students' participation in physical education, development of gross and motor skills, habits of personal hygiene, broad interests, and a healthy aesthetic temperament.

The academic year is divided into two semesters, each nineteen weeks long, with a total of thirty-eight weeks of instruction for the year. In addition, there is one week "in reserve" (similar to "snow days" in American schools) for additional time as needed. The remaining thirteen weeks are for vacations and holidays.

China has centralized curricula for each grade level. The Ministry of Education of the People's Republic of China issues general curricula, and each

Shown here are members of a 2004 "English, Science, and Nature Tour," a popular school activity in the summer.

province, city, and county and local schools administer and implement the curricula. Curricula are given not only in terms of the constituent courses, but also in terms of the number of hours dedicated to each subject. The total schooling hours for the six-year program range from thirty to thirty-three hours per week and for the five-year program from thirty-one to thirty-four hours per week (see tables 8 and 9).

Foreign language is an optional course in primary schools. However, as part of the increasingly developed economic reform, the Chinese government mandates that all primary schools should put forth efforts to start offering English as a second language from the third grade on. Most primary schools in the cities or economically developed areas have already implemented foreign language, mostly English, in curricula starting from the third grade. Some schools even start teaching English in preschool.

The students' excessive repertoire of learning tasks has been a long-term problem in primary and lower secondary schools. According to a survey, 36.7

TABLE 8
Weekly Lesson Timetable for Six-Year Program of Primary Education

Subjects/Activities	Number of Weekly Periods in Each Grade					
Subjects	I	II	III	IV	V	VI
Ideology and moral character education	1	1	1	1	1	1
Chinese language	10	10	9	8	7	7
Mathematics	4	5	5	5	5	5
Society	-	-	-	2	2	2
Nature science	1	1	1	1	2	2
Physical education	2	2	3	3	3	3
Music	3	3	2	2	2	2
Painting	2	2	2	2	2	2
Work (laboring skills)	-	-	1	1	1	1
Subtotal	23	24	24	25	25	25
Activities						
Collective activities	1	1	1	1	1	1
Physical exercise; science, technology, and cultural activities (or special-interest-related activities)	4	4	4	4	4	4
Subtotal	5	5	5	5	5	5
Locally arranged curriculum	2	2	3	3	3	3
Total Weekly Periods Morning/afternoon meetings (ten minutes per day)	30	31	32	33	33	33

Source: IBE, 2002 Curriculum Data Set.

TABLE 9
Weekly Lesson Timetable for Five-Year Program of Primary Education

Subjects/Activities	Number of Weekly Periods in Each Grade				
Subjects	I	II	III	IV	V
Ideology and moral character education	1	1	1	1	1
Chinese language	11	11	9	9	9
Mathematics	5	6	6	6	6
Society	-	-	2	2	2
Nature science	1	1	2	2	2
Physical education	2	2	3	3	3
Music	3	3	2	2	2
Painting	2	2	2	2	2
Work (laboring skills)	-	-	1	1	1
Subtotal	25	26	28	28	28
Activities					
Collective activities	1	1	1	1	1
Physical exercise; science, technology, and cultural activities (or special-interest-related activities)	3	3	3	3	3
Subtotal	4	4	4	4	4
Locally arranged curriculum	2	2	2	2	2
Total Weekly Periods Morning/afternoon meetings (ten minutes per day)	31	32	34	34	34

Source: IBE, 2002 Curriculum Data Set.

percent of students stated that the workload is too much to handle. The endless periods of drill and practice, overloaded courses and assignments, and pressure from competitive examinations have depressed students' learning interests and harmed students' physical and psychological growth. Therefore, character education (quality-oriented education) has become a core of reforms in Chinese education for the twenty-first century. The state Ministry of Education requires schools to lighten the learning load of primary and lower secondary school students. Integrated courses, textbooks, and instruction have been implemented in traditional separate-course curricula; character education is carried out and emphasized in schools to improve all-around development of students.

See also Character Education in Primary and Secondary Schools; Educational Administration; Educational System; Higher-Education Reform; Private Education; Secondary Education; Taiwan, Education Reform in; Teacher Education; Vocational and Technical Training.

Bibliography

International Bureau of Education (IBE), *2002 Curriculum Data Set*, http://www
.ibe.unesco.org/International/Databanks/Dossiers/TChina.pdf, accessed on April 1,
2003; Ministry of Education, PRC, *Education in China* (Beijing: Ministry of Education,
2002); Ministry of Education, *Reform Trends of Education in China from 1998–1999*
(Beijing: Department of International Cooperation and Exchanges, 2000).

Ronghua Ouyang and Dan Ouyang

Print Media

See Media Bodies, Central and Local; Media Distribution; Media Reform; Press
Control; Press Freedom.

Private Education

Private education is a supplementary section of China's educational system
and includes private colleges and universities, elementary, lower secondary
(middle), and upper secondary (high) schools, kindergartens, and private training programs. These schools are administered and supervised by local educational departments, typically at the county level, and are funded by individuals
or social organizations that undertake and sponsor the institutions. By 2001,
China had set up 56,274 private schools and institutions of higher education,
with more than 9 million students at all levels and a teaching faculty of 420,000.
In 2001, there were 44,562 private kindergartens that enrolled 3,420,000 children, 16.9 percent of the total number of kindergarten children across the
country; 4,846 private elementary schools with 1,820,000 students, 1.4 percent
of the national total; 4,571 private middle schools and high schools with
2,328,700 students, 3 percent of the national total; 1,040 private vocational high
schools with 377,300 students, 8 percent of the national total; and 1,202 private
colleges, universities, and institutes with an enrollment of 1,130,400 students
pursuing academic degrees and/or certifications. Private education is a tradition
in Chinese history and has experienced five phases in development since 1949.

1949–1966

In the 1950s, China reorganized its educational system, with the result that
the private schools and higher-education institutions that had existed before
1949 became public. With the increase of the student population in the 1960s,
private schools, particularly at the lower secondary school level, were established in towns and small **cities** to provide educational opportunities to those
whom public schools could not accommodate. However, the number of these
private schools and the capacity of their enrollment were limited.

1966–1976

During the ten years of the **Great Cultural Revolution**, China's educational
system was deeply damaged by the radical movement, and there was no development in private education.

1976–1992

After the Cultural Revolution, education once again received high attention in rebuilding the country's economy, which opened the door for private education. In 1978, because China's focus was shifting to modernization and construction, fostering various talents became an urgent task. A number of private schools were set up in a short time in many cities with government encouragement. In December 1982, the **National People's Congress** approved a new constitution, which stated that "The country encourages collective economic organizations, enterprises, and public institutions and other nongovernmental sectors to initiate various educational undertakings according to the law." Shortly thereafter, thousands of private schools and institutions were established across the country.

1992–1997

China's private education enjoyed rapid development from 1992 to 1997 along with consistent growth in the country's economy and educational market and great support from the central government. The latter, for the first time, adopted the policy of "active encouragement, great support, proper leadership, and effective administration" for private education. Private primary and secondary schools and institutions experienced fast development. By 1995, private colleges and universities alone numbered 1,219, with an enrollment of more than 1 million students in 1996.

1997–Present

Regulations were established that defined a framework for private education. With rapid growth in private education, the central government and local educational departments issued a number of laws to regulate and further stimulate the development of private education. In 1997, the State Council issued Rules of Schools and Institutions Run by Nongovernmental Sectors. These rules were soon followed by regulations issued by provincial educational departments. At the beginning of the new millennium, more than twenty provinces, major cities, and municipalities issued laws to regulate private education with regard to application and approval for new schools and institutions, program assessment and evaluation, and budgeting and managing financial resources. Private education entered a phase of systemic changes.

In December 2002, the National People's Congress passed the Law for the Development of Private Education, the first national law that exclusively appertained to private education, which became effective on September 1, 2003. The law recognizes private education as a beneficial undertaking for society and as a valuable part of China's educational system. It underlines the country's policy on private education as active encouragement, great support, proper leadership, and regulated administration. It states that private education is managed by the related administrative departments at the county or superior levels. The leadership body of a private school or an institution is the board of trustees, which is composed of the sponsor or his/her representative, the principal or president, and faculty representatives. The law also states that faculty members who teach in private schools should enjoy the same legal status to which teachers in public schools are entitled.

Private education in China has two significant characteristics. First, it is a needed supplement and addition to the public educational system. When public schools and institutions cannot provide enough opportunities, the private sector helps tremendously in meeting the demands of a large population. For example, every year private colleges and universities welcome tens of thousands of talented and hardworking students who could not get into the public institutions.

Another characteristic of China's private education is its unique curricula and instructional styles. This is particularly notable in early childhood education and basic education. Many private kindergartens and schools take one or more subject areas as core specializations in the their curricula. These core subject areas include fine arts, music, athletics, and foreign languages.

Private education has now become a dynamic, well-received, and ever-growing element of the Chinese educational system. It offers excellent and unique educational opportunities of different types for individuals at all levels, including early childhood education, basic education, higher education, special education, vocational education, and continuing education. With great enthusiasm from many individuals and social organizations and full support from central and local governments, development and progress in China's private education are taking place, and the system holds promise for greater achievement.

See also Character Education in Primary and Secondary Schools; Educational Administration; Educational System; English Proficiency Levels; Higher-Education Reform; Primary Education; Secondary Education; Taiwan, Education Reform in; Teacher Education; Vocational and Technical Training.

Bibliography

China's Civilian-Run Education in the New Century (Beijing: People's Pictorial, 2002); *Introduction to Education in China* (Beijing: Department of Foreign Affairs of the State Education Commission of the PRC, 1996); *Newsletter of Private and NGO-Sponsored Education* (Beijing: Education Department of the City of Beijing, 2002).

Binyao Zheng

Privately Owned Enterprises (POEs)

Privately owned enterprises (POEs) in China are enterprises that are owned by domestic private entrepreneurs with eight or more employees. This measure leaves out urban proprietors, or *getihu* in Chinese, who are also private entrepreneurs. Moreover, since China's agricultural sector consists predominantly of production units that are family based, the private enterprise classification excludes these units as well, though they are privately owned.

To reflect the development of the private economy, however, the measure of nonpublic enterprises, or enterprises that are neither state nor collectively owned, is more pertinent. Hence both terms, "private enterprises" and "nonpublic enterprises," are used according to their relevance in the context and wherever appropriate. Moreover, since the existence of private enterprises contrasts with publicly owned enterprises primarily in the urban sector, it is the development of urban private enterprises that bears significantly on the development of the private economy.

Private enterprises and proprietors in 1949 produced more than 70 percent of the gross value of industrial output (GVIO), while **state-owned enterprises (SOEs)** produced 26.2 percent. By 1978, the share of all nonpublic enterprises had shrunk to zero, and China's GVIO was produced entirely by SOEs (77.6 percent) and collective-owned enterprises (COEs) (22.4 percent) after two decades of transforming "proprietors toward socialism" and merging private enterprises with public enterprises, the **Great Cultural Revolution**, and other political movements. The economy was predominantly public, not only in the urban sector but also in the rural sector. Then the rural sector started reforms in 1978 by distributing the land back to farmers and practicing the household re-

Mrs. Mingfeng Li owns the Jade Cloud, one of the best restaurants in Kunming.

sponsibility system, which eventually dissolved the **people's communes** and resumed family-based private production. China's agricultural production has since been predominantly private in nature.

In the urban sector, the development of the private economy has met more ideological and structural constraints. The term of "private enterprise" implied a contradiction of China's socialist economy, and thus the topic of private enterprise development was an extremely politically sensitive subject that had led to little development of private enterprises in the 1980s. When private enterprises were allowed to operate, they existed mostly in retail and household-related services. Productions that were considered vital to the national interest, such as automobiles, petroleum and natural gas, telecommunications, public utilities, banking, and insurance, had all been off-limits to private enterprises.

The existing private enterprises have grown in a difficult environment in which they have been discriminated against by policies and in their access to bank loans, land-use rights, import and export rights, distribution channels, issuing corporate bonds, and other areas. When the running shot is fired, the SOEs can have a head-start of one hundred steps, then the foreign enterprises by fifty steps. The opportunity for private enterprises comes last. This is a vivid portrayal of unequal treatment by Liu Yonghao, the chairman and CEO of the well-known privately owned Hope Corporation.

As China's reform deepened, ideological blockage was gradually cleared. China's entry into the World Trade Organization (WTO) gave a further push to the development of private enterprises. Their role in the economy has been further legitimized, and many entry barriers have been broken. At the Fifteenth

Party Congress, the Chinese Communist Party (CCP) upgraded the role of private enterprises as being "supplementary to state enterprises" to that of "equal importance." The Sixteenth Party Congress amended the Party's constitution to open its door to private entrepreneurs and accept them to become new members. This is an unprecedented move that has signaled the green light for an unconstrained development of Chinese private enterprises. The government now officially denounces discrimination against private enterprises in their access to, for example, land-use rights or bank loans.

The improved growth environment, the stronger incentive for private enterprises to survive in the market, and their lighter burden of surplus workers and retirees have led to unprecedented growth of private enterprises, especially since 2002. At the end of 2001, 12.68 million urban and 11.39 million rural people, a total of 24.07 million, were employed by POEs. By the end of June 2002, employment by 2.21 million privately owned enterprises had increased to about 30 million. Moreover, the employment share of all nonstate enterprises, including private enterprises, collectively owned enterprises, proprietors, foreign enterprises, and joint-ownership enterprises, had reached 88.8 percent of all employment (including farming).

The number of private enterprises has also rapidly increased. Beijing, for example, had 150,873 private enterprises by 2002, in addition to 312,932 proprietors, a growth rate over 2001 of 21.54 percent for the former and 20.77 percent for the latter. Shanghai, which has the fourth-largest number of private enterprises among all provinces and municipalities, averaged in 2002 a daily increase of 3.5 newly established POEs.

Private enterprises have especially made headway in foreign trade. By 2002, export value of Shanghai POEs increased by more than 300 percent in compared with the year before. Nationwide, more than 40,000 private firms have obtained export licenses. Growing at a faster pace than those of other types of enterprises, exports by private enterprises comprised 8.6 percent of the national total in 2002. In trucking and freight transporting, there were more than 700,000 nonpublic enterprises, an absolute majority of all firms in the industry.

Private-capital-controlled banks have been increasing rapidly, to a total of about 100 by 2002. They no longer have to exist in the form of urban credit unions or urban cooperative banks. But as of June 2002, China did not have an urban commercial bank of 100 percent private capital, and private banks dealt primarily with small businesses as a result of history, size, and ideological considerations.

Private enterprises can now enter the auto industry without restrictions on what to produce, whether parts or the whole vehicle of any model. Currently, there is only one private automaker, Jili Company in Zhejiang Province. Moreover, the year 2002 saw the first private enterprise ever to obtain, through bidding, the right to operate a gold mine, which suggests the potential breakdown of entry barriers into other similar areas.

Growing at a rate higher than 10 percent annually during 1998–2002, the private sector contributed more to the nation's 7.7 percent average GDP growth rate during this period than the public sector, which grew at 7 percent.

As a result, the share of GDP by the private sector grew from less than one-fourth in 1998 to greater than one-third in 2002. In March 2003, the Deputy Director Qiu Xiaohua of China's State Statistical Bureau predicted that the private sector would grow further at an annual rate of 15 to 20 percent in the next five years.

See also Auto Industry Development; Banking and Financial System Reform; Deng Xiaoping (1904–1997), Reforms of.

Bibliography

Book of Chinese Economic Events on Reforming and Opening, vol. 1 (Beijing: Beijing Industrial University Press, 1993); CCTV English Channel, "Non-Public Sector Boosts China's Economic Growth," http://202.108.249.200/english/news/china/FinanceABusiness/20030304/100336.html; Chen, Aimin, "The Impact of China's WTO Entry: An Analysis *ex ante* and *ex post*," *American Review of China Studies*, fall 2003; Chen, "The Structure of Chinese Industry and the Impact from China's WTO Entry," *Comparative Economic Studies*, spring 2002, 72–98; National Bureau of Statistics, *China Statistical Yearbook* (various issues, 1981–2004) (Beijing: China Statistics Press).

Aimin Chen

Putonghua, Promotion of

China is the world's most populous and fourth-largest country, with fifty-six ethnic groups and hundreds of dialects and ethnic languages. The Han are the largest group, accounting for 95 percent of the population. Major ethnic minorities include the Zhuang, Hui, Miao, Uygur, Tibetan, Mongolian, Yi, and Korean. All the ethnic groups have their own languages that are different from that of the Han, whose language is Chinese. Among the Han Chinese, the language variance is significant. Between different provinces, **cities**, and regions, there are linguistic differences that pose significant barriers to communication.

Therefore, Putonghua, the "common language," has been systematically promoted since 1949 as the official language. The spoken form of Putonghua is the lingua franca for Chinese worldwide. It is based on the dialect spoken in the Beijing area and thus features Beijing pronunciation and usages, in combination with the vocabulary of the Northern dialect group.

The Chinese government has been strongly promoting Putonghua by providing a variety of opportunities and incentives, particularly for minority groups, to learn this standard language. For example, in China's westernmost area, the **Xinjiang** Uygur Autonomous Region, where ethnic minorities constitute more than 60 percent of the total population, Putonghua has been promoted for several decades. A large number of primary and middle schools have set up bilingual education systems where teaching is conducted both in the Uygur languages and in Putonghua.

Various names are given to Putonghua. The official Chinese term is Hanyu Putonghua (Han-language common speech). Another term is Guoyu (the national language), a traditional term from the time before 1949 that is widely used in Taiwan today. In Western countries, Putonghua is often referred to as Mandarin, a misnomer translated directly from the Chinese term Guanhua, "official language (of old imperial China)." Western linguists refer to Putonghua as Modern Standard Chinese, often abbreviated MSC.

The promotion of Putonghua as a national standard began in the early 1950s. In 1951, the Communist Party of China issued a directive that inaugurated a three-part plan for language reform that brought several major changes to the Chinese language. The plan's first objective was to establish a universally comprehensible common language. Second, it introduced simplified written characters; and third, it introduced the romanized transcription Hanyu Pinyin. In 1956, Putonghua became the medium of instruction in all schools nationwide and the standard for communication in government offices. The changes introduced in the 1950s eventually led to today's language differences between the People's Republic of China, Taiwan and Hong Kong, and the Chinese overseas communities.

When the present Putonghua development drive was launched in the late 1990s, the use of a commonly understood language of communication became an important issue for cooperation between the Chinese and the outside world. China's accession into the World Trade Organization (WTO) has further increased the demand for teaching and learning the Chinese language, both in China and abroad. People of the Hong Kong Special Administrative Region (SAR) particularly need Putonghua as a bridge to the mainland. Putonghua has become increasingly popular in Hong Kong during the past few years, so the British Council, which normally promotes British culture, recently began promoting the Chinese language as well.

The popularization of Putonghua is a priority issue in China's two **special administrative regions (SARs)**. Since Hong Kong's and Macao's return to China, mastering China's official language is crucial for effective economic exchanges between the special administrative regions and the Chinese mainland. The government in Hong Kong, for example, promotes Putonghua through "Putonghua Month" activities. This event was introduced in 2002, five years after Hong Kong's return to China. The activities of the annual Putonghua Month are arranged by major organizations and government departments and take place from mid-September to mid-October.

In order to promote Putonghua efficiently, the Chinese government suggests that in China all civil servants should be able to communicate in Putonghua, because they officially represent the image of the Chinese government and are considered executors of the nation's laws. Consequently, all of Beijing's civil servants are expected to pass the Putonghua test before the end of 2004. In Shanghai, China's largest city, about 100,000 civil officials are required to take the test by 2007.

On another front, education is considered an important realm for contributing to the country's language unification through the use of Putonghua in teaching. Because China is becoming a more open and mobile society, the emergence of a common language standard is preventing dialects from being an impediment in people's daily lives. For example, the national minorities in China's various autonomous regions, such as Inner Mongolia and **Tibet**, have their own languages. In these regions, the Chinese government has provided teachers and created the conditions for promoting Putonghua.

At the same time, Putonghua is not being promoted with the intention to make ethnic languages and dialects obsolete. China's National Common Language Law stipulates that every ethnic group has the right and freedom to use and develop its own language, and the languages of the different ethnic groups enjoy equal status. According to China's official language policy, the government's promotion of Putonghua and the standard Chinese script does not mean any restriction on the use and development of ethnic-minority languages.

A Putonghua test for determining a language user's level of competence was implemented by the Chinese government in 1990 as part of the civil service examination, an important means for the promotion of Putonghua. This standardized Putonghua test, "Hanyu Shuiping Kaoshi," is known as the HSK test or also as the Chinese Proficiency Test. It is used for testing the proficiency of nonnative speakers of Chinese, such as foreigners, overseas Chinese, and students from Chinese ethnic-minority groups. It has become the Chinese equivalent of the well-known Test of English as a Foreign Language (TOEFL).

The Chinese Proficiency Test is officially divided into eleven proficiency levels. The top three levels, nine to eleven, are advanced levels, equivalent to the language skills of a Chinese native speaker with a bachelor's degree. Levels six to eight are intermediary—good enough to satisfy the requirements for an ordinary job. Levels one to five are elementary. For example, those seeking to study for a master's degree must pass the Chinese Proficiency Test at level eight. The test is held regularly at test centers in China and overseas. Those who pass are issued a certificate by the State Commission of Chinese Proficiency Test. Beginning in 2001, the Chinese Proficiency Test is given in China three times a year.

According to Chinese official data from 2003, there are forty-seven Chinese Proficiency Test centers in twenty-seven cities in China and fifty-five centers overseas. Since the test was launched in 1990, 400,000 people from more than 100 countries have taken the test, with a passing rate of 75 percent. The number of Chinese Proficiency Test participants has been increasing at an annual rate of 35 percent since 1997.

On January 1, 2001, China enacted a National Common Language Law that stipulates that announcers, anchors, movie actors and actresses, theater performers, teachers, and government employees, as well as members of certain other groups, should pass the Putonghua level test and reach the grade specified by the state. Due to the existing socioeconomic and sociocultural gap between the cities and the countryside, language laws are first being implemented in big cities, with a certain delay in remote or isolated regions, because it is easier to promote Putonghua in urban centers than in rural areas. Many people are not used to communicating in a language different from their local dialect and often are reluctant to accept the common language. Some schools in the countryside, especially those located in remote areas, continue to use local dialects, but this situation is changing due to the government's persistent efforts to promote the standard speech. While the use of local dialects is by no means forbidden in schools and offices, the process of speech standardization is progressing steadily.

See also Chinese Script, Reform of; English Proficiency Levels; Foreign-Language Teaching Methodology; Foreign-Language Training; Hong Kong, Return of.

Bibliography

HSKOnline.com.cn, "An Introduction to HSK Testing," http://www.hsk.com.cn/articles/info.asp?id=99, accessed on November 30, 2004; Xinhua Net, "Shanghai's Civil Servents Will Pass HSK Tests in 2004," http://news.sol.sohu.com/49/17/news200801749.shtml, accessed on November 30, 2004.

Senquan Zhang

R

RCCs

See Rural Credit Cooperatives (RCCs).

Reemployment of Laid-off Workers

Reform and restructuring of China's **state-owned enterprises (SOEs)** have led to massive layoffs of their workers, though the government has largely controlled the pace of this downsizing. "Laid-off workers" refers to those jobless workers who have lost their jobs for more than three months but still maintain a tie with the original firm. The laid-off thus exclude workers who are under training with pay, who are on leave without pay, who take early retirement, who export their services overseas, who engage in various market activities, who maintain an employment relationship with the firm based on an agreement, and who voluntarily become jobless.

At the end of 2002, laid-off workers by SOEs, including SOEs with 100 percent state ownership and those with state controlling shares, amounted to a total of 4.1 million, 1.05 million less than in 2001. The reemployment rate of the laid-off in 2002 was 26.2 percent, and the majority of laid-off workers who enter a reemployment center have been able to obtain unemployment compensation to cover their minimum living, according to a 2003 report by China's Ministry of Labor and Social Security and National Bureau of Statistics.

Regionally, China's old industrial bases and the less developed areas have more laid-off workers. The laid-off workers in the northeastern provinces of Liaoning, Jilin, and Heilongjiang, for example, account for 25 percent of the national total. Structurally, the coal-mining, textile, machinery, and munitions industries have experienced more difficulties in the transition and have laid off more workers, according to *China Labor Statistical Yearbook, 2002*. Demographically, men over the age of fifty and women over forty have comprised most of the urban unemployed and have formed the "unemployed class of forty–fifty," and women are more likely to be laid off than men.

Solving the problem of laid-off workers has been dealt with by the **social security system** and reemployment programs that are run either by the original firms that laid off the workers or by government and social organizations outside the firms. Most SOEs have established reemployment service centers to retrain workers toward their reemployment, and firms with smaller numbers of laid-off workers tend to delegate the service to an existing department such as the human resource department. Two types of workers are eligible to enter reemployment centers: (1) those who were hired before the contract system was initiated in the mid-1980s and are laid off because of poor financial condition of firms and (2) those who were hired under the contract system and are laid off before their contracts expire, but rural migrants with temporary contracts are excluded from this benefit. Reemployment centers disburse minimum living compensations to the laid-off and pay for their pension, medical, and **unemployment** insurance contributions, organize retraining, and guide the laid-off toward reemployment. A laid-off worker can remain in the reemployment center for no more than three years. After three years, the firm can sever its tie and responsibilities with the worker. The jobless worker then must seek help from the social welfare system by collecting unemployment compensation or guaranteed minimum living. Since operation of reemployment centers by original firms increases costs for firms that must downsize to become profitable and is thus unsustainable, the central government in September 2003 stipulated that firms will discontinue establishing reemployment service centers and that those who newly become laid off will stop entering these centers.

In addition to the central government's policies for alleviating poverty of laid-off workers and assisting their reemployment, local government apparatuses, government employment centers, and talent centers, as well as social employment service intermediaries, facilitate reemployment services outside of original firms. Local government apparatuses refer primarily to urban neighborhood or community committees that are under the administration of the Ministry of Civil Affairs and undertake the responsibility of locating suitable jobs and training the unemployed for the jobs. Such local governmental services have become well established in provinces of high unemployment such as Liaoning Province and have become a nationwide trend in helping the unemployed.

Government employment centers and talent centers differ in their operations and functions. While employment centers function as intermediaries for all job seekers, talent centers are primarily for job seekers with higher than a vocational education, certified skilled technical personnel, and other technical and management personnel. Administratively, the Ministry of Labor and Social Security and its branches at various local levels oversee the operation of employment centers, and the Ministry of Human Resources and its above-county-level branches administer talent centers (China Ministry of Labor and Social Security 2001 and 2002). By the end of 2002, ninety **cities** in China had formed an electronic network that disseminates and exchanges up-to-date employment information and publishes quarterly statistical reports on employment demand and supply. At the end of 2002, 26,158 employment intermediaries existed and, during the year, successfully facilitated 13.54 million placements, a 10.2 percent growth over 2001. Of the 26,158 employment intermediaries, 18,010 were owned by the Ministry of Labor and Social Security and facilitated 9.78 million placements. There were twenty-eight national-level talent centers at the end of 2002 (*China Human Resources Daily*, June 23, 2003).

Reemployment assistance policies include the following:

1. Self-employment: Laid-off workers have been encouraged to engage in self-employment through three basic policy-related channels. The first is obtaining a lump-sum settlement payment, meanwhile severing the employment relationship with the original firm. The State Council issued the stipulations On the Operations of Separating the Supplementary from the Principal and Replacing the Redundant Workers in Medium and Large State Enterprises on November 11, 2002. According to the stipulations, a state enterprise can use its net assets to pay a laid-off worker a lump sum to sever his/her employment relationship with the firm. The amount varies among firms and regions depending on firms' financial capability and can often be nominal, but to most laid-off workers, a lump-sum fund can be an important source to start their small businesses as proprietors. The second is favorable tax policies. Laid-off workers who choose to self-employ are entitled for three years to the waiver of a host of taxes, such as operation taxes, city maintenance taxes, income taxes, education support taxes, and various administrative fees such as management, registration, and licensing fees. Moreover, the taxes to be resumed after three-year holiday period will carry a higher deductible level. The third is loan support. According to the Regulations on the Management of Collateralized Small Loans to the Laid-offs issued in December 2002, former laid-off workers in their reemployment businesses can obtain, with guaranteed repayment from an intermediary agency, interest-free loans up to 20,000 yuan for a period of less than two years. The interest costs are born by fiscal sources.

2. Reemployment in service jobs: The China Ministry of Finance and the National Bureau of Taxation coissued a tax policy in 2002, the Fiscal and Taxation No. 208, 2002, Announcement on the Tax Policies Concerning the Reemployment of Laid-off Workers. According to the announcement, newly established permissible (not listed as off-limits by the government) service businesses and retail trade and commercial firms are entitled for three years to the waiver of income, operation, city maintenance, and education support taxes when they employ laid-off workers at least 30 percent of their total employment and sign employment contracts of at least three years with the workers. If the reemployed laid-off workers comprise less than 30 percent of the firms' total employment, the firms are entitled to the waiver of 2 percent of income tax for each 1 percent of reemployed laid-off workers in the firm's total employment. The establishment of the

businesses and the employment of the laid-off must be verified and sanctioned by local labor departments and tax bureaus before the favorable tax policy can be applied. Existing service and retail sales firms that meet the same qualifications are entitled to a 30 percent deduction of income tax for three years.

3. Separating supplementary units from principal units in large and medium-sized state enterprises: The waiver of income tax for three years also applies to state enterprises that reemploy their redundant workers from principal departments, such as factory floors, to supplementary units or service units, such as newly established day-care centers or restaurants that are open to the public as independent commercial units. State enterprises are encouraged to do the separation to enhance efficiency in their main production and reemploy redundant workers in the supplementary units.

4. Direct reemployment assistance: The Stipulation on Reemploying the Laid-off Workers, 2002 No. 20, by the Ministry of Labor and Social Security, governs the operation of governmental assistance to those laid-off workers over forty (women) and fifty (men) years of age who face the most difficulty in becoming reemployed. Direct investment in social services by local governments, including neighborhood committees, has become the most effective way of reemploying this group of unemployed over forty or fifty years of age. Their salaries at the reemployment jobs are often well below the current market level, however, and fiscal subsidies for their social insurance and wages often make up a major part of their total remuneration.

See also Labor Policy, Employment, and Unemployment.

Bibliography

Chen, Aimin, "China's Urbanization, Unemployment, and the Integration of the Segmented Labor Markets," in *Urbanization and Social Welfare in China*, ed. A. Chen, G. G. Liu, and K. H. Zhang (London: Ashgate Publishing, 2003); Ministry of Labor and Social Security, *China Labor Statistical Yearbook, 2002* (Beijing: Labor Press); ———, *Stipulation on the Management of Employment Centers*, December 2002; ———, *Stipulation on the Management of Talent Centers by the Ministry of Personnel*, October 1, 2001; Ministry of Labor and Social Security and State Statistical Bureau, *Statistical Report of the Employment and Social Security Development, 2003*.

Aimin Chen and Jianbing Shao

Reform

See Administrative Reforms (1949–1978); Administrative Reforms after 1978; Adoption, Reform and Practice of; Agricultural Reform; Armed Forces, Reforms of; Banking and Financial System Reform; Chinese Script, Reform of; Deng Xiaoping (1904–1997), Reforms of; Fiscal Policy and Tax Reforms; Health Care Reform; Higher-Education Reform; Housing Reform; Journalism Reform;

Judicial Reform; Land Reform; Media Reform; Social Security Reform; Taiwan, Constitutional Reform in; Taiwan, Education Reform in.

Regional Disparity

See Regions of China, Uneven Development of; Rural-Urban Divide, Regional Disparity, and Income Inequality.

Regions of China, Uneven Development of

Conventionally, China is divided into three regions: eastern (coastal), central, and western. The eastern region has three central municipalities (Beijing, Tianjin, and Shanghai) and nine provinces, Hebei, Liaoning, Jiangsu, Zhejiang, Fujian, Shandong, Guangdong, Guangxi, and Hainan. The central region has nine provinces, Shanxi, Inner Mongolia, Jilin, Helongjiang, Anhui, Jiangxi, Henan, Hubei, and Hunan. The western region is the rest of China and includes Chongqing, Sichuan, Guizhou, Yunnan, **Tibet**, Shaanxi, Gansu, Qinghai, Ningxia, and **Xinjiang.** From the map of China, it is obvious that these three regions are not strictly defined based on actual geographic locations.

In 2000, 536.2 million Chinese lived in the coastal region, 439.4 million in the central region, and 2,867 million in the western region, respectively accounting for 42 percent, 35 percent, and 23 percent of the total population. The coastal region, however, produced 59.4 percent of the nation's GDP, with the other two regions contributing 27 percent and 13.6 percent, respectively. At the provincial level, the five areas with the highest per capita GDP in 2000 were Shanghai (34,547 yuan), Beijing (22,460 yuan), Tianjin (17,993 yuan), Zhejiang (13,461 yuan), and Guangdong (12,885 yuan); all are located in the coastal region. The five areas with the lowest per capita GDP were Guizhou (2,662 yuan), Gansu (3,838 yuan), Guangxi (4,319 yuan), Shaanxi (4,549 yuan), and Tibet (4,559 yuan); all but Guangxi are located in the western region. Therefore, the coastal region is relatively more developed, and regional disparity exists in China.

In a large country with a diversity of local endowments, regional disparity in the course of growth is inevitable. In fact, uneven development is one of China's prominent features, and China has experienced a persistent widening of regional disparity during most years since 1949. The interprovincial relative disparity coefficient of per capita GDP (coefficient of variation) was 65.6 percent during the first five-year period (1952–1957) and rose to 70.9 percent in 1993 and 77 percent in 2000. More specifically, in 1980, per capita GDP for

Uneven regional development is characteristic of China's economic transformation of the last two decades. While most farmers or workers reside in poor housing, most Chinese cities have luxurious apartment buildings like the one shown here.

the eastern, central, and western regions was, respectively, 818, 409, and 370 yuan. Hence per capita GDP for the eastern region was 2 and 2.21 times those for the central and western regions. In 2000, per capita GDP for the three regions was 13,698, 6,045, and 4,734 yuan, respectively. Hence per capita GDP for the eastern region was 2.27 and 2.89 times those for the central and western regions.

Uneven development is also evidenced by the widening income disparity across regions. For urban residents, in 1980, per capita income for the eastern, central, and western regions was 512, 410, and 428 yuan, respectively. Hence per capita income for the eastern region was 1.19 and 1.25 times those for the central and western regions. In 2000, per capita income for the three regions was 7,733, 5,159, and 5,674 yuan, respectively. Hence per capita income for the eastern region was 1.36 and 1.49 times those for the central and western regions. For rural residents, in 1980, per capita income for the eastern, central, and western regions was 248, 190, and 172 yuan, respectively. Hence per capita income for the eastern region was 1.31 and 1.45 times those for the central and western regions. In 2000, per capita income for the three regions was 3,341, 2,071, and 1,531 yuan, respectively. Hence per capita income for the eastern region was 1.61 and 2.18 times those for the central and western regions. It is worth mentioning that per capita income disparity is smaller than per capita GDP disparity because of government efforts on income redistribution.

Many studies have examined China's regional disparity during the last few decades. The general conclusion is that China's regional disparity showed a positive (widening) trend since the early 1950s, with a U-shaped pattern in the 1980s and 1990s. Some scholars have argued that the declining disparity in the 1980s was caused by the agricultural reform, which greatly improved agricultural productivity and relatively benefited the inland regions more than the coastal areas. However, this catch-up was swamped when China started a large-scale urban reform and the government gave more and more favorable policies to the coastal region. Globalization and China's further opening-up make the coastal region more attractive to foreign investment and international trade and lead to a divergence in regional development.

Three economic and institutional factors have contributed to the widening of regional disparity. First, pole growth might be dominant in the early stage of economic reform and development. A concentration of population is conducive to economic development because agglomeration economies in large metropolitan areas reduce the necessary costs of infrastructure and promote the productive efficiency of resource use. Therefore, economic growth begins first and faster at concentrated poles, then spreads outward to peripheral areas. In China, the coastal area is relatively more developed and populous. The pole growth theory predicts that this region will develop faster than the inland regions, at least in the short run. Regional disparity is a direct consequence of the pole growth process.

Second, government economic policies since the 1980s have become a force in widening regional disparities. Since the early 1980s, regional economic policies have moved away from the "even development" strategy, and relatively more government capital has been invested in the eastern region than in the inland regions. The proportion of the total investment in fixed assets that went to the interior regions decreased from 60 percent in 1958–1962, 71 percent in 1966–1970, and 61 percent in 1971–1975 to 55 percent in 1976–1980 and 42 percent in 1986–1990. By 1980, four special economic zones (SEZs) were established along the coast. Later, the concept of SEZ was extended to Hainan and fourteen other coastal cities. The central government not only invested directly in many projects in these areas but also granted these cities many favorable policies such as lower tax rates and more autonomy. The policy advantages helped the coastal region grow faster than its inland counterparts.

Third, the coastal region benefits more from China's economic reform and opening-up. Because the gravity center of the world economy has been shifting from the Atlantic to the Asia-Pacific region, the coastal region has become increasingly important in China's outward-looking development strategy. This is reinforced by the close ties of the coastal region with overseas Chinese, especially with Hong Kong, Macao, and Taiwan. The coastal region develops faster because of its better access to international markets and stronger connection with overseas Chinese.

The **Western Region Development Project**, which started in 2000, aims to reduce China's regional disparity. The future of this project, however, does not look promising. In the 1960s and 1970s, China implemented an "even development" strategy, and the "three-fronts" construction shifted large amounts of resources to the inland regions, especially to Sichuan and Shaanxi Provinces. While emphasizing political and military considerations, the inland-oriented development policy was unsuccessful from the economic point of view, especially in the long run. The new Western Region Development Project will help China reduce its regional disparity only if China's development policies will emphasize economic efficiency and comparative advantages of different regions in terms of ecological conditions, natural resources, access to international markets, and geographic factors. Efficiency, equality, and stability are the three most important purposes of economic development policies.

See also Economic Policies and Development (1949–Present); Growth and Development, Trade-offs of; Hong Kong, Return of; Sustainable Growth and Development.

Bibliography

Jian, Tianlun, Jeffrey D. Sachs, and Andrew M. Warner, "Trends in Regional Inequality in China," *China Economic Review* 1, no. 7 (1996): 1–22; National Bureau of Statistics of the PRC, *China Regional Economy: A Profile of 17 Years of Reform and Opening-Up* (Beijing: China Statistical Press, 1996); National Bureau, *China Statistical Yearbook* (Beijing: China Statistical Press, 2000); Song, Shunfeng, George S-F Chu, and Rongqing Cao, "Intercity Regional Disparity in China," *China Economic Review* 11, no. 3 (2000): 246–261.

Shunfeng Song

Religion and Freedom of Religious Belief

Communist China is not an atheist state. Religion has long played an important role in Chinese life and remains a powerful force. Religious belief has

Since the reforms began in the late 1970s, religious life has returned to rural China. The women in this 2004 photo are worshipping at a local temple; they write their wishes on a prayer bag, which is then burned as an offering to the gods.

persisted throughout the past half century, although believers were forced into hibernation for ten years during the **Great Cultural Revolution (1966–1976)**. Since the late 1970s, the reform and Open Door policy have helped the revival of religion, and new religious sects have come into being.

The Communist revolution and the establishment of the People's Republic of China in 1949 had a significant impact on religion in China, particularly on Christianity. The **Korean War (1950–1953)** further heightened confrontation between China and the West. Foreign missionaries were compelled to leave, and all religions were put under government control. Nevertheless, since 1954, when the first constitution was promulgated, freedom of religious belief has been a constitutional right. Subsequent constitutions again state that citizens enjoy freedom of religious belief and that the state protects proper religious activities. At the same time, the constitutions declare that religion is not permitted to interfere in politics, and it is understood that foreign influence will not be allowed in Chinese religious matters.

In the 1950s, the new regime defined its relationship with religion. The Bureau of Religious Affairs was created within the government and the Department of Religious Work within the Communist Party to implement religious policy. Although the Communist Party regarded religion as the opiate of the people and enforced many policies to eliminate superstitious and sectarian societies, it adopted a cautious line in dealing with well-established faiths. Many religious leaders were assigned titular governmental positions. The Dalai Lama, leader of the Tibetan Buddhists, served as vice president of China and the Panchen Lama as a vice president of the **National People's Congress**. Both Buddhist leader Zhao Puchu and Islamic leader Bao Erhan were vice chairmen of the Chinese People's Political Consultative Conference.

The biggest problem for the government was its relationship with Christianity, which it saw as a vehicle for Western imperialism in China. The government cut Chinese church ties with the foreign churches but at the same time adopted a policy to protect Christian belief. The Three Self Patriotic Movement (TSPM) was established in 1950 with the goals of self-rule, self-support, and self-propagation. The TSPM endeavored to include all Chinese Christians in the task of "socialist construction." However, some Christians refused to conform, such as Ni Tuosheng (known in the West as Watchman Nee) and Wang Mingdao, who supported the independence of Chinese churches from foreign influence but who objected to control by the Communist government. Some nonconformists left China for Hong Kong or overseas, and some were arrested and sentenced to labor reform.

The Great Cultural Revolution (1966–1976) had a disastrous impact on all religious believers. Religions were seen as a part of the Four Olds (old culture, old beliefs, old customs, and old habits) or the remnants of the Old China. Normal religious life was halted, and many churches, monasteries, temples, and mosques were destroyed or converted to secular use. Religious leaders were openly criticized and persecuted. All mention of religion disappeared, and religious artifacts even disappeared from museums. The cult of **Mao Zedong** reached its zenith. Mao became the center of worship, and pictures of Mao were hung everywhere. Mao's "Little Red Book" became holy scripture, and the Mao badge testified to one's personal belief in the great leader.

The death of Mao Zedong marked the end of the Cultural Revolution, but normal religious life was revived only after Deng Xiaoping's reforms. The Party loosened its control over people's lives, and the government adopted a relatively liberal policy toward religion and even utilized religious sites for tourist purposes. Traditional religions began to resurface in Chinese society. To redress the mistakes of the Cultural Revolution, the government allocated funds to rebuild temples, churches, and mosques. Religious texts were again printed, although in limited circulation. New religious communities were organized, and a new generation of scholars specializing in religion was trained. The government officially denominated five religions in China: Buddhism, Daoism, Islam, Catholicism, and Protestantism (treating Catholicism and Protestantism as separate religions rather than as different branches of Christianity).

Although Confucianism is not regarded by the government as a religion, its practices are widespread. Belief in heaven (*tian*) is still held by most Chinese. Ancestor worship, a central tenet of Confucianism, has reemerged as a dominant feature of rural life in the past two decades. Ancestor temples and clan halls can be found in villages in many parts of China. The teachings of Confucius remain central in regulating social relationships.

The revival of Buddhism has been phenomenal. Temples attract millions of believers and visitors. The mercy of Buddha and the Bodhisattvas offers solace to people facing the increasing disparities between rich and poor, blessing their prosperity and their protection. Donations from believers facilitate the construction and maintenance of temples. The government does not have any major conflicts with Buddhism except in the case of Tibetan Lamaism (a form of Buddhism), which has become vital for Tibetan ethnic and cultural identity.

Islamic believers in northwestern China have maintained good relations with the government, which has benefited Islamic ethnic groups such as the Hui and the Uygur with a number of preferential policies. Islamic schools have been established, and measures of local autonomy have been granted. However, major problems still exist in **Xinjiang**, where fundamentalists and radical Muslims seek to form a separate Islamic state.

Daoism is the weakest religion in terms of political influence, although it is the only officially recognized native Chinese religion. One reason for this is that the Daoist doctrine is seen to be too individualistic and antisocial, and its philosophy too abstract. However, Daoist temples continue to attract people who seek a spiritual life closely related to nature.

Christianity has posed the greatest problem for government religious policy in the past two decades. Both Catholic and Protestant churches enjoy favorable treatment, but conversion of young people, establishment of new churches, and relations with the outside world have remained under government control. Despite these limitations, there has been a boom in Christian growth. Millions of Chinese, especially in the rural areas, have been converted. Yet foreign missionaries are not allowed in, and Chinese contact with foreign churches is strictly limited. This poses a critical problem for Catholics, who owe allegiance to the pope. The Vatican and Beijing have appointed rival bishops, but the Chinese government regards as legal only those it appoints. The clash between the two sides often results in the arrest of "illegal" bishops and their coreligionists, which is seen by the international community as persecution and violation of human rights. In recent years, many newly organized churches have refused to register with the government and have become part of the unregistered or so-called underground churches.

Traditional popular religion has also been widely practiced in the past two decades. Fengshui (geomancy) is employed in fortune-telling, and some practitioners make a living by helping people determine the site of their house or by forecasting their future prosperity. Respect for supernatural beings and worship of traditional deities such as the kitchen god and the door god are dominant in the rural areas, especially during festivals.

In the 1990s, a new quasi-religious sect, Falun Gong, was founded by Li Hongzhi. It drew inspiration from Buddhism and Daoism and made the practise of *qigong* (energy exercise) a centerpiece of its teaching. The mass demonstration of Falun Gong adherents in 1999 at Zhongnanhai, the headquarters of the Communist leadership, alarmed the Party, which declared Falun Gong a "highly organized, fully operating and unregistered illegal organization." Li Hongzhi went into exile, and some of his followers were arrested.

It is difficult to estimate the number of religious believers in China, since different sources present different statistics. It is even more difficult to predict future religious trends. As the spiritual crisis of communism, which is admitted by the government, continues, religion will fill the void. It can be predicted that more people will look to religion for spiritual salvation in the new century. They may not hold to one belief, because the Chinese syncretic tradition of choosing and combining whatever is available and practical will give believers more space to select their preferred faith or even several religious faiths at the same time. In a sense, as long as they practice their religion within the framework allowed by the government and as long as their creeds do not pose a threat to the government, they will be allowed to enjoy "the freedom of religious belief" granted as a constitutional right.

See also Confucian Tradition and Christianity; Human Rights Debate; Islam; Jews; Spiritual Life in the Post-Mao Era.

Bibliography

Overmyer, Daniel L., *Religions of China: The World as a Living System* (Prospect Heights, IL: Waveland Press, 1986); Sommer, Deborah, *Chinese Religion: An Anthology of Sources* (Oxford: Oxford University Press, 1995); Thompson, Laurence G., *Chinese Religion: An Introduction*, 5th ed. (Belmont, CA: Wadsworth Publishing Company, 1996); Yang, C. K., *Religions in Chinese Society: A Study of Contemporary Social Functions of Religions and Some of Their Historical Factors* (Prospect Heights, IL: Waveland Press, 1991).

Patrick Fuliang Shan

Renminbi (RMB)

The Renminbi (RMB) is China's legal tender. The name of the currency translates into English as "the people's currency." The basic unit of the currency is the yuan. It is issued and administered by the People's Bank of China (PBC), which is China's central bank.

The use of money in China dates back at least 4,000 years. Cattle, grain, and things of daily use such as silk, pearls, jade, tortoise shells, and seashells, as well as gold and silver, have been used as media of exchange in Chinese history. Paper currencies have been in circulation for more than 1,000 years. With the rise of modern banks, banknotes became popular in recent history. When the victory of Communist forces was in sight in China's civil war after World War II, the PBC was established on December 1, 1948. In the same year, the PBC began to issue RMB. After the founding of the People's Republic of China in 1949, China recalled other forms of currency circulating regionally, and RMB became the sole unified legal currency in China. On March 1, 1955, the PBC issued new RMB at the rate of one yuan to 10,000 yuan of the old RMB. The basic denominations have remained unchanged ever since. While the yuan is the basic unit of RMB, two smaller units are also used: jiao, one-tenth of a yuan, and fen, one-hundredth of yuan. Currently, the RMB is issued in the following denominations: 1, 2, 5, 10, 20, 50, and 100 yuan; 1, 2, and 5 jiao; and 1, 2, and 5 fen.

The RMB was stable in terms of inflation for much of the 1960s and 1970s, the years in which the government set wages and prices under a centrally planned economy. Since China's economic reform began in 1978, price controls have been gradually relaxed, and market forces have played an increasingly dominant role in price determination. Inflation, measured by consumer prices, climbed to double digits at times in the late 1980s and mid-1990s as economic growth accelerated, but it was quickly brought under control in both cases. China has achieved high economic growth while maintaining price stability for more than two decades since 1978.

The value of the RMB in terms of foreign exchange has maintained stability in the past few decades, except for a few discrete changes in its exchange rate with the U.S. dollar. This stability has been attributed largely to China's restrictions on the currency's convertibility. In the years immediately following the founding of the People's Republic of China in 1949, the value of the RMB was determined by price comparison of China's exports, imports, and the purchasing power parity of foreign exchange remittance. But when international trade embargoes were set in place against China and China adopted a Soviet-style centrally planned economy during the two decades after the late 1950s, the exchange rate of the RMB no longer reflected price linkages between China and the rest of the world. At the end of 1980, the exchange rate of the RMB was set at 1.53 yuan per U.S. dollar.

On January 1, 1980, China's State Council introduced "the internal settlement rate" of the RMB at 2.80 yuan to the dollar. China's trading firms used this rate to settle foreign exchange earnings/payments with the government. It was determined by the average cost of foreign exchange earnings from China's exports. The significance of this internal settlement rate was that for the first time, the exchange rate of the RMB reflected to some extent the relative prices between China and its trade partners and corrected, albeit temporarily, the overvaluation of the RMB. This internal settlement rate coexisted with the "official rate" of 1.53 yuan to the dollar, which was still used for nontrade foreign exchange transactions. The Chinese government also introduced the foreign exchange coordination market in 1980, which allowed foreign exchange earners and users (mainly foreign trading firms) to exchange their foreign exchange quotas. The foreign exchange quotas were portions of the foreign exchange earned by Chinese export firms that these export firms could keep for future foreign exchange transactions. The exchange rate of the RMB in the coordination market was allowed to fluctuate around the internal settlement rate by plus or minus 10 percent.

The dual-exchange-rate system—the coexistence of the internal settlement rate and the official rate—lasted until January 1985, when the PBC and other government agencies decided to abolish the internal settlement rate and adjusted the official exchange rate of the RMB to 2.80 yuan to the dollar to reflect domestic inflation. The foreign exchange coordination market remained and expanded as Chinese exporters were given more freedom to keep their foreign exchange earnings. Afterward, the official value of the RMB was adjusted downward a few times until it was settled at 3.71 yuan to the dollar in July 1986 and remained stable at that level until December 1989. Despite the devaluations since 1985, the currency was still considered overvalued as the cost of China's exports kept rising and export firms suffered increasing losses. In 1989, the value of the RMB dropped to as low as 7.2 yuan to the dollar in the foreign exchange coordination market, although it recovered to below 6 yuan to the dollar in the early 1990s. The official exchange rate was adjusted to 4.72 yuan to the dollar in December 1989 and to 5.22 yuan to the dollar in November 1990, bringing the official rates close to the rate that prevailed at the foreign exchange coordination market.

China's foreign exchange regime underwent a major reform in 1994, in tandem with the deepening of its overall economic reform. China adopted a market-based and managed floating exchange-rate system and set a goal for the currency to become convertible for current account transactions. The official exchange rate and the foreign exchange coordination rate were merged to produce a single exchange rate, which was set at 8.7 yuan to the dollar at the beginning of 1994. In April 1994, China's foreign exchange center, located in Shanghai, started operation and marked the beginning of China's interbank foreign exchange market. The value of the RMB appreciated slightly to about 8.3 yuan to the dollar by mid-1995 and stayed at 8.28 yuan to the dollar from September 1998 to September 2003.

During the Asian financial crisis that started in Thailand in 1997, the RMB was under severe pressure to devalue amid sharp declines of several Asian currencies. The RMB remained unchanged and proved to be a pillar of stability in the international monetary system, a stance that won appreciation from China's neighbors and policy makers in the United States and international financial institutions.

China's low labor costs have made China one of the major exporters of labor-intensive products in the world. China has also been one of the major recipients of foreign investments. As a result, China's foreign exchange reserves increased significantly at the beginning of the twenty-first century. By the end of June 2003, China's foreign exchange reserves reached about $350 billion.

These developments have triggered intense debates about the valuation of the RMB since 2002. It is argued that the undervalued RMB may lead to deflation in neighboring countries and has contributed to the U.S. trade deficit with China and millions of jobs lost in the U.S. manufacturing industry. China is being urged to revalue the RMB or let it float in the foreign exchange market.

People on the other side of the debate view these arguments as unjustified economically. First, there have been no sound assessments of a currency's "true" value. The low price of China's exports is a reflection of low wages for Chinese workers rather than undervaluation of the RMB. Given China's restrictions on capital movements, the level of foreign exchange reserves does not reflect the supply of and demand for foreign reserves and, in turn, the value of the RMB. Second, the alleged impact of China's exports on inflation (or deflation) in other countries may not be supported by statistics. China's exports were $266.6 billion in 2001, accounting for about 4.3 percent of the world's total, as compared with 11.9 percent for the United States and 6.6 percent for Japan for the same year. China's exports in 2001 to Japan were less than 1 percent of Japan's gross national income. Third, China's exports depend crucially on the low cost of labor in China and are price sensitive in the world market. Any revaluation of the RMB will not help the U.S. trade deficit, but will depress income for Chinese workers, which is already low by international standards. On the other hand, as China fulfills its World Trade Organization (WTO) commitments to open its market to foreign goods and services, including the financial sector, China may not be able to maintain its trade surplus. Fourth, China's banking sector and its financial markets in general are vulnerable to disturbances. An undue floating of the RMB may cause dramatic financial fluctuations harmful to both the Chinese economy and the international monetary system.

The future value of the RMB will depend on the overall performance of the Chinese economy, the competitiveness of Chinese goods in the world market, and the susceptibility of China's financial market to domestic and international disturbances. As of September 2003, the PBC maintained that while full convertibility of the RMB is the long-term goal, revaluation or immediate convertibility is not appropriate.

See also Banking and Financial System Reform; Credit Spending, Development of; Savings, Pattern of.

Bibliography

Lin, Guijun, *On the Exchange Rate of the RMB* (Beijing: University of International Business and Economics Press, 1997); Xinhua Publishing House and the People's Bank of China, *A History of Chinese Currency* (Beijing: Xinhua [New China] Publishing House, N.C.N., and M.A.O. Management Group, 1983); Yang, Jiawen, "Valuation of the Chinese Currency: A Background Study." Occasional Paper Series, Center for the Study of Globalization, George Washington University, 2003.

Jiawen Yang

Revolutionary Realism and Revolutionary Romanticism

The policy of revolutionary realism and revolutionary romanticism was first put forward by **Mao Zedong**. In March 1958, while discussing how to advance poetry writing in China, Mao said that the content of a poem should be "the unity of realism and romanticism" because people would not be able to compose poems at all if they were too realistic. In May 1958, at the Second Plenary Session of the Eighth Central Committee of the Communist Party, Mao further stated that proletarian literature and art should adopt the creative method of combining revolutionary realism with revolutionary romanticism. For Mao, literature and art should not be bogged down by excessive details, but rather should concentrate on depicting a Communist society that would be brought about by revolution. Zhou Yang, a vice minister of the Culture Ministry at the time, explained Mao's teaching in detail. According to Zhou, Mao's new teaching was the scientific summary of all the experience in literary history and the most appropriate principle based on the needs and characteristics of the times. He also thought that instead of rejecting each other, realism and romanticism should join forces, relying on each other and working in coordination. He believed that without romanticism, realism would easily turn into short-sighted naturalism, and likewise, if romanticism failed to integrate with realism, it would only become swashbuckling talk or fantasy.

At first sight, this policy appeared to be a repetition of Soviet ideas not only because the term "revolutionary romanticism" was originally used in Soviet literary criticism, but also because a few decades earlier, the Russian writer Maxim Gorky had suggested combining realism with romanticism. But in fact, although Mao Zedong applied similar wording, he did not intend to copy the Soviet model; on the contrary, he was trying to lead China in a direction that would be different from the Soviet Union's.

Two important shifts can be found in this new policy. First, China's own literary tradition was emphasized. Zhou Yang understood clearly that the term "revolutionary romanticism" originated in the Soviet Union and that Gorky had once urged linking realism with romanticism, because Zhou himself had introduced both of these ideas to Chinese readers as early as 1933. However, in interpreting Mao's formula in 1958, instead of mentioning the Russians, Zhou sought origins and evidence from Chinese history to defend Mao. He held that more than 1,400 years ago, the well-known Chinese critic Liu Xie had pointed out the necessity of integrating realism with romanticism. Therefore, the Chinese could absorb rich experience from their own history and carry forward the spirit of that experience on the new ideological basis of communism. Zhou's pride in national literature was by no means accidental, but a carefully planned strategy of the Chinese leaders. By 1958, the disagreements between China and the Soviet Union had become more obvious. To show their firm stand as well as their indignation at Nikita Khrushchev's "anti-Marxist" conduct, the Chinese were deliberately seeking a road that would differentiate them from the Russians. Stressing China's own age-old literary heritage seemed to be an effective solution because neither the origin nor the setting of this heritage was dependent on foreign influence. In fact, even the adjective "revolutionary" in Mao's teaching had a symbolic connotation, for to a certain extent, Mao used the word to oppose the "revisionists" in the Soviet Union.

The other important shift in this new policy was the stress on romanticism. As a literary method or mode, romanticism was almost as popular as realism in China after the 1910s, but after 1942, especially in the Communist-controlled Liberated Areas, romanticism became much less preferred because realism was thought to be a better artistic mode in describing reality and encouraging readers to actively involve themselves in society, particularly during the time when China was striving for social changes. Another reason that realism was more welcomed after 1942 is linked to the impact of Mao Zedong's "Talks at the Yan'an Forum on Literature and Art." In his talks, Mao called on Chinese writers to learn from "socialist realism," which was a Soviet literary dogma. As a result, socialist realism not only was held up as a good example for the Chinese to follow in the 1940s, but also was officially announced to be the highest principle for literature and art in China. But in 1958, Mao wished to give romanticism an equal standing with realism. Mao thought then that romanticism would help promote the **Great Leap Forward** movement, which was a nationwide drive launched early in 1958 to accelerate China's already overheated economy. At that time, in order to realize the dream of expanding the capacity of industrial production within the shortest possible time, the Chinese government overstressed ideological power. It was believed that under the leadership of the Communist Party, as long as the Chinese people had revolutionary ideals and enthusiasm, they could perform every kind of miracle and triumph over anything. Some leaders even thought that China had already entered an epoch in which Communist spirit was rising to an unprecedented height, and the Chinese people's selflessness and boundless zeal for developing their country filled them with the vigor of heroism and romanticism. In their eyes, the epoch was so glorious and splendid that realism alone was not enough to portray it.

Only with the assistance of romanticism could the heroic efforts, the dreams for a stronger and richer country, and the magnificent pictures of the "Communist paradise" be fully brought out.

After Mao's new teaching was announced, hot discussions appeared about the difference between revolutionary realism and conventional realism, and the relationship between socialist realism and Mao's "revolutionary realism." Although different views were expressed, it was generally agreed that Mao's instruction was the most progressive method for advancing China's literature and art. The Third National Congress of Literature and Art, which was convened in 1960, further avowed that Mao's saying was completely new and suitable not only for literary and art creation, but also for criticism. By then, as the Sino-Soviet split became more apparent, socialist realism had given way, at least in theory, to Mao's "revolutionary realism and revolutionary romanticism."

The new policy benefited literary and art creation in that it officially encouraged the use of romanticism and raised romanticism's standing, which had been underestimated for years. But in the meantime, the policy also pushed to a new stage the tendency for formalism and bombast that had already emerged in the previous years. What was advocated, fundamentally speaking, was a politics-oriented romanticism rather than an artistic one. Personal vision of reality and free expression of inner emotions in a nonpolitical context—features that one can easily find in most other works of romanticism—were still restricted. In most cases, the imaginative quality of romanticism was given full play to extol the political passion for a utopian Communist society and exaggerate the infinite ideological and creative power of the Chinese people during the Great Leap Forward movement. Consequently, although the total output of writings increased remarkably during this time, much of the quality was sacrificed for quantity. Some works were imbued with superficial descriptions and stereotypical characters; others looked more like political sermons or slogans than anything else.

See also Anticorruption Literature and Television Dramas; Avant-garde Literature; Experimental Fiction; Great Cultural Revolution, Literature during; Intellectuals, Political Engagement of (1949–1978); Intellectuals, Political Engagement of (1978–Present); Literary Policy for the New China; Literature of the Wounded; Misty Poetry; Modern Pop-Satire; Neorealist Fiction and Modernism; Pre–Cultural Revolution Literature; Root-Searching Literature; Sexual Freedom in Literature.

Bibliography

Mao Zedong, *Quotations from Chairman Mao Zedong*, translated by Stuart R. Schram (New York: Frederick A. Praeger, 1967).

Dela X. Jiao

Revolutionary Romanticism

See Revolutionary Realism and Revolutionary Romanticism.

Rhetoric in China's Foreign Relations

China's official rhetoric in foreign affairs can be divided into two major categories: officially publicized rhetoric disseminated through the mass media and private discourse used in negotiation to reach a certain objective. Over the years, China's media and official rhetoric, as well as negotiation language in international relations, has matured. Publicly, while the language that emanates from the Chinese government remains political, strong, and uninformative, private diplomacy and negotiation are accompanied by a flexible language in order to reach desired goals in Chinese foreign affairs. Public rhetoric for Olympics bids, most-favored-nation (MFN) status, World Trade Organization (WTO) admission, human rights, and other high-profile issues demonstrates that the government has become more adept in using public relations to its advantage. For example, while privately releasing individual dissidents under U.S. pressure, Chinese officials have publicly defended China's human rights record and attacked the U.S. human rights record.

China's official rhetoric in international affairs can also be divided into primary and secondary rhetoric. Primary rhetoric expresses China's essential and enduring national interest, such as sovereignty. Beijing's adherence to these principles is always firm and consistent. Peripheral principles and rhetoric are formulated to deal with less substantial issues and secondary goals and can diminish or disappear when the primary goals are achieved. This dual rhetoric enables Beijing to establish a negotiating position to maximize its advantage. Before entering a negotiation, Beijing clearly and often publicly states its primary principles (*yuanzexing*), which are essential and nonnegotiable. Privately, however, what constitutes flexible (*linghuoxing*) and secondary principles is decided. This rhetoric and these issues are more flexible in nature and thus negotiable.

The dual natures of Chinese bargaining communication principles serve to prevent other nations from coercing China into making concessions and provide China with a flexible bargaining tool. An example is the air collision on April 1, 2001, between a Chinese fighter jet and an American spy plane that resulted the loss of the Chinese pilot, Wang Wei, and his jet and the emergency landing in southern China of the American reconnaissance plane. While insisting first with firm language both publicly and privately that the American government apologize to the Chinese people and government for violating Chinese air sovereignty and for killing the Chinese pilot, the Chinese government also flexibly accepted the word "sorry" that carries similar meanings when translated into Chinese because it recognized that the American side would not apologize.

Reality in the U.S.-China relationship is not always as simple as the rhetoric sounds. The bilateral relation and the understanding about it are complex and constantly change. The two nations are neither permanent "friends" nor lasting "enemies," as often portrayed, perceived, and said. Unity is inevitable after long division and division is inevitable after long unity, as the Chinese proverb goes.

Difficulties in U.S.-China relations are often caused by miscommunication, lack of communication, or biased and inflammatory rhetoric that can hurt bilateral relations. Contradictory rhetoric and policies from Washington confuse and upset Beijing, whose behaviors often frustrate Washington. Differences in political systems aside, cultural, rhetorical, and historical differences, as well as public opinion, also influence the relations. The negotiation of such crises as the spy plane incident are as much about symbolism as about substance and as much about rhetoric as about reality. Forcing the Americans to cut their plane into pieces is symbolically important. In the eyes of the Chinese government and public, whose lives are governed by complicated and sophisticated symbolism and face-saving rituals and rhetoric, as a symbol of aggression, the plane was as much a culprit as the crew who flew it. The United States was primarily and realistically interested in getting the crew back and was willing to compromise on symbolism (cutting the plane into pieces).

The uniform way Chinese officials expressed themselves shows that the government still exercises direct control over the political discourse with centralized management and manipulation of "appropriate" and "inappropriate" language formulation. However, the government makes the language of the state the sole legitimate political expression but allows private flexibility to negotiate. Core expression is often formed to guide matters of principle, while flexible discourse is allowed for nonessential issues.

See also Independent Foreign Policy (1982); Jiang Zemin (1926–), Diplomacy of; Sino-American Relations, Conflicts and Common Interests; Sino-American Relations since 1949; Sino-Japanese Relations since 1949; Sino-Russian Relations since 1991; Sino-Soviet Alliance; World Trade Organization (WTO), China's Accession to.

Bibliography

Schoenhals, Michael, *Doing Things with Words in Chinese Politics* (Berkeley: University of California, Institute of East Asian Studies, 1992); Zhao, Quansheng, "Modernization, Nationalism, and Regionalism in China," in *Comparative Foreign Policy: Adaptation Strategies of the Great and Emerging Powers*, ed. Steven W. Hook (Upper Saddle River, NJ: Prentice Hall, 2002).

Yu Zhang

RMB

See Renminbi (RMB).

Root-Searching Literature

Different from the modernism shown in the avant-garde school of Chinese literature and neorealistic fiction during the post–**Great Cultural Revolution** era, root-searching literature mainly seeks changes or innovations in contents rather than change in forms, although stylistic and linguistic considerations are not totally ignored in this type of literary creations. Root-searching literature is mainly based upon a kind of national consciousness, anthropological self root-digging intellectual efforts, and an ethnic and cultural reidentification social process as an ideological reaction to the westernization of China since the beginning of the 1980s. With their fictions and essays, the writers want to bring readers back to their cultural roots and their own identity in this fast-changing China and world that are moving toward Western modernization.

After **Mao Zedong**'s death in 1976, economic reforms and the **Open Door policy** of the Chinese government brought not only Western technology, American, Japanese, and European currencies, the market system, foreign corporations, rock and roll, **Coca-Cola**, McDonald's, Kentucky Fried Chicken, motor vehicles, skyscrapers, and taxis to China, but also Western culture, ways of thinking, and lifeways, including Western literature and arts, to the Central Country of the world (Zhongguo—China). As far as the cultural aspect is concerned, after 1982, Chinese culture started to face a second wave of westernization (the first had followed the May 4 Movement in 1919), during and after which Chinese literature, written language morphology and style, and sociopolitical structures underwent a series of major changes. Political revolution, democracy, social reforms, individualism, socialism, capitalism, liberalism, and colonialism began shaking the traditional Chinese political system and social structure in all psychological, moral, philosophical, and cultural aspects. Literature, as a manifestation of thought, was no exception. As in the case of the New Cultural Movement following the May 4 Movement, the Open Door policy also brought profound changes in Chinese culture. In the last twenty years or so, by comparing the two waves of westernization, Chinese **intellectuals** have realized that Chinese people are facing the shock of the collision between two large cultural systems, Western and Eastern. That is the reason that many Chinese intellectuals, including writers and artists, have been submerging themselves again into long reflection, rethinking, researching, refinding, and redefining their cultural, ethnic, and literal identity. If one considers that both socialism and communism were imported from Western idealism and materialism, the avant-garde school and the neorealism school constitute no exception and manifest westernization in Chinese literature. Therefore, for many people in China, the post-Mao era's Chinese literature has already been cut off from its genetic relations with its motherland's cultural roots. It is important that Chinese writers connect their artistic branches with their cultural roots. If they do not, real Chinese literature with its national and ethnic identity will die soon.

Some Chinese literature critics and writers also compare the status of contemporary Chinese literature with that of Latin American literature, whose important figures and contemporary representatives, like Gabriel García Márquez and Jorge Luis Borges, were successful because their writing was directly related to their root-searching expressions instead of being a mere copy of Western literary styles. In other words, if and only if Chinese literature goes back consciously to its cultural roots, it can be truly recognized and accepted by the world. The so-called modernization of Chinese literature cannot be separated from the root-searching process.

The most influential writers of the root-searching school include Han Shaogong, A Cheng, Jia Ping'ao, Wang Zengqi, Zheng Yi, Zhang Chengzhi, Zhaxidawa (Tibetan), Wure'ertu (Mongolian), and Li Hangyu. Not happy with the Western cultural inundation of Chinese cultural nationalism in the post-Mao era, they are all trying to incorporate certain linguistic, artistic, stylistic, cultural, and ethnic features into their novels, short stories, and essays, although their viewpoints and critiques often vary from person to person.

Unlike other literary categories, the so-called root-searching school does not refer to a specific stylistic structure nor to specific denotative or connotative semantic contents of literature, but to a kind of cultural and artistic conceptualization based on a common ethnic identity. However, China was formed as a unified country from many kingdoms in ancient societies throughout its history. Each geographic location has its own cultural roots. Therefore, root-searching literature also seeks the roots of each locative cultural identity. For instance, Jia Ping'ao focuses on the local flavors of Shangzhou in the central part of China; Li Hangyu puts the locative features of northern Jiangsu Province into his descriptions and also focused on various aspects of ancient Yue culture (in the southeastern part of China) and its folklore; Zheng Yi fills his pages with the cultural aspects of northwestern Shanxi Province; Zhang Chengzhi takes the central Asian grassland as the background of his narratives; Wure'ertu's fictions refer to the Ewenke's hunting culture, and Zhaxidawa tells stories about Tibetan religions and culture.

Besides the regional elements, root-searching literature also displays discussions and concepts of ancient Chinese Taoist and Confucian philosophy and thoughts. A Cheng profoundly roots his writing in Daoism, and Zhang Wei and Jiao Jian have made every effort to mine Confucian ideology through their writing.

The most important well-known root-searching narratives are Han Shaogong's *Yue Lan* (Moon orchid), *Ba Ba Ba* (Daddy-daddy-daddy), *Nu Nu Nu* (Women-women-women), *Gui Qu Lai* (Returning), and *Huo Zhai* (Fire house), and A Cheng's *Qi Wang* (Chess king), *Shu Wang* (Tree king) and *Haizi Wang* (Children king). *Daddy-Daddy-Daddy* describes a prehistoric tribe named Bird where obscurantism dominates both the bossy fellow and the common people. The main character of the story is a man named Binzai who can never grow up, and the only words he can pronounce are "daddy, daddy, and daddy." The only concepts he is able to use to judge about the outside world are "good" and "bad" and "white" and "black." He rejects any ideas from outside the village. Anyone who expresses a foreign, extraneous, and contrary thought is the enemy of Binzai and of everyone in the tribe. In this story, the author strongly criticizes a conservative and obscurantist society. Han Shaogong followed to some extent the Chu culture and civilization (the Chu kingdom was located in the central part of the Yangtse River Valley, and the people were wild and had a strong character) in his writing contents and style.

A Cheng loves Daoism and all kinds of art, painting, and folklore related to Daoism because he grew up in a traditional Chinese intellectual family. In all his stories, readers can easily recognize a strong tendency toward Taoist thoughts. *Chess King* is a story of Wang Yisheng, who dedicates his whole time during the ten years of the Cultural Revolution to playing chess. He does nothing but play the famous Chinese chess with his friends and forgets everything in real life. All his happiness and sadness are related to this board game. Everyone who plays Chinese chess knows that the chessboard is divided by a "river" whose name is Chuhe and by a "frontier" whose name is Hanjie, which symbolize in Daoism the release of souls from purgatory. The "revolutionary" tempests and thousands of vicissitudes that occur every day during the Cultural Revolution cannot move the main character's attention from his game-playing joy. It is only possible for the "King of Chess" to stand aloof in the midst of acute human struggles when Wang Yisheng is playing to defend one side of the Chu River and the Han frontier, which gives him peace, psychological balance, and tranquillity. This life philosophy comes from a Taoist concept of the balance between yin and yang. Some literal critics in China do not like this Taoist way of thinking, because for them, in the face of social struggles, one should fight instead of balancing without action. However, in Daoist philosophy, any fighting is inside balance, and any balance is inside a struggle. Taoist ideas are also hidden in Li Hangyu's narratives, in which cultural romanticism is combined with Taoist balance. Following this balance philosophy, Jia Ping'ao also seeks the balance between the countryside's wild culture and the urban and metropolitan culture in the modernization process of modern China.

Root-searching literature also looks for linguistic purity of the Chinese language. Instead of following Western Indo-European languages' long and "overstuffed" sentential structures, the writers try to use more simplified, concise, and clear typical Chinese linguistic structures.

After 1987, the root-searching school started to decline. Many factors influenced this process. However, the most important reason, perhaps, was that after ten years of searching for cultural roots in their narrative, the root-searching writers finally could not find a way to express themselves in an ideal and self-defined way.

See also Anticorruption Literature and Television Dramas; Avant-garde Literature; Experimental Fiction; Great Cultural Revolution, Literature during; Intellectuals, Political Engagement of (1949–1978); Intellectuals, Political Engagement of (1978–Present); Literary Policy for the New China; Literature of the Wounded; Misty Poetry; Modern Pop-Satire; Neorealist Fiction and Modernism; Pre-Cultural Revolution Literature; Revolutionary Realism and Revolutionary Romanticism; Sexual Freedom in Literature.

Bibliography

Guo Zhigang, and Suen Zhongtian, eds., *Contemporary Chinese Literature—Second Part* (Beijing, China: Higher Education Press, 1993); Jin Han, *Modern Chinese Novels* (Hangzhou, China: Zhejiang University Press, 1997); Zhang Rongjian, ed., *Contemporary Chinese Literature* (Wuhan, Hubei Province: University of Sciences and Technology of Central China Press, 2001); Zhang Rongjian, ed., *Contemporary Chinese Literature— Reference Materials* (Wuhan, Hubei Province: University of Sciences and Technology of Central China Press, 2001); Zhang Weizhong, *Transformations in the New Age Novels and the Chinese Traditional Culture* (Beijing, China: Xuelin Press, 2002).

Zhiyuan Chen

Ru Zhijuan (1925–1998)

Ru Zhijuan was a short-story and prose writer in modern Chinese literature. She was born on September 13, 1925, in Shanghai. Her parents passed away when she was very young, so she lived a hard life with her grandmother during her childhood. In 1943, she joined the army with her elder brother. After transferring to civilian work in 1955, Ru became an editor for *Literature and Art*

Monthly in Shanghai. During 1959 to 1961, when the issues of writing style and subject matter in literary creation were under discussion in China, Ru was criticized for lack of "political orientations" and "lofty images of revolutionary heroes" in her works. During the **Great Cultural Revolution**, because of the sufferings that she was experiencing, Ru swore not to write anymore. However, after 1977, especially in the late 1970s and early 1980s, she not only resumed writing, but also became one of the most active writers in the country. Ru's daughter, Wang Anyi (1954–   ), who started a writing career after the Cultural Revolution, is one of the most prolific and influential novelists in contemporary China.

Ru's first short story, "Lilies" (1958), was a great success because of her vivid depiction of the friendly relationship between a peasant woman and a young soldier. Almost all her works written afterwards, such as "Wish Fulfilled," "When Flowers Bloom in Warm Spring," and "Quiet Obstetrical Hospital," were well received by readers. Her writings in the 1950s and 1960s were rich in lyrical expressions and poetic flavor, but the plots and characters were relatively simple. After 1978, Ru broadened her scope to describe some issues more important to contemporary life and made great efforts to improve her writing techniques. Unlike in her earlier writings, the narrator's voice now became restrained, calm, and serious. Ru preferred to portray diverse and complex social life through a detailed delineation of the inner worlds of her characters. In fact, she was one of the first Chinese writers in the post–Cultural Revolution era who tried to apply such Western techniques as stream of consciousness in her writings. "Wrongly-Edited Story" and "Path on Grassland" are the most representative of her works published after 1978. "Wrongly-Edited Story" showed her profound insight into the history and the present condition of the country and won the National Prize for Best Short Stories in 1979.

Ru's poetic, lyrical, and graceful language style is widely liked by readers. For many years, Ru's "Lilies" and some other short stories were included in the textbooks of elementary and middle schools in China and used as good examples of modern Chinese language.

See also Intellectuals, Political Engagement of (1978–Present); Literary Policy for the New China; Pre-Cultural Revolution Literature.

Bibliography

Ru Zhijuan, *Lilies and Other Stories* (Beijing: International Book Trading Corporation [Guoji Shudian], 1985).

Dela X. Jiao

Rural Administrative Organizations

From 1949 to 1958, rural China was organized in a county-township-village hierarchy line. However, during the era of the **people's communes** between 1958 and 1982, the institutional organization in rural China was restructured to a system of county, commune, brigade, and production team. After 1982, rural China resumed the county-township-village organization.

Under the commune system, counties remained administrative organizations, while communes were "integrated administrative and economic organizations." A county usually consisted of eight to fifteen communes. Depending on the region, each commune consisted of 2,000 to 7,000 households. Communes were divided into brigades, and brigades into production teams. The production team was the basic institutional unit of rural China. In most areas, production teams coincided with natural villages.

People's communes were governed by the commune management council, which was both an organ of the state and a local economic management body. As the organ of the state, the commune management council performed government administrative functions such as fiscal budget control, public security, local infrastructure development, education, health care, and social services; as the local economic management body, it was responsible for carrying out the central government's economic goals and for planning and guiding production within its jurisdiction. Brigades and production teams were governed by brigade management councils and production team councils, respectively. Production teams were the basic units for collective property ownership and accounting. They practiced management of rural daily production and distributed income to rural populations. They were also the basic organizations to implement the government's policies.

China launched its economic reform in 1978. This reform was initiated in the rural areas through the replacement of the commune system with the household responsibility system. This change in economic organization led to a change in rural institutional organizations. Under the household responsibility system, rural individual households became the basic units of production and accounting. The economy of the commune, brigade, and production team collapsed. As early as 1979, a number of provinces started various experiments in separating administration from the communes. In 1982, the Fifth **National People's Congress** passed the current Constitution, which resumed the legal status of townships in China's administrative hierarchy. On October 12, 1983, the Central Committee of the Chinese Communist Party and the State Council issued a notice that started the reestablishment of townships and township governments. By the end of 1984, nationwide township reestablishment was completed, which formally terminated the commune system, and rural China has used the county-township-village organizational structure ever since. To better serve individual farming households, a township is usually smaller than a commune in area and in population. Below townships are villages. In northern China, an administrative village often coincides with a large natural village. However, in densely populated southern China, an administrative village is often an artificial grouping of a number of small natural villages close to each other. In other words, administrative villages replaced brigades in most areas and production teams in others. If an administrative village consists of several small natural villages, the residents in each natural village are organized as a residents' group. The Thirty-sixth Document of the Central Committee of the Chinese Communist Party of 1982 called for experiments in establishing villagers' organizations. In November 1987, the Standing Committee of the National People's Congress passed the Organic Law of Villagers' Committee of the People's Republic of China and put the law into practice the same year.

FIGURE 4
Basic Organizational Structure in Rural China

County→ Township→		Village→Rural Households	
↑ ↑		↑ ↑	
Administrative Organizations		**Communal Organizations**	

After these reforms, the basic organizational structure in current rural China can be simplified as shown in Figure 4. In 2001, there were 40,161 townships and towns in China, under which 709,257 administrative villages existed. By law, the township government is the lowest government authority in China's formal administrative hierarchy, and the villagers' committee is the formal authority of an administrative village. However, the villagers' committee is not a government administrative branch but an authority of the village residents' autonomous organization. Therefore, townships belong to the state administrative organization, while villages belong to society or communal organization. Both townships and villages constitute the primary organizational framework of contemporary rural China. The state-society boundary is blurred at the township-village level.

Towns and townships are administrative organizations at a similar level in China's bureaucratic hierarchy. The difference between a town and a township is that a town is usually where the county government is located. Under the following two circumstances, a township will be restructured as a town: if the township's total population is less than 20,000, but the nonagricultural population in the place where the township government is located exceeds 2,000; or if the township's total population exceeds 20,000, and the nonagricultural population in the place where the township government is located accounts for more than 10 percent of the township population.

A township is governed by the township government. Township governments perform government administrative functions through various executive functions. Two kinds of officials form the power nucleus in a township. One is the township director and deputy directors. The other is the cadres of the township Communist Party. The township director and deputy directors are government executives elected by the township's people's congress and operate under the supervision of the township's people's congress. They are supposed to be in charge of all the administrative affairs of the government. However, in many cases, the real control of a township rests in the hands of the township Party secretary, because most township directors are township Party committee members under the leadership of the Party secretary. They are elected because of the nomination of the township Party committee. The appointment of township government branch chiefs and the recruitment of government staff are also mainly controlled by the township Party committee. Township government officials are government employees and receive formal salary payments from government payrolls.

According to the Organic Law of Villagers' Committee Organization, the villagers' committee is a residents' autonomous organization that represents local residents' interests. Its major responsibilities include maintaining community harmony through activities such as **conflict resolution** and self-education; managing and coordinating village economic activities, public affairs, and welfare; and communicating with township authorities or neighboring villages on behalf of village residents. However, the village committee must perform at least part of the state agent's role as well. Under the vigilant guidance of the township government, village committees have to fulfill certain tasks assigned to them such as levying collections and overseeing birth-control compliance. According to the law, a villagers' committee exercises its power on village affairs by calling for and moderating either all village residents' forums or village residents' representative meetings for decision making. The power and the influence of villagers' committees differ widely, from being virtually invisible in many agriculture-based areas to being all-powerful in newly industrialized areas. The village Party secretary generally has more influence than the director of the villagers' committee. In many villages, the two major positions are actually held by one person. However, in recent years, the power of the village Party secretary has been declining. The director and the members of the villagers' committee receive no formal salaries from the government payrolls, but they may receive some subsidies either from the township government or from the revenues of the villagers' committee generated by the village-owned enterprises.

The director and the members of the villagers' committee are popularly elected by the village residents. Starting in 1994, the election of the villagers' committee has adopted a method of "direct, fair, competitive, and secret ballot," which is aimed at encouraging fair competition. The formal procedure of the election is as follows: prior to the election, all village residents over the age of eighteen register for the election and receive voting certificates, one vote per person; voters nominate the candidates, and the number of nominees should exceed the number of open positions; and voters elect the villagers' committee director and other committee members through secret ballots. This method has effectively reduced the domination of the village Party branch in village elections and other affairs and is viewed as the first step toward a more democratic political system. Since 2001, this method has been experimented with in some township government elections, but only on a small scale. Various new problems related to the direct elections have been reported, such as conflicts between clans in village elections, gang influence and related activities in elections, and domination of wealthy families or local political elites in elections.

See also Agricultural Reform; *Hukou* System; Rural Credit Cooperatives (RCCs); Rural Industrialization; Rural-Urban Divide, Regional Disparity, and Income Inequality; Township and Village Enterprises (TVEs).

Bibliography

Li, Kang, *Rural Community Development in Transitional China* (Beijing: China Science and Technology Press, 1992); O'Brien, Kevin, and Lianjiang Li, "Accommodating Democracy in a One-Party State: Introducing Village Elections in China," *China Quaterly*, 162 (June 2000): 465–490; Oi, Jean, and Scott Rozelle, *Elections and Power: The Locus of Decision-Making in a Chinese Village* (New York: Oxford University Press, 2000).

Hong-yi Chen

Rural Credit Cooperatives (RCCs)

Rural credit cooperatives (RCCs) are part of three official financial institutions in rural China. The other two are the Agricultural Bank of China (ABC) and the Agricultural Development Bank of China (ADBC). In addition, other state-owned commercial banks (SOCBs), such as the Industrial and Commercial Bank of China (ICBC), the Construction Bank of China (CBC), and the Bank of China (BC), also have their branches in rural county towns. Furthermore, nonofficial financial organizations also operate in the rural sector, including rural credit foundations (RCFs), mutual savings associations, the informal sector, and microcredit projects that have developed in recent years to target poverty relief.

Founded in March 1955, the ABC is a state-owned commercial bank that focuses on supporting (1) enterprises, enterprise groups, and large-scale agricultural production bases engaged in primary agricultural production; (2) profit-earning enterprises engaged in primary agricultural production; and (3) development of the social service system. ABC's clients are primarily **township and village enterprises (TVEs)**, supply and distribution cooperative commercial organizations, and private businessmen or individuals. Though defined primarily as a commercial bank, ABC retains some policy lending activity in rural areas, such as agricultural development and poverty relief lending. In 1998, ABC's policy lending amounted to 156,000 million yuan, representing 28 percent of the year's total loans (some 553,800 million yuan) (IFAD 2001). Founded in December 1993, the ADBC, in contrast, is officially a policy bank that engages primarily in lending to enterprises for purchasing and storing grain, cotton, and oil, with reassignment of agricultural development and poverty relief lending to ABC. Both ABC and ADBC also operate in urban areas.

Rural credit cooperatives are nonbank financial institutions that operate only in rural areas. RCCs' mandate is to serve the rural population. RCCs lend for all activities, including production and consumption, to individuals, **privately owned enterprises**, and TVEs. Their main borrowing clients are farmers and TVEs. In more developed rural areas, the township and county enterprises are the majority borrowers. There are about 34,909 rural credit cooperatives across China, with 2.23 trillion yuan (about 272 billion U.S. dollars) in outstanding deposits and 1.61 trillion yuan (about 197 billion U.S. dollars) in outstanding loans, equal to some 11.5 percent and 10.8 percent of the total deposits and loans in China's banking sector. The burden of financial support in the countryside has been borne increasingly by RCCs since 1998, when the four state-owned commercial banks, ICBC, ABC, CBC, and BC, started to withdraw from rural areas to focus on big **cities**. They are the primary source of finance in the countryside, reportedly handling 75 percent of all agricultural loans.

RCCs differ from the ABC and other SOCBs in ownership and management. RCCs are nominally cooperative banks with a certain share of capital from households and are supposedly managed by shareholders. They are single-unit financial organizations, not banks within a banking network that can transfer liquidity and perform cross-subsidization. They provide services that the state commercial banks are reluctant to provide because of higher transaction costs resulting from either small scales or remote locations. Compared to ABC, they have a larger share of time deposits, which also tends to make costs of funds higher. Moreover, they are less equipped with management networking, professional advisory services, and other modern managerial and governance structures.

Cooperatives emerge organically from the share capital mobilized by an interest group for a specific activity. Though they are called rural cooperatives, China's RCCs did not start as member-driven institutions. The RCC system first developed as a part of the collectivization efforts of the government to form cooperatives in all spheres of economic activity and was part of the communes and brigades. In February 1979, at the beginning of the agricultural reform that eventually dissolved the commune and collective system in the rural sector, the RCCs came under the leadership of ABC. As a result of the government's intention of transforming RCCs into real cooperatives, they were decoupled from ABC in 1996 and were put under the regulatory framework of the People's Bank of China (PBC). But the assets of RCCs have grown very large because of government support and patronage, and the share capital contribution from households is minimal. China's RCCs are, therefore, de facto state-owned financial institutions and are cooperatives in name only. Although RCCs are not controlled directly by local governments, their interventions are unavoidable due to the special political, economic, and social conditions in China.

The PBC Cooperative Financial Management Department directly supervises and manages the RCCs. The RCCs in all areas are required to set up county-level apex institutions (*xian lianshe*) to provide a clearinghouse service for the local RCCs. Some apex institutions also handle financial business directly. Currently, regional-level apex institutions (*diqu lianshe*) have been set up in some areas on a trial basis. The apex institutions collect management fees from their affiliates. A law on credit cooperatives has not yet appeared, however.

The PBC appoints the RCC staff and imposes reserve requirements and interest-rate restrictions. RCCs have some flexibility in setting interest rates for lending within a band linked to regulated rates. To encourage competition and allow greater flexibility, the PBC permits RCCs to charge a maximum interest rate of twice the official rate set by the central bank, while banks can charge up to 1.7 times the official rate.

While RCCs share the problem of nonperforming loans (NPLs) with the ABC and other SOCBs, the problem is more severe for the RCCs. At the end of 2002, the NPLs of the RCCs stood at 515 billion yuan (U.S. $62 billion), a staggering 37 percent of their total outstanding loans, according to a *China Daily* report, compared with less than 25 percent for the four SOCBs. Most RCCs are unprofitable. In poor provinces, the bad-loan ratio can be as high as 99 percent. Most RCCs' nonperforming loans date from before the reforms of 1996–1997, and a high proportion of them are regarded as policy loans, that is, loans provided in compliance with instructions given by county and township governments. Loans to TVEs, which have a higher percentage of delinquency than loans to rural households, also represent a high percentage of RCC nonperforming loans (IFAD 2001). Moreover, blind lending in real estate in the early

1990s has also contributed to the NPLs of RCCs. The bad-loan problem and general poor management of the RCCs have led to little confidence of the rural population in the RCCs. Consequently, many borrowers turn to the informal financial sectors or to friends and relatives for their financial needs. This severely limits the function of RCCs in supporting rural development.

The government, including the central bank, has taken actions to restructure the NPLs of RCCs. As a part of restructuring debt-laden RCCs, the China Banking Regulatory Commission, which was set up in April 2003 to take over some regulatory functions of the PBC, is considering drafting a bankruptcy law for small and medium-sized financial institutions.

Rebuilding the rural financial system has been given top priority as China aims to solve its "agricultural problems" to sustain its growth. Developing RCCs into rural cooperative banks is an important step of the reform, which would allow the RCCs to have a combination of a joint-stock structure and cooperative mechanisms and thus lift many geographic and business restrictions previously imposed on them. The State Council approved a pilot reform of rural credit cooperatives in Jiangsu Province in August 2000. Mergers and reorganizations of the RCCs subsequently took place. In 2001, with the approval of the PBC, China's first batch of shareholding rural commercial banks was established in Zhangjiagang, Changshu, and Jiangyin in Jiangsu Province. Moreover, Shanghai plans to create the Third City Commercial Bank via mergers of more than 230 RCCs.

Also as part of the reform, RCCs are required to increase their share capital. The amount of loans to shareholding farmers is required to make up at least 50 percent of the loan portfolio of each RCC. Other reform actions include improving the management of the RCCs by hardening their budget constraints, reducing government intervention, facilitating a professional service and advisory network, and training personnel. To restore the trust of the rural population, the RCCs not only need to restructure their NPLs, but also must have transparent regulations and policies governing their operation. To relieve poverty and promote small businesses in the rural sector, the RCCs must also increase their service products and quality, which have been rudimentary, in order to attract funds scattered in the hands of the rural population. The government and the central bank, meanwhile, must devise tax and industrial policies that encourage deposits into the RCCs and improve microfinancing directly to poor farmers.

See also Agricultural Reform; *Hukou* System; People's Communes/Household Responsibility System; Rural Administrative Organizations; Rural Industrialization; Rural-Urban Divide, Regional Disparity, and Income Inequality.

Bibliography

"Banking Crisis in Rural China Threatens Financial and Political Stability," NewMax.com, October 3, 2000, http:/www.newsmax.com.articles/; "China Outlines Policies Rural CUs, Co-ops," Cuna News Now, December 1, 2003, http://www.cuna.org/newsnow/ 03/international112603-2.html, accessed on November 28, 2004; China Radio International (CRI), "Shanghai to Create 3rd City Commercial Bank Via Merger," http://web12 .cri.com.cn/english/2003/Feb/87104.htm, accessed on December 18, 2004; "China to Delegate Administrative Power of Rural Credit Cooperatives," *People's Daily Online*, August 20, 2003, http://english.people.com.cn/200308/20/eng 20030820_122667.shtml, accessed on November 28, 2004; International Fund for Agricultural Development (IFAD), "Thematic Study on Rural Finance in China within the Framework of IFAD Projects— Main Report," report no. 1147-Cn Rev. 1, December 2001.

Aimin Chen and Junqi Liu

Rural Industrialization

Rural industrialization has been an indispensable part of China's economic development in the last quarter century. According to the National Bureau of Statistics, from 1978 to 2002, the number of rural enterprises increased from 1.52 million to 21.33 million; the number of workers increased from 28.27 million to 132.85 million, or in terms of the percentage of the total rural labor force, from 9.5 percent to 26.8 percent. The share of industry in the total value of gross rural output increased more dramatically. In 1978, only 21.2 percent of the total gross rural output was created by rural enterprises; by 2003, this percentage was raised to 83.68 percent. The output value of the rural industrial sector accounted for only 9.1 percent of the national total in 1978; this figure became 30.9 percent in 2002. Also in 2002, nonfarm income accounted for 54.2 percent of all rural income, compared with only 15.0 percent in 1978.

It is worth keeping in mind that Chinese rural industrialization started even before the rural reform took place. It was a by-product of an otherwise unwise national drive to mechanize agriculture in the early 1970s. The output value of rural industry was increased from 9.25 billion yuan in 1970 to 27.2 billion yuan in 1976, with an average annual growth rate of 25.7 percent. However, it was after the rural reform that rural industry began to gain momentum. Several factors have contributed to the fast growth of the rural industrial sector. The first factor is the rural reform itself, which released a large portion of the rural labor force and enabled the rural population to accumulate the necessary capital to run industry. Starting in the mid-1980s, the dual-track price system also played a significant role because it opened up markets so that rural enterprises had a space to flourish. The heavy-industry-development strategy implemented in the planning era had left a large unfilled market for consumer goods, and rural enterprises were suited perfectly to fill that market. In the coastal areas, rural industrialization has been helped by the influx of a large amount of **foreign direct investment**. Many companies in the Great China Region moved their factories to the Pearl River and Yangtze River deltas, seeking cheap land and labor. The arrival of these companies instantly transformed originally rural villages into booming and noisy industrial towns.

With a high labor/land ratio, the factor endowment in rural China has inevitably led its rural industry to adopt labor-intensive technologies. Compared with the **state-owned enterprises** in the **cities**, rural enterprises use much more labor and much less capital. Per worker net capital stock of the rural enterprises never passed 20 percent of that of the state-owned enterprises in the period from 1978 to 1997. With this light capital-labor structure, rural enterprises have become an important contributor to China's exports. Their share of exports was only 9.2 percent in 1986, but after that year, it kept an average annual growth rate of 20.6 percent in the next ten years and reached 42.9 percent of the country's total exports in 2002.

Another positive effect of the labor-intensive approach has been the enhanced income distribution at the local level. Provinces with a larger rural industrial sector tend to have smaller Gini coefficients. The Gini coefficient, invented by the Italian Statistician Corado Gini, is a number between zero and one that measures the degree of inequality in the distribution of income in a given society. The coefficient would register zero (or minimum inequality) for a society in which each member receives the same income and it would register a coefficient of one (maximum inequality) if one member gets all the income and the rest gets nothing. For example, with 76 percent of the rural output being contributed by the industrial sector, Jiangsu had a Gini coefficient of 0.30 in 1992; in contrast, Ningxia's rural industrial output accounted for only 35 percent of its rural output, and its Gini coefficient was 0.43 in the same year. The rural-urban divide is by far the most significant factor contributing to China's income inequality (standing at 3.1 times in 2003, China's urban-rural income gap is the largest in the world). To the extent that rural industry raises the income of the rural population, it is not a surprising result that provinces with a larger rural industrial sector tend to have more equal income distribution. However, it is an unanswered question whether rural industrialization has contributed to the growing regional income gaps.

From the very beginning, rural industrialization in China has been tied to urban industry. In the early days, the tie was only one way in that technologies were transferred from urban industry to rural industry. In the 1990s, the countryside began to receive factories that were reallocated from cities mainly to evade more and more stringent environmental regulations in the cities. This has brought serious and even disastrous environmental consequences to the recipient regions. Rivers and even underground water are polluted, which threatens the basic life of the rural population.

Rural industry is not always a passive receiver of urban technologies and reallocated factories, though. As the size of rural industry increased, urban industry began to feel competitive pressure, starting in the late 1980s. Rural enterprises have been technically inferior to state-owned enterprises, but the gap has narrowed over time. They were 61 percent less efficient than state-owned enterprises in 1980, but only 41 percent in 1988. On the other hand, rural enterprises are more eager than state-owned firms to seek profit because they are subject to harder budget constraints. Competition from rural industry as well as from private firms in the cities led to massive privatization of the state-owned enterprises, starting in the mid-1990s.

Rural industry itself has experienced dramatic privatization. In the early days, there was a heavy presence of local governments in rural enterprises, either as owners or as providers of direct management. This, together with the extraordinary performance of rural industry, has spurred wide academic interest concerning the relationship between local government ownership and the success of rural industry. Several theories have appeared in academic literature to explain why local government ownership emerged and why it was successful. Most of them treat public ownership as a second-best choice in an imperfect institutional and market environment (e.g., Li 1994; Che and Qian 1998), but some of them resort to the cooperative culture in the Chinese village (Weitzman and Xu 1994). While there are some merits of these theories, the last two decades have shown that their applicability might be limited only to specific periods of time. Even in 1984, 69.3 percent of the rural enterprises were privately owned; in 1997, that figure became 93.6 percent. Vast privatization brought about this trend in the 1990s. Two factors contributed to the start of privatization: market liberalization and the commercialization of the banking sector. Market liberalization gave market access to rural enterprises and rendered unnecessary the role of local governments in providing productive resources. Commercialization of the banking sector hardened the budget constraints of the rural public enterprises and severed the channel for local governments to siphon off financial resources through these enterprises.

Rural industrialization in China is quite uneven across regions. The share of industrial output in total rural output varied from 86 percent in Shanghai to 4 percent in Tibet in 1996. Several factors may have contributed to the huge regional diversity. Initial conditions matter. Rural industrialization is still mainly confined to the coastal areas and the suburban areas in inland provinces. Factor endowments also matter. The provinces that started earlier and have been taking the lead in rural industrialization are those located in the coastal areas where labor is much more abundant relative to land and other natural resources than in the inland areas. Here the relative abundance of natural resources is not a blessing, probably because it leads a region to develop a dependence on resources rather than on innovations.

After two decades of development, rural industry is converging with urban industry in capital intensity and product development. Many enterprises have moved from villages to towns and small cities to get access to better infrastructure, markets, and information. This trend has profound implications for urbanization, the environment, and rural society.

See also Agricultural Reform; *Hukou* System; People's Communes/Household Responsibility System; Rural Administrative Organizations; Rural Credit Cooperatives (RCCs); Rural-Urban Divide, Regional Disparity, and Income Inequality; Township and Village Enterprises (TVEs).

Bibliography

Che, Jiahua, and Yingyi Qian, "Insecure Property Rights and Government Ownership of Firms," *Quarterly Journal of Economics* 113, no. 2 (1998): 467–496; Li, David, "Ambiguous Property Rights in Transition Economies," *Journal of Comparative Economics* 23, no. 1 (1994): 1–19; Lin, Justin, and Yang Yao, "Chinese Rural Industrialization in the Context of the East Asian Miracle," chapter 4 in *Rethinking the East Asian Miracle*, ed. Joseph Stiglitz and Shahid Yusuf (London: World Bank and Oxford University Press, 2001); National Bureau of Statistics of the PRC, *China Economic Yearbook 2003* (Beijing: China Statistics Press); National Bureau of Statistics of the PRC, *China Township and Village Enterprise Yearbook 2003* (Beijing: China Statistics Press); Weitzman, Martin, and Chenggang Xu, "Chinese Township Village Enterprises as Vaguely Defined Cooperatives," *Journal of Comparative Economics* 23, no. 1 (1994): 121–145.

Yao Yang

Rural-Urban Divide, Regional Disparity, and Income Inequality

As much as 62 percent of the Chinese population is still officially identified as "rural," although the majority of them have diversified their occupations among farming and nonfarming jobs. For decades since 1949, rural people in China have been deprived relative to urban dwellers in terms of income, consumption, savings, and welfare allocation, such as education, health care, and housing. The economic reforms since 1979 have not completely changed this deprived position of the rural population in China.

The ratio of urban to rural per capita income has been very high throughout both the planning period and the reform era. The ratio exceeded 3.0 in the mid-1950s, was 2.6 in 1978, and rose to 2.9 in 2001. Great differences exist between rural and urban China not only in income but also in welfare and opportunities for self-fulfillment.

The most important factor that influences a person's educational attainment is whether he or she lives in a rural or an urban area. The standardized mean difference in educational attainment is 4.6 years in favor of urban dwellers. This educational gap has not diminished with time or with economic development. There is evidence that school expenditures per pupil, public subsidy per pupil, and the average quality of teachers are all higher in urban than in rural China. Rural children have been and remain at a disadvantage in education.

There is a considerable gap between urban and rural provision of and access to health services. The rural population is at a disadvantage in both the quantity and quality of health care. Urban medical services had been heavily subsidized such that rural people had to pay more to pick up the tab until radical welfare reform began in urban China in the mid-1990s. In addition, a wide difference exists in mean percentage of income contributed to health needs of urban and rural people. This has resulted in lower health benefits for the rural population. According to the 1990 census of population, the mortality rates for infants and children were 1.60 and 1.81 times higher in the countryside than in the cities, and the premature mortality rate was 1.22 times higher.

Rural China does enjoy more spacious housing than urban China. The ratio of rural to urban living space rose from 2.2 in 1979 to a high of 2.8 in 1993 and fell to 1.65 in 2001. However, the quality of urban housing is much higher than that of rural housing. Most rural dwellings lack modern sanitary facilities, and, in particular, central heating is in short supply in northern regions. In the 1990s, the privatization of urban housing shifted the basis for housing allocation from occupational status to purchasing power. Most urban dwellers who used to pay a small nominal rent for publicly owned housing have the possibility of home ownership. Payments for housing purchases have been subsidized, often on the basis of an individual's favorable job tenure condition and occupational seniority. Rural dwellers through all periods have had to build their houses without any public subsidies.

This huge rural-urban divide has been the direct consequence of China's strategic development plan that was chosen by the Communist government during the three decades after 1949. This centrally controlled strategy, known as "urban-based industrialization," was implemented and assisted by a variety of subsequent policies. In 1953, a system of state-monopolized purchases and

A village in rural China, 2004.

Shanghai nightlife, 2003.

marketing was established to control the food supply. Between 1953 and 1954, a rationing system for grain and other necessities was introduced to control their demand by urban dwellers. By 1957, a combination of household registration, the establishment of the **people's communes**, and urban food rationing had given the state the administrative leverage to curb rural-urban migration. During the people's commune period and through the reform years, the rural sector was expected to be self-reliant and not to be a fiscal burden on the state. Relatively little gross revenue flows down to rural governments, counties, and townships.

The urban-rural income gap is greater in poverty-stricken provinces. Urban incomes are standardized by institutionalized wage scales, whereas rural incomes reflect regional disparities in natural resources and economic opportunities. Both the prevalence of an urban-rural income gap in all provinces and its greater size in the poorer provinces suggest that rural-urban migration is not occurring sufficiently and market forces are not operating effectively to equalize urban and rural incomes.

Urban wage differences that exist among provinces are less likely to reflect local market forces than informal profit sharing between enterprises and their employees. The growing importance of profit-linked payment in urban incomes appears to provide incentives at the enterprise rather than at the individual level. This has segmented the urban labor market by enterprise, area, and economic activity.

The rural wage varies across provinces with respect to rural per capita incomes, which indicates that market forces play an important part in the equation. However, the excess of the rural wage over the rural supply price is probably due to local imitation of the state wage system and rent-sharing and efficiency wage payments by collectively owned and private enterprises.

Much of the considerable inequality of rural income per capita is regional in nature and reflects the uneven development of a vast country. Regional inequality existed even under the egalitarian policies of the prereform period. However, these inequalities have increased significantly since the economic reforms started in 1978. Apparently, in some areas **rural industrialization** has proceeded rapidly, labor shortages have emerged, and rural incomes have risen toward the urban income level. In other areas, rural development is limited, surplus labor is chronic, and the potential economic gain from rural-urban migration is very great.

See also Agricultural Reform; *Hukou* System; Migrant Population; Rural Administrative Organizations; Rural Credit Cooperatives (RCCs); Township and Village Enterprises (TVEs); Urban Households; Urban Housing Privatization; Urbanization and Migration.

Bibliography

Knight, John, and Lina Song, *The Rural-Urban Divide: Economic Disparities and Interactions in China* (Oxford and New York: Oxford University Press, 1999); National Bureau of Statistics of the PRC, *China Statistical Yearbook 2002* (Beijing: China Statistics Press, 2002).

Lina Song

S

SAR

See Special Administrative Region (SAR).

Savings, Pattern of

The Chinese value saving. In Chinese culture, diligence and thrift are traditional virtues, and wasting and luxury are sins. Saving plays an important role in Chinese life. Since the economic reform and **Open Door policy** in the late 1970s, Chinese household savings have increased rapidly. For example, the savings balance of Chinese households in 1978 was 21.06 billion RMB yuan. By July 2003, it was more than 10 trillion, an increase of nearly 500 times in only twenty-five years. The average annual growth rate of savings is about 30 percent. Such a fast rise in more than twenty years is extraordinary not only in the world, but also in Chinese history. This pattern has appeared not only in the savings themselves, but also in the increasing rate of savings. Especially since 1996, the government has taken many measures to slow down the increase of savings so as to promote consumption and expand domestic demand, but savings still increase at a relatively high speed, and the savings rate also continues to rise. This situation, called "the myth of Chinese savings," draws attention from economists.

Before the economic reform and opening to the outside world, the total savings of Chinese households were low. In the 1950s and 1960s, they were less than 10 billion yuan. Even at the end of the 1970s, they were only 28.1 billion yuan. The growth rate of savings was also relatively low. During the decade of the **Great Cultural Revolution (1966–1976)**, the annual growth rate of savings was only about 10 percent.

After the reform and opening policy started, Chinese household savings greatly changed. They increased at a high speed for many years. The period with the fastest increase in household savings was the first decade after the reform and opening, from 1979 to 1988. Savings increased from 28.1 billion yuan in 1979 to 382.22 billion yuan in 1988. In this decade, the growth was relatively smooth and the rate was high. In the next seven years (1989 to 1996), savings increased from 519.64 billion yuan in 1989 to 3,852.08 billion yuan in 1996, with an annual growth rate of about 25 to 35 percent and many more fluctuations. During the next period, 1997 to 2003, the growth rate decreased, with an annual rate ranging between 10 and 20 percent.

Not only did gross household savings increase quickly, but also the rate of savings. Before the economic reform (1956 to 1978), the saving rate was only 6.8 percent, but in the first twelve years after the reform (1979 to 1990), the rate increased to 27.7 percent, about three times higher. According to a World Bank report, in 1980, 1995, and 1997, the domestic saving rates were 35 percent, 42 percent, and 45 percent, respectively.

Structures of savings have also changed. The share of savings by middle- and low-income households has become smaller, and that of high-income households has become larger since the reform and opening. Before the reform and opening, savings were mainly from middle- and low-income households. According to a survey by the People's Bank of China in 1975, workers, cadres (administrators in China, often appointed by the government), technicians, and teachers constituted the largest portion of savers and accounted for more than 80 percent of savings. But in the 1990s, the situation changed greatly. The largest share of savings came from high-income households that made up a small portion of the population. In a survey (Guo 1997) of 3,000 households in 1996, the lowest-income households contributed 8.2 percent, but the highest-income households contributed 43.3 percent of the total savings. Currently the trend continues, and the share of highest-income households in savings is becoming larger.

A disparity has existed between urban and rural household savings, and the disparity has widened since 1984. For example, the ratio of savings from urban households to that from rural households was 5.2 in 1956, 3.9 in 1966, 2.58 in 1979, 1.77 in 1984, 2.86 in 1990, 3.788 in 1995, and 4.315 in 1999. On a per capita basis, the gap has been even greater and has followed the same trend of widening: 12.69 in 1978 and 2.86 in 1990, sharply rising to 8.36 in 1991 and 9.66 in 1999.

The share of savings of households in general has consistently grown since 1979, from 24.4 percent in 1979 to 66 percent in 1989. Savings motives have also changed. Under the planned economy before the reform and opening, the state, including its enterprises, provided a "cradle-to-grave" security system for urban households. It was unnecessary for urban households to worry about their retirement, medical expenditures, and housing. Moreover, households had very little to save at very low incomes. Important motives for saving then were "financing the socialist construction" and "forming a social atmosphere with thrift," which were more political than economic.

After the reform and opening, household incomes rose rapidly. In the 1980s, after the demand for necessities, such as food and clothing, was met, consumers' expenditures turned to durable goods such as color **television** sets, refrigerators, and washing machines. Before the economic reforms began in 1978, the primary motives for a Chinese household to save money were related to adding durable goods, raising children, and events that typically call for extensive spending, such as a wedding or a funeral. Very few households saved for retirement, and even fewer worried about being able to buy their own homes.

The concept of savings has apparently changed since then. A 1991 survey conducted in twenty cities by the People's Bank of China (Xie 1995) on the primary reasons for saving money showed that 19 percent of those people surveyed saved for their children's education, 13 percent saved for buying or constructing homes, and 12 percent saved for retirement. A 2002 survey by the National Statistical Bureau showed that 36.5 percent of the respondents saved for their children's education, 31.5 percent for retirement, 10.1 percent for expenses, 7.2 percent for housing, 5.7 percent for the marriage of their children, and 3.0 percent for **unemployment**. The different savings motives from the 1980s to the 1990s and after reflect the changes in the Chinese economy. Reforms of the "iron rice bowl" (lifelong job security) system, the education system, the medical system, the housing system, and the labor system, for example, greatly increased household expenditures on education, medical care, housing, and retirement. The reforms also brought uncertainties to the lives of urban households and thus affected their savings.

Government policies on savings have also changed in recent years. Before the reform and opening, the governmental policy on household savings was encouraging appropriate savings and keeping savings stable in the long run. The interest rate for savings was higher than other deposit interest rates. In 1988, panic buying occurred in many **cities** because of a continual high inflation rate. The central government took several strong measures to deal with the crisis. One of them was to offer a savings deposit guaranteed against inflation according to the inflation rate issued by the National Statistical Bureau, which started on September 10, 1988. In 1996, the pressure from inflation lessened, and later inflation turned to deflation. The central government decided to cancel the inflation guaranteed saving deposit from April 1, 1996.

See also Banking and Financial System Reform; Credit Spending, Development of; Renminbi (RMB).

Bibliography

Editorial Committee, Ministry of Finance, *China Financial Yearbook* (Beijing: Ministry of Finance Press, 2000); Guo, Cai, "Analysis of Resources and Structures on Chinese Households' Savings," *Journal of Economic Issues*, no. 9 (1997): 28–31; Guo, Kesha, and Dongxia He, "Gaige Yilai Jumin Xiaofei He Chuxu Biandon de Shizheng Fenxi" (An empirical study of changes in household consumption and savings since the reform and opening), *Zhongguo Shehuikexueyuan Xuebao* (Journal of China Academy of Social Science) 2 (1992): 1–10; National Bureau of Statistics of the PRC, *China Statistical Yearbook* (Beijing: China Statistics Press, 2003); People's Bank of China, *Zhongguo Renmin Chuxu Shiye* (The People's Saving in China) (Beijing: China Finance and Economics Press, 1979); *World Development Report, 1997* (Chinese Edition) (Beijing: China Financial and Economic Publishing, 1997): 238; Xie, Ping, "Some Issues on the Marketization of Interest Rate on the Transformation of Chinese Economy" (Zhongguo Jingji Zhuan-gui Zhong de Lilu Shichanghua Wenti), *Economics of Finance and Trade* (Caimao Jingji), no. 8 (1995): 4–9; Yan, Xianpu, "Nine Reasons for the Fast Rise of Chinese House-hold Savings," *Shanghai Securities News*, October 18, 2003.

Qingfei Yin and Jingjian Xiao

Scar Literature

See Literature of the Wounded.

School Enrollment and Employment

Enrollment

China's educational system consists mainly of primary schools, secondary schools (junior middle schools, senior high schools, secondary teacher-training schools, secondary technical schools, secondary-skill workers' schools, and secondary vocational schools), and various institutions of higher education. Because of the implementation of nine-year compulsory education, enrollments at primary schools and lower secondary schools have formed a broad base in the total student enrollment. The enrollment tapers down in number at higher levels. One reason is insufficient resources. The distribution of student enrollment at different levels in 2000 is shown in table 10.

Before the economic reform was launched in 1978, school enrollment planning in higher education was done collaboratively between the central and local governments to reflect future workforce demands and the needs of business enterprises. At that time, higher education in China was fully funded by the government, and universities could earn still more money by enrolling business employees in contracted in-service training programs. During the years of **Mao Zedong**'s rule, school enrollment was limited to qualified students who could present evidence of good political background. The political requirements disqualified many otherwise eligible students from admission until the Entrance Examination of Higher Education Institutions was reinstalled after the **Great Cultural Revolution**. As China becomes increasingly involved in a market economy, any major efforts for enrollment planning become more and more difficult. In fact, in the mid-1980s, some higher-education institutions started allowing some of their graduates to plan for their employment search. When the universities finally stopped enrollment planning based on manpower planning, students began enrolling in

In this 1990 photo, Chinese schoolchildren in the village of Sanchawan read at their desks. © Stephanie Maze/Corbis.

TABLE 10
Student Enrollment in Chinese Schools (2000)

	Number of Schools	*Enrollment*
Graduate schools	738	301,200
Universities (undergraduate)	1,041	5,560,900
Senior secondary schools	14,564	12,012,600
Junior secondary schools	62,704	61,676,500
Secondary technical schools	2,963	4,125,400
Secondary teacher-training schools	683	769,800
Secondary-skill workers' schools	4,098	1,560,500
Secondary vocational schools	8,849	5,032,100
Primary schools	553,622	130,132,500
Kindergarten schools	175,836	22,441,800
Special education schools	1,539	377,600

Source: China Education and Research Network.

programs using their own money and their own free will. In view of the rapidly growing economy, the present enrollment at the higher-education level needs to be raised and diversified to meet the challenge of the twenty-first century.

At the secondary level, school enrollment has been substantially increased by the introduction of the secondary vocational schools to meet the personnel demands of the rapid development of a diverse economy. Contracting with enterprises by offering in-service training of their employees is also increasing the enrollments of secondary technical schools. The high percentages of student enrollment in primary and lower secondary schools are an indication of the overall success of implementing nine-year compulsory education. Exceptions are found in some remote and underprivileged areas where the completion of the compulsory education goals is yet to be evaluated.

Employment

Before 1978, a ruling principle of the Chinese Communist Party was to secure employment for all people. In accordance with this principle, the government operated a planned economy and managed the nation's education accordingly. Under the direction of the central government, graduates of secondary schools and universities were assigned to work either in government offices or in government-owned work units that had been promised their manpower supply. Graduates were given no career choice of their own, but, in return, were guaranteed an "iron rice bowl" (permanent employment) after graduation.

The general preference used to be that the most desirable positions were those associated with the management levels of government entities. Therefore, graduates competed in particular for administrative positions. In the early years, many administrative measures were primarily taken to secure urban employment. The urban residency requirement, for example, under the *hukou system* was paramount for urban employment. These policies never worked very well since they worked against the majority of the people. Rural people secretly immigrated into **cities** as "black inhabitants," simply because cities offered better living conditions and more occupational opportunities.

During the Cultural Revolution, employment policies were made to disparage education and schooling experiences by assigning educated urban youths to participate in the development of rural and remote areas. Many of them were coerced to work in rural regions to "learn from the peasants and workers." This policy, which proved to be unpopular among the peasants and the urban youths because of the large disruption to their way of life, was discontinued soon after 1976.

In the late 1970s, the reinstallation of the university entrance examination served as more than a tool for screening university applicants for admission. The entrance exam has also been recognized as a basic qualification for midlevel management jobs. Youths who have successfully passed the university entrance examination are in a better position to compete in the job market, should they decide not to enroll in universities.

Changes in employment practices at the higher-education level have had a significant impact on the employment trends of the Chinese job market. The first is the phasing out of the tenure system in higher education in 1986. Faculty have been hired on a contract basis at salaries commensurate with their rank and abilities. The second is the abolition of the graduate job assignment system in 1998. Graduates are presently advised by university placement services in their search for jobs.

Since the launching of the economic reform in 1978, China has been faced with increasingly troublesome **unemployment** problems. Because of its huge population, the unemployment problem tends to worsen in the short term. Some new issues have emerged as well:

1. Favorable conditions offered in the **Open Door policy** have served to attract interested investments in China since 1978. Low production costs result in extremely marketable products in the Asian market. These enterprises, whether solely or partly owned by foreign investors, are in a better position to recruit more competent employees by offering attractive salaries and fringe benefits. They are the primary targets of the Chinese school graduates in their job hunt.

2. Government-owned businesses cannot afford many new hires because most such businesses are still operated under the Communist traditional management system. Some of them are in the process of transition to a more efficient operating approach. However, they are stuck with a large population of employees inherited from the old system. Many of these employees lack training and tend to underperform.

3. Chinese graduates today are faced with a new challenge of job hunting. Presently, because of a poor economy and market saturation, many of them will soon become frustrated with the slow job market and choose to go back to school to pursue a higher level of learning.

This is known as "deferred employment" in sociological terminology. These Chinese youths will wait to compete in the job market with higher qualifications at a later time.

See also Character Education in Primary and Secondary Schools; Education Media and Technology; Educational Administration; Educational System; Higher-Education Reform; Management Education; Primary Education; Private Education; Secondary Education; Taiwan, Education Reform in; Teacher Education; United States, Chinese Education in; Vocational and Technical Training.

Bibliography

Huang, B. N., *A Report on the Risks in Chinese Education* (Beijing: Chinese City Press, 1998); Planning and Development Bureau of the Ministry of Education of the PRC, "An overview of China's Education 2000," http://www.edu.cn/20011219/3014655, accessed on December 2, 2004; *A Statistical Report on the Chinese Educational Development in 2000* (Beijing: Department of Education, National Statistics Bureau, and Department of Finance, 2002).

Tak Cheung Chan

Script, Chinese

See Chinese Script, Reform of.

Secondary Education

Secondary education in the People's Republic of China (PRC) consists of schools at two levels: lower secondary schools and upper secondary schools, which are named junior middle schools and senior high schools in the United States. The lower secondary school is a part of compulsory education after **primary education**. It lasts three to four years, with an entry age of twelve or thirteen. Students who have graduated from primary schools may, without examination, advance to the appropriate lower secondary schools. The entry age for general upper secondary schools is fifteen or sixteen, and the duration of study is three years. Graduates of lower secondary schools may enter regular upper secondary schools or specialized secondary schools after passing entrance examinations set by the local education authorities.

Since the enactment of the Compulsory Education Law of the PRC in 1986, Chinese governments at all levels have actively promoted nine-year compulsory education in "6+3" or "5+4" systems and have made remarkable achievements. Throughout the nation, nearly 1,500 counties, **cities**, and municipal districts have basically instituted nine-year compulsory education, covering about 50 percent of the population. The gross enrollment ratio of lower secondary school-age children reached 88.7 percent, and 95.5 percent of primary school graduates continued their study in lower secondary schools. Statistics for 2001 indicated that there were 66,600 lower secondary schools (including 1,065 lower vocational schools) with a total enrollment of 65,143,800, of which 833,300 were enrolled in vocational schools, and there were 3,385,700 full-time teachers (Ministry of Education 2002).

TABLE 11
Weekly Lesson Timetable for Three-Year Program of
Lower Secondary Education

Subjects/Activities	Number of Weekly Periods in Each Grade		
Subjects	I	II	III
Ideology and moral character education	2	2	2
Chinese language	6	6	5
Mathematics	5	5	5
Foreign language (level II)	4	4	4
History	2	3	2
Geography	3	2	-
Physics	-	2	3
Chemistry	-	-	3
Biology	3	2	-
Physical education	3	3	3
Music	1	1	1
Painting	1	1	1
Work skills	2	2	2
Subtotal	32	33	31
Activities			
Collective activities	1	1	1
Physical exercise; science, technology, and cultural activities (or special interest-related activities)	3	3	3
Subtotal	4	4	4
Locally arranged curriculum	-	-	1
Total Weekly Periods Morning/ afternoon meetings (ten minutes per day)	36	37	36

Source: IBE, 2002 Curriculum Data Set.

Upper secondary education consists of regular upper secondary schools, specialized secondary schools, technical worker schools, and upper secondary vocational schools. Regular upper secondary schools are now virtually a staple in large and medium-sized cities and the coastal areas, where the economy is fairly well developed. Nationally, at present only 52.9 percent of lower secondary school graduates can continue their schooling in various types of schools at the upper secondary level. Therefore, the competition is fierce. On January 7, 2000, the Ministry of Education of the PRC demanded that all local education departments take effective actions to lighten primary and lower secondary school students' burden of academic learning as soon as possible in this

TABLE 12
Weekly Lesson Timetable for Four-Year Program of Lower Secondary Education

Subjects/Activities	Number of Weekly Periods in Each Grade			
Subjects	I	II	III	IV
Ideology and moral character education	2	2	2	2
Chinese language	5	5	5	5
Mathematics	5	4	4	4
Foreign language (level II)	4	4	4	4
History	2	3	2	-
Geography	3	3	-	-
Physics	-	-	2	3
Chemistry	-	-	2	2
Biology	2	2	2	-
Physical education	3	3	2	2
Music	1	1	1	1
Painting	1	1	1	1
Work skills	2	2	2	2
Subtotal	30	30	29	26
Activities				
Collective activities	1	1	1	1
Physical exercise; science, technology, and cultural activities (or special interest-related activities)	3	3	3	3
Subtotal	4	4	4	4
Locally arranged curriculum	1	1	3	6
Total Weekly Periods Morning/afternoon meetings (ten minutes per day)	35	35	36	36

Source: IBE, 2002 Curriculum Data Set.

regard. However, statistics for 2001 indicated that upper secondary education had made great progress in China. By the end of 2001, there were 14,907 regular upper secondary schools with a total enrollment of 14,049,700 students, and there were 840,000 full-time teachers. The gross enrollment ratio of the upper secondary age group reached 42.8 percent, and 78.8 percent of upper secondary school graduates could continue their education in higher-education institutions (Ministry of Education 2002).

Specialized secondary schools, technical-worker schools, and vocational schools at the upper secondary level are developing significantly in China. According to the statistics for 2001, there were 13,789 schools with 9,811,800 students who engaged in upper secondary vocational school education. Among

TABLE 13
Weekly Lesson Timetable for Three-Year Program of Upper Secondary Education

Subjects/Activities	Number of Weekly Periods in Each Grade		
Subjects	I	II	III
Ideology and moral character education	2	2	2
Chinese language	5	4	4
Mathematics	5	5	5
Foreign language (level II)	5	5	4
History	3	-	-
Geography	-	2	-
Physics	4	3	4
Chemistry	3	3	3
Biology	-	-	2
Physical education	2	2	2
Music	-	-	-
Painting	-	-	-
Vocational skills	2	2	2
Subtotal	31	28	28
Activities			
Electives (physical exercise; science, technology, cultural activities, or special interest-related courses)	4	4	4
Subtotal	4	4	4
Locally arranged curriculum	-	-	-
Total Weekly Periods Morning/afternoon meetings (ten minutes per day)	35	32	32

Source: State Education Commission, 1989.

them, there were 3,260 specialized secondary schools with a total enrollment of 4,579,800 students; 3,792 skilled-worker schools with a total enrollment of 1,401,000 students; and 6,737 upper secondary vocation schools with a total enrollment of 3,831,000 students (Ministry of Education 2002).

Starting in the lower secondary schools, students in secondary education learn a variety of content-focused subjects such as chemistry, physics, and biology in science and history, geography, and foreign languages in liberal arts. Physical education is also enthusiastically encouraged. Lesson timetables for lower and upper secondary education are presented in tables 11, 12, and 13.

See also Character Education in Primary and Secondary Schools; Education Media and Technology; Educational Administration; Educational System;

Higher-Education Reform; Management Education; Private Education; School Enrollment and Employment; Taiwan, Education Reform in; Teacher Education; United States, Chinese Education in; Vocational and Technical Training.

Bibliography

International Bureau of Education (IBE), *2002 Curriculum Data Set* (http://www.ibe .unesco.org/International/Databanks/Dossiers/TChina.pdf), accessed on April 1, 2003; Ministry of Education, PRC, *Education in China* (Beijing: Ministry of Education, 2002); State Education Commission, *Basic Education of China* (Beijing: Department of Basic Education, 1989).

Ronghua Ouyang and Dan Ouyang

Secret Societies

Secret societies are those social organizations that are illegal and underground and mostly engage in criminal activities. Rampant in China long before the victory of the Communist revolution in 1949, secret societies were effectively eliminated in the early 1950s by the Communist state through sustained and massive campaigns. From then until the mid-1980s, secret societies were nonexistent in China. During this period, the state maintained overall and highhanded administrative control over society via an elaborate network of official organizations such as Communist Party committees and public security bureaus and the so-called mass organizations, including the poor-peasant associations, the Youth League, the Young Vanguards, and the Women Federation. Coupled with this administrative control were the state's persistent efforts to build ideological conformity by indoctrinating people with Communist ideologies and suppressing nonofficial ("feudal and bourgeois") ideas. These efforts were especially successful among young people. Economically, the state dominated all sectors (and enterprises) and monopolized the power of resource allocation, leaving no space for market forces and individual economic initiatives. Economic organizations or work units (e.g., factories in cities and production teams or brigades in the countryside), to which laborers were bound, served simultaneously as social and political institutions and instruments for state control. Under these conditions, Chinese society remained regimented, immobile, and little differentiated. Social order was well maintained, and rates of crime were kept extremely low, although at the price of personal freedoms. Such a society could hardly provide any breeding ground or space for secret societies.

Secret societies began to reemerge in the mid-1980s, when market-oriented economic reforms were well under way, and since have grown rapidly and become a major social phenomenon. Economic reforms have brought about profound socioeconomic and political changes. As the economy became increasingly liberalized, individuals gained enormous freedoms. In the countryside, with the replacement of the collective by the individual household as the basic unit of production, peasants were able to decide their own economic activities, especially how to use their own labor. No longer bound to the land, millions of peasants were constantly on the move in search of new employment opportunities, often in **cities** and coastal regions. Urban residents equally gained the freedom of choice, especially in the area of employment—they could freely choose or change their careers within their native cities or find jobs in other regions. Meanwhile, economic reforms also gave rise to a variety of social problems, the most acute of which were social inequality and **unemployment**. In both rural and urban areas, some people greatly benefited from the reforms and got rich; many others, however, found their economic conditions less improved or unimproved or even worsened, and accordingly they became frustrated and discontented. Most unfortunate were the unemployed, who numbered hundreds of millions and lived in poverty. These changes indicate that society has become highly mobile and greatly diversified and differentiated.

Parallel to this economic liberalization and social transformation was the loosening of the state's administrative and ideological control. Local Party committees, especially in rural areas, became lethargic, mass organizations almost irrelevant, and the Communist ideology obsolete, which combined to undermine the state's capability for social control. As a result, a power vacuum or public space appeared that made it possible for citizens to engage in various nongovernmental activities.

It was against this background of socioeconomic and political changes that secret societies reemerged and thrived. Secret societies existed nationwide, but more were found in the southern part of the country than in the northern part, more in the coastal regions than in the interior, and more in cities than in rural areas. Their number increased steadily in the 1980s and 1990s. Statistics indicate that criminal bands or groups that were ferreted out by the public security authorities numbered 30,476 in 1986, 57,229 in 1988, 100,527 in 1990, 120,000 in 1992, and 150,000 in 1994. Many of these bands were secret societies, which the Chinese authorities categorized as those criminal bands that were well organized, with stable leadership and membership.

Secret societies are of various types. Some of them are foreign originated—organized by members of secret societies from overseas, especially from Hong Kong, Macao, and Taiwan, where secret societies have always been prevalent and never met fatal suppression, as their Chinese counterparts did in the 1950s. As China has become more and more open, foreign secret societies have made increasing efforts to infiltrate China and to found affiliates among the Chinese. These foreign-related secret societies are particularly active in southeastern coastal regions, including Guangdong and Fujian Provinces. In the 1990s, about thirty such secret societies were uncovered in the city of Shenzhen in Guangdong and seventeen in the areas around Fuzhou in Fujian.

Most secret societies are native born—organized by Chinese citizens within China. Among them, some are locally based: their members are locals, and their activities are confined mainly to a local community such as a village, a township, or a city or part of a city. Others are interregional: their members include both locals and outsiders and conduct their activities provincewide or even nationwide, sometimes along railway lines. Especially in the countryside, some secret societies are lineage based: their key members were simultaneously family or clan members or relatives. In big cities, there is yet another type of secret society that is formed by migrants from the same native places. For instance, there was Fuzhou Gang in Shenzhen, Mayang Gang in Guangzhou, and **Xinjiang** Gang in Shanghai. These native-born secret societies and foreign-related ones often collaborate with each other in conducting certain activities such as cross-border smuggling.

Secret society members are generally young. Their ages range from eighteen to thirty-five years old. Most of them are from marginalized **social strata**, including the impoverished, the unemployed, and former convicts, some of whom are so-called habitual criminals. They form or join secret societies primarily for economic purposes—to get rich. From another perspective, these people are the losers in the increasingly competitive labor market. With neither good education nor special expertise, they are unable to find decent careers, but yet are unwilling to do the so-called dirty and hard jobs. To them, the best way to get rich quickly and easily is through illegal activities, which in turn entail collective efforts or partnership.

Secret societies maintain tight organizational structures. A typical secret society has the following organizational features. It has a name, which may be "such and such dare-to-die corps" or may be formed from the name of a certain animal or a place. It has a leader who is accepted by all members as the ablest or toughest, the most experienced, and sometimes the most senior within the society. The leader selects certain members as his deputies and advisers to help him make activity plans. Other members are ranked according to their seniority and ability. The leading figures and backbone members are relatively stable or fixed. A certain division of labor exists among the members: some are responsible for intelligence gathering, some for enforcing the society's rules, and so on. The secret society maintains strict discipline or rules, including absolute obedience to the leader, loyalty to the society, no betrayal, handing in all booty to the leader for distribution, keeping secrecy, no private action in the society's name, and mutual help. Those who break the rules face severe punishments. "Traitors" are to be punished especially severely, often with execution or mutilation. To protect the secrecy of the society, the members use pseudonyms or nicknames. To maintain the society's solidarity, members perform such rituals as making oaths of allegiance and forging sworn brotherhood. The secret society also is armed with various weapons, such as daggers, knives, and even guns, explosives, and bombs.

Secret societies engage in various activities, mostly illegal and criminal, including theft and robbery (sometimes involving cultural relics), blackmail, kidnapping and extorting ransoms, trafficking in drugs, smuggling goods, abducting and selling women and children, organizing prostitution, monopolistically controlling recreational places and marketplaces by force and threats, contracting construction projects by illegal means, and offering unsolicited protection for certain businesses and charging high protection fees. These activities often lead to bloodshed and loss of life of innocent people. Through these activities, many secret society members do get rich. Instead of investing their wealth in proper (legitimate) businesses, they often choose to be obsessed with conspicuous consumption—attending fancy banquets, building luxurious residences, and the like. Committing crimes is also a typical part of their enjoyment.

For self-preservation or protection, many secret societies took pains to build official connections by infiltrating governmental agencies or recruiting governmental personnel by threats or material enticements. More commonly, secret societies chose to bribe local officials, especially those in charge of legal and public security affairs, and gain their sympathy or sponsorship. As a result, some secret society members became local leaders, for example, village and township heads (they achieved this mainly by manipulating local elections); some public security personnel became secret society agents; and many local officials turned a blind eye to secret society activities. This official involvement partly accounted for the rapid growth of secret societies and the prevalence of their activities.

Secret societies functioned to the detriment of the well-being of the general public, disturbing social order and threatening the security of people's life and property. Therefore, they were identified by the state as criminal organizations. The state policy toward them was suppression. One major technique that the state adopted to suppress secret societies was to launch periodic large-scale (sometimes nationwide) campaigns, known as "severe strikes." During these campaigns, tens of thousands of secret societies were destroyed, and many of their key members were executed or imprisoned. However, these campaigns as well as other suppressive measures have fallen short of rooting out secret societies. Many old secret societies have survived the suppression, while new ones have kept rising. The explanation for this tenacity and vitality of secret societies is that the social conditions suitable for their growth have remained and even multiplied.

See also Correction System; Crime Prevention; Judicial Reform; Legal Infrastructure Development and Economic Development.

Bibliography

He Bingsong, "Evolution and Tendency of the Criminal Activities of Secret Societies in Mainland China," *Political and Legal Tribune*, no. 1 (2001); 61–73; Kang, Shuhua, and Shi Fang, "Eliminating Secret and Criminal Forces According to Law," *Law Science Magazine*, no. 3 (2001); 2–5; Zhang, Renshan, *Secret Societies in Contemporary China* (Nanjing: Jiangsu Renmin Chubanshe, 1998).

Yunqiu Zhang

Self-Learning

See Television Institute and Self-Learning.

Service Industries

See World Trade Organization (WTO), Impact of on Service Industries.

Sexual Freedom in Literature

Whereas many contemporary Chinese writers have difficultly attracting a large readership, young women writers have dramatically invigorated Chinese literature since the 1990s. Their writings focus on steamy urban sexual encounters, including their own relationships with single and married men, both Chinese and foreign. Their readers come from all walks of life, particularly from the younger generation, which finds a voice that reflects its own experience. This literary genre, also known as *meinü wenxue* (beauties' literature) by *meinü zuojia* (beautiful writers), has been enormously attractive and has often been featured in the media. However, overly explicit publications have been banned because of their content, which includes casual sex, drugs, prostitution, and suicide. The crackdown apparently has led to pirated and plagiarized versions flourishing on the black market. These works have been translated into many languages and arguably have been studied abroad more fervently than those of other contemporary Chinese writers.

Mian Mian (1970–), the pen name of a Shanghai high-school dropout, is a former drug addict turned dance-party queen and single mother. Her works, which she began writing at seventeen, include *LaLaLa* (1997), a collection of short stories, and *Tang* (Candy, 2000), a novel. Both are semiautobiographical fiction about drugs, promiscuity, and rock music. The author claims, "My autobiography will have to wait until I've been stripped naked as a writer. That is what I'm aiming for." The Chinese government banned *Tang* in 2000 and later all her works, including *Yansuan Qingren* (Acid lover), for "spiritual pollution." Her novel *Women Haipa* (We panic, 2001) was adapted into *Shanghai Panic* (2002) by filmmaker Andrew Yusu Cheng. This work describes young people disillusioned by an AIDS/HIV crisis that is later found to be a false alarm. The film, full of self-indulgent and chaotic scenes that rely heavily on improvisation, was shown at the 2002 Berlin International Film Festival and won the Dragons and Tigers Award for Best New Asian Filmmaker at the 2002 Vancouver Film Festival. Mian Mian herself assumed the roles of screenwriter, actress, and coproducer. In her new Chinese novel *Panda Sex* (2004), she claims to have handled love and sex more maturely.

Zhou Weihui (1972–), pen name Wei Hui, another Shanghai-based writer, has been vying with Mian Mian for fame. Their drawn-out literary catfights provide fodder for heated discussion in many **Internet** chat rooms. A graduate of Fudan University, Wei Hui is known for her autobiographical novel *Shanghai Baobei* (Shanghai baby, 1999). It depicts the adventures of a young Shanghai woman, Coco, named after French fashion designer Coco Chanel. She initially falls in love with the drug-addicted and impotent younger man with whom she lives, then becomes involved with a virile German neo-Nazi who eventually leaves her for Shanghai's decadent underground. The book was banned in China in 2000 after 150,000 copies had been sold. Wei Hui's other works include a collection of two novellas and three short stories titled *Xiang Wei Hui Nayang Fengkuang* (As crazy as Wei Hui), which also made her a lightning rod for establishment critics of the genre.

Zhu Ziping (late 1960s–), pen name Jiu Dan, is a columnist for a Beijing **television** magazine. Her other early novels gained little success, but *Wuya*

(Crows, 2001; translated into English) topped the best-seller list in China and Singapore. *Crows* is a kiss-and-tell novel detailing the lives of mainland Chinese *xiaolongnü* (Little dragon girls) in Singapore. Under the pretext of studying, they become nightclub hostesses, wealthy men's mistresses, or even prostitutes, all of which professions are vividly depicted. When the suspicion that the novel is autobiographical was raised, Jiu Dan insisted that the student prostitution described in *Crows* was based on her knowledge of Singapore, since she had studied there from 1995 to 1997. *Nüren Chuang* (A woman's bed, 2002) is another graphic novel of "prostitute literature" that sparked a great deal of reaction.

Chun Shu (mid-1980s–), a pen name that means "spring tree," is a straightforward writer. Her *Beijing Wawa* (Beijing doll, 2002) is the Beijing equivalent of *Shanghai Baby* and a volume of "punk memoirs." It features urban teenagers from single-child families who are contemptuous of school and indulge their passions. She extensively describes her days spent with sexual partners, listening to rock music, and idling with like-minded friends, as well as her pursuit of art and poetry. Despite the apparent lack of soul-searching in this book, Chun Shu's writing, which rings with greater sincerity, appeals more to readers, given its lessened self-consciousness, than the deliberate writing of *Shanghai Baby*.

Chen Huan (1981–), pen name Shuijing Zhulian, is another fiction writer and poet. At sixteen, she began writing the novel *Kuqi de Wutong* (The weeping wutong tree), which was later published. Since 1999, she has been posting her fiction and essays on the Internet, which has quickly established her reputation. Her recent collection of poetry and prose, titled *Pianyao Zuo Meinü* (I'm determined to be a beauty), is about love, lust, and whirling emotions, as shown in "Intimacy," "The Secrets of the Bedroom," "Love at First Sight," and "Envy." These and many other poems have been translated into English and are available on poetry Web sites.

Li Li (1979–), pen name Muzimei, is an ex–feature writer for *City Pictorial*, a Guangzhou-based magazine that covers popular culture. Muzimei shares her bed-hopping exploits with the world mainly via the Internet. In June 2003, she began posting her sex diary "Yiqing Shu" (Ashes of love) online, which includes detailed records of her own sexual activities. The explicit account of her tryst with a rock star, whose real name was used, posted in November 2003 attracted well over twenty million "netizens" daily. Then she lost her job and closed her Web site; her book of the same title, *Ashes of Love*, a semifictional coming-of-age collection of her diary, poems, and short stories, was subsequently banned. Boasting of having slept with approximately seventy men, including many one-night stands, Muzimei said to the media: "If you want to get an interview, go to bed with me first. The longer you can last in bed, the longer the interview will be."

Gone are the days when Muzimei and other women writers lived awaiting a man or authorities' approval to write. Indeed, they are not shy about standing up to critics. The gallery of their characters is no longer ordered and structured around such themes as revolution or high ideals during the time when one's private life was politicized. These authors have overthrown the dictatorship of constrained writing and have opted for the soberly naturalistic. Their heroines, usually a single woman much like the writer, no longer believe in tears or promises, but follow their own feelings, living as they wish. The rights to love and to initiate physical relationships reflect their equal status in society, and the theme of invigorating amorous relationships strongly marks the works of these women writers. When love and sex, beauty and decadence, attraction and disgust become intertwined, the concepts of right and wrong seem too subjective in a patriarchal society. One might argue that a woman's personal experience in the bedroom is also part of her social experience. These authors' writings may be free of gilded and glorified language, but the style is in step with the times and the narrators' experience. If some scenes are unacceptable, they nonetheless reflect the real decay of society.

Some readers do not think highly of these young women writers and call their works "subliterature," mainly due to the subject matter, but also due to the language, which is deemed too bold, too vivid, or even obscene, with a shared intimacy between the narrator and the author herself. The naturalistic descriptions of sexual experiences and physical torment related to drugs seem particularly intolerable for some. Detractors who dislike the characteristic subjectivity of the "I" in private life—which overrides history, society, and the external world—regard the genre as "private literature" written with the body but not the brain. It is sex, not writing skills, that is used as a shortcut to fame, and the banning of such literature seems legitimate for those concerned that these "bad girls of letters" will cast blight on children and society at large. Another potential problem for male critics is the perception of the female character's triumph in her intimacies, which casts a new light on present-day Chinese women. Though most readers turn to this literature out of curiosity, some admit that the experience of reading these young women writers is awakening, a potential source of discomfort for men.

For better or for worse, intimate autobiographical fiction has become a favored genre. Most of the works by the authors mentioned here have been published in China, many by prestigious presses and literary journals, such as Writers Press, *Shanghai Literature*, and *Harvest*, journals for pure literature. In contrast to the editorial control of conventional print media, Web publication allows for largely unconstrained new voices. The belief that the popularity of a literary work equates with low taste, inferior quality, and commercialization seems questionable.

See also Anticorruption Literature and Television Dramas; Avant-garde Literature; Experimental Fiction; Great Cultural Revolution, Literature during; Intellectuals, Political Engagement of (1949–1978); Intellectuals, Political Engagement of (1978–Present); Literary Policy for the New China; Literature of the Wounded; Misty Poetry; Modern Pop-Satire; Neorealist Fiction and Modernism; Pre–Cultural Revolution Literature; Revolutionary Realism and Revolutionary Romanticism; Root-Searching Literature.

Bibliography

Chun Sue, *Beijing Doll* (New York: Penguin Group Riverhead Books, 2004); Chun Sue, *Beijing Wawa* (Beijing doll) (Huhhot, Inner Mongolia: Yuanfang, 2002); Jiu Dan, *Nüren Chuang* (A Woman's Bed) (Huhhot, Inner Mongolia: Yuanfang, 2002); Jiu Dan, *Wuya* (Crows) (Wuhan, Hubei: Changjiang Wenyi, 2001); Jiu Dan, *Xinjiapo Qingren* (Lovers in Singapore) (Wuhan, [Hubei]: Changjiang Wenyi, 2002); Mian Mian, *Candy*, translated by Andrea Lingenfelter (Boston: Little, Brown, 2003); Mian Mian, *LaLaLa* (Hong Kong: New Century, 1997); Mian Mian, *Tang* (Candy) (Taiwan: Shengzhi, 2000); Mian Mian, *Yansuan Qingren* (Acid lover) (Shanghai: Shanghai Joint, 2000); Muzimei, *Yiqing Shu* (Ashes of love) (Nanchang, Jiangxi: Jiangxi 21st Century, 2003); Shuijing Zhulian [Chen Huan], *Kuqi de Wutong* (The weeping wutong tree) (Beijing: Writers Press, 1999); Shuijing Zhulian, *Pianyao Shi Meinü* (Determined to be a beauty) (Beijing: Jingji Ribao Chubanshe, 2001); Wei Hui, *Shanghai Baby*, translated by Bruce Humes (New York: Simon and Schuster, 2001); Wei Hui, *Shanghai Baobei* (Shanghai baby) (Changchun, Jilin: Chunfeng Wenyi, 1999).

Helen Xiaoyan Wu

Shanghai Communiqué

See Nixon's Visit to China/Shanghai Communiqué (1972).

Sino-American Relations, Conflicts and Common Interests

In recent years, China has demonstrated strong support for the antiterrorist war led by the United States. Economically, China has become a top trade partner. One may not lose sight, however, of the rugged path that the two countries have covered during the past fifty years. In particular, because Taiwan has been a renegade province and has been keeping an ambiguous relationship with the United States, the island has been the source of many recent tensions. Integrating the past into perspective analysis often proves to be helpful for understanding.

As people on both sides readily remember, the Sino-American relationship had a fighting start. In 1949, **Mao Zedong** declared the founding of the People's Republic of China (PRC). Meanwhile, Jiang Jieshi's (Chiang Kai-shek's) Nationalist army fled to Taiwan. The U.S. policy at the time was one of confrontation. Washington refused to recognize the PRC and sent the Seventh Fleet to patrol the Taiwan Strait. The situation escalated when the **Korean War** started in 1950. In addition to sending troops to South Korea, President Harry Truman protected Taiwan and ramped up efforts to upgrade Taiwan's military. China, not willing to tolerate a U.S.-dominated Korea at its doorstep, sent troops to support North Korea and to "defend the motherland." After the war ended with the 1953 armistice, the Sino-American tensions wound down.

Not long after the tensions eased along its northern border, however, China was faced with tensions in the south. After the French withdrew from Vietnam in the 1950s, the United States played an increasingly important role there. In 1965, the United States bombed North Vietnam, and once again China stepped up its military aid to Hanoi. Four years later, President Richard Nixon suspended the patrol by the Seventh Fleet in the Taiwan Strait. The tension wound down again. However, there were two additional factors: (1) the determination of the United States in winning the **Vietnam War** was shaken; (2) a new world relationship was firming up after China withdrew from the Soviet camp in 1960. As the Soviet Union and China fortified their military forces along China's northeastern border, military confrontations kept rising. Apparently, Chinese leaders devised a new set of strategies that would enable the country to thwart Soviet aggressions and later proved to have changed the entire world.

The new strategies started with the **Ping-Pong diplomacy** of 1971, when China invited the U.S. Ping-Pong team to Beijing. The event was soon followed by Secretary of State Henry Kissinger's secret visit to Beijing. In 1972, to the surprise of the entire world, President Richard Nixon met Mao Zedong and signed the Shanghai Joint Communiqué recognizing Taiwan as part of China. Three years later, the new tie was strengthened with President Gerald Ford's visit to Beijing in 1975. Ford was the last U.S. president to meet Mao Zedong, who died in 1976.

With Mao Zedong's passing, China entered a new era under the leadership of Deng Xiaoping, one of unprecedented economic and political reforms. In late 1978, the Chinese Communist Party (CCP) decided to refocus its socialist revolution from ideological control and class struggle to the "Four Modernizations" in industry, agriculture, national defense, and science and technology. On the international front, Deng implemented the Open Door policy that gradually opened up China to the rest of the world. In 1979, the Sino-American diplomatic relationship was resumed. Deng Xiaoping, then China's vice premier, visited Washington to meet with President Jimmy Carter. The Joint Communiqué stated that Washington would maintain only unofficial links with Taiwan. However, in April 1979, the U.S. Congress passed the Taiwan Relations Act, which reaffirmed a commitment to Taiwan and pledged to maintain arms sales to the island. Under strong protest by the Chinese government, in a third joint communiqué signed in 1982, the United States again pledged to gradually reduce arms sales to Taiwan.

In the 1980s, concerns over Taiwan continued to boil in the background as relations improved in the foreground. In January 1984, Premier Zhao Ziyang visited the United States, and President Ronald Reagan paid a return visit in April. During these highest-level meetings, the Chinese side strongly conveyed that Taiwan was the core issue in Sino-American relations. Before long, however, the bilateral relationship was once again put to a serious test. This time, the challenge went beyond the Taiwan issue. In February 1989, President George Bush visited China and invited a prominent Chinese physicist, Fang Lizhi, to a state banquet. In addition to being a famous scientist, Fang was also known for his dissident stance. The rendezvous sent a message to Chinese democratic fighters that the United States was strongly behind them. On June 4 of that year, the Chinese government dispersed student prodemocracy demonstrations in Beijing's Tiananmen Square, using military force. This action resulted in sanctions by the West. However, to the dismay of many, National Security Adviser Brent Scowcroft met Chinese leaders in a secret mission in July to reaffirm relations. The maneuvering of the White House deeply disappointed democratic fighters in China. They felt betrayed, and some claimed that they learned a "cruel political lesson."

After the June 4 event, China's economic reform scaled back. Some Western companies withdrew in anticipation of civil strife. The domestic situation was appeased rapidly, however, under Deng Xiaoping's ironfisted control. In 1991, the U.S. government announced three sanctions against China: (1) suspending exports of satellites and related components, (2) restricting exports of high-speed computers, and (3) prohibiting exports of missile-related products. In the following year, President Bush approved the sale of 150 F-16 fighter jets to Taiwan, overturning a long-term U.S. policy. These pressures could have shut off China's Open Door policy, as many in Congress had warned. However, Deng Xiaoping urged the nation to continue with the reform in a series of speeches given during his 1992 tour of coastal cities. Deng told the nation that China had been poor for too long, and that it was time for the Chinese to get rich. Deng reaffirmed to the world that nothing had changed, except that he did not and would not tolerate instability.

When President Bill Clinton took office in 1993, he was flexible enough to change his earlier campaign stance on human rights. He met President Jiang Zemin at the Asia-Pacific Economic Cooperation (APEC) leadership meeting in Seattle in November. In the following year, he dropped the policy of linking human rights reform to annual renewal of China's most-favored-nation trading status. Meanwhile, in order to balance public opinion, he authorized a private visit to New York in 1995 by Taiwan's president Li Denghui (Lee Teng-hui), reversing a fifteen-year-old policy of denying visas to Taiwanese leaders. China recalled its ambassador to Washington in protest. Furthermore, in March 1996, China stepped up the pressure by holding missile tests near Taiwan in an attempt to influence the island's first direct presidential election. In response, the United States sent two aircraft-carrier battle groups to the area in a show of support. This was certainly not the last opportunity for Washington to demonstrate its keen interest in Taiwan, despite the fact that three communiqués had been signed previously. In March 2000, proindependence politician **Chen Shuibian** won Taiwan's presidential election. When Beijing threatened to attack the island, the United States decided to sell a new military package to Taiwan. However, as Chen Shuibian toned down his independence rhetoric, the crisis stopped escalating.

Two events made the year 2001 memorable for the Chinese. The first one was the crash landing in April of a U.S. spy plane on the Chinese island of Hainan after a collision with a Chinese fighter jet. The Chinese government believed that it had caught the United States redhanded in spying on China, although the United States insisted that the plane was conducting routine missions above international waters. Furthermore, the Chinese government was successful in making the White House change an arrogant rhetoric into a "very sorry" apology. The second memorable event was China's joining the World Trade Organization (WTO) in December after ministers from almost all the WTO's 142 members voted in favor of China's application. In October, President George W. Bush and President Jiang Zemin met for the first time in Shanghai at the Asia-Pacific Economic Cooperation (APEC) summit, at which President Jiang pledged to back the U.S. war on terrorism.

As the Sino-American relationship steps into the twenty-first century, Taiwan continues to be the most difficult issue. In November 2003, the Chinese government warned Taiwan authorities led by Chen Shuibian to immediately stop separatist advocacy for a "referendum" and urged the United States not to support Taiwan's separatism. The winning of reelection by Chen Shuibian in

March 2004, however, seems to promise more troubles ahead both for future Sino-American relationships and for China's plan of peaceful reunification. On the optimistic side, since the United States and China have weathered many storms together in the past, the two countries are likely to maintain generally good terms in the future.

See also Cold War and China; Independent Foreign Policy (1982); Jiang Zemin (1926–   ), Diplomacy of; June 4 Movement; Nixon's Visit to China/Shanghai Communiqué (1972); Sino-American Relations since 1949; Sino-Japanese Relations since 1949; Sino-Russian Relations since 1991; Sino-Soviet Alliance; Taiwan Strait Crisis, Evolution of; United Nations (UN) and China.

Bibliography

"Major Events of China-U.S. Ties," Embassy of the PRC, www.china-embassy.org/eng/zmgx/t35075.htm, accessed on November 30, 2003; "Timeline: US-China Relations," *BBC News*, news.bbc.co.uk/1/hi/world /1258054.stm, accessed on October 29, 2002.

Jing Luo

Sino-American Relations since 1949

Sino-American relations since 1949 can be divided broadly into three periods: (1) 1949 to 1972, (2) 1972 to 1989, and (3) 1989 to the present. The years from 1949 to 1972 were a period of confrontation, with no diplomatic relations between the two nations. Even formal economic and cultural relationships between the two countries were virtually nonexistent. The hostility between the two nations resulted mainly from the continuous U.S. recognition and support of the Kuomintang government in Taiwan. In 1949, when the Chinese Communist Party established the People's Republic of China (PRC) in mainland China, both the new Chinese leaders and American policy makers showed certain signs of seeking accommodation. Nevertheless, deep mutual distrusts and suspicions let the momentary chance quickly slip away. Cold War tensions increasingly separated the two nations. In June 1949, **Mao Zedong** announced his policy of "leaning to one side"—that of the Soviet Union. In February 1950, the Sino-Soviet Treaty of Friendship, Alliance, and Mutual Assistance was concluded. After the outbreak of the **Korean War** in June 1950, any remaining hope for the United States to recognize the PRC vanished. U.S. president Harry Truman ordered the U.S. Seventh Fleet to the Taiwan Strait to prevent a potential PRC attack on Taiwan. Chinese premier **Zhou Enlai** responded by declaring that the U.S. actions constituted armed aggression against the territory of China. Under the umbrella of the United Nations, U.S. troops entered the Korean Peninsula to push North Korean forces to the Chinese border. On October 19, 1950, Chinese troops intervened to aid North Korea. Hot war between China and the United States ensued. Although a cease-fire agreement in Korea was reached in 1953, from Beijing's viewpoint, the United States now regarded China as its major enemy in Asia. The United States had quickly ended the occupation of Japan and had signed the U.S.-Japan Security Treaty in 1951. In early 1954, eight nations, orchestrated by the United States, formed the Southeast Asia Treaty Organization (SEATO). Later in the same year, a mutual defense treaty was signed between the United States and Taiwan, thus completing the encirclement of China.

To cope with U.S. containment, China needed Soviet support. However, the Soviet Union's conduct during the Korean War and, subsequently, Nikita Khrushchev's pursuit of peaceful coexistence with the United States soon convinced Chinese Communist leaders that the Soviet Union could not be relied upon to come to the aid of China when conflicts occurred with the United States. The Chinese decided to take their own initiative in Sino-American relations. In 1954 and 1958, Mao Zedong twice tested U.S. determination to protect Taiwan by ordering the bombing of the offshore islands of Jinmen (Quemoy on Kinmen) and Mazu (Matsu). Faced with the firm stand of the United States and the lack of Soviet backup, Mao had to stop before the crisis went out of control. In April 1955, the PRC offered to have a direct dialogue with the United States. The Americans accepted, and ambassadorial-level talks began in Geneva and then continued in Warsaw. However, talks went on and off for fifteen years without any substantial achievement. The crucial issue was Taiwan. While the Chinese were determined to "liberate" Taiwan, by force or otherwise, the American government's goal was to maintain the status quo by pursuing a "two-China" or "one China, one Taiwan" policy. Therefore, no compromise could be made between the two sides.

As Sino-Soviet divergence began to widen and as the United States appeared more hostile to China than to the Soviet Union in the late 1950s and early 1960s, the PRC decided to pursue an independent foreign policy. In 1964, the Chinese managed to produce their first nuclear bomb to break the American "nuclear monopoly," although the Soviet Union had withdrawn its aid to their project. China began to champion vigorously Third World countries' nationalist movements to position itself as the leader of a worldwide anti-imperialism movement. China also sought to exploit the differences among Western nations to promote anti-American sentiment in the West. In 1964, Beijing established diplomatic relations with France, a breakthrough in its relations with the West.

The increasing deterioration of Sino-Soviet relations in the late 1960s led China to reconsider its U.S. policy. If China equated the Soviet Union with the United States during most of the 1960s and perceived both as menaces to China's security, by the end of the 1960s China had begun to view the Soviet Union as the more dangerous threat of the two. At the same time, exhausted in the **Vietnam War**, America was seeking a way out of Vietnam. Aware of its own limited capability, the United States anticipated Chinese participation in world affairs, especially in Asia and the Pacific, so that a new balance of power could emerge to prevent Soviet expansion.

Sino-American relations entered a new era when President Richard Nixon visited China in February 1972. Three documents concluded in the 1970s between the PRC and the United States constituted their agreement and compromise on the issue of Taiwan. In the Shanghai Communiqué of 1972, the United States acknowledged, "All Chinese on either side of the Taiwan Strait maintain there is but one China and that Taiwan is a part of China" and affirmed its intention to withdraw, in due course, its military from Taiwan. In 1974, the two nations established diplomatic liaison offices in Beijing and Washington, which functioned as de facto embassies. Relations between China and the United States were fully normalized on January 1, 1979. In their joint announcement, the United States agreed to sever diplomatic ties with Taiwan, to abrogate the 1954 U.S.-Taiwan mutual defense treaty, and to withdraw American troops from the island. In 1982, the PRC and the United States signed another joint communiqué in which the latter promised to "reduce gradually its sale of arms to Taiwan, leading over time to a final resolution." In exchange, the former agreed that peaceful reunification with Taiwan was a "fundamental policy."

New relations between China and the United States began to develop rapidly in the 1970s. Nevertheless, it was the 1980s that witnessed tremendous expansion. In the early 1970s, Mao's China turned to a rapprochement with the United States mainly for strategic reasons, regarding America as a counterweight against the Soviet Union. In the 1980s, while realpolitik still played an important part, Chinese leader Deng Xiaoping took much interest in America's role in China's "Four Modernizations." Economic, cultural, and scientific exchanges between China and the United States grew in full swing. American businessmen were eager to enter Chinese markets, and Deng's China developed a strong desire to share American capital, technology, and markets as well. The United States became a leading foreign investor in China. China obtained advanced military technology from the United States. American visitors contributed a significant part to Chinese tourism, and thousands of Chinese scholars and students flocked to the United States to study.

While bilateral exchanges expanded, problems remained. The thorniest was still Taiwan. Shortly after the establishment of diplomatic relations, to soothe both Taiwan and the pro-Taiwan faction in America, the U.S. Congress passed the Taiwan Relations Act of April 1979 to form the quasi-official American Institute on Taiwan. The United States continued to export weapons to Taiwan. From the Chinese standpoint, continued U.S. support for Taiwan created serious problems for China's efforts to reunify Taiwan with the mainland. Other controversies included U.S. criticism of Chinese violation of human rights, alleged Chinese sales of nuclear technology and missiles to Third World countries, and Chinese complaints about American restrictions on trade.

The Tiananmen Square incident of 1989 ushered in a new stage in Sino-American relations. In response to the bloody suppression, Washington quickly imposed a series of economic, political, and military sanctions against Beijing. All high-level exchanges were suspended for a while. The U.S. actions outraged the Chinese government, which indignantly criticized American interference in China's internal affairs. Relations between the two nations declined to the lowest point since the early 1970s. Yet neither of the nations intended to see the free fall of Sino-American relations. Dialogues resumed in the early 1990s.

The Tiananmen incident coincided with the ending of the Cold War. After the collapse of the Soviet Union, the anti-Soviet strategic rationale as a basis for Sino-American collaboration lost its validity. The Tiananmen incident inaugurated a trend that linked human rights closely with America's China policy. Increasingly, the United States demanded Chinese improvement of human rights as a condition for mending and advancing bilateral ties. As the Chinese economy in the post–Cold War era expanded at a remarkable rate, U.S. suspicions of Chinese intentions in world affairs also shaped its policy toward China. Continued U.S. support to Taiwan has been interpreted by China as a U.S. attempt to contain China's growth. In addition, weapons proliferation and trade issues also remain major controversies. In particular, Taiwan president Li Denghui's (Lee Teng-hui's) visit to the United States in 1995, the bombing of the Chinese embassy by U.S. warplanes in Belgrade in 1999, and the U.S. spy plane incident in 2001 all chilled their relationship.

However, a growing realization of China's rise as an important world power has cautioned U.S. policy makers to engage China. They recognize that it is in America's interest to strengthen contacts with China and to promote China's modernization. On the Chinese side, aware that the Sino-American relationship is foremost in its foreign relations, the Chinese government in the last decade has generally pursued a conciliatory policy accompanied by measured counterattack. It has tried to stress common interests, minimize differences, and reduce direct confrontations with the United States wherever possible. Chinese policy has shown considerable achievements. Most of the U.S. sanctions related to the Tiananmen incident have been lifted. Chinese president Jiang Zemin and U.S. president William Clinton visited each other's nation in 1997 and 1998, respectively, the first state visits since 1989. Both leaders expressed a willingness to develop a "constructive strategic partnership." In 1999, the United States and China agreed on terms for China's entry to the World Trade Organization (WTO). In 2000, the U.S. Congress passed the Permanent Normal Trade Relations (PNTR) Act to grant China permanent most-favored-nation status.

The September 11 terrorist attack in 2001 provided an opportunity for both nations to advance their relations. In October 2001, George W. Bush met with Jiang Zemin for the first time in Shanghai at an Asia-Pacific Economic Cooperation (APEC) summit. In making advances toward a global "counterterrorism" alliance, Bush agreed to build a "constructive and cooperative relationship" with China. In 2002, Bush and Jiang paid official visits to each other. China has cooperated with the United States on the issue of North Korea and avoided direct criticism of the U.S.-led war against Iraq in 2003. In June 2003, new Chinese president Hu Jintao met with Bush in Evian, France, to stress the importance of Sino-American relations. Whether strategic considerations after September 11 can become a common ground for stable Sino-American relations remains to be seen. Even so, increasing economic, cultural, and scientific interactions between the Chinese and the Americans have made it abundantly evident that China and the United States are now mutually dependent.

See also Cold War and China; Independent Foreign Policy (1982); Jiang Zemin (1926–   ), Diplomacy of; Nixon's Visit to China/Shanghai Communiqué (1972); One Country, Two Systems; Sino-American Relations, Conflicts and Common Interests; Sino-Japanese Relations since 1949; Sino-Russian Relations since 1991; Sino-Soviet Alliance; Taiwan Strait Crisis, Evolution of; United Nations (UN) and China; World Trade Organization (WTO), China's Accession to.

Bibliography

Chen Jian, *Mao's China and the Cold War* (Chapel Hill: University of North Carolina Press, 2001); Foot, Rosemary, *The Practice of Power: U.S. Relations with China since 1949* (Oxford: Oxford University Press, 1997); Lampton, David M., *Same Bed, Different Dreams: Managing U.S.-China Relations, 1989–2000* (Berkeley: University of California Press, 2001); Sutter, Robert G., *Chinese Policy Priorities and Their Implications for the United States* (Lanham, MD: Rowman & Littlefield, 2000); Yuan, Peng, " 'September 11 Event' vs. Sino-U.S. Relations," *Contemporary International Relations (Xiandai Guoji Guanxi)*, November 2001, http://www.uscc.gov/researchpapers/2000_2003/pdfs/septe.pdf, accessed November 28, 2004.

Jinxing Chen

Sino-Japanese Relations since 1949

Sino-Japanese relations since 1949 can be divided into roughly three periods: (1) 1949 to 1972, (2) 1972 to 1990, and (3) 1990 to the present. During the first period, no official diplomatic relations existed between the two nations. When the People's Republic of China (PRC) was established in 1949, Japan was in the midst of the American occupation after World War II. The San Francisco Conference in 1951 excluded China from participating in the discussion of a peace treaty that formally ended the state of war with Japan. In the

On October 20, 2001, Chinese President Jiang Zemin *(left)* greets Japanese Prime Minister Junichiro Koizumi at the start of the APEC meeting in Shanghai. © Reuters/Corbis.

same year, the United States and Japan concluded the U.S.-Japan Security Treaty. In the Chinese government's view, this was a clear "anti-China" military alliance. Though Japan was not directly involved in the **Korean War**, it provided the base for U.S. military operations against Chinese troops in Korea. The Japanese government also followed the United States in challenging the legitimacy of the Communist government. In 1952, Japan and the Jiang Jieshi (Chiang Kai-shek) government in Taiwan signed a peace treaty that recognized Taiwan as the legitimate government of China.

In 1958, the PRC announced the "Three Political Principles" concerning its relations with Japan. To normalize its relations with China, the Chinese government asserted, Japan would need to change its hostile attitude toward China; Japan would need to cease fashioning the myth of two Chinas; and Japan should not hamper any attempts to normalize Sino-Japanese relations. During the heyday of the Cold War, the Japanese government complied with the U.S. containment policy that made any breakthrough in Sino-Japanese political relations impossible. The Chinese Communist leadership frequently castigated Japan as a "running dog" of U.S. imperialism. It criticized any efforts made by the Japanese government to strengthen its relationship with Taiwan. The extension of the U.S.-Japan Security Treaty in 1970 and the expansion of Japanese military expenditures were regarded by China as attempts to revive Japanese militarism.

Nevertheless, to break its diplomatic isolation, the PRC from the beginning actively engaged in what is called "people-to-people" diplomacy toward Japan. The Chinese government consistently encouraged unofficial commercial and cultural exchanges between the two nations, intending to strengthen pro-Beijing sentiment in Japan. Using nongovernmental organizations, China concluded a series of commercial agreements and cultural exchange programs with Japan. In September 1962, a memorandum on trade was reached between China and Japan. Strongly endorsed by the Chinese government, it also won support from a faction of the Japanese ruling party, the Liberal Democratic Party (LDP) and thus became a significant development in Sino-Japanese relations. In 1964, the two sides agreed to establish permanent trade liaison offices in each capital. This marked the formation of semiofficial relations between the two nations. It was a success of China's diplomatic strategy: to use trade as a lever with which to influence Japanese foreign policy. From 1965 on, Japan became China's top trading partner. It retained its position in Chinese foreign trade even during the turbulent **Great Cultural Revolution** in the late 1960s.

The Sino-American rapprochement in the early 1970s substantially reshaped China's relations with Japan. The announcement in 1971 of Richard Nixon's forthcoming visit to China was a shock to the Japanese government. In 1970 and 1971, Japan faithfully voted with the United States in the United Nations (UN) to oppose the expulsion of Taiwan and the acceptance of the People's Republic of China. The Nixon shock made Japan feel that it was no longer obligated to subjugate its foreign policy to U.S. directives. The "mainstream" faction within the LDP soon turned in favor of establishing formal relations with China. In September 1972, newly selected Prime Minister Kakuei Tanaka visited China. Chinese Premier **Zhou Enlai** and Tanaka signed a joint Sino-Japanese statement that normalized relations. The two sides agreed that China renounced its demand for war indemnities from Japan, while Japan recognized that Beijing was the sole legal government of China, acknowledged that Taiwan was part of China, and terminated the 1952 peace treaty between Japan and Taiwan.

The normalization marked the beginning of a new period in Sino-Japanese relations. During the 1970s, when Sino-Soviet relations remained tense, one of China's goals was to impede potential Soviet-Japanese collaboration. China supported Japan's effort to regain the four northern islands occupied by the Soviet Union at the end of World War II. China vigorously sought a Sino-Japanese treaty of peace and friendship in the hope of, among other goals, forming a partnership against Soviet expansion in Asia. Throughout the negotiations, China insisted that an "antihegemony" clause not only should renounce mutual hegemony aspirations, but also must condemn any other country's hegemony in Asia and the Pacific, which obviously aimed at the Soviet Union. Moscow consequently protested. Japan, though interested in playing the China card in its relations with the Soviet Union, was reluctant to be viewed publicly as an ally with China against the latter. The Sino-Japanese treaty of peace and friendship, concluded in 1978, was a compromise. It included an "antihegemony" clause, but also added another clause that stipulated that the treaty would not affect the relations of either Japan or China with third nations. In October 1978, Deng Xiaoping visited Japan to celebrate the formal ratification of the treaty.

In the economic arena, Sino-Japanese trade expanded after the normalization. In particular, post-Mao China under the leadership of Deng Xiaoping expressed great enthusiasm over the expansion of Sino-Japanese economic exchanges. The annual trade rose from about $1 billion in 1972 to more than $10 billion in 1981. In 1985, it surpassed $20 billion. Japan was China's number one trading partner until 1987, when Hong Kong took its place. In addition, from 1979 to 1988, the Japanese government signed three agreements with China to extend numerous long-term and low-interest loans, totaling $10.1 billion. Also, cultural exchanges between the two nations flourished. Each nation received a large number of visitors from the other, while a greater number of Chinese students studied in Japanese higher-education institutions than in previous periods.

Problems, however, still arose from time to time. In economic relations, China's complaints included trade imbalances in favor of Japan, China's difficulties in penetrating Japanese markets, Japan's unwillingness to share technology with China, and Japanese reluctance to make direct investment in China. In political aspects, China was concerned about what it perceived as Japan's intention to whitewash Japanese past misdeeds. In 1982, Japan's Ministry of Education made changes in school textbooks regarding Japan's war against China in the 1930s and 1940s in which the word "invasion" was altered to "advance." In 1985, Prime Minister Yasuhino Nakasone visited Tokyo's Yasukuni Shrine, the burial place of Japan's military men, including war criminals. These incidents incited strong protests from China.

Overall, the controversies in the 1970s and 1980s did not constitute major obstacles in the development of Sino-Japanese relations. Even the 1989 Tiananmen Square incident did not do much damage to them. Immediately after the incident, under pressure from the United States, Japan suspended its aid to

China, but it did so only temporarily. Bilateral cooperation was resumed a few months later. A Japanese Diet delegation went to Beijing in September 1989, the first high-level official delegation among industrialized nations to visit China since the Tiananmen incident.

The end of the Cold War in the early 1990s inaugurated a new era in Sino-Japanese relations. A new trend has emerged since then. Frequent eruptions of frictions and tensions between the two nations have caused serious concerns among China-Japan watchers. After the demise of the Soviet Union, the two nations' mutual interest in collaboration against Soviet expansion vanished. Instead, the rapid growth of China's economic and military power in the 1990s has aroused Japan's concerns about its own security. China has been worried about increasing Japanese military capabilities. For example, in 1999, China adamantly opposed U.S.-Japanese plans to develop a theater missile defense in East Asia. In particular, with the passage of time, Japan has become less willing to acknowledge its past aggression against China. In the Chinese view, this has revealed Japan's lack of a sense of historical guilt and a dangerous sign of the revival of militarism in Japan. Territorial disputes on islets in the East China Sea have also erupted several times recently, to which no solution has been found yet. On the issue of Taiwan, a strong pro-Taiwan independence view in Japanese society has kept China alert. Economic relations have not been immune from troubles. For example, China has continued to express its disappointment over Japan's reluctance to share its most advanced technology.

Difficulties notwithstanding, observers have also noted the increasing interdependence between China and Japan. Both nations have placed economic development as their first priority, and the two economies have never been so closely intertwined. China depends on Japan for economic assistance, for technology and investment, and as a market, while Japan now not only relies on China as a market and a source of imports, but also as an offshore manufacturing base. Cultural and personnel exchanges have continued to grow rapidly in spite of political differences. Chinese president Jiang Zemin and Premier **Zhu Rongji** visited Japan in 1998 and 2000, respectively. Japanese prime minister Junichiro Koixumi went to China twice, in 2001 and 2002. In the spring of 2003, the eruption of sudden acute respiratory syndrome (SARS) in China brought Japan's quick response. The Japanese government provided the largest direct foreign government aid for combating SARS China had received up to that point. The international community favors a cooperative relationship between China and Japan, because no other nation would benefit from disorder and instability in Asia and the Pacific. Predictably, despite the fact that difficulties between China and Japan will remain, their mutual interest will help keep frictions confined, and cooperation will continue to be a main trend in Sino-Japanese relations.

See also Cold War and China; Independent Foreign Policy (1982); Jiang Zemin (1926–   ), Diplomacy of; Nixon's Visit to China/Shanghai Communiqué (1972); One Country, Two Systems; Sino-American Relations, Conflicts and Common Interests; Sino-American Relations since 1949; Sino-Russian Relations since 1991; Sino-Soviet Alliance; Taiwan Strait Crisis, Evolution of; United Nations (UN) and China; World Trade Organization (WTO), China's Accession to.

Bibliography

Feng, Zhaokui, Liu Shilong, Liu Yingchun, Jiang Peizhu, Jin Vide, and Zhou Yongshang, *Zhanhou Riben Waijiao: 1945–1995* (Postwar Japanese diplomacy: 1945–1995) (Beijing: Social Science Press, 1996); Lin Daizhao, *Zhanhou zhongri guanxishi* (Postwar Sino-Japanese relations) (Beijing: Beijing daxue chubanshe, 1992); Sutter, Robert, "China and Japan: Trouble Ahead." *Washington Quarterly* 25, no. 4 (autumn 2002): 37–49; Whiting, Allen S., *China Eyes Japan* (Berkeley: University of California Press, 1989).

Jinxing Chen

Sino-Russian Relations since 1991

China is the world's most populous country, and Russia is its geographically largest neighbor. The two countries share the longest border in the world. China and Russia have had very complicated and often tumultuous relationships. The **Sino-Soviet alliance** in the 1950s soon gave way to hot disputes in the 1960s. In 1969, the two giant neighbors fought a border war. After Richard Nixon's visit to Beijing in 1972, China and the United States joined their efforts against Soviet expansion. Mikhail Gorbachev came to power in 1985 and initiated serious domestic reforms and foreign policy changes in the Soviet Union. By 1989, the relationship between China and the Soviet Union was fully normalized. Since the breakup of the Soviet Union and the rise of the new Russia in 1991, Beijing has built a strong relationship with Moscow.

In December 1992, Russian president Boris Yeltsin made a state visit to Beijing, and the Russian delegation signed more than twenty documents, among which figures a mutual promise not to enter into any military-political alliance directed against the other state. The Chinese characterized the atmosphere of talks during Yeltin's visits as friendly, open, constructive, and in a spirit of mutual respect, understanding, and trust. In early 1994, Yeltsin sent a letter to Chinese president Jiang Zemin proposing a "constructive partnership" between the two countries geared to the twenty-first century.

President Jiang's visit to Moscow in September 1994 was said to signify a "qualitatively new level of relations" of "constructive partnership." Although the two countries are not in any military alliance, the two sides agreed not to aim nuclear missiles at one another, never to use force against one another, and to limit sharply the number of troops stationed along their border. Yeltsin, during his visit to China in April 1996, described a "partnership directed toward the twenty-first century" between two great nations such that there was "no such pair in the world." Russia reiterated its position that "Taiwan is an inalienable part of Chinese territory." As a quid pro quo, Beijing gave its support to measures and actions adopted by Moscow on the question of Chechnya.

During Jiang's April 1997 visit to Russia, the Chinese president reached new rhetorical heights, describing the visit as one of enormous historic significance. The summit produced a lengthy declaration, "On the Multipolarization of the World and the Establishment of a New International Order." It put the two countries on record as opposing enlarging and strengthening military blocs. The relevant "military blocs" that were being expanded and strengthened at the time, apparently, were the North Atlantic Treaty Organization and the U.S.-Japan alliance. Guests at the formal luncheon held during Yeltsin's November 1997 visit to Beijing witnessed not only a warm embrace but also singing by the two presidents.

From both Beijing and Moscow's perspectives, a strong relationship between the two partners will contribute to building a multipolar world. A joint statement issued in President Vladimir Putin's inaugural trip to Beijing in July 2000 expressed "deep worry" over the U.S. plan to construct a national missile defense. Addressing a particular concern of China, Putin and Jiang voiced a "resolute protest" over any plan to involve Taiwan in any form of the contemplated missile defense system. During Putin's visit, Jiang sought to retain a modicum of balance in Beijing's ties with Washington by stating that Sino-Russian relations were "not an alliance, not confrontational, and not aimed at any third country."

The Treaty on Good Neighborly Friendship and Cooperation was signed during Jiang's trip to Moscow in 2001. This treaty formalized what Putin liked to call their "strategic partnership" while adhering to China's insistence that it not constitute an "alliance." Virtually every Chinese analysis of the Sino-Russian strategic partnership contains a disclaimer to the effect that the "strategic cooperative partnership" is "not confrontational, not an alliance, and is not directed against any third country," but merely involves coordination in confronting foreign pressure in the international sphere or opposing power politics in international affairs.

During the 1996 summit, Yeltsin and Jiang joined the leaders of Kazakhstan, Kyrgyzstan, and Tajikistan in Shanghai to sign a series of confidence-building agreements to reduce military friction at their respective borders. The five nations agreed to exchange information regarding troops and hardware deployments along the border, to limit large-scale exercises within 100 kilometers of the border to one per year, to give advance notice of these exercises, and to invite observers to witness them. These measures reinforced earlier agreements between Beijing and Moscow on military relaxation. Later, the leaders focused on fighting terrorism and the growing threat of secessionist and Islamic extremist movements in central Asia, which China feared might spill over into its **Xinjiang** Autonomous Region. In June 2001, the five became six with Uzbekistan's entry into what was now called the Shanghai Cooperation Organization.

Russia and China share parallel concerns regarding Japan. Both countries are suspicious of Japanese military and economic power in Northeast Asia. Despite the allure of Russia's natural resources, the Japanese have been reluctant investors in the Russian economy because of the Russo-Japanese dispute over the southern Kurile Islands. In the Sino-Russian-Japanese triangle, China has better relations with each of the others than they have with each other.

Mutual economic interests have provided a sound potential basis for amicable Sino-Russian relations. For the Chinese, trade with Russia allows further diversification of their economic ties. Economic ties and joint ventures with the Russians have the particular advantage of giving China's northeastern provinces an economic boost. China's trade with Russia, however, has met with many obstacles and remains less than 3 percent of total Chinese foreign trade. However, by 1993 China had already become Russia's third-largest export market and its second most important supplier of imports.

Sino-Russian military cooperation, especially Russian arms sales to China, expanded in the 1990s. For China, Russia is an attractive supplier because it offers top-of-the-line equipment at favorable prices, and because the Chinese enjoy relatively free access to Russian weaponry, whereas some restrictions still apply to China's arms trade with Western countries. As many as 2,000 Russian technicians and scientists have come to China to assist in the design and production of various defense-related systems. In October 1999, China and Russia agreed to conduct joint training and share information on the formulation of military doctrine. In 2000, China purchased two Russian-built destroyers worth $800 million each.

Beijing and Moscow are still in the process of adjusting their policies toward each other. From Moscow's strategic perspective, Asia has generally gained importance since the end of the Cold War, following secession of the Eastern European satellites, the Baltic states, Ukraine, and Belarus. Though the national identity remains preferentially "Western," Russia now defines itself geopolitically as a land bridge between Europe and Asia. Forming a strategic partnership can strengthen Russia's position in the world community. For Beijing and Moscow, their strategic partnership represents a stable and meaningful commitment to bilateral aid and support, whose content is left vague to allow for unpredictable vicissitudes in the far less structured post–Cold War era. President Putin visited China in December 2002. Such frequent high-level visits have improved mutual understanding and cooperation between China and Russia.

See also Cold War and China; Independent Foreign Policy (1982); Jiang Zemin (1926–   ), Diplomacy of; Nixon's Visit to China/Shanghai Communiqué (1972); One Country, Two Systems; Sino-American Relations, Conflicts and Common Interests; Sino-American Relations since 1949; Sino-Japanese Relations since 1949; Taiwan Strait Crisis, Evolution of; United Nations (UN) and China; World Trade Organization (WTO), China's Accession to.

Bibliography

Dittmer, Lowell, "The Sino-Russian Strategic Partnership," *Journal of Contemporary China* 10, no. 28 (2001): 399–413; Donaldson, Robert H., and Joseph L. Nogee, *The Foreign Policy of Russia: Changing Systems, Enduring Interests*, 2nd ed. (Armonk, NY: M. E. Sharpe, 2002); Mandelbaum, Michael, *The Strategic Quadrangle: Russia, China, Japan, and the United States in East Asia* (New York: Council on Foreign Relations Press, 1995).

Guoli Liu

Sino-Soviet Alliance

The relationship between the Communist Parties of China and the Soviet Union began and ended in discord. For a brief period during the early days of the People's Republic of China, there was an accord between the two based upon strategic and ideological considerations, but this lasted less than a decade, and by the late 1960s there were military clashes along their borders.

As has been well documented, from the 1930s until the founding of the People's Republic in 1949 there were serious disagreements between **Mao Zedong** and Moscow-trained Chinese students over the course of the Chinese revolution. Mao later argued that Stalin had purposely tried to sabotage Maoist strategy in order to forestall a quick Communist victory. Stalin apparently feared Western reaction to a successful socialist revolution in East Asia. Though Mao proudly proclaimed, "We did not listen to him," in 1950 he did sign a Treaty of Mutual Accord that was based upon widespread Soviet assistance to the People's Republic. The idea was to help shape an economic program that was understood as following a Soviet model for economic development. This was characterized by an emphasis upon heavy industry administered through an authoritarian system of "one-man management." The stress was upon technical expertise as opposed to ideological commitment (expert over Red).

China's reliance on the Soviet Union was extensive. By 1956, approximately 166 industrial projects had been completed with Soviet support. According to Soviet reports, as cited by Jürgen Domes (1973), these projects accounted for approximately 30 percent of the pig iron, 30 percent of the synthetic ammonias, 39 percent of the trucks, and 35 percent of the electricity that was being produced in China. In addition, China received more than 24,000 collections of Soviet scientific data, while 10,000 Chinese engineers and technical and skilled workers went to the Soviet Union for training. They were matched by an equal number of Soviet technicians who were sent to China. These joint ventures were the key to China's industrial growth.

At the same time, the leadership did attempt to assert its political independence by removing from control those in Manchuria who seemed to be close to the Soviet Union. The removal of Gao Gang, who had been vice minister in Manchuria, and who had been accused of establishing an "independent kingdom," signified the strengthening of Party control over its domestic affairs. Still, in general, until 1956 China emulated the Soviet model in regard to economic development.

The period between 1956 and 1958 marks a turning point in Sino-Soviet relations. This was due to both foreign and domestic factors. Domestically, having declared a new stage of a "transition to socialism," the leadership launched the now famous movement of "let a hundred flowers bloom, let a hundred thoughts contend." Believing that the contradictions among the people were nonantagonistic, it felt that constructive criticism would aid creativity. The criticism that developed was far greater than the leadership had anticipated, and much of it was aimed at the Soviet Union.

Russia was attacked for having left the industrial base in Manchuria in shambles after World War II. It was denounced for the heavy interest payments on its loans and for having forced China to bear the cost of the **Korean War**. In addition, political economists started to reject the Soviet paradigm. They argued that it exacerbated the distinction between town and countryside and between heavy and light industry and degraded the agricultural sector. Though many suffered for their criticisms in the Anti-Rightist Campaign of 1957, within a year many of these ideas were taken up in the **Great Leap Forward**. Moreover, in late 1955 and in 1956 Mao had already begun to think of amending the Soviet model. The speeches "High Tide of Collectivization" and "On the Ten Great Relationships," with their emphasis on revolutionary consciousness and on the overall need for a more balanced and gradual economic approach, signify what Stuart Schram (1990) has called the beginning of Mao's attempt to sketch in more systematic form a Chinese road to socialism.

This reemergence of Marxist nationalism in China was also a result of Khrushchev's denunciation of Stalin at the Soviet Twentieth Party Congress. Though Mao thought that Stalin saw "things, not people," as he said in "On Dialectics," the Chinese leadership was furious with Khrushchev over his speech, in part because it believed that it was too harsh. Stalin should have been given a 70 percent approval rating, with only 30 percent in the negative. It also felt that it was foolish, because Khrushchev had not anticipated the consequences of the speech. It could be interpreted as giving license to attack Communist parties in general, as was shown by the rebellions in Hungry and Poland. Most important, China felt that it should have been consulted beforehand. The leadership took this as a serious slight and saw it as an example of "great-power chauvinism." This idea that China was considered a second-rate partner intensified after the Tass Communiqué of 1959, in which the Soviet Union seemed to side with India in the India-China border dispute.

The steady deterioration of Sino-Soviet relations led to a full rupture in 1960 during the period of the Great Leap Forward. Though the Soviet model had been criticized as early as 1956, it was not until 1958 that it was discarded. The announcement by Mao that China's revolution would now be "self-reliant" and would no longer "blindly copy" Soviet work inaugurated a sweeping program that aimed at the radical transformation of the economy and society. Declaring that the new task was the "transition from socialism to communism," Mao saw as the basis for this a vast rural communization movement. As is known, the attempt to mobilize peasant labor for innumerable projects in industry and construction led to serious food shortages and a split in the leadership that was revealed at the Lushan Conference in 1959. It was there that Peng Dehuai, China's defense minister, launched an attack on the Great Leap. Peng's criticism occurred after he had met with Khrushchev, who had also publicly criticized the communization movement. Indeed, to show Moscow's displeasure with the abandonment of its economic model, Khrushchev canceled the agreement on nuclear aid that the Soviet Union had been providing.

But Khrushchev went further and in 1960 attempted to stop the Leap altogether by withdrawing Soviet aid and advisers. This occurred after he denounced China at the Romanian Party Congress, an attack that Mao characterized as an attempt to "encircle and annihilate us." Feeling betrayed by the withdrawal of aid and advisers, by the public criticism and the lack of Soviet support on the Indian question, and the Soviet silence on the issue of Quemoy and Matsu, China launched an ideological counteroffensive that attacked all the "revisionists" who were part of the "anti-China" chorus.

This was followed in 1962 by Mao's speech at the 7,000 cadres meeting where he called for the overthrow of the existing Soviet regime. Though this speech was not made public until later, China's position on Soviet revisionism was not hidden. This was made manifest in the polemics on the Soviet Union that were published between 1963 and 1964. Throughout this period, there was a constant theme of the need for vigilance in China against the incursions of Soviet-style revisionism. This in part may be attributed to the influence of Kang Sheng, an expert on Soviet affairs, who, as Kenneth Lieberthal (1993) notes, had been promoted by Mao after Khrushchev's public criticism. Kang was to play a prominent ideological role in combating rightist tendencies during the **Great Cultural Revolution**.

China's charge of "revisionism" was multilayered. It reflected the rejection of a model that seemingly downgraded revolutionary consciousness in favor of the control of bureaucrats and technocrats. Alternatively, to be Red and expert kept a revolution going. Moreover, to imitate the path of another seemingly denied the uniqueness that had shaped Chinese Marxism. That this might be done in favor of the Soviet Union, which clearly insisted upon its national goals above all else, became intolerable to the Chinese leadership. In 1960, Mao complained that the Soviet Union wanted the socialist countries to produce simply to meet Soviet needs. "It's hard," he said "to be the son of a patriarchal father."

The clash between the two socialist nation-states, each with its own definition of revolutionary success, was inevitable. The fact that by the late 1960s Chinese and Soviet troops were firing at each other in border clashes was another form of a virulent dispute that could be traced back to the 1930s, but was exacerbated by Khrushchev's actions. China's charge of revisionism was a result of Soviet attempts to reassert dominance over China's domestic and foreign policies. In the end, there had almost always been conflicting definitions as to national interest. Given this history, forms of accord could only be temporary.

See also Cold War and China; Independent Foreign Policy (1982); Jiang Zemin (1926–   ), Diplomacy of; Nixon's Visit to China/Shanghai Communiqué (1972); One Country, Two Systems; Sino-American Relations, Conflicts and Common Interests; Sino-American Relations since 1949; Sino-Japanese Relations since 1949; Sino-Russian Relations since 1991; Taiwan Strait Crisis, Evolution of; United Nations (UN) and China; Vietnam War; World Trade Organization (WTO), China's Accession to.

Bibliography

Domes, Jürgen, *The Internal Politics of China, 1949–1972* (London: C. Hurst & Co., 1973); Falkin, James, "The Formation and Development of Chinese Political Theory," (doctoral thesis, University of London, 1995); Lieberthal, Kenneth, "The Great Leap Forward and the Split in the Ya'an Leadership," in *The Politics of China, 1949–1989*, ed. Roderick MacFarquhar (Cambridge: Cambridge University Press, 1993); Meisner, Maurice, *Mao's China and After*, 3rd ed. (New York: Free Press, 1999); Schram, Stuart, *The Thought of Mao Tse-tung* (Cambridge: Cambridge University Press, 1990).

James M. Falkin

Social Connections in Transition

For those who have had experience working in China, *guanxi* (connections) may be a familiar term. It refers to social connections that one is surrounded by and has to deal with in business interactions and in daily life as well. *Guanxi* networks entail reciprocity, obligation, and indebtedness in the network connections, as well as a set of aesthetic protocols that come with cultivating these relationships. One way to gain prestige and improve status is to be well versed in situational and relational ethics, that is, to know when and how to use *guanxi* and when and how to pay back the resulting indebtedness. A Chinese individual with a problem, whether it is personal or organizational, naturally turns to his or her relationship network for help. Surely among this array of acquaintances—relatives, classmates, colleagues, neighbors, and friends—is someone who has pull at this hospital, that school, or that regulatory body.

The *guanxi* phenomenon as part of the Chinese tradition dates back to dynastic times. Then, having access to officialdom was very much a matter of recommendations. Hence one source of the modern practice is the heritage of Confucian bureaucracy. However, *guanxi* is by no means unique to China. Japan, Korea, and many other Asian countries that follow the Confucian tradition are known for similar practices. In fact, Western society is hardly without its own concept of "pull" and nepotism. The Chinese, however, have made *guanxi* more routinely and extensively relevant. As is popularly said, if you have *guanxi*, there is little you cannot accomplish; but if you do not, you are likely to run into a series of long lines, tightly closed doors, and a maze of administrative and bureaucratic hassles.

In addition to bureaucracy, *guanxi* has another source buried in the culture: face-saving. To the Chinese, and to most of their Asian brethren, face is serious business. One's prestige and dignity are so important that losing face (*mianzi*) is the worst thing that could happen to a person's status and therefore to his/her own ego. Those who wish to live, work, or do business in China ignore this at their own peril. It is not exaggerating to say that together with money and power, face is one of three key motivators that govern modern Chinese behavior. Losing face is justification for retaliation. As some suggest, the price exacted may be as low as an apology or as high as a corresponding loss of face. In many cases, it is due to the respect of influential figures that business deals or opportunities are born. Westerners may not realize that organizations have face, too. Ministries, corporations, and bureaus all have reputations to worry about; so does the entire country. This is why President George W. Bush was pressed to express regret for the loss of the Chinese pilot, to which he grudgingly adapted, during the spy plane event in 2001. The lesson learned in this case is that without saving face to the Chinese government, it is impossible to build any meaningful connections (*guanxi*).

It is important to note that *guanxi* is not equivalent to corruption. *Guanxi* is too often misunderstood as a form of cronyism and influence peddling. To most Chinese, *guanxi* has its own moral code and serves a necessary social function; that is, it is considered banked credits that can be used at a later date. For that reason, mutual trust is an important part of the accepted relational ethics. Hence the *guanxi* relationship must be set apart from money-based or commodity transactions: *guanxi* is a matter of relationship building, whereas corruption is bluntly taking bribes and like actions. For example, much different from transactional deals typical in corruption cases, *guanxi* may not be readily redeemable, as the latter must be properly maintained in order to be good. A favor is often provided based on no more than the promise of an equivalent return. But one cannot continue to seek favors indefinitely on the basis of a historical debt, because when the debt is judged paid, the sense of obligation may cease. Therefore, not surprisingly, the strongest *guanxi* occurs among both immediate and extended family members or among individuals who have shared deep and meaningful experience—old friends, former classmates, coworkers, and so on. The Chinese in general prefer to do business with people they know, or with friends of friends. It is in this network of security that they typically invest much of their time and energy.

The importance of cultivating *guanxi* seems to fluctuate with the degree of political and social openness. During the rigid state-planned economy under orthodox communism, everything had to be done by resorting to connections, due to insufficiency of supply of virtually any goods and the inefficiency of the rigid bureaucratic system. From food to opportunities for children's schooling, common people widely relied on *guanxi* to get their share of the distribution. Today, while material life has tremendously prospered, in view of fierce competition both domestic and international, *guanxi* can count for a great deal more. Foreign and local companies alike spend heavily to establish and maintain relationships with those who run and influence China's powerful government organizations and state-owned conglomerates. The outsiders count on the *guanxi* they have established to protect themselves from overly burdensome regulations or costly changes in government policy or to prolong the terms of a profitable sweetheart deal.

As many would readily acknowledge, good relationships with the customs bureau, the tax bureau, the local administration for industry and commerce, and the myriad of other regulatory organizations charged with oversight of foreigners and their affairs are as good as gold in China. *Guanxi* gets things moving. However, there is no doubt that it has many shortfalls and can be a formidable barrier. Undeserving people sometimes find refuge through *guanxi*, while critical projects get delayed. While it is not corruption per se, *guanxi* may indeed allow some individuals to get an unlawful edge. Associates of the deposed Beijing mayor Chen Xitong reportedly got away with rampant acts of corruption while he was in power, because his connections at all levels of government agencies were able to broadly conceal his malfeasance. It was only after he was arrested that law enforcement had the courage to clean house in the municipal government, and many were brought to justice. At the level of commoners, a Chinese person is generally far happier to hire a relative than a stranger, because he or she believes that this diminishes the danger of malfeasance. A blood relative, after all, can be counted on, even if he or she is not necessarily 100 percent up to the job; reliability ahead of anything else, as the saying goes.

As industrialization, commercialization, and the legal environment continue to grow in China, some of the infrastructure for a relation-based society will likely disappear. *Guanxi* could lose its preponderance, and people will likely achieve their goals outside the traditional assertive circles. However, most would agree that *guanxi* relationships, with their unique code of ethics, will always be an ingredient in Chinese life, because cultural heritage tends to last for the long run.

See also Social Strata.

Bibliography

Chen, Ming-Jer, *Inside Chinese Business* (Cambridge, MA: Harvard Business Press, 2001); Seligman, Scott D., "*Guanxi:* Grease for the Wheels of China: Chinese Have Raised Connections to an Art," *China Business Review*, September–December 1999: 34–40.

Jing Luo

Social Security Reform

Under the planned economy in the past, China relied on a "cradle-to-grave" **social security system** in which **state-owned enterprises (SOEs)** were solely responsible for their employees' welfare, including lifelong employment, housing, medical expenses, pension, and children's education. China started its social security reform in the early 1980s, in the wake of the economic transition to a market economy. The reform is intended to establish a unified, sustainable, well-functioning, and market-oriented social insurance system that is characterized by multiple funding sources, multitiered security measures, a combination of individual rights and obligations, and socialized management and services.

China's growing elderly population has made social security reform an important issue. Every morning, many retired men and women can be found practicing Tai Chi in city parks.

China's social security system consists of social insurance, social welfare, social relief, and special care of disabled servicemen and family members of revolutionary martyrs. The system includes **old-age insurance**, medical insurance, **unemployment** insurance, work injury insurance, and maternity insurance. It also includes a program of cash assistance to many low-income households, mainly in urban areas.

Pension reform started nationwide in 1991 after a series of experiments. Pension reform was triggered mainly by the financial trouble inherited from an enterprise-based pay-as-you-go system. In 1991, the State Council's Document No. 33 encouraged the establishment of a three-pillar pension system that required individual contributions in addition to enterprise contributions. The three-pillar system is comprised of a defined-benefit public pillar for income redistribution, a mandatorily funded defined-contribution pillar for individual workers, and a voluntary supplement pension pillar managed by individual firms or insurance companies. The 1995 State Council Document No. 6 called for a social system to pool individual accounts. The 1997 State Council Document No. 26 deepened the reform by introducing three important changes: extending the program's coverage to the entire urban labor force, socializing the pension administration service, and unifying pension contribution rates nationwide. Under the program, the public pillar will provide 20 percent of the benefit replacement rate with a 13 percent employers' contribution, and the individual-funded pillar will provide 38.5 percent of that with a 4 percent employees' and 7 percent employers' contribution.

Health insurance reform began in 1988 and ended a free medical system in government institutions and SOEs. In 1998, the government implemented the decision on Establishing the Basic Medical Insurance System for Urban Employees, which mandated a basic medical insurance system for urban employees throughout the country. The reform shifted the responsibility of financing basic health insurance to a wage contribution levied on both employers and employees. At present, about 6 percent of the wage bill of enterprises and 2 percent of personal wages should be paid as part of the medical insurance premiums. Part of the employer contribution is to finance major medical expenses, primarily inpatient services. The rest of the employer's and all of the employee's contributions are deposited in an individual account that each employee can draw on to pay for outpatient services. To support the reform, the government has also initiated a reform of medical institutions and the medicine production and distribution system to ensure better medical service at lower cost and has encouraged enterprises to offer a supplemental health insurance package where conditions permit.

An unemployment compensation system began in 1986, initially to assist laid-off SOE workers through basic living guarantee and reemployment policies. In 1999, the government issued the Regulation on Unemployment Insurance, which aimed at accomplishing the transition of basic living guarantees to the unemployment insurance scheme. The system covers all urban enterprises, institutions, and SOE employees. Enterprises pay 2 percent of their wage bills, and employees pay 1 percent of their wages. The benefit replacement rate is lower than the minimum wage but higher than the minimum living allowance for urban residents. Benefits can continue for up to two years, depending on the length of service prior to the unemployment spell. Eligibility for the unemployment insurance benefit requires that beneficiaries were laid off involuntarily and had contributed insurance premiums for one full year.

Work injury insurance provides cash and in-kind (medical) benefits in the event of work-related diseases, disabilities, and deaths. A reform adopted in 1996 extended coverage to all urban employees, except for employees of government and public institutions. The reforms implement the pooling approach to finance work injury benefits by all employers in a given region.

Maternity insurance covers medical expenses and pays a living allowance to women in childbirth. Coverage and finance are similar to that for health care insurance. Benefits are financed by pooled contributions from covered employers.

Other social security programs include a minimum living guarantee, voluntary rural pensions, and reemployment service centers. In 1998, the government formulated the "two guarantees and three security lines" policy—basic living allowance, unemployment insurance program, and minimum living allowance to protect urban laid-off and vulnerable individuals. The policy provides the most important social protection for Chinese urban workers.

So far, China's social security system applies mainly to government institutions and urban public-owned enterprises. The majority of employees in the private sector are not covered. Rural workers and farmers lack coverage entirely.

Administration of social insurance programs was consolidated in the late 1990s, and various important institutions have been created under the jurisdiction of the Ministry of Labor and Social Security (MOLSS). These include the Social Security Fund Management Center, the social insurance administration agency, and the social security service information network. The government also established the National Council for Social Security Fund, responsible for the operation and administration of the social security fund. On social security law and regulation, the Chinese government is accelerating the pace by drafting a social security law, a pension law, a medical and unemployment insurance law, among other laws and regulations.

See also Privately Owned Enterprises (POEs); State-Owned Enterprises (SOEs).

Bibliography

China State Council, *China Social Security Reform: White Paper* (Beijing: China State Council, April 29, 2002); International Labor Organization, *Review of Social Security Reform in China in 2002*, draft report, March 2002; Mengkui, Wang, ed., *Restructuring China's Social Security System* (Beijing: Foreign Languages Press, 2002).

Vivian Chen

Social Security System

The Chinese social security system includes social insurance, social assistance, social welfare, special care and placement for servicemen in the military, and basic living protections and reemployment for the laid-off works in

state-owned enterprises. Since the 1980s, China has begun to reshuffle its entire social security system in light of the rapid changes that have taken place. The current social security network is quite extensive, but it still covers primarily urban employees, or one-tenth of the total population. Farmers, who make up 60 percent of the population, still live without much protection against aging, sickness, poverty, and **unemployment**.

During the prereform era, employees in urban areas received most of their social insurance benefits, such as pension plans, health care insurance, industrial injury and disability insurance, and childbirth insurance, from their work units. Pension benefits, for example, were based on a pay-as-you-go system that required the younger generation to pay for the older generation. There was no social-pooling mechanism to reduce the risk and to redistribute the benefits equally. Consequently, the program was poorly organized and financed. It ran into serious difficulties in the 1980s for several reasons. First, as a result of enterprise reforms, enterprises must now be responsible for their own profits and losses. Therefore, they could not bear the burden of providing social security entirely by themselves. Second, a large number of workers had reached their retirement age, which put a tremendous financial burden on their former employers. Finally, as the labor market became the major force of labor allocation, portability of employment benefits such as pensions, health care, and unemployment insurance needed to be put in place to ensure labor mobility.

The reforms of the social security system are intended to make the system independent of enterprises and institutions. Risk pooling, portability, and universal coverage are the main focus. All programs are to be funded through individual, enterprise and institutional, and governmental contributions and run with socialized management and services. Currently, only limited benefits are provided to urban residents. The long-term goal of the government is to gradually develop these benefits into a single, standardized, and nationalized social security system for all Chinese laborers, including farmers. Given the sheer size of China's labor force, this goal is indeed very ambitious, and one should not expect to see the system put in place until the middle of this century.

The reform of the pension system began in 1991. Drawing lessons from other industrialized countries, the government's plan is made up of three components: a state-sponsored basic **old-age insurance** system, an enterprise supplementary pension system, and individual retirement savings accounts. Unlike any other state-sponsored pension system in the world, the basic old-age insurance system combines basic mutual assistance funds with mandatory individual accounts. Individual employees contribute about 8 percent of their gross wages to their own individual accounts. Companies and institutions contribute about 20 percent of their employees' total wages to the program. Part of the premium goes to mutual assistance funds, and the rest goes to employees' individual accounts. All funds are to be collected, managed, and distributed through a government management agency at the city or county level. When an employee retires, he or she will draw a pension from both basic pension funds and individual accounts. The contribution an individual made is transferable in that it can be inherited by his or her offspring.

In 1995, the Childbirth Insurance Program was reformulated. Among many generous protections for women in maternity, the most notable one is a ninety-day paid maternity leave. According to related laws, women who are pregnant cannot be laid off or have their wages reduced. In order to encourage women to comply with the one-child policy, many local governments have extended the paid pregnancy leave for up to six months. The insurance also covers the cost of medical services such as examination, delivery, and hospitalization and necessary medicines.

A new experimental Industrial Injuries Insurance Program was launched in 1996. The program covers loss of wages, cost of medical care, family support, and lump-sum compensations due to work-related injuries, disabilities, and death. The rate of the industrial injury insurance premium varies according to different trades and may fluctuate with the situation of the individual enterprise. The rate of premiums is determined on the basis of the level of industrial injury risks and that of occupational danger in different trades. A widow of a deceased worker, for example, can receive up to sixty months' one-time lump-sum wage compensation for the job-related death and 40 percent of her husband's regular wage thereafter. The premium for the insurance program is paid entirely by employers. In 2004, the state formally launched the insurance nationwide. All employers, including individual business owners, must purchase the insurance for their employees.

The reform of medical insurance was based on a similar design. According to the new Basic Medical Insurance Program regulation issued in 1998, employees are required to contribute 2 percent of their wages to their individual medical funds, and employers contribute about 6 percent of their employees' total wages to basic medical funds. The individual medical funds pay for individual employees' routine doctors' visits and prescription drugs, and the basic medical funds pay for employees' major health care costs such as hospitalizations and surgeries. A regional fund management agency manages both types of funds. Compared with the old medical insurance programs, the new insurance program requires a considerable amount of out-of-pocket spending from the insured. To help pay for the costs of catastrophic illnesses, some companies also offer supplemental health insurance programs to cover medical costs in excess of the maximum coverage under the public medical insurance program. In addition, the government has also set up a medical subsidy program for all civil servants.

In 1999, the Unemployment Insurance Program was established to deal with the mounting unemployment problem. Both employees and employers pay for the insurance premium. The length of coverage varies from one to two years, depending on the number of years an employee has contributed to the insurance. As a part of the program, an unemployed worker can also receive a certain amount of medical assistance while he or she is unemployed. However, the unemployment insurance does not cover many temporarily laid-off workers from state firms. Their livelihood is paid for by the provisional reemployment center set up by the government.

According to official statistics, by the end of 2002, 147 million workers and retirees enrolled in the Old-Age Insurance Program, 94 million enrolled in the Basic Medical Insurance Program, 101 million enrolled in the Unemployment Insurance Program, 44 million enrolled in the Industrial Injuries Insurance Program, and 34 million enrolled in the Childbirth Insurance Program. As the programs continue to expand their coverage, the number of those enrolled in each of the programs is expected to grow substantially in the near future. The major challenge to the existing programs is inadequate funds. If no effective means is installed to collect premiums, these programs will become a huge financial burden on the government.

Social assistance and social welfare programs are also important parts of China's social security system. Since the 1980s, poverty has resurfaced among a relatively large part of the population in urban areas. In 1997, China for the first time instituted a minimum living standard security system for urban residents. The new system covers three groups of people: (1) people who have no fixed income, no ability to work, or no legal guardians in the case of the elderly; (2) unemployed workers; and (3) employees and retirees with an income still below the local minimum standard of living. The program is funded through general revenues of the local governments. The actual amount of subsidies is determined according to the cost necessary for maintaining the basic livelihood of the local urbanites. In 2001, more than 11 million people benefited directly from this system nationwide.

The Ministry of Civil Affairs (MCA) administers China's welfare system. In **cities**, several disadvantaged groups are entitled to receive welfare support in the form of assisted living in social welfare homes, old-age homes, sanitariums, and children's welfare homes: elderly widows and widowers who are childless and helpless and living alone, eligible handicapped persons, and orphans. Enterprises are also required to hire handicapped persons. The MCA also administers a special care and placement program designed to compensate or commend the special group of people who have rendered meritorious or military service to the state and society. Potential beneficiaries, such as dependents of fallen servicemen, disabled revolutionary servicemen, and demobilized veterans, receive regular fixed-amount subsidies from the state.

In the rural areas, the government is experimenting with programs to provide old-age insurance to the elderly and a minimum living standard security system to the rural poor. Because of the sheer size of the rural population, these programs will not be likely to be put in place for several decades.

The incremental reforms of China's social security system have created a basic safety network for millions of millions of Chinese. The system helps alleviate the anxiety and insecurity many people have suffered during a period of painful economic transition. This system still has many problems, but the positive impact of these reforms cannot be overstated.

See also Social Connections in Transition; Social Security Reform; Social Strata.

Bibliography

Information Office of the State Council, the People's Republic of China, *Labor and Social Security in China* (Beijing: Information Office of the State Council, the People's Republic of China, 2002); Ministry of Labor and Social Security and Bureau of Statistics, the People's Republic of China, *Statistical Survey of Development in Labor and Social Security (2002)* (Beijing, April 30, 2003).

Baogang Guo

Social Strata

Chinese social strata are in the process of restructuring in response to the rapid economic reform since 1978. Government policies and the market-oriented economy function as the two major forces in bringing about the emergence of the new structure. Layers of this social structure are increasingly visible but not yet definite. Roughly ten social strata are identifiable from the socioeconomic perspective: national and social management, managers, industrial workers, agricultural laborers, private enterprise owners, industrial and commercial individuals, professional technicians, clerks, business service staffs, and urban unemployed, laid-off and half-laid-off vagrants (table 14).

A striking feature of the social strata in twenty-first-century China is the rapid polarization of wealth. In 2000, the combined estimated wealth of the top fifty richest entrepreneurs in China was $10 billion. Number fifty was worth $42 million. On the basis of per capita income differentials, $42 million in China would be the equivalent of roughly $500 million in the United States. The wealthiest had an estimated net worth of $1.9 billion. The average annual wage of industrial and agricultural workers, who accounted for two-thirds of the total population, was well below U.S. $1,000 the same year.

Between the two extremes are the booming but not yet fully developed middle strata, including the majority of private enterprise owners, managers, specialists, professional technicians, and administrators at higher levels. These "career persons" typically have higher-than-average income and higher social prestige and engage in more stable and respected professions. Of these middle-status people, private enterprise owners are gaining wealth faster than others in this process of wealth and political power redistribution. Relatively small in

TABLE 14
Social Strata in China

Composition of China's Workforce, %

	1952	1978	1988	1999
Administrators/managers	0.6	1.2	2.2	3.6
Owners of private enterprises*	0.2	0.0	0.0	0.6
Owners of private enterprises**	4.1	0.0	3.1	4.2
Technicians/specialists	0.9	3.5	4.8	5.1
Office workers	0.5	1.3	3.7	4.8
Business/service workers	3.1	2.2	6.4	12.0
Manufacturing workers	6.4	19.8	22.4	22.6
Agricultural workers	84.2	67.4	55.8	44.0
Unemployed/underemployed	n/a	4.6	3.6	3.1

*Eight or more employees.
**Fewer than eight employees, roughly equivalent to industrial and commercial individuals as mentioned earlier.

Source: Lu Xuryi, Report on a Study of Contemporary China's Social Strata, January 2002.

number, the "social middles" are not forceful enough to stabilize as the new socioeconomic structure.

Another feature of Chinese social strata is the diminishing boundaries between different social statuses that were clearly and rigidly marked in **Mao Zedong**'s time. In the years between 1949 and 1978, society was fragmented into three groups: workers, farmers, and cadres. Disparities in political prestige, income, and attainability of education were obvious and not crossable. For instance, rural farmers were denied any of the medical, food, and housing benefits that the state granted to urban workers, the benefits that could mean life and death in those years of material destitution. The *hukou* **system** bounded farmers to where they were born and prevented them from taking up any other professions or moving to new locations. Workers also had numerous obstacles to overcome. Only a lucky few could manage to enter the elite cadre group. However, disparities in income between and within each social group were historically low, because the New China was founded on the principle of abolishing class differences. Government policies, regulations, and rhetorical propaganda were combined to keep the accumulation and transmission of wealth to a minimum.

This stability within a given stratum began to dissolve in the economic reform. In its place rose social mobility that features another aspect of the twenty-first-century social system. The "contract system with remuneration linked to output," later known as the household responsibility system, freed farmers from their collective ownership of the land and stimulated their incentive for production. The emergence of local **township and village enterprises** expanded their traditional occupation of farming into a variety of occupational possibilities. The loosening of government control in regard to people's geographic mobility further promoted farmers to occupations originally only available to urban residents. All these developments helped diversify the homogeneous group of farmers into different social groups and quickly boosted a considerable number of them into better-off strata.

Market reforms in agriculture were later introduced into industry. Especially under the Open Door policy implemented in the early 1980s, industry began to strengthen and prosper. Consequently, a small group of industrial workers found their way into higher strata. On the whole, however, the status of urban workers, and **state-owned enterprise** workers in particular, has sunk lower in the social structure. State and work-unit subsidies have dropped. State-provided medical insurance has collapsed. Jobs are no longer secured until retirement. Some 20 million urban workers fell into the stratum of laid-off, half-laid-off, and unemployed at the turn of the twenty-first century. A fall in political position and social prestige goes hand in hand with the loss of economic status for industrial workers. Originally the "master" and main pillar of the New China, as the rhetoric went, urban workers find themselves at the mercy of government policies and industrial restructuring.

People with college degrees and higher are labeled **intellectuals**. Traditionally, they were a middle-income group with lower political status than workers, farmers, and administrators. They have managed to maintain the middle position in the contemporary social structure. Socially highly respected, the intellectual stratum does not necessarily have higher incomes.

Social stratification in China manifests itself also in different geographic locations. Middle and upper strata typically concentrate along the eastern coast. The further west the location, the less prosperous people are. Rural areas typically are less well off than urban areas. The per capita annual net income of rural households in 2001 was 2,366.4 RMB yuan, compared with a per capita annual disposable income of urban households of 6859.6 RMB yuan. However, partly because of this inequality, agricultural laborers are also the most mobile at the same time. They make constant efforts to squeeze into other social strata.

Income, occupation, and education are not the only things that count in regard to social status in China. Distribution of strata is uneven across ethnic groups. The five autonomous regions where most minority ethnic groups live accommodate a large proportion of agricultural and other lower-income social groups. Within each autonomous region, counties with minority ethnic concentration are at a greater disadvantage. For instance, out of 104 poverty-stricken villages of Yili Prefecture in **Xinjiang** Autonomous Region, 102 are national minority villages. In Guizhou, another relatively low-income province, 21 out of 31 poverty-stricken villages (*pingkun xian*) are in minority regions and account for half the total minority population in the province.

The stratum of national and social management corresponds roughly to the administrative and management group. They used to be the cream of society in nearly every sense. As a social stratum, their political power remains. However, they typically have fixed incomes, which means limited resources compared with private entrepreneurs. The contrast between their power and their lesser importance in the economic lives of local residents often compels those with greater economic ambition to get out of the stratum and strive for the better-off private enterprise stratum.

At present, the rapid change of the traditional social strata is largely perceived as beneficial to the healthy growth of society. It increases opportunities for the general public and helps make social mechanisms of choice and award the norm, a norm that did not exist in the old times. In this process, new concerns emerge. Official corruption, use of illegal means for wealth acquisition, and theft of public property are rampant, in spite of the government's efforts to get them under control. They help internalize the sharp disparities that exist between the rich and the poor. In addition, the relatively slow growth of farmers' benefits from the reform and millions of layoffs in urban areas make the traditional pillar classes feel deprived rather than benefiting from the change. Some scholars fear that these factors may affect people's confidence in the fairness of the newly emerging social structure. Therefore, social stability will rely mostly on a fair and peaceful redistribution of wealth. An era where the Communist Party governs a privatized society has yet to pan out.

See also Rural-Urban Divide, Regional Disparity, and Income Inequality; Social Connections in Transition.

Bibliography

Deutch Bank Research, The Domestic Political Change, China Special, September 27, 2002, http://www.dbresearch.com/PROD/DBR_INTERNET_EN-PROD/PROD

0000000000046261.pdf, accessed on December 20, 2004. Ge, Daoshun, "Social Strata," in *Transformation of Social Structure*, ed. Lu Xueyi (Beijing: China Social Science Press, 1997); Lu, Xueyi, *Chinese Society in the 21st Century* (Kunming: Yunnan People's Press, 1996); ———*Report on a Study of Contemporary China's Social Strata* (Beijing: Social Sciences Academic Press, 2002); National Bureau of Statistics of the PRC, *China Statistical Yearbook 2002* (Beijing: China Statistics Press, 2002).

Hong Wang

SOEs

See State-Owned Enterprises (SOEs).

Songs of New China

See Folk Music and Songs of New China.

Soviet Union

See Sino-Russian Relations since 1991; Sino-Soviet Alliance.

Special Administrative Region (SAR)

The term "special administrative region" (SAR) refers to Hong Kong after July 1, 1997, and Macao after December 20, 1999. Their formation is the result of the negotiations between the People's Republic of China and Great Britain over the status of Hong Kong and between China and the Portuguese government over the status of Macao. As of 2004, Hong Kong and Macao, two former Western colonies, were the only two special administrative regions in the world. Because Hong Kong SAR was established first, the Macao SAR government follows the example of Hong Kong in both structure and policy.

The Opium War (1839–1842), a result of the conflict between the Chinese imperial government and British merchants over the importation of opium, granted the British Hong Kong Island "in perpetuity" in 1842. In 1860, again as a result of British victory in battle, China ceded Stonecutter's Island and Kowloon Peninsula to Britain. Finally, the third and largest part of what is now known as "Hong Kong," the New Territories, was leased to the British for ninety-nine years under the second Anglo-Chinese Convention of Peking in 1898. The New Territories constitute 89 percent of Hong Kong's area and are agricultural bases important for the survival of Hong Kong. By 1980, the British government felt compelled to do something about the soon-to-expire lease on the New Territories to calm investors. Thus the British government took the initiative in negotiating the future status of Hong Kong.

In their Joint Declaration on the Question of Hong Kong (September 1984), Great Britain and the People's Republic of China stated that Hong Kong would become a "Special Administrative Region" based on "the provisions of Article 31 of the Constitution of the People's Republic of China." Specifically, Hong Kong would function like any other autonomous country in everything but defense and diplomacy, and it would be allowed to maintain its own legal, social, and economic systems for at least fifty years. The Hong Kong people's civil liberties would be guaranteed. The government and legislature of the SAR would be composed of local inhabitants. The legislature would be constituted by elections, and the executive authorities would be accountable to the legislature. Common law would remain in force. The central government in Beijing would not levy taxes on the Hong Kong SAR. Hong Kong would be able to establish economic relations with foreign countries and issue travel documents for entry into and exit from Hong Kong. Administratively, "the chief executive will be appointed by the Central People's Government on the basis of the results of elections or consultations to be held locally. Principal officials will be nominated by the chief executive of the Hong Kong Administrative Region for appointment by the Central People's Government. Chinese and foreign nationals previously working in the public and police services in the government departments of Hong Kong may remain in employment." In addition to Chinese, English may continue to be used by the government and in the courts. The Sino-British Joint Liaison Group was created to oversee the transition of Hong Kong to Chinese rule.

The Basic Law, often referred to as a "miniconstitution" for Hong Kong, serves as a legal code to translate the principles of the Sino-British Joint Declaration into daily practices. In 1985, China formed a Basic Law Drafting Committee under the direction of the **National People's Congress**. Among the ninety-five members, fifty-nine were from the mainland, and twenty-three are from Hong Kong. In addition, China also established a 180-member Consultative Committee of Hong Kong composed of people from all walks of life in an attempt to confer political legitimacy on the Basic Law. The Hong Kong SAR Executive Council is composed mainly of businessmen. Tung Cheehwa is the current chief executive.

The Hong Kong Special Administrative Region is a unique political entity in China's history. It is different in many respects from China's thirty provinces, and its strategic importance to China is manifested in many aspects. First, being a regional business and financial center, Hong Kong remains an indispensable window for China on the global market of information, technology, and finance. Second, its role of financier for China's reform is extremely important. As the region's headquarters for many major international banking corporations from Western countries, Hong Kong remains one of the biggest sources of loans to China, as well as one of the biggest investors in China. Third, Hong Kong has been one of the largest trading partners of China by virtue of its state-of-the-art facilities in banking, finance, insurance, telecommunications, and shipping. Fourth, its role as the "middleman" in commodity and service trade is indispensable for China's economic development. China's indirect trade via Hong Kong has always far exceeded its direct trade with Hong Kong. Finally, with a population of 6.5 million with high per capita income and consumption power, Hong Kong remains a significant client for Chinese exports.

Since the SAR's birth, Hong Kong people have experienced its special status every day. Residents do not pay taxes to China. The civil service remains effective and clean. The media is free from government control. The Falun Gong cult, banned on the mainland, remains legal in Hong Kong SAR. International human rights organizations continue to operate without interference from the

Hong Kong government. Hong Kong is still the most globalized city in Asia and has been actively participating in such international organizations as the World Trade Organization (WTO), Asia-Pacific Economic Cooperation (APEC), and the World Customs Organization.

But there have also been some setbacks in the past six years, such as the Hong Kong government's decision in 1999 to seek from Beijing a reinterpretation of the Right of Abode Clause in the Basic Law and the recent denial of entry to a human rights activist. Also, there are signs that PRC officials pressured local media and warned about Falun Gong activities in Hong Kong. Beijing also sent out an early endorsement of the incumbent chief executive in 2002 to discourage other candidates from seeking office. Overall, however, Hong Kong's transition from a British colony to a People's Republic of China special administrative region has been a smooth and positive one. With some notable exceptions, China has kept its promise to respect Hong Kong's autonomy. At the same time, the Hong Kong people have demonstrated their continuing commitment to their unique way of life and institutions.

Shortly after the 1984 Hong Kong agreement, the Macao question was settled following the Hong Kong model. In April 1987, the Portuguese agreed to return Macao to China in 1999, and Macao would also become an SAR of China. Edmund Ho Hua Wah is the chief executive of Macao SAR.

See also Administrative Structure of Government; Hong Kong, Return of; One Country, Two Systems; Tibet; Xinjiang.

Bibliography

Chung, Jae Ho, and Shiu-hing Lo, "Beijing's Relations with the Hong Kong Special Administrative Region: An Inferential Framework for the Post-1997 Arrangement," *Pacific Affairs* 68, no. 2 (summer 1995): 167–186; Hsiung, James C., ed., *Hong Kong, the Super Paradox: Life after Return to China* (New York: St. Martin's Press, 2000); "Joint Declaration of the Government of the United Kingdom of Great Britain and Northern Ireland and the Government of the People's Republic of China on the Question of Hong Kong," December 19, 1984.

Ting Ni

Special Education

Special education is both an important and a challenging part of basic education in the People's Republic of China (PRC). During the past fifty years, the Chinese government has continuously attached great importance to special education. The state has not only issued a whole set of laws and regulations that make explicit stipulations on safeguarding the rights to education of the disabled, but has also formulated a series of both general and specific policies for reforming and developing special education and has earmarked special funds for this purpose. In the early 1950s, special education became a part of basic education in the central government's decision on the reform of the education system in China. In 1986, the state issued the Compulsory Education Law of the People's Republic of China to institute that "all children who have reached the age of six shall enroll in school and receive compulsory education, regardless of sex, ethnicity, or race" (Ministry of Education 2002, 3). In November 1988, the Ministry of Education (formerly the State Education Commission), the Ministry of Civil Administration, and the China Association for the Handicapped jointly sponsored the first national conference on special education. At the conference, scholars called for an active and steady development of education for disabled children, which laid a solid foundation for special education. Therefore, by 2000, most blind, deaf, and mentally retarded children were offered the opportunity to attend schools. In the 1990s, the Law on the Protection of the Disabled and the Regulations on Education of the Disabled were promulgated to further promote and strengthen special education.

As a result, special education in schools has developed rapidly. According to statistics, in 1948, there were only forty-six special education schools with a total enrollment of 2,380 disabled students. The number of special education schools jumped to 375 with a total enrollment of 40,000 students in 1985 and 886 special education schools with a total enrollment of 85,000 students in 1991 (Qian 2001). By 2001, there were 1,531 special education schools for blind, deaf, or mentally retarded children and about 5,400 special education classes attached to regular schools. The total number of special education students was more than 386,400 (Ministry of Education 2002). In addition, a large number of disabled children and teenagers attended regular schools. Special education schools and classes for the disabled are widely distributed in China's education system. Statistics show that by 1999, in mainland China there were 28 special schools for the blind, 871 schools for the deaf, 163 schools for those who were blind and deaf, 473 schools for mentally retarded children, and more than 10,000 special classes for the disabled within regular schools (Qian 2000). Currently, there are more than 1,700 rehabilitation institutions where 70,000 deaf children have been trained or are receiving training in mainland China, and there are also more than 1,000 vocational training institutions for the disabled. In Taiwan, there are 16 special education schools and about 2,000 special education classes for approximately 40,000 disabled students; in Hong Kong, there are about 70 special education schools with an enrollment of about 10,000 students; and in Macao, there are 354 disabled children receiving special education (Qian 2001).

According to the law, any district with a population of 40,000 or more must establish one school dedicated to special education (Jin 2000). The schools for special education in China aim at enabling disabled children to successfully develop morally, intellectually, physically, aesthetically, and in work experience. In the meantime, according to the needs and characteristics of disabled children, training effects their physical recovery with a view to compensating for and rectifying their psychological and physiological defects and thus improving their ability to take care of themselves and fit themselves into the social environment. To help the disabled become capable of taking a job and be self-reliant, diverse vocational or technical training is conducted in most special education schools. For the blind, training is mainly given in the area of massage and knitting work. For the deaf, the training is largely concerned with carpentry, sewing, painting, industrial art, or typing. China is forming a special education system from early childhood education and basic elementary and secondary education to higher education for the disabled. The schools for special education are becoming a backbone of the special education system in addition to the special education classes in regular schools. Meanwhile, reforms of special education in theory, curriculum, and strategies of instruction are being carried out. Integration of special education into regular education has been proposed and started.

However, special education in China is comparatively less developed than other forms of education. China is a large country with a population of 1.3 billion people. There is no doubt that special education for the disabled is a great challenge to its nine-year compulsory education. According to the census of 1987, China had a population of 1 billion people, and 51,640,000 people were disabled. The number of disabled children between the ages of six and fourteen was about 6,250,000 (Qian 2000). By the end of 2000, China's population reached 1.3 billion. Calculations indicated that China would have about 67,132,000 disabled people, and among them 8,125,000 disabled children should be able to receive compulsory education. In fact, the number of disabled children receiving compulsory education is far more than 8,125,000 because the definition of special education in China only includes education for physically disabled children. If those children who have special learning needs or disabilities or need emotional support are added, the number of children between the ages of six and fourteen with special needs is approximately 22,000,000.

See also Character Education in Primary and Secondary Schools; Education Media and Technology; Educational Administration; Educational System; Higher-Education Reform; Management Education; Primary Education; Private Education; School Enrollment and Employment; Secondary Education; Taiwan, Education Reform in; Teacher Education; United States, Chinese Education in; Vocational and Technical Training.

Bibliography

Jin, Xibin, *Administration System of Special Education in China*, 2000, http://www.isec2000.org.uk/abstracts/papers_x/xibin.htm, accessed on April 1, 2003; Ministry of Education, PRC, *Education in China* (Beijing: Ministry of Education, 2002); Qian, Zhiliang, *Report on Education of the Disabled Youths in China*, 2000, http://www.bnu.edu.cn/centers/tejiao/lsyxz.htm, accessed on April 1, 2003; Qian, *Special Education in China*, 2001, http://www.edu.cn/20010827/208334.shtml, accessed on April 1, 2003; State Education Commission, *Basic Education of China* (Beijing: Department of Basic Education, 1989).

Ronghua Ouyang and Dan Ouyang

Spiritual Life in the Post-Mao Era

China has long been a nation with a wide range of religions. Before the founding of the People's Republic of China (PRC) in 1949, there were four major religions, Buddhism, Daoism, Islam, and Christianity, among which Daoism was a Chinese native religion. Buddhism, which originated in India and was introduced into China at the end of the Han dynasty, was greatly influenced by Chinese traditional culture, so Chinese Buddhism was not quite the same as that in India. As a Western religion, Christianity came to China in the Tang dynasty, but was not successful in achieving an enduring and wide recognition. Islam began to appear in the north of China in the seventh century and gained continuous acceptance among the Islamic minority. Confucianism, although strictly speaking hardly a religion, enjoyed dominance over other beliefs. Scholars therefore often summarize Chinese traditional culture as *Ru, Fo*, and *Dao*, that is, Confucianism, Buddhism, and Daoism. From this historical perspective, one might say that people in ancient China led a very spiritual life. Indeed, the crucial figures of Confucianism, such as Confucius himself, Mencius, and Zhu Xi, all vigorously stressed the spiritual level of life.

With the founding of the PRC, the religious life of the Chinese people almost came to a halt. Marxism replaced all other philosophies as well as religions, and the Chinese people were forced to pursue a so-called proletarian way of life, while anyone with any appreciation of an alternative lifestyle would be accused of harboring a bourgeois taste. In order to create a brand-new, socialist culture of proletariats, religions of all kinds, native or imported, were indiscriminately treated as heresies or superstitions and vehemently debased. Christianity, which had been at odds with Chinese culture for almost 1,500 years, was linked to imperialism. As a result, in the 1950s, Western missionaries were driven out of China; only native bishops or priests were appointed. Confucianism and other Chinese traditional cultural values and beliefs met a similar fate, because they were all treated as part of feudal elements to be discredited and prohibited.

In addition to Marxism and later Leninism, the idolization of Mao's thoughts was transformed into a quasi-religious fervor. Gradually, Maoism became the yardstick for almost everything. Mao's books were accepted as the Chinese "Red Bible," and Mao himself became the spiritual leader for millions of people. If there were any religion, Maoism was the religion; if there were any god, Mao himself was the god.

The death of Mao marked a great transition of Chinese society and the spiritual life of the Chinese people. Not only was Confucianism actively reevaluated, but freedom of religion was also acknowledged—at least, it can be found in the Constitution. It must be noted that there has been no fundamental change in the Communist Party's attitude toward religion. First, it still holds that religion is like opium for the human spirit. In order to weaken religion's influences, it tried to inoculate the Chinese, especially the young people, with the teaching of dialectical materialism, historical materialism, and ideas of atheism and urged them to establish a scientific Weltanschauung. From a historical materialism point of view, for example, the Party wants to convince its audience that religion is only a product of certain historical periods: it ceases to exist when certain conditions are no longer available. Second, the Party tries hard to win over government-sanctioned religious organizations and establishments. One strategy is to define a religion and its activities along the line of "patriotism." According to the Party's view, or policy, to be exact, the so-called patriotic organization acts as a bridge between the government and the Chinese religious world. In other words, the Party wants to foster an alliance with the religious organization through which the Party's religious policy can be carried out and religious activities can be "normalized" and/or controlled. Third, because of the existence of numerous religious organizations and establishments within its borders, the government is concerned about the potentially subversive role these organized entities and their gatherings might play. In light of these concerns, the government finds it of paramount importance to put all religious activities under control.

Although the Chinese people cannot enjoy religious freedom as much as most westerners can, since the death of Mao, ordinary people have been able to choose their own religious beliefs at their own will. Party members, however, are not allowed to have faith in or association with any religion. Statistics show that there are about 100 million converts of all kinds of religions, 85,000 religious locations (churches, temples, and the like), and 3,000 religious organizations or establishments. About 300,000 people take religious positions. Seventy-four colleges or institutes that focus on religious studies and personnel training are directly or indirectly affiliated with and/or sponsored by different religious organizations.

The following statistics give an overall picture of religion in China. There are about 13,000 Buddhism temples within its borders, of which about 3,000 are Tibetan temples. About 200,000 monks and nuns reside in temples, of whom 120,000 are Tibetan-branch lamas and nuns. There are also about 10,000 *biqius* (monks) and presbyters who belong to the Pali branch of Buddhism. There are about 1,500 Taoist temples in China with 25,000 Daoists who belong to the Qian (Heaven) school and the Kun (Earth) school. Islam is mainly preached among Huizu (Chinese Muslims), Uygur, and some other ethnic groups that represent a significant Islamic population. The total population of these minorities is only about 18 million. Currently, there are about 30,000 mosques in China, with about 40,000 imams and other religious leaders.

The number of Christians has increased noticeably. In 1950, there were about 4 million Christians (3 million Catholics and 1 million Protestants) in China. In 1982, according to the government, there were 3 million Protestants and about 3 million Catholics. There were probably another million or more that could be counted if one added "secret Christians," those who were never baptized but were believers in their own ways. Yet the church grew slightly faster than the growth of the general population, and nearly doubled during that time. According to the latest statistics, there are currently about 10 million Christians in China, with about 18,000 preachers. They share 12,000 churches or chambers and 25,000 religious gathering locations.

There are various religious associations in China, such as the Buddhism Association, the Daoism Association, the Islam Association, and the Christian Association. The government seems to have more confidence in the native religion, Daoism, and Buddhism, which has almost achieved a native status by adapting itself to Chinese culture, but it is more cautious and skeptical about Christianity, the Western religion still considered incommensurate with Chinese cultural values.

The statistics given here, according to which there are about 100 million believers, suggest that the spiritual life of the Chinese may be quite rich, and

China may be ranked among the countries with the biggest number of believers. Nevertheless, these statistics need to be treated with extra caution if reality is factored in. From a Western point of view, one can be surprised to discover that it is very hard to find a true believer in China. There are two reasons. One is that religion is still discriminated against in Chinese society. Any public identification with a certain religion can make an individual an outcast. Religion and religious activities are rather "invisible" in China.

The other is that many Chinese believers—due to Chinese cultural influence—demonstrate too many pragmatic concerns in their religious beliefs. One can find that many Chinese bow before any god they happen to encounter and burn joss sticks in any god's presence. For many Chinese, religion is just an exterior existence that has little or nothing to do with the soul or spirit. This Chinese cultural influence that makes a Chinese believer unique in a westerner's eyes can be explained from a Chinese approach to Daoism, Buddhism, and Confucianism. What Daoism "preaches" is the way for longevity, what Buddhism cares about are earthly sufferings, and what Confucianism concerns most is ethics and the code of social conduct. Clearly, they are all practical religions when compared with Judaism and Christianity.

Aside from the growing number of believers, there is a consensus that Chinese today in general are suffering from what scholars call a "belief crisis." In the first thirty-some years of the last five decades under the Communist regime, Maoism accounted for all the spiritual life of the Chinese, but soon after Mao's death people found that Maoism was fundamentally flawed, and the mansion of belief collapsed overnight. Left with a void in their beliefs, many Chinese turned to making money. With no proper gods to worship, they became true believers in "materialism": when one is in possession of money, one is in possession of everything. That is why people say that in the post-Mao era, China has been transformed into a nation without any beliefs. One result of economic reform is that many people are economically rich but spiritually poor.

See also Confucian Tradition and Christianity; Islam; Jews; Religion and Freedom of Religious Belief.

Bibliography

Ren, Yanli, ed., *Basic Knowledge of Chinese Catholicism* (Beijing: Religious Culture Press, 2000); *Selected Documents of Religious Works* (Beijing: Religious Culture Press, 1995).

Yihai Chen

State-Owned Enterprises (SOEs)

State-owned enterprises (SOEs) in China are owned by governments at different levels. Enterprises directly under the central government represent the highest level of government ownership, and the ranks decline to the provincial governments, municipal governments, and county-level governments. Technically, Chinese state-owned enterprises are also known as enterprises

Recent mass layoffs have forced people to seek other opportunities, such as opening the type of family restaurant shown here.

owned by the people (*quan min suo you zhi*). The state, or the government, thus serves on behalf of the people as the owner, or the principal, and the firms' managers are the agents.

State enterprises at the establishment of the People's Republic of China in 1949 produced 26.2 percent of the gross value of industrial output (GVIO), while private enterprises and proprietors produced more than 70 percent. By 1978, shares of all nonpublic enterprises had shrunk to zero, and China's GVIO was produced entirely by SOEs (77.6 percent) and collectively owned enterprises (COEs) (22.4 percent) after two decades of transforming "proprietors toward socialism" and merging private enterprises with public enterprises, the **Great Cultural Revolution**, and other political movements. Then came the period of opening-up and economic reforms in 1978.

Before the reform, state enterprises took orders from the government on what and how much to produce and then delivered the products at government-set prices. Market signals and consumer preferences were largely ignored. Within enterprises, employees had implicitly been guaranteed lifetime employment and a safety net of medical care, child care, housing, and retirement benefits. Many enterprises functioned as small societies and owned and operated hospitals, schools, housing departments, child care centers, and other service units. Moreover, employee remuneration was not tied to performance. As a result, Chinese state enterprises suffered from an antiproductivity macroenvironment and incentive crises within the firm. The economy was on the verge of bankruptcy at the end of the Cultural Revolution and before the reform.

The economic reform that was launched in 1978 first emphasized giving autonomies back to firms and tying remuneration to performance. Then the government instituted a "two-track system" in which SOEs must first fulfill the production quota and sell at the government-set prices and then could produce beyond quota and sell at market prices. Price controls have been gradually relaxed and now no longer exist except in a very few areas such as grain price supports. Other reform measures undertaken have included the contract responsibility system, leasing of enterprises, share system experimentation, corporatization, and allowing multiple ownerships of firms.

Steeper reforms toward privatization have taken place since the government decided to "let go of the small and hold on to the large," which was reemphasized by the Fifteenth Party Congress as a landmark strategy in the reform of state enterprises. By 2000, more than 80 percent of small and medium-sized enterprises completed their transformation through ownership diversification, which includes restructuring, mergers, leasing, contracting, joint-stock companies, and bankruptcies. Publicly listed companies are mostly large ones. In 2002, the government started to allow cross-national mergers between foreign and Chinese state enterprises and thus opened a new channel of reforming state enterprises.

To clear the entanglement of poorly performing state enterprises and bad-debt-ridden state banks, the government in 1999 also set up four state asset management companies, China Cinda, China Oriental, China Great Wall, and China Huarong, to purchase, manage, and dispose of the bad loans of four state banks (including their branches everywhere in the country). Instead of paying banks interest, the debtor enterprise pays dividends to the asset company. These loans are then sold as initial public offerings or transfers of ownership. The first transfer of ownership through auction was carried out by China Cinda in 2002. The debt-equity-swap scheme allows enterprises in question a fresh start without the burden of heavy debts, on the one hand, and allows banks to strengthen their balance sheets, on the other. Through the debt-equity swap, the four state banks have gotten rid of 1,400 billion yuan of nonperforming loans and have lowered their ratios of nonperforming loans.

The reforms have brought marked changes to the state sector. First, the share of GVIO produced by state enterprises decreased from 77.6 percent in 1978 to 18.05 percent in 2001. Second, SOEs have been consolidating through mergers, bankruptcies, and regrouping. The number of industrial SOEs declined from 118,000 in 1995 to 46,800 in 2001, while the size of employment per firm grew from 373 persons in 1995 to 528 in 2001. Third, China's state enterprises have nearly completed separating themselves from the social functions of providing housing, day care, hospitals, and schools for their employees. Fourth, as a generic term, "state enterprises" now often refer to SOEs with 100 percent state ownership and state-holding enterprises with mixed ownership. The government has also relaxed the restriction that the state in a state-holding enterprise must hold more than 50 percent of the shares (or the absolute majority) to a plurality. The proportion of GVIO produced by state-owned and state-holding enterprises in 2001 was 44.43 percent.

Regionally, the burden of the state enterprise problem is more prominent in old industrial centers such as Wuhan, Chongqing, Xi'an, Shengyang, and Harbin and in hinterland provinces. In locales such as Shanghai and Beijing, where state enterprises dominated but nonstate enterprises have developed most rapidly, the incremental nonstate economy has made the state enterprise problem much less pronounced. This is an apparent example of "incremental economy" at work. China's strategy of gradualism refers in large part to letting the state enterprises gradually recede from the economic stage either through direct privatization or by being minimized by the incremental nonstate-sector development.

Chinese state enterprises reportedly improved their profitability in three of the four years from 1999 to 2002. The improvement may be a short-term phenomenon, as many would argue, but it may also represent real economies that arise from changes in corporate governance and ownership structure, as many would counterargue. Regardless, China's state enterprises today face greater challenges to their survival because of fierce competition from both domestic private enterprises and foreign firms. Many entry barriers to previously state-monopolized industries such as telecommunications, banking, automobiles, insurance, and public utilities have been broken following China's entry into the World Trade Organization (WTO). Private enterprises have gained an unprecedented favorable developmental environment since the Sixteenth Congress of the Communist Party of China.

While China's inefficient SOEs will eventually disappear from the market, the pace at which this can happen may be slowed by ideological constraints, as well as feasibility conditions. The most important condition that will make free exit by SOEs more feasible is the establishment of a **social security system** that can provide for the unemployed and laid-off workers from the SOEs. According to the Chinese government, such a system is nearly established and is now able to provide current unemployed and laid-off urban workers with a "guaranteed minimum living."

See also Privately Owned Enterprises (POEs); World Trade Organization (WTO), China's Accession to.

Bibliography

Book of Chinese Economic Events on Reforming and Opening, vol. 1 (Beijing: Beijing Industrial University Press, 1993); Chen, Aimin, "Inertia in Reforming China's State-Owned Enterprises: The Case of Chongqing," *World Development* 26, no. 3 (March 1998): 479–495; National Bureau of Statistics of the PRC, *China Statistical Yearbook* (various issues, 1981–2004) (Beijing: China Statistics Press).

Aimin Chen

Statistics

See Consumption Patterns and Statistics of Living Conditions; Disease and Death Rates.

Suicide in China

Suicide has emerged as an increasingly serious social issue in China today because of the astonishing rates reported from the largest population in the world and the high risks for rural young women. Studies of Chinese suicide have been on the rise in the past two decades, partially because of the ever-growing availability of Chinese suicide data. In 1987, the World Health Organization (WHO), for the first time in history, publicized the Chinese vital statistics, including those for suicide, in its *World Health Statistics Annual*. In the past twenty years or so, researchers inside and outside of China have also obtained suicide data from various local governments in China, although suicide is still a politically sensitive topic in the nation.

Suicide Rates in China

A 1995 "World Mental Health Report" put the overall suicide rate in China at 17.1 per 100,000 population (Murray and Lopez 1996b). Other research conducted at the Harvard School of Public Health reported the Chinese suicide rate as 30.3 per 100,000 (Murray and Lopez 1996a). In a more recent study by Phillips, Li, and Zhang (2002), the Chinese suicide rate was reported as 22.2 per 100,000 population. Since the average of suicide rates in the world is 10.7, all these estimates of Chinese suicides are comparatively high. On the basis of Murray and Lopez's analysis, China, with 21.5 percent of the world's population, accounts for a staggering 43.6 percent of the 786,000 suicides worldwide, and suicide takes more than 330,000 Chinese lives each year (Brown 1997).

Easy access to lethal pesticides and lack of medical facilities have been blamed as the most prominent reasons why suicide rates are high in China. Nearly all rural households store pesticides, which make suicide means all too readily available in the Chinese countryside ("China: Suicide Riddles" 1997). Handguns, which are a primary means of suicide in the West, are not available to Chinese civilians and account for only about 0.1 percent of Chinese suicides (Zhang 1996). Although pesticides are usually less violent and less efficient than guns, they can be an effective means of suicide if they are easily available and if few hospitals are equipped to treat patients who have ingested them. No reliable figures yet exist for the ratio of attempted suicides to completed suicides in China. The difference between China and other countries may lie less in a higher rate of attempted suicide than in a higher rate of attempted suicides that succeed because of ineffective remedial action ("China: Suicide Riddles" 1997).

Gender Differences

Unlike any other country in the world, the suicide rate for Chinese women is about 40 percent higher than that for Chinese men: for each 100 male suicides, there are about 139 female suicides in China ("China: Suicide Riddles" 1997; Maris 1992; Phillips and Liu 1996). *The Global Burden of Disease*, a study conducted by the World Bank, the World Health Organization, and Harvard University, credits China with 56.6 percent of all female suicides worldwide, an astonishing figure since only 21 percent of the world's female population lives in China. The study also found that the rate of suicide among

Chinese women is nearly five times the world average (Macleod 1998). China is the only country in the world where women's suicides outnumber men's suicides. Explanations for the unique gender difference are many, but most have concentrated on the lower status of Chinese women, love, marriage, marital infidelity, family problems, and methods Chinese women use to commit suicide.

Rural versus Urban Differences

Contrary to the common belief that urbanization is bad for mental health and increases suicide rates, in China, rural people commit more suicides (Brown 1997; Pritchard 1996), and the rural rate is nearly three times the urban rate ("China: Urban Riddles" 1997). In other words, for each urban suicide, there are 2.77 rural suicides (Brown 1997). Although about 70 percent of the Chinese population lives in rural areas, rural people account for about 93 percent of suicides in the nation (Phillips and Liu 1996). These observations are in contrast to the situation in Western nations, where suicide has come to be associated with city dwelling (Brown 1997; Kowalski Faupel, and Starr 1987). Previous researchers have suggested two explanations for this unique difference between the rural and urban suicide rates: easy accessibility to the means in the countryside and the rural Chinese culture.

Age Differences

Suicide rates usually increase with age, but there are exceptions. Girard (1993) suggested four patterns of suicide rates as a function of age: upward sloping, downward sloping, bimodal, and convex. The upward-sloping pattern is a simple monotonic line of suicide rates going up steadily with increased age. The downward-sloping pattern has a peak suicide rate before the age of thirty-five, and the rate then goes down as age increases. The bimodal pattern has two peaks of suicide rates, one around the ages of twenty-five to thirty-four and the other over seventy-five. The convex pattern is an inverted U shape with a peak in suicide rates between thirty-five and seventy-four years of age (Girard 1993). The Chinese suicide pattern is generally a bimodal one (Ji 2000; Ji, Kleinman, and Becker 2001; Phillips, Li, and Zhang 2002; Zhang 2000), but the first peak of suicide rates is between fifteen and twenty-four instead of around the ages of twenty-five to thirty-four, as found in other societies (WHO 1995; Zhang 2000). Among young adults fifteen to thirty-four years of age, suicide is the leading cause of death, accounting for 19 percent of all deaths in this age group (Phillips, Li, and Zhang 2002). The rural population as reviewed earlier contributes substantially to the tremendously high rates of suicide by young people.

Culture Theory of Suicide

The uniqueness of Chinese suicide is that women commit more suicides than men, while the reverse is true in all other nations and areas of the world. Another characteristic of Chinese suicide is that rural rates are usually three to four times the urban rates. In the rural areas of China, young women aged between fifteen and thirty-four are at high risk. Therefore, rural young women constitute a special demographic group in China that is the most vulnerable to suicide. To account for this unique phenomenon, it is necessary to understand the environment and the culture this specific population is living in.

Unlike the Western world, where more than 90 percent of completed suicides had suffered mental disorders such as major depression and schizophrenia, less than half of the Chinese suicides had records of mental diseases prior to the suicidal event. Many of the risk factors from the West also exist in Chinese culture, such as lack of social support, stressful life events, and relative economic deprivation. However, some suicide buffers in the West can be risk factors in China, such as religion/religiosity and marriage for women. Further, the suicide rates in Chinese rural areas have increased due to the easy availability of suicidal means such as pesticides and the lack of medical facilities to rescue a suicide attempter.

One popular explanation for the high suicide rate among Chinese women is their low status in society. However, lower social status is not always associated with high suicide rates. In America, the suicide rate in the black population is much lower than that among whites. Also, Chinese women are not alone in the world in having lower social status; gender inequality exists in other cultures such as Japan, India, and the Muslim world. Women in these societies appear not to be at higher risk of suicide than men.

Researchers have found that gender ratios (men to women) of suicide rates are as high as 4 or 5, while those in Asian areas are about 1 or 2. The Chinese ratio of less than 1 (usually .80) is first a reflection of Asian culture and then of factors particular to China and Chinese culture. Confucianism, which advocates *xiao* (filial piety), may work against a filial man's suicide, especially when his parents are still alive. On the other hand, Confucianism's views on gender inequality and downgrading women may have contributed to women's suicide in the Confucian nations and areas in Asia. Thus Confucian ethics for men and values for women may account for the very low gender ratios of suicide rates in Asian areas.

But what has made China reverse the ratio so that women commit more suicides than men? The only difference between China and other Asian areas (Hong Kong and Taiwan) and nations (Japan, Korea, Vietnam, Singapore, and others) is in the political ideologies. China is now the only place where Communist ideologies rule. Gender equality, equal pay for equal work, the same opportunities for education, and the ideal egalitarianism of Chinese communism have provided Chinese women with beautiful pictures of life. However, Confucianism, deeply rooted in Chinese minds, especially of those less educated in the rural areas, still places women at the bottom of the social ladder. The discrepancies between the Communist ideals and the Confucian expectations may have created a frustrating and even hopeless situation among the rural young women, and it is this frustration and hopelessness that may have led women to suicide.

See also Taiwan, Suicide in.

Bibliography

Brown, Phyllida, "No Way Out," *New Scientist* 153, no. 2074 (March 22, 1997): 34; "China: Suicide Riddles," *Economist*, November 8, 1997, 45; Girard, Chris, "Age, Gender, and Suicide: A Cross-National Analysis," *American Sociological Review* 58, no. 4 (1993): 553–574; Ji, Jianlin, "Suicide Rates and Mental Health Services in Modern China," *Crisis* 21, no. 3 (2000): 118–121; Ji, J., A. Kleinman, and A. E. Becker, "Suicide in Contemporary China: A Review of China's Distinctive Suicide Demographics in Their Sociocultural Context," *Harvard Review of Psychology* 9, no. 1 (2001): 1–12; Kowalski, Gregory S., Charles E. Faupel, and Paul D. Starr, "Urbanism and Suicide: A Study of American Counties," *Social Forces* 66, no. 1 (1987): 85–101; Macleod, Lijia, "The Dying Fields," *Far Eastern Economic Review*, April 23, 1998, 62–63; Maris, Ronald, "Suicide," in *Encyclopedia of Sociology*, vol. 4 (New York: Macmillan, 1992); Murray, Christopher, and Alan Lopez, *The Global Burden of Disease* (Geneva, Switzerland: World Health Organization, 1996a); Murray and Lopez, *Global Health Statistics: A Compendium of Incidence, Prevalence, and Mortality Estimates for over 200 Conditions* (Cambridge, MA: Harvard University Press, 1996b); Phillips, M. R., X. Li, and Y. Zhang, "Suicide Rates in China, 1995–99," *Lancet* 359 (2002): 835–840; Pritchard, C., "Suicide in the People's Republic of China Categorized by Age and Gender: Evidence of the Influence of Culture on Suicide," *Acta Psychiatrica Scandinarica* 93 (1996) 362–367; World Health Organization, *World Health Statistics Annual* (Geneva, Switzerland: WHO, 1988–1995); Zhang, Jie, "Suicide in Beijing, China, 1992–1993," *Suicide and Life-Threatening Behavior* 26, no. 2 (1996): 175–180; Zhang, "Understanding Chinese Suicide with a Comparison of National Data," *American Review of China Studies* 1, no.1 (2000): 9–29; Zhang, Jie, and Jin Shenghua, "Determinants of Suicide Ideation: A Comparison of Chinese and American College Students," *Adolescence* 31 (1996): 451–467.

Jie Zhang

Sun Li (1913–)

Sun Li is a well-known novelist and prose writer in modern China. He was born on April 6, 1913, in Anping County, Hebei Province. In his early teens, he was influenced by Lu Xun (1881–1936) and some other modern Chinese writers. Upon graduation from middle school, Sun left his hometown for Beijing and worked there for a few years. In 1936, he returned to Hebei Province and taught at an elementary school. He went to Yan'an in 1944 and worked and studied at Lu Xun Institute of Literature and Art. After 1949, he first worked at *Tianjin Daily* and then ceased writing for many years because of illness. After 1977, he was mainly engaged in writing prose essays and literary reviews.

Sun's writing career can be traced back to the 1940s. While he was in Yan'an, he published several stories, including "Hehuadian Lake" and "Luhuadang Marsh," that immediately caught the attention of Chinese readers. *Changeable Situations* was written in the early 1950s. This novel concentrated on the life of five families during the early stage of the Anti-Japanese War (1937–1945) and meticulously presented both the living conditions and the inner world of different social strata at that time. Although the historical background of the novel was the traumatic war, Sun's main focus was not on the cruel and bloody scenes of battles, but rather on the ideological changes and the awakening of his characters. Moreover, he used a calm and humorous tone to depict the plots and characters. The year 1956 saw the publication of his novelette *Stories of the Tie and Mu Families*. In this work, through the friendship and breaking-up of two families, Sun unfolded the profound impact that the agricultural cooperative movement exerted upon the countryside and the Chinese peasantry in the early 1950s.

Sun's best-known anthology is *Scenes of Baiyangdian Lake* (1958). This collection of short stories and prose essays was devoted to rural life during the Anti-Japanese War, the War of Liberation (1945–1949), and the early 1950s. The pictures of the times and history, the poetic and graceful language, and the vividly portrayed characters resonated in the hearts of many readers.

In almost all his works, Sun strove to seek and present the true, the good, and the beautiful in society. He paid great attention to exploring his characters' innermost souls and the progress of the times, not through certain significant social events, but through certain ordinary things or daily household affairs. He preferred to structure his plots according to the developments of his characters' emotions and personality, and this attempt eventually added a touch of prose writing to his fiction. Sun's unique style is so widely accepted that it has become a banner of a new literary school in modern Chinese literature, the Hehuadian school. Sun also published some anthologies after 1977; however, they are not as influential as his early writings.

See also Anticorruption Literature and Television Dramas; Avant-garde Literature; Experimental Fiction; Great Cultural Revolution, Literature during; Intellectuals, Political Engagement of (1949–1978); Intellectuals, Political Engagement of (1978–Present); Literary Policy for the New China; Literature of the Wounded; Misty Poetry; Modern Pop-Satire; Neorealist Fiction and Modernism; Pre–Cultural Revolution Literature; Revolutionary Realism and Revolutionary Romanticism; Root-Searching Literature; Sexual Freedom in Literature.

Bibliography

Guo, Zhigang, *Biography of Sun Li* (Chongqing: Chongqing People's Publishing House, 1955).

Dela X. Jiao

Sustainable Growth and Development

In 1979, China set a goal to reach a per capita income of $800 and total GDP of 200 percent greater than the level of 1980 and has achieved both. Now it aims to build a "comprehensively well-off society" (*quan mian xiao kang she hui*) in which per capita GDP will not only reach $3,000, but will also do so in a less skewed distribution. This "comprehensively well-off society," as well as an even more comprehensively better-off society beyond the set income level of $3,000, requires two essential elements: sustaining economic growth and maintaining equitable distribution, or, simply put, it requires sustainable growth and development. How China can reach this goal is an issue of extreme broadness that is approached here from an economics point of view.

The busy streets of Shanghai (shown here) and other cities are where Chinese economic development has been most dramatic and sustained over the last two decades.

The growth of the economy must come from the urban and rural sectors that form the substance of the economy. In the urban sector, the most pressing economic problem is further reform of the state enterprises and the development of private enterprises, because this structural change has been the driving force for China's growth in the past two decades. China has remarkably reduced the role of the state sector. In 1978, when economic reform started, China's industrial structure was one of complete dominance by public enterprises. By 2001, the share of gross value of industrial output (GVIO) produced by state enterprises of 100 percent state ownership had quickly shrunk to 18.05 percent, whereas private enterprises had regained their ground and produced one-third of the nation's GDP in 2002. Despite the achievements, however, private businesses in the urban sector are still effectively supplementary to **state-owned enterprises (SOEs)** and face entry barriers to industries that are considered vital to the national economy and continue to be dominated by the state, such as petroleum, automobiles, banking and financial institutions, public utilities, communications, and publishing. The government's recent permissions for private enterprises to enter some industries that had been off-limits to them are to some extent symbolic gestures. It has remained a fact that private businesses encounter the most difficulties in obtaining bank loans and other forms of financing. Moreover, private enterprises have been smaller in size measured by both assets and employment, which has prevented them from becoming publicly listed and from entry into industries that require scale economies. Meanwhile, the reform of SOEs encounters much resistance within firms and ideological barriers from the government. The **corporate governance** structure under the drive to build a modern enterprise system is characterized by continuing heavy government interference, on the one hand, and "insider control," on the other hand.

In the rural sector, the "*san nong* problem" (the "three ag problem") is widely being acknowledged as the most pressing issue. It refers to the problem of agriculture as a sector (*nongye*), agricultural (or rural) place as a residential area (*nongcun*), and the agricultural population (*nongmin*). This problem arises because the sector has a low level of mechanization and massive disguised unemployment; it has been the most closed sector and thus the most vulnerable to international competition following China's World Trade Organization (WTO) entry; and the urban-rural income disparity, measured by the ratio of urban per capita disposable income to rural per capita net income, has worsened from 2.57 in 1978 to 3.0 in 2002. Solving the problem implies that China's agricultural sector needs to restructure and become more competitive internationally, that China's countryside needs to industrialize and urbanize, and that China's agricultural population needs to catch up with its urban counterpart in income distribution. To cope with the "three ag problem," restructuring toward idiosyncratically Chinese and higher-value-added products, developing processing industries, and providing agricultural support have been emphasized by governments at all levels. Land policies have become more flexible, at least in practice, and land contracts with farmers have recently been lengthened to thirty years. Measures have also been taken to directly raise rural incomes. The government, for example, has launched the "return cultivated land to forest" (*tuigeng huanlin*) program and has begun to implement a nationwide reform in the rural sector to reduce levies of taxes and fees that have burdened farmers and become a severe source of social instability. But such efforts are only a start. The most challenging task toward solving the problem is to accelerate the pace of urbanization and create an estimated minimum of 15 million nonfarm jobs a year, according to one estimate, for the next thirty years in order to eliminate disguised rural unemployment. Unless the rural sector catches up with the urban sector, sustainable growth and development are in jeopardy.

Meanwhile, a set of special establishments is required to ensure the growth of the rural and urban sectors in an efficient and equitable fashion that stresses the two essential functions of resource allocation and income distribution. Among the components of this supporting system is establishing an effective **social security system**. In the transition from a socialist economy to a market economy, the system is needed to socialize the responsibilities of China's state enterprises so that failing enterprises can exit the industry or be privatized. The lack of such a system in the past has been responsible for the continued operation of China's money-losing enterprises and for restricted labor mobility because employees have been reluctant to leave their current jobs, to which their social benefits are tied. The system also helps redistribute income and reduce poverty.

Progress has been made in establishing the social security system. Currently, socialized pension disbursement, in which retirees collect their pension at local banks and post offices, has reached almost all of the approximately 33 million urban retirees. Moreover, most SOEs have stopped operating housing, day care, schools, and hospitals. China's urban housing market has developed rapidly in recent years, and private home buyers have formed the majority of the demand. In the urban sector, the "guarantee of minimum living"(*di bao*), which provides merely enough for the recipient to be fed and clothed without provision for housing, education of children, medical expenses, and heating in northern China, has reached almost 100 percent of urban residents in need of welfare. But the system is severely underfunded if the implicit promises of housing, medical care, and retirement made to many urban workers are taken into account and is virtually nonexistent in the rural sector. Out of the total rural population of more than 700 million, only 4.04 million residents have been helped by some kind of social welfare funding, primarily those who are jobless, disabled, and without children or family members to support them. This lack of a social welfare system in the rural sector is another source of inequality between China's urban and rural sectors beyond income differentials. Moreover, state enterprises are hardly free to quit their businesses, and many urban employees who have been laid off have been left without proper care because of lack of contract enforcement and orderly legal and social services.

Establishing an integrated and efficient labor and resource market is also essential because it directly affects the way resources are allocated, and current inefficiencies in this market are responsible for many of the problems in the two main sectors. In the urban sector, the resource market lends little support to the development of private enterprises in obtaining land-use rights and bank loans, becoming publicly listed, and issuing corporate bonds. Between urban and rural sectors, immobility of labor has been the main culprit in the dichotomous development of the two sectors and the "three ag problem." The banking sector, while unsupportive of private enterprises, is notoriously bad debt ridden and entangled deeply in the problems of state enterprises. The capital market is largely symbolic, with around 1,300 firms, almost all state owned and publicly listed, and private enterprises are largely not allowed to issue bonds. The **labor market** is young, and market services, information flow, and job retraining for the laid-off are limited discrimination is rampant, and mobility is restricted. In fact, the segmentation of the market between the urban and rural sectors is primarily responsible for the dichotomous development of the two sectors and the increasing urban-rural income disparity.

Finally, efficient functioning of these elements directly involves the shifting and changing role of the government. The Chinese government, in addition to its normal functions in any economy, needs to further withdraw from the management of state enterprises, service private enterprises, support the agriculture sector, smooth labor market transactions, and establish an effective social security system. Meanwhile, the government must be supervised by the legal system to carry out its role properly, and the supervisory function of the legal infrastructure must first be initialized by the government as well. Moreover, during China's economic transition, where the lack of laws and regulations and their enforcement, as well as the lack of policy transparency, is a common phenomenon, establishing an effective legal system is of special urgency for the market to function efficiently. Banning discrimination against women and rural migrants in the labor market, for example, is not only necessary as a matter of justice, but also beneficial for achieving greater labor mobility and more efficient allocation of resources. The arbitrary leving of fees and taxes by local officials, which has so pervasively burdened and angered rural residents that it has become a source of not only rural poverty but also social instability, must be banned and new tax laws made. The system is also indispensable for safeguarding the property rights of private entrepreneurs and consumers, outlawing piracy of state assets, and fighting corruption.

In short, China has achieved remarkably in each of the areas discussed here, but much remains to be done. Sustainable growth and development of the Chinese economy depend on how further progress is made in these areas.

See also Agricultural Reform; Banking and Financial System Reform; Legal Infrastructure Development and Economic Development; Regions of China, Uneven Development of; Rural-Urban Divide; Urban Housing Privitization.

Bibliography

Chen, Aimin, "The Structure of Chinese Industry and the Impact from China's WTO Entry," *Comparative Economic Studies*, spring 2002, 72–98; Chen, "Urbanization and Disparities in China: Challenges of Growth and Development," *China Economics Review* 13, no. 4 (2002): 407–411.

Aimin Chen

T

Taiwan, Constitutional Reform in

Constitutional reform has been an important part of Taiwan's democratization since the 1980s. The original Constitution of the Republic of China was created in 1947 when the civil war between the Kuomintang (KMT, or Nationalist Party) government and the Chinese Communist Party was under way. During the first session of the National Assembly in March 1948, many Assembly members argued that the new constitution authorized too little power for the president, who was Jiang Jieshi (Chiang Kai-shek) at the time, to deal with the civil war. They established some Temporary Provisions Effective during the Period of National Mobilization for Suppression of the Communist Rebellion and froze parts of the Constitution effective after May 9, 1948, giving the president special power to deal with "emergencies."

After 1949, the KMT government retreated to Taiwan with the Temporary Provisions. The provisions required the president to call a special session of the National Assembly before December 25, 1950, to discuss the changes to the Constitution, but the **Korean War** cut that effort short. It was not until February 19, 1954, that the National Assembly ever got a chance to call its second session. At the meeting, it was agreed that the Temporary Provisions should be extended, and a bill was passed with the following major points:

1. The president has the authority to issue "emergency orders" without approval from the legislative branch of government.
2. The National Assembly gives up its power to create and amend the Constitution and allows the president to decide what is necessary.
3. The two-term limit on the president is no longer binding.
4. The president has the power to create his National Security Council (NSC) to propose and supervise major national policies.

The Jie Yan Fa (martial law) dominated the period. On December 10, 1948, the KMT government announced martial law throughout China. The next year, Taiwan was also under martial law. This martial law denied many constitutional freedoms, such as personal liberty, freedom of travel and press, and freedom of assembly and organization. The KMT government insisted that it was an absolute necessity to strengthen national security in the face of a pending Communist invasion and to prevent the Taiwan independence movement. Taiwan's survival was the biggest issue, and without it there was little room to talk about democracy.

It was not until 1987 that the KMT government decided to lift martial law. Many factors caused this change. People had gotten used to the local elections that never stopped even during the martial law era. Taiwan's economic takeoff also brought about wealth, as well as political consciousness. Taiwan's comparatively high education level enabled people to have better organizational ability. International development also helped. After the United States formalized its relationship with mainland China (1979), the pro-Taiwan force in the U.S. Congress passed the Taiwan Relations Act to help Taiwan, but even this friendly act showed signs of Americans' unhappiness with the lack of civil rights in Taiwan. The democratic reforms that were going on in neighboring countries such as South Korea also put pressure on the Taiwanese leaders. Mainland China's policy change from the earlier "We must liberate Taiwan!" to "peaceful unification" (though it never excluded military action) also started the "thaw" of the confrontation across the Taiwan Strait and gave the Taiwanese government more room to consider lifting martial law.

But the biggest force behind the decision was the development of Taiwan's political opposition. During the martial law era, these groups had gained strength through local elections. In the late 1970s, softened government policies allowed the publication of many political journals and most street demonstrations. The opposition strongly challenged the KMT in the 1980 election and in September 1986 even established a new party, the Democratic Progressive Party (DPP). This development forced the KMT government to think about political liberalization.

The KMT leaders' determination to change from authoritarian rule also played an important role. They were already talking about lifting martial law and the ban on political parties before the DPP was born. After the DPP's establishment, the government did not suppress it and instead tried to establish communication with it. On October 15, 1986, the KMT Central Committee under President Jiang Jingguo passed a new National Security Act and a modified Civil Organization Act. In late June 1987, the Legislative Yuan officially declared the end of martial law, and the Executive Yuan also announced the end of more than thirty executive orders associated with martial law.

In March 1990, some National Assembly deputies proposed increasing the authority and funding of the Assembly. To many people, the deputies were increasing their own power without popular support. In March 1990, Taipei students started a demonstration and called for disbanding the Assembly, the end of the Temporary Provisions, and a National Affairs Conference to schedule Taiwan's democratic reform. On March 21, they even started a hunger strike. The government quickly backed down and agreed to call the conference, which officially opened on June 24, signaling a very important beginning of Taiwan's political reform.

The representatives from the KMT, the DPP, nonpartisan groups, and academics at the conference discussed two important issues: amplifying constitutional rule and unifying the country. They reached a few consensuses, including the end of "the Period of National Mobilization for Suppression of the Communist Rebellion," the repeal of the Temporary Provisions, and the authority of the National Assembly to carry out constitutional reform. They also set up the procedure for reform: the first phase of reform would concentrate on the agenda, while the second would carry out the revision of the Constitution. During the National Affairs Conference (NAC), more than 100 discussion sessions were held that involved more than 13,000 people from different ranks. But the ruling KMT and the opposition DPP could not reach agreement on many issues. For example, the KMT insisted that the NAC was only a form of consultation, while the DPP argued that the NAC agreements should have binding power on the government.

The first phase of reform started in April 1991, but soon the DPP representatives decided that the amendments presented by the KMT could not represent the DPP's ideas. They threatened to give up negotiation and called for mass demonstrations. The threat forced the KMT to include some of the DPP's ideas in the KMT plans. By April 22, ten amendments had passed the Assembly, and on April 30, President Li Denghui officially announced the abolition of the Temporary Provisions and the adoption of the new amendments to the Constitution, which have the following major points:

1. They establish the procedure of elections for all representatives in the government to reflect the political reality in Taiwan.
2. They set up agendas for the second National Assembly meeting on constitutional reforms.
3. They modify the procedure of the president's emergency executive orders—he must present them to the Legislative Yuan for approval.
4. They finalize the "sunset" procedure for the National Security Council and the Bureau of National Security.

Heated debates never stopped. The KMT insisted that the purpose of the reform was to amend the Constitution, while the DPP held that the Constitution needed to be rewritten. This of course reflected the ideals of the two parties: unification of China versus Taiwan independence. The most controversial issue was the National Security Council, a superagency in charge of all systems of Taiwan's military, police, intelligence, and secret services. According to the new amendment, the NSC was to be put under the president. This not only greatly increased his power but also made the NSC avoid supervision by the Legislative Yuan.

The 1991 year-end National Assembly election gave the KMT a landslide victory and the necessary overwhelming majority (three-fourths) to enable it to lead the next phase of reform. On March 20, 1992, the Second National Assembly started, and conflict soon developed. The DPP representatives repeatedly interrupted the meeting and even engaged the KMT members in fist fights. On April 16, the DPP mobilized a large-scale demonstration in Taipei. On May 4, the DPP delegation simply walked out of the meeting. The remaining KMT members continued the meeting and on May 7, passed eight more constitutional amendments.

The second phase of reform increased the power of the National Assembly to approve presidential nominations to the Judicial, Examination, and Control Yuan. It also decided, starting from 1996, that the president would be elected directly by voters, not the National Assembly anymore. Though the president's term shrank from six to four years, he enjoyed more power: he could nominate more officials in the central government. The reform also increased the difficulties of presidential impeachment: one-sixth of the National Assembly's members could propose the impeachment, but they needed a two-thirds majority to start it. It also changed the organizations and the functions of other branches of the government. Because the National Assembly only set the general idea of direct election but never explained how to implement it, a third constitutional reform was needed.

The third phase of constitutional revision began in March 1994. The KMT quickly established the so-called KMT Eight Points, which called for maintaining the five-power structure of the government, with necessary adjustments, and no major change to the Constitution, only a few minor amendments. The DPP also presented its own Six Points, mostly in opposition to the KMT proposals. Conflict immediately emerged. The DPP members again interrupted the meeting, sometimes physically. When the meeting was ready to vote, the DPP representatives withdrew from the meeting in protest of the "abusive KMT majority." The KMT members, on July 29, quickly passed another ten amendments, and Li Denghui announced their adoption on 1 August.

The third revision combined the eighteen earlier amendments into the ten new ones. They included the direct election of the president by 1996, the creation of the positions of president and vice president in the National Assembly, and adjustments to the National Assembly's authority—the power to fill the vice president's vacancy, to propose the impeachment of the president, to discuss and approve the proposed presidential impeachment by the Control Yuan, to amend the Constitution and to approve the constitutional revision proposals by the Legislative Yuan, and to (dis)approve the president's nominations.

There was much criticism. Because the presidential and vice presidential candidates pair themselves up to run and the pair that receives the most votes wins the election, it becomes possible for the so-called minority president to be elected due to coalitions and alliances among weaker political groups, since only a simple majority is required. Also, the president has the power to nominate four out of five branches of the government (the Executive, Judicial, Control, and Examination Yuans), which gives him more power and creates a conflict of interest. He also becomes the chairman of the National Security Council, and the head of the Executive Yuan is the vice chairman. The president has great power and does not have to be responsible to the legislative body, while the head of the Executive Yuan (the vice chair of the council), who has to respond to the Legislative Yuan, has little power in the council.

President Li Denghui called a National Development Conference (NDC) in December 1996 that attracted more than 170 representatives from different groups. Many critics suspected Li Denghui's intention. He seemed to be in a hurry to move the presidency toward a position as both the head of the nation and the highest executive officer of the government, something in contradiction with the current Constitution. He also seemed worried about the challenge from Taiwan's provincial government.

At the conference, the KMT leadership encountered new problems. The **New Party (NP)**, a group of former KMT members who had split from the party earlier, challenged KMT ideas, including the KMT definition of "central government system," the election procedure, and the elimination of the provincial government. The NP members specifically insisted on a minimum of constitutional revision to keep the document's authority and continuity. They demanded that the head of the Executive Yuan have the power of cosignature with the president and that the National Security Council be put under the Executive Yuan. After unsuccessful negotiations with the two major parties, the New Party decided to boycott the conference.

Bypassing the New Party, the KMT and DPP passed twenty-two reform consensuses. These include the presidential power to appoint the head of the Executive Yuan without approval from the Legislative Yuan and the power to disband the Legislative Yuan, and the Executive Yuan head's power to ask the president to disband the Legislative Yuan (though the Legislative Yuan could also raise a nonconfidence vote against the head of the Executive Yuan). They agreed to freeze the provincial election, reform the current election procedures, and promote "positive" communication among political parties.

The Legislative Yuan's power is reduced. The president can appoint, not nominate, the head of the Executive Yuan. Even if the Legislative Yuan is determined to remove the executive head, the president can simply appoint another "his man." He can also disband the Legislative Yuan when he feels it "necessary." The power of the Executive Yuan as the "highest executive branch" of the government is disappearing since the head of the Executive Yuan has no power of his own. The president also obtained the new power to nominate members of the Judicial, Control, and Examination Yuan.

After the National Development Conference, the fourth revision of the Constitution started on May 5, 1997, in which conflicts among different parties and among different factions of each party dominated the debate. Within the KMT, criticism never stopped on the top leaders' predesigned plans. The DPP leadership also faced challenges from within the party, with two versions of reform plans. The New Party kept up its criticism of both the KMT and DPP plans. Outside the meeting, concerned citizens organized demonstrations in protest of political parties' "using constitutional reform to expand their power." To put things under control, top leaders of the KMT and DPP tried to discipline their party members. Using a "big stick plus carrot" approach, they finally silenced most critics. The two big parties also coordinated their actions to defeat other opposition groups. Seeing their opposition collapsing, the New Party representatives issued a statement on July 18, declaring their refusal of the KMT-DPP amendments and collectively walked out of the conference. The KMT and DPP members quickly passed eleven new constitutional amendments, ending the fourth try at constitutional revision.

After four revisions, Taiwan's constitutional structure moved increasingly from the earlier "cabinet system" toward the "presidential system," abandoning the principle "the president rules but does not administer; the head of the Executive Yuan administers but does not rule." This change makes the president replace the head of the Executive Yuan as the "highest executive officer," while the Legislative Yuan has very little means to handle the situation. Besides, the president also gains authority to disband the legislative body and control over personnel issues in four of the five branches of the central government, and there is nobody to check and balance his power. In September 1999, the Third National Assembly made another try, modifying some of the constitutional amendments passed earlier. Since 1999, a few more minor changes have been made, some of them seemingly aimed at mending the loopholes left by earlier revisions. Though the changes have moved far beyond the original goal of "minor revisions," discussions on further reform have been going on into the new century. People in Taiwan are still trying to make their constitutional rule really work.

See also Chen Shuibian (1950–   ); Minority Women in Xinjiang and Taiwan; Taiwan, Development of Democracy in; Taiwan, Economic Transition of; Taiwan, Education Reform in; Taiwan, Ethnicity and Ethnic Policies of; Taiwan, Financial Relations with the Mainland; Taiwan, Income Distribution in; Taiwan, Labor and Labor Laws; Taiwan, Suicide in; Taiwan, Trade Relations with the Mainland; Taiwan Strait Crisis, Evolution of.

Bibliography

Chin, Ko-Lin, *Heijin: Organized Crime, Business, and Politics in Taiwan* (Armonk, NY: M.E. Sharpe, 2003); Roy, Denny, *Taiwan: A Political History* (Ithaca, NY: Cornell University Press, 2003).

Xiansheng Tian

Taiwan, Development of Democracy in

One of the most dramatic sociopolitical changes in East Asia in the late twentieth century was a full-scale democratic transition in Taiwan. In the mid-1980s, the signs of political liberalization began to appear when the ban on opposition political parties was lifted and the system of direct and open election for political offices was introduced at local levels and was made open to all political parities. By the early 1990s, the open election system was extended to the selection of all the members of the Legislative Yuan. Soon after that, the system expanded even further to include competetive races for high-ranking government officials such as Taiwan's provincial governor and the mayors of Taipei and Kaohsiung, the two key cities in Taiwan. In the spring of 1996, Taiwan held a popular presidential election, the first in the history of Taiwan, to have its president elected by open ballot. At the dawn of the twenty-first century, Taiwan appears to have an entirely new sociopolitical landscape characterized by an open and free society with a contesting multiparty system operating through an effective mechanism of direct elections. The highlight of this transition was marked by the triumph of the Democratic Progressive Party (DPP) in the 2000 presidential election that peacefully put an end to the rule of the Kuomintang (KMT), the Nationalist Party, over Taiwan during the past fifty years. Under Huntington's procedural definition of democracy, the change in Taiwan is indeed very impressive in terms of interparty contests and popular participation in voting. With the amendment of the Constitution that ensures a free press and free speech, Taiwan is obviously among those regions in the world that ride on what Huntington depicts as "the third wave" of democratization (Huntington 1991).

While the dramatic democratic change in Taiwanese society is acclaimed, it has also been noticed in recent years that Taiwan's democracy is increasingly engulfed in an ethnonationalist movement called "Taiwanization" that seeks to break away from the domain of "one China." Taiwan's current status as a de facto independent sovereign state is a historical outcome of the Chinese civil war in the late 1940s in which Communist forces under **Mao Zedong** overthrew the Nationalist rule over China and drove Jiang Jieshi (Chiang Kai-shek) and his followers to the offshore island of Taiwan. Yet despite their separate political entities, the two governments across the Taiwan Strait have long declared that there is only one China and have placed unification on their political agenda. Until the late 1980s, the Taiwanese authorities under the rule of Jiang Jieshi and then his son had never given up their claims to legitimate representation of the whole of China, including both Taiwan and mainland China. Taiwan's consensus with mainland China over "one China" status has also gained long-term recognition from the U.S. government since 1972, when Richard Nixon visited China, and has further been observed by many other countries in the world. Throughout the 1990s, the shared support for "one China" in Taiwan collapsed under the growing Taiwanization movement, encouraged by the then president, Li Denghui (Lee Teng-hui), who succeeded Jiang Jingguo (Chiang Ching-kuo) after the latter's death. In 2000, the Taiwanization movement gained more force and popularity when the proindependence DPP became the ruling party.

Closer examination reveals that Taiwan's journey to democracy does not involve restructuring political institutions alone. It also embraces the ethnonationalist agenda to break away from the historically established "one China" consensus. Because of this hybrid nature of political development, Taiwan's democracy cannot be studied with an eye only to institutional reforms. The complicity of Taiwanization in the advance to democracy should also be taken into account. Such an examination shows how Taiwan's ongoing democratic consolidation is fraught with daunting challenges down the road.

First, democracy and Taiwanization can hardly play complementary roles to each other. Theoretically and empirically, democracy and ethnonationalism are two separate concepts and realities. Democracy is the legitimate ideal of a modern state, or what Montesquieu and Rousseau described as a set of liberal values and norms that embody "the general will of the people." Democracy, in other words, upholds the interests and welfare of all people within a nation-state. Ethnonationalism is a social movement with the political agenda of attaining self-determination or independence for one particular group only. Not surprisingly, as world history shows, democracy is not an inherent companion of ethnonationalism, and neither is the rise of ethnonationalism a product of democratization. In fact, ethnocentrism is a natural enemy of a civil society—the cornerstone of democracy—because ethnocentrism breeds hostility toward out-groups. This is particularly true when national identity is built upon one ethnic affinity so that other, different ethnic groups are shut out of the democratic process (Markoff 1996). This problem has already begun to emerge in today's Taiwanese society, where the so-called indigenous Taiwanese oppose the Chinese from the mainland. Paradoxically, while democratization is serving as a stabilizing force to bring peace and prosperity to society, Taiwanization stands in the way as a countervailing force to undermine the progress of democratic transition.

Another daunting challenge facing Taiwan is its inescapable fate of being bound by the "one China" factor, which revolves around the sensitive relations between Taiwan and mainland China. The risk posed by Taiwanization to a smooth democratic consolidation is the unyielding threat from mainland China, which holds unification with Taiwan as its ultimate national goal, particularly now that China is rising as a strong political and economic power in the region. The issue is not that undemocratic China would not tolerate democratic Taiwan, but that the conceptual ambiguity that overlaps democracy and Taiwanization makes Beijing discount Taiwan's democratization. What it sees happening in Taiwan are rulers attempting to use democratic legitimation as a shield against unification and as an excuse to negate the cultural and ancestral roots shared by all people on both sides of the Taiwan Strait. What really concerns Beijing is not a localized democracy in Taiwan, but the island's attempt to break away from the commonly held consensus of "one China." Naturally, China is determined to prevent Taiwan from achieving independence. Geopolitically, China's rising status as a superpower will undoubtedly make it difficult for Taiwan to gain worldwide support for its move toward independence. Therefore, a full-scale ethnonationalist mobilization will create problems for the people in Taiwan because it will harm their peaceful democratic consolidation.

The future of Taiwan may depend much on its success at achieving democratic consolidation rather than establishing an independent "Taiwan Republic." The pursuit of the latter could turn into a bumpy journey leading to nowhere but a destination of uncertainty. World history shows that a misguided ethnonationalist movement could disrupt a progressive democratic transition and even reverse the process. If Taiwan's democracy is subordinated to Taiwanzation, the prospects for a stable society may be hampered. The overarching geopolitical power of China would augur more tensions and the threat of war for Taiwan. When democracy cannot ensure social stability and reduce the anxiety of its people, it will naturally lose its appeal to the general populace. Furthermore, because of the lack of historical evidence, it would be very difficult for the Taiwanese authorities to make a legitimate claim that the Taiwanese identity is a unique cultural heritage.

A promising prospect for Taiwan's democratic transition is to adhere to the "One China" policy. By engaging in direct unification negotiations with mainland China, Taiwan's democracy will have its full potential on display, and this will lead to a positive change in the future relations between Taiwan and China. Further, Taiwan still holds its competitive geopolitical edge, which does not lie in its drive toward independence but in its position as a de facto independent territorial entity in relation to China. Unlike Hong Kong and Macao, both of which are within China now, Taiwan is not a colony to be negotiated between China and a third-party country. Also, Taiwan is one of the strongest free-market economies in Asia, for it is not only highly modernized but has an advanced industrial/manufacturing base, and its trading economy is the world's fourteenth largest. Most important, the ongoing democratization will garner greater international support and put Taiwan in a better position to negotiate with Beijing for its future. It would be hard to imagine that China could get away with world condemnation if it attacks Taiwan without any legitimate reasons to justify the war.

In conclusion, all advantages from unification may not necessarily accrue to mainland China, because the Beijing authority would be under increased pressure to make more concessions to Taiwan to come closer to Taiwan's demands. In fact, the whole process of negotiation would speed up political reforms in mainland China, where some incremental changes toward democracy have taken place in recent years. As some scholars have rightly pointed out, the most viable solution to preventing belligerent confrontation between Taiwan and mainland China depends on the progress of democracy in both places.

See also Chen Shuibian (1950–   ); Minority Women in Xinjiang and Taiwan; New Party (NP) (Taiwan); Taiwan, Constitutional Reform in; Taiwan, Economic Transition of; Taiwan, Education Reform in; Taiwan, Ethnicity and Ethnic Policies of; Taiwan, Financial Relations with the Mainland; Taiwan, Income Distribution in; Taiwan, Labor and Labor Laws; Taiwan, Suicide in; Taiwan, Trade Relations with the Mainland; Taiwan Strait Crisis, Evolution of.

Bibliography

Huntington, Samuel P., *The Third Wave: Democratization in the Late Twentieth Century* (Norman: University of Oklahoma Press, 1991); Markoff, John, *Waves of Democracy: Social Movement and Political Change* (Thousand Oaks, CA: Pine Forge Press, 1996).

Jieli Li

Taiwan, Economic Transition of

When Jiang Jieshi's (Chiang Kai-shek's) Nationalist government moved to Taiwan, its economy was characterized by high inflation, low productivity, and an influx of population from the mainland. About 2 million people moved across the strait from the mainland. In 1948, the inflation rate reached 1,145 percent. Only a few industries remained from the heavy bombing of Allied forces during the war, including sugar refining and some textile manufacturing. The first thing the Taiwanese government did after the move was to carry out land reform, which limited rent to a maximum of 37.5 percent of crops, distributed public land, and purchased and resold land from large landlords. The government also introduced a new monetary system and initiated interest-rate, foreign exchange, and trade controls. The inflation rate was reduced to 181 percent in 1949. U.S. aid poured in to help the Taiwanese economy's recovery and future takeoff. From 1951 to 1965, economic and military aid from the United States averaged U.S. $100 million a year, 36.8 percent of its total annual investment. Much of the aid was used in infrastructure and the agricultural sectors. Farmers were supplied with fertilizer, seeds, pesticides, training, and tax credits. The growth rate of real GDP reached 12 percent in 1952.

In 1953, the Taiwanese government implemented its First Four-Year Economic Plan. Its emphasis on an import-substitution policy aimed at making Taiwan self-sufficient by producing inexpensive consumer goods, processing imported raw materials, and restricting other imports. By 1959, 90 percent of exports were agriculture or food related. Increased production and higher income resulted in low inflation and capital accumulation, because importing food was unnecessary. Realizing Taiwan's narrow domestic market, the Taiwanese government adopted a second policy of export promotion in the late 1950s and continued it throughout the 1960s. From 1961 to 1964, Taiwan's exports averaged a growth rate of 31 percent per year. The economic growth rate rose steadily and in 1964 reached a double-digit figure (12.6 percent) for the first time since 1952.

With the Fourth Four-Year Economic Plan in 1965, Taiwan began its first economic plan without economic aid from the United States. In 1966, the share of heavy industry in total industrial output reached 52 percent, exceeding that of light industry for the first time. By 1968, the output of the manufacturing industry hit 24 percent, for the first time exceeding the share of the agriculture industry (22 percent). At the same time, Taiwan's economy became increasingly dependent on the United States and Japan. Its share of exports to the United States hit 26 percent and its share to Japan was 18 percent by 1967. Taiwan also began a continuous trade surplus with the United States in 1968.

The 1970s were a period in which Taiwan experienced major political and economic turmoil. Taiwan was replaced by mainland China in the United Nations in 1971. Its diplomatic relations with Japan, the Philippines, and the United States were terminated in 1972, 1975, and 1978, respectively. However, mainly pushed by its expanding exports, Taiwan's economy garnered four continuous years of double-digit growth rates at the beginning of the 1970s. That growth was abruptly terminated by the first oil crisis in 1974. The huge oil import burden caused the economy's growth to drop to a creeping 1.2 percent. Taiwanese manufacturers took advantage of low wage costs and chose to engage in labor-intensive industries, becoming very competitive in the global market. Taiwan quickly secured an international reputation as an exporter to the world. As a result of minimal government intervention in the functioning free markets and the government's export promotion policy, Taiwan's economy produced a large number of small and medium-sized businesses, many of which were primarily run to serve global markets. A globalized industrial structure dominated by small and medium-sized businesses thus became a major characteristic of Taiwan's economy.

In the late 1970s and early 1980s, the Taiwanese government initiated the program of second import substitution, under which capital- and technology-intensive domestic products were to replace similar imports. In 1976, the government also started "Ten Major Construction Projects," then "Twelve Major Construction Projects," to expand the island's industrial base and infrastructure, such as power plants, steel mills, petrochemical complexes, railroads, and highways, and to focus on agricultural, social, and cultural development. The economic growth rate bounced back quickly to the range of 8 to 9 percent.

By the mid-1980s, the Taiwanese government was faced with increasing dissatisfaction among its trading partners, which resulted from the enormous trade surpluses that accompanied Taiwan's rapid growth in exports. Taiwanese businesses were under severe competition from other developing countries, which had begun to follow the examples of "little dragons of Asia" and had switched to export expansion to join the global competition. The Taiwanese government was forced to adopt the policy of "liberalization, internationalization, and institutionalization," abolish the interest-rate and exchange-rate controls that had been in place for many years, and upgrade Taiwan's industry. During the past dozen years or so, Taiwan has virtually eliminated all nontariff trade barriers, and tariffs have dropped to levels the same as or lower than those of developed countries. Taiwan has also lifted restrictions on foreign participation in such service industry sectors as finance, insurance, shipping, food and beverages, and retailing. Restrictions have also been lifted on Taiwanese people traveling abroad. Foreign direct investment is welcome, and restrictions on foreign financial investments have been relaxed. Foreigners can currently invest in up to 30 percent of the overall valuation of the Taiwanese stock market and are expected to be able to invest without any restriction soon.

After the mid-1980s, the Taiwanese economy moved from a period of high growth rates to a time of moderate growth rates, then gradually slowed down. The average rate of growth during the thirty years from the 1960s to the end of the 1980s showed an impressive upswing. Between 1962 and the end of the 1980s, Taiwan's economy witnessed the most rapid growth in its history: an average annual rate of nearly 10 percent, more than twice the average economic growth rate of industrialized countries during this period. The trend gradually slowed down as the Taiwanese economy entered the 1990s and finally recorded its first negative growth rate in 2001 when worldwide recession hit its major industrialized economic partners.

The economy of Taiwan shifted from reliance on agricultural exports in the 1950s to light manufacturing in the 1960s and 1970s and to high-technology and chemical product exports in the 1980s and 1990s. By 1995, technology-intensive products constituted 46.7 percent of exports. This is a reflection of great change in Taiwan's economic structure since the 1960s. In 1965, the agriculture sector absorbed 46.5 percent of total employment, industry 22 percent, and the service sector 31 percent. By 1989, the agriculture sector declined to 15 percent, the industry sector increased to 41 percent, and the service sector jumped to 44 percent. The trend was then a further decline in agriculture and a small drop in industry, but a steady increase in the service sector. In 2000, the three sectors' shares of employment were 8 percent, 37 percent, and 55 percent, respectively. The trend is even more dramatic if one examines the changes in the total output structure. After a decline in agriculture's share and an increase in industry's share in earlier years, both sectors were of the same importance in the total output in 1960, each accounting for 27 percent. By 2000, agriculture dropped to 2 percent, industry rose to 32 percent, and the service sector shot up to 66 percent.

A new and significant economic trend that began in the 1980s was the rise of investments by the Taiwanese business community in mainland China. After the Emergency Decree was lifted in 1986, nongovernment civilian contacts between Taiwan and mainland China were allowed. Taiwan businesses were increasingly interested in the mainland market. By the end of 2000, 47,000 Taiwan business firms had invested in the mainland. The total investment reached more than $17.1 billion, according to official Taiwan statistics. Mainland China's statistics indicated a much higher figure of $26.4 billion. Taiwan's Central Bank even estimated the total amount in the range of $100 billion. The sharp increase of Taiwanese exports to mainland China that began in 1990 also increased Taiwan's dependence on the mainland market. In 1990, Taiwan's exports to the mainland were worth $4.4 billion, 6.5 percent of its total exports. By 2001, the share had shot up to 17.9 percent. One-fifth of its products are sold to the mainland. The total amount of trade between Taiwan and the mainland hit $30.5 billion in 2000, 396 times the amount in 1979. Taiwan has become the fifth-largest trade partner and the second-largest import market for mainland China. Mainland China, in turn, has become the second-largest export market and the largest source of trade surplus for Taiwan. Mainland China will continue to play a more important role in Taiwan's future economic development.

See also Chen Shuibian (1950–   ); Minority Women in Xinjiang and Taiwan; New Party (NP) (Taiwan); Taiwan, Constitutional Reform in; Taiwan, Development of Democracy in; Taiwan, Education Reform in; Taiwan, Ethnicity and Ethnic Policies of; Taiwan, Financial Relations with the Mainland; Taiwan, Income Distribution in; Taiwan, Labor and Labor Laws; Taiwan, Suicide in; Taiwan, Trade Relations with the Mainland; Taiwan Strait Crisis, Evolution of.

Bibliography

Chen, Kongli, ed., *A Compendium of Taiwan History* (Beijing: Jiuzhou Book Press, 1996); Chow, Peter C. Y., ed., *Taiwan in the Global Economy: From an Agrarian Economy to an Exporter of High-Tech Products* (Westport, CT: Praeger, 2002); Chu, Yun-Peng, and Sheng-Cheng Hu, *The Political Economy of Taiwan's Development into the 21st Century* (London: Edward Elgar Publishing, 1999); Directorate-General of Budget, Accounting, and Statistics, Executive Yuan, Taiwan, ed., *The Social and Economic Indicators—Annual Observations*, updated May 28, 2002; Metraux, Daniel, *Taiwan's Political and Economic Growth in the Late 20th Century* (Lewiston, NY: Edwin Mellen Press, 1991).

Zuohong Pan

Taiwan, Education Reform in

In the past fifty years, Taiwan has carried out a number of educational reform movements. Generally speaking, the reforms have involved three significant

In this 1991 photo, a teacher at the Taipai Language Institute instructs her student in the Taiwanese language. © Bohemian Nomad Picturemakers/Corbis.

sectors: the school system, government involvement, and recruitment of students. However, education reform is a never-ending process that must always move forward to meet citizens' expectations and the government's goal of a better future.

The basic framework for the current school system in Taiwan was formed in 1922. The central government extended compulsory education from six to nine years (six years of elementary school and three years of junior high school) in 1968. For the economic development of labor-intensive industries, junior vocational schools were terminated and senior vocational schools were fully supported by the government. In the 1970s, to meet the urgent need for manpower, many two-year junior colleges or five-year technical ones were established. Because of the transformation of the economic structure from labor-intensive industries to capital- and technology-intensive ones, public four-year technical institutes were set up to meet the higher-level need for manpower. Currently, the school system in Taiwan is six years of primary school, followed by three years of junior high school. Afterward, a three-year senior high school, a vocational school, or a five-year technical school are the choices available for students. Postsecondary education includes three years of junior college or four years, usually, of college/university, with the exception of departments such as dental and medical science, which take six and seven years, respectively. Between 1987 and 1997, the number of universities and colleges increased from twenty-eight to sixty-seven, and student enrollments rose from less than 200,000 to more than 380,000. In 1999, there were a total of 463,575 university students at both undergraduate and postgraduate levels.

Multilevel control over the contents of education such as teaching materials, the curriculum, and teachers gave rise to a crisis of monotony and homogeneity in national education. Unified textbooks as approved by the Ministry of Education made the contents of learning rigid and unchanging, and there was no opportunity to update and self-adjust or quickly reflect the needs of society and the times. The curriculum criterion was also overly detailed and gave teachers little flexibility. Teaching leaned abnormally toward education in bookish knowledge. Cramming to make grades caused students to lose curiosity and interest in learning.

After the enactment of the Civil Organization Law in 1989, the civil education reform movement began to flourish and managed to overcome resistance by the Taiwanese education authorities. After different opinions were expressed, persons of many different affiliations united to form an organization called 410 Education Reform League. President Li Denghui (Lee Teng-hui) appointed Nobel Prize winner Dr. Y. Z. Lee as the director of the Council on Education Reform, which was affiliated with the Executive Yuan. The council was officially set up on November 21, 1994, as a two-year temporary institution. Its main task was to propose a plan for education reforms in five reports, including the concluding report issued in December 1996. Five directions for reform actions were declared: deregulating education, helping every student learn, broadening the channels for student recruitment, promoting educational quality, and establishing a lifelong learning society. Prominent civil organizations, the Ministry of Education, and the Council on Education Reform were the three main systemic forces to advocate educational reforms. In the 1990s, the Ministry of Education, under the influence of education pressure groups and educators, opened up the textbook market to the private sector and separated the processes of editorship and assessment. In 1996, permission was given for all primary school textbooks to be written and compiled by more than ten private publishers. As of 2001 the National Institute of Compilation and Translation (NICT) ceased to compile primary school textbooks. The Ministry of Education also allowed private organizations to compile and publish textbooks of nonexamination subjects for junior secondary schools in 1998 and textbooks of the six remaining restricted subjects of senior secondary schools in 1999. The Ministry of Education (2000) promised to give schools and publishers more freedom to develop school-based curricula, as the newly designed national Provisional Curriculum has been introduced gradually into primary schools and junior secondary schools between 2001 and 2004.

Equality of education is the long-term goal of the government. Many efforts have been made to achieve this goal. The first focus is on opportunities for entrance at every school level. The school district recruits pupils for compulsory education. Beyond that, from senior high school to graduate school, entrance examinations are used to screen for qualified students. This examination system has a long and deep-rooted history in Chinese culture and has been retained up to the present. Entrance examinations have advantages, such as fairness and effectiveness in the selection of a talented young generation. However, their side effect is that the screening process often leads to the exclusion of talented students who cannot perform very well on typical pencil-and-paper tests. Besides, the fairness of the examination has become a debated issue, for the examination may benefit only the middle and upper classes, while it may adversely affect culturally and economically disadvantaged children whose parents cannot afford to hire tutors or send children to cram schools to prepare for school entrance examinations. To lessen the negative effects, a new college student recruiting system was proposed by the Center for College Entrance Exams (CCEM), a support organization that is half official and half civilian. The new system adopts a combination of recommendation and examination that is used as a parallel system to the traditional exam venue. The recruitment process comprises two stages. At the first stage, the student takes a general test that is given by CCEM; at the second stage, the student takes a test given by the department in which s/he wishes to enroll. The student needs to show his/her capabilities in order to pass the requirements set by the department. This system has been in force for less than ten years. Since the traditional College Joint

Entrance Exam has been criticized, the CCEM is revising the existing system and is also investigating alternative systems to recruit students.

In addition to the college entrance system, the high-school joint entrance examination is also a focus for improvement. First, a project of "Selection of Secondary Education Tracks" according to students' own wishes was proposed, with the purpose of lessening the burden for students of the college entrance examinations. The junior high school grade point average (GPA) is used as the criterion for entry to high school. However, because of weaknesses of the design of the project, the outcome is unsatisfactory. In 2001, the Joint Public Senior High School Entrance Exams were eliminated, and a multiroute program to enter senior high school was implemented, allowing junior high graduates to enter high schools through assignment, application, or selection by recommendation. However, junior high graduates must still pass the Basic Achievement Tests for Junior High Students (BAT). After obtaining a BAT score, students can file applications, be selected by recommendation, or get assigned based on their BAT score.

The basis for the government's establishment of control over enrollment is estimation of human resource needs. The aim of this control is chiefly to prevent a proliferation of schools so as to guarantee education quality. The comprehensive aim is to control the total number of college students at the number needed for economic development. However, because of people's eagerness to be free from government control, deregulation has become a hot issue. It seems that there is a tendency to believe that the less control the government has, the better education will develop.

See also Chen Shuibian (1950–); Minority Women in Xinjiang and Taiwan; New Party (NP) (Taiwan); Taiwan, Constitutional Reform in; Taiwan, Development of Democracy in; Taiwan, Economic Transition of; Taiwan, Ethnicity and Ethnic Policies of; Taiwan, Financial Relations with the Mainland; Taiwan, Income Distribution in; Taiwan, Labor and Labor Laws; Taiwan, Suicide in; Taiwan, Trade Relations with the Mainland; Taiwan Strait Crisis, Evolution of.

Bibliography

Clark, Nick, "Education in Taiwan," http://www.wes.org/ewenr/oznov/Practical.htm, accessed on December 2, 2004; Kuo, J. Y. "Educational Reform in Taiwan," in *Taiwan in the Twenty-first Century* ed., Xiaobing Li and Zuohong Pan, 130–150. (Lanham, MD: University Press of America, 2003); Yu, C., and H. L. Pan, "Educational Reforms with Their Impacts on School Effectiveness and School Improvement in Taiwan, R.O.C.," *School Effectiveness and School Improvement* 10, no. 1 (March 1999): 72–86.

Janet Yun Wei Kuo

Taiwan, Ethnicity and Ethnic Policies of

Several levels of ethnic distinction have long existed among the peoples of Taiwan. "Aborigines" is the preferred English appellation of the indigenous ethnic groups. The broad spectrum of Taiwanese Aborigines encompasses several languages and cultures. Languages of the various Aborigine groups, many of which are now extinct, are classified as Formosan. Their languages belong to the Austronesian language family. By the end of the twentieth century, Aborigines generally had been integrated with other groups and described themselves in terms of their cultural traditions rather than linguistic distinctiveness. Nevertheless, the historically derived division of Aborigines into plains and mountain groups based on linguistic and geographic origins remains a common approach.

Taiwan's Aborigines and their descendants have been subjected to multiple colonial projects since the early seventeenth century. The Dutch controlled southwestern Taiwan from 1624 to 1661, when they were ousted by the Ming dynasty general Zheng Chenggong's Chinese loyalist army. The Dutch had used the Plain-Aborigine militia to help control the fast-growing Han population and meet the need to produce agricultural surpluses. The Zheng regime was the first Han regime to control the island, bringing about a drastic reduction in access to power by the Aborigines who resided in the plains. Under the Qing dynasty's rule of Taiwan (1683–1895), officials viewed the Aborigines as "barbarians." They were categorized into two groups: the "wild" or "raw" Aborigines (living in the high central mountains, on the eastern plain, and on smaller coastal islands) who adopted few or no Han customs, and the "civilized" or "cooked" Aborigines (living on the western plain and in the western foothills of the central mountains) who adopted much of the Han culture, including the Chinese language. Under the Japanese colonial government (1895–1945), Taiwan continued to use these pejorative labels for the Aborigines.

"Han" is the term used in the Mandarin Chinese language for those whom most Americans think of as ethnic Chinese. The Confucian ideology that dominated imperial China held that Han identity was dependent on culture. In other words, people were Han if they practiced Han customs. Most Han, however, claimed to be Han on the basis of ancestry. Hoklo and Hakka are two regional varieties in Taiwan of the Han ethnicity. Many of their customs differ widely. Their spoken dialects, Minnan (also called Taiwanese) and Kejia, respectively, are mutually unintelligible. Although the Han demonstrate enormous social, cultural, and linguistic varieties, as a whole, they clearly belong to one ethnic group. The Hoklo have always constituted the great majority of Han in Taiwan.

Mainlanders—around 1 to 2 million of them—came to Taiwan between 1945 and 1949 with Jiang Jieshi (Chiang Kai-shek) and his Nationalist government. They constituted only about 15 percent of Taiwan's population, but this minority group possessed ruling power in Taiwan for a prolonged period of time. Under the Nationalist martial law rule (1949–1987), the mainlanders, who controlled the government, treated the Hoklo and the Hakka together as "Taiwanese." Two major ethnic issues have emerged in the relationship between Taiwanese (natives) and Chinese mainlanders (recent immigrants). One serious question is how political power should be properly shared and distributed. Because Taiwan was only one of the thirty-five Chinese provinces claimed by the Nationalists, limited political access, unfavorable to the Taiwanese, was legitimized. Language and class differences are the other serious issues between native Taiwanese and immigrant Chinese. The prevailing language among Taiwanese is a Fukienese dialect, which was suppressed by the ruling class, who speak Mandarin Chinese. Speaking the local dialect was treated as a symbol of low social class.

Since their arrival in 1949, the immigrant Chinese have been the dominant social class in Taiwan. Because they were selected from the upper class of mainland China, their levels of education and wealth were much higher than those of native Taiwanese. Thus political power, educational prestige, and economic wealth were all concentrated in the hands of the mainlanders. Nevertheless, the progression of the Taiwanese economy in the last forty years has gradually lessened the class dominance of the immigrant Chinese. The government now provides compulsory education up to the ninth grade. Currently, more than 50 percent of high-school students go to college. The education gap between the mainlanders and the natives has narrowed rapidly.

As the class gap between the natives and the mainlanders narrows, the differentials in political power have become an important issue. The mainlanders saw their political dominance gradually eroding under the Li Denghui (Lee Teng-hui) administration. An obvious example is the termination of the lifelong tenure system of the National Assembly and the Legislative Yuan (the legislative government branch) in 2000. People in Taiwan are well aware of the strong linkages between politics and economic interests. To guarantee their continued economic interests, the natives have to ensure a strong grip on future political events. In Taiwanese, the gaining of more political representation by the Taiwanese is often referred to as the "redistribution of political resources." However, from the viewpoint of the mainlanders, political power is the last resource they have. The relative advantages in education and other social class dimensions have rapidly diminished. In addition, they have lost dearly in the economic competition because the majority of the mainlanders do not own real estate. To the mainlanders, their gradually diminishing role in the political arena will mean the end of their dominance in Taiwanese society.

See also Chen Shuibian (1950–   ); Minority Women in Xinjiang and Taiwan; New Party (NP) (Taiwan); Taiwan, Constitutional Reform in; Taiwan, Development of Democracy in; Taiwan, Economic Transition of; Taiwan, Education Reform in; Taiwan, Financial Relations with the Mainland; Taiwan, Income Distribution in; Taiwan, Labor and Labor Laws; Taiwan, Suicide in; Taiwan, Trade Relations with the Mainland; Taiwan Strait Crisis, Evolution of.

Bibliography

Brown, M. J., "The Cultural Impact of Gendered Social Roles and Ethnicity: Changing Religious Practices in Taiwan," *Journal of Anthropological Research* 59 (2003): 47–67; Brown, "Reconstructing Ethnicity: Recorded and Remembered Identity in Taiwan," *Ethnology* 40, no. 2 (spring 2001): 153–164; Li, Wenlang, "Ethnic Competition and Mobilization in Taiwan's Politics," *Journal of Northeast Asian Studies* 12 (spring 1993): 59–71.

Janet Yun Wei Kuo

Taiwan, Financial Relations with the Mainland

In 1987, Taiwan's government deregulated the control of foreign exchange, which led to a rapid increase in outward investment by Taiwanese entrepreneurs. In the late 1980s, Taiwan's outward investment mainly focused on the United States and the member countries of the Association of Southeast Asian Nations (particularly the Philippines, Indonesia, Thailand, Malaysia, and Vietnam, hereafter ASEAN-5). By the 1990s, Taiwan's investors rapidly shifted their attention to mainland China. These investors were primarily attracted by China's cheap labor, the most important reason, and the potential local market, the second most important reason.

In addition, the Chinese government promulgated several regulations and laws to attract and protect Taiwan's investment in China. In order to attract Taiwanese enterprises, China's State Council promulgated the Regulations for Encouraging Investment by Taiwan Compatriots in July 1988. China offered preferential treatment, and numerous **cities** and provinces set up special investment zones that granted Taiwan-invested enterprises (TIEs) many privileges, including tax exemption or reduction. In March 1994, China's **National People's Congress** promulgated the Taiwan Compatriot Investment Protection Law of the People's Republic of China. Furthermore, in December 1999, China's State Council issued the Implementing Rules for the Taiwan Compatriot Investment Protection Law of the People's Republic of China.

At the same time, Taiwan's government gradually relaxed the regulations on cross-strait economic exchange at a crucial moment (1987–1988) when Taiwanese exports were suffering due to a strong New Taiwan dollar, the high cost of labor, and environmental controversies. Along with the relaxation of foreign exchange controls, Taiwan's government liberalized its China policy by nullifying martial law and allowing Taiwanese to visit China. In October 1990, Taiwan's Ministry of Economic Affairs (MOEA) formally lifted the ban on indirect investment in China by promulgating the Regulations on Indirect Investment and Technology Cooperation with the Mainland Area.

Although investment from Taiwan to China began to increase rapidly in the late 1980s, Taiwan's Investment Commission did not compile formal statistics until 1991. According to Taiwan's official figures, in 1991, Taiwan's outward **foreign direct investment (FDI)** into China was only $17 million. Since 1992, however, China has become the largest recipient of Taiwan's outward investment. In 1993, the numbers increased dramatically to nearly $3.2 billion, which was 66 percent of Taiwan's total FDI for that year. By the end of 2002, Taiwan's cumulative FDI in China was $26.6 billion, or 43.4 percent of total Taiwanese outward FDI. In just one decade, China became the destination of the most cumulative outward FDI of Taiwan.

Overall, Taiwan's FDI in the late 1980s and early 1990s involved mainly small to medium-sized labor-intensive enterprises that were looking for overseas manufacturing bases, most of which focused on China as well as ASEAN-5. After the mid-1990s, Taiwan's FDI in China involved more and more large enterprises with high capital and technology intensities, companies that were looking for both overseas manufacturing bases and access to China's huge potential market. For instance, in 1995, only 14 percent of Taiwan's information technology products were produced in China; in 2002, 47 percent were produced in China.

Taiwan's official figures considerably underestimate the extent of Taiwan's real investment in China because many Taiwanese businesses began in the mid-1990s to invest in China through their holding companies in Third World tax-exempt countries, such as the Virgin Islands and the Cayman Islands. For instance, Peng Fai-nan, governor of Taiwan's Central Bank, estimated that by the end of 2002, the real figure of Taiwan's cumulative investment in China was about U.S. $66.8 billion.

As a result, scholars usually use China's official data on Taiwan's investment in China because it is mandatory for TIEs to register their investments with the Chinese government. According to China's statistics, the first TIE in China opened in 1983. By 1991, Taiwan's total realized investment in China was $844 million divided among 3,446 projects, with a cumulative contracted amount of $2.78 billion and an average contracted amount of $0.81 million per project. Since 1991, Taiwan's investment in China has been increasing dramatically, with an average annual contracted amount of $5.3 billion or an average realized amount of $2.9 billion. By the end of 2002, Taiwan's cumulative contracted investment in China was $61.5 billion in 55,691 projects, of which $33.1 billion was actually utilized, with an average contracted amount of $1.1 million per project; the average project size has grown by about 37 percent.

In addition, as of March 2003, the share of Taiwan's cumulative realized investment in China was 7.4 percent of total FDI in China. Taiwan was the fourth-largest source of FDI in China, next to Hong Kong (45.6 percent), the United States (8.9 percent), and Japan (8.2 percent). Nevertheless, Chinese figures may have underestimated Taiwan's real investment in China because many Taiwanese businesspeople began to invest in China through their holding companies in British Central America in the mid-1990s. The Virgin Islands (part of British Central America) was the fifth-largest investor in China by March 2003, with cumulative realized FDI of $25.9 billion, or 5.6 percent of China's total FDI.

There are no available Chinese data on Taiwan's investment in China by industry, and thus this entry relies on Taiwan's official data. As of April 2003, according to Taiwan's MOEA Investment Commission, Taiwan's total investment in China included $9.7 billion (31.3 percent) in electronics and electrical appliances, $2.7 billion (8.8 percent) in basic metals and metal products, $2.2 billion (7 percent) in plastic products, $2 billion (6.4 percent) in chemicals, $1.8 billion (5.8 percent) in food and beverage processing, $1.7 billion (5.6 percent) in precision instruments, $1.6 billion (5 percent) in nonmetallic minerals, $1.2 billion (4 percent) in transportation equipment, $1.2 billion (3.9 percent) in textiles, and $1 billion (3.4 percent) in machinery equipment. As of April 2003, Taiwan's investment was focused in the manufacturing industry, which accounted for 96 percent of Taiwan's total investment in China.

As of April 2003, the geographic distribution of Taiwan's cumulative investment in China was $12.3 billion (39.6 percent) in Jiangsu (including Shanghai), $9.8 billion (31.6 percent) in Guangdong, $2.9 billion (9.4 percent) in Fujian, $1.8 billion (5.7 percent) in Zhejiang, $1.5 billion (5 percent) in Hebei (including Beijing), and $543 million (1.8 percent) in Shandong. According to Taiwan's statistics, these six coastal provinces comprised 93 percent of Taiwan's total cumulative investment in China.

In addition, TIEs tend to partner with local and foreign enterprises when they invest in China. According to a 1996 report by Taiwan's MOEA, which included a sample size of 1,312 companies, 36 percent of TIEs established joint ventures with other partners. Fifty-six percent (multiple choices) of TIEs who entered joint ventures cooperated with local Chinese enterprises, 35 percent cooperated with Chinese local governments, and 28 percent cooperated with foreign enterprises.

According to a 1999 report by Taiwan's MOEA, which included a sample size of 1,627 companies, 38 percent of TIEs established joint ventures with other partners. Fifty-nine percent of these TIEs held less than a 50 percent share in the joint ventures. Thirty-one percent (multiple choices) of these TIEs cooperated with local Chinese enterprises, 20 percent cooperated with Chinese local governments, and 26 percent cooperated with foreign enterprises.

In regard to other capital flow between Taiwan and China, the Taiwanese government began to compile statistics on individual remittances to China (including household remittances, donations, and other transfer payments, but excluding travel expenditures) on May 21, 1990, and on both Taiwan business remittances to China and remittances from China to Taiwan on July 29, 1993. In 1993, Taiwan remitted $254 million to China, and China remitted $26 million to Taiwan. In 2002, Taiwan remitted $2.5 billion to China, and China remitted $2.3 billion to Taiwan. As of April 2003, Taiwan had remitted a cumulative $11.2 billion to China, and China had remitted a cumulative $6.9 billion to Taiwan.

Nevertheless, the Taiwanese government's figures hardly tell the truth of capital flow across the Taiwan Strait. For example, Taiwan's Central Bank estimated in late 2000 that Taiwan's total capital flow to China was around $70 billion, of which $40 to $50 billion was Taiwan's FDI in China. That is, in 2000 Taiwan might have remitted as much as $20 to $30 billion in total to China, including portfolio flows to China.

See also Chen Shuibian (1950–   ); Minority Women in Xinjiang and Taiwan; New Party (NP) (Taiwan); Taiwan, Constitutional Reform in; Taiwan, Development of Democracy in; Taiwan, Economic Transition of; Taiwan, Education Reform in; Taiwan, Ethnicity and Ethnic Policies of; Taiwan, Income Distribution in; Taiwan, Labor and Labor Laws; Taiwan, Suicide in; Taiwan, Trade Relations with the Mainland; Taiwan Strait Crisis, Evolution of.

Bibliography

Chung-Hua Institution for Economic Research, *Dalu ji Liangan Jingji Qingshi Baogao (1997/1998)* (Report on the economic situation of mainland China and the two sides of the Taiwan Strait [1997/1998]) (Taipei: Mainland Affairs Council, 1999); Kao, Charng, *Dalu Jinggai yu Liangan Jingmao Guanxi* (Mainland economic reforms and cross-strait economic relations), 2nd ed. (Taipei: Wu-Nan, 1999); Ministry of Economic Affairs (Taiwan), *Zhizaoye Duiwai Touzi Shikuang Diaocha Baogao* (The investigation report on outward investment of manufacturing industry) (Taipei: Ministry of Economic

Affairs), various issues; 1997–2003; Taiwan Economic Research Institution, ed., *Cross-Strait Economic Statistics Monthly* (Taipei), various issues, 1996–2003.

Chenyuan Tung

Taiwan, Income Distribution in

Taiwan's income distribution has been a special phenomenon in the history of economic development in that the inequality of income among citizens showed a declining trend during the whole period of industrialization. The income distribution in Taiwan was affected by the definition of property rights in the process of industrialization in a manner that was different from the way commonly used in Western countries and resulted in the divergence from the generally accepted hypothesis of Simon Kuznets (1995) that industrialization would be accompanied by a trend of increasing income disparity during its early and middle stages and decreasing disparity during the later stage.

Taiwan's independent industrialization began in the early 1950s and lasted into the late 1980s. Taiwan became a newly industrial economy in the 1990s, and the significance of the problem of income distribution in the economy was diluted after this. During industrialization, Taiwan successfully reduced its Gini coefficient and Oshima index, which are utilized in theoretical analyses of income distribution to show the degree of income disparity, from 55.8 and 20.5 in 1953 to 44.0 and 9.0 in 1959, 32.1 and 5.3 in 1964, 29.4 and 4.6 in 1970, 28.7 and 4.4 in 1974, 27.7 and 4.2 in 1980, 28.7 and 4.4 in 1984, and 29.9 and 4.9 in 1988. There was a slight rise in both figures in the 1980s. The change displayed a pattern contrary to the theory of Simon Kuznets. Simultaneously, industrialization and economic growth maintained stable and high rates in Taiwan. For instance, the proportions of the agricultural and industrial sectors in the total economy were changed from 32 and 22 percent in 1953 to 26.4 and 27.1 percent in 1959, 24.5 and 30.4 percent in 1964, 15.5 and 36.8 percent in 1970, 12.4 and 40.7 percent in 1974, 7.7 and 45.8 percent in 1980, 6.3 and 46.2 percent in 1984, and 5 and 44.8 percent in 1988. Meanwhile, the growth rates of GDP reached 5.1, 6.3, 12.2, 11.4, 1.2, 7.3, 10.6, and 7.8 percent, respectively.

The direct cause of decreasing income disparity in Taiwan during its industrialization was the gradual alteration of income proportions of people at different levels. First, poor people's income level rose at a rate of 260 percent from the 1950s to the 1980s. The middle class with midlevel incomes, 60 percent of all households, received only 35 percent of all income in the 1950s but 54 percent in the 1980s. The share of the richest people in total income declined from 60 percent in the 1950s to 38 percent in the 1980s.

However, the fundamental reason for the change of Taiwan's income distribution was the proper definition of property rights with oriental social characteristics. First, land property rights in Taiwan were defined by the "Reform of Farming Land" in the 1950s and the 1960s. The first step of the reform was to reduce the rent burden of the tenant farmers under the old ownership by decreasing the previous rent rate of 57 percent on average to a uniform rent of 37.5 percent and fixing the rent period at six years or more by a formal contract instead of an uncertain period by an oral contract. This measure raised and stabilized the income expectation of the tenants and gave incentives for production and investment. In the three years after the reform, three-fourths of the increased income was invested into production. The second step was the sale of public-owned farming land, 22 percent of all the farming land in Taiwan, to tenant farmers at a low price with a quota of a maximum of three acres per farming family. The price level was 2.5 times the annual output of the land and could be paid over ten years in installments without interest, which meant that a tenant farmer could obtain the land by paying a rent of 25 percent for ten consecutive years. The final step was to institute "farmland owned by farmers." The government first bought surplus farmland from landlords who were legally permitted to own and cultivate up to three acres per family and then sold the farmland to tenant farmers in the same way as the sale of public land. Property rights—especially the right of utilization of farmland owned by cultivating farmers—constitute the core of Taiwan's rural economic success.

Second, the principle of defining capital property rights in Taiwan was "encouraging competition and protecting development." The government adopted policies to support private enterprises and industries that included the establishment of the China Productivity Center, the Industry of Handmade Goods Promotion Center, and the China Technological Service in order to provide professional training, guidance in production techniques and product designs, and other services. The government also carried out a policy of privatization of state-owned enterprises, set up uniform taxing ratios for private and public firms, and reduced entry barriers to industries that had previously been controlled by governments to encourage fair competition. In this way, the government replaced entry permits for some industries with uniform standards of quality and operation evaluations. The government also made an effort to establish a good business environment for private firms, for example, by building some public enterprises to produce products or services that private firms were not willing or able to provide, carrying out the construction of infrastructure, and reducing the very high rate of inflation to around ten percent. The responsibilities and rights of private capital were clearly defined, and the right of profit was especially defined and protected.

Third, the rights of labor property were defined in rural and urban areas. The rights of rural labor were defined as follows: (1) Every rural laborer in the farming family had his or her ownership of land after the reform of farmland. (2) He or she had the right to choose a career or kind of work in a labor market and could work in any year in one, two, or several fields of work as a full-time or part-time employee in each field. (3) Everyone had the right to move from one place to another, for example, from a rural to an urban area or from an inland to a coastal area—as indicated in the theory of dualism, the right of mobility of rural laborers was one of the necessary conditions for industrialization. (4) Everyone had the right of access to social education. Although basic education was traditionally stressed in Taiwan, the government conducted some special policies to promote the education of rural laborers. (5) The rural laborer had the right to own, accumulate, and invest money or material property. Because of the farmland reform and the growth of farming production or other production, rural laborers had more and more income and wealth. The government did not levy high taxes on rural income but encouraged farmers to own and save more with favorable terms on interest and loans to farmers.

In urban areas, around 30 percent of laborers worked in large enterprises and were protected by company regulations as well as government regulations on large enterprises. Their rights of labor property were embodied in the normal wage and salary payments, working conditions, and fair treatment in daily work that were provided by the enterprises, most of them with public ownership. However, nearly 70 percent of urban employment took place in private middle-sized and small firms that had characteristics of the traditional family economy. The government took the responsibility of protection of the basic rights of common employees or self-employed workers. In addition, the rights of laborers were also protected, to a certain extent, by the traditional practice in these businesses. This combination of formal and informal definitions of property rights was reflected in several ways: (1) Employees had the right to learn about the profitability of the firm through enforcing the routine of business transparency in middle-sized and small firms. Firms in Taiwan were relatively small, with less than ten employees for small firms, and most of the full-time or part-time employees were relatives, friends, or neighbors, so the employees would know to a great extent the performance of the business and the level of reasonable compensation for themselves. (2) Employees had access to technical or professional training in their firms. This right was provided by the traditional routines of apprenticeship and the tradition of "learning through working" in Chinese firms and by the Factory Act, which was enforced in the 1960s. (3) If a worker found a better job than the one he or she already had, he or she could change his or her employer and residence place to take the new job. (4) Employees had the right to enjoy a reduction of taxes in many realms.

The proper definition of property rights altered the distribution of component incomes. Profit-style incomes, namely, net agricultural income, net business operation income, and partly net professional income, played a critical role in raising the income level of poor families and forming the large group of the middle class, reducing the total income inequality during the rapid economic development, and creating the economic miracle of "growth with equity" in Taiwan.

However, since around the beginning of the 1990s, when the people of Taiwan generally became richer, with a per capita GNP of U.S. $8,111, and the government had more fiscal resources, the government has changed its focus from encouraging private economic development to bureaucratic political benefits. The private capital rights of property were injured because the government did not allow private capital to legally invest abroad and to build a more sophisticated domestic financial system. It also did not permit private enterprises to trade freely with firms of mainland China to pursue their comparative advantages. As a result, much capital transferred from substantive industries to overgrown bubble sectors such as stock exchange markets, estate markets, and the gambling industry, while many middle-aged and older workers with low skills found very limited opportunities to get a job, and the jobless rate of Taiwan grew from 1.3 to 3 percent during the decade of the 1990s.

Nevertheless, the information technology industry was strongly supported by the government with tax reductions and subsidies, and the income of people working there rose rapidly. Meanwhile, the government also failed to renew the rights of property for landowners and laborers and delayed necessary urbanization and economic modernization as a whole in Taiwan. Therefore, income inequality rose on the Oshima index from 4.9 in 1989 to 5.5 in 1999, and the growth rate fell from 8.15 percent annually in the 1980s to 6.35 percent in the 1990s.

See also Chen Shuibian (1950–   ); Minority Women in Xinjiang and Taiwan; New Party (NP) (Taiwan); Taiwan, Constitutional Reform in; Taiwan, Development of Democracy in; Taiwan, Economic Transition of; Taiwan, Education Reform in; Taiwan, Ethnicity and Ethnic Policies of; Taiwan, Financial Relations with the Mainland; Taiwan, Labor and Labor Laws; Taiwan, Suicide in; Taiwan, Trade Relations with the Mainland; Taiwan Strait Crisis, Evolution of.

Bibliography

Kuznets, S., "Economic Growth and Income Inequality," *American Economic Review* 46, no. 2 (March 1955): 1–28; Yu, Zongxian, ed., *Taiwan de Suode Fenpei* (Income distribution in Taiwan) (Taipei: Lianjing Publishing Co., 1983).

Cheng Wang

Taiwan, Labor and Labor Laws

Taiwan achieved tremendous economic and political development in the second half of the twentieth century, transforming itself from an agricultural society into one of the world's leading industrialized entities. Taiwan has an area of about 36,179 square kilometers with a population of 23 million and comparatively poor supplies of natural resources. Since the early 1950s, however, Taiwan's economy has been growing at an average rate of 8.4 percent annually, one of the best in the world. Taiwan claims that its GNP per capita reached $14,188 in the year 2000, while its Gini coefficient remained as low as 0.371. Traditional Confucian ethics, family-clan unity, an educated labor force, women's participation in the "satellite factory" system, and government policies all played important roles in Taiwan's success stories.

A well-educated labor force is Taiwan's most important asset. Traditional Confucianism advocates diligence, frugality, and universal nondiscrimination in education. After Japan's occupation of Taiwan in 1895, the educational focus began to move from the traditional emphasis on Confucian ideals to the Japanese version of Western-style education, which put more stress on science and practical knowledge. Girls were also encouraged to take advantage of educational opportunities. In 1902, the student enrollment in Taiwan was only 3.21 percent of the school-age population. By 1945, the percentage had reached 71.31 percent (male, 80.86 percent, versus female, 60.94 percent). More important, people's attitude began to change from favoring intellectuals over manual labor toward an emphasis on scientific techniques, machine technology, and modern business practice. A new labor force able to read and write, calculate, apply technology to production, and manage business with more emphasis on economic factors had formed.

After the Nationalist (Kuomintang, KMT) government retreated to Taiwan in 1949, its efforts to promote education continued. The government made it one of its most important tasks that the education system receive necessary funding. The percentage of educational expenditure in Taiwan's GNP increased from the 1950s to the 1990s. In 1951, that percentage was 1.73 percent (NT$4.4 billion). By 1998, it had reached 6.55 percent (NT$557 billion). Today Taiwan has more than 7,700 schools (elementary schools through universities) with a student body of more than 5 million. In 1998, about 365,000 students graduated from middle school. Among them, about 340,000 entered high schools and special trade schools (94 percent of the total). Among the 84,000 high-school graduates, about 56,000 (67.5 percent) continued into higher education. Members of this well-educated young generation are prepared when they get into the job market, a plus for Taiwan's economic development.

Along with government-sponsored industrial projects, numerous satellite factories (family-based and run, export-oriented businesses) played important roles in the economic takeoff. Answering the government slogan "Living Rooms as Factories," tens of thousands of ordinary people, especially women, joined this effort. During the 1960s and 1970s, these workers sacrificed greatly while contributing to the economic growth, enduring long and hard work days, low pay, and a labor system strategically controlled by the factory owners through ethnic and kinship systems (paternalism) to suppress any union activities.

Government policies also contributed to Taiwan's economic miracle. Much emphasis was given to labor's education. In the 1960s, the government required all laborers to attend at least six years of school. In 1968, the government extended this compulsory education to nine years, which greatly boosted the labor force's quality. The government also made other adjustments to its economic policies to meet the challenges, such as gradually replacing central planning with a market economy. Taiwan also introduced an Open Door policy to promote international trade, first developing labor-intensive industries (1950s–1960s) and later on moving gradually into capital-intensive industries (since the 1980s). A policy of light industry first, heavy industry later also led to a healthy transition for the island's economy.

Along with Taiwan's economic development, an industrial working class emerged. However, Taiwan's labor force never formed a real movement. Taiwan's working class avoided antagonistic relations with capitalists because most of the workers were working in small satellite factories, which are based on family members' cooperation in most cases. The high turnover rate and the family-centered business that functioned under effective paternalism prevented the formation of a true proletariat and a working-class consciousness. The political environment before 1987 was also not favorable for any labor movement. The martial law of the KMT government did not encourage labor unions, and strikes were forbidden. There was indeed a Chinese Federation of Labor (CFL), but more than half of its officers were ruling KMT members, the funding of the federation mostly came from government grants, and it never called any strike. It did not truly represent Taiwanese workers' interests and did little in terms of collective bargaining. The dominance of management, frequently backed by the government, was obvious in Taiwan.

However, membership in Taiwan's unions is comparatively high. For example, union membership in 1987 was 1.87 million. Many so-called friendship associations also appeared, mostly because of workers' dissatisfaction with the government-sponsored unions. There is also an independent association of unions called the Taiwanese Association for Labor Movement. By the early 1990s, about 34 percent of workers belonged to unions, though the 1975 Labor Union Law still put many restrictions on the labor movement. For example, craft and industrial local unions could only be formed at the individual enterprise, which effectively curbed the effort to create any national-level industrial unions. A true labor movement did not arise in Taiwan until after 1987.

In 1987, the KMT government finally lifted martial law, and strikes became legal. In the late 1980s and the early 1990s, a moderate wave of strikes did take place involving Taiwan's railroad system, bus service, postal service, and other industries, but they were mostly about workers' rights rather than wages. Since 1987, more than 1,200 industrial unions and more than 2,300 craft guilds have formed. A Labor Party and a Workers Party also came into being (1987 and 1989, respectively), although they never won the support of the majority of Taiwanese workers because of their liberal ideals.

The Taiwanese government has always tried to promote harmonious relations between management and labor. The 1984 Basic Labor Standards Law shows that government indeed was aiming at cooperation between the two. The purposes of the law were to provide minimum standards of labor conditions, protect workers' rights and interests, strengthen the labor-management relationship, and promote social and economic development. Taiwan's leaders, despite party affiliation, generally agree that a harmonious relationship between labor and management is essential for maintaining a high level of productivity and indeed the very existence of any enterprise in Taiwan.

The Taiwanese government has paid much attention to the creation of new labor laws. By the summer of 2002, the government had passed more than seventy different laws and regulations in regard to labor-management relations, working conditions, benefits and welfare, labor insurance, labor safety and health, professional training and examination, employment services, workers with disabilities, and other issues. According to these laws, an industrial union is required in any factory with more than thirty workers. All workers over the age of sixteen have the right to join the union, though there is no penalty for not joining. The laws also provide comprehensive guarantees and rights to workers, such as injury compensation and minimum wages. Workers, after working in the firm for a certain length of time, are eligible for benefits and protections. After working for the firms for fifteen years or more and reaching age fifty-five, workers are entitled to their pensions. The problem, however, that is many firms in Taiwan never last that long and many employers never pay enough to the retirement fund to meet the required amounts.

In spite of the numerous problems, Taiwan has made very impressive progress in many aspects of labor relations. According to the data provided by the Council of Labor Affairs, the labor force in Taiwan has experienced big changes both in quantity and quality: the number of people in employment increased from 3,473,000 in 1960 to 9,491,000 in 2000 (about 60 percent male and 40 percent female); about 70 percent of males and 46 percent of females are in the labor force. Those with postsecondary education rose from 3 percent in 1964 to 27 percent in 2000. While employees in the service sector increased from 29 percent to 55 percent and in industries from 21 percent to 37 percent, labor involved in agriculture decreased from more than 50 percent to 8 percent from 1960 to 2000. The unemployment rate has remained low (about 2 percent), though it began to rise after 1995 because of structural changes and recent worldwide economic recessions. Employees' income has also been increasing. In 1960, the average monthly income was NT$8,847. By 2000, it reached NT$41,874. At the same time, the average working hours per month decreased, from 215 hours (1980) to 190 hours (2000). Because of the government's emphasis on a safe working environment, accidental deaths on the job dropped significantly, from 871 in 1989 to 647 in 2000. To help labor deal with changing demands on the job, the government established thirteen public professional training centers across the island. The retraining programs helped more than 675,000 people in the year 2000. By May 2002, several new laws were put into practice, including the new Sexual Equality in Labor Act and a renewed Labor Insurance Act. The former is actually a copy of the sexual equality law in most developed countries: besides establishing the equal-job, equal-pay principle, it deals with issues like equal treatment in promotion and prevention of sexual harassment. The Labor Insurance Act covers payments for unemployment, new job training, health insurance during the unemployed period, and other unemployment issues.

To meet the challenges of the twenty-first century, the Taiwanese government has set up new goals for its efforts to maintain Taiwan's economic momentum: prepared labor, safe working environment, and humane working conditions. So far, Taiwan is striving vigorously to conquer its problems and keep up its efforts to play an active role in the world economy.

See also Chen Shuibian (1950–); Minority Women in Xinjiang and Taiwan; New Party (NP) (Taiwan); Taiwan, Constitutional Reform in; Taiwan, Development of Democracy in; Taiwan, Economic Transition of; Taiwan, Education Reform in; Taiwan, Ethnicity and Ethnic Policies of; Taiwan, Financial Relations with the Mainland; Taiwan, Income Distribution in; Taiwan, Suicide in; Taiwan, Trade Relations with the Mainland; Taiwan Strait Crisis, Evolution of.

Bibliography

Chin, Ko-Lin, *Heijin: Organized Crime, Business, and Politics in Taiwan* (Armonk, NY: M. E. Sharpe, 2003); Roy, Denny, *Taiwan: A Political History* (Ithaca, NY: Cornell University Press, 2003).

Xiansheng Tian

Taiwan, Suicide in

In 1964, the suicide rate in Taiwan reached its peak at 18.7 suicides per 100,000 people. Throughout the late 1960s and 1970s, suicide rates gradually declined to less than 10 suicides per 100,000 people. In the 1980s, suicide rates started to rise and reached their highest point in 1985 at 11.9 suicides per 100,000 people. The late 1980s through the mid-1990s saw another decline in suicide rates, but from the mid-1990s until the present, suicide rates have risen steadily. The upward trend of suicide rates, together with other social, cultural, and economic factors, is alarming. The Taiwan government acknowledges that suicide is a major public health issue, along with socioeconomic and cultural concerns. From 1999 to 2001, suicide was one of the ten leading causes of death in Taiwan, and it became the third most common cause of death in 2001.

For years, scholars have recognized that suicide carries social and cultural meanings. Research links suicide to economic, political, social, and cultural, as well as psychological, factors. For example, a time-series study correlated the suicide rate in Taiwan with divorce, female labor-force participation, and unemployment (Lester and Yang 1995), which have all reached record-high levels in recent years. However, male and female suicide rates may respond differently to divorce, labor-force participation, and unemployment. For example, according to a report by the *People's Daily* in 2001, more than half of all men who committed suicide were unemployed, while half of all women who took their own lives were housewives ("Taiwan" 2001). Therefore, suicide in any society has to be understood at both individual and societal levels in relation to social and cultural conditions in that particular society.

At the societal level, Durkheim was one of the first sociologists to link suicide directly with social and cultural conditions in a society. In his study of suicide (1897/1951), Durkheim, back in 1897, indicated that suicide is an index of societal well-being. He identified social integration as the social force that affects suicide rates in a society. According to Durkheim, extremely high or low degrees of social integration may cause suicide. Normally, married people should have a lower rate of suicide than single or divorced people. But for traditional marriage, which tends to be highly integrated, married people could actually have a higher rate of suicide than married people in a nontraditional marriage setting.

Family affiliation is paramount in traditional Chinese culture. In support of Durkheim's theory, many researchers over the years have found empirical evidence that links family attachments, socioeconomic conditions of family life, and divorce to suicide rates (Goldsmith et al. 2002). For example, divorce causes suicide rates to go up in Taiwan. However, the association is much stronger for women than for men. In general, the higher the divorce rates, the higher the suicide rates for both men and women. The trend seems to suggest that family is a stronger predictor of suicide for women than for men, even though women may have an overall lower rate of suicide than men do.

Divorce affects suicide rates uniquely in Taiwan when compared with suicide rates in other countries. Women in Taiwan today are still by and large financially dependent upon their husbands. When they are divorced, some women could become financially destitute. Taiwan's divorce law on marital property does not provide divorced people the protections offered in other countries such as the United States. Therefore, divorce poses financial hardships for women. On the other hand, divorce affects Taiwanese men in a very different way. As Kposowa (2000) states, divorce doubles the chance that a man will commit suicide since he considers divorce as a failure.

Not only does divorce raise suicide rates for both men and women, but parenthood in Taiwan also is a good predictor. In the past, whenever suicide rates went up, so did crude birth rates. Hence, contrary to evidence from other countries, marriage with children produces higher rates of suicide than marriage without children in Taiwan. Researchers (Lester and Yang 1995; Li 2003) confirm that high suicide rates correlate with high crude birth rates in Taiwan. However, there seems to be a reverse correlation between suicide rates and crude birth rates beginning from 1980 and continuing to the present. The upward trend in suicide rates in most recent years seems to be accompanied by a drop in crude birth rates in Taiwan. This latest trend in suicide is more in accordance with findings from other countries that suggest that married people, especially mothers, have a decreased risk of suicide. If this is the case, having children may serve as a buffer to self-destruction in Taiwan today, as it does in other countries.

Economic factors such as labor-force participation, unemployment, and socioeconomic disadvantage all influence suicide probability. Most people have attributed the rising suicide rates in Taiwan to an economic slowdown and a sharp increase in unemployment. For example, the unemployment rate today is about 5 percent in Taiwan. Among the poorest section of the population, the unemployment rate is around 15 percent. Unemployment rates significantly affect suicide rates, especially among men.

Labor-force participation also affects suicide rates. However, male labor-force participation is linked to higher male suicide rates in Taiwan, while female labor-force participation reduces female suicide rates.

Socioeconomic disadvantage is another strong predictor for suicide. For example, unemployment, downward mobility, reduced income, and divorce all can translate into a loss in one's socioeconomic status. Economic distress has been linked to higher suicide rates.

Society-wide economic downturns also can affect suicide probability. Years after the devastating earthquake that struck Taiwan on September 21, 1999, and left tens of thousands of people either dead, seriously injured, or homeless, Taiwan still feels economic aftershocks. Suicide rates soared in the months after the earthquake because many could not either afford to rebuild their homes or find jobs after the quake.

Culture affects how people perceive suicide. Although suicide exists across nations, there are great variations in rates of suicide depending on cultural values and social structures. Some cultures may actually encourage suicide, while others strictly prohibit it. For example, in traditional Chinese culture, suicide committed because of loyalty was morally acceptable; at times, such suicides were even glorified. The cultural dynamics of suicide could also play a role in suicidal behavior (Xiao 2001). For example, traditional Chinese culture viewed suicide as an acceptable means of communication or coping in certain situations, a view that might encourage suicidal behavior. Far more women than men in Taiwan contemplate or attempt suicide, and the majority of callers to suicide help lines are women who simply want to talk to someone about their problems (Chang 1997).

Suicide has to be understood at the individual level too. Depression, substance abuse, and mental illness, all can heighten suicidal tendency. In Taiwan, for example, depression is increasingly common. Doctors there attribute depression to the rise of chronic illness, alcoholism, and drug abuse. The first peak age for depression is about thirty-five. Women who are starting menopause and men who are retiring also are more likely to suffer from depression. A large number of people who commit suicide are psychiatrically ill, with depression being the major factor. Other factors such as chronic illness, disability, and aging also increase suicidal tendency (Chang 1997).

See also Chen Shuibian (1950–   ); Minority Women in Xinjiang and Taiwan; New Party (NP) (Taiwan); Suicide in China; Taiwan, Constitutional Reform in; Taiwan, Development of Democracy in; Taiwan, Economic Transition of; Taiwan, Education Reform in; Taiwan, Ethnicity and Ethnic Policies of; Taiwan, Financial Relations with the Mainland; Taiwan, Income Distribution in; Taiwan, Labor and Labor Laws; Taiwan, Trade Relations with the Mainland; Taiwan Strait Crisis, Evolution of.

Bibliography

Chang, Chiung-fang, "A Silent Protest—Suicide in Taiwan," *Sinorama*, March 1997; Durkheim, Emile, *Suicide: A Study in Sociology* (New York: Free Press, 1997); Goldsmith, S. K., T. C. Pelimar, A. M. Kleinman, and W. E. Burney, eds., "Reducing Suicide: A National Imperative," A Report by the National Institute of Mental Health, 2002; Hoyer, G., and E. Lund, "Suicide among Women Related to Number of Children in Marriage," *Archives of General Psychiatry* 50 (1993): 134–137; Kposowa, Augustine J., "Marital Status and Suicide in the National Longitudinal Mortality Study," *Journal of Epidemiology and Community Health* 54, no. 4 (2000): 254–261; Lester, David, and Yang Bijou, "Do Chinese Women Commit Fatalistic Suicide?" *Chinese Journal of Mental Health* (1995); Li, Liying, "Suicide in Taiwan," in *Taiwan in the Twenty-first Century*, ed. Xiaobing Li and Zuohong Pan (Lanham, MD: University Press of America, 2003); "Taiwan Posts Highest Suicide Rate in Nine Years," *People's Daily Online*, March 29, 2001, http://english.people.com.cn/english/200103/29/eng20010329_66374.html, accessed on December 2, 2004.

Liying Li

Taiwan, Trade Relations with the Mainland

Because of political and military hostilities, economic exchange between Taiwan and mainland China was virtually nonexistent between 1949 and 1979. On January 1, 1979, after adopting reforms and the **Open Door policy** in late 1978, China proposed establishing three links (direct trade, postal exchange, and transportation links) between Taiwan and China. In 1980, China organized a mission to Hong Kong and purchased $80 million worth of Taiwanese products. In the same year, to further encourage trade, China announced a tariff-free policy on Taiwan-made imported goods. However, the zero tariff policy lasted for only one year.

Beijing's initiatives received no response from Taipei until the mid-1980s. For the first time in 1985, Taiwan responded to China's request for cross-strait trade by announcing the Noninterference Principle of Indirect Exports to the Mainland. From then on, cross-strait trade started to grow rapidly along with China's increasing economic reforms and Taiwan's gradual relaxation of limits on cross-strait economic interaction. Nevertheless, Taiwan's imports from China are still under regulations. Only 53.9 percent (or 5,777 items) of 10,724 Harmonized Tariff Schedule (HTS) system–coded ten-digit trade commodities were permitted to be imported from China to Taiwan by December 2000 and 77.5 percent (or 8,306 items) by September 2003.

Statistics on trade between Taiwan and China should include transit exports (reexports) to China via Hong Kong and other places, transshipments (goods are consigned directly from Taiwan to a buyer in China, though the goods are transported via Hong Kong), transit shipments (goods do not change vessels and simply pass through Hong Kong on their way to China), direct trade (small-scale trade often conducted by fishermen, legal for China, but illegal according to Taiwan's regulations), and smuggling (illegal for both Taiwan and China). Some portion of Taiwan's exports to northern China pass through Japan and Korea, in particular through Japan's Ishigaki-jima (Shiyuan Islands).

Taiwan's Mainland Affairs Council (MAC) estimates that Taiwan's exports to China are equal to transit trade plus the difference between Taiwan's exports to Hong Kong and Hong Kong's imports from Taiwan. This estimate should be better than the figures from China's customs service because China's figures do not take different types of Taiwanese exports to China into account and thus underestimate the total amount. Because MAC has provided a consistent series of estimates for bilateral trade between Taiwan and China since 1981, scholars usually adopt its estimated figures.

According to MAC's estimates, Taiwan's indirect trade with China via Hong Kong was only $460 million in 1981 and $279 million in 1982. Thereafter, cross-strait trade increased tremendously to $3.9 billion in 1989, $17.9 billion in 1994, $31.2 billion in 2000, and $37.4 billion in 2002. Between 1981 and 2002, Taiwan's trade with China increased 134-fold.

In addition, Taiwan has enjoyed a continuous and large trade surplus with China for the past two decades. In 1981, Taiwan ran a trade surplus of $310 million, with $385 million of exports to China and $75 million of imports from China. In 1989, Taiwan ran a trade surplus of $2.7 billion, with $3.3 billion of exports to China and $587 million of imports from China. In 2002, Taiwan ran a trade surplus of $21.6 billion, with $29.5 billion of exports to China and $7.9 billion of imports from China.

Since 1993, China has become Taiwan's third-largest trading partner, after the United States and Japan. In 2002, Taiwan's trade with the United States, Japan, and China was $44.9 billion, $39.3 billion, and $37.4 billion, respectively. In addition, China has also become Taiwan's second-largest export market, next to the United States, since 1993. In 2002, China became Taiwan's largest export market for the first time. According to MAC's estimate, in 2002, Taiwan's exports to China (excluding Hong Kong), the United States, and Japan were $29.4 billion, $26.7 billion, and $12 billion, respectively.

In comparison, between 1990 and 1999, Taiwan was China's fourth-largest trading partner, next to Japan, the United States, and Hong Kong. Between 2000 and 2002, Taiwan was China's fifth-largest trading partner, next to Japan, the United States, Hong Kong, and Korea. In 2002, China's trade with Japan, the United States, Hong Kong, Korea, and Taiwan was $101.9 billion, $97.2 billion, $69.2 billion, $44.1 billion, and $37.4 billion, respectively. In addition, since 1993 Taiwan has also become China's second-largest supplier (Japan has been its largest supplier). In 2002, China's imports from Japan and Taiwan were $53.5 billion and $29.5 billion, respectively.

According to Taiwan's customs statistics, Taiwan's exports to China were concentrated in four of the twenty-two sections in the HTS system: section 7 (plastics and rubber), section 11 (textiles), section 15 (base metals), and section 16 (machinery, mechanical appliances, electrical equipment, parts, and accessories). These four sectors included 61 percent of Taiwan's total exports to China in 1992, 75 percent in 1994, 77 percent in 1996, and 79 percent in 1998. Moreover, between 1992 and 1998, the merchandise structure of Taiwan's exports to China was similar to that of Taiwan's total exports, and these four sections were also the four largest sections of Taiwan's overall exports.

In particular, the share of both section 15 and section 16 has been increasing exponentially. In 1992, section 15 represented 5 percent of Taiwan's total exports to China and section 16 represented 25 percent. In 1998, section 15 represented 13 percent of Taiwan's total exports to China and section 16 represented 33 percent. These two sections accounted for about 46 percent of Taiwan's total exports to China in 1998. By contrast, section 12 (footwear, headgear, and artificial flowers) accounted for 16 percent of Taiwan's total exports to China in 1992, but then declined dramatically to 2 percent by 1998.

This trend is closely related to Taiwan's investment in China. In the late 1980s and early 1990s, most of Taiwan's investment in China was in the plastics, shoe, textile, and apparel industries (sections 7, 11, and 12). By the mid-1990s, the bulk of Taiwan's investment in China was concentrated in base metals industries and electronic and electric appliances (sections 15 and 16). Indeed, Taiwan's exports were mostly driven by Taiwan's investment in China.

According to Taiwan's customs statistics, the merchandise structure of Taiwan's imports from China was also concentrated in four of the twenty-two sections in the HTS system: section 5 (mineral products), section 6 (products of chemical or allied industries), section 15 (base metals), and section 16 (machinery, mechanical appliances, electrical equipment, parts, and accessories). These four sectors accounted for 61 percent of Taiwan's total imports from China in 1992, 61 percent in 1994, 69 percent in 1996, and 73 percent in 1998. These four sections were also the four largest sections of Taiwan's overall imports between 1992 and 1998.

In particular, section 16 (machinery, mechanical appliances, electrical equipment, parts, and accessories) has increased rapidly, from 0.3 percent of Taiwan's total imports from China in 1992 to 37 percent in 1998. In addition, section 15 and section 16 accounted for about 57 percent of Taiwan's total imports from China in 1998. By contrast, in 1992, section 2 (vegetable products) accounted for 15 percent of Taiwan's total imports from China but then declined sharply to 3 percent in 1998. Furthermore, section 5 (mineral products) also declined from 28 percent of Taiwan's total imports from China in 1992 to 9 percent in 1998. Overall, Taiwan's imports from China are no longer China's basic agricultural and industrial raw materials, but products closely related to Taiwan's investment in China (sections 15 and 16).

Finally, trade between Taiwan and China has been characterized by intraindustry trade (IIT), which refers to simultaneous exports and imports of commodities in the same industry or production group during a given time. The IIT index measures the degree of intraindustry trade and varies between 0 (complete interindustry trade) and 100 (complete intraindustry trade). On the basis of the HTS classification, the IIT index for the manufacturing industry of trade between Taiwan and China increased from 16 in 1992 to 30.4 in 1998.

See also Chen Shuibian (1950–); Minority Women in Xinjiang and Taiwan; New Party (NP) (Taiwan); Taiwan, Constitutional Reform in; Taiwan, Development of Democracy in; Taiwan, Economic Transition of; Taiwan, Education Reform in; Taiwan, Ethnicity and Ethnic Policies of; Taiwan, Financial Relations with the Mainland; Taiwan, Income Distribution in; Taiwan, Labor and Labor Laws; Taiwan, Suicide in; Taiwan Strait Crisis, Evolution of.

Bibliography

Chung-Hua Institution for Economic Research, *Dalu ji Liangan Jingji Qingshi Baogao (1997/1998)* (Report on the economic situation of mainland China and the two sides of the Taiwan Strait [1997/1998]) (Taipei: Mainland Affairs Council, 1999); Naughton, Barry, *The China Circle: Economics and Electronics in the PRC, Taiwan, and Hong Kong* (Washington, DC: Brookings Institution Press, 1997); Taiwan Economic Research Institution, ed., *Cross-Strait Economic Statistics Monthly* (Taipei) (various issues, 1996–2003); Tung, Chen-yuan, "China's Economic Leverage and Taiwan's Security Concerns with Respect to Cross-Strait Economic Relations," Ph.D. dissertation, Johns Hopkins University, 2002, pp. 18–90; Wang, Zhi, and G. Edward Schuh, "Economic Integration among Taiwan, Hong Kong, and China: A Computable General Equilibrium Analysis," *Pacific Economic Review* 5, no. 2 (June 2000): 229–262.

Chenyuan Tung

Taiwan Strait Crisis, Evolution of

The Taiwan Strait is a body of water off China's southeast coast and separates the island of Taiwan (Formosa) from mainland China. The strait ranges around 120 to 145 miles in width. After the Chinese Communist Party (CCP) won the civil war (1946–1949) and founded the People's Republic of China (PRC) on the mainland on October 1, 1949, the Republic of China (ROC) moved its seat of government across the Taiwan Strait to the island of Taiwan. From then on, the Taiwan Strait became a battleground between the Chinese Communists and the Nationalists (Kuomintang, KMT) in reshaping their domestic military and political struggle and was the center of a series of international crises between the PRC and the United States during and after the Cold War.

On October 24–26, 1949, the People's Liberation Army (PLA) launched an amphibious offensive campaign against Jinmen (Quemoy or Kinmen), one of several offshore islands in the Taiwan Strait. The landing failed after the PLA lost 9,086 men on Jinmen. The failure of the 1949 Jinmen landing delayed China's plan to attack Taiwan. **Mao Zedong**, chairman of the CCP, ordered the

As Chinese Communist forces approach the Tachen Islands in February 1955, school children are evacuated to Taiwan. © Bettmann/Corbis.

PLA to be better prepared for its cross-strait operations. In December, Mao paid a visit to Moscow and convinced Joseph Stalin, the Soviet leader, to support a new Chinese naval force. Stalin agreed to provide gunships and naval equipment valued at U.S. $150 million, half of the loan Mao received from the Soviet Union. In May, the Chinese Air Force established its first division with fifty Soviet-made fighters and bombers in Nanjing in southeastern China. On June 8, the PLA General Staff reported its Taiwan campaign preparation to the Third Plenary Session of the CCP Seventh National Congress in Beijing.

The **Korean War** broke out on June 25, 1950. It changed the nature of the struggle in the Taiwan Strait. On June 27, President Harry Truman announced that the U.S. Navy Seventh Fleet would be deployed in the Taiwan Strait to prevent the Chinese Communists from attacking Nationalist Taiwan. The presence of the Seventh Fleet transformed the Chinese domestic struggle into an international confrontation between China and the United States. This new challenge in the Taiwan Strait forced the PLA to postpone its attack plan.

The United States officially committed itself to the defense of Taiwan during the 1954–1955 Taiwan Strait crisis. After the Korean armistice was signed in 1953, the PLA resumed its offensive activities in the Taiwan Strait. On September 3, 1954, its artillery troops began heavy shelling upon Jinmen and Mazu (Matsu). On that day, 7,000 shells fell on Jinmen. Because of the severity of the bombardment, a landing on these offshore islands seemed imminent. To support the KMT defense of the Taiwan Strait, President Dwight Eisenhower sent a large naval force to the area in September. The United States was on the brink of war over the Taiwan Strait with China just one year after the Korean armistice. On December 2, the United States and the ROC concluded the Mutual Defense Treaty. The crisis escalated when the PLA landed on Yijiangshan Island on January 18, 1955, and then occupied ten other islands off the eastern coast. The U.S. Congress passed the Formosa Resolution by a vote of 409–3 in the House on January 25 and 85–3 in the Senate on January 28 and authorized the president to deploy U.S. forces for the defense of Taiwan "to include the securing and protecting of such related positions and territories of the area now in friendly hands." In the spring, the Eisenhower administration began a highly charged nuclear threat against the Chinese Communists' further operations in the strait. On April 23, PRC premier **Zhou Enlai** dramatically announced that the Chinese people and their government wanted "no war with the United States in the strait," and that the Chinese government was willing to open negotiations to relax tension. The 1954–1955 crisis did not cause a war between the PRC and the United States. On August 1, 1955, the Chinese-American ambassadorial talks began.

China and the United States went to the brink of war again during the 1958 Taiwan Strait crisis. To stop KMT raids on the mainland, the PLA began another large-scale bombardment of Jinmen, 30,000 shells on the first day, August 23, 1958. The PLA's constant shelling overwhelmingly silenced KMT return fire and halted Taiwan's supply shipments to Jinmen. On September 7, seven American warships (two cruisers and five destroyers) commenced escort of two KMT supply ships. That day the PLA decided not to attack the supply escort. However, on September 8, the PLA bombed another joint fleet that included four KMT ships and five American ships. Meanwhile, U.S. airplanes began to escort KMT shipments to Jinmen. By October 5, the KMT resumed subdued transportation from Taiwan to Jinmen. The PLA's blockade of Jinmen was strong but futile. Taiwan showed no signs of withdrawing its garrison from the island. Mao and the Central Military Commission (CMC) designed a new plan to slow down the shelling and leave the offshore islands in the KMT's hands as a burden for America. Mao called his new policy the "noose strategy." This strategy meant that Beijing would let Taiwan keep Jinmen as long as the Americans occupied Taiwan. Beijing, however, could use the islands as the rope noose to serve its own goals in the international arena in that U.S. protection of Taiwan and Jinmen had put a noose around the United States' neck. In October, the tension in the Taiwan Strait began to ease.

In 1962, the PLA commenced another heavy shelling in the Taiwan Strait. China could now bombard Jinmen to put pressure on America or stop the bombardment to relax tension as an effective means to deal with America and Taiwan in the international arena. Then Beijing ordered the PLA batteries on the front not to shell Jinmen on even-numbered days, while a continued shelling on odd-numbered days would be limited by certain conditions. Thereafter, the shelling became symbolic, a political instrument in the Cold War. The PLA shelling continued from August 1958 to January 1, 1979, when the PRC and the United States normalized their diplomatic relations. The bombardment of Jinmen, which lasted more than twenty years, was the longest sustained artillery warfare in world military history.

The crisis in the Taiwan Strait has continued since the Cold War ended in 1990. In March 1996, China employed military instruments again in the strait in order to prevent ROC president Li Denghui's reelection, which might turn Taiwan's independence ideas into a reality. From March 8 to March 15, the PLA launched three missile tests near Taiwan. One of the missile test areas was only eight miles off the Taiwan coast. From March 12 to March 20, the PLA conducted large-scale naval, air, and landing exercises near Jinmen and Mazu. The KMT government declared that it had made all necessary preparations to deal with the possible Communist invasion. The United States also immediately became involved in the 1996 Taiwan Strait crisis. The U.S. government accused China of being reckless and provocative. President Bill Clinton sent two battle groups headed by the U.S. aircraft carriers *Independence* and *Nimitz* to the area near Taiwan to monitor China's military actions. It was the largest U.S. naval movement in the Asia-Pacific region since the **Vietnam War**. The Chinese government warned the United States not to send its warships into the Taiwan Strait. The United States refused to make any promises. This constituted the first military confrontation in the strait between the two countries since President Richard Nixon's visit to China in 1972. On March 23, Taiwan's presidential election took place, and Li won a landslide victory. On March 25, China ended its third round of military exercises. But the 1996 Taiwan Strait crisis brought the Sino-American relationship down to another low point, and the sources of the hostility, tensions, and confrontations in the Taiwan Strait are far from over. The crises in the Taiwan Strait have often damaged the relationship between China and the United States and poisoned cross-strait communication and negotiations between China and Taiwan.

See also Chen Shuibian (1950–); Cold War and China; Minority Women in Xinjiang and Taiwan; New Party (NP) (Taiwan); Sino-American Relations, Conflicts and Common Interests; Sino-American Relations since 1949; Taiwan, Constitutional Reform in; Taiwan, Development of Democracy in; Taiwan, Economic Transition of; Taiwan, Education Reform in; Taiwan, Ethnicity and Ethnic Policies of; Taiwan, Financial Relations with the Mainland; Taiwan, Income Distribution in; Taiwan, Labor and Labor Laws; Taiwan, Suicide in; Taiwan, Trade Relations with the Mainland.

Bibliography

Accinelli, Robert, *Crisis and Commitment: United States Policy toward Taiwan* (Chapel Hill: University of North Carolina Press, 1996); Li, Xiaobing, "PLA Attacks and Amphibious Operations during the Taiwan Strait Crises of 1954–55 and 1958," in *Chinese Warfighting: The PLA Experience since 1949* ed. Mark Ryan, David Finkelstein, and Michael McDevitt (Armonk, NY: M. E. Sharpe, 2003); Li, Xiaobing, Xiaobo Hu, and Yang Zhong, *Interpreting U.S.-China-Taiwan Relations* (Lanham, MD: University Press of America, 1998); Mao Zedong, *Mao's Manuscripts since the Founding of the PRC*, vols. 4–10, 1954–1963 (Beijing: CCP Central Archives and Manuscripts Press, 1990–1995); Zhao, Suisheng, ed., *Across the Taiwan Strait* (New York: Routledge, 1999).

Xiaobing Li

Tax Reform

See Fiscal Policy and Tax Reforms.

Teacher Education

China has a population of 1.3 billion, and its teacher education serves the largest **educational system** in the world. In 2001, China had 491,300 elementary schools with 125.43 million students, 66,600 lower secondary schools (middle schools) with 65.14 million students, 14,900 upper secondary schools (high schools) with 14 million students, and 21,800 vocational secondary schools holding 9.81 million students. To meet the demands for more and better-qualified teachers, China has exerted great efforts in developing its teacher education. The central government considers teacher education its top priority in the entire educational system. By 2000, China had set up 1,200 teacher education institutions at various levels with an enrollment of more than 1.5 million teacher candidates. Statistics indicated that in 2001 China had 5.8 million elementary-school teachers (with a student/teacher ratio of 22.21:1), 3.4 million middle-school teachers (with a student/teacher ratio of 19.03:1), and 840,000 regular high-school teachers (with a student/teacher ratio of 15.87:1).

The teacher education institutions in China consist of independent public universities, colleges, and schools responsible for teacher preparation at different levels. There are three levels of institutions and schools: (1) teachers' universities and colleges that offer four-year programs and produce upper secondary school teachers; (2) teacher training institutes that offer three-year programs and develop lower secondary school teachers; and (3) teachers' schools that usually have three- or four-year programs at the secondary level and prepare elementary-school and kindergarten teachers. In addition, there are specialized teacher-training schools to provide training for specialized teachers to teach special subjects, such as those in **special education** and vocational education.

Teacher education in China has a very competitive admission process. Teachers' universities, colleges, and institutes enroll new students through the national entrance examination that covers three required subjects (Chinese language and literature, mathematics, and foreign language) and two elective subjects. Biology and chemistry may be selected by science-major candidates, and history and geography by liberal arts–major candidates. Art-, music-, and physical education–major candidates must take additional examinations in specialized areas. Recently, the practice of interviewing candidates has been added to the standardized entrance examinations to evaluate a candidate's learning motivation, appearance, communication skills, and special talents in arts, music, and athletics. Although at this present time, this additional process is still in its trial phase and has been adopted by only a few top schools in the nation, it is likely to be adopted in the near future as standard procedure by teacher education programs throughout the country. The departments of education at the provincial and local levels develop their own entrance examinations to recruit students for local teachers' schools. Since the end of the 1990s, more and more top upper secondary school graduates have chosen teaching as their profession because of increasingly recognized social status, tremendous pay raises, and housing benefits for teachers.

The curricula of teacher education at the higher-education level are very content oriented. The student focuses on one subject area of teaching and pursues systematic and in-depth learning. However, all students are required to take a number of general core courses that include educational theories, psychology, educational technology, foreign language, and field teaching practice. The Ministry of Education leads the centralized curricula planning and development. The centralized curricula cover the science of education, early childhood education, special education, **educational administration**, educational psychology, educational technology, Chinese language and literature education, education in languages and literatures of the minority nationalities, foreign-language education (English, Russian, Japanese, and so on), moral and political education, mathematics education, computer science education, physics education, chemistry education, biology education, geography education, history education, music education, fine-arts education, and physical education.

In addition to the regular teacher education institutions, China has established a nationwide network of in-service training to enhance teachers' qualifications at all levels. Statistics indicated that in 2001 there were 122 educational colleges at the provincial level with an enrollment of 304,400 in-service teachers from lower and upper secondary schools, and there were 1,866 teacher-training schools at the county level with an enrollment of 192,800 in-service elementary and kindergarten teachers. Moreover, **television** universities, evening universities (usually located at regular institutions), and universities by correspondence also offer in-service teacher trainings. Television universities and universities by correspondence have established thousands of tutoring stations across the nation. The stations are not only places for tutoring, but are also used to conduct series of workshops to provide opportunities for face-to-face communication and discussion between students and instructors. These various training programs provide teachers with sufficient opportunities to meet the national standards for obtaining academic degrees and teaching certifications. They also provide teachers with a lifelong learning environment to update their knowledge and skills for the best practices in education.

The teacher institutions share specific responsibilities for the in-service training. The Ministry of Education runs six key teachers' universities in six geographic regions, each of which offers in-service training to administrators and faculty members from other teacher education institutions in that region. These universities also provide training for upper secondary school teachers and principals. The teachers' colleges and universities run by provinces and major cities offer in-service training for lower and upper secondary school teachers, while teachers' schools at the county level, kindergartens, and elementary schools provide in-service training to teachers.

Since the mid-1980s, comprehensive reform has taken place in China's teacher education. Changes have focused on curricula design for wider coverage, pedagogical approaches for effective instruction, and textbooks and other resources for curricula update and enrichment. The reform has also emphasized candidate recruitment to deal with teacher shortages, teacher placement to bring school systems and graduates together, and candidates' targeted knowledge, creativity, and teaching skills, a significant step forward at the beginning of the twenty-first century to raise the standards for teaching certifications. These new standards expect upper secondary school teachers to hold bachelor's or higher degrees, lower secondary school teachers to hold bachelor's degrees, and elementary and kindergarten teachers to have certifications from a three-year teacher education program at the higher-education level.

See also Character Education in Primary and Secondary Schools; Education Media and Technology; Higher-Education Reform; Management Education; Primary Education; Private Education; School Enrollment and Employment; Secondary Education; Taiwan, Education Reform in; United States, Chinese Education in; Vocational and Technical Training.

Bibliography

General Survey of Education in China (Beijing: Department of Foreign Affairs of the State Education Commission of the People's Republic of China, 1997); Ministry of Education, PRC, *Education in China* (Beijing: Ministry of Education, 2002); *The Ninth Five-Year Plan for Educational Development and the Long-Range Development Program toward the Year 2010* (Beijing: State Education Commission of the People's Republic of China, 1996).

Binyao Zheng

Telecommunications Industry

In March 2002, China's telecommunications market surpassed that of the United States and became the world's largest telephone network in terms of both capacity and subscriber base, with 190 million fixed-line subscribers and 160 million mobile-phone subscribers. This remarkable achievement changed the landscape of the global telecommunications market.

When the People's Republic of China (PRC) was founded in 1949, the country of more than 500 million people had only 263,000 telephones with a switchboard capacity of 310,000 lines. Teledensity (telephone main lines per 100 residents) was only 0.05. More than 90 percent of counties in China had no telecom facilities at all.

In the first two-thirds of the PRC's history, telecommunications development tailed national economic growth for most years. While the size of the economy multiplied 6.5 times in real terms, the switchboard capacity increased to only 2.5 times the base-year level. As a result, toward the end of the **Great Cultural Revolution (1966–1976)**, China's teledensity was only 0.3. The snail-pace growth was largely due to the low priority given to the telecom sector in the heavy-industry-biased development plans during the **Mao Zedong** era (1950s–1970s).

When China launched its economic modernization program with market-oriented reforms in the late 1970s, the telecom sector stood as a glaring

Telephone booths like this are found on most street corners in major Chinese cities.

bottleneck in the economy. This situation caused grave concerns to policy makers. The government then introduced a series of policy stimuli and reforms to promote the industry.

In the prereform years, the state-owned post and telecom enterprises (PTEs) were considered "nonprofit institutions." The telecom sector was placed under a rigid, semimilitary administrative structure under the Ministry of Post and Telecommunications (MPT). The system was highly centralized, with little autonomy and financial accountability at the local enterprise level. The MPT was dissolved in the period from 1969 to 1973, and the telecom sector was put under the regional military administrations. From 1973 to 1979, provincial and municipal governments controlled the media. The fragmented administrative structure caused many coordination problems.

In 1979, the State Council reestablished the MPT's role as the dominant central planner of nationwide post and telecom development. Local PTEs were put under the "dual leadership" of provincial governments and the MPT, and the latter was the main supervisor. Operational business decisions were delegated with the introduction of primary financial accountability at the local level. By the mid-1980s, all the PTEs started to operate on a system of contractual responsibility in which their earnings were linked to the revenues of their own operation and the national network. In this hierarchic regime, the MPT set or capped service prices and tariffs, while output (communication traffic) maximization became the main business objective for the PTEs, which were strongly motivated to expand local infrastructure to overcome supply capacity constraints.

From the 1980s to the 1990s, the telecom sector received various financial stimuli from the state. In the early 1980s, a policy of "three 90 percents" was adopted: 90 percent of profit was retained by the MPT (in other words, the tax rate was 10 percent, well below the 55 percent tax rate for other industries before 1994); 90 percent of foreign exchange (hard-currency) earnings were retained by the MPT; and 90 percent of central government investment was not considered repayable loans. PTEs also enjoyed favorable interest rates when they borrowed from state banks. The preferential "three 90 percents" policy provided favorable conditions for the sector's expansion until 1994, when a major fiscal monetary reform unified corporate tax rates, simplified the tax levy structure, and moved the Chinese currency toward current account convertibility. Other preferential policies included decentralizing telecom investment financing to the local level through various fund-raising schemes, allowing a faster pace of capital depreciation in the postal and telecom sector, granting the most preferential zero rate for telecom projects when the "coordinating tax for directions of fixed capital investment" was levied in the 1990s, authorizing PTEs to charge telephone subscribers expensive installation fees, granting preferential tariff rates to the import of telecom equipment, and opening the telecom equipment manufacturing sector to foreign investment.

In the decade after 1984, these favorable policies accelerated switchboard capacity growth by leaps and bounds. The average annual growth rate of main telephone lines from 1988 to 1991 was twice the rate of GDP growth and accelerated above 30 percent after 1992. In the first half of the 1990s, China installed more than 73 million phone lines, more than all the rest of the developing world combined. The investment boom was mainly financed through three sources: the installation fee collected from the users (40 percent); domestic and foreign government loans (30 percent); and PTEs' profits and capital depreciation (30 percent). Throughout the 1990s, the growth rate of telephone lines consistently exceeded that of GDP, three to four times higher on average. From 1985 to the end of 2002, switchboard capacity leaped from 5.5 million lines to 283.6 million lines, the number of fixed-line phone subscribers increased from 2.7 million to 214.4 million, and teledensity rose from below 0.6 to 16.8.

Backed by strong state support and preferential policies, the MPT-controlled business empire enjoyed the status of a privileged monopoly in its heyday. However, with increasing participation of non-MPT investors in infrastructure construction and rising demand for better and more telecom services, the call for competition became increasingly compelling in the 1990s and eventually made its way to the official agenda. Competition first arrived in China's telecom equipment market in 1988 when the MPT delegated decisions regarding procurement, operations, network development, and financing to local PTEs. The terminal equipment market was deregulated to allow the PTEs and service users to make purchasing choices freely among competing domestic and foreign equipment suppliers.

Over the years, several government ministerial branches developed a number of nonpublic/dedicated communication networks (outside the MPT-managed public network) for their own interior uses. The jurisdiction of these ministerial branches over these dedicated networks was beyond the MPT's domain. In 1993, the State Council formally deregulated the paging service market and very small aperture terminal (VSAT) communications by authorizing the MPT to license these service suppliers. Jitong Communications Company, set up by the State Economic and Trade Commission, was the first major value-added network operator that entered the market in June 1993. Later that year, the State Council awarded a basic telecom license to China United Telecommunications Corporation (Unicom), which was set up by three powerful ministries and thirteen major state-owned companies. After the entry of these new players, China Telecom, the MPT-controlled monopoly, faced increasing challenges to its dominance over the telecom market (Mueller and Tan 1997).

At first, policy coordination between the MPT and non-MPT interests was carried out by the State Council at the superministerial level through ad hoc administrative intervention or arbitrated negotiations. In March 1998, the Ministry of Information Industry (MII) was created at the Ninth **National People's Congress** to replace the MPT and become the regulatory authority of the info-communications industry. By early 1999, the business interests of the former MPT were regrouped and incorporated into two separate business entities, China Post and China Telecom. A year later, China Telecom experienced its first divestiture, which divided major chunks of its assets between China Telecom, which owned the nationwide fixed-line public network and provided long-distance and local fixed-line services, and China Mobile, which offered mobile telecom services. With transferred assets and managerial personnel from the former China Telecom and backed by favorable policy support, China Unicom was soon beefed up as an effective and aggressive rival to China Mobile in mobile telecommunications.

From 1999 to 2001, two more powerful players, China Railcom, backed by the Ministry of Railway, and China Netcom Corporation, backed by the Chinese Academy of Sciences and several other government departments, entered the arena. Both had plans to operate and develop their own nationwide broadband network projects. In early 2000, the MII licensed China Telecom, Unicom, Jitong, and Netcom to compete in the **Internet** protocol telephone market. Later that year, the State Council promulgated the Telecommunications Regulations as a preliminary regulatory framework.

At the end of 2001, China joined the World Trade Organization (WTO) as its 143rd member. As part of its commitments to the organization, China lifted its long-standing ban on foreign equity investment in the telecom service business. Foreign companies were allowed to enter China's telecom market through joint ventures with indigenous partners, while foreigners' capital shares were permitted to rise gradually up to 49 percent for basic fixed-line and mobile telecom services and up to 50 percent for paging and value-added services by the end of 2003.

Meanwhile, the State Council ruled favorably for the second divestiture of China Telecom, the fixed-line telecom monopoly. This divestiture, completed in May 2002, transferred China Telecom's network of ten provincial regions in northern China to Netcom and restructured the latter to China Netcom Corporation (CNC), which also took over Jitong. The postdivestiture (new) China Telecom retains the remaining network of twenty-one provincial regions in the rest of China. Since then, the telecom market has been shared by six corporations, China Telecom, CNC, China Mobile, China Unicom, China Railcom, and China Satcom (set up in December 2001).

The industry's regulatory framework still lacks legal basis due to the absence of a telecommunications law, which has been drafted for years but has yet to be proposed for approval to the National People's Congress, China's legislature. Drastic industrial restructuring and uncertainty of regulatory reform have clouded business prospects in a market where the hypergrowth period is nearing its end. In a state-ownership-dominated industrial structure, business interests continue to intertwine with political influences. Despite that, progress has been made toward a rule-based regulatory framework and business environment. The Tenth Five-Year Plan (2001–2005) drafted by the MII predicts that the growth rate of the telecommunications industry will continue to beat the overall economic growth rate in the near future.

See also Television; Television Institute and Self-Learning.

Bibliography

Lu, Ding, "China's Telecommunications Infrastructure Buildup: On Its Own Way," in *Deregulation and Interdependence in the Asia-Pacific Region*, ed. Takatoshi Ito and Anne O. Krueger, 371–414 (Chicago: University of Chicago Press, 2000); Lu, Ding, and C. K. Wong, *China's Telecommunications Market: Entering a New Competitive Age* (Cheltenham, UK: Edward Elgar, 2004); Mueller, Milton, and Zixiang Tan, *China in the Information Age: Telecommunications and the Dilemma of Reform* (Westport, CT: Praeger, 1997).

Ding Lu

Television

In the approximately forty years since television emerged in China, Chinese television has become one of the largest, most sophisticated, and influential television systems in the world. The country's first TV station, Beijing Television, began broadcasting on May 1, 1958. Within just two years, dozens of stations were set up in major cities such as Shanghai and Guangzhou, though most stations had to rely on planes, trains, or cars to transport video files. The first setback for Chinese television came in the early 1960s when the Soviet Union withdrew economic aid from China. Many TV stations were closed. The second setback was caused by an internal factor, the **Great Cultural Revolution** from 1966 to 1976. Television's regular telecasting was forced to a halt in January 1967 by the leftists of the Chinese Communist Party. Television stations were changed to a new revolutionary direction as a weapon for class struggle and anti-imperialism, antirevisionism, and anticapitalism.

In the late 1970s, with the end of the Great Cultural Revolution and the start of the country's reform, television became the most rapidly growing medium. On May 1, 1978, Beijing Television changed to China Central Television (CCTV) as the country's only national network, with the largest audience body in the world. From the 1980s throughout the 1990s, television underwent swift development. The total number of TV stations once reached more than 1,000, with one national network, dozens of provincial and major city networks, and hundreds of regional and local ones. The government reregulated

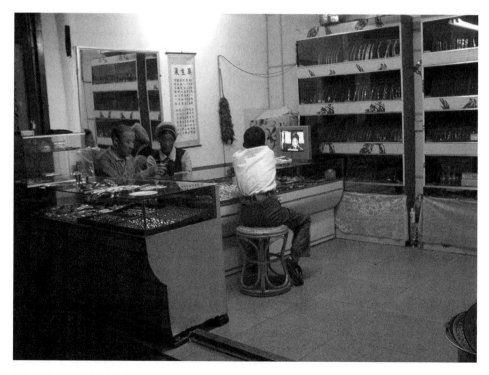

Televisions are becoming more common sights in modern China. In this 2004 photo, a jewelry store employee passes the time watching television.

TV development when it became out of control and chaotic in the late 1990s. In 2000, China had a total of 651 programming-generating TV stations, 42,228 TV transmitting and relaying stations, and 368,553 satellite-TV receiving and relaying stations. With 270 million TV sets, China has become the nation with the most TV sets in the world. Statistically, presently every Chinese family owns a TV set, and the penetration rate of television has reached 92.5 percent, covering a population of 1 billion.

Television broadcasting technology has also developed very quickly. Both cable television and satellite television have developed rapidly. Except at the central level, thousands of cable services were established in all provinces, major cities, and especially at the county level during the 1980s and 1990s. A few major stations have also started using high technology for production and broadcasting, such as virtual field production technology and high-definition technology. Digital broadcasting technology has been set as one priority of China's Tenth Five-Year Plan from 2001 to 2005. However, the only form of television in China is state ownership. No private-ownership or foreign-ownership television is permitted. Without government permission, receiving foreign TV programming via satellite is still illegal and prohibited.

The media theories that underpin Chinese television broadcasting come directly from Marxist-Leninist doctrine. **Mao Zedong** further embellished Marx's idea of the importance of superstructure and ideological state apparatus and Lenin's concept of the importance of propaganda and media control. The current leadership of the Communist Party follows Mao's course and requires that broadcasting must keep in line with the Party and serve the Party's main tasks voluntarily, firmly, and in timely fashion. Under these guidelines, television is used by the Party and the state to impose ideological hegemony on the society. The Party and the central government set the tone of propaganda for television. Although TV stations provide news, entertainment, and education programs, television's first function is to popularize Party and government policies and motivate the masses in the construction of Communist ideology. The Communist Party is actually the owner, the manager, and the practitioner of television. All TV stations are under the dual jurisdiction of the Communist Party's propaganda department and the government's radio and television bureaus at different levels. The self-censorship policy has long been extensively used. While routine material does not require approval from Party authorities, important editorials, news stories, and sensitive topics all require prior endorsement by Party authorities.

In general, television programming consists of five categories: news programs, documentary and magazine programs, education programs, entertainment programs, and service programs. Among the total broadcasting hours, roughly 10 percent are news programs, 10 percent are documentary and magazine programs, 2 percent are education programs, 60 percent are entertainment programs, and 18 percent are service programs and advertising. Although entertainment programs occupy the bulk of the total broadcasting hours, before the reform in the late 1970s there were not many real entertainment programs. In those years, most entertainment programs were old films of revolutionary stories, with occasional live broadcasts of modern operas about model workers, peasants, and soldiers. Newscasts were mostly what the

Party's official newspapers and the official news agencies reported. Production capability was low, production quality was poor, equipment and facilities were simple, and broadcasting hours, transmitting scales, and channel selections were limited.

Nevertheless, television production and programming have developed explosively in the last twenty years. Many taboos have been eliminated, restrictions have been lifted, and new production skills have been adopted. Entertainment programs in the form of TV plays, soap operas, Chinese traditional operas, game shows, and domestic and foreign feature films have become routine. News programs have also changed substantially and expanded enormously. International news coverage and live telecasts of important news events are now often seen in news programs, and education programs have received special treatment from the government.

Television production capability also has been remarkably enhanced since the reform. CCTV has expanded from two channels in 1978 to twelve channels in 2002, and most provincial and major city networks have also increased broadcasting channels and offered more programs. Broadcasting hours have increased considerably as well. In an average week of the year 1980, 2,018 hours of programs were broadcast. The number went up to 7,698 in 1985, 22,298 in 1990, and 83,373 in 2000, a 3.5-fold increase in five years, an 11-fold expansion in ten years, and a 41-fold explosion in twenty years.

The most important token of the internationalization of Chinese television is the change in programming importation. Importation before the reform was quantitatively limited and ideologically and politically oriented. From the late 1950s to the late 1970s, only the national network was authorized to import TV programs under tight control and close surveillance of the Party and the government. Few programs were imported from Western countries, and these few were restricted only to those that exemplified that "socialism is promising, capitalism is hopeless." During the reform period, the ban was gradually lifted. Today, central, provincial, regional, and even local television stations are all looking to other countries, mostly Western nations, as a source of programs. Moreover, import channels, import purposes, import criteria, import formats, and import categories have all changed, expanded, or developed significantly. In the early 1970s, imported programming occupied less than 1 percent of the total programming nationwide. The figure jumped to 8 percent in the early 1980s, 15 percent in the early 1990s, and around 25 percent in 2000.

Efforts have also been made to expand exportation of China-produced TV programs to other countries. Programs produced by major TV stations have entered the global TV program market. In addition, CCTV and a few other major Chinese TV stations have established joint-venture businesses with television stations in North America, South America, Europe, Asia, and Oceania to broadcast programs via satellite. CCTV's International Channel and English Channel are now broadcast via satellite and are available in most countries across the world.

The most significant change in Chinese television is commercialization. Advertising was halted for three decades following the Communist Party's ascent to power in 1949, but both domestic and foreign advertising were resurrected in the late 1970s. Throughout the 1980s, television's revenue from advertising increased at an annual rate of 50 to 60 percent. In the 1990s, television became the most commercialized and market-oriented medium and attracted a large portion of advertising investment from both domestic and foreign clients. Presently, the majority of programming revenue, ranging from 90 percent as the highest to 40 percent as the lowest, is being funded by advertising and other commercial activities. In 2000, the nationwide total TV advertising revenue was 16,891 million Chinese yuan, 23.7 percent of China's total advertising revenue.

Overall, under the modernization policy, the **Open Door policy**, the marketization policy, and the decentralization policy, in the last two decades television in China has become a very popular medium, a very technologically advanced broadcast system, and a highly professionally performed service. Television's function has evolved from a single-purpose one for political and ideological propaganda only to a multipurpose one for serving both the Party and the government and society and the public as well.

See also Commercial Advertising, Policies and Practices of; Internet; Media Bodies, Central and Local; Media Distribution; Media Reform; Telecommunications Industry; Television Institute and Self-Learning.

Bibliography

Hong, J., "China's Dual Perception of Globalization and Its Reflection on Media Policies," in *The New Communications Landscape: Demystifying Globalization*, ed. G. Wang, 288–306 (London: Routledge, 2000); Hong, *The Internationalization of Television in China: The Evolution of Ideology, Society, and Media since the Reform* (Westport, CT: Praeger, 1998); Hong, "The Transition of China's Media Import Policy in the 1990s: Continuities, Discontinuities, and New Trends," in *Transition towards Post-Deng China*, ed. X. Hu and G. Lin, 171–194 (Singapore: Singapore University Press, 2001).

Junhao Hong

Television Institute and Self-Learning

The Television Institute is an important part of adult and higher education in the People's Republic of China (PRC). The institute delivers its instruction mainly through **television**, radio, and modern advanced technology. Established in 1979 with the strong backing of President Deng Xiaoping, the institute has grown rapidly. The China Television Institute has become the largest distance education system in the world, with an enrollment of 1.3 million students. Within twenty years (1979–1999), this giant education system had educated more than 2.6 million university undergraduates and 1 million senior college students and had certified 3.5 million nonmajor students in the humanities, natural sciences, and other disciplines. The national television normal colleges had served about 710,000 normal-school graduates and 550,000 normal-college graduates and had provided training for more than 2 million in-service teachers and 1 million principals from elementary, lower secondary, and upper secondary schools (Ministry of Education 2002).

In the beginning, the Television Institute system in China aimed to meet the needs of those who did not get the chance to be formally enrolled in regular universities and colleges. Later it served all students nationwide as long as they wanted to pursue further education. Now it consists of Central Television University, state television universities, and city or local branches. Central Television University is directly under the leadership of the Ministry of Education and coordinates 44 state television universities, 841 city branches, and 1,742 county centers, and leads the development of curriculum, faculty training, and candidate testing (Bian 2001). Each state television university or local branch has its own responsibility for running instruction and management to meet state and local needs. In 1999, the national fixed assets of the China Television Institute were more than 5 billion Chinese yuan, and the library collections contained about 240 million hard copies of books and materials, 2 million audiocassette tapes, and 1.7 million videotapes.

As the largest distance education system in the world, the China Television University is involved in distance instruction and learning, planning and organizing under central leadership, and operating and managing at different levels. The Chinese government strongly supports this education giant by investing in and establishing a dependable and reliable satellite broadcasting and receiving system. Central Television University programs are delivered to all corners of the nation through three television channels. There are 8,000 hours of instructional programs on the air annually. The Central Television University also provides state television universities and local branches/centers with different instructional resources and supplementary materials at different levels through Vertical Blanking Interval (VBI) data net. Since 1999, the Central Television University has implemented **Internet** use into distance education and has increasingly developed computer-assisted instruction. The goal is for China to activate a national satellite education net, establish a dynamic and interactive distance education system, and integrate an advanced computing network with the instruction and management of the television institute by 2006.

Tuition and related fees for instructional materials and activities are not the same within the television institute system. Each state television university has its own standards for tuition and fees. Generally, tuition and fees are collected on the basis of an academic semester or year. Tuition for a junior college student currently ranges from 1,100 to 1,500 Chinese yuan per year. The total is about 3,300 to 4,500 Chinese yuan to complete a program within three years and 5,000 to 6,000 Chinese yuan for a four-year degree (Bian 2001).

The students of the China Television Institute system are enrolled in degree and nondegree programs. Those in degree programs must pass a national entrance examination, although each state television university may have its own admission criteria. Those students in nondegree programs can waive the entrance examination; however, they must have an upper secondary school diploma or an equivalent diploma from a technical school and pay tuition and related fees. The majority of students in either of the two programs are young adults from twenty to thirty-five years old, some are older (forty to fifty years old), and a few are over the age of sixty.

The Television Institute system in China offers both junior college and senior college degrees. The curriculum covers various subject areas, including economics, law, education, literature, history, science, technologies, agriculture, medical science, and business management. Instructional quality is heavily stressed with a "Five Unities" approach: unified curricula, unified syllabus, unified textbooks, unified examinations, and unified assessments. In addition to instruction via television, radio, and computer networks, self-studies, tutorials, questions-and-answers, and practice are also widely used in both teaching and learning. Of course, self-learning is key for a student of the Television Institute. He or she sets up his or her learning schedule according to the requirements of the specific program and instruction plan. The assessment of the degree of knowledge acquired depends on the completion of course assignments, projects, papers, and a final examination. Course assignments, projects, and papers are evaluated as prerequisites of the final examination and are proportionally weighted for course credits. Upon the completion of course work, each student participates in field practice training for three to four weeks and completes the program with a capstone project or final paper within the following four to eight weeks. The topic of the capstone project or final paper is selected under the guidance of the instructor, monitored and evaluated by a project committee, and defended by the learner. A learner can also depend on his or her self-learning without being enrolled in the Television Institute system. Upon completion of required courses through self-study, he or she can apply to take the national graduation examination for the diploma and degree in a specific major area. Both the Television Institute and the self-learning system have greatly promoted lifelong learning in Chinese higher education today.

See also Higher-Education Reform; Telecommunications Industry.

Bibliography

Bian, Qingli, *China Television Education*, 2001, http://www.edu.cn/20010827/208332.shtml, accessed on April 1, 2003; "Introduction to China Central Radio and TV University (CCRTVU), People's Republic of China," http://www.logos-net.net/ilo/150_base/en/init/chn_2.htm, accessed on April 1, 2003; Liu, Aoping, "Self-Learning and Examination in Higher Education," 2001, http://www.edu.cn/20010827/208331.shtml, accessed on April 1, 2003; Ministry of Education, PRC, *Education in China* (Beijing: Ministry of Education, 2002).

Ronghua Ouyang and Dan Ouyang

Theater in Contemporary China

Contemporary Chinese theater can mean indigenous operatic forms, West-imported theatrical genres, or hybridizations of the two. The Chinese theater history since 1949, when the People's Republic of China (PRC) was founded, has witnessed a government-sponsored movement to reform traditional forms and introduce the Western models in line with Mao's cultural policy of "using the ancient to serve the present and the foreign to serve the domestic." While efforts in the 1960s to "modernize" traditional operas can be seen as motivated by ideological reasons, they can also be seen as an attempt to render ancient forms responsive to present reality. Governmental patronage was also seen in the establishment of a nationwide network of academies and schools to train

Classic dance performances, like the one shown here, have become popular entertainment in modern Chinese theater.

professional performers and specialists in Western forms such as spoken drama (Stanislavskian realism), opera (bel canto), and ballet (Russian). One side effect was that Chinese theater was invariably institutionalized. Performances were offered exclusively by state-owned companies. Professional training could only be pursued in state academies and schools. Not surprisingly, contents of theatrical works, if not directly decided on by the state in each case, were chosen by companies themselves in careful conformity with generally received standards of political correctness.

A new leaf was turned when China embarked on the modernization program in the late 1970s. As a consequence of the switch to a market-oriented economy, institutionalized theater companies have diminished in numbers and size and have staged fewer shows than before as government subsidies have continued to dwindle. The need of most provincial and national companies to fend for themselves has ushered in a period of commercialization. Less ideologically committed and hardly mindful of politics, many of them have undertaken to pander to popular taste by having recourse to such elements as song, dance, and amours for the purpose of profit. Chinese contemporary theater, hitherto heedful of Marx, has become attentive also to mammon. In a related way, the government has adopted a more broad-minded attitude toward cultural production. It advocates a policy of both promoting the "key theme" and encouraging "diversification." Productions that play on "key themes" are expected to uplift people's minds and pick up people's spirits, that is, promote a positive attitude toward present life. They tend to be tailor made for special days on the Chinese political calendar and often with a view to winning official awards.

As a result of the nation's opening to the West, the first phase of Chinese theatrical "diversification" saw a spate of productions of works by such Western masters as Shakespeare, Brecht, Beckett, Büchner, Pinter, Ionesco, Genet, and O'Neill, as well as applications of Western ideas of theater. A more profound impact of Western theater on Chinese artists was evidenced in the emergence of "experimental theater," the most prominent figure of which was Gao Xingjian. Directed ingeniously by Lin Zhao Hua in the country's most prestigious institutionalized company, the Beijing People's Art Theatre, the three plays Gao composed before his departure for Paris in 1988 may be seen as having been inspired by theater of the absurd, Brecht, and Artaud.

In the last decade, professional theater artists in major cities have concentrated their creative energy on aesthetic pursuits. The most noticeable accomplishment has been increased visual appeal of the stage. Important stage designers include Yi Liming, Liu Yuansheng, Liu Xinglin, Huang Haiwei, Gao Guangjian, and Li Zeng. Another area that has attracted many aspiring artists is theatrical kinetics. Serious choreographic work started only after 1949. The Russian model of classical ballet introduced in the 1950s dominated dance training for a long time and left an omnipresent stamp. Chinese choreographers, however, have been seeking a Chinese idiom for this imported form either by availing themselves of stylized operatic movements of traditional operas and vernacular dances or by turning to ancient murals and sculptures. Having returned in 1996 from studies and performances in the United States, Jin Xing delighted audiences with the *Half Dream* and *Red and Black* series as well as *Tipsy Concubine*, the first full-length Chinese dance theater work. In these works, she blended her Chinese experience with her modern dance training with varying degrees of success. In spite of occasional flashes of talent and imagination, a coherent, consistent, original dance vocabulary is yet to emerge for full-fledged dance theater works. However, welcome results have been achieved by stage directors Xu Xiaozhong and Zha Lifang, who have incorporated elements of folk dance and traditional operatic movement in productions of plays like Xu's *Shangshuping Chronicles* and Zha's *Stirrings in a Cesspool*.

The most aesthetically accomplished artist may be the director Lin Zhao Hua, whose diverse productions are characterized by precise acting, fluid narration, refined staging, and thematic clarity. The most popular one may be Meng Jinghui. His works are marked by a joie de vivre and playful irreverence that have won the hearts of young audiences.

Exposure to the international theater scene has had such artists as Western-trained director Chen Shizhen and designer Huang Haiwei to reexamine Chinese heritage from new perspectives acquired via contact with modern Western theater. Energized by searing visual effects and mesmerizing ritual dances from their native Hunan Province, their intercultural production of *Bakchai* by the Beijing Peking Opera Troupe was a triumph of visual and physical theater. Their large-scale international project *Peony Pavilion*, staged in New York and Paris, was a multinight saga to the accompaniment of an orchestra of period instruments, in authentic costume and a setting that recreated a traditional water pavilion. The extravaganza did not pretend to be an archeological endeavor. It was a carefully employed stratagem to reposition Chinese artists in the time of cultural globalization by emphasizing the uniqueness of a Chinese idea of theater.

Patronage offered by Western foundations and festivals has given rise to a new type of theatrical productions. While some critics argue that these productions are symptomatic of postcolonialism because they are made to order and meant for export only, others choose to see overseas sponsorship as an opportunity for individual artists from different cultural backgrounds to meet each other in search of new art forms and deepened understandings.

Taking advantage of the lack of censorship of the stage and fighting against the lack of access to the resources of professional companies, independent theater began to emerge in the early 1990s. Mo Sen's ensemble may be seen as the flagship of the marginalized independent theater, although his last work was staged in 1997. Although there is little evidence that Mo Sen, who did his apprenticeship with Lin Zhaohua, has been sufficiently exposed to Western theater or commands a good understanding of Western avant-gardism, he has repeatedly paid homage to such figures as Suzuki, Grotowski, Brook, and the Living Theatre. Mo Sen's real innovation lies in the alternative he offers to the professionalism of institutionalized theater and an interdisciplinary approach that opens up theater to artists from other fields. While his use of nonprofessionals, disregard of academy aesthetics, reliance on visual and physical expressiveness, and use of nondramatic text may impress a sophisticated audience as an amalgam of performance art, installation, physical theater, and other forms, such a work as *File Zero* still remains a unique, powerful, and more-than-realistic exploration of the sense of alienation in a metropolis.

The fate of spoken drama has always been bound with the political life of the nation. When students first imported spoken drama into China, this Western form was welcomed as a forum to discuss ways to amend social maladies and in itself as a means to effect social reform. Its supposed virtue was its powerful engagement with pressing issues that were facing the nation. Recent Chinese history has witnessed the persistence of this power. It had its time of glory when plays by Su Shuyang and Li Longyong that drew on recent political events and depicted the experiences of ordinary people in cataclysmic times packed playhouses everywhere. In the mid- and late 1980s, when public expectations for socialist democracy and national prosperity were raised, plays by Sha Yexin, Liu Shugang, and Wang Peigong about people's aspirations and disappointments struck chords of sympathy in massive audiences. In 1999, Tian Qin Xin's dramatization of *Scenes of Life and Death*, a thought-provoking and emotive study of gender, class, and nation against the background of China's Anti-Japanese War (1937–1945), Huang Jisu and Meng Jinhui's free adaptation of Dario Fo's *Morte accidentale di un anarchico*, a biting satire against corruption, and the collaborative production *Che Guevara*, a plea for a fairer society, have succeeded in pushing theater into the focus of attention for **intellectuals** for the first time in the past twenty years. The latest heartening news is the tremendous increase in theatrical creations on college and university campuses, in part due to the governmental efforts to install art disciplines in university education. Campus theater seems to be gathering momentum for original playwriting and turning away from masterpieces. Even though it is often found lacking in technical competence and aesthetic polish, it testifies both to an absorption with the newly discovered individual and to an alertness to Chinese and world politics.

See also Anticorruption Literature and Television Dramas; Avant-garde Literature; Experimental Fiction; Folk Songs and Music of New China; Great Cultural Revolution, Literature during; Intellectuals, Political Engagement of (1949–1978); Intellectuals, Political Engagement of (1978–Present); Literary Policy for the New China; Literature of the Wounded; Misty Poetry; Modern Pop-Satire; Neorealist Fiction and Modernism; Pre–Cultural Revolution Literature; Revolutionary Realism and Revolutionary Romanticism; Root-Searching Literature; Sexual Freedom in Literature.

Bibliography

Lau, Joseph S. M., and Howard Goldblatt, eds., *The Columbia Anthology of Modern Chinese Literature* (New York: Columbia University Press, 1995); Mackerras, Colin, *The Chinese Theatre in Modern Times, from 1840 to the Present Day* (Amherst: University of Massachusetts Press, 2000); Meng Jing Hui, ed., *Files on Avant-garde Theatre* (Beijing: Writers Press, 1999); Wei Li Xin, ed., *Playmaking: Playmakers Talking* (Beijing: Culture and Art Press, 2003).

Lin Shen

"Three Prominences," Principle of

Put forward by Jiang Qing in association with Yu Huiyong during the late 1960s, the principle of "three prominences" (*san tuchu*) was promulgated as the foundation of all literary works during the **Great Cultural Revolution** (although it was found to be completely inapplicable to poetry). It required all writers, scriptwriters, and directors to follow the same principle: of all the characters, stress the positive ones; of the positive characters, stress the heroic ones; of the main heroic characters, stress the principal hero/heroine.

The Eight Model Theatrical Works (*yangbanxi*) that served as the sole fare for China's theatergoing public during the Cultural Revolution were the most affected by the principle of "three prominences." Later variants and transplants of the model works during that period were all in compliance with this principle. Under the direct supervision of Jiang Qing, all of them placed concentric emphasis on the story's characters. In other words, in characterization and presentation, the most heroic character(s) received the primary focus. All the characters, including the villains, gave prominence to the good characters. They, in turn, gave prominence to the heroic characters, who, in their turn, yielded to the main hero.

Zhiqu Weihushan (Taking Tiger Mountain by strategy) is an example of how these model theatrical works were guided by the principle of "three prominences." The story was about a People's Liberation Army (PLA) scout, Yang Zirong, on a mission to penetrate the bandits' lair on top of a mountain in northeastern China after the end of the war against Japan. On the way up the mountain, Yang Zirong encountered a tiger and killed it. On the mountain, he successfully disguised himself as one of the bandits, won their trust, and finally defeated the bandits with his comrades. The play was first produced in 1958 by the Shanghai Beijing Opera Troupe. In that original version, the hero Yang Zirong was portrayed in a way that was strongly reminiscent of the martial hero Wu Song in *Water Margin*, who also killed a tiger in his drunkenness, but the script was revised drastically in the next few years in accordance with the principle of "three prominences." As the main hero, Yang Zirong received all the prominence, and the spotlight followed him wherever his position was on the stage. He was always standing upright, fearless in face of the tiger, and was the very embodiment of wisdom, courage, and determination among the bandits. Scenes that did not fit with the "three prominences" principle were deleted. Secondary heroic characters like the hunter and his daughter were brought in to highlight Yang's integration with and reliance on the people. Negative characters disappeared more and more into the dark. They all had a stooping posture and had to look at Yang with their faces tilted upward when they spoke to him. Following the principle of "three prominences," instead of trying to blend in with his company on the mountain, as was portrayed in the earlier versions, Yang held himself apart through contrasts in makeup and posture.

To Chinese audiences used to exaggerated characters and painted face performance, the application of red makeup for highlighting heroes and green for denigrating villains was not a problem. The use of dramatic pauses in the action to allow the hero or heroine to strike a pose was also fully within the tradition. Therefore, despite all the technical difficulties involved in adapting traditional techniques to portray contemporary life, the theory of "three prominences" on the whole was not considered to be completely out of keeping with the spirit of traditional Chinese theater.

In the world of fiction, Hao Ran's works constitute an excellent example of adhering to the principle of "three prominences." Two of his novels, *Yan Yang Tian* (Bright sunny sky) and *Jin Guang Da Dao* (The road of golden light), were made into films and became very influential as models for younger writers. The name of the hero Gao Daquan in *The Road of Golden Light*, meaning "tall, big, and whole," spoke of the qualities such a hero held: good-looking, generous, honest, reasonable, and level-headed. He always took the correct political line. To the Party he was loyal and submissive; to his antagonists he was implacable. Whether such a character was true to life or not was of secondary importance: it was designed as a model rather than a realistic hero.

Hao Ran's third novel, *Sons and Daughters of Xisha*, has been considered a perfect example of the principle of "three prominences" in action. The heroine of the novel, A Bao, was beautiful and unflinching and had great faith in Party policies, socialism, and the development of Xisha. She was made prominent by heroic secondary characters such as He Wangli and Zheng Taiping who also supported Party policies and socialism, but who occasionally wavered slightly or were caught in a minor contradiction, which only served to thrust A Bao forward. These secondary characters, in turn, were foregrounded by the negative characters One-Eyed Crab, a former owner of the fishing fleet, and Big Pumpkin, leader of the Saigon troops. In the novel, conflicts and contradictions were created as challenges for heroes and heroic characters to respond to. The plot was only used as a means to advance characterization by showing how heroic thought and action could overcome any obstacle.

The imposition of the principle of "three prominences" on all literary works during the Great Cultural Revolution resulted in exaggeration and stereotyping of characters, action, rhetoric, and situation. Middle-ground characters no longer existed, and the audience was presented with an unambiguous polarization of good and evil. The principle was denounced with the ending of the Cultural Revolution, but its influence was still felt in the late 1970s and early 1980s.

See also Great Cultural Revolution, Literature during; Theater in Contemporary China.

Bibliography

McDougall, Bonnie S., ed., *Popular Chinese Literature and Performing Arts in the People's Republic of China, 1949–1979* (Berkeley: University of California Press, 1984); McDougall, Bonnie S., and Kam Louie, *The Literature of China in the Twentieth Century* (London: Hurst & Company, 1997).

Xiaoling Zhang

Tibet

In 1951, the People's Liberation Army entered Tibet, marking the year of "peaceful liberation." On May 23, 1951, the Agreement on Measures for the Peaceful Liberation of Tibet (hereafter referred to as the "Seventeen-Article Agreement") was signed by the Central People's Government and the local government of Tibet. The People's Liberation Army subsequently entered Tibet to safeguard its borders. The Seventeen-Article Agreement affirmed the necessity of reforming the social system of Tibet. The Central People's Government suppressed a rebellion in 1959 that was suspected of separatism. The same year, the fourteenth Dalai Lama escaped into India. The democratic reform and **land reform** were carried out under the direction of the central government, which aimed at abolishing the feudal serf owners' right to own land and the serfs' and slaves' personal bondage to the feudal serf owners. The government's *White Paper* (2001) stated, "The reform liberated Tibet's millions of serfs and slaves politically, economically, and spiritually, making them masters of the land and other means of production, giving them personal and religious freedom, and realizing their human rights. The reform greatly liberated the social productive forces in Tibet, and opened up the road toward modernization."

In 1961, a general election was held in Tibet. Former serfs and slaves were given "democratic rights to being their own masters" in the election of power organs and governments at all levels in the region. Many emancipated slaves took up leading posts at various levels in the region. In September 1965, the First People's Congress of Tibet was convened, at which the founding of the Tibet Autonomous Region and the Regional People's Government was officially proclaimed.

While Tibet is integrated into China as an autonomous region, its spiritual leaders, represented by the Dalai Lama, have been at odds with the central government. Traditionally, the Dalai Lama and the Panchen Lama are venerated as the supreme spiritual leaders. The Dalai Lama is worshipped as the incarnation of the compassionate Buddha, and the Panchen Lama, as the incarnation of Amitabha or the meditative Buddha, is worshipped second only to the Dalai Lama. During the period when the fourteenth Dalai Lama was in exile, the tenth Panchen Lama was worshipped as the spiritual authority in Tibet until his passing in 1989. The process of selecting the eleventh Panchen Lama was conducted in 1995. The process reflected influence from the central government when Beijing overrode the living Dalai Lama's candidate. The final election was decided through a drawing of lots among three candidates. Beijing claimed that the method was a traditional and conventional measure to determine the reincarnation when controversies arose. President Jiang Zemin presented a plaque bearing the inscription "Protect the country, benefit the people" to the eleventh Panchen Lama, a five-year-old boy by the name of Gyaincain Norbu, born in Lhari in 1990, to commemorate the occasion. More controversy is expected when the time comes to select the Dalai Lama's successor when he dies. While Beijing believes that the Dalai Lama's reincarnation will be in China, the Dalai Lama believes that he will be born outside China if contradictions continue.

The Dalai Lama has vigorously campaigned since the late 1980s for his political agenda, which holds that Beijing should relax its grip over his homeland. His plan rejected by the central government in 1987, the Dalai Lama proposed five-point peace proposals calling for the demilitarization of Tibet and talks about its future. In 1988, the Dalai Lama urged the central government to grant Tibet autonomy under the title of **special administrative region (SAR)**, the same status as that Hong Kong would later enjoy. In the framework of SAR, Tibet would be able to run its own affairs in every aspect save defense and foreign affairs. The Dalai Lama was awarded the Nobel Peace Prize in 1989 for his efforts on behalf of his countrymen, some of whom were of radical tendency at the time. In a similar effort, despite his residence in Tibet, the Panchen Lama had voiced his complaint in a report of 70,000 words in 1962 to Premier **Zhou Enlai** that chronicled the sufferings of the masses and suggested how Beijing might relieve them. Because of that, the Panchen Lama was labeled an enemy of the people and urged to do self-criticism. It is believed, however, that the Panchen Lama's complaint resulted in the granting of autonomous region status later in 1965.

In the 1990s, it was clear that the Dalai Lama's and Panchen Lama's spiritual institution weakened as Beijing intensified its modernization of Tibet. As indicated in the government's *White Paper* (2001) from 1994 to 2001, the central government had directly invested a total of 4.86 billion yuan in sixty-two projects. Fifteen provinces and municipalities and the various ministries and commissions under the State Council had also given aid gratis for the construction of 716 projects and had contributed a total of 3.16 billion yuan. More than 1,900 cadres were sent from all over the country to assist in Tibet's construction. As a result, "the production and living conditions in Tibet have been greatly improved and its social and economic developments revved up." Moreover, Tibet is reported to have promoted all-around reform in its economic and technological systems, adjusted its economic structure and mechanism of enterprise operation and management, set up a complete social security system, enlarged its scope of opening-up, and actively encouraged and attracted funds from both home and abroad for its economic construction. According to statistics listed in the *White Paper*, from 1994 to 2000, the gross domestic product (GDP) in Tibet increased by 130 percent, or a yearly increase of 12.4 percent, a change from the situation in which Tibet had lagged behind the other parts of China in the GDP growth rate for a long time in the past. Urban residents' disposable income per capita and the farmers and herdsmen's income per capita increased by 62.9 percent and 93.6 percent, respectively, and the impoverished population decreased from 480,000 in the early 1990s to just over 70,000.

Modernization projects created jobs that attracted not only Tibetans, but also migrant workers from other provinces. The "modern industrial system with Tibetan characteristics" has produced nationally famous brand names, such as Lhasa Beer, Qizheng Tibetan Medicine, and Zhufeng Motorcycles. In particular, transportation modernization is leading the way in Tibet's integration into so-called modern civilization. A highway network now extends in all directions with Lhasa as the center, including such trunk roads as the Qinghai-Tibet, Sichuan-Tibet, **Xinjiang**-Tibet, Yunnan-Tibet, and China-Nepal highways, 15 main highways, and 375 branch highways. These roads total 22,500 kilometers and reach every county and more than 80 percent of the townships in the region. The two civil airports in Tibet, Gonggar Airport in Lhasa and Bamda Airport in Qamdo, operate domestic and international routes from Lhasa to Beijing, Chengdu, Chongqing, Xi'an, Xining, Shanghai, Deqen, Kunming, Hong Kong, and Kathmandu. Meanwhile, a 1,080-kilometer petroleum pipeline has been built from Golmud in Qinghai Province to Lhasa, the highest-altitude pipeline in the world. It carries more than 80 percent of the petroleum transported into the region. In June 2001, construction was started on the 1,925-kilometer Qinghai-Tibet Railway. By 2004, two-thirds of the railway had been completed.

According to the *White Paper*, by 2001, telecommunications had developed at a fast pace. With Lhasa as the center, and including cable and satellite transmission together with program-controlled switching systems, digital and mobile communications covered all of Tibet. By the end of 2000, the total installed capacity of fixed telephones reached 170,200 dwellings and offices where 111,100 telephones were installed. In addition, there were also nine **Internet** Web sites and 4,513 users during the period.

The booming of the service industry has reportedly contributed to Tibet's modernization. Service-related jobs offered opportunities to the female population in Tibet and let them walk out of the house for the first time in generations. Before the launch of economic reforms in 1978, Tibetan women had virtually never been able to receive school education. A recent report by Xinhuanet claims that by 2003, more than 110,000 Tibetan women had mastered some practical skills through attending training opportunities. Women technical workers now make up 43 percent of the region's technical workforce.

Technological progress has made business expansion and profit making more easily achievable. The *Beijing Times* (March 31, 2004) reported that Qoinpe Cering, a former poor Tibetan farmer in a small village of Xigaze City, became the first billionaire in the autonomous region through hard work in the construction industry and set up a model for many others to follow.

Overall, economic modernization is rapidly transforming Tibet from a closed society into a dynamic part of the national economy. Tibetans' educational level and their living standards have tremendously improved. It is a fact that geographic boundaries warrant no protection any longer for the traditional way of life. Because of the economic invasion from the rest of the country and the migration of Tibetan young people to large Chinese **cities**, it is increasingly difficult to preserve "Tibetan identity." With respect to religious freedom, for example, whether one labels it "interference" or "sponsorship," the central government's influence is strong. The government invests generously in restoring damaged Buddhist shrines, for example, and many monks are listed on the government's payroll. As Tibet has joined the mainstream economic boom, ethnic conflicts have subsided. Nevertheless, occasional outbursts of demonstrations in Tibet, such as one in 1988, constantly prompt the government to deeply probe the nationalist mood and complaints by Tibetans, because territorial integrity has always been of primary concern to the central government.

See also Regions of China, Uneven Development of.

Bibliography

Dalai Lama, *Freedom in Exile: The Autobiography of the Dalai Lama Re-issued ed.* (San Francisco: Harper, 1991); Hutchings, Graham, *Modern China: A Guide to a Century of Change* (Cambridge, MA: Harvard University Press, 2001); *White Paper on Tibet's March toward Modernization (Parts I, II, III)*, August 11, 2001, *Embassy of the People's Republic of China in the United States of America*, http://www.china-embassy.org/eng/zt/zgxz/News%20About%20Tibet/default.htm, accessed on December 2, 2004; Xinhuanet, *More Tibetan Women Find Employment*, http://www.humanrights-china.org/news/2003-8-27/rdgz200382774655.htm, accessed on December 3, 2004.

Jing Luo

Tobacco Industry

China is by far the largest producer of tobacco products in the world. In 1996, China produced 1,712.5 billion cigarettes, far more than the next largest producer, the United States, which made 760 billion in 1996. In recent years, China's cigarette output has been controlled at around 1,725 billion a year, more than 30 percent of the world's supply. China is also unmistakably the largest cigarette consumer in the world, burning more than 30 percent of the world's cigarettes in recent years. Based on the author's interview with officials of the industry, in 1996, 1,663 billion cigarettes were smoked. It was estimated that 320 to 340 million people in China smoke.

China, however, does not play a significant role in the importing and exporting of tobacco products. Its tobacco industry serves mainly its huge domestic market. In 1996, for example, it exported 65.75 billion cigarettes and imported 16 billion. Duties on foreign cigarettes have been 200 percent, and most foreign cigarettes found their way to the Chinese markets through smuggling.

Nevertheless, aggressive advertising has clearly made the presence of foreign brands felt in China.

The importance of the tobacco industry lies in its role in fiscal revenues. The industry has always been a major contributor to government coffers. It has led all the industries in China in profit and tax remittances since 1989. In recent years, the revenues collected from this industry have accounted for 11 percent of the total government revenues of the nation. In 1996, for instance, it remitted to the government more than 83 billion yuan in profits and taxes. There is no evidence that the Chinese government curbs the tobacco industry through economic measures, such as imposing taxes.

Given its importance to fiscal revenues, the tobacco industry, especially cigarette manufacturing, has always been tightly controlled by governments. In 1981, the State Council ordered the tobacco industry to be monopolized and established the China National Tobacco Corporation (CNTC). Two years later, the State Council promulgated the Tobacco Monopoly Regulations and established the State Tobacco Monopoly Administration (STMA) as the regulatory agency. In 1991, the **National People's Congress** passed the Tobacco Monopoly Law, which has since become the legal foundation of state monopolization of tobacco procurement, manufacturing, and distribution in China.

Research shows that about one-half of the male population of China smokes. The man shown here is smoking a water pipe.

The STMA and CNTC have their branches at the provincial, prefecture/city, and county/township levels. Currently, there are thirty-one provincial tobacco monopoly administrations (TMAs), more than 300 prefecture and city branches, and more than 1,800 county/city branches. The industry now has 178 cigarette manufacturers and more than 2,000 wholesale companies. It boasts of employing a total of 540,000 people, of whom 280,000 are in cigarette manufacturing and more than 200,000 in distribution and wholesale. There is no direct control over cigarette retailing, which has been mostly individual and family businesses. The number of retailers is estimated at 3.6 million. Similarly, tobacco growing is not nationalized. The STMA simply sets national plans for the total acreage for tobacco farming and allots quotas to concerned provinces, which further break the quotas down to prefectures and counties. In addition, the CNTC provides seeds and technical guidance to growers. The procurement of leaves, however, is centralized, and prices are set by the STMA and CNTC. Because of poor statistics in the rural areas, the STMA does not have a good estimate of the number of tobacco growers. It is generally believed that the figure is somewhere between 10 and 20 million households. In 1996, the total output of tobacco leaves was around 2.5 million metric tons.

Because tobacco businesses are cash cows for governments, one cannot have a full picture of the industry without understanding the fiscal system in

China and the taxes on cigarettes. In 1980, China began implementing a fiscal responsibility system, under which adjacent levels of governments signed a revenue-sharing contract and each level then was responsible for the finance of the programs assigned to it. The contract specified that taxes and profits collected from provinces and localities were to be divided into two parts, the central fixed revenues, which were to be remitted entirely to the central government, and the local revenues, which were subject to sharing. In 1994, a fiscal reform instituted a tax-sharing system in an attempt to strengthen the central government's ability to collect and retain tax revenues. Under the new system, taxes are divided into three categories, the central, the local, and the shared taxes. The central taxes are collected and retained by the central government, the local taxes, by the local governments, while the shared taxes are divided between the central and local governments in accordance with proportions specified by the tax code. Prominent among the central government taxes is the newly created consumption tax levied in addition to the value-added tax (VAT) on eleven goods, including tobacco products, alcohol, and cosmetics. Cigarettes are taxed at 40 percent. Another central tax that is relevant to tobacco products is the special agriculture product tax levied on seven high-profit-margin products, including tobacco leaves. The leaves are taxed at the highest rate of 31 percent. Of the shared taxes, the most important one is the VAT, levied on all stages of commercial activities from industrial processing through wholesale and retail. The basic VAT rate is 17 percent. The central government takes three-quarters of VAT revenues, while the rest goes to local governments. The local taxes include business taxes, income taxes, profit remittances from local enterprises, and others.

Taxes on tobacco products have been the highest among those on all products in China, and the price-cost margins for tobacco products, especially cigarettes, are extremely large, due to state monopolization of the industry. It is no wonder that local governments have strong incentives to develop cigarette manufacturing in their jurisdictions, either through direct investment or subsidization. With the backing of local governments, the tobacco industry experienced a rapid growth in the 1980s and mid-1990s in quantity as well as quality. The total output of cigarettes increased from 852 billion in 1981 to 1,736 billion in 1993, at an average rate of more than 8 percent per year. Had the STMA not enforced a cap on the total output, the output would have continued to grow. The quality of tobacco products was greatly improved as well, especially in the early 1990s. For instance, while filter-tip cigarettes accounted for only 5.8 percent of the total output in 1982, they rose to 93.5 percent in 1996. Production technologies were substantially updated, largely through importing entire production lines.

However, expansion of cigarette production in the 1980s finally resulted in excess supply. In 1990, cigarette prices started to slide nationwide for the first time. Toward the mid-1990s, one-third of the total production capacity had to be idled, while total inventories accumulated up to 150 billion, nearly 10 percent of the annual output. Concerned with prospective declines in remittances of taxes and profits, the STMA took a number of measures in 1992 and again in 1997 to tighten control over the total output. In recent years, the

STMA has managed to contain the total output at the 1993 level, around 1,725 billion a year.

Heavy government involvement has created and protected grossly inefficient firms. Because tobacco businesses generate a huge amount of revenues, governments of almost all provinces rushed into cigarette manufacturing, regardless of the availability of resources and expertise. The result was striking gaps in efficiency across provinces. In 1994, the most efficient manufacturers contributed nearly forty times more profits and taxes than the least efficient ones, with the former making 32.00 yuan per carton, while the latter made only a little more than 0.80 yuan. The lion's share of the revenue contributions was made by a very small number of firms. In 1996, for example, the average remittance of taxes and profits per carton was 7.50 yuan. However, of the 144 centrally owned plants, only 19 contributed above the average, 116 plants made payments below the average, and 9 had zero or negative taxes and profits combined. If performance was measured in after-tax profits, the average profit per carton was 0.92 yuan in 1996. Only seventeen plants made profits higher than the average, and sixty-eight made losses. If the province-owned plants were included, loss-making firms reached 55 percent, and a quarter of the firms in the industry made losses more than 0.40 yuan per carton, according to Tobacco Economic Information (1997). The STMA pushed for cross-provincial mergers in 1980s but failed, because the local governments resisted such mergers.

The development pattern of the tobacco industry in the past two decades since the reforms began in the early 1980s is not unique. Other industries, including consumer electronics, home appliances, **telecommunications**, automobiles, iron and steel, and airlines, have similar experiences. Competition among different jurisdictions broke up the state monopoly in many industries and brought about rapid growth. However, many of these industries have suffered from obstacles and inefficiencies typical of governmental involvement.

See also Disease and Death Rate; Health Care Reform.

Bibliography

China State Administration of Tobacco Monopoly, *Tobacco Economic Information*, Beijing, February 1997; Zhou, Huizhong, "Fiscal Decentralization and the Development of the Tobacco Industry in China," *China Economic Review* 11, no. 2 (December 2000): 114–133.

Huizhong Zhou

Township and Village Enterprises (TVEs)

Township and village enterprises (TVEs) as a sector have become an important pillar of China's national economy and the mainstay of its rural economy. By 2000, this sector contributed about one-third of China's GDP, nearly 50 percent of its total industrial growth, and more than 60 percent of rural economic growth. It supplied 40 percent of China's merchandise for export and provided 20 percent of total tax revenues. Moreover, TVEs employed 127 million people by the end of 2000, about 50 percent of the rural surplus labor force. The proportion of money from TVEs in the annual income of the average farmer reached 34 percent in the same year.

TVEs originated from China's rural subsidiary production. When rural communization was introduced in 1958, these subsidiary productive businesses were turned over to the communes and became commune enterprises. To respond to the central government's call for developing industries in the communes, many new enterprises were established as commune enterprises or brigade enterprises for the purpose of promoting agricultural mechanization and rural industrialization, particularly in the early 1960s following the **Great Leap Forward** movement. When the commune system was abolished by the rural economic reforms launched in 1978, the commune and brigade enterprises became collective enterprises owned by townships and villages. After the Third Plenum of the Thirteenth Central Committee of the Chinese Communist Party (CCP), more rural enterprises, including individual and private enterprises, were established between 1978 and 1984. In 1984, the central government decided to change the title of "commune and brigade enterprises" to "township and village enterprises." The scope of this sector was expanded to include four types of rural enterprises: township enterprises that are collectively owned by township residents, village enterprises that are collectively owned by village residents, joint-household enterprises, and individual and private enterprises. Rural enterprises that are jointly owned by townships, villages, rural households, and rural individuals with other owners such as **state-owned enterprises** or other collective enterprises, other individuals, and foreigners are also included in this sector.

During the early stage of the TVE movement, the main objectives of establishing rural enterprises were to provide employment opportunities to local surplus labor and to generate revenues to support agricultural production. Local government leaders were the most enthusiastic initiators and promoters of the development of this sector. However, being concerned about the possible competition of TVEs with state-owned sectors for raw materials and markets, the central government was hesitant to encourage the expansion of this sector in general. It adopted a guideline of "local inputs, local processing, and local markets" and attempted to restrict TVEs mainly to subordinate businesses serving agricultural production and other industrial sectors. This guideline was abandoned in 1984. The 1984 Number 1 and Number 4 Documents of the Central Committee of the CCP confirmed that the TVE sector is an important part of the national economy. These documents led to a drastic development of this sector in the second half of the 1980s. It became a key catalyst of rural economic growth. However, during the macrorectification period of 1989 to 1991, TVEs as a sector faced severe financial hardship. The sector's growth slowed down, and profitability declined. Many firms were closed, and millions of workers returned to agricultural production. This situation was changed after the Third Plenum of the Fourteenth CCP Central Committee held in 1993. This plenum once again confirmed that the development of the TVE sector is a necessary path to make the rural economy prosper, to increase rural income, and to promote national economic growth. On January 1, 1997, the PRC Law of Township and Village Enterprises was put into effect.

There are several models in TVE development. The most significant ones include the Sunan model, the Wenzhou model, and the Jinjiang model. The Sunan model refers to the TVE development style in the suburb of three southern Jiangsu Province cities, Wuxi, Suzhou, and Changshu, and their neighboring areas. Collective enterprises dominated the sector in this region and had a close relationship with large urban industrial enterprises. Local governments were directly involved in the establishment and management of these industry-oriented collective enterprises. The Wenzhou model refers to the TVE development style in the city of Wenzhou in Zhejiang Province and its neighboring areas. Household businesses and private enterprises dominated the sector. Division of labor, specialized production, and well-developed markets for production factors were the salient features of this model. The Jinjiang model, also known as the Quanzhou model, refers to the TVE development style in Jinjiang County of Fujian Province. Foreign investment from local overseas emigrants and joint ventures dominated the sector. Export-oriented production and advanced technologies, management, and marketing are significant in this model.

The form of governance in the TVE sector has been evolving. In its early stage, except for a few individual or private enterprises, most TVEs were under the direct control of local governments. Local government leaders participated in and dominated the establishment, management, and development of these enterprises and also enjoyed full rights over the profits generated by them. The contractual responsibility system was adopted first in Wuxi in 1983 and later spread nationwide. Under this system, the firm's employees as a collective, or the firm's manager as an individual, signed responsibility contracts with the local government. After certain financial responsibilities were fulfilled, the residual profit was shared by the local government and the firm's employees or the manager. Since 1993, leasing has become prevalent in many areas, especially for small and medium-sized enterprises. Local governments collect a fixed amount of rent under this system and grant full management and profit rights to the leaseholders. In the late 1990s, a significant portion of TVEs, mainly small and medium-sized enterprises, were privatized through auction. During the same period, another portion of TVEs, large and profitable enterprises in particular, were transformed into share-cooperative enterprises. Despite the encouragement of the central government, however, share-cooperative enterprises accounted for a small portion of this sector in 2000.

Significant disparities in TVE development exist between eastern coastal regions and central and western regions. Since the full marketization of China's economy in the late 1990s, TVEs have faced tremendous pressure from competition. The problems of this sector in industrial structure, management, capability in research and development (R&D), and overall quality have become salient. Its institutional advantage has been weakened, and its economic efficiency has been declining.

See also Rural Administrative Organizations; Rural Credit Cooperatives (RCCs); Rural Industrialization; Rural-Urban Divide, Regional Disparity, and Income Inequality.

Bibliography

Byrd, W., and Q. Lin, eds., *China's Rural Industry: Structure, Development, and Reform* (New York: Oxford University Press, 1990); Chen, H., *The Institutional Transition of China's Township and Village Enterprises: Market Liberalization, Contractual Form Innovation, and Privatization* (Aldershot, England; Brookfield, CT: Ashgate Press, 2000); Ma, R., C. Huang, H. Wang, and M. Yang, eds., *Investigations on China's Township and Village Enterprises in the 1990s* (Hong Kong: Oxford University Press, 1994).

Hong-yi Chen

Trade Relations with the United States

Trade relations between China and the United States date back to the early days of the independence of the United States. At the end of World War II, the United States was China's leading trade partner. But after the People's Republic of China was founded in 1949, trade between the two countries dried up very quickly. Since then, sanctions against China have been part of U.S.-China economic and trade relations, although the sanctions have assumed different forms and taken on different levels of severity at different times.

The United States imposed selective controls on trade with China as soon as the Communist forces began to win the civil war early in 1949. U.S. export controls were then gradually tightened until a total embargo was set in place against China by the United States following the outbreak of the **Korean War**. The United States was also instrumental in creating the Coordinating Committee on Multilateral Export Controls (COCOM), composed of representatives of the North Atlantic Treaty Organization (NATO) countries and Japan, to supervise an embargo that was imposed against China by the United Nations. By 1951, there was virtually no trade between China and the United States.

In 1971, China resumed its seat in the United Nations. In 1972, U.S. president Richard Nixon made his historic visit to China. In the wake of these ice-breaking events, COCOM agreed to loosen its export controls and allow China to be treated the same as the Soviet Union. Thereafter, the United States permitted its citizens to make purchases from China and pay for them in dollars. U.S. exports, instead of being under a total embargo, were under the same export-control restrictions as sales to the Soviet Union. After a hiatus of more than twenty-years, trade between China and the United States began to grow. Total trade between the two countries expanded from nothing to $2.4 billion in 1979, the year in which the two countries formally established diplomatic relations.

On July 7, 1979, the two governments signed the Trade Relations Agreement, which accorded each other most-favored-nation treatment (MFN, now called normal trading relations, NTR) on a reciprocal basis. In the following years, numerous specific agreements were concluded, including the Textile Trade Agreement, the Agreement on Avoidance of Double Taxation, and the Agreement on Civil Aviation and Sea Transportation. In the meantime, three joint working committees were established (on commerce and trade, on science and technology, and on economic affairs), and these have been regarded as effective mechanisms to promote dialogue between the two countries.

Starting in 1981, China was given access to higher levels of U.S. technology than the Soviet Union. In December 1985, COCOM adopted a "green line" policy toward China, which gave preferential licensing treatment, as compared with other COCOM-proscribed countries, to twenty-seven categories of controlled items for exports to China. Internally, China's economic reform provided an impetus to the country's international trade. Labor-intensive industries, such as textiles, garments, toys, and other light industrial goods, developed rapidly and became the driving forces for China's exports. China's total exports reached more than $40 billion and total trade topped $80 billion in 1988. Sino-American trade increased to more than $10 billion in that year.

After the Tiananmen Square incident in the early summer of 1989, the United States imposed broad sanctions against China, including a suspension of official and military exchanges between the two governments, a prohibition on U.S. trade financing and investment insurance for China-related projects, and an embargo on exports to military and police entities in China. The United States started to link China's MFN status to human rights. After that, China's MFN status with the United States was subject to annual review by the U.S. Congress, although China was never denied this status. In the aftermath of the Tiananmen Square incident, China took bolder steps in its economic reform and **Open Door policy**. Dramatic measures were taken to move **state-owned enterprises** toward a market economy, to encourage foreign economic cooperation, and to attract foreign investment. China's international trade continued to grow. Trade between China and the United States surpassed $50 billion in 1994. In tandem, U.S. investment in China increased from a mere $284 million in 1989 to about $2.5 billion in 1994.

The 1990s were riddled with trade conflicts as well as political skirmishes between the two countries, but progress was often made to avert trade wars. In January 1992, the United States and China signed the U.S.-China Memorandum of Understanding (MOU) on intellectual property rights (IPR), which resolved the U.S. Trade Representative's Special 301 Investigation on China's inadequate protection of U.S. intellectual property. Pursuant to this MOU, China improved its laws governing IPR protection during the following two years and joined the Berne Copyright and Geneva Phonograms Conventions. An IPR enforcement agreement was signed between the two countries on February 25, 1995, that was designed to address enforcement problems, particularly the protection of copyrighted works and trademarks, and increased market access for products based on intellectual property.

China was one of the twenty-three original signatories to the General Agreement on Tariffs and Trade (GATT), the predecessor of the World Trade Organization (WTO), in 1948. However, it lost its GATT membership in 1950. In 1986, China formally requested resumption of its seat in the GATT and embarked on a strenuous road of negotiations with GATT/WTO member countries for fifteen years until China finally joined the WTO in December 2001. The United States had considerable leverage over the decision, and China's negotiations with the United States were at center stage of this prolonged negotiation process. In the process, China made continuous efforts and commitments to meet the requirements of the negotiating parties, including tariff reductions and greater market access for foreign goods and services. On November 15, 1999, the two countries reached a bilateral agreement on China's accession to the WTO. The U.S. House of Representatives passed legislation (H.R. 4444) to grant permanent normal trade relations (PNTR) with China on May 24, 2000. The U.S. Senate voted to the same effect on September 19, 2000. On October 10, 2000, President Bill Clinton signed the PNTR legislation into U.S. law (P.L. 106-286). This ended the annual review of China's NTR status in the United States.

China became a major trade partner of the United States at the turn of the twenty-first century by all broad measures. According to U.S. statistics for 2004, China was the second-largest U.S. import supplier after Canada; the fifth-largest purchaser of U.S. exports after Canada, Mexico, Japan, and the United Kingdom; and the third-largest trade partner for the United States in total trade (exports plus imports) after Canada and Mexico. U.S. exports to and imports from China accounted for 2.07 percent and 8.58 percent of its total exports and imports, respectively, in 2000. The United States is in a more prominent position in China's international trade. The United States was China's top export market and third import source, accounting for 20.93 percent and 8.98 percent of China's total exports and imports, respectively, in 2000.

Trade between China and the United States is complementary, typifying the classical comparative advantages of industrial and developing countries. Low labor costs have made China one of the major sources for low-priced manufactured products in the world and in the United States in particular. China's exports to the United States are composed mainly of miscellaneous manufactured articles such as toys and games, clothing and apparel, footwear, telecommunications equipment, sound recording and reproduction equipment, and electrical machinery. Major categories of U.S. exports to China include chemical products (fertilizers), transportation equipment (mainly aircraft and aircraft parts), cereals and cereal preparations, textile fibers, and telecommunications and sound equipment. China has become an increasingly important market for U.S. agricultural exports as well.

Trade statistics differ markedly between reports by the two countries. According to U.S. statistics, exports of the United States to China were in the range of $16.19 billion, while imports from China were around $100.02 billion in 2000. As a result, the U.S. suffered a trade deficit of $83.83 billion. However, China reports that its exports to and imports from the United States were $52.16 billion and $22.34 billion, respectively, in 2000, yielding a trade deficit of $29.79 billion for the United States. The discrepancy in statistics is partly due to inconsistencies in statistical methods adopted by the two countries, particularly in accounting for transshipments through Hong Kong and other intermediaries.

The growing U.S. trade deficit with China has become a major issue between the two countries. U.S. economic sanctions against China, particularly restrictions on exports to China, China's low labor costs, the value of the Chinese currency, and the migration of other countries' manufacturing facilities to China are among the factors that have often been cited as contributing to the U.S. trade deficit.

See also June 4 Movement; Nixon's Visit to China/Shanghai Communiqué (1972); Sino-American Relations, Conflicts and Common Interests; Sino-American

Relations since 1949; U.S. Legislation on China-Related Issues; World Trade Organization (WTO), China's Accession to.

Bibliography

Askari, Hossein, John Forrer, Hildy Teegen, and Jiawen Yang, *Case Studies of U.S. Economic Sanctions: The Chinese, Cuban, and Iranian Experience* (Westport, CT: Praeger, 2003); Cohen, Jerome A., Robert F. Dernberger, and John R. Garson, *China Trade Prospects and U.S. Policy* (New York: Praeger, 1971); Yang, Jiawen, "Some Current Issues in U.S.-China Trade Relations," *Issues and Studies* 34, no. 7 (July 1998): 62–84.

Jiawen Yang

Trade Unions

The freedom of association is one of the core labor standards protected by the International Labor Organization (ILO) conventions. China is a rather peculiar case in this regard. On the one hand, China has the largest trade-union system in the world, and its unionization rate is among the highest. On the other hand, China allows only one official union in each workplace. No independent union outside the official union network is allowed. China insists that ILO conventions on trade unions accept the practice of the unitary form of the union system; China therefore does not violate labor's freedom of association.

The All-China Federation of Trade Unions (ACFTU) was founded in 1925. After the founding of the People's Republic of China in 1949, the ACFTU was given a semiofficial status. It governs all trade-union organizations in China. By the end of 2002, it had 586,000 grassroots trade unions and 131.5 million union members. While private companies still are not fully unionized, the overall labor participation rate in unions is fairly high. The ACFTU holds its national meeting every five years. The standing committee is its Executive Committee, which is elected by the delegates at the national meeting. Its chairman is normally a member of the Politburo of the Chinese Communist Party (CCP).

The Chinese Trade Union Act, which was adopted in 1992 and amended in 2001, legally defines the monopolistic position of the ACFTU. According to the law, a workplace with more than twenty-five employees should establish a union, but only one union is allowed in each workplace. All unions must join the ACFTU. Employers are required to contribute 2 percent of the company's total wages paid to workers to the union and to provide necessary office space for union activities. Regional unions control many resources, such as clubs, recreation centers and rehabilitation facilities, art performance teams, newspapers, colleges or training facilities, and business entities.

Although the ACFTU is claimed to be a voluntary mass organization, in reality it serves many official roles: it is a peripheral organization of the CCP and a state apparatus of labor administration. This dual-function model makes the union function not just as a typical labor union or an interest group. It weakens the role of unions since the interests of the state are not necessarily the same as the interests of the workers. For example, it has been reported that some union leaders take an active role in helping enterprises fulfill production tasks, but sometimes at the expense of workers' welfare, safety, and hygiene.

Chinese trade unions are closely associated with and controlled by the CCP. The Leninist "transmission belt" theory holds that the union is a bridge that links the Party and labor. It represents the interests of the Party and the state and implements their policies. At the same time, the union is also responsible for mobilizing workers to carry out the Party's policies. Rather than articulating and representing the interests of its members, it aggregates the political interests of a variety of labor groups and filters the information flow. This type of Party-union relations serves the goals of the authoritarian corporatist policy that is aimed at extending the state's control over all social interests.

The Trade Union Act stipulates four primary tasks for the unions: preservation, education, participation, and representation. The primary task of the trade union is to preserve the overall national interests of all people, as well as the interests of labor. These dual preservations tie unions to the state and the Party and prevent unions from becoming a true, independent voice of labor. The lack of independence and the close tie to the Party have compromised the unions' ability to represents the interests of the workers in case of labor disputes. For many years, the internal debates on unions' role never ceased. Many union leaders wanted to change the union to be solely a workers' representative body. The efforts to do so, however, were quickly suppressed.

Unions play an important role in labor education. For the Party and the state, unions are an important tool in extending their political propaganda and mass mobilization. Unions help transmit important Party and state policies through workplace meetings and union-controlled media. Unions are also responsible for occupation training, retraining of laid-off workers, and cultural and recreational activities. By 2002, labor unions owned more than 39,000 labor cultural centers and clubs of various types, 52,000 sport facilities, and 2,400 educational facilities, including 89 colleges.

Like many corporatist organizations in China, the trade union is also a part of the system of labor administration. Union leaders are considered "cadres" of the state and receive administrative salaries and benefits based on their administrative ranks. They help formulate laws and regulations and implement them through their own networks of local trade unions. They even have the power of interpreting laws and administrative regulations. At the factories, they also organize production. In recent years, as the number of retirees has increased, the unions have been given the responsibility for the management of retirees. In addition, unions sponsor mutual cooperative insurance, organize a system of labor protection inspectors, participate in the mediation of labor disputes, and provide legal assistance for laborers involved in court battles.

Under the corporatist state policy, unions are allowed to actively participate in the political and economic decision-making process. In 2001, a national consultation conference of the ACFTU, the National Association of Entrepreneurs (NAE), the National Chamber of Commerce, and the Ministry of Labor (MOL) was established to consult on key labor issues. A similar system has been established at the provincial level and in all counties as well. Moreover, a system of joint conferences of local unions and local labor administrative agencies is also being promoted. By law, labor unions are a mandatory party of the labor dispute mediation process.

Trade unions can also represent workers in democratic management. Chinese laws prescribe two types of workplace democratic management: one is through the **workers' congress**, and the other is through the trade union. Enterprises have the right to determine which one to use. In places where unions are authorized to represent workers in collective bargaining and to sit on boards of trustees or supervisors, unions have to call union representative meetings to discuss important decisions made by management.

In recent years, trade unions have begun to play active roles in collective bargaining, consultations, contract negotiations, and the settlement of labor disputes. Trade unions conduct negotiations on workers' behalf with management over issues that concern workers' interests, especially wages and terms of collective agreements. As of the end of June 2002, this practice had expanded to 635,000 enterprises and covered more than 80 million workers. Union representatives usually chair the enterprise-level mediation committees and sit on district- and city-level arbitration committees. By the end of June 2002, 155,022 trade-union-affiliated labor law supervision organizations had been formed, of which 139,856 were operated by enterprise-level trade unions, and they had settled 50,786 law-breaching cases and reported 14,782 government-related institutions. More than 643,000 trade-union-based labor-protection supervision committees had been established at the enterprise level by the end of June 2002.

Not all trade unions, especially at the enterprise level, are able to conduct their work effectively on behalf of workers. Many of them are subject to various constraints and remain inactive. One major constraint is the lower quality or incompetence of union leaders. Some union chairs lack the basic knowledge and expertise on union work and know hardly anything on how to bargain with employers. Sometimes, management outmaneuvers them. The effectiveness of union leaders is further compromised by the vulnerability of their personal interests to encroachments from management. Enterprise-level union leaders are first of all enterprises' employees and only work for unions concurrently or on a part-time basis. This put them in a dilemma. As employees, they have to succumb to the authority of their employers; yet as union leaders, they are obligated to speak for workers, who are usually against employers' wishes or interests and could easily incur revenge such as dismissals. However, union leaders would risk alienating workers and even being blamed by the latter as siding with employers if they shied away from expressing concerns over workers' interests. On balance, they seem more worried about potential retaliation by employers, especially about being fired. Labor laws do prohibit employers from firing union leaders, but the labor laws are rarely fully observed by nonstate sectors.

See also Labor Market; Labor Market Development; Labor Policy; Labor Policy, Employment, and Unemployment; Labor Relations; Labor Rights; Migrant Population; State-Owned Enterprises (SOEs), Reemployment of Laid-off Workers; Unemployment.

Bibliography

ACFTU, *Blue Paper on the Protection of Labor's Legal Rights by the Chinese Trade Union*, February 2003, http://www.acftu.org.cn, accessed on December 3, 2004;

All-China Federation of Trade Unions Policy Research Office. *Chinese Trade Unions Statistics Yearbook* (Beijing, Labor Press, 2000);———, *Chinese Trade Unions Yearbook* (Beijing: Labor Press, 2000); Fong, Tongqing, *The Fate of Chinese Labor: Labor's Social Actions since the Reform* (Beijing: Social Science Documents Press, 2002); Liu, Wenhua, Ma Te, Liu Zheng, and Wang Yongting, *Circumvention of the Conflict between the WTO and Labor Legal System of China* (Beijing: China City Press, 2001).

Yunqiu Zhang and Baogang Guo

TVEs

See Township and Village Enterprises (TVEs).

U

UN

See United Nations (UN) and China.

Unemployment

Before the start of the economic reforms, unemployment (*shiye*) ideological had been labelled a phenomenon of capitalist economies. The calculation of official unemployment is based on the number of registered unemployed persons in urban areas, which includes primarily laborers newly entering the market and excludes laid-off workers. The official rate of unemployment in China has been relatively low, but it increased steadily from around 2 percent in the early 1990s to 3 percent in the late 1990s and further to 3.6 percent in 2001.

The Chinese government today still prefers the term *xiagang*, which is a Chinese style of laying off workers and transitioning from disguised unemployment to explicit unemployment. No longer employed in the main production lines, *xiagang* workers usually maintain a relationship with their enterprises for retirement, health care, and housing benefits. Some are enrolled in retraining programs, some are engaged in sideline production, and the remainder are on extended unpaid leave. Except those who agree to take extended leave without pay, *xiagang* workers are paid reduced wages at various scales depending on the capability of their enterprises. There is an overestimation of the amount of *xiagang* and an underestimation of the amount of unemployment because many who have lost their jobs permanently are still registered as *xiagang*.

A more realistic measure calculates unemployment as all jobless workers who are actively seeking work, including those registered in the official statistics and those who have been laid off and have not found new jobs. According to this measure, urban unemployment in China in 1998 was around 7 to 8 percent, of which 3.1 percent was officially registered unemployment and 3.9 to 4.9 percent was *xiagang* workers who had not found jobs. The official news media have been quoting the urban unemployment rate as 8 percent, though the rate of just more than 3 percent may still appear in the official statistical yearbook.

Yet another measure of unemployment includes disguised unemployment. Disguised unemployment refers to a scenario where marginal productivities are lower than remuneration. Estimates of the total surplus workforce vary among researchers. Ballpark figures centered around 50 million in urban areas and 130 million in rural areas in 1998. Comparing these redundant labor forces with the total labor forces of 200 million in urban areas and 500 million in rural areas yields an urban unemployment rate of about 25 percent, a rural rate of 26 percent, and a nationwide rate of 25.7 percent. Some of the disguised unemployed today may have become either fully employed or released into explicit unemployment.

The sources of China's unemployment are manifold. First, systemic changes, that is, the reforms of the state sector, have released a large number of disguised unemployed into explicit unemployment. By the end of 1999, mergers and bankruptcies, as well as debt-equity swaps, had led to the closures of 435 large and medium-sized enterprises and the layoffs of 11 million workers, of whom only about 5 million found new jobs, for example. Moreover, government apparatuses at all levels as well as state-owned higher-education and research institutions have cut their personnel by a total of more than 3 million jobs. Unemployment from this sector may accelerate as more state enterprises are allowed to go bankrupt over time. China's urban collectively owned enterprises (COEs) had, by the end of 1999, collectively cut 14.35 million jobs, or 45.6 percent of their total employment in 1995.

The second source is the off-land labor force. Rural laborers in China had been tied to their land because policies had prevented them from entering the **cities**. The gradual relaxation of migration restrictions and the transition from an agrarian to an industrialized economy have led to a continuing influx of around 100 million rural migrant laborers into urban areas, which has made the disguised rural unemployment visible. This process will continue following China's entry into the World Trade Organization (WTO), which will cause the displacement of still more rural labor.

The third source can be called "structural unemployment." The structural changes that have accompanied China's transition from a planned to a market economy and from a lower to a higher development stage have resulted in considerable reallocations of labor. Massive overcapacities in the auto and textile industries led to unemployment of tens of thousands of workers in the 1990s, for example. Reallocation of labor from the traditional manufacturing industries to tertiary and high-tech industries, which is taking place at a higher pace than that experienced by industrialized market economies because of China's later entry into the world economic community, also creates another source of structural unemployment. China's traditional industries such as machinery, munitions, and technologically outdated textile industries have suffered the most in the process. Closures of thousands of **township and village**

enterprises (TVEs) because of environmental concerns and the government's crackdown on the "five small"—small glass plants, small cement plants, small oil refineries, small power plants, and small steel plants—have left millions jobless.

The fourth source is frictional unemployment related particularly to China's **labor market** being young and job opportunities are missed because of noneconomic reasons. In this newborn market, the service intermediaries are severely underdeveloped. The media are ineffective in carrying job ads. Local job centers provide services primarily to college graduates and professionals; laid-off workers struggle to find the new jobs; and migrant rural labor rely on relatives and village neighbors to find jobs for them in the cities. These limitations constrain the speed at which the unemployed can find matching jobs and thus make unemployment unnecessarily higher. Another institutional barrier is China's enterprise-linked safety net. Since employee pensions, medical benefits, unemployment compensation, and housing are linked closely to individual enterprises, workers often prefer taking a pay cut or early retirement or, once they are laid off, waiting to be reemployed within the same firm to finding a job elsewhere, thus significantly slowing turnover and labor mobility. Moreover, the lack of home ownership and an underdeveloped private rental housing market makes it physically difficult for one to relocate to a new place for reemployment.

The distribution of unemployment is by no means even. Regionally, areas with greater shares of **state-owned enterprises**, such as Shenyang, Wuhan, Chongqing, and Harbin, are more burdened with the problem of unemployment. Women are more victimized by the changing labor market, and female employment has been continuously declining since 1995 and is currently lower than the 1985 level. Among different age groups, men over the age of fifty and women over forty have comprised most of the urban unemployed and formed the "unemployed class of forty-fifty."

One phenomenon that puzzles many is the concurrent increase in urban unemployment, officially reported at 8 percent, with continuing healthy economic growth at a rate of around 8 percent since the late 1990s and at an average of around 10 percent since 1978. Solving the puzzle in the Chinese case is actually easy after examining the sources of unemployment discussed here. Economic growth has turned some disguised unemployment into full employment and some into explicit unemployment. Although the growing economy has been able to create more jobs, the rate of new job creation has not been able to catch up with the new labor-force formation and newly emerging explicit unemployment from the disguised unemployment.

The government has become more concerned with the unemployment issue, which can become a major source of social unrest. Government-sponsored job retraining and placement centers have sprung up all over the country. Urban laborers can track job openings not only through the **Internet** but also through cell phones. Rural migrants, however, still rely more on their relatives and other social connections for locating a job in the city.

The most important development is unemployment compensation through the **social security system**. In the urban sector, the "guarantee of minimum living" (*di bao*), which provides merely enough for the recipient to be fed and clothed without provision for housing, education of children, medical expenses, and heating in northern China, has reached almost 100 percent of urban residents in need of welfare. The system, which provides a bare minimum to the urban unemployed at a controlled rate, is virtually nonexistent in the rural sector, however. Out of the total rural population of more than 700 million, only 4.04 million residents have been helped by any kind of social welfare funding, let alone unemployment compensation. Redundant rural labor must continue to remain as disguised unemployment and bring down the average pay of every family member who forms the production unit. Rural disguised unemployment will, therefore, remain for a longer period than in the urban sector. While the government needs to expand the social security system to the rural sector to improve the equity situation, the biggest challenge is creating nonfarm jobs. The late professor Gale Johnson of the University of Chicago pointed out that each year during the next three decades, at least 15 million nonfarm jobs must be created to permit the farm labor force to decline by 3 percent annually and to provide jobs for the new entrants into the rural labor force.

See also Labor Policy, Employment, and Unemployment; Reemployment of Laid-off Workers.

Bibliography

Chen, Aimin, "Analysis of Unemployment and Labor Market Development in China," paper presented at the International Symposium on 21st-Century China and Challenge of Sustainable Development, September 3–5, 1999, Washington, DC; Chen, "Assessing China's Economic Performance in 1978–2001: Material Attainments and Beyond," seminar paper, April 23, 2003, Indiana State University; Johnson, D. Gale, "Can Agricultural Labor Adjustment Occur Primarily through Creation of Rural Nonfarm Jobs in China?" in *Urbanization Transformation in China*, ed. A. Chen, G. G. Liu, and K. H. Zhang (Aldershot: Ashgate Publishing Limited, 2004); Wang Yuguo, and Aimin Chen, ed., *China's Labor Market and Problems of Employment* (Chendu, China: Southwestern University of Finance and Economics Press, June 2000).

Aimin Chen

Unfinished Demographic Transition

Demographic transition conventionally refers to a process whereby a country moves from high birth and death rates to low birth and death rates, with an interstitial spurt in population growth. However, demographer John R. Weeks (2002) argues that demographic transition does not occur alone. Demographic transition is not one process but a set of intertwined transitions. That is, demographic transition goes along with a group of other transitions that accompany demographic transition and are considered an integral part of it. This set of transitions includes epidemiological transition, fertility transition, age transition, family transition, and urban transition. According to this reformulated perspective, China's demographic transition is not yet finished.

Epidemiological transition describes a long-term shift in health and disease patterns that has brought down death rates from high levels in which people die young, primarily due to communicable diseases, to low levels with deaths concentrated among the elderly, who die from degenerative diseases. On the basis of this definition, China has obviously completed this transition. Among the ten major diseases in urban China in 1957, for example, three were infectious: "acute infectious diseases" ranked second, or 7.93 percent, "tuberculosis (TB)" ranked third, or 7.51 percent, and "other non-pulmonary tuberculosis" ranked tenth, or 1.98 percent. In general, respiratory diseases were the number-one killer among all diseases. In comparison, of the first ten major diseases by 2000, none was infectious. Eight of the ten belonged to degenerative diseases, and two fell into the category of social causes. The first three degenerative diseases for urban areas were "malignant tumor," "cerebrovascular disease," and "heart trouble," which together accounted for about 63.4 percent of the total deaths. Similar findings were observed for the rural areas for the same period.

Fertility transition refers to the shift from natural fertility to controlled fertility, that is, the shift from high fertility to low fertility through birth control. There are three indicators to illustrate this transition: total fertility, contraceptive prevalence, and induced abortion. In the 1950s and 1960s, for example, China's total fertility was as high as five or six children per woman. By 2000, the total fertility dropped to below two. The overall contraceptive prevalence rate for the entire country in 1982 was 69 percent. By 2002, it rose to 83 percent. Correspondingly, the rate of induced abortion went as high as 30 percent in the 1970s. Although not an encouraging approach to reduce fertility, induced abortion serves as an option in practicing birth control and reflects the degree of controlled fertility among married couples in the country. This suggests that the status of fertility in China has shifted from the absence of birth control to deliberate contraceptive use. People's reproductive behaviors are increasingly regulated by their demands. Natural fertility has been replaced by controlled fertility. As a result, a shift from high fertility to low fertility has been taking place, and the transition in fertility has been accomplished. The declining birth rates and total fertility rates during the last half of the twentieth century in China have provided solid evidence of this trend.

While China has obviously succeeded in both epidemiological and fertility transitions, the age transition is still under way. By definition, age transition refers to a shift from a young age population structure to an old age population structure. Whether a population is considered "young" or "old" depends on the proportion of people at different ages. According to the conventional measures, while a population with about 35 percent or more of its people under the age of fifteen is "young," a population with about 12 percent or more of its people aged sixty-five or older is "old." In between, a population with 34 percent or less of its people under the age of fifteen or a population with 11 percent or less of its people aged sixty-five or above represents the "middle." Under this definition and these measures, China basically belonged to a "young" age structure in the 1950s, 1960s, and 1970s. The percentage of the age group zero to fourteen was about 36.28 percent in the first census of 1953, 40.69 percent in the second of 1963, and 33.59 percent in the third of 1982. The corresponding percentages of the age group sixty-five years and above were 4.41 percent, 3.56 percent, and 4.91 percent, respectively. Since the third census of 1982, however, a fairly big change has taken place in the country's age composition. The percentage of the age group zero to fourteen in the total population has been dropping steadily, while that of the age group sixty-five or older has been going up. By the fourth census of 1990, the percentage of the youth dropped to 27.69 percent of the total population, while that of the old went up to 5.57 percent. A recent estimate is that this percentage for the young was 24.30 percent in 2002, whereas that of the old was 7.40 percent. These data suggest that China's age transition is far from being completed but is still in process.

The salient characteristics of the family transition in China are increasing age at first marriage, a low divorce rate, reduced family size, and a transition from extended families to nuclear ones. From the 1940s to the 1980s, the mean age at first marriage for women in China increased slowly but steadily. In the country as a whole, the mean age at first marriage in 1940 was 18.21. By 1982, it went up to 22.66, an increase of 4.45 years. For urban areas, it increased by 6.2 years, from 18.73 in 1940 to 24.93 in 1982. For rural areas, it went up 3.95 years, from 18.12 in 1940 to 22.07 in 1982. As for the divorce rate, China has a much lower one than those of Western countries. For example, according to data for 1998, the divorce rate for the country was 1.9 per 1,000 married couples. In comparison, the United States has a steady divorce rate of 50 percent. Though the average family size in China has fluctuated over the decades, it has been reduced during the past fifty years, from 4.33 in the first census of 1953 to 3.44 in the fifth census of 2000, a reduction of about 0.89 person per family.

With respect to family structure, China underwent dramatic changes during the period from 1940 to 1982. In general, the proportion of single-family and nuclear-family households went up, while that of extended-family households went down. This tendency was reflected by the changes in the percentages of one-generation households, two-generation households, and three-and-above-generation households. For example, in the 1930s, one-generation households were only about 2.52 percent of the total, two-generation households accounted for about 48.93 percent, and three-and-above-generation households represented about 48.53 percent. By 1982, however, one-generation households rose to 13.74 percent, and two-generation households rose to 67.46 percent, while three-and-above-generation households dropped to 18.76 percent. All these statistics show that China's families are in an ongoing transition.

In urbanization, the last of the set of transitions, China lags far behind. Demographic transition theory predicts that due to different paces of declining death and birth rates, there will be overpopulation in rural areas, which will lead to rural-urban migration and accelerate the urbanization process. However, this prediction does not hold true in China. As in the assumption of the theory, the different paces of mortality and fertility produced a spurt of births in rural China during the late 1950s, all of the 1960s, and the early 1970s. From 1966 to 1976 alone, 360 million newly born babies were added to the total population. Unlike the assumption of the theory, however, the spurt of the rural population did not lead to a rapid migration transition toward urban areas. This happened primarily for two major reasons: the lack of nonagricultural job opportunities and inadequate infrastructure in urban areas, and a strictly restrictive rural-urban migration policy set up by the state government that strove to slow population growth in the largest **cities** while allowing continued increases in medium-sized and small urban centers. Consequently, rural-urban migration has been quite limited, and the urbanization process is slow. In 1949, for example, the percentage of people living in urban areas was 10.64 percent. The rate fluctuated from 12.02 percent to 16.84 percent in the years between 1963 and 1971 and then rose to 19.39 percent in 1980. By 2001, the rate was 36 percent, far below the world average of 46 percent.

This discussion suggests that China's demographic transition is unfinished despite the transitions in fertility and epidemiological diseases. Of the other three transitions, two stand out and deserve attention for policy implications. The first is age transition and concerns the issue of the elderly. It is apparent that care for the elderly by families, by the state, and by a combination of the two is far from being effective in China. In view of China's vast rural elderly population, it would be unrealistic to rely solely on the state government for social welfare security in the short run. The second is urbanization transition and concerns rural-urban migration. It is not yet clear how to resolve the issue of the surplus rural population: whether to transfer it into cities so as to speed up the urbanization process by changing dramatically the given urbanization policy, or simply to absorb it into the local areas so as to expand the small or medium-sized cities, as proposed by the state. In addition, due to its recent accession to the World Trade Organization in the new era, China is not only being swiftly swept into the international trade system but is also involved in the globalization drive, in which its policies on rural-urban migration and urbanization and its old-age security system are bound to be impacted and reshaped. China stands in a new world era in which it has to re-invent itself in almost every aspect.

See also Disease and Death Rates; Social Connections in Transition; Social Strata; Urbanization and Migration; World Trade Organization (WTO), China's Accession to.

Bibliography

Ji, Jianjun, "An Assessment of Demographic Transition in China," *Journal of Developing Societies* 19, no. 1 (2003): 1–25; Weeks, John R., *Population: An Introduction to Concepts and Issues*, 9th ed. (Belmont, CA: Thompson Wadsworth Learning, 2004).

Jianjun Ji

United Nations (UN) and China

China's relations with the United Nations (UN) can be divided into two major periods: the preentry period (1949–1971) and the postentry period (1971–present). Between 1949 and 1971, the Republic of China (ROC) in Taiwan retained its seat in the UN. The People's Republic of China (PRC) conducted a long campaign to win entry into the UN. However, the intensity of its interest in entry changed at different times. The PRC's attitude toward the UN passed through the stages of optimism, disappointment, antagonism, and revived enthusiasm.

UNITED NATIONS (UN) AND CHINA

China was one of the original members of the UN and one of the five permanent members of the Security Council. The UN was created at a time when the Kuomintang (KMT) government was the sole legitimate government of China. The Chinese Communist Party (CCP) at the beginning showed an active attitude toward the UN. In April 1945, **Mao Zedong** extended his full endorsement to "the establishment of an organization to safeguard international peace and security after the war." The Chinese Communist representative Dong Biwu was among China's delegation to the founding conference in San Francisco and signed the UN Charter.

After the formation of the PRC in October 1949, the CCP maintained its positive attitude toward the UN and attempted to take Taiwan's seat. In November 1949, Premier **Zhou Enlai** informed the UN that the PRC had repudiated the legal and factual status of the KMT government. The communications from Beijing to the UN in the next few years clearly revealed its interest in the PRC's entry. Influenced by the United States, nevertheless, the UN continued to recognize the legitimacy of the ROC based in Taiwan. In January 1950, the Soviet Union submitted a formal proposal to the Security Council to expel the ROC and to accept the PRC. The motion was defeated. In July and September of the same year, India twice proposed similar resolutions, which were rejected by the General Assembly as well. The outbreak of the **Korean War** and the subsequent Chinese military involvement evaporated any hope for China's quick entry into the UN. In February 1951, the General Assembly adopted a resolution to condemn China's "aggression" against Korea. Between 1951 and 1961, every year when a resolution to seat the PRC and to expel the ROC was proposed, the General Assembly, under the influence of the United States, simply adopted a moratorium to postpone consideration of the issue. The PRC in the 1950s continued to express its support for the principles of the UN Charter, but it developed a policy of "work and wait." It began to work on Afro-Asian countries to win their endorsement and waited for a change of the majority's view within the UN. This policy worked well. The votes in the UN in favor of seating the PRC between 1954 and 1960 rose from some 18 percent of the total to nearly 35 percent.

Facing the rising signs favorable to Beijing within the UN, the United States in 1961 took a new position, arguing that the issue of representation of China was a substantive question, which required a two-thirds vote of the General Assembly to make a change. This new U.S. tactic to block the PRC's entry into the UN helped harden Beijing's attitude toward the UN. The PRC's comments on the UN turned negative. In January 1965, Indonesia, led by Sukarno, withdrew from the UN to protest the admission of what he perceived to be the neocolonialist Malaysian regime to the Security Council. This event spurred the PRC to make a radical shift in its policy toward the UN. Zhou Enlai hailed Sukarno's decision as a "revolutionary action." Siding with Indonesia, the PRC claimed that the UN had "degenerated into a dirty international political stock exchange in the grip of a few big powers." The Chinese government went so far as to suggest that either the UN must rid itself of U.S. domination and reorganize itself, or a new revolutionary UN must be set up to replace it. The campaign did not last long, because it received little attention from other nations. Preoccupied with fervent domestic affairs, because the **Great Cultural Revolution** soon broke out, Chinese leaders' interest in either the UN or its substitute declined considerably during the next few years.

The PRC's revived interest in gaining entrance to the UN in the late 1960s reflected a significant change in its global strategy. In order to deal with the Soviet threat and to break out of China's diplomatic isolation, Chinese leaders launched a major drive to form diplomatic relations with an increasing number of nations. Along with its conciliatory approach toward the United States, China resumed its efforts to win support for its bid for a UN seat. In 1970, the majority of the UN members turned in favor of Beijing. The United States proposed dual representation between Beijing and Taiwan, but when President Richard Nixon's scheduled visit to Beijing was announced, the U.S. proposal completely lost its persuasiveness. On October 25, 1971, the UN General Assembly passed a resolution by a decisive vote of 76 to 35, with 17 abstentions, to admit the PRC and expel Taiwan.

The year 1971 marked a beginning in China's new relations with the UN. The PRC's entrance demonstrated a wide international recognition of Beijing as the sole legitimate government of China. It allowed Beijing access to a paramount stage of world politics. However, in the 1970s, China's participation in UN activities was limited. Twenty-two years of exclusion, its ideological commitment, and its suspicions of manipulation by two superpowers contributed to China's reservations on many UN activities. China treated the UN as a global forum rather than an international instrument for world peace. The General Assembly and Security Council gave China opportunities to present itself as a strong advocate of the causes of Third World countries. For example, in 1974, Deng Xiaoping went to the UN General Assembly to address the international community on Mao Zedong's three-worlds theory. Chinese diplomats in the UN did not hesitate to speak of high principles and criticized imperialism, capitalism, racism, and hegemonism. China also supported UN system reform and a new international economic order. Despite its revolutionary rhetoric, however, China was cautious on specific issues and joined only eight organizations in the UN system by the end of the 1970s.

The late 1970s witnessed a shift in China's foreign policy. Consistent with Deng Xiaoping's reform policy, the Chinese government took a more pragmatic approach in the hope of obtaining UN aid for its modernization drive. China began participating more fully in UN activities in the 1980s and joined virtually all specialized organizations in the UN system. In 1978, China shifted from aid giving to aid seeking and requested assistance from the United Nations Development Program (UNDP). By 1992, the UNDP had funded more than 400 Chinese projects totaling $273.6 million, thus making China the largest single recipient of UNDP assistance. China's position on UN peacekeeping shifted from opposition to participation, and China started paying its share of UN peacekeeping expenses. China began to be fully involved in the human rights arena as well. In 1979, it felt confident enough to send its observer to the Human Rights Commission. In 1981, it became a full member. China no longer strongly advocated UN system reform; rather, it preferred to maintain the UN system for its own advantage.

The confusion of the post–Cold War world has urged China to increase its involvement with the UN. China has participated in discussion of a full range of items on the UN agenda, including human rights, disarmament, peacekeeping, economic development, environmental development, science and technology, and legal issues. China has continued to benefit from grants, loans, and other economic assistance from the UN. China has fully utilized its status as one of the five permanent members of the Security Council to make sure its interests are protected. In 1990, Beijing chose to abstain when the Security Council voted for the resolution that authorized the use of force against Iraq. In 1991, China backed a UN peace plan for Cambodia, despite its association with the Khmer Rouge. In return, the United States and other Western nations relaxed their tough sanctions that had been in place since the Tiananmen incident in 1989. Facing severe criticism after the Tiananmen incident, China decided not to shy away from the human rights issue and became more engaged in the subject with the UN. Its persistent lobbying efforts, along with other tactics, have paid off. In 2002, the United States and its allies, after a decade's pursuit, ceased sponsoring a resolution that condemned China for human rights abuse at the UN Human Rights Commission. More active also in the Middle East than in the past, China joined the UN weapons inspection mission in Iraq. Chinese forces played peacekeeping roles in more than ten nations. In 2003, China dispatched 175 peacekeeping soldiers to the Congo, the largest peacekeeping operation China had ever conducted.

The UN has become increasingly important for China. The UN is China's front line in battling Taiwan's plan for independence. In 1997, China exercised its veto power for the first time to block a peacekeeping resolution on Guatemala for its support of Taiwan's reentry into the UN. In 1999, it did the same thing to Macedonia, which had just established official ties with Taiwan. The UN is indispensable in China's combat against the "unipolar" U.S. foreign policy since the end of the Cold War. China has championed a multipolar world order and emphasized the UN's authority in the international arena. Nevertheless, consistent with its overall global strategy, China has maintained a low posture on sensitive, controversial issues. Though it opposed the U.S.-led war against Iraq in 2003, China positioned itself behind France and Russia and let them take the lead. National self-interest is the key to understanding China's performance in the UN. China's involvement will increase in the years to come, but its approach will remain pragmatic.

See also Cold War and China; Independent Foreign Policy (1982); Rhetoric in China's Foreign Relations; Sino-Soviet Alliance; Taiwan Strait Crisis, Evolution of.

Bibliography

Kent, Ann, *China, the United Nations, and Human Rights: The Limits of Compliance* (Philadelphia: University of Pennsylvania Press, 1999); Kim, Samuel S., "China and the United Nations," in *China Joins the World: Progress and Prospects*, ed. Elizabeth Economy and Michel Oksenberg, 42–89 (New York: Council on Foreign Relations Press, 1999); Kim, *China, the United Nations, and World Order* (Princeton, NJ: Princeton University Press, 1979); Weng, Byron S. J., *Peking's UN Policy: Continuity and Change* (New York: Praeger, 1972).

Jinxing Chen

United States

See Adoption, American Families and; Korean War (1950–1953); Nixon's Visit to China/Shanghai Communiqué (1972); Ping-Pong Diplomacy; Sino-American Relations, Conflicts and Common Interests; Sino-American Relations since 1949; Taiwan Strait Crisis, Evolution of; Trade Relations with the United States; United States, Chinese Education in; United States, Chinese in; U.S. Legislation on China-Related Issues; Vietnam War.

United States, Chinese Education in

Chinese education in the United States started in the mid-nineteenth century as a literacy program for the early immigrants who came as railway laborers. To serve the needs of those early immigrants, Chinese-language schools (then called Chinese heritage community language schools) were established. Language classes in Cantonese were offered to residents in Chinatown in a number of large cities in the United States. In 1905, the emperor of the Qing dynasty (1644–1911) dispatched his secretary of justice to the United States to identify and assess the needs of Chinese communities in the United States. In his report, the secretary recommended that the Chinese government fund the establishment of formal Chinese-language schools in Chinese communities. As a result of joint efforts from both the Chinese consulate and local Chinese charities, more Chinese schools were established in big cities like San Francisco, New York, and Chicago.

The relaxation of immigration regulations in 1965 resulted in a new wave of Chinese immigration from Hong Kong and Taiwan. Motivated by a strong desire to preserve their Chinese heritage, these Chinese established family-oriented schools in which they taught their own youngsters, which later were merged into more community-oriented schools, partly because of the limited resources of family education and partly because of growing needs for a more robust curriculum in Chinese education.

Chinese education in the United States has witnessed a rapid growth in the past three decades. In a report of 1995 by the National Council of Associations of Chinese Language Schools, approximately 82,675 students were taking courses in 634 Chinese schools across the country. The growth of Chinese education, accompanied by a rapid expansion of Chinese schools, has brought changes in curriculum, school management, and the delivery system.

Curriculum

Unlike the Chinese schools in the late nineteenth century whose educational mission was to teach early immigrants basic reading and writing skills, schools in the twentieth century, particularly the late twentieth century, strove to preserve the Chinese heritage for the next generation, and this approach continues in the twenty-first century. The curriculum is broadly defined as an overall effort to cultivate student abilities to appreciate Chinese culture and tradition. This effort is particularly evident in the courses offered and the textbooks used for Chinese education.

Realizing the diverse needs of learners, the modern Chinese schools offer a variety of courses to students ranging from Chinese language to arts, literature, and traditional holidays. For example, the Chinese schools in the Dallas–Fort Worth area offer more than twenty Chinese courses that include Chinese language, literature, Chinese painting, traditional dance, abacus, and calligraphy.

Unlike the schools in the nineteenth century where textbooks were compiled by teachers, Chinese schools in the twentieth century took a more systemic approach in textbook adoption based on (*a*) curriculum goals and objectives, (*b*) developmental level, and (*c*) costs. Most Chinese schools adopt textbooks published either in mainland China or in Taiwan. Interestingly, some government organizations in China, such as the Office of Overseas Affairs under the State Department of the People's Republic of China, have expressed their interest in Chinese education in the United States and have sponsored a program to provide free textbooks to students in Chinese schools in the United States.

School Management

Chinese schools in the United States can be divided into four categories: (*a*) church-run schools, (*b*) for-profit schools, (*c*) nonprofit schools, and (*d*) public schools. The majority of Chinese schools are either for-profit or nonprofit schools. There are some church-run schools and a few public schools. For-profit schools include mostly kindergartens, child care centers, and tutorial programs for secondary school students such as SAT II: Chinese with Listening tutoring. Nonprofit schools consist of those operated by volunteers and those run by voluntary administrators and board members with the assistance of a small, partially compensated teaching staff. School boards in nonprofit schools are established to make policies and directives regarding school administration, teaching, pedagogy, and textbook adoption. Small schools may have no school board; medium and large schools may have a school board that consists of anywhere from three to thirty people. The principal is responsible for overall operation of the school. In small schools where there is no school board, the principal is often burdened with both teaching and administrative duties. In medium and large schools, the administrative structure is often comparable to that of an accredited school.

Course Delivery

Most courses in Chinese schools are taught in traditional classrooms that are rented through churches, nonprofit organizations, or community colleges. Recent studies show that there is a trend to use the **Internet** to deliver Chinese courses. For example, the Southern California Council of Chinese Schools provides an online homework site so the students can access lecture notes, assignments, and supplementary materials after school. The University of California at Davis has set up a Study Chinese Online Web site that provides synchronous and asynchronous Chinese learning environments for students.

Visibility of Chinese Education in the United States

Chinese education has increased its visibility in the United States in recent years. A growing number of students of Chinese descent and American students are taking Chinese in U.S. colleges and universities. In 1994, the American College Board introduced the SAT II: Chinese with Listening, which measures the language abilities of all students who have taken two to four years of Chinese in an American high school. Some public schools grant credit to students for classes taken at Chinese-language schools. Of the 189 Chinese schools in California, 166 are eligible for credit transfer. So far, 37 Chinese schools have been granted credit-transfer status. The San Francisco Bureau of Education offers multiple foreign-language tests at the end of the school year. A student enrolled in a Chinese-language school is eligible for five credits upon passing the test.

In 1994, the National Council of Associations of Chinese Language Schools (NCACLS) was established. The NCACLS consists of eleven council members from ten states and regions, including California, Colorado, Michigan, Illinois, Dallas–Fort Worth, New England, and northwestern regions. A nonprofit organization, the NCACLS has played an important role in promoting Chinese education in the United States. It provides services to teachers and schools with regard to teaching, textbook adoption, school management, and other matters. The National Council holds an annual meeting to discuss issues regarding policies, school management, teaching, and curriculum development in Chinese schools.

Chinese education in the United States has evolved from private, one-room schools to a system that comprises dynamic and creative institutions that serve thousands of students across the country. Driving for a high standard, Chinese schools have redesigned their curricula to meet the needs of a new generation of students of Chinese descent. Improvements has been made in several areas, such as school management, course delivery, and pedagogy. Twenty-first-century Chinese education continues to seek national recognition through its effort to preserve and disseminate Chinese culture and tradition in the United States.

See also Adoption, American Families and; Korean War (1950–1953); Nixon's Visit to China/Shanghai Communiqué (1972); Ping-Pong Diplomacy; Sino-American Relations, Conflicts and Common Interests; Sino-American Relations since 1949; Taiwan Strait Crisis, Evolution of; Trade Relations with the United States; United States, Chinese in; U.S. Legislation on China-Related Issues.

Bibliography

Chao, T. H., *Chinese Heritage Community Language Schools in the United States*, Office of Educational Research and Improvement of U.S. Department of Education (ERIC Document Reproduction Service No. ED. 409744, 1997); Ye, W., *Seeking Modernity in China's Name: Chinese Students in the United States*, 1900–1927 (Stanford, CA: Stanford University Press, 2001).

Robert Zheng

United States, Integration of Chinese Immigrants

Overseas Chinese in the United States are composed of three different groups, American born, naturalized, and permanent residents. As an ethnic group, overseas Chinese have lived and worked in the United States for more than two centuries. They have sacrificed and contributed to the building of the nation and have served as a bridge between the United States and China.

National and cultural identity has always been a challenge to immigrants in the United States. Chinese Americans, in particular, are conscious of both their Chinese cultural heritage and their American national identity. According to the 2000 U.S. census, there are 2,734,841 people of Chinese ancestry in the total U.S. population of 281.4 million. Overseas Chinese came from China and different parts of the world, such as Singapore, Cuba, Peru, and Canada.

Overseas Chinese have brought tremendous economic contributions. Early Chinese immigrants to the United States were generally from the Pearl River delta areas of Taishan, Kaipin, Xinhuei, Heshan, and Enping in southern China. Some of them came through Canada and South America. Although most of them were laborers who worked as farmers and industrial workers, there were also doctors, merchants, artisans, teachers, and students. Early Chinese immigrants also worked in mines during the gold rush era in the 1840s. In the 1860s, they contributed greatly to the construction of the transcontinental railroad that linked the East to the West and became vital in the economic development of the United States. Small businesses such as Chinese laundries and restaurants provided services for the convenience of people's daily life. However, Chinese settlement and adaptation have not had smooth sailing all along.

As early as the late nineteenth century, Chinese in the United States brought cases to the Supreme Court to protest against their unequal treatment because of their race and ethnicity. Cultural ignorance and racial prejudice in conjunction with institutionalized anti-Chinese rhetoric made it almost impossible for the Chinese to come to the United States and to stay. On May 6, 1882, Congress passed the Chinese Exclusion Act, which legally prohibited Chinese from freely entering the United States. The Chinese Exclusion Act was the first national legislation that banned immigrants on an ethnic basis. For decades after the 1882 Chinese Exclusion Act, more laws and regulations were imposed. The quota system of the 1924 immigration law declared Chinese already residing in the United States ineligible for citizenship. Local laws that prohibited Chinese from buying land and owning property were also enacted.

Despite the social hostility and political antagonism, overseas Chinese pursued racial equality through judicial processes. More than 9,200 Chinese immigrants filed civil suits against the exclusion laws between 1882 and 1905. They petitioned American authorities for their constitutional right to live and to work in the United States. They also rallied and participated in mass demonstrations to express their opposition to restrictive legislation publicly.

Engagement rather than disengagement became the strategy of overseas Chinese to integrate themselves into mainstream American life as citizens. While Chinese were forced into isolation as a consequence of exclusion laws, their conscious decisions to participate in political, economic, and social events rose, particularly during the Great Depression, which also helped them form a new dual identity as Chinese Americans. They formed their own labor organizations and took part in American labor-union movements at large to protect their economic interests. Their involvement in local and national political campaigns demonstrated their insistence on political democracy and their intention to be included in the system.

World War II provided a tremendous impetus for overseas Chinese to realize their goals. Even before the Pearl Harbor attack, Chinese Americans joined the American military forces to support the Anti-Japanese War in China. In addition, they donated millions of dollars for civilian relief. More Chinese Americans joined the army when Japan attacked the United States. Many laid down their lives. Their contributions to the United States and to the war effort were recognized by society and eventually led to the repeal of the Chinese exclusion laws in 1943.

Cultural diversity has been another front where overseas Chinese brought about many changes. The Chinese maintained their language and culture and contributed to the mosaic of American cultures. After-school programs such as Chinese-language learning, Chinese painting, and calligraphy, as well as Chinese martial arts, are popular and are shared by all ethnic groups.

The new immigration laws of the 1960s opened the door to better immigration opportunities. Intellectuals, scientists, technical personnel, and businessmen composed a large portion of the immigrants. Good education and skills make it easier for them to integrate into American society. Like their predecessors, the younger generation is hardworking and proachieving. Many overseas Chinese have become leaders in politics, science, architecture, sports, education, and business. Gary Locke, for example, who was born in Seattle, Washington, in 1950, became the first Chinese American state governor (in Washington) in 1996. Elaine L. Chao (1953–) was appointed as secretary of labor by President George W. Bush, thus becoming the first Chinese American woman to join the U.S. cabinet. Architect I. M. Pei (1917–), famous for his sharp and geometric designs, received both the American Institute of Architects Gold Medal in 1979 and the Pritzker Architecture Prize in 1983. David Ho (1952–) was named *Time* magazine's man of the year in 1996 for his discovery of the replication of HIV in the human body and his "cocktail" treatment of AIDS.

Through centuries of struggle, overseas Chinese as a whole have risen from lower levels of American society to the middle class. From being restaurant owners and laundry workers, they are stepping into leadership in virtually all areas of modern society.

See also Adoption, American Families and; Korean War (1950–1953); Nixon's Visit to China/Shanghai Communiqué (1972); Ping-Pong Diplomacy; Sino-American Relations, Conflicts and Common Interests; Sino-American Relations since 1949; Taiwan Strait Crisis, Evolution of; Trade Relations with the United States; United States, Chinese Education in; U.S. Legislation on China-Related Issues.

Bibliography

Tsai, Shi-shan Henry, *The Chinese Experience in America* (Bloomington: Indiana University Press, 1986); Wong, K. Scott, and Sucheng Chan, eds., *Claiming America: Constructing*

Chinese American Identities during the Exclusion Era (Philadelphia: Temple University Press, 1998).

Jingyi Song

U.S. Fulbright Scholars in China

See Fulbright Scholars in China (1979–1989).

U.S. Legislation on China-Related Issues

The numerous bills passed in the U.S. Congress on China since 1949 have profoundly influenced U.S. foreign policy toward China during that period. Since the Congress is representative as well as legislative, the major bills it has passed also reflect the sentiments and interests of certain groups. It is important to note at the outset, however, that Congress passes four types of legislative measures: bills, joint resolutions, concurrent resolutions, and simple resolutions. For the sake of reference, each of these forms is briefly explained.

A bill that originates in the House of Representatives or the Senate is designated by the letters "H.R." or "S." followed by its sequence number. It becomes a law only after it is passed in both chambers and signed by the president. Then the bill receives a public law number, for example P.L. 108-1, which refers to the first bill enacted in the 108th Congress. A joint resolution is similar to a bill, since it also becomes law after the same treatment. A joint resolution is designated "H.J. Res." or "S.J. Res." with a number following it, depending on which chamber it originates from. When Congress seeks other measures where the authority of law is not necessary, it uses concurrent resolutions and simple resolutions. A concurrent resolution is designated "H. Con. Res." or "S. Con. Res." A simple resolution is "H. Res." or "S. Res." The fact that neither of them becomes law does not mean that they are less important. They are used for expressing facts, opinions, and other purposes of either of the two houses. Finally, each Congress has a two-year term numbered in order, for example, the 108th Congress (2003–2004). In this discussion, some key legislative measures on China selected for their historical significance are chronologically organized around four historical events: the Cold War, the diplomatic normalization, the Tiananmen event, and the 9/11 terrorist attack.

The Cold War

Before 1949, U.S. policy toward China was ambivalent. The Truman administration had long been against American intervention in the Chinese civil war (1946–1949) and an American commitment to defend Taiwan, an offshore island where the Nationalist Chinese sought refuge after their defeat. Nevertheless, congressional opposition to New China remained strong. After the **Korean War** broke out in mid-1950, the 82nd Congress (1951–1952) passed H. Res. 77 and S. Res. 35 to label China an aggressor. It then resisted China's seating in the United Nations (UN) and refused to recognize the Chinese government. Its expressed opposition was attached to foreign aid appropriation acts from 1950 through 1970.

By the mid-1960s, the United States had increased its military involvement in Vietnam, where Chinese soldiers were also found to be manning antiaircraft guns and building roads for North Vietnam. Despite the mutual hostility, a series of congressional hearings and debates shaped the perspective of U.S.-China relations with the theme of "containment without isolation." Nevertheless, no major bill or resolution was passed to articulate this theme. In retrospect, the lack of China-related bills during this period suggested the troubled bilateral relations and the general lack of congressional interest in China.

Diplomatic Normalization

The 92nd Congress (1971–1972) passed S. Con. Res. 38 in 1971 to commend President Nixon's intended trip to China to seek normalization. A new era in U.S.-China relations began when Nixon went to China in 1972. In the following year, the 93rd Congress (1973–1974) enacted S. 1315 (P.L. 93-22) to extend diplomatic privileges and immunities to the Liaison Office of China. In 1979, the 96th Congress (1979–1980) passed H. Con. Res. 31 to express the sense of Congress that the United States welcomed the establishment of full diplomatic relations with China. In 1980, the 96th Congress approved H. Con. Res. 204, which granted most-favored-nation (MFN) trade status to China (nondiscriminatory treatment of the products of China) and thus made China the third Communist recipient after Romania and Hungary. In 1983, H. J. Res. 315 was passed by the 98th Congress (1983–1984), which requested that the president negotiate the creation of a U.S.-China student exchange program. In 1985, the 99th Congress (1985–1986) approved S. J. Res. 238 (P.L. 99-183), which provided for the sale of nuclear fuel, equipment, or technology to China for peaceful uses. This trade agreement was the first one regarding nuclear fuel between the United States and a Communist country.

The normalization of relations, however, did not divert Congress from its concerns about many other issues relating to China. To voice its condemnation of China's human rights violations, the 100th Congress (1987–1988) in 1987 passed S. Con. Res. 73 to call on the president to place the Chinese human rights situation on the agenda of the UN Commission on Human Rights. The 101st Congress (1989–1990) in 1989 passed H. Con. Res. 80 to demand that China stop forced abortion for the one-child-per-family program. To pursue its good relations with Taiwan, the 96th Congress (1979–1980) in 1979 passed H. Con. Res. 31 to renew its friendship with Taiwan and look forward to full diplomatic relations with it. To oppose China's missile transfer and nuclear proliferation, S. J. Res. 238 (P.L. 99-183) included articles restricting the use of nuclear fuel for peaceful purposes. In addition, H. Con. Res. 207 of the 100th Congress (1987–1988) in 1987 urged the administration to inform the Chinese government that the continued transfer of Silkworm missiles to Iran might seriously jeopardize U.S.-China relations.

Tiananmen Event (1989)

The Tiananmen event from April to June 4, 1989, enraged both Democrats and Republicans on Capitol Hill and prompted them to condemn strongly the Chinese government's crackdown on prodemocracy protesters in Beijing's

Tiananmen Square. In May 1989, the 101st Congress (1989–1990) passed H. Con. Res. 131, 132, 134, and 136 to protest and register their anger. Afterwards it targeted renewal of China's MFN status as a punishment. According to the Jackson-Vanik amendment of 1974, the MFN status of China was subject to annual renewal, which was contained in an annual presidential waiver subject to congressional disapproval. The 101st Congress (1989–1990) in 1990 passed H. J. Res. 647 to revoke the MFN status of China. Then it passed H.R. 2624 to prohibit the export of satellites intended for launch from launch vehicles owned by China. It also passed H.R. 2722 to grant permanent residence status to certain nonimmigrant natives of China.

The stage of bilateral tensions set by the Tiananmen mass movement remained through most of the 1990s. The policy of engagement that both the George H. W. Bush and Bill Clinton administrations pursued was scrutinized and criticized by members of Congress, who came to the conclusion that China could not be democratic and would become a big threat to America. The active 105th Congress (1997–1998) took up a package of bills as an alternative to the Clinton administration's failed "engagement" policy. It set the goal of promoting freedom in China by addressing all facets of U.S.-China relations, including prison conditions and prison labor exports (H.R. 2195, H.R. 2358), coercive abortion practices (H.R. 2570), abuses of religious freedom (H.R. 967, H.R. 2431), missile proliferation (H. Res. 188), Radio Free Asia to China (H.R. 2232), and China's military and intelligence services (H.R. 2647, H.R. 2190).

A breakthrough occurred in the 106th Congress (1999–2000) that led to an end of the Tiananmen Square sanctions. It finally ended the annual renewal process for extending MFN status (later renamed normal trade relations, NTR) to China by passing H.R. 4444. On December 11, 2001, China joined the World Trade Organization and received permanent NTR from the United States. The disappearance of the annual debate over NTR disabled Congress from using it as a vehicle for regularly reexamining China.

The 9/11 Terrorist Attack

The terrorist attack on September 11, 2001, against the United States seriously affected its China policy. The U.S. government came to see China as a potential ally in the war against terror. Meanwhile, Congress has been preoccupied with homeland security and wars in Afghanistan and Iraq. On the whole, Congress has been less vocal and less legislatively active on China, but the relationship has never recovered fully from the 1989 Tiananmen mass movement. Against this background, the 107th Congress (2001–2002) enacted H.R. 428 (P.L.107-10) to authorize the president to seek observer status for Taiwan in the World Health Assembly. The 108th Congress (2003–2004) enacted H. J. Res. 2 (P.L. 108-7) to appropriate funds to support democracy, human rights, and rule-of-law programs in China, Hong Kong, and **Tibet**.

See also Adoption, American Families and; June 4 Movement; Nixon's Visit to China/Shanghai Communiqué (1972); Ping-Pong Diplomacy; Sino-American Relations, Conflicts and Common Interests; Sino-American Relations since 1949; Taiwan Strait Crisis, Evolution of; Trade Relations with the United States; United States, Chinese Education in; United States, Chinese in.

Bibliography

CQ Press, *Congress and the Nation*, vols. 1–10; Dumbaugh, Kerry, *China and the 105th Congress: Policy Issues and Legislations, 1997–1998*, Congress Research Service Report for Congress, October 21, 1999, http://www.pennyhill.com/china/r130350 .html, accessed on December 6, 2004; Legislative Citations at http://thomas.loc.gov/.

Yan Bai

Urban Households

Urban Chinese families and households are undergoing a transition. Economic reforms since the early 1980s have changed the urban economy and culture, and tumultuous population changes in recent decades have greatly reduced China's fertility rates. These changes have had such a profound impact on urban Chinese families and marriage that China amended its 1980 marriage law in 2001.

There have been significant changes in marriage rates and age at first marriage. The number of marriages has gradually declined in recent years, while the number of divorces is skyrocketing. Since the early 1980s, the number of couples seeking divorce has almost quadrupled. According to the Chinese Civil Ministry ("Divorce Rate" 2002), in 1990, 9.51 million couples married, and 800,000 couples divorced. In 1995, 9.34 million couples married, and 1.05 million couples divorced. In 2000, 8.48 million couples married, and 1.21 million couples divorced. Overall, between 1990 and 2000, the number of marriages decreased by more than 10 percent, while the number of divorces increased by 50 percent ("Divorce Rate" 2002).

Today, both men and women marry at a later age. China has the world's highest minimum legal age for marriage: for men, twenty-two; for women, twenty years of age (Mackay 2000). But female mean age at first marriage has risen significantly during the 1990s. In 1950, the female mean age at first marriage was about seventeen; it was about twenty in 1970. In 1979, it rose significantly to twenty-three (Lee and Wang 1999, 66–68). In 2002, the average age at first marriage for women was about twenty-two. Evidence suggests that the rising age at first marriage in recent decades has contributed to a reduction in fertility.

There have been major changes in family formation and residential patterns. Although no single pattern in family organization is emerging in China, one thing is certain: there are more nuclear families in Chinese **cities** today, mainly because of the implementation of the one-child-per-couple population policy in the late 1970s. About 60 percent of urban households are nuclear families with three to four family members (Chen 2003). Another common type consists of a married couple with their children and one or more grandparents. Together, these types of family account for more than 90 percent of all Chinese urban households (Unger 1993, 27). The other families are a mix of extended families and single-person households, as well as nonfamily households.

Married couples are less likely to live with their parents. The emerging norm is that young people start saving to buy their own houses as soon as they start working. Some, if not many, of them are able to buy a house or find affordable housing when they get married or even before they are married. In addition, hundreds of thousands of young migrant workers in cities live in rental housing away from their rural hometown. As a consequence, the traditional patrilocal family pattern is gradually disappearing.

Divorce has become increasingly common in urban China since the early 1980s. Numerous reasons have been cited for the soaring divorce rate. Among them are extramarital affairs, bigamy, domestic violence, financial stress, and health issues such as AIDS. People tend to stress quality of marriage, rather than just being married.

Extramarital affairs and domestic violence have become major social issues. Concubines were once common during pre-Communist China. After economic reforms in the early 1980s, the practice resurfaced and became fashionable for a growing number of men, especially in certain cities in China. Increasing physical mobility, such as rural-to-urban and urban-to-urban migration, has contributed to the rise of family instability.

Domestic violence has been steadily rising in Chinese cities during recent decades. About one-third of Chinese families experience domestic violence, mostly in the form of wife abuse. However, husband abuse by wives is also said to be on the rise and may be unreported since men may be too embarrassed to report or speak about it ("Marital Problems" 2003).

Economic reforms since the early 1980s have crushed the "iron rice bowl" (lifelong job security) that existed under **Mao Zedong's** Communist rule. The competitive nature of the economy has created tremendous financial pressures for families and households in China.

AIDS is becoming a health issue in today's China. The spread of AIDS in China is very different from that in other countries, such as the United States. In the United States, AIDS is more common among gay communities and among lower-income racial and ethnic populations. AIDS in China is more likely to occur among urban middle-class, well-to-do businessmen. Some businessmen, when away on business trips, patronize local bathhouses where the risk of AIDS infection is high. Many persons infected with HIV are married and have families. HIV carried by married men could have a far-reaching impact on urban households if left unchecked.

Divorce is much easier to obtain legally today. Socially, divorce does not carry the same kind of social stigma as in the past. Once considered shameful and almost unthinkable, divorce is tolerated and accepted. Instead, people have a higher expectation of their marriages. For example, the majority of people today disapprove of a marriage without love. The quality of one's sex life is discussed more openly and is considered an important part of a happy marriage.

Remarriage is more common among men than among women. Few widowed or divorced women remarry, mainly because eligible men are in short supply. Middle-aged single, divorced, or widowed men today prefer much younger women in their twenties or early thirties. Therefore, middle-aged women have a difficult time finding a mate. In demography, this phenomenon is called "marriage squeeze" (Weeks 2001, 383), which implies an imbalance between the number of men and women of marriageable ages. The burden of "marriage squeeze" falls disproportionately on Chinese women and poor men. Not only do men bypass older women to marry much younger ones, but violence against women such as kidnapping and trade of women has become more prevalent. For men, about one in five may not find a wife if the current sex ratio continues.

Future trends and challenges in Chinese urban households include celibacy, sterility, single parenthood, and care of the elderly. More and more Chinese urban youth accept the idea of being single; some have already chosen to be single. For those who have a partner, cohabitation is more accepted among urban young people. The traditional norm about women's virginity has eroded. More young people opt for trial marriage before they commit themselves. Although it is hard to gauge the extent of cohabitation, as more people become able to afford to buy houses or to rent, many may choose cohabitation in the future.

The one-child-per-couple population-control policy has been effective in limiting urban couples to only one child, and many young people are choosing to have children later in their life. In addition, some urban youth choose not to have children at all.

If the current trend in divorce continues, single parenthood and single-parent households are bound to rise. At this time, most people still have other family members who could help take care of the children, so single parenthood has yet to become a major social problem in China. Out-of-wedlock births may also become an issue in the future.

Care of the elderly is likely to become a challenge. Because most families today have only one child, every couple would eventually have two sets of parents to look after. The fast pace of urban life further exacerbates the heavy burden of care of the elderly for future generations. Therefore, adult care facilities have become more common in recent years. However, it is still difficult to make members of the Chinese older generation accept the idea of spending their older years in a nursing home.

In 2001, China revised and implemented its new marriage law. One of the goals of the new law is to curb adultery and domestic violence ("China to Amend" 2000; "Public Replies" 2001). The law also guarantees family and marital rights and seeks to preserve stable families. However, the rising divorce rate is only one of the forces that transform urban families and households in China today. Demographic and social factors such as the imbalanced sex ratio and discrimination against women must also be addressed in order to guarantee a stable family life for all.

See also AIDS, Prevention of; Marriage and Divorce; Rural-Urban Divide, Regional Disparity, and Income Inequality; Urban Housing Privatization; Urbanization and Migration.

Bibliography

Chen, Xinxin, "Marriage and the Family in China," Women's Institute, All-China Women's Federation, 2003; "China to Amend Marriage Law," *People's Daily Online*, March 12, 2000, english.people.com.cn/english/200003/12/eng2000312N102.html, accessed on December 5, 2004; "Divorce Rate in China Will Increase, *People's Daily Online*, April 21, 2002, english.people.com.cn/200204/21eng20020421_94459.shtml, accessed on December 5, 2004; Lee, Z. James, and Wang Feng, *One Quarter of Humanity: Malthusian Mythology and Chinese Realities, 1700–2000* (Cambridge, MA: Harvard University Press, 1999); Mackay, Judith, *The Penguin Atlas of Human Sexual Behavior* (New

York: Penguin, 2000); "Marital Problems, Domestic Abuse Plague China's Women," *People's Daily Online*, March 9, 2003, english.people.com.cn/english/200303/09/eng20030309_112987.shtml, accessed on December 5, 2004; "Public Replies to New Marriage Law," *People's Daily Online*, March 2, 2001, english.people.com.cn/english/200103/02/eng20010302_63845.html, accessed on December 5, 2004; Unger, Jonathan, "Urban Families in the Eighties: An Analysis of Chinese Surveys," in *Chinese Families in the Post-Mao Era*, ed. Deborah Davis and Stevan Harrel (Berkeley: University of California Press, 1993); Weeks, John R., *Population: An Introduction to Concepts and Issues*, 8th ed. (Belmont, CA: Wadsworth Publishing Co., 2001).

Liying Li

Urban Housing Privatization

Privatization has been a crucial part of China's urban housing reform. It refers to the increasing role of the private sector in housing investment and the growth of private housing ownership.

Housing Investment

In the mid-1950s, China established a socialist model of urban housing provision in which the state took on the primary responsibility for housing investment. The state housing was provided through **state-owned enterprises (SOEs)**. State investment in urban housing was carried out by the allocation of capital construction investment (CCI) to SOEs. The latter constructed housing on land obtained from local governments and then assigned the houses to the workers. In 1979, more than 90 percent of all urban housing investment was financed by centrally planned state and local budgets.

In 1979, the state began to encourage work units to invest in housing through so-called self-raised funds—funds raised by work units themselves. After fulfilling tax requirements and turning over assigned profits to the state, work units were allowed to retain a certain proportion of their revenues for housing investment. They were also allowed to collect money from workers to finance housing projects. As a result, housing investment was decentralized. By 1988, state and local government budgets contributed only 22 percent to total urban housing investment, while work units financed 52 percent through retained earnings. This decentralization in investment was a major reason for the housing investment and construction boom that occurred in the 1980s.

Privatization of urban housing investment progressed faster in the 1990s and was evidenced by the increasing role of the nonpublic sector in housing provision. According to the 1997 *China Real Estate Market Yearbook*, housing investment from the nonpublic sector accounted for almost half of total housing investment in 1996. Of the nonpublic housing investment, 16.1 percent came from foreign-funded enterprises, 15.5 percent came from enterprises owned by investors from Hong Kong, Macao, and Taiwan, and 17.6 percent came from the domestic nonpublic sector. In 1986, China had 1,704 real-estate companies. In 1999, the number increased to 25,762. These real-estate enterprises together employed 0.88 million workers. Among these enterprises, 7,370 were state-owned enterprises, 4,127 were collective-owned enterprises, and 4,340 were enterprises funded from Hong Kong, Macao, Taiwan, and other countries. From 1987 to 1998, more floor space of residential buildings was furnished by individuals in **cities** and towns than by the state capital construction and urban collective-owned units. In Shanghai, the percentage of commodity housing construction in total housing construction increased from 13.5 percent in 1989 to 76.5 percent in 1998. The nonpublic sector is clearly playing a more important role in urban housing investment.

Housing Allocation and Purchases

Before the housing reform, housing provision was treated as a social welfare service. Allocation was based on occupational rank, seniority, number of family members working in the same work unit, and family size. It did not have a direct link with the tenants' income and gave priority to those with the highest status. Therefore, power and personal status were essential for access to more and better housing. Unequal distribution and corruption in the allocation of housing caused serious complaints from the general public.

Since the onset of housing reform, allocation of urban housing or housing purchases has been gradually privatized. China started to privatize urban housing in 1979 in four cities by selling new housing units to individuals at full construction cost. In the late 1980s, the government started to sell existing public housing at subsidized rates. By the end of 1997, about 60 percent of the public housing stock in major Chinese cities had been sold to individuals. In mid-1998, China finally decided to end the welfare housing system.

Even in the 1990s, however, a small proportion of commodity housing was directly purchased by individuals, due to several factors. In Shanghai, for example, 85 percent of commodity housing was sold to work units in 1990 and 75 percent in 1993. In Beijing, government institutions and work units purchased 75 percent in 1996 and 72 percent in 1997 of the total commodity housing. Chinese scholars argued that the constraint on cash wages and the nature of socialism had driven work units to provide in-kind benefits to their workers. Work units, still subject to "soft budgeting," increasingly siphoned whatever funds were available into consumption. Urban housing was one such consumption good. Therefore, when housing became commercialized, work units were happy to buy apartments for their workers.

The pattern changed dramatically when China decided to end the welfare housing system in mid-1998. As a result, the proportion of commodity housing sold directly to individuals increased from 13.96 percent in 1986 to 28.72 percent in 1990 and 80.08 percent in 1999. Clearly, housing allocation is becoming more market oriented, and the private sector is playing a more important role in the urban housing market. In Shanghai, for example, 74,583 commodity housing units were sold in 1998. Among these, 9,971 units were purchased by work units, only 13.4 percent. The remaining 64,612 units were directly purchased by individuals, 86.6 percent of the total transactions.

Several recent developments have contributed to the privatization of urban housing allocation/purchase. First, rents of public housing have been gradually raised over the years. This change gives urban residents more incentive to purchase houses by themselves. Second, the Chinese government proposed three different price mechanisms to promote housing sales. (1) Market prices are applied to high-income commodity housing buyers. (2) The government initiated the so-called comfort housing project or economical housing in February 1995 to sell commodity housing to low- and middle-income families at prices based on housing costs. Central legislation requires that all real-estate companies must include at least 20 percent economy housing in their development plan for low- and middle-income families. (3) A standard price that took costs and affordability into consideration was applied to public housing from 1994 to 1999. This was the main way in which public housing was sold through work units. For new housing, the standard price included only construction costs and compensation for land requisition, dismantling old housing, and moving its tenants. For older housing already allocated through the work unit, the price was equivalent to replacement costs, discounted on the basis of quality, depreciation, and environment. The standard price was subsidized by the state in the form of exemptions from taxes, forgone profits, and absorption of the expense of public facilities. Third, China introduced a housing accumulation fund in 1991 in Shanghai and later made it a major national policy. Employees and employers both contribute a portion of the employees' salaries to individuals' accounts at the wholly funded housing provident funds, which can be used for house purchases, mortgage payments, and large-scale home improvements. By the end of September 1999, 60.67 million workers had participated in this program, with a total contribution of 161 billion yuan to the fund and a loan of 32 billion yuan from the fund. Participants enjoy some advantages compared with other commercial housing loans, such as lower interest rates and easier applications. Fourth, mortgage financing, though still in its primitive stage, helps urban households purchase commodity housing. By the end of 1996, banks had lent about 50 billion yuan to individuals for their housing purchases. In May 1998, the People's Bank issued an important regulation on individual housing loans. According to the regulation, home buyers need to make a down payment of at least 30 percent of the selling price, and the maximum loan period is twenty years (which was extended to thirty years in 1999). In 2003, the mortgage interest rate was 5.04 percent for the first unit and 5.76 percent for other units. Mortgages have become an option for home finance and have helped many urban households in their home purchases.

By the end of 2002, more than 80 percent of all public housing had been sold to urban residents, and 82 percent of urban housing was privately owned. Many urban families, 9.6 percent, owned two or more housing units. In 2002, the average national price was 2,227.1 yuan per square meter for urban commodity housing, with the highest, 4,517.2 yuan, in Beijing, the second-highest, 3,836.9 yuan, in Shanghai, and the lowest, 904 yuan, in Jiangxi Province. More than nine-tenths (90.5 percent) of urban commodity housing was sold directly to individuals. In 2003, the national per capita living space was 14.9 square meters (22 square meters of construction area), which was more than four times the level of 3.6 square meters in 1978. More and more families are selling homes for larger and newer ones. In Nanjing in the first half of 2003, more than 50 percent of sales were for secondhand housing units. In Guangzhou, this proportion increased from 9.1 percent in 1999 to 18.3 percent in 2000, 29.5 percent in 2001, and 34.6 percent in 2002. It is interesting to note that in many cities a large proportion of housing is not purchased by local residents. In Sanya, Hainan, only 20 percent of housing units sold in 2003 were purchased by Sanya residents. In Shanghai, 53 percent of housing transactions in 2003 were made to people out of Shanghai. Most such housing purchases are for investment.

See also Hong Kong, Return of; Rural-Urban Divide, Regional Disparity, and Income Inequality; Urbanization and Migration.

Bibliography

China Real Estate Market Yearbook Compiling Group, *China Real Estate Market Yearbook* (Beijing: China Planning Press, 1997); Liang, Yongping, *Looking Forward Monetary Distribution of Housing* (Beijing: China Price Press, 1998); National Bureau of Statistics of the PRC, *China Statistical Yearbook* (Beijing: China Statistical Press, 2000); Shanghai Statistical Bureau, *1999 Shanghai Real Estate Market* (Beijing: China Statistical Press, 1999).

Shunfeng Song

Urbanization and Migration

Urbanization refers both to aspects of urban population growth and to urban place expansion. The latter is a spatial measure, which, in China, is indicated by the administrative adjustment of rural villages to townships and towns, and of towns to urban **cities**. China has upgraded many towns to urban cities and rural townships to towns. The number of cities increased from 450 in 1989 to 663 in 2000. The number of towns increased from 2,176 at the beginning of the reform in the late 1970s to 20,374 in 2001.

At the core of spatial adjustment is the growth of the nonagricultural population, which is, therefore, the most important measure of urbanization. In addition to natural growth, the urban nonagricultural population in China grows when people change their household registration (or *hukou* **system**) status from rural agricultural population to urban nonagricultural population. This happens when people retire from military service and remain legally in the cities, when college graduates of rural origin remain in the cities, and when city limits expand to include areas that were previously rural. Moreover, since 1984, peasants who set up businesses in small cities and towns have been granted urban nonagricultural *hukou* provided they are responsible for their food grain. Furthermore, rural migration into the cities has contributed directly and significantly to the growth of the urban nonagricultural population.

Currently, the urban population includes those living in the cities and towns who engage in nonagricultural activities and their families, plus the qualified floating population. As a ratio of urban to total population, China's official urbanization rate by the end of 2000 was calculated at 36.22 percent and by the end of 2001 at 37.66 percent. Although this rate has more than doubled 1978's rate of 17.92 percent, China's urbanization is said to have lagged behind the world's average urbanization rate of 50 percent, as well as China's own industrialization rate of 51.1 percent and the rate of nonagricultural employment of 50 percent in 2001.

Many factors have contributed to the lower ratio of urbanization in China. The first and foremost responsible factor is China's many decades of the *hukou*, or household registration, system. The system has artificially separated the urban from the rural population by restricting the freedom of changing status and migrating, primarily from the rural into the urban sector. As a result, the system not only has impeded the process of urbanizing the population but also has statistically left uncounted the considerable nonfarming population that has failed to obtain urban *hukou*. Second, the dichotomous development of the rural and urban sectors has also led to a segmented labor market in which rural migrant labor has been discriminated against, discouraging many from attempting to become urban. Moreover, before 1978, China's industrial policy had emphasized the development of heavy industry instead of labor-intensive light industry and had thus created limited nonfarm jobs to absorb rural surplus labor. In this respect, the inherited imbalance continues to be of significance today. Furthermore, many rural residents who have been working at nonagricultural jobs have chosen not to become urban to maintain their land, because of nostalgia, and for other reasons.

In the midst of China's rapid economic development and globalization, accelerating the pace of urbanization has become an urgent issue. Urbanization is the most important way to absorb rural surplus labor, estimated to be around 150 million persons, to raise rural income that has fallen farther behind the urban level and has caused a widened urban-rural income disparity, and to promote social stability, aggregate domestic demand, and ultimately, **sustainable growth and development**.

Rural-to-urban migration has contributed significantly to China's urbanization, as previously mentioned. Rapid migration started in the early 1980s as a "tidal wave" of rural migrant workers into the cities and experienced three phases the early to mid-1980s, the late 1980s to the 1990s, and during the period from 1997 to 2002. The rapid increase in the number of migrant workers, from more than 40 million workers in 1997 to 94 million in 2002, was a record and the number will increase at the rate of 4 to 5 million annually in the foreseeable future. According to data released recently by the China State Statistical Bureau (CCTV, March 22, 2004), in 2003 a total of 98 million rural workers were employed or seeking jobs in the urban sector. Among them, 65.7 percent were male, and 34.3 percent were female. With an average age of 29.5 years, 73.8 percent of these rural migrant workers belonged to the better-educated rural labor force with more than a middle-school education, 54.5 percent of them landed stable jobs in the city, 42 percent had unstable jobs, and 3.5 percent were still seeking jobs.

China's rural-urban migration has been attributed to both "pulling factors" (such as higher incomes and better job, education, and other opportunities) in the cities and "pushing factors" (such as poorer living conditions, lower incomes, and poorer job and education opportunities) in the countryside. Among the factors, the urban-rural income disparity is the most important driving force. Measured by the ratio of per capita urban disposable income to per capita rural net income, the disparity in 1978 was 2.57, and it widened each year after 1999, reaching 3.11 in 2002. It has been reported that in 2002, migrant workers' remittances back home, if all rural migrant workers were duly paid as promised, should have contributed 300 yuan to per capita rural net income. Without this source of income, rural income would have experienced a negative growth.

Geographically, migrants from Henan, Sichuan, Hunan, Anhui, Hubei, Jiangxi, and Chongqing accounted for 61.6 percent of the total (CCTV, March 22, 2004), and Beijing, Shanghai, and other eastern coastal cities have hosted most migrants because of their more rapid economic development that has created suitable jobs and a demand for rural migrant labor. For a similar reason, migrants to cities of medium and large sizes account for 70 percent, while small cities and townships have hosted only 30 percent of total migrants. Occupationally, rural migrants have entered industries that require low education and skills and have low entry barriers, such as the construction, extracting, textile, and service industries. In 2002, more than 90 percent of construction jobs, more than 80 percent of jobs in the extracting industry, and about 70 to 80 percent of textile jobs were held by rural migrants. Food retailing, housekeeping, security guard, and other types of service jobs are also mostly held by rural migrants.

Rural-urban migration has contributed significantly not only to raising rural income but also to the economic growth of Chinese cities. Widespread restrictions and discrimination against rural-urban migration have existed, however, thanks to many decades of dichotomous development and separation between the two sectors. Urban residents in the early and mid-1980s deemed rural migrants a "wolves" and then, in the late 1980s and most of the 1990s, became dependent on many of their services. Since the late 1990s more urban residents have become sympathetic, understanding, and receptive of rural migrants. Accordingly, government policies toward rural migrants have been primarily regulating, supervising, and restricting in nature. To work and legally continue their residency in the cities, rural migrants must obtain three official documents, an employment permit, a temporary resident certificate, and proof of compliance with the family-planning policy. The government listed thirteen industries and 203 types of jobs to be off-limits to rural migrant labor. Although these job restrictions as a government policy were officially lifted in Beijing, they have been replaced by "qualification" restrictions instead. In addition to entry barriers, rural migrants also enjoy fewer labor rights and welfare provisions and must pay higher fees for the education of their children.

As China urbanizes rapidly, barriers of entry and communication have gradually come down. Provinces and cities with less population pressure have published policies to eliminate discrimination and restrictions. The stipulation On How to Better Manage and Service Rural Migrants with Their Entry into the Cities and Job Hunting, issued on January 5, 2003, by the State Council, addresses specifically the change of government function from one of regulating and supervising to that of servicing and assisting. This stipulation is considered a very important landmark of policy transition toward safeguarding the constitutional rights of rural migrant workers.

See also International Migration and Overseas Chinese; Migrant Population; Rural-Urban Divide, Regional Disparity, and Income Inequality; Urban Housing Privatization.

Bibliography

Chen, Aimin, "China's Urbanization, Unemployment, and the Integration of the Segmented Labor Markets," in *Urbanization and Social Welfare in China*, ed. A. Chen, G. G. Liu, and K. H. Zhang (Aldershot, Hampshire, UK: Ashgate Publishing, 2004); Chen, Aimin, and N. Edward Coulson, "Determinants of Urban Migration: Evidence from Chinese Cities," *Urban Studies* 39, no. 12 (2002): 2189–2198; Chen, Yongjun, and Aimin Chen, eds., *An Analysis of Urbanization in China* (Guandong, China: Xiamen University Press, June 2002); *China Report* CCTV 4, January 22, 2003; Wang, Yuguo, and Aimin Chen, eds., *China's Labor Market and Problems of Employment* (Chengdu, China: Southwestern University of Finance and Economics Press, 2000).

Aimin Chen

Urban-Rural Divide

See Cities; Regions of China, Uneven Development of; Rural Industrialization; Rural-Urban Divide, Regional Disparity, and Income Inequality; Urban Housing Privatization; Urbanization and Migration.

V

Vietnam War

As an important player in the Vietnam War, China provided military, economic, and diplomatic support that was vital to North Vietnam's final victory in 1975. The establishment of the People's Republic of China (PRC) in 1949 was an encouragement to Ho Chi Minh, who subsequently sought aid from his personal friend **Mao Zedong**. American weapons captured in the Chinese civil war and the **Korean War**, along with Chinese-made equipment and other forms of aid, were sent to North Vietnam and assisted Ho in defeating the French at Dian Bien Phu in 1954. The North Vietnamese victory raised in the minds of American policy makers the fear that one Asian country after another would fall into the Communist camp. The so-called domino theory was used to justify increasing American involvement in Southeast Asia. To contain the spread of communism into South Vietnam, the United States first sent military advisers and then dispatched troops to support the government there.

China's support to North Vietnam was not based only on shared ideological grounds; geopolitical realities were just as important. A Vietnam either recolonized by France or taken over by America would be a threat to China. Mao's determination to support the oppressed nations also played a part in his thinking. Mao's personal friendship with the North Vietnamese leadership was indispensable to his commitment. Chinese propaganda always portrayed the North Vietnamese as "comrades and brothers" and "beloved little brothers," whose ties with China were "as close as lips and teeth."

Mao, however, always intended to avoid a direct confrontation with the United States. The horrendous casualties China suffered in the Korean War, China's domestic problems such as the economic difficulties of the late 1950s and the early 1960s, and the sheer technological superiority of American military power kept Mao from directly challenging the United States. After 1966, the power struggle within the Chinese Communist Party, as expressed in the

Great Cultural Revolution, further focused Chinese attention on internal priorities.

The Chinese provided the Vietnamese with substantial amounts of food, arms, and other supplies. Mao was determined to keep North Vietnam in the battle. When the Americans sharply escalated their involvement in the war in 1965, the Chinese pledged to "give help to Vietnam without pause, without reservation, and by all possible means." In June 1965, China sent troops into North Vietnam, where they were to act as a reserve should the United States invade the North. During the next seven years, more than 300,000 Chinese soldiers were stationed there. While the ground forces did not go to the front, Chinese air defense units, according to a Chinese source, were involved in 2,153 engagements in which they downed 1,707 enemy aircraft and damaged 1,608. The Chinese railway corps laid 117 kilometers of track and relaid a further 363. Other Chinese military units that specialized in communications, logistical operations, engineering, road building, and minesweeping all served there. During the war, more than 1,100 Chinese military lost their lives and 4,200 were wounded. China provided three-quarters of the total military aid given to the North Vietnamese. For the entire period from 1949 to 1975, it is estimated that the total amount of aid given by China to North Vietnam amounted to $20 billion.

During the war, the whole Chinese nation was mobilized in a "resist America, aid Vietnam" campaign. Newspapers provided daily reports of the heroic Vietnamese struggle and the global protest against the war. Movies about Vietnamese heroes were shown in theaters to foster revolutionary fervor. People were taught to sing songs to show their brotherly affection for the Vietnamese people. Ho Chi Minh appeared as "Uncle Hu (Ho)" for Chinese children. (Since Ho's first wife was Chinese, this title was quite appropriate.) Mass demonstrations that championed North Vietnam and denounced American imperialism were a regular part of urban life.

China also made a significant contribution to the war, as American scholars have observed, by acting as a deterrent to any U.S. invasion of the North. Mao assured Ho that in the event of an American ground assault on the North, China would order its troops to join the Vietnamese on the battlefield. Thus President Lyndon B. Johnson kept the level of U.S. military actions within certain limits in order not to provoke direct Chinese involvement in the war. U.S. troops seldom crossed the seventeenth parallel, though their bombing targeted key areas in the North. China's determination to keep the war confined to the South enormously benefited Ho Chi Minh.

Despite the apparent Chinese–North Vietnamese solidarity in battle, there existed a number of serious differences between the two sides. These went back to 1954, when China pressed Ho Chi Minh to accept the Geneva accords that ended the war against France. Vietnam was split into a Communist North and non-Communist South, despite the North Vietnamese belief that control of the whole of the country was within their reach. Subsequently, China opposed Vietnamese plans to build an Indochinese Federation, which in China's view would be dominated by Vietnam. Once the war against the Americans was under way, Hanoi rejected China's counsel that North Vietnam conduct Maoist guerrilla warfare rather than conventional warfare. Vietnamese Communist leader Le Duan once bluntly declared that Vietnam's military strategy should be one of offense, not defense, and that Vietnam must make its own decision. Finally, the Vietnamese still harbored historical resentments of past Chinese colonial rule. After all, the Chinese were not to be excluded from Le Duan's reference to foreign aggressors.

In the early 1960s, the growing rift between China and the Soviet Union put North Vietnam in an awkward position. The Vietnamese had to move carefully between their patrons to avoid offending either of them. China became less willing to facilitate the transport of Soviet aid across China. A Soviet proposal in 1965 to establish an air corridor over China was abruptly refused by Mao, who considered it a pretext for Soviet intrusion. Instead, China permitted a railway corridor for the delivery of Soviet supplies, but the Vietnamese saw this as less advantageous to their national liberation struggle. From 1965 to 1968, Chinese pressure on North Vietnam to fight on instead of holding peace talks generated further differences with the Vietnamese. In 1968, North Vietnam entered into negotiations with the United States without first consulting China. After Ho Chi Minh's death in 1969, North Vietnam moved closer to the Soviet Union, which further provoked Beijing. Although China continued to provide support, relations with Vietnam began to cool. Hanoi saw the marked improvement of relations between China and the United States in 1972 in the wake of Richard Nixon's visit as tantamount to betrayal on China's part.

As the American menace receded after 1973, border disputes and differences over Indochina caused a rapid deterioration in the Vietnam-China relationship. In the Chinese view, North Vietnam was an ingrate that was challenging China under Soviet protection; for the Vietnamese, however, China became "the Northern threat," replacing America as the enemy. At least 100 border skirmishes occurred in 1974. The deteriorating relationship, along with Vietnam's persecution of its ethnic Chinese and its invasion of Cambodia in late 1978, induced China to take military steps in 1979. This punitive action, termed a "self-defense counterattack," was intended to answer Vietnamese provocations. During this brief war, the far north of Vietnam that had escaped American bombing suffered much devastation. Chinese forces in turn took heavy losses in the face of unexpectedly strong Vietnamese resistance before withdrawing.

The brief war of 1979 was a grievous misfortune for both China and Vietnam, not only because of the material and human losses suffered by both nations, but also because it brought years of earlier cooperation to such a dispiriting conclusion. The war showed that American concerns about the domino theory were misplaced, since two Communist countries, one of which had just attained national liberation, were now in conflict with each other. Each valued its own national interests much more than the common Communist ideology.

As Vietnam's neighbor, China, from geopolitical considerations, had felt that it could not stand by while Vietnam was engaged in a war that might endanger its own security. The Chinese "tightened their belts" to contribute to North Vietnam's survival. Their continuing military, economic, and diplomatic aid was crucial to the victory won by the North. Since the late 1970s, however, the Vietnamese have charged that Chinese assistance intended to keep Vietnam in the war was given in order to exhaust the United States by bleeding Vietnam. References to Chinese aid have disappeared from Vietnamese historical writing, and China is now portrayed as having been an impediment to the reunification. For their part, the Chinese have lamented the loss of Chinese lives and the expenditure of so many resources for so little in return.

In the course of thirty years of war against Japan, France, and the United States, nationalism came to stand above all else for the Vietnamese. Assertion by China of its own interests, whether in regard to the immediate region or in regard to the Soviet Union or the United States, inevitably conflicted with Vietnam's highly charged nationalism. The clashes that resulted from self-centered national pursuits ultimately turned the Vietnam War into an unexpectedly bitter memory for both Chinese and Vietnamese.

See also Nixon's Visit to China/Shanghai Communiqué (1972); Ping-Pong Diplomacy; Sino-American Relations since 1949; Sino-Soviet Alliance; Zhou Enlai.

Bibliography

Duiker, William J., *Ho Chi Minh* (New York: Hyperion, 2000); Karnow, Stanley, *Vietnam: A History* (New York: Viking Press, 1983); Kissinger, Henry, *White House Years* (Boston: Little, Brown, 1979); Young, Marilyn B., *The Vietnam Wars, 1945–1990* (New York: Harper Perennial, 1991); Zhai, Qiang, *China and the Vietnam Wars, 1950–1975* (Chapel Hill: University of North Carolina Press, 2000).

Patrick Fuliang Shan

Vocational and Technical Training

China's vocational education is mainly composed of advanced vocational schools, secondary technical schools, skilled workers' schools, vocational lower secondary schools, job-training centers and other technical training schools for adults, and training institutions run by social forces or individuals. In short, they are secondary vocational and technical schools and higher vocational and technical colleges. Vocational and technical schools are divided into junior and senior levels. Junior secondary vocational and technical training refers to education and training after primary school. It is a part of the nine-year compulsory education in China. Its students are primary school graduates or youths with equivalent cultural knowledge. The schooling usually takes three to four years to complete. Senior secondary vocational and technical training is comparable to education and training at the upper secondary school level. It mainly enrolls lower secondary school graduates. The schooling usually lasts four years, but sometimes three years. A few specialty schools are also open to upper secondary school graduates, and the schooling for this group lasts two years. Senior secondary technical schools and normal schools commonly train secondary-level specialized workers and elementary-school teachers. All graduates are expected to master the basic knowledge, theory, and skills of their specialty in education in addition to the academic curricula required for upper secondary school students. The senior secondary vocational schools develop skilled workers who are capable of practicing and operating in production activities. The schooling of secondary vocational schools lasts three years. Higher vocational college is a part of higher education for adults and lasts two to three years. It mainly enrolls graduates from regular upper secondary schools and senior secondary vocational and technical schools and those who are currently in the labor force. Higher vocational college aims at training practices-oriented and craft-oriented high-level graduates for the needs of economic construction.

Since 1949, the People's Republic of China has adjusted, reformed, and improved the development of vocational and technical education. Vocational and technical training is viewed as a parallel education system to the regular secondary and higher education in China. Statistics showed that there were only 561 secondary vocational and technical schools with an enrollment of 77,000 students in the early 1950s. Thousands of vocational schools were set up to meet the needs of economic expansion. More agricultural and other vocational schools were developed in the 1960s. Although the **Great Cultural Revolution (1966–1976)** seriously affected the development of vocational and technical education, in the early 1980s, China entered a new historical era of reform and opened its door to the world. During the fifteen years between 1980 and 1995, the enrollment of secondary vocational and technical school students increased from 19 percent to 56 percent of all the students in senior secondary education. By 1998, there were altogether 17,090 secondary vocational schools with a total enrollment of 11,460,000 students. The number of vocational and technical colleges reached 101 with a total enrollment of 149,000 students. By the end of 2001, vocational and technical education at both the secondary and higher-education levels had significantly improved. The number of senior secondary vocational and technical schools reached 22,949 with a total enrollment of 13,052,800. At the higher-education level, more than 13 million people had received higher education through state-administered examinations for self-taught learners (Ministry of Education 2002).

Vocational and technical training has played an increasingly important role in Chinese education. Besides the training conducted and managed by the Departments of Education and Labor, outside enterprises at different levels are also encouraged to provide their own employees with vocational and technical training for life learning. In 1997, while the Departments of Education and Labor trained 3 million people through 2,800 employment-training centers, enterprises provided 30 million people with employment training through 20,000 employee-training centers. Statistics for 2001 showed that there were 11,500 technical training schools for staff and workers at the secondary school level and 496,384 technical training schools for peasants across the nation. Basic statistics of vocational and technical training in China are shown in table 15.

During the past fifty years, especially the last twenty years, China has paid much attention to teacher training for vocational education to improve the quality of vocational and technical training. Regular higher-education institutions have taken the lead. In 1989, more than 160 regular colleges and universities developed programs and established departments, specialties, or classes devoted to the training of vocational education teachers, with a total enrollment of 21,000 students. The Chinese government has also been making an effort to establish teacher-training bases for vocational and technical education.

TABLE 15
Basic Statistics of Vocational and Technical Training in Secondary Education in China (2001)

	Schools	Graduates (Thousands)	Entrants (Thousands)	Enrollment (Thousands)	Teaching Faculty, Staff, and Workers (Thousands)	
					Total	Teaching Faculty Only
I. Specialized secondary schools (total)	3,260	1,502.9	1,276.8	4,579.8	429.0	230.0
Secondary technical schools	2,690	1,224.6	1,081.5	3,917.4	352.8	184.4
Secondary normal schools	570	278.3	195.3	662.4	76.2	45.6
II. Skilled workers' schools*	3,792	646.2	503.8	1,401.0	239.6	140.0
III. Vocational schools (total)	7,802	1,665.0	1,850.2	4,664.3	430.1	305.9
Junior vocational schools	6,737	1,419.8	1,550.5	3,831.0	NA	268.6
Senior vocational schools	1,065	245.2	299.7	833.3	NA	37.3
IV. Correctional work-study schools	76	4.0	4.3	8.5	2.6	1.5
V. Specialized secondary schools for adults	4,113	906.3	621.1	1,891.6	182.1	105.1
VI. General secondary schools for staff, workers, and peasants	3,906	399.7	504.2	507.6	27.7	16.0

* The data for skilled workers schools are based on the statistics of 1999.

Source: Statsistics of the Ministry of Education, PRC (July 2002).

Vocational and technical colleges that are affiliated with higher-education institutions have set up 14 training bases, and central and local government have set up more than 200 bases. As a result, a network of training bases has been created in China to meet the needs of teacher training for vocational education at different levels. Vocational and technical training in China has produced a great team of graduates for Chinese economic reform in the twenty-first century. Its 30,850,000 graduates between the years 1980 and 1997 are now playing a significant role in China's modernization and civilization.

See also Character Education in Primary and Secondary Schools; Education Media and Technology; Educational Administration; Educational System; Higher-Education Reform; Management Education; Primary Education; Private Education; School Enrollment and Employment; Secondary Education; Taiwan, Education Reform in; Teacher Education; United States, Chinese Education in.

Bibliography

Department of International Cooperation and Exchanges, *Vocational Education in China* (Beijing: Ministry of Education, 2001), http://www.edu.cn/20010827/208328 .shtml, accessed on April 1, 2003; Ministry of Education, PRC, *Education in China* (Beijing: Ministry of Education, 2002).

Ronghua Ouyang; edited by Dan Ouyang

W

War to Resist U.S. Aggression and Aid Korea

See Korean War (1950–1953).

Wei Wei (1920–)

Wei Wei is a prose writer, novelist, and reportage writer. His original name was Hong Jie. He was born on March 6, 1920, into a poor family in Henan Province. He joined the army when the Anti-Japanese War broke out in 1937. Later he went to Yan'an. From 1939 to 1949, Wei was mainly engaged in poetry writing. After 1949, he published many poems and reportage articles. Since Wei long served in the army, most of the themes of his writings concern military life.

During the War to Resist U.S. Aggression and Aid Korea (1950–1953) (the **Korean War**), Wei went to Korea three times to observe and learn the life of Chinese soldiers there. As a result of his visits, he wrote a number of works about the war, such as *Young People, Let Your Youth Be More Beautiful* and *Forward, My Motherland. Who Are Our Most Beloved Ones?* in which Wei stated that Chinese soldiers are the most beloved people, received a nationwide warm welcome. The internationalist enthusiasm and commendation for the Chinese army expressed in this work greatly inspired the Chinese people in the 1950s. In addition, because of its well-knit structure and graceful language, *Who Are Our Most Beloved Ones?* has long been included in elementary- and middle-school textbooks and used as a good example of writing a prose essay.

The publication of his three-volume novel *The East* (1978) marked a new stage in Wei's writing career. Wei started this gigantic project as early as 1959, but he was not able to finish it until 1974 because he ceased working on it for eight years during the **Great Cultural Revolution**. *The East* once again focused on the hard struggles of the Chinese people during the War to Resist U.S. Aggression and Aid Korea. Compared with his earlier writings, the scenes and spectacles in this monumental work were much broader, and the characters were elaborated with much more mature techniques. Because most of the novel was composed before the Cultural Revolution, sometimes Wei was not able to really break through the writing taboos and the stereotypical tradition of war fiction that was imposed upon Chinese writers at that time, but undoubtedly, *The East* is still one of the best war novels published in the post–Great Cultural Revolution era. It won the first Maodun Prize for Literature in 1982.

In both Wei's prose essays and reportage articles, one can always find enthusiastic emotions, inspiring high spirits, and a description of the features of his time. In fact, his works are often regarded as "fiery fervent poems." Wei is a versatile writer gifted in many ways. In addition to prose essays, reportage articles, and novels, he also wrote an opera, *Attacking Invaders* (1952), the scenario *Red Storm* (1956), and *Biography of Deng Zhongxia* (1980).

See also Anticorruption Literature and Television Dramas; Avant-garde Literature; Experimental Fiction; Great Cultural Revolution, Literature during; Intellectuals, Political Engagement of (1949–1978); Intellectuals, Political Engagement of (1978–Present); Literary Policy for the New China; Literature of the Wounded; Misty Poetry; Modern Pop-Satire; Neorealist Fiction and Modernism; Pre–Cultural Revolution Literature; Revolutionary Realism and Revolutionary Romanticism; Root-Searching Literature; Sexual Freedom in Literature.

Bibliography

Lau, Joseph S. M., and Howard Goldblatt, eds., *The Columbia Anthology of Modern Chinese Literature* (New York: Columbia University Press, 1995).

Dela X. Jiao

Welfare Attainments since 1978

It is well known that considerable changes have taken place in China since 1978 when the country started economic reforms and opening-up to the world. The issue of what has been achieved and what these achievements imply for the well-being of the Chinese people can be addressed from the aspects of material and cultural attainments that apparently enhance economic welfare, as well as from the impacts of such factors as political and macroeconomic stability and personal freedoms.

First, economic welfare can be indicated by material attainments, which, in turn, can be measured by a set of variables presented here. China's real GDP from 1978 to 2001 on average grew 9.46 percent annually, and its real GDP per capita on average grew 8.11 percent annually during the same period. At these growth rates, China's aggregate economic power in 2001 was 792.2 percent of that in 1978, and the purchasing power of each citizen in 2001 was 596.1 percent of that in 1978. This growth performance allowed China to become the third-largest economy in the world, measured in purchasing power parity.

Along with the income growth, the share of expenditures on food in the budget shrank, as the general relationship between food consumption and income growth would suggest. From 1978 to 2001, this share among rural residents declined from 67.7 percent to 47.7 percent and among urban residents from 57.5 percent to 37.9 percent. Meanwhile, per capita annual consumption increased from 437 yuan in 1985 to 3,611 yuan in 2001, and per capita savings increased from 153 yuan to 5,780 yuan during the same period. While the higher growth of savings suggests greater wealth of the Chinese people, it is also a result of decreased job security and the absence of a well-established **social security system**, which have created rising uncertainty in Chinese people's lives.

China also achieved remarkably in housing, transportation, communications, education, and medical care between 1985 and 2001. Per capita housing, measured in square meters of floor space, doubled in urban areas and nearly doubled in the rural sector; transportation capability as measured by bus/population ratio increased 159 percent, as measured by motorcycle/household ratio increased 224 percent, and as measured by automobile/population ratio increased even more, though official data are not yet available; the number of **television** sets, an indicator of durable goods consumption, increased nearly 800 percent in rural areas and more than 600 percent in urban areas, and 92.9 percent and 94.2 percent of the population were reached by radio and television broadcasts, respectively.

In addition to the material attainments, the Chinese population has become better educated and healthier. From 1985 to 2001, enrollment of school-age children increased from 96 percent to 99.1 percent; the ratio of university students to population more than tripled; the ratios of hospital beds and medical doctors to population increased modestly, though quality of medical care may have increased, as evidenced in part by the longer life expectancy of the Chinese population, which increased from 68 years in 1982, according to *China Statistical Yearbook 1996*, to 71.0 in 1996, while the world's average in 1999 was 66.5, according to *China Statistical Yearbook 2001*. Finally, the illiteracy rate of the population decreased from 33.58 percent in 1964 to 22.81 percent in 1982 and further to 6.72 percent in 2000, according to *China Statistical Yearbook 2002*.

What does China's growth pattern imply dynamically? According to Robert Fogel, a Nobel laureate in economics, if China achieves its target growth rate of 8 percent per year, then by 2035, China's GDP will reach about 74 trillion dollars, which is about 60 percent more than the entire income of the world in 2001, while the GDPs in the United States and the European Union, if they grow at 3.5 percent per annum, will be 32 and 30 trillion dollars, respectively. Economist Fogel believes that during the past quarter century, researchers have focused on how Europe and the United States have been influencing Chinese culture by bringing Western technologies and ways of life to China; that it is likely that within a generation, the reverse process will unfold in a powerful way (Fogel 2003).

Because other factors than material and cultural attainments also affect economic welfare, the effects of political and macroeconomic stability, as well as economic and political freedom, on the economy and the welfare of Chinese people are obvious. China has achieved high growth while maintaining relative economic and political stability. While nominal GDP during the period from 1978 to 2001 experienced ups and downs, real GDP and real GDP per capita not only remained positive throughout the period, but also displayed a rather smooth pattern. Politically, except for the 1989 Tiananmen Square incident, there was relatively little turmoil, and the transitions of leadership were smooth. During this period, China experienced two major economic declines, one in 1990 and 1991 and the other in 1998 and 1999, though China maintained positive growth even during these two periods. While domestic political instability was to blame for the 1990–1991 decline, the downturn of 1998–1999 was primarily caused by the external shock of the Asian financial crisis. In other words, from 1978 to the present, China's economy has by and large been free from the sort of disastrous political turmoil that it experienced before 1978 and that led to its near collapse. The absence of political turmoil is perhaps the most important reason for the high economic growth. The fade-out of the memories of frequent political movements before 1978 is a positive contributing factor to the economic well-being of most citizens, as most Chinese people who experienced both periods, before and after 1978, can attest.

Private businesses and consumers have benefited from the political and macroeconomic stability. Firms need no longer worry about whether making a profit today will be politically incorrect tomorrow, and consumers can be assured that more goods will be on the shelves of stores. These assurances, in turn, make production planning easier, reduce transaction costs, and thus raise economic efficiency. Moreover, firms and consumers no longer fear accumulating wealth that, in the past, could become a catalyst for political condemnation. While enhanced economic efficiency resulting from reduced uncertainty has mostly been captured in the higher GDP and income figures, alleviated psychological stress, which can also bring economic welfare, is not accounted for in these figures.

Moreover, firms and consumers alike have enjoyed more economic freedoms, including autonomies for businesses on what to produce, how to produce, and what price to charge and choices for consumers on what to buy, how much to buy, and what types of jobs to hold. Gone are production quotas, set prices, rationed consumption, and administratively assigned jobs. The government has receded from the private lives of citizens, and Chinese people are living a considerably less politically stressed life, which, in addition to the better nourishment and medical maintenance of the population, may have also contributed to the longer life expectancy of the population.

See also Old-Age Insurance; Social Security Reform.

Bibliography

Chen, Aimin, "Assessing China's Economic Performance in 1978–2001: Material Attainments and Beyond," seminar paper, April 23, 2003, Indiana State University; Fogel, W. Robert, "Foreword," in *Urbanization and Social Welfare in China*, ed. Aimin Chen, Gordon G. Liu, and Kevin Zhang (Aldershot, Hampshire, UK: Ashgate Publishing, 2003); National Bureau of Statistics of the PRC, *China Statistical Yearbook* (various issues, 1981–2004) (Beijing: China Statistics Press).

Aimin Chen

Western Region Development Project

On January 19, 2000, the Leading Committee for Developing the Western Region of the State Council was set up in Beijing, with Premier **Zhu Rongji** as the chair and the first ministers of eighteen major ministries and commissions under the State Council as the members. The formation of the high-powered committee showed the determination of the Chinese government to develop the poor and backward interior areas and signified the beginning of a shift in focus of economic development from the eastern to the western region.

The western region includes eleven provinces and one metropolitan city, **Xinjiang**, Gansu, Qinghai, Ningxia, Shaanxi, **Tibet**, Sichuan, Yunnan, Guizhou, Quangxi, Inner Mongolia, and Chongqing. Because of the coast-oriented development strategy in the early years of economic reform, the landlocked western region has been lagging far behind other parts of the country, and thus regional disparities have been widening at an alarming rate. The western region currently accounts for 70 percent of China's land area and 20 percent of China's population, but only 18 percent of China's GDP.

To narrow the economic disparities between the western and the eastern coastal regions was the main motivation for the Chinese government to reorient its development strategy toward the poor western region, because the widening regional disparities contradict the socialist principle of "prosperity for all" and thus threaten the legitimacy of the Communist regime. However, the policy shift was motivated by other concerns as well, such as reduction of overcapacity pressures on the coast by shifting investments into the western region, boosting domestic demand by raising the living standard of the poorest residents in the western region, reduction of ethnic tensions that had been rising among ethnic groups in the western region, and protection of the environment that had been deteriorating because of excessive logging and reclaiming of wastelands in the western region.

The western region is characterized by a harsh physical environment and poor infrastructure. Therefore, the first priority of the westward drive is to speed up the construction of infrastructure. The focus is on the development of highways, railways, airports, natural gas pipelines, electric networks, telecommunications, broadcasting and television, and facilities for water resource utilization. The construction of highways and roads will focus on national highways and eight transprovincial main roads in the western region. The construction of railways will focus on railways that link individual provinces within the western region, that link the western region to the eastern region, and that link the western region to neighboring countries in central Asia (particularly Kyrgyzstan and Uzbekistan). The construction of natural gas pipelines will focus on pipelines that connect the western region to the eastern coastal region.

The western region is a vital part of China's ecological system. The two largest rivers in China, the Yangtze River and the Yellow River, originate from the western region. Excessive logging and reclaiming of wastelands in the upper reaches of the two rivers have led to serious soil erosion and water losses and, therefore, frequent floods and dry-ups in the two rivers. Thus the second priority of the westward drive is to protect the ecological environment. The government will provide farmers with grains and nursery-grown plants so as to encourage them to turn farmlands back into forests or grasslands. Mountain passes will be sealed for afforestation. In the upper reaches of the Yangtze River and the upper and middle reaches of the Yellow River, logging in natural forests will be forbidden, and lumber markets will be closed down. A total of 6 million hectares of natural preservation zones will be built up in the western region, particularly in the Qinghai-Tibet Plateau, the headstream areas of the Yangtze River and the Yellow River, the mountain and valley areas in the southwestern provinces, and the highland and desert areas in Xinjiang and Inner Mongolia. In the next five years, the natural preservation zones in the western region will increase so rapidly that they will account for 8.5 percent of China's total land area.

The western region is nevertheless abundant in natural resources such as natural gas, hydroelectric power, salt, nickel, and platinum. It is also rich in tourism resources, and it has seven world-class cultural heritage sites selected by the United Nations Educational, Scientific, and Cultural Organization. Thus the third priority is to adjust industrial structure so that the western provinces focus on the development of geographic-specific industries with prospective markets, as well as industries in which the western provinces have an advantage. The exploitation of natural resources, husbandry, forestry, plantation of herbs and green foods, and the tertiary industry (particularly tourism) will be among the priority sectors for development and will become new growth points in the western region.

Apart from a few exceptions such as Shaanxi Province, Sichuan Province, and Chongqing City, science, technology, and education are extremely underdeveloped in the western region. Thus the fourth priority of the westward drive is to accelerate the development of science, technology, and education and speed up the nurturing of talents. In addition to the introduction of advanced technology and trained personnel from abroad and other parts of the nation, scientific and technical resources in local munitions enterprises, research institutes, and universities and colleges should be utilized and developed to their full potential. Attention will also be given to the development of education in poor areas at various levels to improve the quality of the labor force.

To reach these goals in the development of the western region, the Chinese government decided to grant preferential policy treatment to the western region. On August 28, 2001, the general office under the Leading Committee for Developing the Western Region of the State Council issued Suggestions on the Implementation of the Policy Measures for the Grand Development of the Western Region. This document officially endorsed a number of new policies in favor of the western region with regard to state investments, arrangement of construction projects, fiscal transfers, financial support, improvement of "soft environments" for investment, taxation, the use of land, mineral resource exploration, reform in the price and fee systems, foreign investments, foreign trade, regional cooperation, introduction of talents, development of science and technology, and development of education, culture, health, and other public services. It is expected that as the grand plan of developing the western region evolves, the western region will be granted more and more preferential policy measures, and it thus will provide increasing opportunities for investors.

See also Regions of China, Uneven Development of.

Bibliography

Tian, Xiaowen, "China's Drive to Develop Its Western Region (I): Why Turn to This Region Now?" in *China's Economy into the New Century: Structural Issues and Problems*, ed. John Wong and Lu Ding, 237–256 (Hackensack, NJ: World Scientific, 2002); Tian, "China's Drive to Develop Its Western Region (II): Priorities in Development," in *China's Economy into the New Century: Structural Issues and Problems*, ed. John Wong and Lu Ding, 257–272 (Hackensack, NJ: World Scientific, 2002).

Xiaowen Tian

Western-Style Fast Food

See Fast Food (Western Style), Integration of.

Women, Role as Mothers

The subservient Chinese women during the early 1900s, with bound feet, would have found it difficult to imagine Chinese women's emancipation as it exists today. Until half a century ago, Chinese women had obediently followed the Confucian principles that positioned women as inferior to men. The Communist revolution in 1949 brought many changes to China, among which was women's emancipation. Since then, traditional Confucian ethics have been challenged successfully by Western political philosophies, especially Marxism.

Since 1949, China has undergone traumatic developments through the destruction of Chinese tradition by political movements. During the **Great Leap Forward** from 1958 to 1960, women started to leave their homes and enter society to join the workforce, a trend that continued during the **Great Cultural Revolution** from 1966 to 1976. During this period, China was mobilized to abolish the tradition represented by the "Four Olds"—old customs, old habits, old culture, and old thinking.

Because the modern mothers of today's China were born after the Cultural Revolution and grew up while family planning and the economic reform were being started in 1978, there is a significant difference between them and the mothers of the previous generation who were still confined by the old tradition. The political campaigns of the one-child policy and the economic reform effected dramatic changes in women's lives. One child per couple

A Muslim family in Lan Zhou, Gansu Province.

became the standard family size in urban areas, while a flexible family-planning policy was implemented in rural areas and for ethnic minorities. Thus mothers in urban areas developed a lifestyle quite different from that of the countryside.

In the **cities**, a mother nowadays takes care of a comparatively small family, often composed of only three people: herself, her husband, and their child. During the week when both parents work, the child attends a day-care center, starting at preschool age. However, there are exceptions: some grandparents may help take care of the grandchild. By contrast, in the countryside, a woman is, by tradition, married into the husband's family and lives with his parents as an additional family member. Because of the limited child care facilities in rural areas, usually the husband's mother assumes the role of a baby-sitter.

Basically, modern mothers living in urban areas tend to have a single child, whether a boy or girl. However, women living in rural areas are still striving, under traditional social pressure and also because of the labor-intensive nature of farming, to have a son. If their first child is a girl, it is likely that the mother will try to have a second child, hopefully a boy. The attitude of urban women toward childbearing is changing, and so is the attitude of Chinese farmers toward raising multiple children. A survey conducted in 2000 in several Chinese big cities showed that almost 20 percent of women did not want a child even if they were to marry. The traditional views of "raising children as a hedge against old age" and "more sons, more blessings" are fading away. A 2001 survey showed that Chinese farmers are now likely to have fewer children—as many as 85 percent of farmers were against multiple births.

The emancipation movements in modern China have empowered women to make their own choices in life. Women who used to be content with a steady family income now are not satisfied to be just caregivers for their husbands and children, but also want to improve their own individual life quality within a happy marriage. While marriages were very stable in the 1950s and the 1960s, the marriage quality was low. Now, women have high expectations from marriage.

Family ties have always played a major role in Chinese society, and a divorce used to be considered a loss of face. In a survey of Beijing youth conducted in 2000, up to 90 percent of youngsters would accept divorce in case the marriage partners became unhappy with each other. In the past, if there happened to be a marital problem, the authorities would try, through persuasion and education, to prevent the couple from getting a divorce. Along with recent social and economic changes, the government policy has loosened up, and the official view regarding divorce has changed. The divorce rate is rising, and rates in cities are higher than in the countryside. In an era of expanding opportunities for women, in most cases the demand for a divorce is initiated by the woman. According to an official estimate in 2002, some two million couples per year will join the ranks of the divorced. Because young Chinese are very different from the older generation and care more about the quality of their marriage than about traditional opinions, more and more couples prefer divorce to an unhappy marriage. The high and growing rate of divorce in China reflects the modern urban woman's notion of mastering her own fate and at the same time is a reflection of women's new social and economic freedom.

China's family planning with its one-child policy has resulted in delayed marriages, late childbearing, and fewer children. This has freed modern mothers, especially those in urban areas, from the burden of housework, and their goals in life have become quite different from those of the mothers of previous generations who had four, five, six, and sometimes more children. Furthermore, the new social structure facilitates more freedom for modern mothers. Besides kitchen modernization and the availability of appliances that provide women with convenience and thus more freedom, social development in modern China offers a flexible solution for working mothers.

With well-equipped kindergartens and a booming domestic service market, more and more mothers can now enjoy work and family life at the same time. In most cities, children over two years of age can receive good care and all the necessary early childhood training at child centers close to home. Alternatively, domestic helpers are available and can be found through community service centers. A mother can always have a helper to take her child to and from kindergarten or school, go grocery shopping, and prepare food. Thus, even with a busy work schedule, mothers have more time for themselves, and this also applies to grandmothers; thanks to a modernized lifestyle, a Chinese grandmother no longer has to be a full-time baby-sitter. Because Chinese mothers are no longer enslaved by the burden of frequent childbearing and other heavy family responsibilities, their general health has improved, and more of their attention has also been paid to the well-being of the children.

Although modern mothers have taken up various jobs and proved to be as competent and successful as men, some mothers have started to follow the trend of reviving traditional values, another aspect of modernization that is due to the recent economic reform and the social changes it effected. These sociocultural and socioeconomic changes have influenced women's attitudes as mothers and wives. In today's social context, many modern women consider housekeeping as one of the most important obligations they should fulfil—a revival of traditional values. As women's status rises, they become more independent and have more choices in life; some of them react to this by quitting their jobs and going home to concentrate on raising a family. While professional women are playing an increasingly important role in social and economic life, nowadays women's work at home is also widely acknowledged and appreciated. In this recent trend, the modern opinion holds that by rearing children and doing housework, a woman also contributes to society. Some modern mothers accept the different roles of men and women and are willing to play their role at home to improve the quality of family life. Housekeeping is considered hard work, but is also viewed as important and a kind of "art"—not an easy task if one wants to do it well. This new trend of accepting a more supportive role in the family does not diminish the rising status of women in China and the increasing role they play in a full range of social activities.

However, although women are devoted to and get due respect for their role as wives and mothers, not many are willing to give up their job and return to their small home world for good. Women enjoy their jobs despite the chores that keep them busy at home. Most women want to keep their jobs even after improving their financial circumstances. Many Chinese nowadays believe that the success and happiness of a woman lie in the combination of a well-established career and a happy family life, and most women spend their life-time balancing the two.

See also Great Cultural Revolution, Impact of on Women's Social Status; Marriage and Divorce; Minority Women in Xinjiang and Taiwan; Women, Social Status of.

Bibliography

Barlow, Tani, ed., *Gender Politics in Modern China: Writing and Feminism* (Chapel Hill, NC: Duke University Press, 1993); Cheung, Fanny, *Engendering Hong Kong Society: A Gender Perspective of Women's Status* (Hong Kong: Chinese University Press, 1997); Honig, E., and Hershatter, G., *Personal Voices: Chinese Women in the 1980s* (Stanford, CA: Stanford University Press, 2003); People's Daily Online, "More Than a Third of Chinese Engineers Are Female," http://english.people.com.cn/200411/05/eng20041105_162910.html, accessed on December 7, 2004; People's Daily Online, "Wedding Revolution Sweeps China," http://english.people.com.cn/200410/13/eng20041013_160113.html, accessed on December 7, 2004; Yan, Y., *Private Life under Socialism: Love, Intimacy, and Family Change in a Chinese Village, 1949-1999* (Stanford, CA: Stanford University Press, 2003).

Senquan Zhang

Women, Social Status of

Significantly improved, women's social status in China since the establishment of the People's Republic of China (PRC) contrasts sharply with the situation under the old regime. However, in recent years, women have suffered some nefarious conditions that previously had existed only before 1949.

Women's social position in China before 1949 was largely one of obedience, obeisance, passivity, seclusion, and instrumentality, a condition worse than women's overall status worldwide. Men were considered the superior sex, and women largely existed for men's needs and the related social values system. One primary goal of a woman's life was to give birth to sons, so that the legacy under the father's name was carried on.

A virtuous and properly bred woman before 1949 was expected to adhere to an elaborate set of Confucian precepts and disciplines. Among these precepts and disciplines were "the Three Obediences" and "the Four Virtues," as catalogued in *Nu er Jing* (cited in Headland 1914, 69–80), or the *Bible for the Daughter.* "The Three Obediences" were (1) the obedience to the authority of the father and the elder brothers when the woman was young, (2) the obedience to the authority of the husband when the woman was married, and (3) the obedience to the authority of sons when the woman was widowed.

A practice that lasted for thousands of years in Chinese history and epitomized the secondary and oppressed position of women was foot-binding. The purpose was the "gradual confinement and silencing of the female body" (Croll 1995, 20). The practice of binding women's feet effectively crippled women's physical mobility and their mental aspirations for the external world and "manly affairs." This practice confined women to the single choice of household duties,

Mrs. Liwei Gong, shown here with her daughter Xindi, is, like her husband, a professor at the Tsinghua and Peking Universities.

such as serving the daily needs of their husbands and bearing and rearing children.

The Communist takeover of China and the establishment of the PRC in 1949 greatly ameliorated women's condition. Maoist culture advocated egalitarianism between men and women. **Mao Zedong** himself claimed that women hold up half of the sky and that times have changed women can do the same as men. Mao initiated an institutional and legal framework for the protection of the rights and interests of women. The legal basis for this protection is provided in China's Constitution, which establishes women's equal status with men in political, economic, cultural, social, and family life. More specific laws were also instituted to protect and promote women's rights, including the Marriage Law, the Law of Inheritance, the Civil and Criminal Law, and the Law of the People's Republic of China on the Protection of the Rights and Interests of Women. In addition to laws, agencies were also established for the specific purpose of protecting women, including the Committee for Women and Children's Work (under the State Council, China's highest executive branch) and the All-China Women's Federation.

Since the beginning of the PRC, women have achieved much more participation in social and political spheres, although still not at the same level as men. In the highest legislative branch, women members constituted more than 21 percent of the total Eighth **National People's Congress (NPC)** convened in 1993 and more than 12 percent of the Standing Committee, the permanent body of the NPC. In 1993, women made up more than 32 percent of all employees working in government organizations. That year, the various ministries and commissions under the State Council had sixteen female ministers and vice ministers, and the nation had eighteen female provincial governors and deputy governors. In the nation's some 500 **cities**, more than 300 women have been elected mayor or deputy mayor. In the legal profession, there were 21,012 women judges and 4,512 women lawyers in 1992. Women members make up 14 percent of the Communist Party's general membership ("White Paper" 1994).

In the social sphere, women's equal rights to education and scientific research have not been transformed into reality. The implementation of the Compulsory Education Law has helped increase the attendance rate for girls in the seven- and eleven-year-old groups to more than 96 percent. The percentages of females in middle schools, colleges, and graduate schools, however, only reached 43.1, 33.7 and 24.8 percent, respectively in the mid-1990s. The majority of school dropouts are females, and about 70 percent of illiterates nationwide are females ("White Paper" 1994).

Efforts since the founding of the PRC have also enhanced equal opportunity for women in employment. In the 1990s, women accounted for 44 percent of the total number of employees in the urban labor force and 50 percent of the rural work force ("White Paper" 1994). Article 12 of the new Labor Law of the PRC, which became effective on January 1, 1995, stipulates that workers shall not be discriminated against on account of nationality, race, sex, or religious belief. The new law also gives female workers special labor protection during their menstrual, pregnancy, and one-year breast-nursing periods (Articles 58, 59, 60, and 62). It also guarantees no less than three months of maternity leave (Labor Law 1994, Article 62).

However, after the advent of China's **Open Door policy** in the late 1970s, an emphasis on the materialistic side of life emerged in China. Women are experiencing some nefarious conditions that previously had existed only before 1949. Discrimination and oppression against women are forbidden by the law. However, in real life, discrimination and oppression against women exist insidiously, in that the duplicity between the legal rhetoric and the social practice often camouflage discrimination and oppression.

In the workplace, despite constitutional protection of women in terms of employment and work, discrimination against women still exists. These workplaces include both **state-owned enterprises** and privately owned businesses, whose job advertisements sometimes flagrantly state that only men are eligible for application. Many work units (known as *danwei* in Chinese) prefer to hire men because men do not have the trouble of pregnancy and maternity leave. Hiring women will obligate the work unit to grant them paid maternity leaves.

Sources indicate that 70 percent of laid-off workers from factories are women. Women are hired into inferior positions even when they are better qualified than men. More than 70 percent of job-seeking urban people are women ("White Paper" 1994). The growing rural surplus labor force may further stratify gender inequality in rural areas. Women have not achieved equal pay for equal work. A 1990 survey revealed that compared to the wages of men, urban women and rural women received only 77.4 percent and 81.4 percent of the pay given to men, respectively. Women also face compulsory early retirement ("Protection" 1994).

Conditions of women migrant workers in some urban places are lamentable. China's Open Door policy and its focus on economic development have produced and strengthened the social phenomenon of rural migrant workers in urban China. Millions of farmers temporarily migrate to urban China to seek jobs. Some one-third of all rural migrant workers are women, but in some places, especially in the export-oriented special economic zones of southern China, women comprise more than 70 percent of the migrant workforce. Rural migrant women form the backbone of the workforce in the textile industry, manufacturing industries, domestic services such as baby-sitting and cleaning, and prostitution. Many forms of policing and regulation make life much harder for migrant workers, including women workers. Journalistic portrayals of female migrant victims are common. Women are abused, beaten, and sexually harassed by men and male employers.

In some illegal social practices, women are treated as commodities and objects of abuse, mostly for commercial returns. Many women are believed to be sold into slavery in China each year. Some women do manage to escape, but others are often ashamed to return to their families.

The phenomenon of "second wife" (*er nai*) may also be becoming a unique and widespread social practice in China. Under the influence and pressure of new economic mores and commercial values, women and women's sexuality have been exploited by the new affluent male business class. Countless "second wives," for the return of financial benefits, are deprived of socially and legally endorsed rights and dignity.

Victims of rape, besides suffering physically and psychologically from the act of rape itself, also suffer from social prejudice. Many see raped women as "unclean" in person, "indecent" in character, "loose" in behavior, or "improper" in dress. In 1994, one-quarter of the younger women and almost one-half of the older women thought that a woman would rather die than be raped. Society's attitude toward rape victims has kept women from reporting rape. There are also reports of cases where female political prisoners are sexually offended and attacked in various ways, including being put in men's prison cells and gang-raped by them. Overall, while women's social status has tremendously improved under the Communist regime, much remains to be done to protect their rights.

See also Confucian Tradition and Christianity; Great Cultural Revolution, Impact of on Women's Social Status; Marriage and Divorce; Minority Women in Xinjiang and Taiwan; Women, Role as Mothers.

Bibliography

Croll, E., *Changing Identities of Chinese Women: Rhetoric, Experience, and Self-Perception in Twentieth-Century China* (Hong Kong: Hong Kong University Press, 1995); Headland, I. T., *Home Life in China Today* (London: BBC, 1914); Huang, C., "China Statement," presented at the fifty-sixth Session of the UN Commission on Human Rights, March 19–April 27, 2001, Geneva, Switzerland; "The Labor Law of the PRC," *BBC Summary of World Broadcasts*, July 6, 1994; "Protection of Women's Rights Draft Law Discussed," *FBIS China Report* 27 (April 2, 1994); "White Paper on the Situation of Chinese Women," Xinhua News Agency, June 11, 1994.

Xinan Lu

Workers

See Labor Market; Labor Market Development; Labor Policy; Labor Policy, Employment, and Unemployment; Labor Relations; Labor Rights; Migrant Population; Reemployment of Laid-off Workers; Trade Unions; Unemployment; Workers' Congress.

Workers' Congress

The workers' congress is an enterprise-level institution with the proclaimed goal of facilitating workers' democratic participation in the enterprise's management and protecting workers' economic interests. The system was borrowed from the Soviet Union and was first established in the northeastern part of China prior to the founding of the People's Republic of China (PRC) in areas controlled by the Chinese Communist Party (CCP). After 1949, the system was promoted throughout the country. After 1957, the enterprise CCP committees took control of all workers' congresses. In 1980, Polish workers engaged in a serious confrontation with the ruling Communist Party in Poland and were eventually responsible for the downfall of the Communist government. This event sent an alarming signal to high-ranking Chinese leaders. They believed that the lack of workers' participation in workplaces was one of the major factors that contributed to the workers' rebellion. Consequently, China strengthened its efforts to promote workers' congresses. In 1986, the Chinese State Council issued a new regulation on the establishment of workers' congresses. Most **state-owned enterprises** began to restore the system. The number of enterprises that have the congresses established has fluctuated over the years due to the restructuring of the state-owned enterprises. Under the current law, only state enterprises are required to establish workers' congresses, but private- and foreign-owned companies are also encouraged to endorse this mechanism of workplace participation.

According to China's labor laws, a workers' congress meets at least once every six months. It elects a labor-union committee to serve as its standing committee. The workers' congress functions under the CCP's leadership; workers directly elect its delegates; and the labor-union committee serves as the congress's working organ in charge of its routine duties. Laws also grant the workers' congress the following rights or powers: (1) to examine and make suggestions on production plans or policies formulated by the management; (2) to approve or reject programs made by management concerning workers' immediate interests such as wage readjustment, distribution of bonuses, labor protection, and rewards and penalties; (3) to decide on matters related to workers' welfare, including the use of welfare funds and housing allotment; (4) to evaluate and supervise the performance of management; and (5) to elect or recommend candidates for managerial personnel and to select workers as members of the board of directors.

The role of the workers' congress has changed over time. During the period from the mid-1950s to the late 1970s, the workers' congress remained powerless and played only a symbolic role, since under the then prevailing command economic system, all important decision-making powers regarding business

operation and workers' interests were concentrated in the government, especially the central government. The role of the workers' congress was further
compromised and even rendered irrelevant by the fact that the labor relationship was almost uninfected by tensions or conflicts over such matters as wages
and welfare, due to the implementation of the egalitarian system of distribution. The primary function of the workers' congress was to foster state-
sponsored projects such as political studies and labor emulation rather than
safeguard workers' interests. In the chaotic years of the **Great Cultural Revolution (1966–1976)**, the workers' congress virtually ceased to function.

Since the early 1980s, with the deepening of market-oriented economic reforms, the workers' congress has received increasing attention from the
regime and has begun to gain substantial influence. A series of laws and government regulations have been promulgated (e.g., the Regulation on the Workers' Congress in State-Owned Enterprises, the Enterprise Law of the People's
Republic of China, the Trade Union Law of the People's Republic of China, and
the Labor Law of the People' Republic of China). These laws stress the popular
or "democratic" nature of the workers' congress as an authentic labor institution and reassert and expand its rights and roles. The All-China Federation of
Trade Unions (ACFTU), in cooperation with other government agencies, has
vigorously promoted reinvigoration of the workers' congress in previously
state-owned enterprises and formation of the workers' congress in newly
founded enterprises, including private ones. By the end of June 2002, workers'
congresses existed in 327,000 state-owned enterprises and in about 60,000
private ones. The ACFTU also has endeavored to create favorable conditions or
channels for the participation of the workers' congress in the decision-making
process of the enterprise. Behind this emphasis on the workers' congress were
the profound changes in labor-management relations brought about by economic reforms: with the diminishing of direct government intervention and
the evolving of state-owned enterprises into independent economic entities,
labor and management became distinct interest groups, and their relationship
became essentially antagonistic. Keenly concerned with maintaining stability
of production and society, the regime deemed it imperative to prevent or reduce tensions in labor relations. One measure the regime adopted to achieve
this goal was to strengthen the role of the workers' congress and thereby get
workers involved in the management of enterprises.

With legal and governmental backing, the workers' congress has, since the
early 1980s, gained substantial influence over management, notably in state-
owned enterprises. Since 1998, the workers' congress has also been active in
promoting transparency of enterprise policies and democratic review of enterprise leaders. These two measures are considered by the government to be
the most important extension of labor's role in democratic management in
workplaces. The transparency requirement demands that the management dis-
close nonclassified information such as business operation, managers' use
of company funds and facilities, and the allocation and use of welfare funds.
The congress also oversees the payment of the company's contribution to retirement, unemployment, health, accident, and maternity insurance funds
sponsored by the state. The democratic performance reviews allow workers
and staff to have a say in the promotion and demotion of management teams.

In state enterprises, this review process can lead to the removal of the manager of the enterprise. As of June 2002, the workers' congress had conducted regular evaluation of managerial performance in 186,000 state-owned enterprises, resulting in the promotion or demotion and even dismissal of some managerial personnel; it had reviewed managers' reports on the use of hospitality funds in 188,000 state-owned enterprises; it had gained a presence on the board of directors and thus participated in the policy-making process by selecting "worker-directors" in 38,350 state-owned enterprise; and it had monitored managers' personal conduct and matters concerning workers' immediate interests under the system of "making the affairs of the enterprise public" in 251,000 enterprises. In addition, the workers' congress also participated, via the **trade union**, in negotiations with management over terms of collective agreements. Through these activities, the workers' congress functioned to express and defend workers' interests and helped ease tensions in labor relations. The workers' congress is also responsible for the election and removal of the workers' representatives on the governing board, but the existing laws do not specify the numbers on the role of the workers' representatives in these decision-making bodies.

On the one hand, the workers' congress has become an integral part of China's economic system and has served as a useful channel for labor participation in enterprise administration. On the other hand, however, it has been subject to a variety of constraints. The workers' congress has so far played an important role only in state-owned enterprises, while in private enterprises it generally has exerted no influence. Even in many state-owned enterprises, the workers' congress has succumbed to formalism and inactivity, which have resulted primarily from management's unwillingness to share its power with workers.

The disadvantages the workers' congress has suffered also have to do with the inadequacy of the Chinese legal system. While the law has granted a wide range of rights to the workers' congress, it has given equally extensive powers to managers over production and workers, and it has not stipulated what penalties would be meted out to managers if they ignore the workers' congress. Managers have proved ready to capitalize on this legal loophole in asserting their own power. In addition, because large numbers of unprofitable state-owned enterprises have been edging toward bankruptcy since the 1990s, their managers are more concerned with the survival of the enterprises than with the rights of the workers' congress; and workers, preoccupied with job security, equally show little interest in these rights. The rise of stockholders' meetings also poses another challenge. Since stockholders own many public and private companies, they have a legal right to participate in the making of companies' decisions as well as business plans. This new form of control by investors will compete with the workers' congress for decision-making powers. How the two can exist side by side remains to be seen.

See also Labor Market; Labor Market Development; Labor Policy; Labor Policy, Employment, and Unemployment; Labor Relations; Labor Rights; Migrant Population; State-Owned Enterprises (SOEs), Reemployment of Laid-off Workers; Unemployment.

Bibliography

ACFTU, *Blue Paper on the Protection of Labor's Legal Rights by the Chinese Trade Union*, February 2003, http://www.afctu.org.cn, accessed on December 6, 2004; *China Labor Statistical Yearbook* (various issues, 1995–1999) (Beijing: Labor Press); Feng, Tongqing, *The Fate of Chinese Labor: Labor's Social Actions since the Reform* (Beijing: Social Science Documents Press, 2002); *Survey of the Status of Chinese Staff and Workers in 1997* (Beijing: All-China Federation of Trade Unions Policy Research Office, 1999).

Yunqiu Zhang and Baogang Guo

World Trade Organization (WTO), China's Accession to

It was a long march for China to become a member of the World Trade Organization (WTO). China formally applied to resume its original contracting party status in the General Agreement on Tariffs and Trade (GATT), the predecessor to the WTO, in July 1986. A GATT Working Party was appointed in June 1987, and the first meeting of the Working Party took place in February 1988. China met several dozen times with the WTO Working Party and conducted extensive bilateral negotiations on WTO entry with the United States and other major trading partners. After fifteen years of onerous and sometimes dramatic bargaining, China finally became the 143rd member of the WTO on December 11, 2001, receiving formal approval at the WTO Annual Meeting of Ministers in Doha, Qatar. In the end, the full Protocol of Accession became a 1,500-page document that incorporated thousands of lines of tariffs and other specific

Chinese Foreign Trade Minister Shi Guangsheng signs the membership document at a November 11, 2001, ceremony recognizing China's accession to the WTO. © Reuters/Corbis.

agreements. The process for China's WTO accession negotiations set a record in bilateral and multilateral negotiations in the world. The accession of China to the WTO has had profound impacts on the Chinese economy and the world economy as well.

The WTO is based on the premise of free trade among its member countries. Each member country should have an open market in which private and foreign enterprises can trade freely without much governmental intervention. The major challenge China faced in the negotiations was how to transform its centrally planned economy to a free-market economy to meet this premise. China's quest for WTO membership was a process with much pain, but not without many gains. The quest became an impetus for China to speed up its ongoing privatization of **state-owned enterprises** and the establishment of a free and open market. In fact, by 2001, mostly under pressure from the developed countries led by the United States, China had sufficiently achieved progress in privatization, trade liberalization, and economic globalization to meet WTO requirements.

First, China pragmatically moved away from its centrally planned economy toward a market economy. In 1986, the year China applied for WTO membership, state-owned enterprises produced 62 percent of China's total industrial output, whereas nonstate enterprises (including collectively owned, individually owned, and foreign-owned business entities) contributed the other 38 percent. In 2000, the state-owned enterprises accounted for merely 27 percent of total industrial output, whereas the nonstate enterprises accounted for 73 percent (*China Statistical Yearbook*, 2001). The non-state-owned sectors have replaced the state-owned sector as the major driving force for the rapid growth of the Chinese economy. More and more state-owned enterprises have been privatized through stock sharing, joint venture, merger, and acquisition. It is expected that the private sector will further grow and contribute even more to total industrial output.

Second, China achieved major progress in trade liberalization. To comply with WTO rules and to give foreign companies greater access to its markets, China systematically reduced its tariff barriers. Tariffs were reduced from 56 percent on average in 1982 to 23 percent in 1996 and to only 15 percent by 2001, which was about the levels in Mexico and Brazil. China has also committed to further cut tariffs to an average rate of 10 percent by 2005, the tariff level maintained by most developing countries. In addition to tariff reduction, China gradually lowered its nontariff barriers. It progressively removed limitations on trading rights—rights to import and export goods, which were traditionally the most important nontariff barriers. Over time, it established transparent eligibility standards for applying for trading licenses for both state and private companies. The number of companies that had trading rights dramatically increased from less than 1,200 in 1986 to more than 35,000 in 2001, which created a competitive market in trading services. Meanwhile, fewer goods were subject to trading rights restrictions—licensing and quotas. For example, by 2000 there were only fifty products, with a volume of less than 4 percent of total exports, that were subject to export controls through designated trading institutions.

Third, China also made major improvements in complying with the National Treatment Rule, which is one of the WTO's most important nondiscrimination principles. China has gradually relaxed restrictions on market entry for enterprises with foreign capital investment. Increasingly, foreign enterprises have been permitted to sell their goods and services in Chinese markets. More and more foreign banks and insurance companies have been allowed to enter the financial and insurance markets. The discriminatory pricing policies against foreigners have also been removed. For example, the double-standard pricing system for transportation was eliminated in 1997.

Another important aspect of China's bid to join the WTO that resulted in positive policy changes is intellectual property rights (IPR) protection. International pressure to protect foreign intellectual property rights helped China establish its IPR legal system and set up rules for the market economy. After the serious efforts of the government in the last decade or so, the IPR legal system and the practice of IPR protection have been significantly improved.

Overall, the fifteen-year quest for WTO membership presented a historic opportunity for China to privatize its economy and liberalize its trading regime. The performance of the free market was remarkable. Real GNP grew by an average of more than 9 percent annually, and China's share of world trade grew faster than that of any other country in the world, rising from 0.6 percent in 1977 to more than 4 percent in 2002.

However, China's economic and trade reforms before its WTO entry were extraordinary but incomplete. Substantial elements of market protection remain, especially in foreign firms' access to its service industries. In the final negotiations, China made far-reaching commitments in its accession protocol to ensure further opening of its markets to foreign competition and to fully comply with WTO rules and provisions. China was also pressed to accept discriminatory treatment in two important areas, safeguards and antidumping. Under the safeguards provision, the United States and other countries can unilaterally impose restrictions on goods imported from China for twelve years from the time of its accession. Under the antidumping provision, the United States and other WTO members have broad discretion in initiating antidumping investigations against Chinese firms for fifteen years, simply based on the assumption that China is still a nonmarket economy. At least in the short run, these provisions are quite burdensome on China and Chinese companies.

Chinese decision makers undertook these commitments as costs paid for WTO membership. China expects that its WTO membership will lead to high economic efficiency, a sustainable high rate of growth, and other benefits in the future. Since its WTO entry, China has been actively taking legislative and administrative actions to fulfill its commitments, and the performance of the Chinese economy has been encouraging.

See also Agriculture, Impact of WTO Accession on; World Trade Organization (WTO), Impact of on Service Industries.

Bibliography

Lardy, Nicholas R., *Integrating China into the Global Economy* (Washington, DC: Brookings Institution Press, 2002); World Trade Organization, *Report of the Working Party on the Accession of China*, October 1, 2001, http://docsonline.wto.org/DDFDocuments/t/WT/ACC/CHN49.doc accessed on December 7, 2004; Yin, Jason Z.,

"China: How to Fight the Antidumping War?" *China and Global Economy* 4 (2003): 51–59; Yin, "The WTO: What Next for China?" in *Dilemmas of Reform in Jiang Zemin's China*, ed. Andrew J. Nathan and Zhaohui Hong, 91–106 (Boulder, CO: Lynne Rienner, 1999).

Jason Z.Yin

World Trade Organization (WTO), Impact of on Service Industries

China joined the World Trade Organization (WTO) as its 143rd member in December 2001. China's commitments in joining the WTO have a direct impact on service sectors. The equation seems to be changing in banking, insurance, telecommunication, capital markets, legal services, and transportation services.

Banking

Since the mid-1980s, China has transformed its banking sector from a centrally planned socialist monobank regime to a fractional-reserve banking system under the supervision of the People's Bank of China (PBC), the central bank. Banking assets have expanded by about 35 percent annually and have become the major source of business finance. The banking sector, however, dominated by major state-owned commercial banks, is burdened by large amounts of nonperforming loans, lower-than-required capital, inadequate risk-management capacity, and overstaffing problems.

China started a trial policy of attracting foreign investment in the banking sector as early as 1982. Before 1995, there were thirteen **cities** where banks were allowed to receive foreign investment. After 1996, China allowed foreign-invested banks to conduct local currency (RMB) business, but imposed restrictions on business scale, number, and quotas of those banks. By the end of 2000, thirty-two foreign banks in Shanghai and Shenzhen had been approved by the PBC to engage in RMB business. On the eve of China's accession to the WTO, foreign financial institutions were allowed to set up and run operational financial subsidiaries in all cities. By mid-2002, there were 167 foreign commercial financial institutions (excluding insurers), of which 147 were branches, 7 were joint-venture banks, 6 were wholly foreign-owned banks, and 7 were foreign-invested financial companies.

Following China's WTO commitment, the State Council promulgated at the end of 2001 the revised edition of Regulations on the Administration of Foreign Financial Institutions and relevant Detailed Rules for Implementation. Since then, these changes have taken and continue to take place. Foreign banks have been allowed to run foreign exchange businesses without any limitation on geographic areas and clients. Such restrictions have been removed as those on business scale, number, and quotas of foreign-invested financial institutions for their entry into the market of RMB business. The Chinese partners in the joint-venture banks or financial companies no longer have to be financial institutions. Foreign financial institutions were allowed to conduct transactions with the local corporate sector in RMB starting in December 2003. Foreign banks that will conduct transactions with local households in local currencies will be under way starting in December 2006, and all the restrictions on the geographic areas and clients will be removed thereafter.

Insurance

In 1992, China began to open its insurance market conditionally by allowing foreign insurers to establish branches and joint ventures in Shanghai on a trial basis. In 1995, the trial was expanded to Guangzhou. By the end of 2001, a total of twenty-nine foreign insurers had set up forty-four operational institutions. Foreign insurance institutions mainly focus on property insurance and related credit and liability insurance of foreign-invested enterprises, life insurance of foreign individuals, and reinsurance of these businesses.

On China's accession to the WTO, the State Council issued Regulations on Administration of Foreign Insurance Companies (effective February 1, 2002), which specify qualifications, procedures, business scope, and legal liability for foreign firms to invest in the insurance business. In accordance with China's WTO commitments, foreign nonlife insurers have been permitted to be established as branches or as joint ventures with up to 51 percent foreign ownership. By the end of 2003, foreign nonlife insurers were to be permitted to be established as wholly owned subsidiaries. Foreign life insurers have been permitted up to 50 percent foreign ownership in a joint venture. For large-scale commercial risks and international marine, aviation, and transport insurance and reinsurance, upon accession, joint ventures with foreign equity of up to 50 percent were permitted. By the end of 2004, the foreign equity share was increased to 51 percent, and by the end of 2006, wholly foreign-owned subsidiaries will be permitted.

Telecommunications

Before China's accession to the WTO, **telecommunications industry** had been a forbidden area for foreign equity investment. China committed itself to gradually loosen its restrictions on geographic areas, the ratio of foreign investment, and business scope within five years after the accession. To specify the requirements and procedures for foreign firms to invest in telecom enterprises, the Ministry of Information Industry and the Ministry of Foreign Trade and Economic Cooperation (MOFTEC) jointly issued Regulations on Administration of Foreign-Invested Telecommunications Enterprises in December 2001. In April 2002, the ban on foreign investment in the telecommunications industry was lifted in the revised edition of Catalog Guiding Foreign Investment in Industries. Foreign companies have been allowed to enter China's telecom market through joint ventures with indigenous partners, while foreigners' capital shares are permitted to rise incrementally up to 49 percent for basic fixed-line and mobile telecom services and up to 50 percent for paging and value-added services by the end of 2003.

Capital Market

China's capital market has developed very quickly. The first stock was issued in 1985, and the national stock market was launched in 1990. In only ten years, the capitalization of China's equity market rose from virtually zero to nearly 50 percent of GDP by the year 2000.

China's stock market has been segmented into two submarkets. A shares, denominated in Chinese currency, can be held and traded by domestic/indigenous institutional and individual investors. B shares, denominated in U.S. dollars and Hong Kong dollars, used to be legally held and traded by foreign investors only. When China's accession to the WTO was imminent, the government permitted local investors with foreign currency deposits to purchase B shares in February 2001. This caused the immediate increase of B-share prices and significantly reduced the price differentials between A and B shares. Thanks to foreign exchange controls, the market for B shares is still technically separated from the A-share market.

On the eve of China's accession to the WTO, the China Securities Regulatory Commission (CSRC) and MOFTEC jointly announced a policy change to allow enterprises with foreign investment to be listed in the A-share market. The new rule also allows foreign-invested enterprises to accept and transfer non-circulation stocks of listed companies in China.

China's WTO commitments required the government to allow joint ventures to underwrite A shares and to underwrite and trade B shares within three years of WTO accession. The government is also committed to permitting joint ventures with 33 percent foreign ownership to engage in fund management businesses upon accession, with the ownership ceiling rising to 49 percent by the end of 2004. To fulfill these commitments, the CSRC issued Rules for Establishment of Securities Companies with Foreign Investment and Rules for Establishment of Fund Management Companies with Foreign Investment on June 1, 2002 (effective July 1, 2002).

Legal Services

Under China's WTO agreement, foreign law firms can provide legal services only in the form of representative offices. By the end of 2002, 110 offices of those legal firms had been set up in China. After China's entry into the WTO, the State Council promulgated Regulations on Administration of Representative Offices of Foreign Legal Firms in China. The regulations removed the restrictions on geographic areas and permitted each foreign legal firm to set up more than one representative office, in accordance with China's commitments.

Transportation

In container transportation and seaport development and operations, China has encouraged foreign investment mainly in the form of preferential tax policies and land leasing. China's WTO entry is expected to lead to a stronger growth of demand for sea transportation and a boom of foreign investment in coastal ports. In accordance with China's WTO commitments, MOFTEC promulgated Regulations on Foreign-Invested International Freight Forwarding Agencies at the end of 2001 to allow foreign investors to establish cooperative international freight-forwarding agencies and to set up wholly foreign-owned international freight-forwarding agencies within three years after WTO entry.

The State Council issued the Regulations on Marine Transport at the end of 2002 to specify the principles for foreign-invested companies dealing with marine transport and auxiliary services. For air transport, the Provisional Regulations on Foreign-Invested Civil Aviation further loosened the requirements for foreign investors that wished to be engaged in civil aviation.

In addition to these service sectors, within months before or after it joined the WTO, China opened to foreign investors such areas as accounting, assets evaluation, publishing, printing, architecture, real estate, property management, audiovisual production, catering, entertainment, maintenance, consultation, advertising, medical care, leasing, commercial inspection, engineering design, and tourist agencies. Some of these decisions were direct results of WTO commitments, and some were indirectly related (Sun 2002). In particular, to raise the standard of China's certified public accountant system and to narrow the gap between China's accounting and auditing system and the international counterpart, China has allowed internationally renowned accounting firms to partner with China's counterparts to set up accounting firms. Meanwhile, as a WTO member, China has to install a framework of laws and regulations at all levels of government to govern trade in goods and services according to WTO principles of transparency and national treatment. This has led to revision and promulgation of relevant laws and regulations that have clarified the market accession conditions for foreign investors in many industries, including the service industries.

See also Agriculture, Impact of WTO Accession on; World Trade Organization (WTO), China's Accession to.

Bibliography

Sun Peng, "Current Situation and Prospects of Opening-up in China's Service Industry," 2002, http://www.fdi.gov.cn, accessed December 8, 2004; World Trade Organization, *Protocol on the Accession of the People's Republic of China*, WTO document code WT/L/432, 2001; World Trade Organization, *Report of the Working Party on the Accession of China: Schedule of Specific Commitments on Services*, October 1, 2001, http://docsonline.wto.org/ DDFDocuments/t/WT/ACC/CHN49.doc, accessed December 7, 2004.

Ding Lu

WTO

See Agriculture, Impact of WTO Accession on; World Trade Organization (WTO), China's Accession to; World Trade Organization (WTO), Impact of on Service Industries.

X

Xinjiang

Known today as Xinjiang Uygur Autonomous Region, with a total area of 1.6649 million square kilometers, Xinjiang accounts for one-sixth of China's territory and is the largest of China's provinces. In ancient times, Xinjiang was China's major corridor to central Asia. It was an important section of the ancient Silk Road and a meeting place for the ancient Chinese, Persian, and Turkic empires. By the end of the nineteenth century, Xinjiang had thirteen ethnic groups, including Uygur, Han, Kazakh, Mongolian, Hui, Kirghiz, Manchu, Xibe, Tajik, Daur, Uzbek, Tatar, and Russian. The Uygurs formed the majority. The 2003 government *White Paper* indicates that in 2000 the region had a population of 19.25 million, including 10.9696 million people from forty-seven ethnic groups. An intensive migration program has obviously changed the demographic landscape.

As the main passageway and hub for economic and cultural exchanges, Xinjiang has always been a region where a number of religions exist side by side. Before **Islam** was introduced into Xinjiang, there had been Zoroastrianism, Buddhism, Daoism, Manichaeism, and Nestorianism in the region. After the introduction of Islam in the eighth century, Xinjiang became a predominantly Muslim region.

Xinjian has always had a rugged fusion with the central government. In 1757, the Qing imperial court crushed the long-standing Junggar separatist regime in the Northwest. Two years later, it quelled a rebellion launched by the Islamic Aktaglik sect leaders Burhanidin and Hojajahan and thus consolidated its military and administrative jurisdiction over all parts of the region. Following the Opium War of 1840, Xinjiang was subject to aggression from tsarist Russia and other powers. In 1884, the Qing government formally established a province in the western regions and renamed the area Xinjiang (meaning "the new dominion"). Frequent rebellions remained unsuccessful until 1944, when

Uygurs took advantage of the turmoil generated by World War II to establish the East Turkistan Republic (ETR). On September 25, 1949, **Mao Zedong**'s troops moved into Xinjiang peacefully and put an end to the ETR, making the East Turkistan forces flee abroad.

After that, separatism remained dormant, particularly under Mao's stern rule, until the 1990s, when the regional control relaxed due to increased economic and trade activities. Since then, militant separatists have been responsible for numerous sabotage activities, including violent demonstrations and car bombings in the provincial capital Urumqi and in Kashgar, Xinjiang's second-largest city. Xinjiang's governor Ablait Abdureschit was reported to confirm that since the start of the 1990s, there have been a few thousand incidents of terrorist activity, such as assassinations and explosions. Dissent in the mass mentality is also strong.

There are three main sources for the widespread dissent, according to analysts. The first one is ethnicity and culture based. Many Uygurs see themselves as physically and culturally different. Additionally, they speak a "foreign language" that most Han Chinese do not speak. However, it is the second source that is believed to yield more serious consequences: the Uygurs feel discriminated against. When large corporations arrive in Xinjiang to mine minerals and drill for oil, they share few jobs with Uygurs. The **unemployment** rate among the Uygurs was above 70 percent in 2000, according to one report, while that of the Han Chinese in the region was less than 1 percent. Cultural differences may have contributed to this discrepancy, because most Uygurs engage in farming and trade of art crafts. Their general education level is lower than that of the Han Chinese. Other than the economic disparity, a deeper concern among the Uygurs is that the fast-developing industrialization by the Han Chinese will eventually push them out of their homeland. The third source is the instigation from terrorist groups in central Asian countries. The central government has a growing concern over foreign influences.

In handling insurgence by militant groups, the Chinese government has always been merciless. However, if the government had been under tremendous pressure from human rights groups before, the 9/11 bombing of the World Trade Center seemed to have provided a window for a wide-scale crackdown. Reports indicate that the Chinese government has taken advantage of the opportunity to deeply infiltrate the region and round up terrorist suspects. The Chinese security forces were able to identify and arrest groups and individuals, for example, who had ties with and received training in al-Qaeda camps run by Osama Bin Laden.

The Chinese government has vowed on many occasions never to let Xinjiang get out of hand. This is easily understood, because any local independence would result in a domino effect. **Tibet**, Inner Mongolia, and Taiwan are regions that have been hotbeds for separatism, and China wants to avoid what happened to the former Soviet Union. However, most analysts believe that the ETR separatists are unlikely to succeed because of lack of support and powerful suppression worldwide. Moreover, the business world considers dealing with a unified China more favorable than a fragmented China. Some believe that even Muslim countries, such as Iran and Pakistan, would find little interest in backing Uygur separatists because these countries largely rely on China's weapons sales and business trade.

While the fusion has been a difficult one, the Chinese government has long found the ultimate solution through modernization and migration. According to the governmental *White Paper*, in the past half century, Xinjiang's economy and social undertakings have advanced by leaps and bounds. The GDP of Xinjiang was 148 billion yuan in 2001; taking price rises into account, this was 42.9 times that of 1952, with an annual growth rate of 8 percent. The per capita GDP rose from 166 yuan in 1952 to 7,913 yuan in 2001. There was almost no modern transport prior to the founding of New China. In little more than fifty years, Xinjiang has witnessed a drastic change in the communications and transport industry. By 2001, the region's operating railway lines totaled 3,010.4 kilometers, and highways had been extended to 80,900 kilometers. The highway that runs through the Taklimakan Desert is a long-distance graded highway, the first one in the world built on shifting sands. There are also ninety-two airlines that radiate from the regional capital Urumqi to sixty-five cities in other parts of the country and abroad and to twelve prefectures and cities within the autonomous region. The total length of the air routes is 161,800 kilometers.

According to the *White Paper*, Xinjiang has built a number of digital microwave trunk circuits and optical cable trunk lines. A direct distance dialing (DDD) telephone network now links all the cities and counties in Xinjiang with the rest of China. The local data communications network and multimedia communications network have developed rapidly, and a mobile-phone network is now in place to cover the whole region. By 2001, Xinjiang had trade relations with 119 countries and regions. Nearly 1,000 commodity items in twenty-two categories were on the export list. Among them, 10 export commodities earned more than U.S. $10 million each. The total value of Xinjiang's exports and imports amounted to U.S. $1.77 billion in that year. In 2001, the average net income per capita in the rural areas of Xinjiang was 1,710.44 yuan, which was more than what was needed for food and clothing. The average annual salary of an urban employee was 10,278 yuan. Urban residents, as a whole, led comfortable lives.

The *White Paper* indicates that the number of primary schools in the region increased from 1,335 in 1949 to 6,221 in 2001, middle schools from 9 to 1,929, and regular institutions of higher learning from 1 to 21. The ratio of the educated population of the region has grown remarkably, and the proportion of illiteracy among the young and middle-aged has dropped to less than 2 percent. In addition, health facilities have been improving. All the eighty-five counties (cities) of the region have hospitals, sanitation and antiepidemic stations, and health centers for women and children. Each township has a hospital, and each village a clinic. Many difficult and complicated illnesses can be treated within the region. Endemic and contagious diseases that afflicted people of all ethnic groups in the past have been basically wiped out. The *White Paper* also indicates that the implementation of a more liberal childbirth policy for ethnic minorities than for the Han people has promoted the growth of the population of ethnic minorities. In 2001, the natural population growth of ethnic minorities was 13.04 per thousand, whereas that of the Han was 8.25 per thousand. The first national census, conducted in 1953, showed that the combined population of ethnic minorities in Xinjiang was 4.54 million, while the figure had risen to 10.9696 million according to the fifth national census in 2002.

Politically, the central government focuses on promoting local support from within the Uygur communities. The *White Paper* indicates that there are as many as 348,000 ethnic-minority cadres today, 51.8 percent of the total number of cadres in the autonomous region. Meanwhile, the number of women ethnic-minority cadres has exceeded 46 percent of the total number of women cadres in the whole region. The proportions of ethnic-minority deputies in the total number of Xinjiang's deputies to the **National People's Congress** in all previous terms have all exceeded 63 percent.

In the religious domain, the central government is reportedly active in providing financial sponsorship. Every year, the government allocates specialized funds for the maintenance and repair of major mosques, monasteries, and churches. Moreover, the government attracts religious figures to administrative posts. According to the *White Paper*, more than 1,800 religious personages in Xinjiang have been elected to posts in people's congresses and committees of the Chinese People's Political Consultative Conference (CPPCC) at all levels and have participated in deliberation and administration of state affairs on behalf of religious believers and in exercising supervision over the government in respect to the implementation of the policy of freedom of religious belief. In order to standardize operations of religious activities, Xinjiang has established an Islamic college that specializes in training senior clergymen. Overall, with strict control, on the one hand, and economic expansion and migration, on the other, it is likely that the central government will maintain stability in Xinjiang for a prolonged period of time.

See also Hong Kong, Return of; One Country, Two Systems; Regions of China, Uneven Development of; Rural-Urban Divide, Regional Disparity, and Income Inequality; Western Region Development Project.

Bibliography

Hasan, Nader, "China's Forgotten Dissenters: The Long Fuse of Xinjiang," *Harvard International Review* 20, no. 4 (fall 2000); *White Paper on History, Development of Xinjiang (Parts 1–10)*, Xinhua News Agency May 26, 2003, http://news.xinhuanet.com/english/2003-05/26/content_887198.htm, accessed on December 6, 2004.

Jing Luo

Y

Yang Mo (1914–1995)

The novelist Yang Mo was an important figure in modern Chinese literature. Although her novel *The Song of Youth* was later criticized during the **Great Cultural Revolution**, it was one of the best-known and most influential literary expressions of official ideology in the 1950s.

Yang Mo was born into a scholar's family on September 25, 1914, in Beijing. Because of the decline of her family, she later had to drop out of school. To resist an arranged marriage, she left her family to make a living independently. She became a member of the Communist Party in 1936. After 1937, Yang joined the Communist-led guerrilla war against the Japanese. After 1943, she served as editor and then as chief editor for several newspapers. In 1952, she became a screenwriter in the Central Film Bureau. Five years later, she transferred to Beijing Film Studio and worked as a screenwriter there. In 1963, she became a board member of the Association of Chinese Writers.

Yang's writing career can be dated back to 1934. In her early years, she wrote mainly short stories, novelettes, and prose essays. Yang's best-known work was her novel *The Song of Youth*. Begun as early as 1951, the novel was first published in 1958, and a revised edition appeared in 1960. The novel concentrated on the patriotic students' movements that occurred between 1931 and 1935. Through a detailed description of a group of young **intellectuals**, Yang brought out the frustration, hesitation, awakening, and rebellion of those young people against the traditional boundaries, as well as the sharp class and national contradictions that existed during the turbulent 1930s. Yang used her own experience as a creative source for the portrayal of her female protagonist, Lin Daojing, and of some Communists who sacrificed their lives to the cause of revolution.

Since the 1950s, *The Song of Youth* has occupied an important place in modern Chinese fiction because it was the first novel in post-1949 China that focused on different types of intellectuals, especially on the life of some progressive intellectuals during the 1930s. A more important reason for its significance is that the novel depicted, in depth, the process of Lin Daojing's search for her ideals and how, under the influence of some Communists, she gradually changed from a "petty bourgeois intellectual," who had fought against her family and society for her own personal interests, into a Communist. To a great extent, the theme that Yang strove to convey in the novel was in agreement with the mainstream ideology of the 1950s: intellectuals will find their real creativity by joining the Communist revolution and by being part of the nation's construction. In 1959, Yang wrote a scenario based on *The Song of Youth* that was immediately made into a feature film. The film was introduced to the public as part of the celebration of the tenth anniversary of the founding of the People's Republic of China. Ironically, the Communist revolution changed targets routinely. Both the novel and the film were criticized as "poisonous weeds" during the Cultural Revolution of the 1960s, and Yang was labeled a "counterrevolutionary writer."

After the Cultural Revolution, Yang published more works, including the short-story anthology *The Red Morningstar Lilies* (1978), the novel *Dawn Is Breaking* (1980), and the long reportage *Vindicating Myself: My Diary* (1985). However, none of her writings after the 1970s was as popular as *The Song of Youth*.

See also Anticorruption Literature and Television Dramas; Avant-garde Literature; Experimental Fiction; Great Cultural Revolution, Literature during; Intellectuals, Political Engagement of (1949–1978); Intellectuals, Political Engagement of (1978–Present); Literary Policy for the New China; Literature of the Wounded; Misty Poetry; Modern Pop-Satire; Neorealist Fiction and Modernism; Pre–Cultural Revolution Literature; Revolutionary Realism and Revolutionary Romanticism; Root-Searching Literature; Sexual Freedom in Literature.

Bibliography

Yang Mo, *Yang Mo Wen Ji* (Selection of Yang Mo's writings) (Beijing: Shi Yue Wen Yi Chu Ban She [October Publications], 1992–1993).

Dela X. Jiao

Yang Shuo (1913–1968)

The novelist Yang Shuo was one of the best and most influential prose writers in modern China. Born on April 28, 1913, in Shandong Province, Yang's original name was Yang Yujin. He changed his name to Yang Shuo in 1937 and used this name for the rest of his life. After the Anti-Japanese War broke out in 1937, he joined the revolution and went to Yan'an for the first time. He returned to Yanan in 1942. During the War of Liberation (1945–1949), as a special correspondent, he took part in the famous battle the Ping-Jin Campaign. When the War to Resist U.S. Aggression and Aid Korea (the **Korean War [1950–1953]**) broke out, Yang went to Korea with a volunteer team. During his four-year stay there, Yang wrote many works about the war. When the war was over, the

Korean government awarded him a second-class merit medal for his contributions. Yang held many official posts as well, including vice chairman of the Foreign Literatures Committee of the Association of Chinese Writers.

Yang's literary career began in the 1930s. Before 1950, he published some reportage essays and novelettes, most of which were about the life of soldiers and workers. After 1949, his writing career entered a new stage. His novel *Three-Thousand-Mile Land* (1952) was one of the most important works in Chinese fiction during the early 1950s; it was also the first work that depicted on a large scale life during what the Chinese called the War to Resist U.S. Aggression and Aid Korea. The novel portrayed in depth how a Chinese volunteer team composed of railroad workers helped the Koreans protect bridges, and praised the friendship between the Chinese and Korean people. The theme of the novel, as Yang himself clearly stated, was that Chinese workers love their own country, their people, justice, and peace.

Especially after 1956, Yang was mainly engaged in prose writing. While writing a prose essay, he often attempted to create an artistic conception that traditionally one could expect to find only in a poem, because he believed that good prose should be as graceful and meaningful as a poem. He devoted great attention to the structure of his prose as a whole and the use of analogy or metaphors. He preferred to apply a language that was based on the spoken Mandarin, and he frequently merged that language with classical Chinese and foreign words or phrases. He loved to express his inner feelings and ideals through the exquisite elaboration of natural scenery. Because of his constant efforts in these respects, Yang developed a unique writing style that was very resplendent and elegant. For years, many of his prose essays, such as "The Red Leaves on the Xiangshan Mountain" and "On the Top of Taishan Mountain," have been included in textbooks for elementary- and middle-school students, and they have been widely used as good examples of standard Chinese language. Yang also published a number of works for children. His "Snowflakes" came in first for the Prize of the National Children's Literature in 1980.

See also Anticorruption Literature and Television Dramas; Avant-garde Literature; Experimental Fiction; Great Cultural Revolution, Literature during; Intellectuals, Political Engagement of (1949–1978); Intellectuals, Political Engagement of (1978–Present); Literary Policy for the New China; Literature of the Wounded; Misty Poetry; Modern Pop-Satire; Neorealist Fiction and Modernism; Pre–Cultural Revolution Literature; Revolutionary Realism and Revolutionary Romanticism; Root-Searching Literature; Sexual Freedom in Literature.

Bibliography

Yang Shuo, *A Selection of Prose Pieces*, translated by Li Yu-hwa (Beijing: Foreign Languages Press, 1980).

Dela X. Jiao

Z

Zhou Enlai (1898–1976)

At the founding of the People's Republic of China (PRC) in 1949, Zhou Enlai served as premier of the Government Administrative Council (the State Council since September 1954). He also served as minister of foreign affairs before 1958, vice chairman of the Party Central Committee, vice chairman of the Central Military Commission, and chairman of the Chinese People's Political Consultative Conference. While Zhou served in a variety of capacities, he is most remembered as the founder of New China's diplomacy.

Zhou Enlai was one of the few founding leaders of the PRC who was trained in both traditional Chinese education and Western education. Born in a rich gentry's family in Jiangsu Province, Zhou Enlai attended the well-known Nankai School of Tianjin and graduated in 1917. He went to Japan and later France for further studies. During his stay in France, he joined the Chinese Communist Party (CCP) in 1922 and started his revolutionary career. In 1924, he was the director of the Political Department of the Huangpu Military Academy under Jiang Jieshi (Chiang Kai-shek), who was the president of the academy. After the failure of the first cooperation between the Communists and the Nationalists in April 1927, Zhou Enlai organized the Shanghai Workers' Armed Uprising and the Nanchang Uprising against the Nationalist regime. Zhou Enlai joined the Red Army's 1934 Long March to break out of Jiang Jieshi's fierce blockade and bombardment of the Jiangxi Red Base. His support ensured that **Mao Zedong** was elected chairman of the Party at the Zunyi meeting held in January 1935, a position that Mao held until he passed away in 1976.

Zhou first demonstrated his diplomatic talent in 1936 when Jiang Jieshi was kidnapped in Xi'an by two of Jiang's favorite generals, Zhang Xueliang and Yang Hucheng. The generals' intention was to force Jiang Jieshi into joining forces with the Communists and to resist the Japanese. Holding on to the principle of "cleaning the house first, fighting foreign aggressors second," Jiang was unwilling to give up his plan of wiping out the Communists. Zhou was able to convince Jiang, however, to put national interests before partisan hatred and to establish a united front with the Communists. Subsequently, Zhou represented the CCP to work for the United Front in the ruling area of the Kuomintang (KMT). The successful coalition won the nation's sympathy for the Communists, as well as a critical window for the Red Army to develop.

Throughout the Anti-Japanese War (1937–1945) and the civil war (1946–1949), Zhou Enlai lobbied domestic democratic parties as well as foreign governments and organizations to win their support for the newly founded Communist country. Zhou directed the drafting of the Common Program under which democratic parties work with the Communist Party through the Political Consultative Conference. In February 1950, Zhou assisted Mao Zedong in negotiating with Stalin to establish the Treaty of Friendship and Mutual Assistance. In June 1950, through Zhou Enlai's persistence, the United Nations agreed to let the Chinese delegation attend the UN Security Council, during which the Chinese delegation accused the United States of armed aggression into China's Taiwan in November. During the **Korean War**, Zhou Enlai was responsible for negotiations with the UN and the final signing of the armistice.

Although China was a poor Communist country and under a Western embargo, Zhou Enlai was able to turn weakness into strength and to exercise China's influence in world matters. His best-known diplomatic policy was his **Five Principles of Peaceful Coexistence**, brought forward in 1953. The principles include mutual respect for one another's sovereignty and territorial integrity, mutual nonaggression, mutual noninterference into one another's internal affairs, equality and mutual benefit, and peaceful coexistence. These principles became the foundation of Chinese diplomacy and were routinely written into diplomatic agreements with China. When Zhou Enlai brought the Five Principles to the Geneva Conference in April 1954 and to the **Bandung Conference of 1955**, they were applauded by the Third World nations.

During the 1950s and early 1960s, Zhou Enlai traveled far and wide among developing nations to build a united front against the two superpowers. Before China's breakup with the Soviet Union, Zhou worked extensively with governments of the Soviet bloc. After the breakup, which led China into a deep isolation, Zhou focused on building alliances with neighboring Asian countries and African countries. He paid visits to twenty-eight Asian and African countries, including Egypt, Algeria, Ghana, Guinea, Mali, and Pakistan, between late 1956 and early 1964. Following Mao Zedong's strategy of divide and conquer, Zhou did not ignore the building of relationships with developed countries such as Japan. He creatively explored multiple venues of contact that ranged from establishing full diplomatic relations (e.g., with France) and governmental relationships (e.g., with Japan) to nongovernmental relationships (e.g., with Britain) and relationships at the level of chargé d'affaires (e.g., with the Netherlands).

While the two superpowers were, by definition, the worst exploiters of the world and hence the number one enemy of poor nations, Zhou Enlai was able to narrow the target down to China's most dangerous enemy, the Soviet Union. In a bold move and to the surprise of the world, Zhou invited the Ping-Pong team of the United States to visit China in 1971, an event that was later known as **Ping-Pong diplomacy**. In 1972, President Richard Nixon paid his visit to Mao Zedong in Beijing. The Shanghai Joint Communiqué, which recognized Taiwan as part of China's territory, was signed during that visit. Thanks to the improved Sino-American relationship, the pressure from the Soviets receded. When China entered the post-Mao era, following Zhou Enlai's Five Principles, it was able to improve its relationships with its northern neighbor, which resulted in reallocation of valuable resources from military buildup to the "Four Modernizations."

Zhou Enlai is remembered by many world leaders as a diplomat of insight and ingenuity. Henry Kissinger, for example, is deeply impressed with Zhou Enlai's photographic memory and appropriate handling of Sino-American relationships. In addition to being a brilliant diplomat, Zhou Enlai is also fondly remembered by the Chinese people for his diligent effort in skillfully correcting Mao Zedong's mistakes during the **Great Cultural Revolution** and in cutting down the devastations of the **Gang of Four**. However, Zhou Enlai's prolonged political career has also attracted suspicion on how much more he could have done but failed to do to save the nation from the Great Cultural Revolution. Nevertheless, for most Chinese people, Zhou Enlai always worked for the good of the nation heart and soul until his death. Though he, too, was attacked, Zhou never completely lost his prestige, and his protective shadow saved many from persecution and destruction.

See also Nixon's Visit to China/Shanghai Communiqué; Sino-American Relations since 1949; Taiwan Strait Crisis, Evolution of; Vietnam War.

Bibliography

Han, Suyin, *Zhou Enlai and the Making of China, 1898–1976* (New York: Hill and Wang, 1994); Kampen, Thomas, *Mao Zedong, Zhou Enlai, and the Evolution of the Chinese Communist Leadership* (Honolulu: University of Hawaii Press, 2000); Zhou, Enlai, *Selected Works of Zhou Enlai* (Oxford: Pergamon Press, 1981).

Jing Luo

Zhu Rongji (1928–   )

Premier of the People's Republic of China (PRC) State Council and Standing Committee member of the Political Bureau of the Fifteenth Chinese Communist Party Central Committee, Zhong Rongji has left a reputation as China's "economic tsar," "rectifier," and, for foreign leaders, "a senior political figure to do business with." Zhong is a pragmatist who gets things done in a no-nonsense style and who charms with his wit, urbanity, and intelligence. Zhu was nominated premier of the State Council by President Jiang Zemin and confirmed by the Ninth **National People's Congress (NPC)** on March 17, 1998, at the NPC First Session, a position that he maintained until the Tenth NPC held in March 2003.

Zhu Rongji was born in 1928 in Changsha of Hunan Province to an intellectual family. Although his ancestors were once wealthy landowners, the death of his father before he was born reduced the family to poverty. Zhu was able to educate himself and won a scholarship to China's prestigious Qinghua University, where he studied electrical engineering. After graduating in 1951, he worked as deputy director of the Production Planning Office of the Planning Division of the Department of Industry of the Northeast. By 1957, he had become deputy division head of the General Office of the Director in the State Planning Commission. The trouble came when he criticized **Mao Zedong**'s "irrational high growth" policies in 1958. Zhu was labeled a "rightist," dismissed from office, and sent to work as a teacher at a cadre school. After he had done his time there in 1962, he worked as an engineer for the National Economy Bureau of the State Planning Commission until 1969. Politically rehabilitated by Deng Xiaoping at the onset of the economic reforms in 1978, Zhu went to work for the State Economic Commission (SEC) as division chief of the Bureau of Fuel and Power Industry and deputy director of the Comprehensive Bureau from 1979 to 1982. He then became director of the SEC's Bureau of Technical Information and a member of the commission. By 1983, he had been promoted to vice minister of the SEC, where he remained until 1987. He was mayor of Shanghai from 1988 to 1991 before he took on the vice premier position in the central government. In the midst of his other activities, Zhu became the director of the Institute of Economic Management at Qinghua University in 1994.

Zhu Rongji was the foremost architect of China's economic reforms. He was credited for orchestrating the soft landing of China's overheated economy in the mid-1990s through the devaluation of China's currency in 1994, tax reform, interest-rate cuts, and lowering of inflation. In 1992, Zhu took tough macroeconomic control measures to curb runaway real-estate development, an excessive money supply, soaring inflation, and a chaotic financial market. Appointed as governor of the People's Bank of China (PBC), Zhu straightened out the financial sector. His leadership prevented a bubble economy and encouraged projects in transport, energy, agriculture, and other sectors that were likely to drive economic development. Thanks to his efforts, China's economy maintained a respectable growth while neighboring economies drifted into recession in the late 1990s. The low inflation enabled the country to weather the Asian financial crisis in 1997 without having to further devalue its currency, which contributed to saving the regional economy from a further downward spiral.

Dubbed "one-chop Zhu," because approving business deals during the 1980s normally required scores of chops and seals, Zhu waged war on bureaucracy from the early years when he was mayor of Shanghai (1988–1991). After becoming premier in 1998, he launched a massive streamlining of China's bloated government bureaucracy in which he removed half of Chinese officials from their posts and trimming **state-owned enterprises** in large part through substantial layoffs of redundant employees and through debt-for-equity swaps. In essence, Zhu's measures redefined the economic relationship between the citizen and the state. In the past, the state-owned economy had provided life-term employment and little incentive to seek improvement. Zhu's reforms included abandoning government ownership over all but the strategic heights of the economy. He privatized housing and moved toward a commercially viable banking system. Meanwhile, he continued to push for a further opening-up drive to lure Western investment, thus creating a competitive environment that forced Chinese enterprises to improve.

A dedicated reformist, Zhu firmly pushed for China's entry into the World Trade Organization (WTO) in the late 1990s. He was convinced that joining the WTO would make Chinese enterprises more dynamic and also help effectively thwart bureaucracy as well as conservative ideology. After all, the WTO entry would be a step closer to bringing Chinese people's living standards in line with those of the Western nations. Once again, due to Zhu's efforts in negotiating forcefully with the United States, China finally secured a deal to enter the WTO in 2001.

Zhu Rongji has been frequently compared to ex-premier **Zhou Enlai** with respect to effectiveness, resourcefulness, and friendliness, and with Russia's Mikhail Gorbachev with respect to dedication to economic reforms. Analysts believed, however, that Zhu was a moderate reformist who would be unlikely to push democratic reforms beyond the boundary. Zhu made it clear in an interview with CNN during his visit to Washington in 1999 that China would stick to the one-party system, because only the Communist Party and socialism could save China. With regard to the 1989 Tiananmen incident, Zhu's view was that the demonstrators ignored the law and were confused over what democracy was all about. However, with respect to human rights, Zhu's opinion seems to differ widely from those of conservative Chinese leaders. Zhu acknowledged that China shares the same concepts of human rights as the West, despite the fact that the Chinese system has its weaknesses. Zhu believes that the difference is mostly in implementation of human rights due to China's lack of trained lawyers and the lower educational level in general of its people.

Zhu demonstrates a great deal of optimism and confidence, because he believes that much improvement has already been achieved compared with early years; hence there is much to be proud of. Indeed, his success as Shanghai's mayor in preventing a crisis in Shanghai in 1989 when students demonstrated in sympathy with the Tiananmen protesters proved his administrative competence in handling crisis differently from the measures adopted in Tiananmen Square. Meanwhile, Zhu's record also proves his firm commitment to the supremacy of the Communist Party.

Zhu Rongji's contribution to the reforms played a crucial role without which China could not have achieved as much. To the world, as analysts suggest, Zhu, like Zhou Enlai, seemed an expert, a pragmatist, and a doer rather than an ideological dreamer or a dull Stalinist. To his countrymen, Zhu's image is that of one of the most capable leaders who rectified wrong policies, scourged the ailing economic sectors, and transformed the country into an unprecedented economic prosperity.

See also June 4 Movement; World Trade Organization (WTO), China's Accession to.

Bibliography

Hutchings, Graham, *Modern China: A Guide to a Century of Change* (Cambridge, MA: Harvard University Press, 2001); "Zhu Rongji," *People's Daily English Edition*, http://english.peopledaily.com.cn/data/people/zhurongji.shtml, accessed on December 8, 2004.

Jing Luo

SELECTED BIBLIOGRAPHY

Abdulgani, Roeslan. *The Bandung Connection: The Asia-Africa Conference in Bandung in 1955*. Singapore: Gunung Agung, 1981.

Accinelli, Robert. *Crisis and Commitment: United States Policy toward Taiwan*. Chapel Hill: University of North Carolina Press, 1996.

All-China Federation of Trade Unions Policy Research Office. *Chinese Trade Unions Statistics Yearbook*. Beijing: Labor Press, 2000.

———. *Chinese Trade Unions Yearbook*. Beijing: Labor Press, 2000.

Allen, Kenneth, Dean Cheng, David Finkelstein, and Maryanne Kivlehan. *Institutional Reforms of the Chinese People's Liberation Army: Overview and Challenges*. Alexandria, VA: CNA Corporation, 2002.

Ashton, Basil, Kenneth Hill, Alan Piazza, and Robin Zeitz. "Famine in China, 1958–1961." *Population and Development Review* 10, no. 4 (December 1984).

Askari, Hossein, John Forrer, Hildy Teegen, and Jiawen Yang. *Case Studies of U.S. Economic Sanctions: The Chinese, Cuban, and Iranian Experience*. Westport, CT: Praeger, 2003.

Bai Shouyi. *Zhongguo Huijiao xiaoshi* (A brief history of Islam in China). Yinchuan: Ningxia Renmin Chubanshe, 2000.

Barmé, Geremie R. *In the Red: On Contemporary Chinese Culture*. New York: Columbia University Press, 1999.

Barnett, A. Doak. *The Making of Foreign Policy in China: Structure and Process*. Boulder, CO: Westview Press, 1985.

Baum, Richard. *Burying Mao: Chinese Politics in the Age of Deng Xiaoping*. Princeton, NJ: Princeton University Press, 1994.

Bodde, Derk, and Clarence Morris. *Law in Imperial China*. Philadelphia: University of Pennsylvania Press, 1973.

Bureau of the Census. *1990 Census of Population and Housing*. Washington, DC: Bureau of the Census, 1993.

Burgess, Robin. "Access to Land and Hunger: Opening the Black Box in China." Working paper, Department of Economics, London School of Economics, 2003.

Burns, John P. "China's Administrative Reform for a Market Economy." *Public Administration and Development* 13 (1993): 345–360.

Byrd, William A. *The Market Mechanism and Economic Reform in China*. Armonk, NY: M. E. Sharpe, 1991.

Caiden, Gerald E. *Administrative Reform*. Chicago: Aldine Publishing Co., 1969.

Chan, M.W.L. "Management Education in the People's Republic of China." In *Management Issues in China*, ed. D. Brown and R. Potter, 1: 237-257. London and New York: Routledge, 1996.

Chang, Chiung-fang. "A Silent Protest—Suicide in Taiwan." *Sinorama*, March 1997. http://www.taiwaninfo.org/info/sinorama/en/8603/603112c1.html, accessed December 23, 2004.

Chang, Ch'un-ch'iao. *On Exercising All-around Dictatorship over the Bourgeoisie*. Beijing: Foreign Languages Press, 1975.

Chang, Gene, and Guangzhong James Wen. "Communal Dining and the Causation of the Chinese Famine of 1958-1961." *Economic Development and Cultural Change*, October 1997, 1-34.

Che, Jiahua, and Yingyi Qian. "Insecure Property Rights and Government Ownership of Firms." *Quarterly Journal of Economics* 113, no. 2 (1998): 467-496.

Cheek, Timothy. *Mao Zedong and China's Revolutions: A Brief History with Documents*. Boston and New York: Bedford/St. Martin's, 2002.

Chen, Aimin. "Assessing China's Economic Performance in 1978-2001: Material Attainments and Beyond." Seminar paper, April 23, 2003, Indiana State University.

———. "China's Urbanization, Unemployment, and the Integration of the Segmented Labor Markets." In *Urbanization and Social Welfare in China*, ed. A. Chen, G. G. Liu, and K. H. Zhang. London: Ashgate Publishing, 2003.

———. "Inertia in Reforming China's State-Owned Enterprises: The Case of Chongqing." *World Development* 26, no. 3 (March 1998): 479-495.

———. "The Structure of Chinese Industry and the Impact from China's WTO Entry." *Comparative Economic Studies*, spring 2002, 72-98.

———. "Urbanization and Disparities in China: Challenges of Growth and Development." *China Economics Review* 13, no. 4 (2002): 407-411.

Chen, Albert H. Y. "The Developing Theory of Law and Market Economy in Contemporary China." In *Legal Developments in China: Market Economy and Law*, ed. Wang Guiguo and Wei Chenying, 3-22. Hong Kong: Sweet & Maxwell, 1996.

Chen Jian. *Mao's China and the Cold War*. Chapel Hill: University of North Carolina Press, 2001.

Chen, Jiwen. "The Amended PRC Patent Law." *China Business Review*, July–August 2001: 38-41.

Chen, Kaige. "Discussing Film with Dadaozhu." *Dang Dai Dian Ying* (Modern films) Beijing: no. 6 (1989).

Chen, Kongli, ed. *A Compendium of Taiwan History*. Beijing: Jiuzhou Book Press, 1996.

Chen, Lidan. *Marxian Journalism*. Beijing: China Radio and Television Press, 1998.

Chen Minzhi and Ding Dong, eds. *Gu Zhun Riji* (The diaries of Gu Zhun). Beijing: Jinji Ribao Chubanshe (Economic Daily Press), 1997.

Chen, Xinxin. "Marriage and the Family in China." Women's Institute, All-China Women's Federation, 2003.

Child, J. *Management in China during the Age of Reform*. Cambridge: Cambridge University Press, 1994.

China and Great Britain. "Joint Declaration of the Government of the United Kingdom of Great Britain and Northern Ireland and the Government of the People's Republic of China on the Question of Hong Kong." December 19, 1984.

China People's Bank. *Zhongguo Xiaofei Xindai Fazhan Baogao* (Report of consumer credit development in China). *Jingrong shibao* (Finance times), February 10, 2002.

Chinese Trade Unions Statistics Yearbook. China Bureau of Statistics, 2000.

Chow, Gregory. *China's Economic Transformation*. Malden, MA: Blackwell, 2002.

Chow, Peter C. Y., ed. *Taiwan in the Global Economy: From an Agrarian Economy to an Exporter of High-Tech Products*. Westport, CT: Praeger, 2002.

Chu, Leonard. "Continuity and Change in China's Media Reform." *Journal of Communication* 44, no. 3 (summer 1994): 4–21.

Chu, Yun-Peng and Sheng-Cheng Hu. *The Political Economy of Taiwan's Development into the 21st Century*. London: Edward Elgar, 1999.

Chung, Jae Ho, and Shiu-hing Lo. "Beijing's Relations with the Hong Kong Special Administrative Region: An Inferential Framework for the Post-1997 Arrangement." *Pacific Affairs* 68, no. 2 (summer 1995): 167–186.

Chung-Hua Institution for Economic Research. *Dalu ji Liangan Jingji Qingshi Baogao (1997/1998)* (Report on the economic situation of mainland China and the two sides of the Taiwan Strait [1997/1998]). Taipei: Mainland Affairs Council, 1999.

CNNIC. *Survey Report on Internet Development in China*. Beijing: CNNIC, January 11, 2003.

Cohen, Jerome A., Robert F. Dernberger, and John R. Garson. *China Trade Prospects and U.S. Policy*. New York: Praeger, 1971.

Cohen, Warren. *America's Response to China*. 4th ed. New York: Columbia University Press, 2000.

Compiling Group. *China Labor and Social Security Yearbook*. Beijing: Zhongguo Laodong Shehui Baozhang Chubanshe, 2001.

Copper, John F. *Taiwan: Nation-State or Province?* Boulder, CO: Westview Press, 1996.

Croll, E. *Changing Identities of Chinese Women: Rhetoric, Experience, and Self-Perception in Twentieth-Century China*. Hong Kong: Hong Kong University Press, 1995.

Dalai Lama. *Freedom in Exile: The Autobiography of the Dalai Lama*. San Francisco: Harper, 1991.

Das Gupta, Monica, Jiang Zhenghua, Li Bohua, Xie Zhenming, Woojin Chung, and Bae Hwa-Ok. "Why Is Son Preference So Persistent in East and South Asia? A Cross-Country Study of China, India and the Republic of Korea." Working paper 2942. World Bank, 2003.

Deng Xiaoping. *Selected Works of Deng Xiaoping*. Beijing: Foreign Languages Press, 1994 and 1995.

Dittmer, Lowell. *Liu Shaoqi and the Chinese Cultural Revolution*. Armonk, NY: M. E. Sharpe, 1998.

———. "The Sino-Russian Strategic Partnership." *Journal of Contemporary China* 10, no. 28 (2001): 399–413.

Domes, Jürgen. *The Internal Politics of China, 1949–1972*. London: C. Hurst & Co., 1973.

Donaldson, Robert H., and Joseph L. Nogee. *The Foreign Policy of Russia: Changing Systems, Enduring Interests*. 2nd ed. Armonk, NY: M. E. Sharpe, 2002.

Dong, Xiao-yuan. "Two-Tier Land Tenure System and Sustained Economic Growth in Post-1978 Rural China." *World Development* 24, no. 5 (1996): 915–928.

Duiker, William J. *Ho Chi Minh*. New York: Hyperion, 2000.

Durkheim, E. *Suicide: A Study in Sociology*. New York: Free Press, 1951 [1897].

Economic Research Service, USDA. "China's Fruit and Vegetable Sector: A Changing Market Environment." *Agricultural Outlook*, June–July 2001, 10–13.

Economy, Elizabeth, and Michel Oksenberg, eds. *China Joins the World: Progress and Prospects*. New York: Council on Foreign Relations Press, 1999.

Falkin, James. "The Formation and Development of Chinese Political Theory." Doctoral thesis, University of London, 1995.

Fan, C. C. "The Vertical and Horizontal Expansions of China's City System." *Urban Geography* 20 (1999): 493-515.

Faust, John R., and Judith F. Fornberg. *China in World Politics*. Boulder, CO: Lynne Rienner, 1995.

Feng, Peter. *Intellectual Property in China*. Hong Kong: Sweet & Maxwell Asia, 1997.

Feng Zhaokui. *Zhanhou Riben Waijiao, 1945-1995* (Postwar Japanese diplomacy, 1945-1995). Beijing: Zhongguo Shehui Kexue Chubanshe, 1996.

Feng Tongqing. *The Fate of Chinese Labor: Labor's Social Actions since the Reform*. Beijing: Social Science Documents Press, 2002.

Foot, Rosemary. *The Practice of Power: U.S. Relations with China since 1949*. Oxford: Oxford University Press, 1997.

Franz, Uli. *Deng Xiaoping*. English translation by Tom Artin. New York: Harcourt Brack Jovanovich, 1988.

Fu Tongxian. *Zhongguo Huijiao shi* (A history of Islam in China). Taipei: Taiwan Shangwu Yinshuguan, 1969.

Gao, Shangquan. *China's Economic Reform*. London: Macmillan, 1996.

Garver, John W. *Foreign Relations of the People's Republic of China*. Englewood Cliffs, NJ: Prentice Hall, 1993.

Gates, David, and Jason Z. Yin. "Energy Development Strategy in China's Urbanization." In *An Analysis of Urbanization in China*, ed. Yongjun Chen and Aimin Chen, 393-398. Xiamen City: Xiamen University Press, 2002.

Gernet, Jacques. *China and the Christian Impact: A Conflict of Cultures*. Cambridge: Cambridge University Press, 1990.

Goldman, Merle. *Sowing the Seeds of Democracy in China: Political Reform in the Deng Xiaoping Era*. Cambridge, MA: Harvard University Press, 1994.

Goldsmith, S. K., T. C. Pelimar, A. M. Kleinman, and W. E. Burney, eds. "Reducing Suicide: A National Imperative." A Report by the National Institute of Mental Health, 2002.

Goldstein, Jonathan, ed. *The Jews of China*. 2 vols. Armonk, NY: M. E. Sharpe, 2000.

Government Information Office. *Chen Shui-bian*. Taipei: Government Information Office, Republic of China, 2004.

Guo Zhigang and Sun Zhongtian, eds. *Contemporary Chinese Literature—Second Part*. Beijing: Higher Education Press, 1993.

Guttentag, Marcia, and Paul F. Secord. *Too Many Women? The Sex Ratio Question*. Thousand Oaks, CA: Sage Publications, 1983.

Hamilton, Gary G., ed. *Cosmopolitan Capitalists: Hong Kong and the Chinese Diaspora at the End of the Twentieth Century*. Seattle: University of Washington Press, 1999.

Hamrin, Carol Lee, and Timothy Cheek, eds. *China's Establishment Intellectuals*. Armonk, NY: M. E. Sharpe, 1986.

Han Suyin. *Zhou Enlai and the Making of China, 1898-1976*. New York: Kodansha America, 1995.

Hao, Tiechuan. "Quanli Shixian de Chaxu Geju" (Variations in the realization of citizen rights). *China Social Sciences* 5 (2002): 112-128.

Hao, Zhidong. *Intellectuals at a Crossroads: The Changing Politics of China's Knowledge Workers*. Albany: State University of New York Press, 2003.

Harding, Harry. *A Fragile Relationship: The United States and China since 1972*. Washington, DC: Brookings Institution, 1992.

Hasan, Nader. "China's Forgotten Dissenters: The Long Fuse of Xinjiang." *Harvard International Review*, 22, no. 3 (fall 2000): 38.

He, Biqing. "*Zhongguo Xiaofei Xindai yu Jiaoyu Chanye de ke Chixu Fazhan*" (The sustainable development of Chinese consumer credit and educational industry). *Yue Gang ao Jiage* (Pricing news of Guangdong, Hong Kong, and Macao), August 20, 2000.

He, Zhou, and Huailin Chen. *The Chinese Media: A New Perspective*. Hong Kong: Pacific Century Press, 2002.

Hong, Junhao. *The Internationalization of Television in China: The Evolution of Ideology, Society, and Media since the Reform*. Westport, CT: Praeger, 1998.

———. "The Role of Media in China's Democratization." *Media Development* 49, no. 1 (2000): 18–22.

Horsley, Jamie P. "Village Election—Training Ground for Democracy." *China Business Review*, March–April 2001.

Hoyer, G., and E. Lund. "Suicide among Women Related to Number of Children in Marriage." *Archives of General Psychiatry* 50 (1993): 134–137.

Hsiung, James C., ed. *Hong Kong, the Super Paradox: Life after Return to China*. New York: St. Martin's Press, 2000.

Hu, Xiaobo, and Gang Lin. *Transition towards Post-Deng China*. Singapore: National University Press of Singapore, 2001.

Huang, Quanyu, Joseph Leonard, and Tong Chen. *Business Decision Making in China*. New York: International Business Press, 1997.

Huang Xianwen. *Last Night's Stars: Chinese Film History of the 20th Century*. Hunan: Hunan People's Publishing, 2002.

Huntington, Samuel P. *The Third Wave: Democratization in the Late Twentieth Century*. Norman: University of Oklahoma Press, 1991.

Hutchings, Graham. *Modern China: A Guide to a Century of Change*. Cambridge, MA: Harvard University Press, 2001.

Information Office of the State Council, People's Republic of China. *Labor and Social Security in China*. Beijing: Information Office of the State Council, People's Republic of China, 2002.

Jencks, Harlan. *From Muskets to Missiles: Politics and Professionalism in the Chinese Army, 1945–1981*. Boulder, CO: Westview Press, 1982.

Jian, Tianlun, Jeffrey D. Sachs, and Andrew M. Warner. "Trends in Regional Inequality in China." *China Economic Review* 1, no. 7 (1996): 1–22.

Jin Han. *Modern Chinese Novels*. Zhejiang: Zhejiang University Press, 1997.

Joffe, Ellis. *The Chinese Army after Mao*. Cambridge, MA: Harvard University Press, 1987.

Johnson, D. Gale. "The Future of the Agricultural Sector." In *The Globalization of the Chinese Economy*, ed. S. Wei, G. J. Wen, and H. Zhou. Cheltenham, UK: Edward Elgar, 2002.

Kahin, George McTurnan. *The Asian-African Conference: Bandung, Indonesia, April 1955*. Ithaca, NY: Cornell University Press, 1956.

Kampen, Thomas. *Mao Zedong, Zhou Enlai, and the Evolution of the Chinese Communist Leadership*. Honolulu: University of Hawaii Press, 2000.

Karnow, Stanley. *Vietnam: A History*. New York: Viking Press, 1983.

Kemenade, Willem van. *China, Hong Kong, Taiwan, Inc.: The Dynamics of a New Empire*. New York: Vintage Books, 1998.

Kent, Ann. *China, the United Nations, and Human Rights: The Limits of Compliance*. Philadelphia: University of Pennsylvania Press, 1999.

Kim, Samuel S. "China and the United Nations." In *China Joins the World: Progress and Prospects*, ed. Elizabeth Economy and Michel Oksenberg, 42–89. New York: Council on Foreign Relations Press, 1999.

———. *China, the United Nations, and World Order*. Princeton, NJ: Princeton University Press, 1979.

Kirsch, Ottfried, Johannes Wörz, and Jürgen Engel. *Agrarian Reform in China*. Berlin: Verlag für Entwicklungspolitik, Breitenbach, 1994.

Kissinger, Henry. *White House Years*. Boston: Little, Brown, 1979.

Kposowa, Augustine J. "Marital Status and Suicide in the National Longitudinal Mortality Study." *Journal of Epidemiology and Community Health* 54, no. 4 (2000): 254–261.

Kung, James. "Egalitarianism, Subsistence Provision, and Work Incentives in China's Agricultural Collectives." *World Development* 22, no. 2 (1994): 175–187.

Lam, Tong. "Identity and Diversity." In *China beyond the Headlines*, ed. T. B. Weston and L. M. Jensen. Lanham, MD: Rowman & Littlefield, 2000.

Lam, Willy Wo-Lap. *The Era of Jiang Zemin*. Singapore: Prentice Hall, 1999.

Lampton, David M. *Same Bed, Different Dreams: Managing U.S.-China Relations, 1989–2000*. Berkeley: University of California Press, 2001.

Lan, Zhiyong. "Federalism and the Central-Local Relations in the People's Republic of China." *Journal of Public Budgeting, Accounting, and Financial Management* 15, no. 3 (2003): 426–454.

Lardy, Nicholas R. *Integrating China into the Global Economy*. Washington, DC: Brookings Institution Press, 2002.

Lau, Joseph S. M., and Howard Goldblatt, eds. *The Columbia Anthology of Modern Chinese Literature*. New York: Columbia University Press, 1995.

Law Yearbook of China. Beijing: Law Yearbook of China Publishing House, 1987–2001.

Lee, Z. James, and Wang Feng. *One Quarter of Humanity: Malthusian Mythology and Chinese Realities, 1700–2000*. Cambridge, MA: Harvard University Press, 1999.

Lester, David, and Bijou Yang. "Do Chinese Women Commit Fatalistic Suicide?" *Chinese Journal of Mental Health* 8 (1995): 23–26.

Levine, Marvin J. *Worker Rights and Labor Standards in Asia's Four New Tigers: A Comparative Perspective*. New York: Plenum Press, 1997.

Li, David. "Ambiguous Property Rights in Transition Economies." *Journal of Comparative Economics* 23, no. 1 (1994): 1–19.

Li, Heng. "Men Outnumber Women, Population Structure Worries China." *People's Daily Online*, September 27, 2002.

Li, Kang. *Rural Community Development in Transitional China*. Beijing: China Scientific and Technology Press, 1992. http://english.people.com.cn/200209/27/eng 20020927_104013.shtml, accessed December 23, 2004.

Li, Liying. "Suicide in Taiwan." In *Taiwan in the Twenty-first Century*, Lanham, MD: University Press of America, 2003.

Li, Xiaobing. *Peasant Soldiers: Chinese Military in the Changing World*. Lexington: University Press of Kentucky, 2004.

———. "PLA Attacks and Amphibious Operations during the Taiwan Strait Crises of 1954–55 and 1958." In *Chinese Warfighting: The PLA Experience since 1949*, ed. Mark Ryan, David Finkelstein, and Michael McDevitt. Armonk, NY: M. E. Sharpe, 2003.

Li, Xiaobing, Xiaobo Hu, and Yang Zhong. *Interpreting U.S.-China-Taiwan Relations*. Lanham, MD: University Press of America, 1998.

Li, Xiaobing, and Hongshan Li, eds. *China and the United States: A New Cold War History*. Lanham, MD: University Press of America, 1998.

Li, Xiaobing, Allan Millett, and Bin Yu. *Mao's Generals Remember Korea*. Lawrence: University Press of Kansas, 2001.

Liang, Yongping. *Looking Forward Monetary Distribution of Housing*. Beijing: China Price Press, 1998.

Liang, Zai. "Demography of Illicit Emigration from China: A Sending Country's Perspective." *Sociological Forum* 16, no. 4 (2001): 677–701.

Lieberthal, Kenneth. "The Great Leap Forward and the Split in the Ya'an Leadership." In *The Politics of China, 1949–1989*, ed. Roderick MacFarquhar. Cambridge: Cambridge University Press, 1993.

Lin Daizhao. *Zhanhou Zhongri Guanxishi* (Postwar Sino-Japanese relations), Beijing: Beijing daxue chubanshe, 1992.

Lin, Guijun. *On the Exchange Rate of the RMB*. Beijing: University of International Business and Economics Press, 1997.

Lin, Justin Y. "Rural Reforms and Agricultural Growth in China." *American Economic Review* 82, no. 1 (1992): 34-51.

Lin, Shuanglin. "China's Government Debt: How Serious?" *China: An International Journal* 1, no. 1 (2003): 73-98.

Lipman, Jonathan N. *Familiar Strangers: A History of Muslims in Northwest China*. Seattle: University of Washington Press, 1997.

Liu Shaoqi. *Selected Works of Liu Shaoqi*. Beijing: Foreign Languages Press, 1984.

Liu, Wenhua and Ma Te. *Circumvention of the Conflict between the WTO and the Labor Legal System of China*. Beijing: China City Press, 2001.

Lu, Ding. "Revamping the Industrial Policies." Chapter 2 in *The Globalization of the Chinese Economy*, ed. Shang-Jin Wei, G. J. Wen, and H. Zhou. Cheltenham, UK: Edward Elgar, 2002.

Lu, Zhigang and Shunfeng Song. "China's Regional Disparities in 1978-2000." Paper presented at the Western Social Science Association 45th Annual Conference, Las Vegas, Nevada, April 2003.

Luo, Jing. "China: Cities vs. the Countryside." *World and I*, October 2001, 20-25.

———. "A Comparative Study of Tongyong Pinyin and Hanyu Pinyin—A Few Considerations on Chinese Romanization." In *Taiwan in the Twenty-first Century*, ed. Xiaobing Li and Zuohong Pan, 49-69. Lanham, MD: University Press of America, 2003.

Luo, Jing, and Zhao Dengming. "Three Models of Foreign Language Reading Comprehension and Their Application in the Instruction of College Level English." *Journal of the Northwest Normal University of China* 36, no. 5 (1999): 98-102.

Lynch, D. *After the Propaganda State: Media, Politics, and "Thought Work" in Reform China*. Stanford, CA: Stanford University Press, 1999.

Lyons, Thomas P. *Economic Integration and Planning in Maoist China*. New York: Columbia University Press, 1987.

Ma Debo and Dai Guangxi. *The Art of Directing: A Study of Five Top Directors of the Beijing Film Co*. Beijing: China Film Publishing, 1994.

Ma Licheng and Ling Zhijun. *Jiaofeng: Dangdai Zhongguo Sanci Sixiang Jiefang Shilu* (Crossing swords: A truthful report on the three thought liberation campaigns in contemporary China). Beijing: Jinri Zhongguo Chubanshe (Today's China Press), 1998.

MacFarquhar, Roderick. "The Succession to Mao and the End of Maoism, 1969-82." In *The Politics of China, 1949-1989*, ed. Roderick MacFarquhar. Cambridge: Cambridge University Press, 1993.

Mackay, Judith. *The Penguin Atlas of Human Sexual Behavior*. New York: Penguin, 2000.

Mackerras, Colin. *The Chinese Theatre in Modern Times, from 1840 to the Present Day*. Amherst: University of Massachusetts Press, 2000.

Mackerras, Colin, and Amanda York. *The Cambridge Handbook of Contemporary China*. Cambridge: Cambridge University Press, 1991.

Mandelbaum, Michael. *The Strategic Quadrangle: Russia, China, Japan, and the United States in East Asia*. New York: Council on Foreign Relations Press, 1995.

Mann, James. *About Face: A History of America's Curious Relationship with China from Nixon to Clinton*. New York: Vintage Books, 2000.

Mao, Tse-Tung. *Quotations from Chairman Mao Tse-Tung*. Stuart R. Schram, ed. New York: Frederick A. Praeger, 1967.

Markoff, John. *Waves of Democracy: Social Movement and Political Change*. Thousand Oaks, CA: Pine Forge Press, 1996.

Meisner, Maurice. *Mao's China and After.* 3rd ed. New York: Free Press, 1999.

Metraux, Daniel. *Taiwan's Political and Economic Growth in the Late 20th Century.* Lewiston, NY: Edwin Mellen Press, 1991.

Ministry of Economic Affairs (Taiwan). *Zhizaoye Duiwai Touzi Shikuang Diaocha Baogao* (The investigation report on outward investment of the manufacturing industry). Taipei: Ministry of Economic Affairs, various issues, 1997–2003.

Ministry of Labor and Social Security. *China Labor Statistical Yearbook.* Beijing: Labor Press, 1995–1999.

Ministry of Labor and Social Security. *Stipulation on the Management of Employment Centers.* December 2002.

Ministry of Labor and Social Security and Bureau of Statistics, People's Republic of China. *Statistical Survey of Development in Labor and Social Security (2002).* Beijing, April 30, 2003.

Nathan, Andrew J., and Robert S. Ross. *The Great Wall and the Empty Fortress: China's Search for Security.* New York: W. W. Norton, 1997.

National Bureau of Statistics of the PRC. *National Labor and Social Security Yearbook.* Beijing: China Statistics Press, 1999.

Naughton, Barry. *The China Circle: Economics and Electronics in the PRC, Taiwan, and Hong Kong.* Washington, DC: Brookings Institution Press, 1997.

O'Brien, Kevin, and Lianjiang Li. "Accommodating Democracy in a One-Party State: Introducing Village Elections in China." *China Quarterly* 162 (June 2000): 465–490. 2000.

Oi, Jean, and Scott Rozelle. *Elections and Power: The Locus of Decision-Making in a Chinese Village.* New York: Oxford University Press, 2000.

Pan Guang. *Youtairen zai Zhongguo: The Jews in China.* Beijing: Wuzhou Chuanbo Chubanshe (China Intercontinental Press), 2001.

Pan, Lynn, ed. *The Encyclopedia of the Chinese Overseas.* Cambridge, MA: Harvard University Press, 2000.

Pei, Minxin. "Citizens v. Mandarins: Administrative Litigation in China." *China Quarterly* 152 (1997): 831–862.

Peters, Richard, and Xiaobing Li. *Voices from the Korean War.* Lexington: University Press of Kentucky, 2003.

Pollay, R. W., D. K. Tse, and Z. Wang. "Advertising, Propaganda, and Value Change in Economic Development: The New Culture Revolution in China and Attitudes toward Advertising." *Journal of Business Research* 20, no. 2 (1990): 83–95.

Poston, Dudley L., Jr., Michael Xinxiang Mao, and Mei-Yu Yu. "The Global Distribution of the Overseas Chinese around 1990." *Population and Development Review* 20 (1994): 631–643.

Powers, Patrick. "Distributing in China: The End of the Beginning." *China Business Review* 28, no. 4 (July–August 2001).

The Public Security Bureau. *Regulations on the Security and Management of Computer Information Networks.* Beijing: The Public Security Bureau, December 11, 1997.

Pyle, David J. *China's Economy: From Revolution to Reform.* London: Macmillan, 1997.

Ren, Xiao. *China's Administrative Reform.* Zhejian, China: Zhejian People's Press, 1998.

Ren, Yanli, ed. *Basic Knowledge of Chinese Catholicism.* Beijing: Religious Culture Press, 2000.

Schoenhals, Michael. *Doing Things with Words in Chinese Politics.* Berkeley: Institute of East Asian Studies, 1992.

Schram, Stuart. *Mao Tse-tung.* New York: Simon and Schuster, 1966.

———. *The Thought of Mao Tse-tung.* Cambridge: Cambridge University Press, 1990.

Selected Archives of the People's Republic of China, 1949–1952. Beijing: China Urban Society Economic Press, 1990.

Shambaugh, David. *Modernizing China's Military: Progress, Problems, and Prospects.* Berkeley: University of California Press, 2002.

Shanghai Statistical Bureau. *1999 Shanghai Real Estate Market.* Beijing: China Statistical Press, 1999.

Shapiro, Sidney, ed. *Jews in Old China: Studies by Chinese Scholars.* New York: Hippocrene Books, 2001.

Shirk, Susan L. *How China Opened Its Door: The Political Success of the PRC's Foreign Trade and Investment Reforms.* Washington, DC: Brookings Institution, 1994.

Shu, Xiaoming. *Zhongguo Dianying Yishiu Shi Jiaocheng* (A course in the history of the Chinese film art). Beijing: China Film Publication, 1996.

Situ, Yingyi, and Weizheng Liu. "The Criminal Justice System of China." In *Comparative and International Criminal Justice Systems,* ed. Obi N. Ibnatius Ebbe. 2nd ed. Boston: Butterworth-Heinemann, 2000.

Song, Shunfeng, and George S-F Chu. "Social Security Reform in China: The Case of Old-Age Insurance." *Contemporary Economic Policy* 15 (1997): 85-93.

Song, Shunfeng, George S-F Chu, and Rongqing Cao. "Intercity Regional Disparity in China." *China Economic Review* 11 (2000): 246-261.

Song, Shunfeng, and Kevin Honglin Zhang. "Urbanization and City Size Distribution in China." *Urban Studies* 39, no. 12 (2002): 2317-2327.

Spence, Jonathan. *Mao Zedong.* New York: Viking, 1999.

State Family Planning Commission. *Population and Family Planning Law.* Beijing: State Family Planning Commission, September 1, 2002.

Su, Shanxiao. *The Government Structure of the People's Republic of China, 1949-1990.* Beijing: China Economics Press, 1993.

Sutter, Robert G. *Chinese Policy Priorities and Their Implications for the United States.* Lanham, MD: Rowman & Littlefield, 2000.

"Taiwan Posts Highest Suicide Rate in Nine Years." *People's Daily Online,* March 29, 2001. http://english.people.com.cn/english/200103/29/eng20010329_66374, html, accessed December 2, 2004.

Terrill, J. Richard. *World Criminal Justice Systems, a Survey.* 4th ed. Cincinnati: Anderson Publishing Co., 1999.

Tien, Hung-mao, and Yun-han Chu. *China under Jiang Zemin.* Boulder, CO: Lynne Rienner, 2000.

Tse, D. K., R. W. Belk, and N. Zhou. "Becoming a Consumer Society: A Longitudinal and Cross-Cultural Content Analysis of Print Ads from Hong Kong, the People's Republic of China, and Taiwan." *Journal of Consumer Research* 15, no. 4 (1989): 457-472.

Tung, Chen-yuan. "China's Economic Leverage and Taiwan's Security Concerns with Respect to Cross-Strait Economic Relations." Ph.D. dissertation, Johns Hopkins University, 2002.

Turner, Karen G., James V. Feinerman, and R. Kent Guy. *The Limits of the Rule of Law in China.* Seattle: University of Washington Press, 2000.

Tyler, Patrick. *A Great Wall: Six Presidents and China: An Investigative History.* New York: Public Affairs, 1999.

Wang Aiwen. *An Examination of the Evolution of Social and Labor Relations.* Beijing: Hongqi Chubanshe, 1993.

Wang, Enbao. *Hong Kong, 1997: The Politics of Transition.* Boulder, CO: Lynne Rienner, 1995.

Wang, Fei-Ling. *China's Hukou System: Organization through Division and Exclusion.* Stanford, CA: Stanford University Press, 2004.

———. "Reformed Migration Control and the New List of the Targeted People: China's *Hukou* System in the 2000s." *China Quarterly* (2003-2004): 115-132.

————. "Stratification and Institutional Exclusion in China and India: Administrative Identification versus Social Barriers." In *Local Governance in China and India: Rural Development and Social Change*, ed. Richard Baum and Manoranjan Mohanty. New York: Sage, 2004.

Wang, Kui Hua. *Chinese Commercial Law.* Oxford: Oxford University Press, 2000.

Wang, Yuguo, and Aimin Chen, eds. *China's Labor Market and Problems of Employment*, Chendu, China: Southwestern University of Finance and Economics Press, June 2000.

Wang, Zhi, and G. Edward Schuh. "Economic Integration among Taiwan, Hong Kong, and China: A Computable General Equilibrium Analysis," *Pacific Economic Review* 5, no. 2 (June 2000): 229–262.

Warner, M. *The Management of Human Resources in Chinese Industry.* New York: St. Martin's Press, 1995.

Weisert, Drake. "Coca-Cola in China: Quenching the Thirst of a Billion." *China Business Review* 28, no. 4 (July–August 2001): 52–55.

Weitzman, Martin, and Chenggang Xu. "Chinese Township Village Enterprises as Vaguely Defined Cooperatives." *Journal of Comparative Economics* 23, no. 1 (1994): 121–145.

Weng, Byron S. J. *Peking's UN Policy: Continuity and Change.* New York: Praeger, 1972.

White House Facts Sheet. "Summary of U.S.-China Bilateral WTO Agreement." 2000. http://www.uschina.org/public/wto/ustr/generalfacts.html, accessed December 23, 2004.

Whiteley, A., S. Cheung, and S. Zhang. *Human Resource Strategies in China.* Singapore: World Scientific Publishing Company, 2000.

Wilson, Dick, ed. *Mao Tse-tung in the Scale of History.* Cambridge: Cambridge University Press, 1977.

Wong, Yiu-chung. "Captive Colony." In *Global Issues: China*, 9th ed. 199–201. Guilford, CT: McGraw-Hill/Dushkin, 2002.

World Bank. *Global Development Finance, 1997.* Oxford: Oxford University Press, 2002.

World Trade Organization. *Report of the Working Party on the Accession of China: Schedule of Specific Commitments on Services*, October 7, 2001. http://docsonline.wto.org/DDFDocuments/t/WT/ACC/CHN49.doc, accessed December 7, 2004.

Xin, Chunying. "What Kind of Judicial Power Does China Need?" *International Journal of Constitutional Law* 1, no. 1 (Oxford University Press and New York University School of Law, 2003).

Xin Meng. *Labor Market Reform in China.* Cambridge: Cambridge University Press, 2000.

Xinhua Publishing House and the People's Bank of China. *A History of Chinese Currency.* Beijing: Xinhua (New China) Publishing House, N.C.N., and M.A.O. Management Group, 1983.

Xiong, Huayuan. *Zhou Enlai Wanlong Zhi Xing* (Zhou Enlai attended the Bandung Conference). Beijing: Zhongyang wenxian chubanshe, 2002.

Xu, Dashen. *Factual Records of the People's Republic of China.* Changchun, China: Heilongjiang People's Press, 1994.

Xu, Guangqiu. "Anti-American Nationalism in China: Causes and Formation." In *Image, Perception, and the Making of U.S.-China Relations*, ed. Hongshan Li and Zhaohui Hong. Lanham, MD: University Press of America, 1998.

Xu Xiao, Ding Dong, and Xu Youyu, eds. *Yu Luoke Yizuo yu Huiyi* (Yu Luoke's works and recollections). Beijing: Zhongguo Wenlian Chubanshe (Chinese Literature and Art Association Press), 1999.

Xu, Xin. *The Jews of Kaifeng, China: History, Culture and Religion.* Jersey City, NJ: KTAV Publishing House, 2003.

———. *Legends of the Chinese Jews of Kaifeng.* Hoboken, NJ: KTAV Publishing House, 1995.

Yang, Dali L. *Calamity and Reform in China.* Stanford, CA: Stanford University Press, 1996.

Yang, Jiawen. "Some Current Issues in U.S.-China Trade Relations." *Issues and Studies* 34, no. 7 (July 1998): 62–84.

———. "Valuation of the Chinese Currency: A Background Study." Occasional Paper Series, Center for the Study of Globalization, George Washington University, 2003.

Yao, Wen-yuan. *On the Social Basis of the Lin Piao Anti-Party Clique.* Beijing: Foreign Languages Press, 1975.

Yin, Jason Z. "The WTO: What Next for China?" In *Dilemmas of Reform in Jiang Zemin's China*, ed. Andrew J. Nathan and Zhaohui Hong, 91–106. Boulder, CO: Lynne Rienner, 1999.

Yin, Jason, and David Gates. "Automobile and Fuel Industries." In *The Globalization of the Chinese Economy*, ed. Shang-jin Wei, James G. Wen, and Huizhong Zhou, 82–99. London: Edward Elgar, 2002.

Yin, Jason Z., Shuanglin Lin, and David F. Gates, eds. *Social Security Reform: Options for China.* Singapore: World Scientific, 2000.

Young, Marilyn B. *The Vietnam Wars, 1945–1990.* New York: Harper Perennial, 1991.

Yu, Tzong-shian. *The Story of Taiwan: Economy.* Taipei, Taiwan: Government Information Office, 1998.

Yu, Yongding, Zheng Bingwen, and Song Hong, eds. *The Research Report on China's Entry into WTO: The Analysis of China's Industries.* Beijing: Social Sciences Documentation Publishing House, 2000.

Yuan, Peng. " 'September 11 Event' vs. Sino-U.S. Relations." *Modern International Relations* (Xiandai Guoji Guanxi), November 2001.

Zhai, Qiang. *China and the Vietnam Wars, 1950–1975.* Chapel Hill: University of North Carolina Press, 2000.

Zhang Chengzhi. *Xinling shi* (A History of the Soul). Guangzhou: Guangdong Huacheng Chubanshe, 1991.

Zhang, Jie, and Xiaobing Li, eds. *Social Transition in China.* Lanham, MD: University Press of America, 1998.

Zhang Rongjian, ed. *Contemporary Chinese Literature.* Beijing: University of Sciences and Technology of Central China Press, 2001.

———, ed. *Contemporary Chinese Literature—Reference Materials.* Beijing: University of Sciences and Technology of Central China Press, 2001.

Zhang Sui. *Youtaijiao yu Zhongguo Youtairen* (Judaism and Chinese Jews). Shanghai: Sanlian Shudian (Sanlian Books Shanghai Branch), 1991.

Zhang Weizhong. *Transformations in the New Age Novels and the Chinese Traditional Culture.* Beijing: Xuelin Press, 2002.

Zhang, Y., and B. D. Gelb. "Matching Advertising to Culture: The Influence of Products' Use Conditions." *Journal of Advertising* 25, no. 3 (1996): 29–46.

Zhang, Yimou. "Questions and Answers." *Guangming Daily* (Shanghai), March 15, 1988.

Zhao, Quansheng. *Interpreting Chinese Foreign Policy.* New York: Oxford University Press, 1996.

———. "Modernization, Nationalism, and Regionalism in China." In *Comparative Foreign Policy: Adaptation Strategies of the Great and Emerging Powers*, ed. Steven W. Hook. Englewood, NJ: Prentice Hall, 2002.

Zhao, Suisheng, ed. *Across the Taiwan Strait.* New York: Routledge, 1999.

Zhao, Yuezhi. *Media, Market, and Democracy in China: Between the Party Line and the Bottom Line.* Urbana: University of Illinois Press, 1998.

Zhou Enlai. *China and the Asian-African Conference* (Documents). Beijing: Foreign Languages Press, 1955.

———. *Selected Works of Zhou Enlai.* New York: Elsevier Science, 1981.

Zhou, Huizhong. "Fiscal Decentralization and the Development of the Tobacco Industry in China." *China Economic Review* 11, no. 2 (December 2000): 114–133.

Zweig, David. *Internationalizing China: Domestic Interests and Global Linkages.* Ithaca, NY: Cornell University Press, 2002.

INDEX

Bold page numbers indicate the location of main entries. The letter *t* following a page number denotes a table, while the letter *f* denotes a figure.

ABOUT THE EDITORS AND CONTRIBUTORS

EDITOR

Jing Luo, Ph.D.
Associate Professor of French and Chinese,
Bloomsburg University of Pennsylvania

ASSOCIATE EDITORS

Aimin Chen, Ph.D.
Professor of Economics, Indiana State
University

Baogang Guo, Ph.D.
Assistant Professor of Political Science,
Dalton State College

Ronghua Ouyang, Ed.D.
Associate Professor of Education, Kennesaw
State University

Shunfeng Song, Ph.D.
Professor of Economics, University of
Nevada

CONTRIBUTORS

Yan Bai, Ph.D.
Political Science Department, Ferris State
University

Richard C. K. Burdekin, Ph.D.
Chair, Department of Economics, Claremont
McKenna College

Tak Cheung Chan, Ph.D.
Professor of Education Leadership,
Coordinator of Doctoral Program,
Kennesaw State University

Changfu Chang, Ph.D.
Assistant Professor of Communication,
Millersville University of Pennsylvania

Aimin Chen, Ph.D.
Professor of Economics, Indiana State
University

Hong-yi Chen, Ph.D.
Professor of Economics, Soka University of
America

Jinxing Chen, Ph.D.
Assistant Professor of History, Edgewood
College

Vivian Chen, Ph.D.
Senior Economist/Team Manager, United
States Department of Labor

Yihai Chen, Ph.D.
Associate Professor, Department of Chinese
Language and Literature, Yancheng Teachers
College, China

Zhiyuan Chen, Ph.D.
Associate Professor of Linguistics,
Appalachian State University

James M. Falkin, Ph.D.
Lecturer in Political Science, College of
Staten Island, City University of New York

Yi Feng, Ph.D.
Dean, School of Politics and Economics,
Claremont Graduate University

Steve Gentner
Holder of Bachelor of Science in
Mathematics, Bloomsburg University

Baogang Guo, Ph.D.
Assistant Professor of Political Science,
Dalton State College

Zhidong Hao, Ph.D.
Assistant Professor, Contemporary China
Studies Program, and Director, Social
Science Research Center in Contemporary
China, University of Macau

Wei He, Ph.D.
Assistant Professor, School of Business,
Indiana State University

Junhao Hong, Ph.D.
Associate Professor and Ph.D. Advisor,
School of Informatics, State University of
New York at Buffalo

Jianjun Ji, Ph.D.
Assistant Professor of Sociology, University
of Wisconsin at Eau Claire

Wenshan Jia, Ph.D.
Assistant Professor of Communication and
Asian Studies, State University of New York
at New Paltz

Dela X. Jiao, Ph.D.
Lecturer in Chinese, Baruch College and
City University of New York

Xudong Jin, M.A.
Associate Director of Libraries and Head of
Technical Services, Ohio Wesleyan
University

Jennifer Kessler
Undergraduate Geology Major, Bloomsburg
University

Janet Yun Wei Kuo, M.A.
Holder of Master of Arts in Journalism

Zhiyong Lan, Ph.D.
Professor of Public Administration, School
of Public Affairs, Arizona State University

Haizheng Li, Ph.D.
Assistant Professor, School of Economics,
Georgia Institute of Technology

Jieli Li, Ph.D.
Associate Professor of Sociology, Ohio
University

Liying Li, Ph.D.
Associate Professor, Department of
Sociology/Anthropology, Southwest
Missouri State University

Xiaobing Li, Ph.D.
Professor of History, University of Central
Oklahoma

Xiaoxiao Li, M.A.
Associate Editor, American Review of China
Studies, Research Fellow, Western Pacific
Institute, University of Central Oklahoma

Zai Liang, Ph.D.
Associate Professor of Sociology, State
University of New York at Albany

Shuanglin Lin, Ph.D.
Lindley Professor of Economics, University
of Nebraska, Omaha

Gordon G. Liu, Ph.D.
Director of Graduate Studies, University of
North Carolina at Chapel Hill
Pharmaceutical Studies and Evaluative
Sciences

Guoli Liu, Ph.D.
Associate Professor of Political Science,
College of Charleston

Junqi Liu, Ph.D.
Professor of Finance, Associate Dean,
College of Economics, Liaoning University,
China

Lu Liu, M.A.
Doctoral Candidate, Purdue University

Ding Lu, Ph.D.
Associate Professor of Economics, National
University of Singapore

Hong Lu, Ph.D.
Assistant Professor, Department of Criminal
Justice, University of Nevada

Xinan Lu, Ph.D.
Assistant Professor and Cochair, Thurgood
Marshall Mentoring Program, Shippensburg
University of Pennsylvania

Jing Luo, Ph.D.
Associate Professor of French and Chinese,
Bloomsburg University of Pennsylvania

Ting Ni, Ph.D.
Assistant Professor of History, St. Mary's
University

Dan Ouyang
Marketing Major, Emory University

Ronghua Ouyang, Ed.D.
Associate Professor of Education, Kennesaw
State University

Zuohong Pan, Ph.D.
Associate Professor of Economics, Western
Connecticut State University

Patrick Fuliang Shan, Ph.D.
Assistant Professor of History, Grand Valley
State University

Jianbing Shao
Instructor of Management, School of
Business, Liaoning University, China

Jian Shen, M.A.
CEO, Beijing Jicai Pharmaceutical
Technology Ltd., Nanjing Zinox
Pharmaceutical Ltd.

Lin Shen, Ph.D.
Professor of Theatre Studies, Director of the
Research Institute, Central Academy of
Drama, Beijing

Jingyi Song, Ph.D.
Assistant Professor of History, Department
of Humanities and Languages, State
University of New York at Old Westbury

Lina Song, Ph.D.
Reader in China Studies, School of Sociology
and Social Policy, University of Nottingham

Shunfeng Song, Ph.D.
Professor of Economics, University of
Nevada

Xiansheng Tian, Ph.D.
Associate Professor of History, Metropolitan
State College of Denver

Xiaowen Tian, Ph.D.
Centre for International Business, University
of Leeds

Chenyuan Tung, Ph.D.
Assistant Research Fellow, Institute of
International Relations, National Chengchi
University, Taiwan

Cheng Wang, Ph.D.
Researcher, Institute of Economics, Chinese
Academy of Social Sciences

Fei-Ling Wang, Ph.D.
Associate Professor, Sam Nunn School of
International Affairs, Georgia Institute of
Technology

H. Holly Wang, Ph.D.
Associate Professor of Economics,
Washington State University

Hong Wang, Ph.D.
Assistant Professor, Department of Speech
and Theater Arts, Shippensburg University
of Pennsylvania

James Wen, Ph.D.
Associate Professor, Department of
Economics, Trinity College, Hartford, CT

Helen Xiaoyan Wu, Ph.D.
Senior Lecturer, Department of East Asian
Studies, University of Toronto

Yinghui Wu, Ph.D.
Professor of Ethnology, Dean of the Institute
of Chinese and International Studies, Dean
of the Institute of Southeast Asia, Director
of the Office of International Affairs, Yunnan
Normal University, Kunming, China

Jingjian Xiao, Ph.D.
Professor of Family Economics, Department
of Human Development and Family Studies,
University of Rhode Island

Guangqiu Xu, Ph.D.
Associate Professor of History, Friends
University

Jiawen Yang, Ph.D.
Associate Professor of International
Business and International Affairs, George
Washington University

Xiaosi Yang, Ph.D.
Lecturer in Philosophy, Lake Forest College

Yao Yang, Ph.D.
Professor, China Center for Economic
Research, Beijing University, China

Jason Z. Yin, Ph.D.
Associate Professor of Management and
International Business, Chairman of the
Management Department, Stillman School
of Business, Seton Hall University

Qingfei Yin, Ph.D.
Associate Professor, School of Mathematics
Science and Computing Technology, Central
South University, China

Hong Zhang, Ph.D.
Associate Professor of History, University of
Central Florida

Jie Zhang, Ph.D.
Professor of Sociology, Director of Center
for China Studies, Department of Sociology,
State University of New York College at
Buffalo

Kevin Honglin Zhang, Ph.D.
Associate Professor of Economics, Illinois
State University

Senquan Zhang, Ph.D.
Associate Professor, Department of
Languages and Asian Studies, Nagoya
University of Commerce and Business, Japan

Xiaoling Zhang, Ph.D.
Lecturer, Institute of Contemporary Chinese
Studies, University of Nottingham

Youde Zhang, Ph.D.
First Vice Provost, Shanghai University, China

Yu Zhang, Ph.D.
Assistant Professor, Department of
Communication, State University of New
York at Geneseo

Yunqiu Zhang, Ph.D.
Assistant Professor of History, North
Carolina A&T State University

Zhiming Zhao, Ph.D.
Assistant Professor and Coordinator,
Linguistics Minor Program, Department of
Anthropology, State University of New York
at Geneseo

Binyao Zheng, Ph.D.
Associate Professor of Educational
Psychology, Department of Secondary and
Middle Grades Education, Kennesaw State
University

Robert Zheng, Ph.D.
Assistant Professor, Instructional and
Learning Technology Program (ILT),
Department of Psychological Studies in
Education, College of Education, Temple
University

Huizhong Zhou, Ph.D.
Professor of Economics, Western Michigan
University

Mei Zhou, B.A.
Assistant Research Fellow, Western Pacific
Institute, University of Central Oklahoma,
Former Deputy Director, High-tech Center
of Xinjiang, China